Marijuana and the Cannabinoids

FORENSIC
SCIENCE AND MEDICINE

Steven B. Karch, *MD,* SERIES EDITOR

HERBAL PRODUCTS: *TOXICOLOGY AND CLINICAL PHARMACOLOGY, SECOND EDITION,* edited by ***Richard L. Kingston and Timothy S. Tracy,*** *2007*

CRIMINAL POISONING: *INVESTIGATIONAL GUIDE FOR LAW ENFORCEMENT, TOXICOLOGISTS, FORENSIC SCIENTISTS, AND ATTORNEYS, SECOND EDITION,* by ***John H. Trestrail, III,*** *2007*

FORENSIC PATHOLOGY OF TRAUMA: *COMMON PROBLEMS FOR THE PATHOLOGIST,* by ***Michael J. Shkrum and David A. Ramsay,*** *2007*

MARIJUANA AND THE CANNABINOIDS, edited by ***Mahmoud A. ElSohly,*** *2006*

SUDDEN DEATHS IN CUSTODY, edited by ***Darrell L. Ross and Theodore C. Chan,*** *2006*

THE FORENSIC LABORATORY HANDBOOK: *PROCEDURES AND PRACTICE,* edited by ***Ashraf Mozayani and Carla Noziglia,*** *2006*

DRUGS OF ABUSE: *BODY FLUID TESTING,* edited by ***Raphael C. Wong and Harley Y. Tse,*** *2005*

A PHYSICIAN'S GUIDE TO CLINICAL FORENSIC MEDICINE: *SECOND EDITION,* edited by ***Margaret M. Stark,*** *2005*

FORENSIC MEDICINE OF THE LOWER EXTREMITY: *HUMAN IDENTIFICATION AND TRAUMA ANALYSIS OF THE THIGH, LEG, AND FOOT,* by ***Jeremy Rich, Dorothy E. Dean, and Robert H. Powers,*** *2005*

FORENSIC AND CLINICAL APPLICATIONS OF SOLID PHASE EXTRACTION, by ***Michael J. Telepchak, Thomas F. August, and Glynn Chaney,*** *2004*

HANDBOOK OF DRUG INTERACTIONS: *A CLINICAL AND FORENSIC GUIDE,* edited by ***Ashraf Mozayani and Lionel P. Raymon,*** *2004*

DIETARY SUPPLEMENTS: *TOXICOLOGY AND CLINICAL PHARMACOLOGY,* edited by ***Melanie Johns Cupp and Timothy S. Tracy,*** *2003*

BUPRENORPHINE THERAPY OF OPIATE ADDICTION, edited by ***Pascal Kintz and Pierre Marquet,*** *2002*

BENZODIAZEPINES AND GHB: *DETECTION AND PHARMACOLOGY,* edited by ***Salvatore J. Salamone,*** *2002*

ON-SITE DRUG TESTING, edited by ***Amanda J. Jenkins and Bruce A. Goldberger,*** *2001*

BRAIN IMAGING IN SUBSTANCE ABUSE: *RESEARCH, CLINICAL, AND FORENSIC APPLICATIONS,* edited by ***Marc J. Kaufman,*** *2001*

TOXICOLOGY AND CLINICAL PHARMACOLOGY OF HERBAL PRODUCTS, edited by ***Melanie Johns Cupp,*** *2000*

CRIMINAL POISONING: *INVESTIGATIONAL GUIDE FOR LAW ENFORCEMENT, TOXICOLOGISTS, FORENSIC SCIENTISTS, AND ATTORNEYS,* by ***John H. Trestrail, III,*** *2000*

MARIJUANA AND THE CANNABINOIDS

Edited by

Mahmoud A. ElSohly, PhD

The School of Pharmacy, The University of Mississippi;
ElSohly Laboratories Inc., Oxford, MS

HUMANA PRESS ✱ TOTOWA, NEW JERSEY

999 Riverview Drive, Suite 208
Totowa, New Jersey 07512

www.humanapress.com

Production Editor: Melissa Caravella

Cover design by Patricia F. Cleary

Cover Illustration: Medical *Cannabis* cultivar (Fig. 1, Chapter 1; *see* complete caption on p. 3).

For additional copies, pricing for bulk purchases, and/or information about other Humana titles, contact Humana at the above address or at any of the following numbers: Tel.: 973-256-1699; Fax: 973-256-8341, E-mail: orders@humanapr.com; or visit our Website: www.humanapress.com

This publication is printed on acid-free paper. ∞
ANSI Z39.48-1984 (American National Standards Institute) Permanence of Paper for Printed Library Materials.

Printed in the United States of America. 10 9 8 7 6 5 4 3 2 1

eIBSN 1-59745-947-8

Library of Congress Cataloging-in-Publication Data

Marijuana and the cannabinoids / edited by Mahmoud A. ElSohly.
p. ; cm. -- (Forensic science and medicine)
Includes bibliographical references and index.
ISBN 1-58829-456-0 (alk. paper)
1. Cannabinoids. I. ElSohly, Mahmoud A. II. Series.
[DNLM: 1. Cannabinoids. 2. Cannabis. QV 77.7 M33515 2006]
QP801.C27M355 2006
615'.7827--dc22

2006012285

Preface

Although primarily used today as one of the most prevalent illicit leisure drugs, the use of *Cannabis sativa* L., commonly referred to as marijuana, for medicinal purposes has been reported for more than 5000 years. Marijuana use has been shown to create numerous health problems, and, consequently, the expanding use beyond medical purposes into recreational use (abuse) resulted in control of the drug through international treaties.

Much research has been carried out over the past few decades following the identification of the chemical structure of THC in 1964. The purpose of *Marijuana and the Cannabinoids* is to present in a single volume the comprehensive knowledge and experience of renowned researchers and scientists. Each chapter is written independently by an expert in his/her field of endeavor, ranging from the botany, the constituents, the chemistry and pharmacokinetics, the effects and consequences of illicit use on the human body, to the therapeutic potential of the cannabinoids.

***Mahmoud A. ElSohly,* PhD**

Contents

Preface v
Contributors ix

Chapter 1

Cannabis and Natural *Cannabis* Medicines

Robert C. Clarke and David P. Watson *1*

Chapter 2

Chemistry and Analysis of Phytocannabinoids and Other *Cannabis* Constituents

Rudolf Brenneisen *17*

Chapter 3

Chemical Fingerprinting of *Cannabis* as a Means of Source Identification

Mahmoud A. ElSohly, Donald F. Stanford, and Timothy P. Murphy *51*

Chapter 4

Marijuana Smoke Condensate: *Chemistry and Pharmacology*

Hala N. ElSohly and Mahmoud A. ElSohly *67*

Chapter 5

Pharmacology of Cannabinoids

Lionel P. Raymon and H. Chip Walls *97*

Chapter 6

The Endocannabinoid System and the Therapeutic Potential of Cannabinoids

Billy R. Martin *125*

Chapter 7

Immunoassays for the Detection of *Cannabis* Abuse: *Technologies, Development Strategies, and Multilevel Applications*

Jane S-C. Tsai ***145***

Chapter 8

Mass Spectrometric Methods for Determination of Cannabinoids in Physiological Specimens

Rodger L. Foltz ***179***

Chapter 9

Human Cannabinoid Pharmacokinetics and Interpretation of Cannabinoid Concentrations in Biological Fluids and Tissues

Marilyn A. Huestis and Michael L. Smith ***205***

Chapter 10

Medical and Health Consequences of Marijuana

Jag H. Khalsa ***237***

Chapter 11

Effects of Marijuana on the Lung and Immune Defenses

Donald P. Tashkin and Michael D. Roth ***253***

Chapter 12

Marijuana and Driving Impairment

Barry K. Logan ***277***

Chapter 13

Postmortem Considerations

Steven B. Karch ***295***

Chapter 14

Cannabinoid Effects on Biopsychological, Neuropsychiatric, and Neurological Processes

Richard E. Musty ***303***

Index ***317***

Contributors

RUDOLF BRENNEISEN, PhD • Department of Clinical Research, Laboratory for Phytopharmacology, Bioanalytics and Pharmacokinetics, University of Bern, Bern, Switzerland

ROBERT C. CLARKE, BA • International Hemp Association, Amsterdam, The Netherlands

HALA N. ELSOHLY, PhD • National Center for Natural Products Research, Research Institute of Pharmaceutical Sciences, The School of Pharmacy, The University of Mississippi, Oxford, MS

MAHMOUD A. ELSOHLY, PhD • National Center for Natural Products Research, Research Institute of Pharmaceutical Sciences, The School of Pharmacy, The University of Mississippi; ElSohly Laboratories Inc., Oxford, MS

RODGER L. FOLTZ, PhD • Center for Human Toxicology, University of Utah, Salt Lake City, UT

MARILYN A. HUESTIS, PhD • Chemistry and Drug Metabolism, Intramural Research Program, National Institute on Drug Abuse, National Institutes of Health, Baltimore, MD

STEVEN B. KARCH, MD • Consultant Pathologist/Toxicologist, Berkeley, CA

JAG H. KHALSA, PhD • Chief, Medical Consequences Branch, Division of Pharmacotherapies and Medical Consequences of Drug Abuse (DPMCDA), National Institute on Drug Abuse, Bethesda, MD

BARRY K. LOGAN, PhD • Washington State Toxicologist and Director of Forensic Laboratory Services Bureau, Washington State Patrol, Seattle, WA

BILLY R. MARTIN, PhD • Louis and Ruth Harris Professor and Chair, Department of Pharmacology and Toxicology, Virginia Commonwealth University, Richmond, VA

TIMOTHY P. MURPHY, BA • ElSohly Laboratories Inc., Oxford, MS

RICHARD E. MUSTY, PhD • Department of Psychology, University of Vermont, Burlington, VT

LIONEL P. RAYMON, PharmD, PhD • Kaplan Medical, Pharmacology Chair and Department of Pathology, Miller School of Medicine, University of Miami, Miami, FL

MICHAEL D. ROTH, MD • Professor of Medicine, Division of Pulmonary and Critical Care, Department of Medicine, David Geffen School of Medicine, University of California at Los Angeles, Los Angeles, CA

MICHAEL L. SMITH, PhD, DABFT • Division of Forensic Toxicology, Office of the Armed Forces Medical Examiner, Rockville, MD

DONALD F. STANFORD, MS • National Center for Natural Products Research, Research Institute of Pharmaceutical Sciences, School of Pharmacy, The University of Mississippi, Oxford, MS

DONALD P. TASHKIN, MD • Professor of Medicine, Division of Pulmonary and Critical Care, Department of Medicine, David Geffen School of Medicine, University of California at Los Angeles, Los Angeles, CA

JANE S-C. TSAI, PhD • Director, Research and Development, Roche Diagnostics, Indianapolis, IN

H. CHIP WALLS, BS • Technical Director, Forensic Toxicology Laboratory, Miller School of Medicine, University of Miami, School of Medicine, Homestead, FL

DAVID P. WATSON • CEO, HortaPharm BV, Amsterdam, The Netherlands

Chapter 1

Cannabis and Natural *Cannabis* Medicines

Robert C. Clarke and David P. Watson

1. Introduction

Cannabis plants produce many compounds of possible medical importance. This chapter briefly explains the life cycle, origin, early evolution, and domestication of *Cannabis*, plus provides a brief history of drug *Cannabis* breeding and looks into the future of *Cannabis* as a source of medicines. *Cannabis* is among the very oldest of economic plants providing humans with fiber for spinning, weaving cloth, and making paper; seed for human foods and animal feeds; and aromatic resin containing compounds of recreational and medicinal value. Human selection for varying uses and natural selection pressures imposed by diverse introduced climates have resulted in a wide variety of growth forms and chemical compositions. Innovative classical breeding techniques have been used to improve recreational drug forms of *Cannabis*, resulting in many cannabinoid-rich cultivars suitable for medical use. The biosynthesis of cannabinoid compounds is unique to *Cannabis*, and cultivars with specific chemical profiles are being developed for diverse industrial and pharmaceutical uses.

2. Life Cycle and Ecology

Cannabis is an annual crop plant propagated from seed and grows vigorously when provided an open sunny location with light well-drained soil, ample nutrients, and water. *Cannabis* can reach up to 5 m (16 ft.) in height in a 4- to 8-month spring-to-autumn growing season. Feral *Cannabis* populations are frequently found in association with human habitation. Disturbed lands such as active and disused farm fields, roadsides, railways, trails, trash piles, and exposed riverbanks are ideal habitats for

From: *Forensic Science and Medicine: Marijuana and the Cannabinoids*
Edited by: M. A. ElSohly © Humana Press Inc., Totowa, New Jersey

wild and feral *Cannabis* because they provide open niches exposed to adequate sunlight.

Seeds usually germinate in 3–7 days. During the first 2–3 months of growth, juvenile plants respond to increasing day length with a more vigorous vegetative growth characterized by an increasing number of leaflets on each leaf. Later in the season (after the summer solstice), shorter days (actually longer nights) induce flowering and complete the life cycle. *Cannabis* begins to flower when exposed to short day lengths of 12–14 hours or less (long nights of 10–12 hours or more) depending on its latitude of origin. However, a single evening of interrupted darkness can disrupt flowering and delay maturation. Conversely, a day or two of short day length can induce flowering that may be irreversible in early-maturing varieties. If an individual plant grows with sufficient space, as in seed or resin production, flower-bearing limbs will grow from small growing points located at the base of the leaf petioles originating from nodes along the main stalk. The flowering period is characterized by leaves bearing decreasing numbers of leaflets and an accompanying change from vegetative growth and biomass accumulation to floral induction, fertilization, seed maturation, and resin production *(1)*.

Cannabis is normally dioecious (male and female flowers developing on separate plants), and the gender of each plant is anatomically indistinguishable before flowering. However, Mandolino and Ranalli *(2)* report success using random amplified polymorphic DNA analysis to identify male-specific DNA markers, and female-associated DNA polymorphisms were also described by Hong et al. *(3)*. The floral development of male and female plants varies greatly. Whereas male flowers with five petals and prominent stamens hang in loose clusters along a relatively leafless upright branch, the inconspicuous female flowers are crowded into dense clusters along with small leaflets at the base of each larger leaf along the branch (*see* Fig. 1). Pollen grains require air currents to carry them to the female flowers, resulting in fertilization and consequent seed set. Viable pollen can be carried by the wind for considerable distance *(4)*; the male plants cease shedding pollen after 2–4 weeks and usually die before the seeds in the female plants ripen. Pollen has been frozen and successfully used for seed production up to 3 years later.

The single seed in each female flower ripens in 3–8 weeks and will either be harvested, be eaten by birds or rodents, or fall to the ground, where they may germinate the following spring. This completes the natural 4- to 6-month life cycle. A large female plant can produce up to half a kilogram of seed. *Cannabis* seeds are a balanced source of essential fatty acids and easily digestible proteins and are suitable for use as whole foods and dietary supplements. Essential fatty acids have been shown to have many important physiological roles, and hemp seed oil is a valuable nutraceutical *(5)*. Recent research has confirmed that topical application of hemp seed oil is effective in treating ear, nose, and throat ailments *(6)*.

3. Field Crop Production

When industrial hemp crops are grown for fiber or seed, both male and female plants are usually left standing in the field until harvest. Most medical *Cannabis* is grown for its psychoactive resin by a different technique. In the early 1970s, a handful

Fig. 1. Medical *Cannabis* cultivars grown in the United Kingdom by GW Pharmaceuticals, which form the basis for GW's development of prescription medicines. The larger inflorescence **(A)** is a cannabidiol (CBD)-rich cultivar containing only traces of Δ^9-tetrahydrocannabinol (THC), and the smaller inflorescence **(B)** is a THC-rich cultivar containing only traces of CBD.

of North American illicit marijuana cultivators began to grow *sinsemilla* (Spanish for "without seed") marijuana that within a few years became the predominant style of North American and European marijuana production. The sinsemilla effect is achieved by eliminating male plants from the fields, leaving only the unfertilized and therefore seedless female plants to mature for later flower and/or resin harvest.* In lieu of setting seed in the earliest flowers, the female plants continue to produce additional flowers covered by resin glands, which increases the percentage of psychoactive and medically valuable Δ^9-tetrahydrocannabinol (THC) or other cannabinoids in these flowers. Yields of terpenoid-rich essential oils produced in the resin glands along with the closely related terpenophenolic cannabinoids are also significantly raised in seedless flowers *(7)*. Throughout the 1980s, the vast majority of domestically produced North American and European drug *Cannabis* was grown from seed in outdoor gardens, but during the 1990s the popularity of growing sinsemilla in greenhouses and indoors under artificial lights grew rapidly.

4. Greenhouse and Grow Room Production

Most *Cannabis* presently used for medical purposes is grown indoors under artificial lights. Modern indoor growers most often grow their own clones under halide and sodium vapor light systems set up in attics, bedrooms, or basements. Crops grown from seed are typically made up of large male and female plants that require a lot of space and exhibit a wide range of physical and biochemical characteristics. A *Cannabis* breeder relies on this variation as genetic potential for improving varieties, whereas a drug *Cannabis* producer wants a profitable and uniform crop and uses female clones to improve grow room yields. Consequently, vegetative production of female clones and the production of seedless flowers preclude the possibility of seed production and variety improvement. Vegetatively propagated crops are preferred because indoor garden space is limited, only female *Cannabis* plants produce resin of medical value, and it is both inconvenient and expensive to purchase reliable drug *Cannabis* seed. In addition, the legal systems of many nations penalize growers of more plants (vegetative, male or female) with harsher penalties. Under artificial growing conditions, crops are reproduced vegetatively by rooting cuttings of only select female plants, transplanting, and inducing flowering almost immediately so that the mature crop is short and compact. Cuttings of one plant are all genetically identical members of a single clone, so they will all respond in the same way to environmental influences and will be very similar in appearance. When environmental influences remain constant, the clone will yield serial crops of nearly identical uniform seedless females each time it is grown.

Female "mother" plants used for cutting stock must be maintained in a constantly vegetative state under 18-hour or longer day lengths or they will begin to flower. Serial cuttings can be removed, rooted, grown under long day length, and used to replace older mother plants indefinitely. If the mother plants remain free of viruses or other pathogens, there is no loss of vigor after multiple rounds of vegetative propaga-

---

*This technique was first encountered by British working in India, but we are unsure of its history prior to 1800.

tion. Serially propagated clones have been maintained for more than 20 years. Whenever flowering plants are required, small rooted cuttings (10–30 cm tall) are moved into a flowering room with a day length of 10–13 hours to mature in 7–14 weeks.*

Vegetatively produced plants can fully mature when they are less than 1 m (3 ft.) tall and form flowers from top to bottom and look like a rooted branch from a large plant grown from seed. The length of time between the induction of flowering and full maturity of the female floral clusters depends largely on the variety being grown and the day length. Some cultivars mature much more quickly than others, and plants tend to be shorter when mature than those of slower-ripening varieties. *Cannabis* plants mature faster when they are given shorter day lengths of 10 hours, but most cultivars have an optimum day length requirement for maximum flower production in the shortest time—around 12–13 hours. Under ideal environmental conditions and expert management, yields of dried flowers commonly reach 400 g/m^2 per crop cycle. As a result of multiple cropping four or five times per year, total annual yields can add up to more than 2 kg of dried flowers per square meter.

In vitro techniques combined with low temperatures would allow long-term storage of wide varieties of living germplasm and could be an important storage technique for germplasm collections and breeders. Several research groups have reported success with vegetatively reproducing and initiating shooting in undifferentiated callus tissue and rooting of branch tips. The induction of rooting in callus and branch tips is straightforward. However, inducing shoots in callus tissue has proven more problematic and needs additional improvement *(2,8)*. Further research and commercial applications of in vitro techniques are expected in the near future.

5. Resin Gland Anatomy and Development

As resin gland development commences, the medically important cannabinoids and the associated terpenes begin to appear. Although the cannabinoids are odorless, terpenes are the primary aromatic principles found in the essential oil of *Cannabis (9,10)*. Most interesting economically and medically are the cannabinoid-rich terpenoid secretions of the head cells of glandular hairs densely distributed across the myriad surfaces of the female flowers. Male plants are of no consequence in medicine production because they develop few glandular trichomes and consequently produce few cannabinoids or terpenes. Solitary resin glands most often form at the tips of slender stalks that form as extensions of the plant surface and glisten in the light. The cluster of one to two dozen glandular head cells atop each stalk secretes aromatic terpene-containing resins with very high percentages of cannabinoids (>80%) that collects in vesicles under a thin membrane surrounding the secretory head cells. The secreted resin component is in large part physically segregated from the secretory cells *(11)*. This isolates the resin from the atmosphere as well as membrane-bound enzyme systems within the secretory cells, possibly protecting the terpenes and cannabinoids from oxidative degradation and enzymatic change. At the base of each cluster of resin head

**Cannabis* breeders maintain male clones in the same way and induce them to flower whenever pollen is required to produce seed. However, males are often more difficult than females to maintain in the vegetative state.

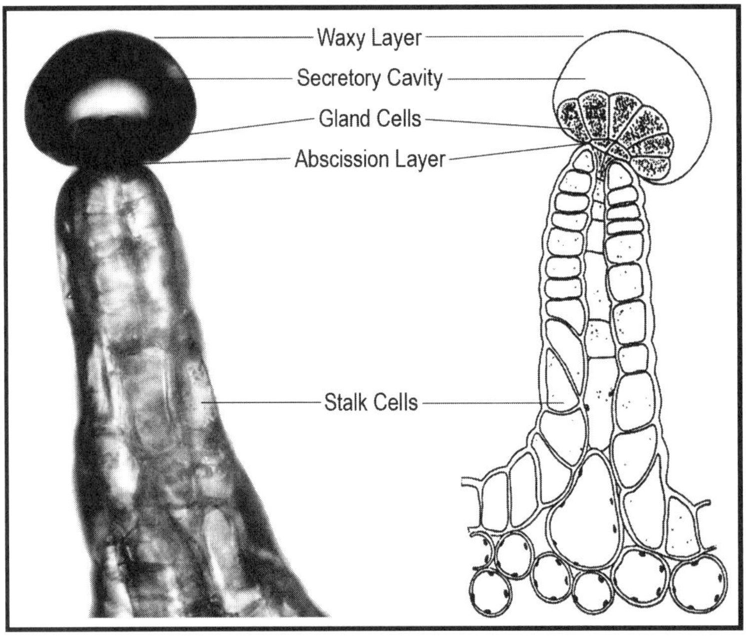

Fig. 2. Microscope photograph and drawing of a *Cannabis* resin gland. The secretory head cells are easily visible within the transparent blister of cannabinoid and terpenoid-rich resin. (Photo courtesy of David Potter, drawing from ref. *14*.)

cells lies an abscission layer allowing the resin gland and secreted resin to be easily removed by mechanical means (*see* Fig. 2). Hashish or charas is simply millions of resin glands that have been rubbed, shaken, or washed from fresh or dry plants and compressed into a dense mass *(11)*.

Resin glands containing cannabinoids and terpenes may have an adaptive significance in reducing insect and fungal attack *(12)*. However, *Cannabis* crops are subject to infestation by a wide variety of pests *(13)*, particularly under greenhouse and grow room conditions.

6. Cannabinoid and Terpenoid Biosynthesis

It is not surprising that cannabinoids are produced along with terpenoid compounds. Terpenes comprise a large group of compounds synthesized from C_{10} isoprene subunits. Monoterpenes (C_{10}) and sesquiterpenes (C_{15}) are the classes most commonly found in *Cannabis*. Terpenoids are the primary aromatic constituents of *Cannabis* resin, although they constitute only a small percentage of organic solvent extracts. Cannabinoids are terpenophenolic compounds chemically related to the terpenoid compounds as the ring structure is derived from a geranyl pyrophosphate C_{10} terpenoid subunit. Cannabinoids make up a large portion of the resin and can make up as much as 30% by weight of dried flowering tops. Cannabinoids are not significantly present in extracts prepared by steam distillation *(15)*.

Our basic understanding of the biosynthesis of the major cannabinoids comes largely from the research of Yukihiro Shoyama and colleagues at Kyushu University in Japan *(16,17)*. Cannabinoid biosynthesis begins with the incorporation of geranyl pyrophosphate (a terpenoid compound) with either a C_{10} polyketide for the propyl (C_3 side chain) or a C_{12} polyketide for the pentyl (C_5 side chain) cannabinoid series into either cannabigerovarin (CBGV) or cannabigerol (CBG), respectively. Research by Etienne de Meijer at HortaPharm B.V. in the Netherlands shows that there is a single allele (Pr) controlling the propyl pathway to CBGV and another allele (Pe) controlling the pentyl pathway to CBG. The biosyntheses of THC, cannabidiol (CBD), and cannabichromene (CBC) (or tetrahydrocannabivarin [THCV], cannabidivarin [CBDV], or cannabichromavarin [CBCV]) are controlled by a suite of three enzymes, each controlled by a single allele: T, D, and C, respectively. The three enzymes can likely use either propyl CBGV or pentyl CBG for the propyl and pentyl pathways, depending on which substrate is available. This hypothesis was verified by Flachowsky et al. *(18)*. Continued research by de Meijer et al. *(19)* (*see* Fig. 3) has shown that CBD and THC biosynthesis are controlled by a pair of co-dominant alleles, which code for isoforms of the same synthase, each with a different specificity for converting the common precursor CBG into either CBD or THC. The group also identified by random amplified polymorphic DNA analysis three chemotype-associated DNA markers that show tight linkage to chemotype and co-dominance.

7. Medical Values of Terpenes

The terpenoid compounds found in *Cannabis* resin are numerous, vary widely among varieties, and produce aromas that are often characteristic of the plant's geographic origin. Although more than 100 different named terpenes have been identified from *Cannabis*, no more than 40 known terpenes have been identified in a single plant sample, and many more remain unnamed *(11)*. Terpenes are produced via multibranched biosynthetic pathways controlled by genetically determined enzyme systems. This situation presents plant breeders with a wide range of possible combinations for developing medical *Cannabis* varieties with varying terpenoid profiles and specifically targeted medical uses. Preliminary breeding experiments confirm that the terpenoid profiles of widely differing parents are frequently reflected in the hybrid progeny.

Only recently have *Cannabis* essential oils become economically important as flavorings and fragrances *(17)*. Early *Cannabis* medicines were formulated from alcoholic whole flower or resin extracts and contained terpenes, although they were not recognized to be of medical importance. Several of the monoterpenes and sesquiterpenes found in *Cannabis* and derived from other botanical and synthetic sources are used in commercial medicines. Other as-yet-unidentified terpenes may be unique to *Cannabis*. The highly variable array of terpenoid side-chain substitutions results in a range of human physiological responses. Certain terpenes stimulate the membranes of the pulmonary system, soothe the pulmonary passages, and facilitate the absorption of other compounds *(15)*. Terpenoid compounds are incorporated into pulmonary medical products such as bronchial inhalers and cough suppressants. Casual studies indicate that when pure THC is smoked, it produces subjectively different effects than it does when combined with trace amounts of mixed *Cannabis* terpenes. Clinical trials

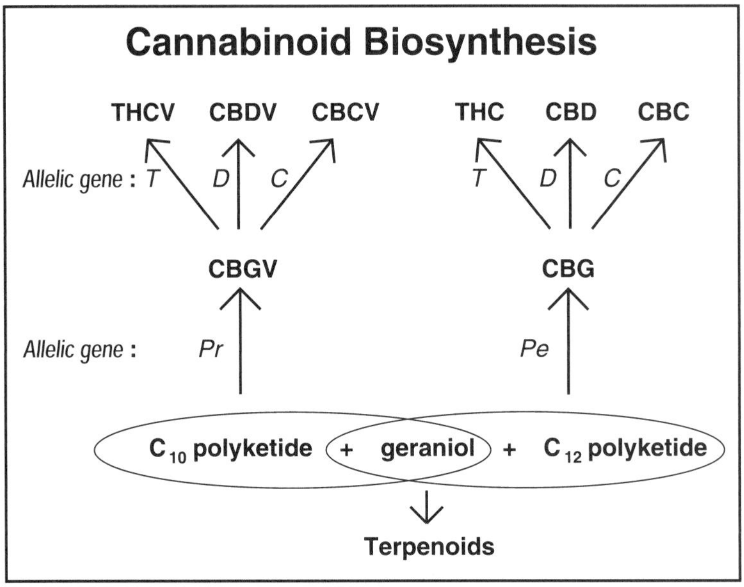

Fig. 3. Cannabinoid biosynthesis is mediated by enzymes controlled by individual genes *(16–18)*. Terpenoid biosynthesis also begins along the same general pathway by utilizing geraniol molecules directly. THCV, Δ^9-tetrahydrocannabivarin; CBVD, cannabidivarin; CBCV, cannabichromavarin; THC, Δ^9-tetrahydrocannabinol; CBD, cannabidiol; CBC, cannabichromene; CBGV, cannabigerovarin; CBG, cannabigerol. (Adapted from ref. *19*.)

using whole plant extracts of known cannabinoid content and varying terpenoid profiles will determine whether terpenoid compounds have an effect on the pharmacokinetics of the cannabinoids.

8. Cannabis's *Origin, Domestication, and Dispersal*

Cannabis originated either in the riverine valleys of Central Asia or in northern South Asia along the foothills of the Himalayas and was first cultivated in China on a large scale for fiber and seed production and soon after in India for resin production. Various cultures have traditionally used *Cannabis* for different purposes. European and East Asian societies most often used *Cannabis* for its strong fibers and nutritious seeds. Species of *Cannabis* from these regions are usually relatively low in THC (average <1% dry weight), with a CBD content averaging about twice as high.* African, Middle Eastern, South Asian, and Southeast Asian cultures used *Cannabis* widely for its psychoactive properties and to a lesser extent for fiber and food. The vast majority of races from these regions are high in psychoactive THC (often 5–10%) with widely varying CBD content (0–5%). Early on, traders spread the South Asian section of the *Cannabis* gene pool far and wide from eastern Africa to Sumatra and eventually to the

*THC is the primary psychoactive compound produced by *Cannabis*, and nonpsychoactive CBD is the other most common naturally occurring cannabinoid.

semi-tropical New World. Central Asian hashish varieties, popularly called "indicas," were introduced to the West much more recently. Drug *Cannabis* use was adopted by indigenous cultures in many of these locations, and highly psychoactive races evolved. All modern drug varieties used as medical *Cannabis* are derived from these two traditional drug variety gene pools.

Certainly, the enchanting psychological and effective medical effects realized from smoking or eating *Cannabis* resins, along with its value as a food and fiber plant, have increased predation by humans, encouraged its early domestication as a crop plant, and hastened its dispersal worldwide first into natural and, more recently, into artificial environments.

9. The Cannabis *Species Debate*

Twentieth-century taxonomists have variously characterized *Cannabis*. Although all taxonomists recognize the species *Cannabis sativa*, Small and Cronquist *(20)* subdivided *C. sativa* into two subspecies, each with two varieties based largely on cannabinoid content and traditional usage. Schultes et al. *(21)* divided *Cannabis* into three separate species: *C. sativa*, *C. indica*, and *C. ruderalis*. Several other researchers do not preserve *C. ruderalis*, but recognize both *C. sativa* and *C. indica (22,23)*. We consider *C. sativa* to include all wild, hemp, and drug *Cannabis* races, with the possible exception of those traditionally used for hashish production in Central Asia. These morphologically and chemically distinct Central Asian races deserve the separate specific name of *C. afghanica* following the variety name for *C. indica* determined by Vavilov and Bukinich *(23)*. Some Chinese races may also deserve taxonomic distinction separate from either *C. sativa* or *C. indica (24)*. Validation of these theories awaits further chemotaxonomic and genetic research.

In all of these taxonomic interpretations, *C. sativa* represents the largest and most diverse taxon and is commonly referred to by marijuana breeders and growers, as well as medical *Cannabis* users, as "sativa." *C. afghanica* is commonly known as "indica" (*see* Fig. 4). Individual plants of these hashish varieties have their own distinctive acrid organic aromas and are often rich in CBD as well as THC. The wide variety of morphological, physiological, and chemical traits encountered in *Cannabis* has proven very attractive to plant breeders for years.

10. Drug Cannabis *Breeding*

During the early 1960s, marijuana cultivation came to North America. At first, *Cannabis* seeds found in illicit shipments of marijuana were simply casually sown by curious smokers. Early marijuana cultivators tried any available seed in their efforts to grow potent plants outdoors that would consistently mature before killing frosts. Because most imported marijuana contained seeds, many possibilities were available. Early-maturing northern Mexican varieties proved to be the most favored, as they consistently matured at northern latitudes. The legendary domestic *Cannabis* varieties of the early and mid-1970s (such as Polly and Haze) resulted from crosses between early-maturing Mexican or Jamaican races and more potent, but later-maturing, Panamanian, Colombian, and Thai races.

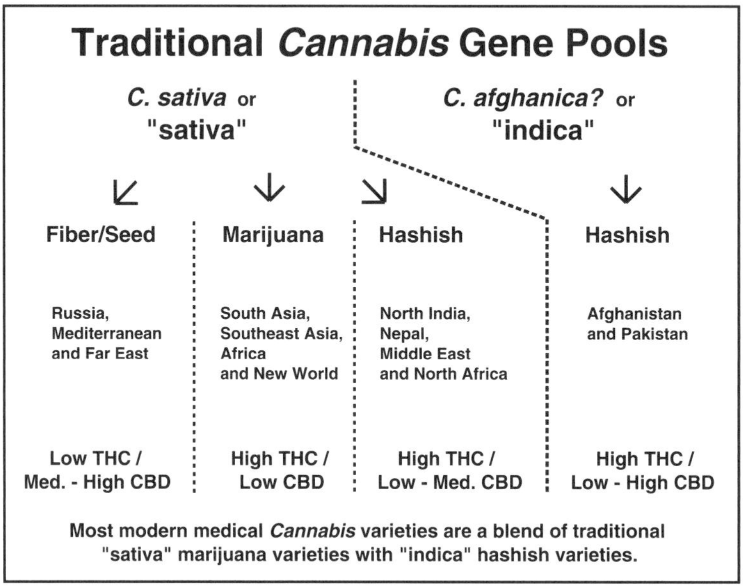

Fig. 4. The four major *Cannabis* gene pools originate either from *C. sativa,* which comprises the vast majority of naturally occurring hemp and drug landraces (adapted from ref. *25*) or from *C. afghanica* from Central Asia, which has become a component in many modern drug *Cannabis* cultivars *(11).* THC, Δ^9-tetrahydrocannabinol; CBD, cannabidiol.

Initially, the new *Cannabis* varieties were aimed at outdoor growing. Soon others were specially developed for greenhouse or artificial light growing, where the plants are sheltered from autumn cold and the growing season can be extended by manipulating day length, allowing later-maturing varieties to finish. Once varieties that would mature under differing conditions were available, pioneering marijuana breeders continued selections for potency (high THC content with low CBD content) followed by the aesthetic considerations of flavor, aroma, and color. Continued inbreeding of the original favorable crosses resulted in some of the "super-sativas" of the 1970s, such as Original Haze, Purple Haze, Pollyanna, Eden Gold, Three Way, Maui Wowie, Kona Gold, and Big Sur Holy Weed.

11. The Introduction of Indica

Indica plants are characterized as short and bushy with broad, dark green leaves, which make them somewhat harder to see from afar. They nearly always mature quite early outdoors, from late August to early October, often stand only 1–2 m (3–6 ft.) tall at maturity, and produce copious resin-covered flowers and leaflets. At least several dozen introductions of indica were made during the middle to late 1970s. Afghani No.1 and Hindu Kush were among the early indica introductions that gained notoriety and are still available today. Following the Soviet invasion of Afghanistan in 1979, many additional introductions were made from Afghanistan and northwestern Pakistan.

Marijuana breeders intentionally crossed varieties of early-maturing indica with their later-maturing sativa varieties to produce early-maturing hybrid crosses (matings of parents from different gene pools), and soon the majority of cultivators began to grow the newly popular indica × sativa hybrids. Many of the indica × sativa hybrids were vigorous growers, matured earlier, yielded well, and were very potent. Skunk No. 1 is a good example of a hybrid expressing predominantly sativa traits, and Northern Lights is a good example of a hybrid expressing predominantly indica traits. By the early 1980s, the vast majority of all domestic sinsemilla in North America had likely received some portion of its germplasm from the indica gene pool, and it had become difficult to find the preindica, pure sativa varieties that had been so popular only a few years earlier.

However, the negative characteristics of reduced potency (lower THC content); slow, flat, sedative, dreary effect (high CBD content); skunky, acrid aroma; and harsh taste quickly became associated with many indica × sativa hybrids. To consumers, who often prefer sativas, indica has not proven itself to be as popular as it is with growers. Also, the dense, tightly packed floral clusters of indica tend to hold moisture and to develop gray mold (*Botrytis*), for which the plants have little natural resistance. Mold causes significant losses, especially in outdoor and glasshouse crops, and was rarely a problem when only pure *C. sativa* varieties were grown. In addition, fungal contamination of medical *Cannabis* could prove a serious threat to pulmonary or immunocompromised patients. Although consumers and commercial cultivators of the late 1970s initially accepted indica enthusiastically, serious breeders of the late 1980s began to view indica with more skepticism. Although indica may currently appear to be a growing bane for *Cannabis* connoisseurs, it has certainly been a big boon for the average consumer, bringing more potent and medically effective *Cannabis* to a wider audience. Indica × sativa hybrids have proven to be well adapted to indoor cultivation where mold is rarely a problem. Indica × sativa varieties mature quickly (60–80 days of flowering), allowing four to five harvests per year, and can yield up to 100 g of dry flowers on plants only 1 m (3 ft.) tall. *C. sativa* varieties are too gangly and tall and take too long to mature to make them desirable for the indoor grower. On the other hand, sativas have unique cannabinoid and terpenoid profiles producing effects considered superior by many medical *Cannabis* users.

Political pressure on marijuana cultivators across North America forced many drug *Cannabis* breeders to relocate to the Netherlands, where the political climate was less threatening. During the 1980s, several marijuana seed companies appeared in the Netherlands, where cultivation of *Cannabis* for seed production and the sale of seeds were tolerated. To North American and European cultivators, this meant increased availability of exotic high-quality drug *Cannabis* seeds and presented yet more possibilities to find varieties that were the most medically effective for individual indications and patients. *Cannabis* seed sales continue in the Netherlands today.

12. Advances in Medical Cannabis *Research*

Cannabis available to the medical user comes in two commonly available types. Marijuana (domestically produced or imported *Cannabis* flowers) is nearly always grown from high-THC varieties (up to 30% dry weight in trimmed female flowers) and contains very little CBD. Very high THC with negligible CBD profiles of modern sinsemilla varieties result from marijuana growers sampling single plants and making seed selections from vigorous individuals with high levels of psychoactivity. Unique individuals may also be vegetatively propagated, thereby fixing the high-THC genotype in the clonal offspring.

Commercially available imported hashish or charas (compressed *Cannabis* resin) is collected from varieties that are predominantly THC (up to 10%) but that often contain up to 5% CBD as well. Imported hashish is produced by bulk processing large numbers of plants. Growers rarely make seed selections from individual, particularly potent plants, and therefore without human intervention the CBD content tends to be closer to that of THC. Hashish cultivars are usually selected for resin quantity rather than potency, so the farmer chooses plants and saves seeds by observing which ones produce the most resin, unaware of whether it contains predominantly THC or CBD. Populations grown from imported indica seeds contain approx 25% plants that are rich in CBD with little THC, 50% that contain moderate amounts of both CBD and THC, and 25% that contain little CBD and are rich in THC.* Marijuana breeders utilized only the high-THC indica individuals in crosses, thereby promoting high THC synthesis and suppressing CBD.

CBD is suspected of having modifying physiological and psychological effects on the primary psychoactive compound THC, and in a medical setting it may also have useful modulating effects on THC or valuable effects of its own. However, analytical surveys of 80 recreational and medical *Cannabis* varieties in the Netherlands *(26)* and 47 samples in California *(27)* show that nearly every sample contained predominantly THC with little if any CBD or other cannabinoids. Higher levels of THC (and other medically effective cannabinoid and terpenoid compounds) in medical *Cannabis* are healthier for patients using smoked *Cannabis* because they can smoke less to achieve the same dosage and effect. Recently developed mechanical resin-collecting techniques combined with high-potency Western cultivars are used to make very potent and pure hashish of more than 50% THC and almost no CBD (*see* Fig. 5).

Proponents of medical *Cannabis*, especially traditional hashish users, claim that the additional benefits of herbal preparations are a result, at least in part, of the presence of other cannabinoids such as CBD. Because THC (with traces of CBD) is the prominent cannabinoid found in most domestically produced North American and European marijuana and hashish, how will medical users gain legitimate legal access to other potentially effective cannabinoids?

13. The Future of Medical CANNABIS

Cannabis breeders are continually searching for new sources of exotic germplasm and will develop new varieties that will prove particularly effective as medicines.

*The ratio of THC to CBD usually approached 1:1 in populations unselected for cannabinoid content, and the amounts of cannabinoids are rather low. Industrial hemp varieties have been selected for unnaturally low levels of THC (European Union regulations stipulate <0.3% dry weight) and much higher levels of CBD, whereas sinsemilla varieties have been selected for unnaturally high levels of THC (>20% dry weight) at the expense of CBD.

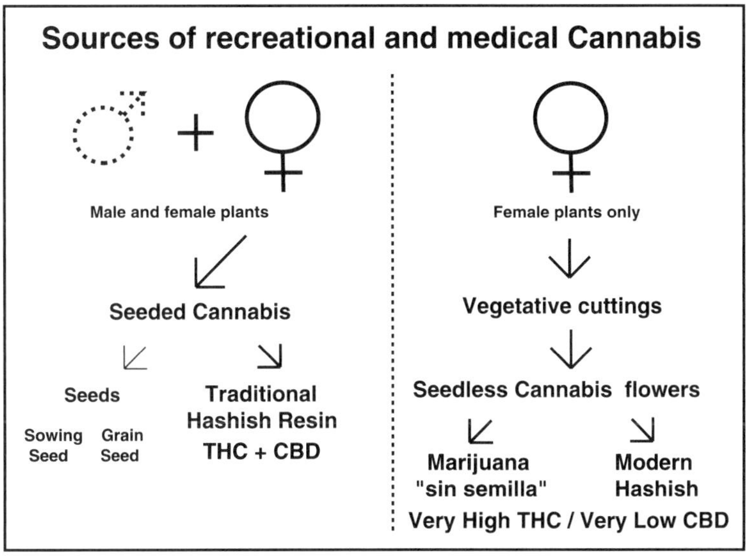

Fig. 5. Both recreational and medical *Cannabis* typically originate from either seeded plants used primarily for traditional hashish production or seedless plants grown primarily for "sinsemilla" marijuana and occasionally for modern hashish production. THC, Δ^9-tetrahydrocannabinol; CBD, cannabidiol.

Pure indica varieties are still highly prized breeding stock, and new indica introductions from Central Asia are occasionally received. Sativa varieties from Mexico, South Africa, and Korea are gaining favor with breeders because they mature early but do not suffer from the drawbacks of many indicas. Recently, *Cannabis* breeders have become more interested in variations in subjective effects between different clones and are developing varieties with enhanced medical efficacy based on feedback from medical *Cannabis* users.

Genetic modification has also reached *Cannabis*. Researchers in Scotland have successfully transferred genes for gray mold resistance to an industrial hemp variety *(28)*. Because *Botrytis* is one of the leading pests of *Cannabis*, causing crop loss and contaminating medical supplies, the transfer of resistance into medical varieties would be of great value. In addition, other agronomically valuable traits may also be transferred to *Cannabis*, such as additional pest resistance, increased yields of medically valuable compounds, tolerance of environmental extremes, and sexual sterility. However, so far the acceptance of genetically modified (GM) organisms has been timid. The European Union, for example, has installed strict regulations to prevent the accidental release of GM crop plants, and production of GM *Cannabis* in the European Union may be impractical. *Cannabis* presents a particularly high risk for transmitting genetically modified genes to industrial hemp crops and weedy *Cannabis* because it is wind-pollinated. If sterile female GM clones could be developed and used for production, then gene transfer would be blocked. Genes coding for cannabinoid biosynthesis might also be transferred from *Cannabis* to less politically sensitive organisms.

GW Pharmaceuticals Ltd. in the United Kingdom is engaged in the development of prescription medicines derived from *Cannabis* and, as part of its research program to develop novel cannabinoid medicines, supports an ongoing breeding project to develop high-yielding *Cannabis* cultivars of known cannabinoid profile. The aims of this research are to create varieties that produce only one of the four major cannabinoid compounds (e.g., THC, CBD, CBC, CBG, or their propyl homologs) as well as selected varieties with consistently uniform mixed cannabinoid and terpenoid profiles. These uniform profiles allow for the formulation of nonsmoked medicinal products, which can meet the strict quality standards of international regulatory authorities. A sublingual spray application of plant-derived THC and CBD began clinical trials for relief of multiple sclerosis-associated symptomology in 1999. These clinical trials have gone on to include patients with neuropathic pain and cancer pain.

14. Conclusion

Cannabis has had a long association with humans, and anecdotal evidence for its medical efficacy is plentiful. Since the 1970s, modern North American and European drug *Cannabis* varieties have resulted largely from crosses made by clandestine breeders between South Asian sativa marijuana varieties that spread early throughout South and Southeast Asia, Africa, and the New World and Central Asian indica hashish varieties. These hybrid varieties are now commonly used in Western societies for medical *Cannabis*.

Largely as a response to increased law enforcement and the limited commercial availability of high-quality medical grade *Cannabis*, patients growing their own plants and self-medicating is a trend rapidly spreading across North America, Europe, and around the globe. The political climate surrounding medical *Cannabis* legislation has become more informed, compassionate, and lenient. *Cannabis* cultivation for personal medical use will eventually be legalized or tolerated in many jurisdictions, if not by the public openly favoring legalization, then by increasing governmental awareness of the inefficiency inherent in attempted prohibition of a popular and effective medicine.

Pharmaceutical research companies are developing new natural cannabinoid formulations and delivery systems that will meet government regulatory requirements. As clinical trials prove successful and the understanding of *Cannabis*'s efficacy and safety as a modern medicine spreads, patients can look forward to a steady flow of new *Cannabis* medicines providing effective relief from a growing number of indications.

References

1. Clarke, R. C. (1981) *Marijuana Botany*, Berkeley: Ronin Publishing.
2. Mandolino, G. and Ranalli, P. (1999) Advances in biotechnological approaches for hemp breeding and industry, in *Advances in Hemp Research.* (Ranalli, P. ,ed.), Haworth Press, New York, pp. 185–211.
3. Hong, S., Song, S-J., and Clarke, R. C. (2003) Female-associated DNA polymorphisms of hemp (*Cannabis sativa* L.) *J. Indust. Hemp* **1,** 5–9.
4. Small, E. and Antle, T. (2003) A preliminary study of pollen dispersal in Cannabis sativa in relation to wind direction. *J. Indust. Hemp* **8,** 37–50.
5. Deferne, J-L. and Pate, D. W. (1996) Hemp seed oil: a source of valuable essential fatty acids. *J. Int.Hemp Assoc.* **3,** 1, 4–7.

6. Grigoriev, O. V. (2002) Application of hempseed (*Cannabis sativa* L.) oil in treatment of ear, nose and throat (ENT) disorders. *J. Indust. Hemp* **7,** 5–15.
7. Meier, C. and Mediavilla, V. (1998) Factors influencing the yield and the quality of hemp (*Cannabis sativa* L.) essential oil. *J. Int. Hemp Assoc.* **5,** 16–20.
8. Liu, Y. and Tang, X. (1984) Green seedling of hemp acquired by tissue culture. *China's Fibre Crops* **2,** 19, 29 [in Chinese].
9. Hendriks, H., Malingre, T. M., Batterman, S., and Bos, R. (1978) The essential oil of *Cannabis sativa* L. *Pharm. Weekbl.* **113,** 413–424.
10. Ross, R. A. and ElSohly, M. A. (1996) The volatile oil composition of fresh and air-dried buds of *Cannabis sativa L. J. Nat. Prod.* **59,** 49–51.
11. Clarke, R. C. (1998) *Hashish!*, Red Eye Press, Los Angeles.
12. Pate, D. W. (1994) Chemical ecology of *Cannabis. J. Int. Hemp Assoc.* **1,** 29, 32–37.
13. McPartland, J., Clarke, R. C., and Watson, D. P. (2000) *Hemp Diseases and Pests,* CAB International, Wallingford, UK.
14. Briosi, G. and Tognini, F. (1894) Intorno alla anatomia della canapa (*Cannabis sativa* L.) parte prima—organi sessual, *Atti dell' Instituto Botanico di Pavia*, Serie I, Vol. 3.
15. McPartland, J. and Mediavilla, V. (2002) *Cannabis and Cannabinoids: Pharmacology and Therapeutic Potential (*Grotenhermen, F. and Russo, E., eds.), Haworth Integrative Healing Press, New York, pp. 401–409.
16. Taura, F., Morimoto, S., Shoyama, Y., and Mechoulam, R. (1995) First direct evidence for the mechanism of delta-1-tetrahydrocannabinol acid biosynthesis. *J. Am. Chem. Soc.* **117,** 9766–9767.
17. Taura, F., Morimoto, S., and Shoyama, Y. (1996) Purification and characterization of cannabidiolic-acid synthase from *Cannabis sativa* L. Biochemical analysis of a novel enzyme that catalyzes the oxidocyclization of cannabigerolic acid to cannabidiolic acid. *J. Biol. Chem.* **271,** 17411–17416.
18. Flachowsky, H., Schumann, E., Weber, W. E., and Peil, A. (2000) AFLP-marker for male plants of hemp (Cannabis sativa L.) Poster presented at the 3rd Bioresource Hemp Symposium, Wolfsburg, Germany, September 13–16.
19. de Meijer, E. P. M., Bagatta, M., Carboni, A., et al. (2003) The inheritance of chemical phenotype in *Cannabis sativa* L. *Genetics* **163,** 335–346.
20. Small, E. and Cronquist, A. (1976) A practical and natural taxonomy for *Cannabis. Taxon* **25,** 405–435.
21. Schultes, R. E., Klein, W. M., Plowman, T., and Lockwood, T. E. (1974) *Cannabis*: an example of taxonomic neglect. *Botanical Museum Leaflets, Harvard University* **23,** 337–364.
22. Serebriakova, T. I. (1940) Fiber plants, in *Flora of Cultivated Plants.* Vol.4, Part1 (Wulff, E. V., ed.), State Printing Office, Moscow and Leningrad [in Russian].
23. Vavilov, N. and Bukinich, D. D. (1929) Agricultural Afghanistan. *Bull. Appl. Bot. Genet. Plant Breed.*Supp. **33,** 378–382, 474, 480, 584–585, 604.
24. Hillig, K. W. and Mahlberg, P. G. (2004) Genetic evidence for speciation in *Cannabis* (Cannabaceae). *Genet. Resources Crop Evol.* **52,** 161–180.
25. de Meijer, E. P. M. (1999) *Cannabis* germplasm resources, in *Advances in Hemp Research* (Ranalli, P., ed.), Haworth Press, New York, pp. 133–151.
26. HortaPharm, personal communication (1998) HortaPharm BV develops industrial Cannabis cultivars and provided the starting materials GW Pharmaceuticals breeding project in the United Kingdom.
27. Gierenger, D. (1999) Medical *Cannabis* potency testing. *Bull. Multidisc. Assoc. Psychedel. Stud.* **9,** 20–22.
28. MacKinnon, L. (2003) Genetic transformation of *Cannabis sativa* Linn: a multi purpose fibre crop, doctoral thesis, University of Dundee, Scotland.

Chapter 2

Chemistry and Analysis of Phytocannabinoids and Other *Cannabis* Constituents

Rudolf Brenneisen

1. The Chemistry of Phytocannabinoids and Noncannabinoid-Type Constituents

1.1. Phytocannabinoids

1.1.1. Introduction

The *Cannabis* plant and its products consist of an enormous variety of chemicals. Some of the 483 compounds identified are unique to *Cannabis*, for example, the more than 60 cannabinoids, whereas the terpenes, with about 140 members forming the most abundant class, are widespread in the plant kingdom. The term "cannabinoids" represents a group of C_{21} terpenophenolic compounds found until now uniquely in *Cannabis sativa* L. *(1)*. As a consequence of the development of synthetic cannabinoids (e.g., nabilone *[2]*, HU-211 [dexanabinol; ref. *{3}*, or ajulemic acid [CT-3; ref. *4*]) and the discovery of the chemically different endogenous cannabinoid receptor ligands ("endocannabinoids," e.g., anandamide, 2-arachidonoylglycerol) *(5,6)*, the term "phytocannabinoids" was proposed for these particular *Cannabis* constituents *(7)*.

1.1.2. Chemistry and Classification

So far, 66 cannabinoids have been identified. They are divided into 10 subclasses *(8–10)* (*see* Table 1).

From: *Forensic Science and Medicine: Marijuana and the Cannabinoids*
Edited by: M. A. ElSohly © Humana Press Inc., Totowa, New Jersey

Table 1
Cannabinoids

Compound	Structure	Main pharmacological characteristics
	Cannabigerol class	
Cannabigerolic acid (CBGA)	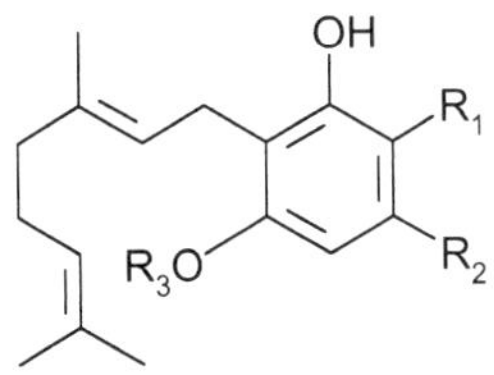 R_1 = COOH, R_2 = C_5H_{11}, R_3 = H	Antibiotic
Cannabigerolic acid monomethylether (CBGAM)	R_1 = COOH, R_2 = C_5H_{11}, R_3 = CH_3	
Cannabigerol (CBG)	R_1 = H, R_2 = C_5H_{11}, R_3 = H	Antibiotic Antifungal Anti-inflammatory Analgesic
Cannabigerol monomethylether (CBGM)	R_1 = H, R_2 = C_5H_{11}, R_3 = CH_3	
Cannabigerovarinic acid (CBGVA)	R_1 = COOH, R_2 = C_3H_7, R_3 = H	
Cannabigerovarin (CBGV)	R_1 = H, R_2 = C_3H_7, R_3 = H	

(continued)

1. Cannabigerol (CBG) type: CBG was the first cannabinoid identified *(11)*, and its precursor cannabigerolic acid (CBGA) was shown to be the first biogenic cannabinoid formed in the plant *(12)*. Propyl side-chain analogs and a monomethyl ether derivative are other cannabinoids of this group.
2. Cannabichromene (CBC) type: Five CBC-type cannabinoids, mainly present as C5-analogs, have been identified.
3. Cannabidiol (CBD) type: CBD was isolated in 1940 *(13)*, but its correct structure was first elucidated in 1963 by Mechoulam and Shvo *(14)*. Seven CBD-type cannabinoids with C1 to C5 side chains have been described. CBD and its corresponding acid CBDA

Table 1 *(continued)*

Compound	Structure	Main pharmacological characteristics
	Cannabichromene class	
Cannabichromenic acid (CBCA)	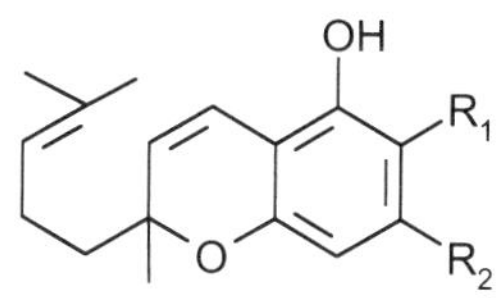 R_1 = COOH, R_2 = C_5H_{11}	
Cannabichromene (CBC)	R_1 = H, R_2 = C_5H_{11}	Anti-inflammatory Antibiotic Antifungal Analgesic
Cannabichromevarinic acid (CBCVA)	R_1 = COOH, R_2 = C_3H_7	
Cannabichromevarin (CBCV)	R_1 = H, R_2 = C_3H_7	
	Cannabidiol class	
Cannabidiolic acid (CBDA)	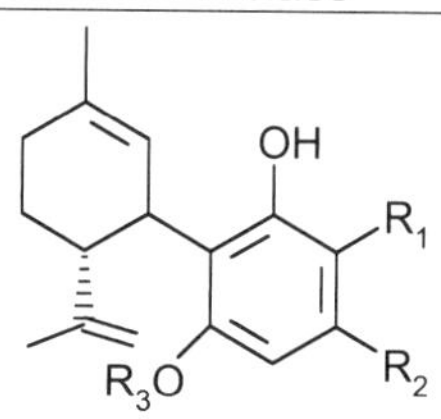 R_1 = COOH, R_2 = C_5H_{11}, R_3 = H	Antibiotic
Cannabidiol (CBD)	R_1 = H, R_2 = C_5H_{11}, R_3 = H	Anxiolytic Antipsychotic Analgesic Anti-inflammatory Antioxydant Antispasmodic

(continued)

are the most abundant cannabinoids in fiber-type *Cannabis* (industrial hemp). Isolated in 1955, CBDA was the first discovered cannabinoid acid.

4. Δ^9-Tetrahydrocannabinol (THC) type: Nine THC-type cannabinoids with C1 to C5 side chains are known. The major biogenic precursor is the THC acid A, whereas

Table 1 ***(continued)***

Compound	Structure	Main pharmacological characteristics
Cannabidiol monomethylether (CBDM)	R_1 = H, R_2 = C_5H_{11}, R_3 = CH_3	
Cannabidiol-C_4 (CBD-C_4)	R_1 = H, R_2 = C_4H_9, R_3 = H	
Cannabidivarinic acid (CBDVA)	R_1 = COOH, R_2 = C_3H_7, R_3 = H	
Cannabidivarin (CBDV)	R_1 = H, R_2 = C_3H_7, R_3 = H	
Cannabidiorcol (CBD-C_1)	R_1 = H, R_2 = CH_3, R_3 = H	
Delta-9-tetrahydrocannabinol class		
Delta-9-tetrahydrocannabinolic acid A (THCA-A)	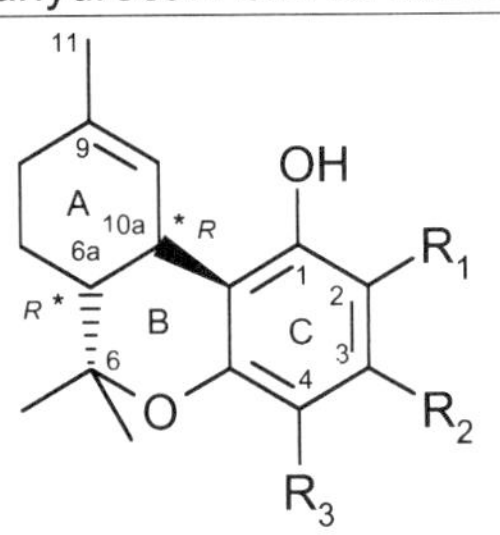 R_1 = COOH, R_2 = C_5H_{11}, R_3 = H	
Delta-9-tetrahydrocannabinolic acid B (THCA-B)	R_1 = H, R_2 = C_5H_{11}, R_3 = COOH	

(continued)

THC acid B is present to a much lesser extent. THC is the main psychotropic principle; the acids are not psychoactive. THC (6a,10a-*trans*-6a,7,8,10a-tetrahydro-6,6,9-trimethyl-3-pentyl-6H-dibenzo[*b,d*]pyran-1-ol) was first isolated in 1942 *(15)*, but the correct structure assignment by Gaoni and Mechoulam took place in 1964 *(16)*.

Table 1 *(continued)*

Compound	Structure	Main pharmacological characteristics
Delta-9-tetrahydrocannabinol (THC)	R_1 = H, R_2 = C_5H_{11}, R_3 = H	Euphoriant Analgesic Anti-inflammatory Antioxidant Antiemetic
Delta-9-tetrahydrocannabinolic acid-C_4 (THCA-C_4)	R_1 = COOH, R_2 = C_4H_9, R_3 = H or R_1 = H, R_2 = C_4H_9, R_3 = COOH	
Delta-9-tetrahydrocannabinol-C_4 (THC-C_4)	R_1 = H, R_2 = C_4H_9, R_3 = H	
Delta-9-tetrahydrocannabivarinic acid (THCVA)	R_1 = COOH, R_2 = C_3H_7, R_3 = H	
Delta-9-tetrahydrocannabivarin (THCV)	R_1 = H, R_2 = C_3H_7, R_3 = H	Analgesic Euphoriant
Delta-9-tetrahydrocannabiorcolic acid (THCA-C_1)	R_1 = COOH, R_2 = CH_3, R_3 = H or R_1 = H, R_2 = CH_3, R_3 = COOH	
Delta-9-tetrahydrocannabiorcol (THC-C_1)	R_1 = H, R_2 = CH_3, R_3 = H	

(continued)

5. Δ^8-THC type: Δ^8-THC and its acid precursor are considered as THC and THC acid artifacts, respectively. The 8,9 double-bond position is thermodynamically more stable than the 9,10 position. Δ^8-THC is approx 20% less active than THC.

Table 1 ***(continued)***

Compound	Structure	Main pharmacological characteristics
Delta-7-*cis*-iso-tetrahydrocannabivarin	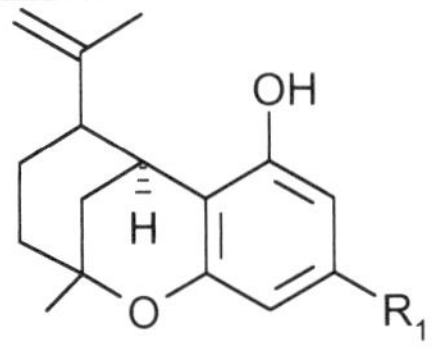 $R_1 = C_3H_7$	
Delta-8-tetrahydrocannabinol class		
Delta-8-tetrahydrocannabinolic acid (Δ^8-THCA)	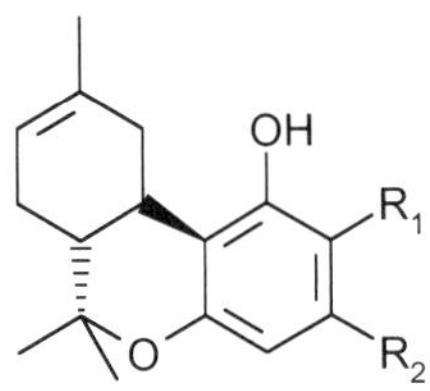 $R_1 = COOH$, $R_2 = C_5H_{11}$	
Delta-8-tetrahydrocannabinol (Δ^8-THC)	$R_1 = H$, $R_2 = C_5H_{11}$	Similar to THC (less potent)
Cannabicyclol class		
Cannabicyclolic acid (CBLA)	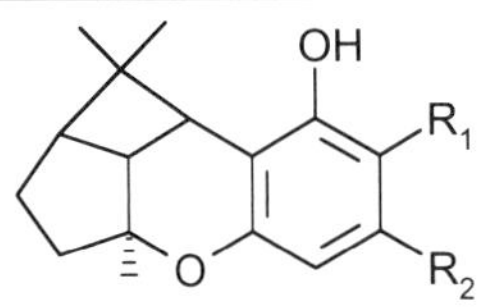 $R_1 = COOH$, $R_2 = C_5H_{11}$	
Cannabicyclol (CBL)	$R_1 = H$, $R_2 = C_5H_{11}$	
Cannabicyclovarin (CBLV)	$R_1 = H$, $R_2 = C_3H_7$	

(continued)

6. Cannabicyclol (CBL) type: Three cannabinoids characterized by a five-atom ring and C_1-bridge instead of the typical ring A are known: CBL, its acid precursor, and the C_3 side-chain analog. CBL is known to be a heat-generated artifact from CBC.
7. Cannabielsoin (CBE) type: Among the five CBE-type cannabinoids, which are artifacts formed from CBD, are CBE and its acid precursors A and B.

Table 1 ***(continued)***

Compound	Structure	Main pharmacological characteristics
	Cannabielsoin class	
Cannabielsoic acid A (CBEA-A)	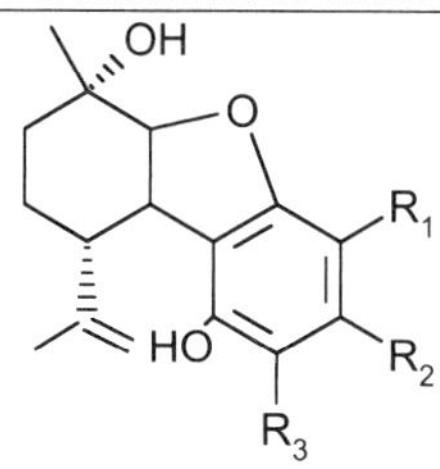 R_1 = COOH, R_2 = C_5H_{11}, R_3 = H	
Cannabielsoic acid B (CBEA-B)	R_1 = H, R_2 = C_5H_{11}, R_3 = COOH	
Cannabielsoin (CBE)	R_1 = H, R_2 = C_5H_{11}, R_3 = H	
	Cannabinol and cannabinodiol class	
Cannabinolic acid (CBNA)	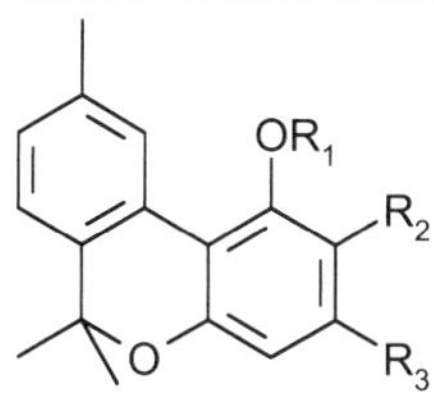 R_1 = H, R_2 = COOH, R_3 = C_5H_{11}	
Cannabinol (CBN)	R_1 = H, R_2 = H, R_3 = C_5H_{11}	Sedative Antibiotic Anticonvulsant Anti-inflammatory

(continued)

8. Cannabinol (CBN) and Cannabinodiol (CBND) types: Six CBN- and two CBND-type cannabinoids are known. With ring A aromatized, they are oxidation artifacts of THC and CBD, respectively. Their concentration in *Cannabis* products depends on age and storage conditions. CBN was first named in 1896 by Wood et al. *(17)* and its structure elucidated in 1940 *(18)*.

Table 1 ***(continued)***

Compound	Structure	Main pharmacological characteristics
Cannabinol methylether (CBNM)	$R_1 = CH_3$, $R_2 = H$, $R_3 = C_5H_{11}$	
Cannabinol-C_4 (CBN-C_4)	$R_1 = H$, $R_2 = H$, $R_3 = C_4H_9$	
Cannabivarin (CBV)	$R_1 = H$, $R_2 = H$, $R_3 = C_3H_7$	
Cannabinol-C_2 (CBN-C_2)	$R_1 = H$, $R_2 = H$, $R_3 = C_2H_5$	
Cannabiorcol (CBN-C_1)	$R_1 = H$, $R_2 = H$, $R_3 = CH_3$	
Cannabinodiol (CBND)	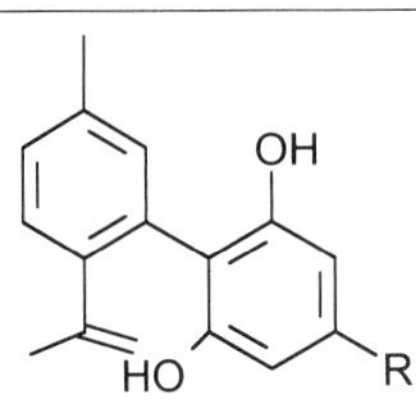 $R = C_5H_{11}$	
Cannabinodivarin (CBVD)	$R = C_3H_7$	

(continued)

9. Cannabitriol (CBT) type: Nine CBT-type cannabinoids have been identified, which are characterized by additional OH substitution. CBT itself exists in the form of both isomers and the racemate, whereas two isomers (9-a- and 9-b-hydroxy) of CBTV were identified. CBDA tetrahydrocannabitriol ester (ester at 9-hydroxy group) is the only reported ester of any naturally occurring cannabinoids.
10. Miscellaneous types: Eleven cannabinoids of various unusual structure, e.g., with a furano ring (dehydrocannabifuran, cannabifuran), carbonyl function (cannabichromanon, 10-oxo-δ-6a-tetrahydrocannabinol), or tetrahydroxy substitution (cannabiripsol), are known.

Table 1 *(continued)*

Compound	Structure	Main pharmacological characteristics
	Cannabitriol class	
Cannabitriol (CBT)	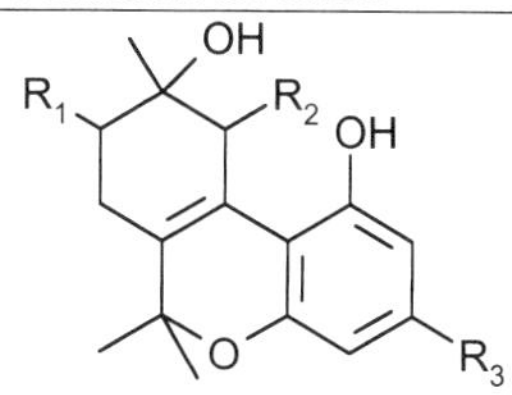 $R_1 = H, R_2 = OH, R_3 = C_5H_{11}$	
10-Ethoxy-9-hydroxy-delta-6a-tetrahydrocannabinol	$R_1 = H, R_2 = OC_2H_5, R_3 = C_5H_{11}$	
8,9-Dihydroxy-delta-6a-tetrahydrocannabinol	$R_1 = OH, R_2 = H, R_3 = C_5H_{11}$	
Cannabitriolvarin (CBTV)	$R_1 = H, R_2 = OH, R_3 = C_3H_7$	
Ethoxy-cannabitriolvarin (CBTVE)	$R_1 = H, R_2 = OC_2H_5, R_3 = C_3H_7$	
	Miscellaneous cannabinoids class	
Dehydrocannabifuran (DCBF)	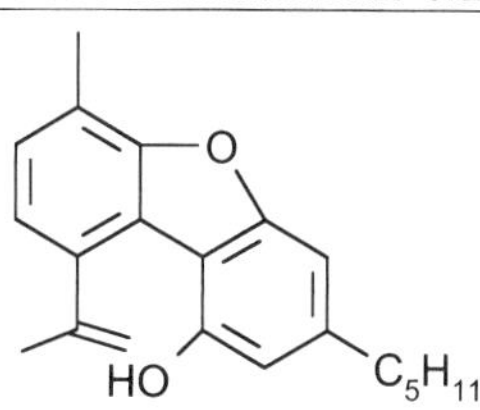	

(continued)

1.1.3. THC Potency Trends

From 1980 to 1997, a total of 35,213 samples of confiscated *Cannabis* products (*Cannabis*, hashish, hashish oil) representing more than 7717 tons seized in the United States were analyzed by gas chromatography (GC) *(19)*. The mean THC concentration increased from less than 1.5% in 1980 to 4.2% in 1997. The maximum levels found were 29.9 and 33.1% in marijuana and sinsemilla *Cannabis*, respectively. Hashish

Table 1 *(continued)*

Compound	Structure	Main pharmacological characteristics
Cannabifuran (CBF)	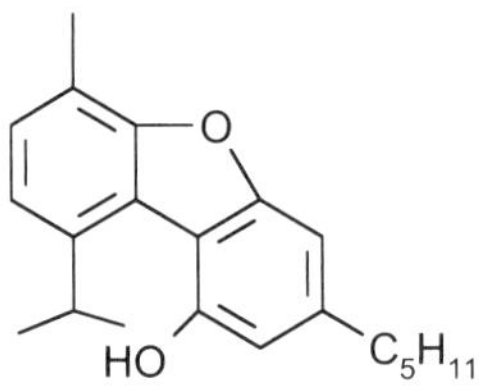	
Cannabichromanon (CBCN)	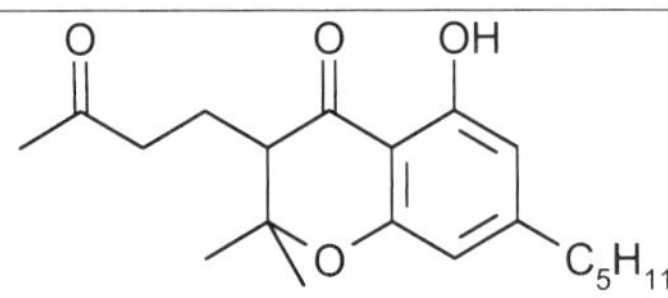	
Cannabicitran (CBT)	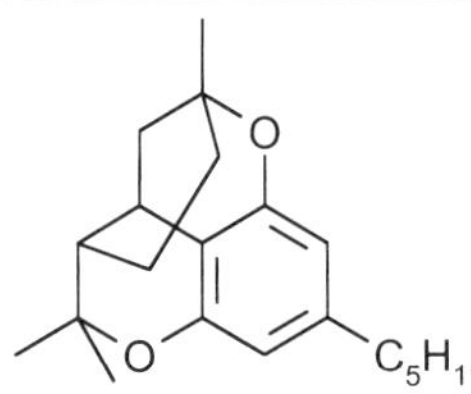	
10-Oxo-delta-6a-tetrahydrocannabinol (OTHC)	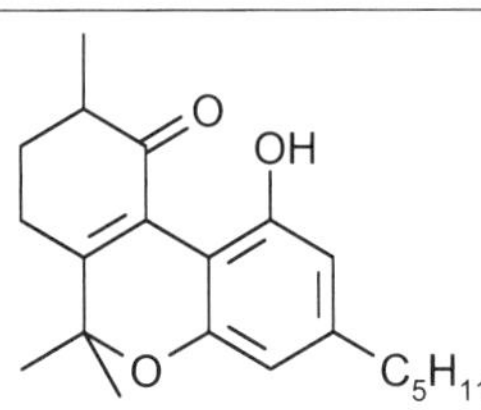	
Delta-9-*cis*-tetrahydrocannabinol (cis-THC)	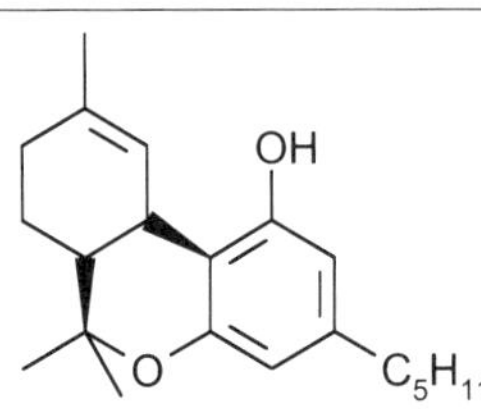	

(continued)

and hashish oil showed no particular potency trend. The highest THC concentrations measured were 52.9 and 47.0%, respectively. Two studies performed in Switzerland from 1981 to 1985 *(20)* and 2002 to 2003 *(21)* found mean THC concentrations in marijuana samples of 1.4 and 12.9%, respectively. Maximum levels were 4.8 and 28.4%, respectively. Reasons for this enormous increase in potency include progress in breed-

Table 1 ***(continued)***

Compound	Structure	Main pharmacological characteristics
3,4,5,6-Tetrahydro-7-hydroxy-alpha-alpha-2-trimethyl-9-n-propyl-2,6-methano-2H-1-benzoxocin-5-methanol (OH-iso-HHCV)	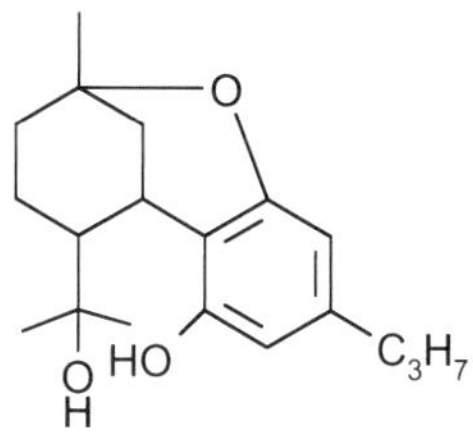	
Cannabiripsol (CBR)	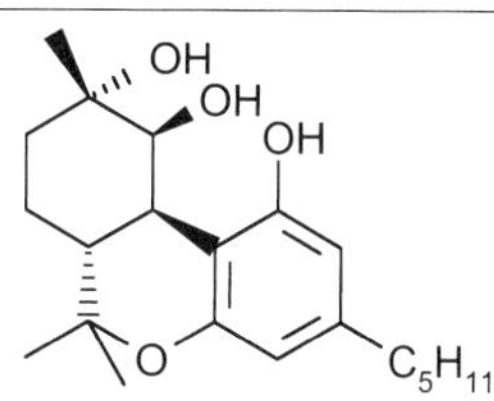	
Trihydroxy-delta-9-tetrahydrocannabinol (triOH-THC)	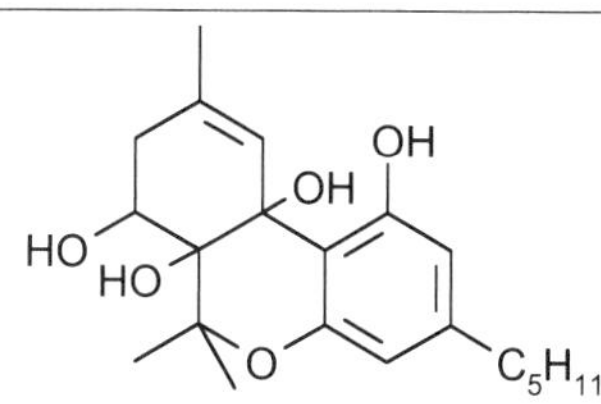	

ing, the tendency to cultivate under indoor conditions, and the worldwide access to and exchange of seeds originating from high-THC cultivars via the Internet *(22)*.

1.1.4. THC in Hemp Seed Products

The presence of THC in hemp seed products is predominantly the result of external contact of the seed hull with cannabinoid-containing resins in bracts and leaves during maturation, harvesting, and processing *(23–25)*. The seed kernel is not entirely free of THC but contains, depending on the hemp variety, less than 0.5 μg/g. Studies on hemp oil conducted in the United States, Germany, and Switzerland have shown THC levels from 11 to 117, 4 to 214, and up to 3568 μg/g, respectively *(24,26–28)*. These high levels were attributed to seeds from THC-rich, "drug-type" varieties, and the lack of adequate cleaning procedures. In recent years, more careful seed drying and cleaning have considerably lowered the THC content of seeds and oil available in the United States *(23,24)*. However, oils and hulled seeds containing 10–20 and 2–3 μg/g THC, respectively, are still found on the US market.

1.2. Noncannabinoid-Type Constituents

1.2.1. Terpenoids

The typical scent of *Cannabis* results from about 140 different terpenoids. Isoprene units (C_5H_8) form monoterpenoids (C_{10} skeleton), sesquiterpenoids (C_{15}), diterpenoids (C_{20}), and triterpenoids (C_{30}; *see* Table 2). Terpenoids may be acyclic, monocyclic, or polycyclic hydrocarbons with substitution patterns including alcohols, ethers, aldehydes, ketones, and esters. The essential oil (volatile oil) can easily be obtained by steam distillation or vaporization. The yield depends on the *Cannabis* type (drug, fiber) and pollination; sex, age, and part of the plant; cultivation (indoor, outdoor etc.); harvest time and conditions; drying; and storage *(29–31)*. For example, fresh buds from an Afghani variety yielded 0.29% essential oil *(32)*. Drying and storage reduced the content from 0.29 after 1 week and 3 months to 0.20 and 0.13%, respectively *(32)*. Monoterpenes showed a significantly greater loss than sesquiterpenes, but none of the major components completely disappeared in the drying process. About 1.3 L of essential oil per ton resulted from freshly harvested outdoor-grown *Cannabis*, corresponding to about 10 L/ha *(29)*. The yield of nonpollinated ("sinsemilla") *Cannabis* at 18 L/ha was more than twofold compared with pollinated *Cannabis* (8 L/ha) *(30)*. Sixty-eight components were detected by GC and GC/mass spectrometry (MS) in fresh bud oil distilled from high-potency, indoor-grown *Cannabis (32)*. The 57 identified constituents were 92% monoterpenes, 7% sesquiterpenes, and approx 1% other compounds (ketones, esters; refs. *9* and *32*). The dominating monoterpenes were myrcene (67%) and limonene (16%). In the essential oil from outdoor-grown *Cannabis*, the monoterpene concentration varied between 47.9 and 92.1% of the total terpenoid content *(29)*. The sesquiterpenes ranged from 5.2 to 48.6%. The most abundant monoterpene was β-myrcene, followed by *trans*-caryophyllene, α-pinene, *trans*-ocimene, and α-terpinolene. "Drug-type" *Cannabis* generally contained less caryophyllene oxide than "fiber-type" *Cannabis*. Even in "drug-type" *Cannabis*, the THC content of the essential oil was not more than 0.08% *(29)*. In the essential oil of five different European *Cannabis* cultivars, the dominating terpenes were myrcene (21.1–35.0%), α-pinene (7.2–14.6%), α-terpinolene (7.0–16.6%), *trans*-caryophyllene (12.2.–18.9%), and α-humulene (6.1–8.7%; ref. *33*). The main differences between the cultivars were found in the contents of α-terpinolene and α-pinene.

Other terpenoids present only in traces are sabinene, α-terpinene, 1,8-cineole (eucalyptol), pulegone, γ-terpinene, terpineol-4-ol, bornyl acetate, α-copaene, alloaromadendrene, viridiflorene, β-bisabolene, γ-cadinene, *trans*-β-farnesene, *trans*-nerolidol, and β-bisabolol *(29,32,34)*.

1.2.2. Hydrocarbons

The 50 known hydrocarbons detected in *Cannabis* consist of *n*-alkanes ranging from C_9 to C_{39}, 2-methyl-, 3-methyl-, and some dimethyl alkanes *(10,35)*. The major alkane present in an essential oil obtained by extraction and steam distillation was the *n*-C_{29} alkane nonacosane (55.8 and 10.7%, respectively). Other abundant alkanes were heptacosane, 2,6-dimethyltetradecane, pentacosane, hexacosane, and hentriacontane.

Table 2
Terpenoids of the Essential Oil From *Cannabis*

Compound	Class[a]	Structure	Percentage	
			Ref. *32*	Ref. *29*
Myrcene	M	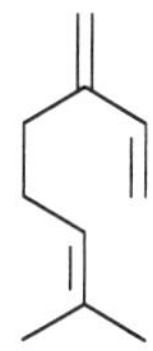	32.9–67.1	29.4–65.8
Limonene	M	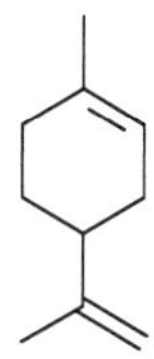	16.3–17.7	0.9–1.5
Linalool	M	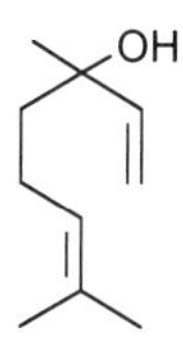	2.8–5.1	0.002
trans-Ocimene	M	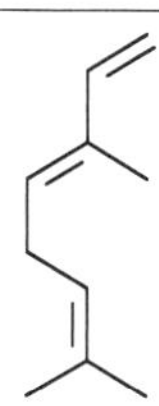		2.3–5.7

(continued)

1.2.3. Nitrogen-Containing Compounds

Cannabis sativa L. is one of the rare psychotropic plants in which the central nervous system activity is not linked to particular alkaloids. However, two spermidine-type alkaloids (*see* Table 3) have been identified among the more than 70 nitrogen-containing constituents. Other nitrogenous compounds found are the quartenary bases choline, trigonelline, muscarine, isoleucine betaine, and neurine. Among the 8 amides are, for example, *N-trans*-feruloyltyramine, *N-p*-coumaroyltyramine, and *N-trans*-caffeoyltyramine (*see* Table 4). Five lignanamide derivatives have been isolated, including cannabisin A, B, C, and D (*see* Table 5).

Twelve simple amines, including piperidine, hordenine, methylamine, ethylamine, and pyrrolidine, are known. The three proteins detected are edestin, zeatin, and

Table 2 *(continued)*

Compound	Class[a]	Structure	Percentage	
			Ref. *32*	Ref. *29*
beta-Pinene	M	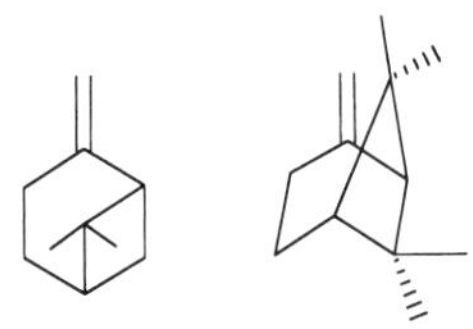	2.2–2.5	1.3–1.6
alpha-Pinene	M	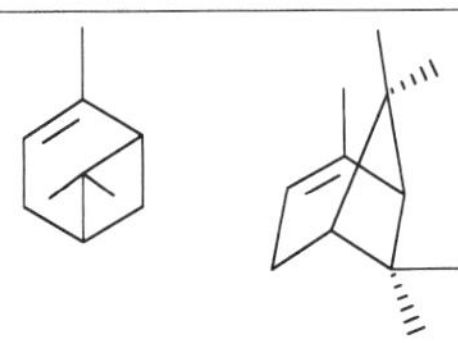	1.1–1.6	6.0–8.4
beta-Caryophyllene	S	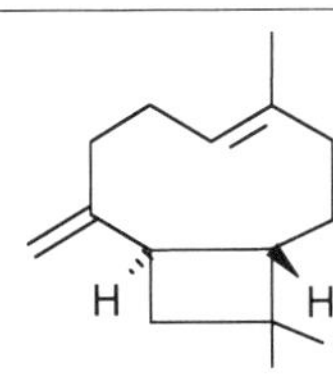	1.3–5.5	19.5–31.4
delta-3-Carene	M	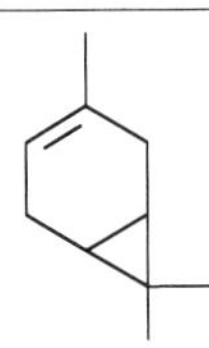		0.8–1.0
trans-gamma-Bisabolene	S	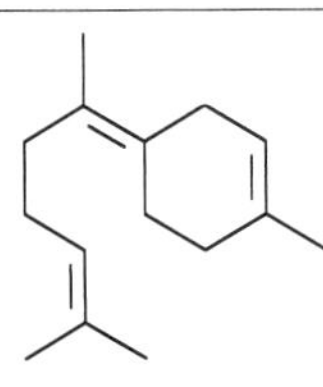	0.7–3.9	

(continued)

zeatinnucleoside; the six enzymes are edestinase, glucosidase, polyphenoloxydase, peptidase, peroxidase, and adenosine-5-phosphatase. The 18 amino acids are of a structure common for plants.

1.2.4. Carbohydrates

Common sugars are the predominant constituents of this class. Thirteen monosacharides (fructose, galactose, arabinose, glucose, mannose, rhamnose, etc.), two disaccharides (sucrose, maltose), and five polysaccharides (raffinose, cellulose, hemicellulose, pectin, xylan) have been identified so far. In addition, 12 sugar alcohols

Table 2 *(continued)*

Compound	Class[a]	Structure	Percentage	
			Ref. *32*	Ref. *29*
trans-alpha-Farnesene	S	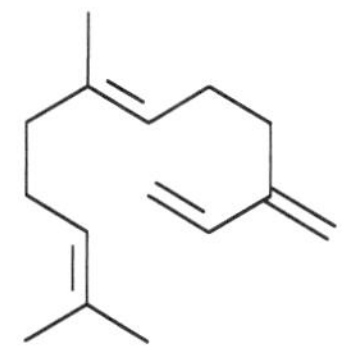	0.6–2.7	
beta-Fenchol	M	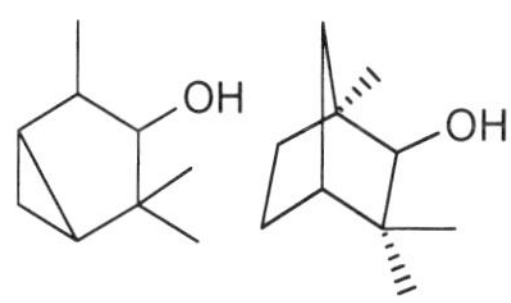	0.4–1.0	
beta-Phellandrene	M	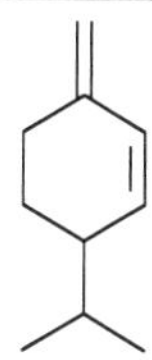		0.4
alpha-Humulene (alpha-Caryophyllene)	S	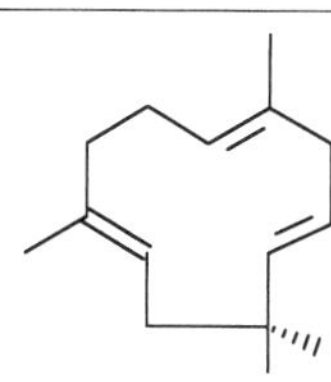	0.3–2.1	3.3–3.4
Guajol	S	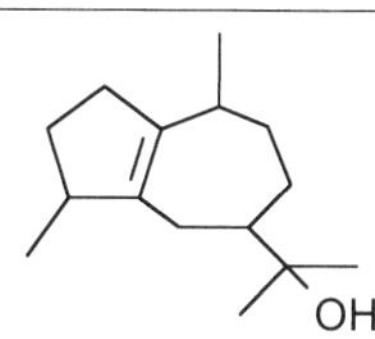	0.3–1.8	
alpha-Guaiene	S	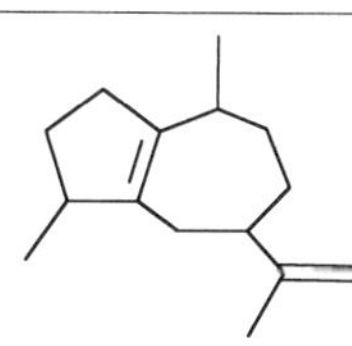	0.3–1.2	

(continued)

and cyclitols (mannitol, sorbitol, glycerol, inositol, quebrachitol, etc.) and two amino sugars (galactosamine, glucosamine) were found.

1.2.5. Flavonoids

Twenty-three commonly occurring flavonoids have been identified in *Cannabis*, existing mainly as C-/O- and *O*-glycosides of the flavon- and flavonol-type aglycones

Table 2 ***(continued)***

Compound	Class[a]	Structure	Percentage	
			Ref. *32*	Ref. *29*
alpha-Eudesmol	S	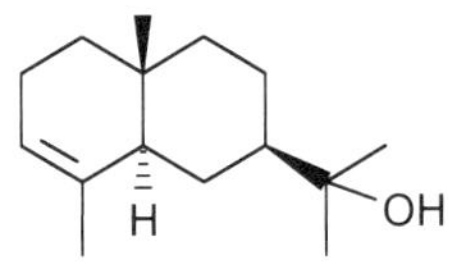	0.2–1.4	
Terpinolene	M	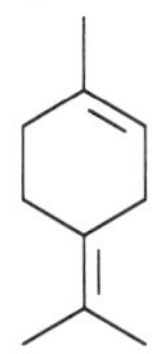	0.2–1.1	3.4–5.6
alpha-Selinene	S	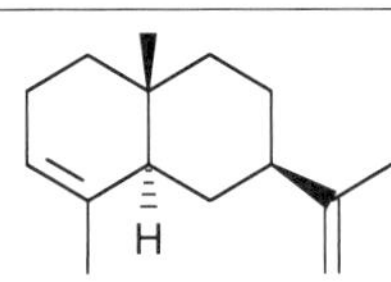	0.2–0.7	
alpha-Terpineol	M	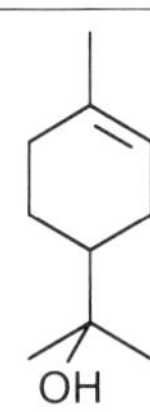	0.2–0.5	
Fenchone	M	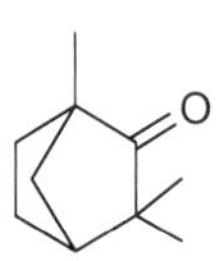 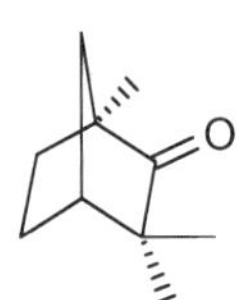	0.2–0.4	
Camphene	M	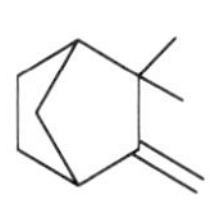 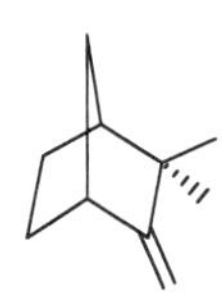	0.2–0.4	

(continued)

apigenin, luteolin, quercetin, and kaempferol (*see* Table 6; ref. *36*). Orientin, vitexin, luteolin-7-*O*-glucoside, and apigenin-7-*O*-glucoside were the major flavonoid glycosides present in low-THC *Cannabis* cultivars *(37)*. The cannflavins A and B are unique to *Cannabis (38,39)*.

1.2.6. Fatty Acids

A total of 33 different fatty acids, mainly unsaturated fatty acids, have been identified in the oil of *Cannabis* seeds. Linoleic acid (53–60% of total fatty acids), α-

Table 2 *(continued)*

Compound	Class[a]	Structure	Percentage	
			Ref. *32*	Ref. *29*
cis-Sabinene hydrate	M	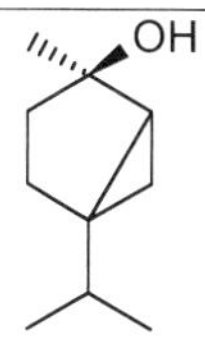	0.2–0.5	
cis-Ocimene	M	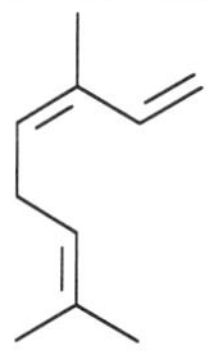	traces–0.2	0.2–0.3
beta-Eudesmol	S	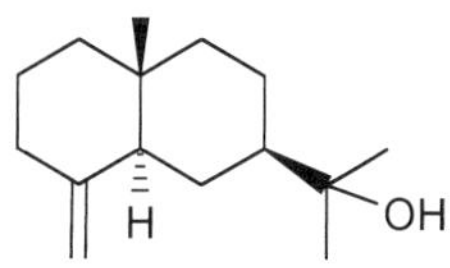	0.1–1.1	
beta-Selinene	S	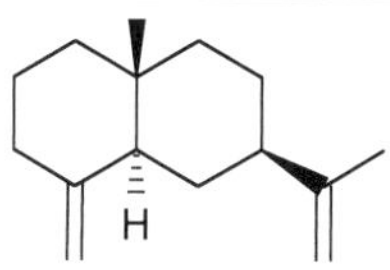	0.1–0.6	0.2–0.4
alpha-*trans*-Bergamotene	S	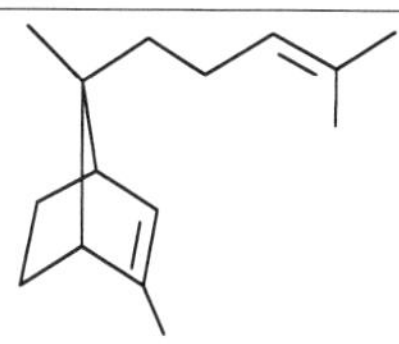	0.1–0.5	0.4–0.6
gamma-Eudesmol	S	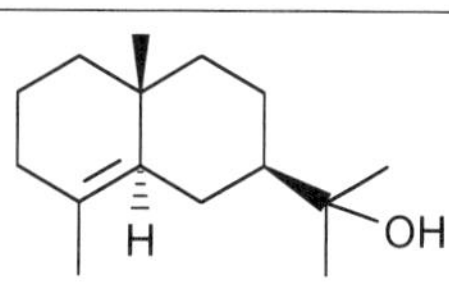	0.1–0.5	
Borneol	M	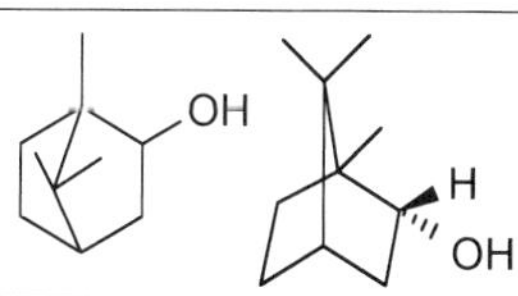	0.1–0.3	0.008

(continued)

linolenic acid (15–25%), and oleic acid (8.5–16%) are most common (*see* Table 7) *(40)*. Other unsaturated fatty acids are γ-linolenic acid (1–4%), stearidonic acid (0.4–2%), eicosanoic acid (<0.5%), *cis*-vaccenic acid, and isolinolenic acid. The saturated fatty acids are palmitic acid (6–9%), stearic acid (2–3.5%), arachidic acid (1–3%), behenic acid (<0.3%), myristic acid, lignoceric acid, caproic acid, heptanoic acid, ca-

Table 2 *(continued)*

Compound	Class[a]	Structure	Percentage Ref. *32*	Percentage Ref. *29*
cis-beta-Farnesene	S	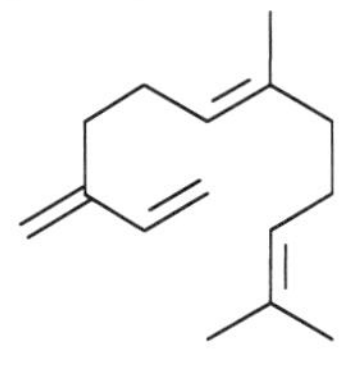	0.1–0.3	0.6–0.9
gamma-Curcumene	S	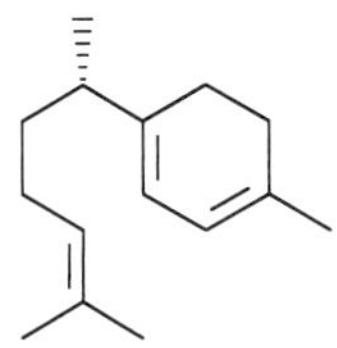	0.1–0.3	
cis-gamma-Bisabolene	S	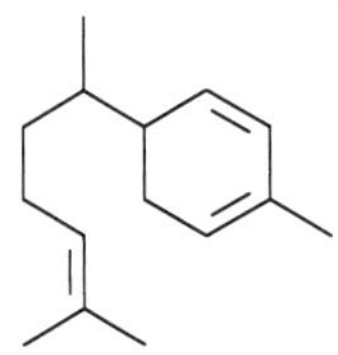	0.1–0.3	
alpha-Thujene	M	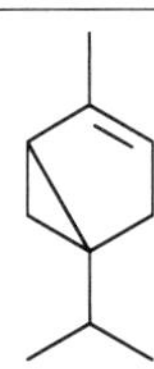	0.1–0.2	
epi-alpha-Bisabolol	S	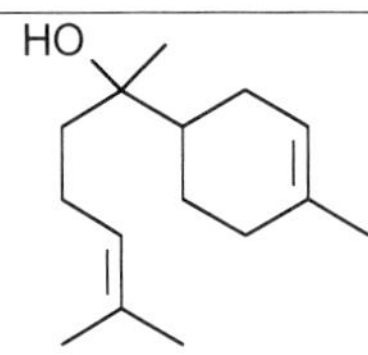	0.1–1.2	
Ipsdienol	M	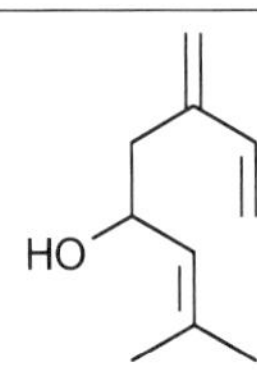	traces–0.1	

(continued)

prylic acid, pelargonic acid, capric acid, lauric acid, margaric acid, and isoarachidic acid. The fatty acid spectrum of *Cannabis* seeds does not significantly vary in oil produced from drug (THC) or low-THC (hemp, fiber) type *Cannabis (41)*. For the THC content of *Cannabis* seeds and seed oil, *see* Section 1.1.4.

Table 2 ***(continued)***

Compound	Class[a]	Structure	Percentage	
			Ref. *32*	Ref. *29*
alpha-Ylangene	S	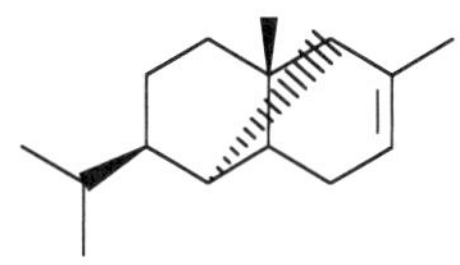	traces–0.1	
beta-Elemene	S	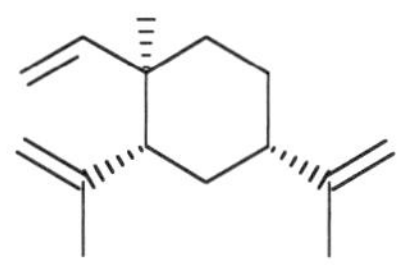	traces–0.2	
alpha-*cis*-Bergamotene	S	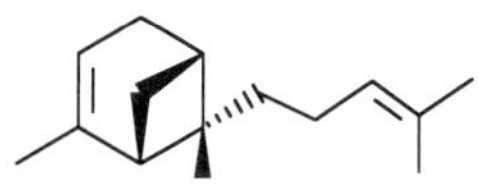	traces–0.6	
gamma-Muurolene	S	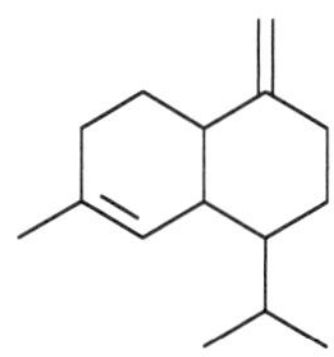	traces–0.1	
alpha-Cadinene	S	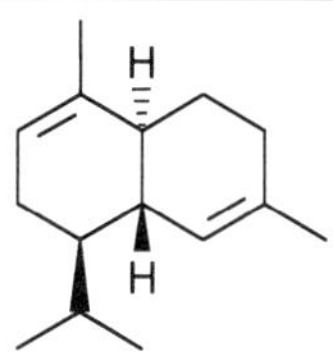	traces–0.1	
alpha-Longipinene	S	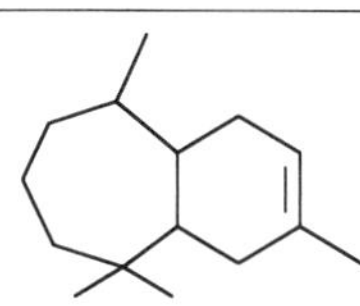	traces–0.1	
Caryophyllene oxide	S	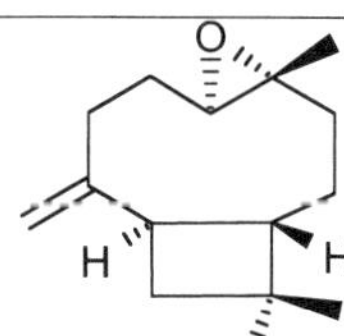	traces–0.8	

[a]M, monoterpene; S, sesquiterpene.

1.2.7. Noncannabinoid Phenols

Thirty-four noncannabinoid phenols are known: nine with spiro-indan-type structure (e.g., cannabispiran, isocannabispiran), nine dihydrostilbenes (e.g., cannabistilbene-

Table 3
Spermidine Alkaloids

Compound	Structure
Cannabisativine	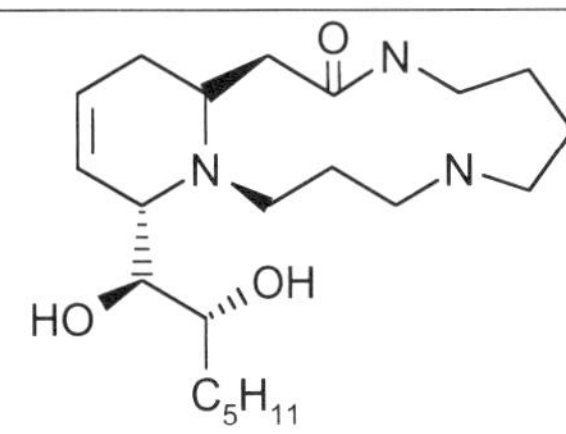
Anhydrocannabisativine	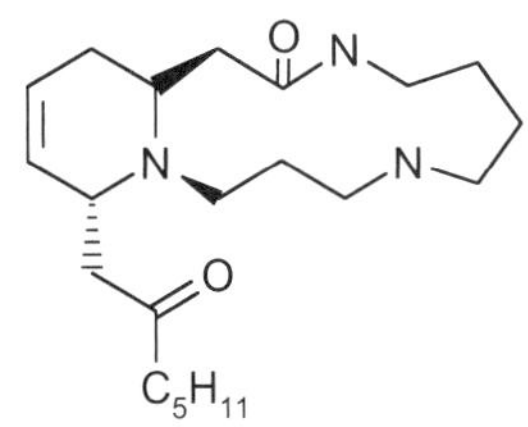

Table 4
Amides

Compound	Structure
N-trans-Feruloyltyramine	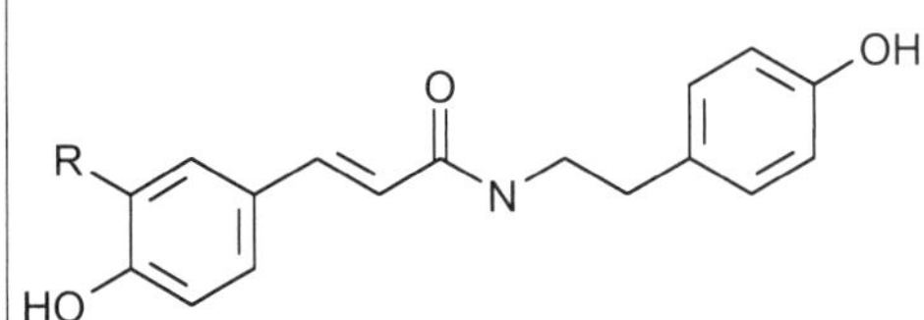 R = OCH_3
N-p-Coumaroyltyramine	R = H
N-trans-Caffeoyltyramine	R = OH

I, -II), three dihydrophenanthrenes (e.g., cannithrene-1, -2), and six phenols, phenol methylethers, and phenolic glycosides (phloroglucinol glucoside; *see* Table 8).

1.2.8. Simple Alcohols, Aldehydes, Ketones, Acids, Esters, and Lactones

Seven alcohols (e.g., methanol, ethanol, 1-octene-3-ol), 12 aldehydes (e.g., acetaldehyde, isobutyraldehyde, pentanal), 13 ketones (e.g., acetone, heptanone-2, 2-methyl-2-heptene-6-one), and 21 acids (e.g., arabinic acid, azealic acid, gluconic acid) have been identified.

Table 5
Lignanamide Derivatives

Compound	Structure
Grossamide	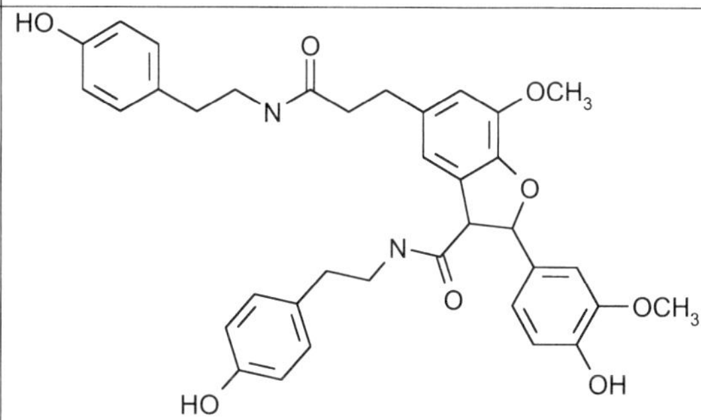
Cannabisin-A	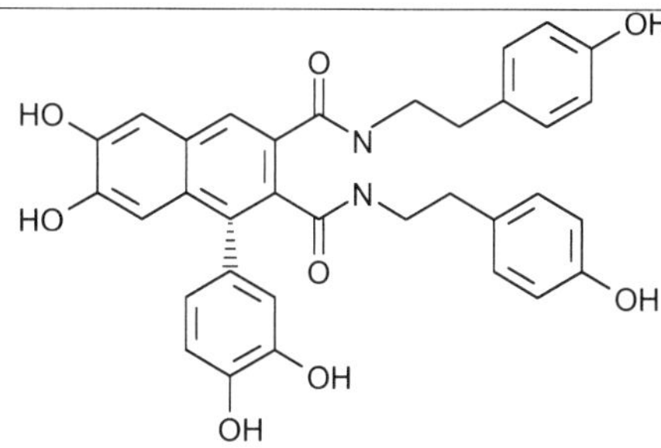
Cannabisin-B	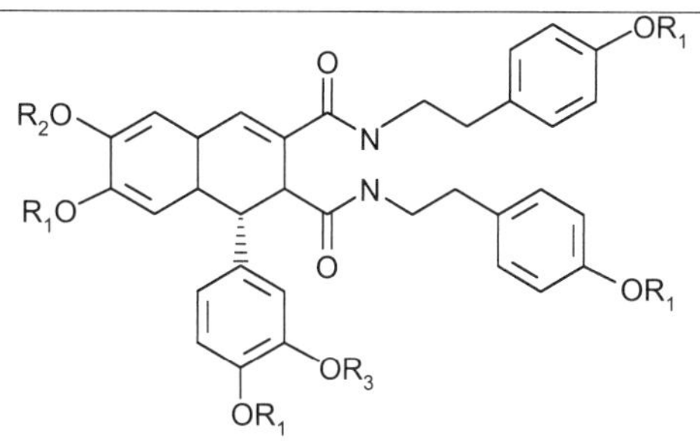 $R_1 = R_2 = R_3 = H$
Cannabisin-C	$R_1 = R_3 = H$, $R_2 = CH_3$
Cannabisin-D	$R_1 = H$, $R_2 = R_3 = CH_3$

1.2.9. Other

Among the 11 phytosterols known are campesterol, ergosterol, β-sitosterol, and stigmasterol. Vitamin K is the only vitamin found in *Cannabis*, whereas carotene and xanthophylls are reported pigments. Eighteen elements were detected (e.g., Na, K, Ca, Mg, Fe, Cu, Mn, Zn, Hg).

Table 6
C- and O-Glycosides Forming Flavonoid Aglycones and C-Glycosides

Compound	Structure
Apigenin	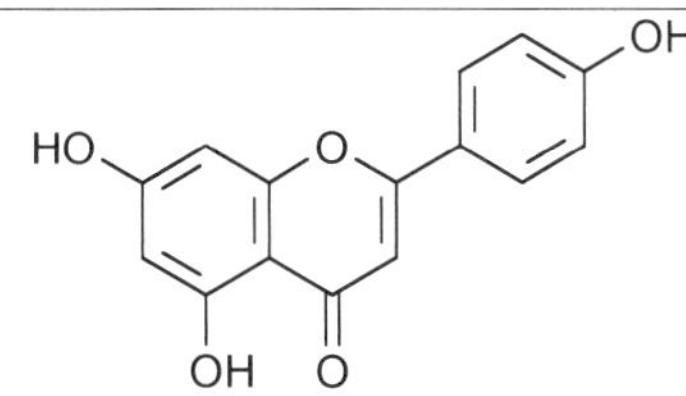
Luteolin	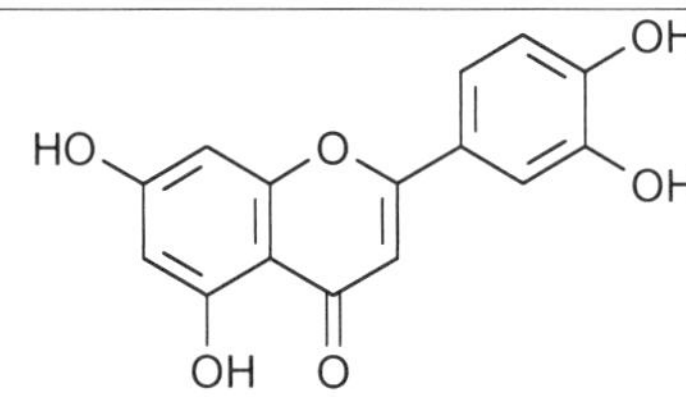
Kaempferol	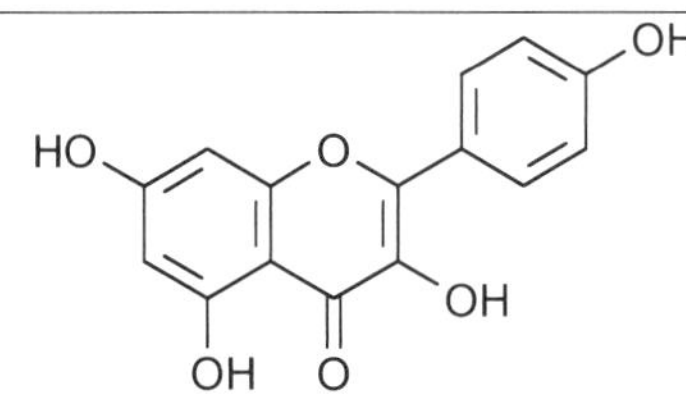
Quercetin	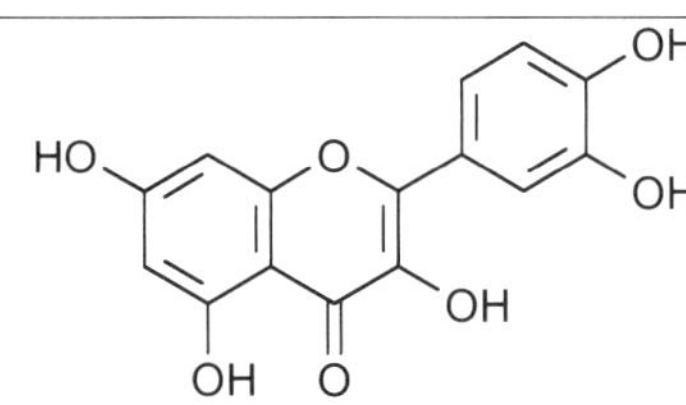

(continued)

1.3. Pharmacological Characteristics of Cannabinoids and Other Cannabis Constituents

THC is the pharmacologically and toxicologically most relevant and best studied constituent of the *Cannabis* plant, responsible for most of the effects of natural *Cannabis* preparations *(42)*. (A MEDLINE search covering the period 1993–2003 and using the keywords "tetrahydrocannabinol" and "pharmacology" produced about 1000 citations.) THC mainly acts through binding to the CB-1 receptor (see Chapter 6). The natural (-)-*trans* isomer of THC is 6- to 100-fold more potent than the (+)-*trans* isomer. A review of the pharmacology, toxicology, and therapeutic potential of *Cannabis*, cannabinoids, and other *Cannabis* constituents is given in refs. *43–53*. It is claimed that *Cannabis* as a polypharmaceutical herb may provide two advantages over

Table 6 *(continued)*

Compound	Structure
Orientin	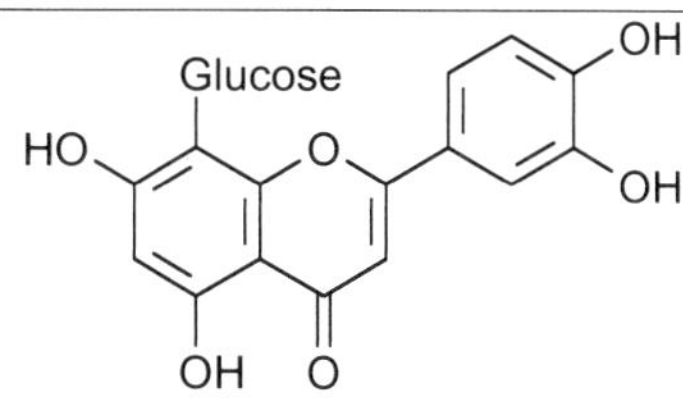
Vitexin	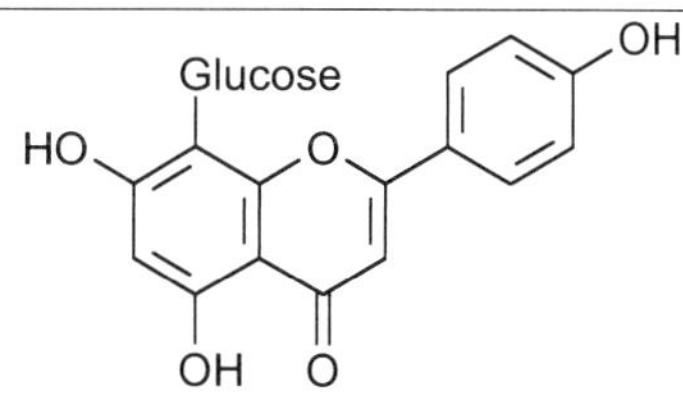
Cannflavin A	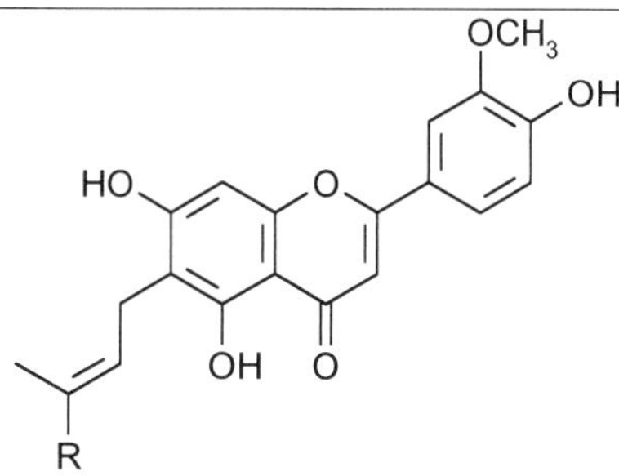 R = $H_2C\text{-}CH\text{=}C\text{-}(CH_3)_2$
Cannflavin B	R = CH_3

single-ingredient synthetic drugs: (1) the therapeutic effects of the primary active *Cannabis* constituents may be synergized by other compounds, and (2) the side effects of the primary constituents may be mitigated by other compounds *(34)*. Thus, *Cannabis* has been characterized as a "synergistic shotgun," in contrast, for example, to dronabinol (synthetic THC, Marinol®), a single-ingredient "silver bullet" *(54)*. A recent study compared the subjective effects of orally administered and smoked THC alone and THC within *Cannabis* preparations (brownies, cigarettes; refs. *55* and *56*). THC and *Cannabis* in both application forms produced similar, dose-dependent subjective effects, and there were few reliable differences between the THC-only and whole-plant conditions.

CBD is the next-best phytocannabinoid after THC. An overview of the pharmacology and clinical relevance of CBD can be found in refs. *34*, *57*, and *58*. Of clinical relevance could be its reported ability to reduce anxiety and the other unpleasant psychological side effects of THC. Among the underlying mechanisms is the potent inhibition of the cytochrome P450 3A11, which biotransforms THC to the fourfold more psychoactive 11-hydroxy-THC *(59)*.

Table 7
Unsaturated Fatty Acids From *Cannabis* Seed Oil

Compound	Structure
Linoleic acid	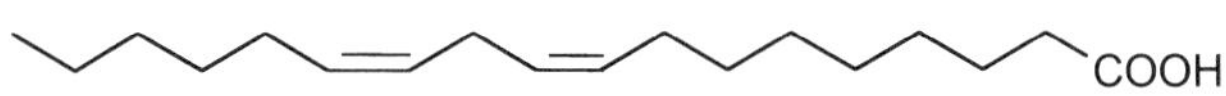
alpha-Linolenic acid	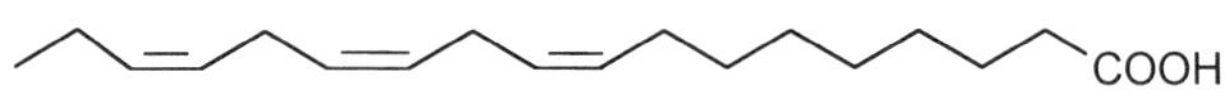
Oleic acid	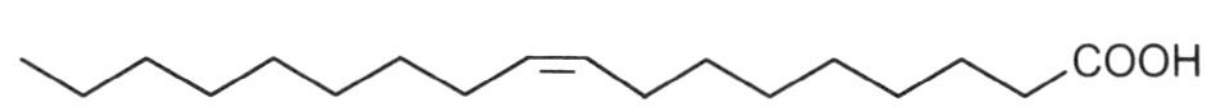

It has been suggested that the terpenoid constituents of *Cannabis* modulate THC activity, for example, by binding to cannabinoid receptors, modulating the THC receptor affinity, or altering its pharmacokinetics (e.g., by changing the blood–brain barrier; ref. *60*). Whereas the anti-inflammatory and antibiotic activity of *Cannabis* terpenoids is known and has been used therapeutically for a long time, the serotonergic effect at 5-HT$_{1A}$ and 5-HT$_{2A}$ receptors of the essential oil, which could explain *Cannabis*-mediated analgesia and mood alteration, has only recently been demonstrated *(61)*. β-Myrcene, the most abundant monoterpene in *Cannabis*, has analgesic, anti-inflammatory, antibiotic, and antimutagenic properties (34). β-Caryophyllene, the most common sesquiterpene, exhibits anti-inflammatory, cytoprotective (gastric mucosa), and antimalarial activity. The pharmacological effects of other *Cannabis* terpenes are discussed by McPartland and Russo *(34)*.

Apigenin, a flavonoid found in nearly all vascular plants, excerts a wide range of biological effects, including many properties shared by terpenoids and cannabinoids. It selectively binds with high affinity to benzodiazepine receptors, thus explaining its anxiolytic activity *(62)*. The pharmacology of other *Cannabis* flavonoids is reviewed in ref. *34*.

2. ANALYSIS OF PHYTOCANNABINOIDS

Instrumental methods are most often used for the identification, classification (e.g., fiber type, drug type), and individualization (e.g., source tracing) of *Cannabis* plants and products. Because of the complex chemistry of *Cannabis*, separation techniques, such as GC or liquid chromatography, often coupled with MS, are necessary for the acquisition of the typical chemical profiles and the sensitive, specific, qualitative, and/or quantitative (e.g., THC potency) determination of *Cannabis* constituents. However, especially for screening purposes and on-site field testing, noninstrumental techniques like thin-layer chromatography (TLC) and color reactions are helpful, too.

Table 8
Noncannabinoid Phenols

Compound	Structure
Cannabispiran	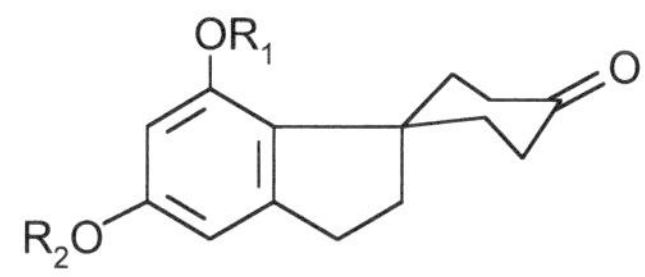 $R_1 = H$, $R_2 = CH_3$
Isocannabispiran	$R_1 = CH_3$, $R_2 = H$
Cannabistilbene-I	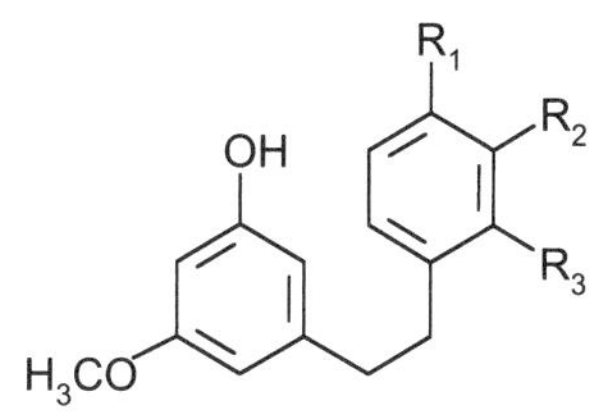 $R_1 = OH$, R_2 = isoprenyl, $R_3 = H$
Cannabistilbene-II	$R_1 = OCH_3$, $R_2 = OH$, $R_3 = OCH_3$ or $R_1 = OCH_3$, $R_2 = OCH_3$, $R_3 = OH$
Cannithrene-1	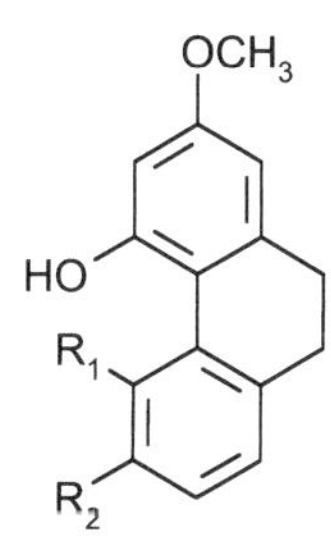 $R_1 = H$, $R_2 = OH$
Cannithrene-2	$R_1 = OH$, $R_2 = OCH_3$

2.1. Microscopy

Identifying a plant sample as *Cannabis sativa* L. is the first step. The botanical identification of plant specimens consists of physical examination of the intact plant morphology and habit (leaf shape, male and female inflorescenses, etc.) followed by the microscopical examination of leaves for the presence of cystolith hairs *(22,63–69)*. The very abundant trichomes, which are present on the surface of the fruiting and flowering tops of *Cannabis*, are the most characteristic features to be found in the microscopic examination of *Cannabis* products (not liquid *Cannabis*, hashish oil). Sometimes microscopic evidence is still available in smoked *Cannabis* residues.

2.2. Color Reactions

It must be stressed that positive reactions to color tests are only presumptive indications of the possible presence of *Cannabis* products or materials containing *Cannabis* products. A few other materials, often harmless and uncontrolled by national legislation or international treaties, may react with similar colors to the test reagents. It is mandatory for the laboratory to confirm such results by the use of an alternative technique, which should be based on MS *(70)*. The most common color spot tests include those developed by Duquenois and its modifications *(70–74)*. A study of 270 different plant species and 200 organic compounds has shown that the Duquenois–Levine modification is most specific *(71)*. The fast blue B salt test is the most common color reaction for the visualization of TLC patterns but may also be used as spot test on a filter paper *(70)*.

2.3. Chromatographic Techniques

2.3.1. Thin-Layer Chromatography

One- and two-dimensional TLC is suited for the acquisition of qualitative cannabinoid profiles from plant material *(70,73,75,76)*. Fast blue salt B or BB are used for visualization and result in characteristically colored spot patterns *(68)*. For quantitation, instrumental TLC coupled to densitometry is necessary. High-pressure TLC and overpressured layer chromatography have been developed for the reproducible and fast determination and isolation of neutral and acidic cannabinoids *(77–79)*.

2.3.2. Gas Chromatography, Gas Chromatography/Mass Spectrometry

GC with flame ionization or MS detection is now the best established method for the analysis of *Cannabis* and its products *(25,32,70,77,80–92)*. Derivatization is necessary (e.g., silylation or methylation) when information about cannabinoid acids, the dominating cannabinoids in the plant (*see* Section 1.1.), is required. The total cannabinoid content, i.e., the amount of neutral cannabinoids plus the neutral cannabinoids formed by decarboxylation of the acidic cannabinoids, is determined when the GC analysis is performed without derivatization *(89)*. GC/MS is the method of choice for creating *Cannabis* profiles and signatures (chemical fingerprints), a tool for attributing the country of origin, the conditions of cultivation (indoor, outdoor), an so on (*see* Chapter 3; refs. *21* and *87*).

2.3.3. High-Performance Liquid Chromatography

High-performance liquid chromatography makes possible the simultaneous determination of neutral and acidic phytocannabinoids without derivatization. Reversed-phase columns and preferably solvent programmed gradient systems are required for the separation of major and minor cannabinoids and their corresponding acids, e.g., for chemotyping (CBD-, THC, CBD/THC-type etc.), estimating the age (ratio acidic/neutral cannabinoids) of *Cannabis*, studying the effect of manufacturing processes and storage conditions, batch comparison, or direct quantification of THC in aqueous herbal preparations (e.g., *Cannabis* tea) *(81,82,93–98)*. Detection is usually performed by UV *(70,80,87,98–101)* and diode array photometers *(93)*, as well as by fluorescence, electrochemically *(102)*, and, recently, MS (103).

2.3.4. Other Techniques

The applicability of capillary electrochromatography with photodiode array UV detection for the analysis of phytocannabinoids has been demonstrated *(104)*. Supercritical fluid chromatography coupled to atmospheric pressure chemical ionization/MS is characterized by shorter analysis times than GC or high-performance liquid chromatography and does not require derivatization *(105)*.

2.4. DNA Testing

After a *Cannabis* sample has been identified and classified, it may become important to individualize the specimen for forensic and intelligence purposes *(22)*. Tracing the source of origin can be performed on a chemical, e.g., by using chromatographic–spectroscopic profiles (*see also* Chapter 3) or a genetic base. For DNA profiling *(22,106–110)*, the following techniques are used: randomly amplified polymorphic DNA *(111)*, amplified fragment length polymorphism *(112)*, short tandem repeats *(113,114)*, inter-simple sequence repeats *(115)*, internal transcribed spacer II *(116)*, and microsatellite markers *(117)*. An overview and description of the different DNA testing methods is given in ref. *22*.

References

1. Mechoulam, R. and Gaoni, Y. (1967) Recent advances in the chemistry of hashish. *Fortschr. Chem. Org. Naturst.* **25**, 175–213.
2. Ward, A. and Holmes, B. (1985) Nabilone. A preliminary review of its pharmacological properties and therapeutic use. *Drugs* **30**, 127–144.
3. Mechoulam, R., Lander, N., Breuer, A., and Zahalka, J. (1990) Synthesis of the individual, pharmacologically distinct, enantiomers of a tetrahydrocannabinol derivative. *Tetrahedron Asymmetry* **1**, 315–318.
4. Burstein, S. H., Audette, C. A., Breuer, A., et al. (1992) Synthetic nonpsychotropic cannabinoids with potent antiinflammatory, analgesic, and leukocyte antiadhesion activities. *J. Med. Chem.* **35**, 3135–3141.
5. Di Marzo, V. and Fontana, A. (1995) Anandamide, an endogenous cannabinomimetic eicosanoid: 'killing two birds with one stone'. *Prostaglandins Leukot. Essent. Fatty Acids* **53**, 1–11.
6. Devane, W. A., Hanus, L., Breuer, A., et al. (1992) Isolation and structure of a brain constituent that binds to the cannabinoid receptor. *Science* **258**, 1946–1949.
7. Pate, D. (1999) Anandamide structure-activity relationships and mechanisms of action on intraocular pressure in the normotensive rabbit model, PhD thesis, University of Kuopio, Kuopio, Finland.
8. Turner, C. E., Elsohly, M. A., and Boeren, E. G. (1980) Constituents of Cannabis sativa L. XVII. A review of the natural constituents. *J. Nat. Prod.* **43**, 169–234.
9. Ross, S. A. and ElSohly, M. A. (1995) Constituents of Cannabis sativa L. XXVIII—A review of the natural constituents: 1980–1994. *Zagazig J. Pharm. Sci.* **4**, 1–10.

10. ElSohly, M. (2002) Chemical constituents of Cannabis, in *Cannabis and cannabinoids—Pharmacology, Toxicology and Therapeutic Potential* (Grotenhermen, F. and Russo, E., eds.), Haworth Press, New York, pp. 27–36.
11. Gaoni, Y. and Mechoulam, R. (1964) The structure and synthesis of cannabigerol, a new hashish constituent, in *Proc. Chem. Soc.*, London, p. 82.
12. Shoyama, Y., Yagi, M., Nishioka, I., and Yamauchi, T. (1975) Biosynthesis of cannabinoid acids. *Phytochemistry* **14**, 2189–2192.
13. Adams, R., Hunt, M., and Clark, J. (1940) Structure of cannabidiol, a product isolated from the marihuana extract of Minnesota wild hemp. I. *J. Am. Chem. Soc.* **62**, 196–199.
14. Mechoulam, R. and Shvo, Y. (1963) Hashish—I. The structure of cannabidiol. *Tetrahedron* **19**, 2073–2078.
15. Wollner, H., Matchett, J., Levine, J., and Loewe, S. (1942) Isolation of a physiologically active tetrahydrocannabinol from Cannabis sativa resin. *J. Am. Chem. Soc.* **64**, 26–29.
16. Gaoni, Y. and Mechoulam, R. (1964) Isolation, structure and partial synthesis of an active constituent of hashish. *J. Am. Chem. Soc.* **86**, 1646–1647.
17. Wood, T., Spivey, W., and Easterfield, T. (1896) XL. Charas. The resin of Indian hemp. *J. Chem. Soc.* **69**, 539.
18. Adams, R., Baker, B., and Wearn, R. (1940) Structure of cannabinol III. Synthesis of cannabinol, 1-hydroxy-3-n-amyl-6,6,9-trimethyl-6-dibenzopyran. *J. Am. Chem. Soc.* **62**, 2204–2207.
19. ElSohly, M., Ross, S., Mehmedic, Z., Arafat, R., Yi, B., and Banahan, B.F., 3rd (2000) Potency trends of delta-9-THC and other cannabinoids in confiscated marijuana from 1980–1997. *J. Forens. Sci.* **45**, 24–30.
20. Brenneisen, R. (1986) The cannabinoid content in Cannabis products confiscated in Switzerland. *Arch. Kriminol.* **177**, 95–104.
21. Brenneisen, R. and Meyer, P. *Swiss Cannabis Profiling Project*, University of Bern and Swiss Federal Office of Public Health (unpublished data).
22. Miller Coyle, H., Palmbach, T., Juliano, N., Ladd, C., and Lee, H. C. (2003) An overview of DNA methods for the identification and individualization of marijuana. *Croat. Med. J.* **44**, 315–321.
23. ElSohly, M. (2003) Practical challenges to positive drug tests for marijuana. *Clin. Chem.* **49**, 1037–1038.
24. Leson, G., Pless, P., Grotenhermen, F., Kalant, H., and ElSohly, M. A. (2001) Evaluating the impact of hemp food consumption on workplace drug tests. *J. Anal. Toxicol.* **25**, 691–698.
25. Ross, S. A., Mehmedic, Z., Murphy, T. P., and Elsohly, M. A. (2000) GC-MS analysis of the total delta9-THC content of both drug- and fiber-type cannabis seeds. *J. Anal. Toxicol.* **24**, 715–717.
26. Bosy, T. Z. and Cole, K. A. (2000) Consumption and quantitation of delta-9-tetrahydrocannabinol in commercially available hemp seed oil products. *J. Anal. Toxicol.* **24**, 562–6.
27. Mediavilla, V., Derungs, R., Känzig, A., and Mägert, A. (1997) Qualität von Hanfsamenöl aus der Schweiz. *Agrarforschung* **4**, 449–451.
28. Lehmann, T., Sager, F., and Brenneisen, R. (1997) Excretion of cannabinoids in urine after ingestion of cannabis seed oil. *J. Anal. Toxicol.* **21**, 373–375.
29. Mediavilla, V. and Steinemann, S. (1997) Essential oil of Cannabis sativa L. strains. *J. Int. Hemp Assoc.* **4**, 80–82.
30. Meier, C. and Mediavilla, V. (1998) Factors influencing the yield and the quality of hemp (Cannabis sativa L.) essential oil. *J. Int. Hemp Assoc.* **5**, 16–20.
31. Lehmann, T. (1995) Chemical profiling of Cannabis sativa L., PhD thesis, University of Bern, Dep. of Pharmaceutical Sciences, Bern, Switzerland.
32. Ross, S.A. and ElSohly, M. A. (1996) The volatile oil composition of fresh and air-dried buds of Cannabis sativa. *J. Nat. Prod.* **59**, 49–51.

33. Novak, J., Zitterl-Eglseer, K., Deans, S. G., and Franz, C. M. (2001) Essential oils of different cultivars of Cannabis sativa L. and their antimicrobial activity. *Flavour Fragr. J.* **16**, 259–262.
34. McPartland, J. M. and Russo, E. B. (2001) Cannabis and cannabis extracts: greater than the sum of their parts? *J. Cann. Therap.* **1**, 103–132.
35. Hendriks, H., Malingré, T. M., Batterman, S., and Bos, R. (1977) Alkanes of the essential oil of Cannabis sativa. *Phytochemistry* **16**, 719–721.
36. McPartland, J. and Mediavilla, V. (2002) Noncannabinoid components, in *Cannabis and Cannabinoids—Pharmacology, Toxicology, and Therapeutic Potential* (Grotenhermen, F., and Russo, E., eds.), Haworth Press, New York, pp. 401–409.
37. Vanhoenacker, G., Van Rompaey, P., De Keukeleire, D., and Sandra, P. (2002) Chemotaxonomic features associated with flavonoids of cannabinoid-free cannabis (Cannabis sativa subsp. sativa L.) in relation to hops (Humulus lupulus L.). *Nat. Prod. Lett.* **16**, 57–63.
38. Barrett, M. L., Scutt, A. M., and Evans, F. J. (1986) Cannflavin A and B, prenylated flavones from Cannabis sativa L. *Experientia* **42**, 452–453.
39. Barrett, M. L., Gordon, D., and Evans, F. J. (1985) Isolation from Cannabis sativa L. of cannflavin—a novel inhibitor of prostaglandin production. *Biochem. Pharmacol.* **34**, 2019–2024.
40. Leson, G., Pless, P., and Roulac, J. (1999) *Hemp Foods and Oils for Health*, Hemptech, Sebastopol, CA.
41. Ross, S., ElSohly, H., ElKashoury, E., and ElSohly, M. (1996) Fatty acids of cannabis seeds. *Phytochem. Anal.* **7**, 279–283.
42. Grotenhermen, F. (2002) Effects of Cannabis and the cannabinoids, in *Cannabis and Cannabinoids—Pharmacology, Toxicology, and Therapeutic Potential* (Grotenhermen, F. and Russo, E., eds.), Haworth Press, New York, pp. 55–65.
43. Grotenhermen, F. and Russo, E. (eds.) (2002) *Cannabis and Cannabinoids—Pharmacology, Toxicology, and Therapeutic Potential*, Haworth Press, New York, p. 439.
44. Iversen, L. (2003) Cannabis and the brain. *Brain* **126**, 1252–1270.
45. Croxford, J. L. (2003) Therapeutic potential of cannabinoids in CNS disease. *CNS Drugs* **17**, 179–202.
46. Kumar, R., Chambers, W., and Pertwee, R. G. (2001) Pharmacological actions and therapeutic uses of cannabis and cannabinoids. *Anaesthesia* **56**, 1059–68.
47. Hirst, R. A., Lambert, D. G., and Notcutt, W. G. (1998) Pharmacology and potential therapeutic uses of cannabis. *Br. J. Anaesth.* **81**, 77–84.
48. Ashton, C. H. (1999) Adverse effects of cannabis and cannabinoids. *Br. J. Anaesth.* **83**, 637–49.
49. Williamson, E. M. and Evans, F. J. (2000) Cannabinoids in clinical practice. *Drugs* **60**, 1303–1314.
50. Campbell, F. A., Tramèr, M. R., Carroll, D., Reynolds, D. J., Moore, R. A., and McQuay, H. J. (2001) Are cannabinoids an effective and safe treatment option in the management of pain? A qualitative systematic review. *Br. Med. J.* **323**, 13–16.
51. Tramèr, M. R., Carroll, D., Campbell, F. A., Reynolds, D. J., Moore, R. A., and McQuay, H. J. (2001) Cannabinoids for control of chemotherapy induced nausea and vomiting: quantitative systematic review. *Br. Med. J.* **323**, 16–21.
52. Walker, J. M. and Huang, S. M. (2002) Cannabinoid analgesia. *Pharmacol. Ther.* **95**, 127–135.
53. Voth, E. A. and Schwartz, R. H. (1997) Medicinal applications of delta-9-tetrahydrocannabinol and marijuana. *Ann. Int. Med.* **126**, 791–798.
54. McPartland, J. M. and Pruitt, P. L. (1999) Side effects of pharmaceuticals not elicited by comparable herbal medicines: the case of tetrahydrocannabinol and marijuana. *Altern. Ther.* **5**, 57–62.

55. Wachtel, S. R., ElSohly, M. A., Ross, S. A., Ambre, J., and de Wit, H. (2002) Comparison of the subjective effects of delta-9-tetrahydrocannabinol and marijuana in humans. *Psychopharmacology* **161**, 331–339.
56. Hart, C. L., Ward, A. S., Haney, M., Comer, S. D., Foltin, R. W., and Fischman, M. W. (2002) Comparison of smoked marijuana and oral Delta(9)-tetrahydrocannabinol in humans. *Psychopharmacology* **164**, 407–415.
57. Mechoulam, R., Parker, L. A., and Gallily, R. (2002) Cannabidiol: an overview of some pharmacological aspects. *J. Clin. Pharmacol.* **42**, 11S–19S.
58. Consroe, P. (1998) Brain cannabinoid systems as targets for the therapy of neurological disorders. *Neurobiol. Dis.* **5**, 534–551.
59. Bornheim, L. M., Kim, K. Y., Li, J., Perotti, B. Y., and Benet, L. Z. (1995) Effect of cannabidiol pretreatment on the kinetics of tetrahydrocannabinol metabolites in mouse brain. *Drug Metab. Dispos.* **23**, 825–831.
60. Meschler, J. P. and Howlett, A. C. (1999) Thujone exhibits low affinity for cannabinoid receptors but fails to evoke cannabimimetic responses. *Pharmacol. Biochem. Behav.* **62**, 473–480.
61. Russo, E. (2001) Hemp for headache: an in-depth historical and scientific review of cannabis in migraine treatment. *J. Cann. Ther.* **1**, 21–92.
62. Salgueiro, J. B., Ardenghi, P., Dias, M., Ferreira, M. B., Izquierdo, I., and Medina, J. H. (1997) Anxiolytic natural and synthetic flavonoid ligands of the central benzodiazepine receptor have no effect on memory tasks in rats. *Pharmacol. Biochem. Behav.* **58**, 887–891.
63. Mitosinka, G. T., Thornton, J. I., and Hayes, T. L. (1972) The examination of cystolithic hairs of Cannabis and other plants by means of the scanning electron microscope. *J. Forens. Sci. Soc.* **12**, 521–529.
64. Thornton, J. I. and Nakamura, G. R. (1972) The identification of marijuana. *J. Forens. Sci. Soc.* **12**, 461–519.
65. Gigliano, G. (2001) Cannabis sativa L.—botanical problems and molecular approaches in forensic investigations. *Forens. Sci. Rev.* **13**, 2–17.
66. Stearn, W. T. (1970) The Cannabis plant: botanical characteristics, in *The Botany & Chemistry of Cannabis* (Joyce, C. and Curry, S., eds.), J. & A. Churchill, London, p. 1.
67. Nordal, A. (1970) Microscopic detection of Cannabis in the pure state and in semi-combusted residues, in *The Botany & Chemistry of Cannabis* (Joyce, C. and Curry, S., eds.), J. & A. Churchill, London, pp. 61–68.
68. Petri, G., Oroszlan, P., and Fridvalszky, L. (1988) Histochemical detection of hemp trichomes and their correlation with the THC content. *Acta Biol. Hung.* **39**, 59–73.
69. Bruni, A., Barni Comparini, I., and Menziani Andreoli, E. (1983) A histofluorescent procedure for identifying marijuana cannabinoids. *Experientia* **39**, 886–888.
70. United Nations (1987) *Recommended Methods for Testing Cannabis,* ST/NAR/8, Division of Narcotic Drugs, United Nations, New York.
71. Bailey, K. (1979) The value of the Duquenois test for cannabis—a survey. *J. Forens. Sci.* **24**, 817–841.
72. Butler, W. (1962) Duquenois-Levine test for marijuana. *J. Assoc. Off. Anal. Chem.* **45**, 597–600.
73. Tewari, S. N. and Sharma, J. D. (1982) Spot tests for cannabis materials. *Bull. Narc.* **34**, 109–112.
74. Pitt, C. G., Hendron, R. W., and Hsia, R. S. (1972) The specificity of the Duquenois color test for marihuana and hashish. *J. Forens. Sci.* **17**, 693–700.
75. Mali, B. D. and Parulekar, P. P. (1988) Diazotized dapsone as a reagent for the detection of cannabinoids on thin-layer chromatographic plates. *J. Chromatogr.* **457**, 383–386.

76. Baker, P. B., Gough, T. A., and Taylor, B. J. (1980) Illicitly imported Cannabis products: some physical and chemical features indicative of their origin. *Bull. Narc.* **32**, 31–40.
77. Debruyne, D., Albessard, F., Bigot, M. C., and Moulin, M. (1994) Comparison of three advanced chromatographic techniques for cannabis identification. *Bull. Narc.* **46**, 109–121.
78. Pothier, J., Galand, N., and Viel, C. (1992) Rapid characterization of stupefacient and toxic substances by pressurized thin-layer chromatography. *J. Toxicol. Clin. Exp.* **12**, 495–501.
79. Oroszlan, P., Verzar-Petri, G., Mincsovics, E., and Szekely, T. (1987) Separation, quantitation and isolation of cannabinoids from Cannabis sativa L. by overpressured layer chromatography. *J. Chromatogr.* **388**, 217–224.
80. Ferioli, V., Rustichelli, C., Pavesi, G., and Gamberini, G. (2000) Analytical characterisation of hashish samples. *Chromatographia* **52**, 39–44.
81. Debruyne, D., Moulin, M., Bigot, M. C., and Camsonne, R. (1981) Identification and differentiation of resinous cannabis and textile cannabis: combined use of HPLC and high-resolution GLC. *Bull. Narc.* **33**, 49–58.
82. Tsatsakis, A. M., Tutudaki, M., Stiakakis, I., Dimopoulou, M., Tzatzarakis, M., and Michalodimitrakis, M. (2000) Characterisation of cannabis plants phenotypes from illegal cultivations in Crete. *Boll. Chim. Farm.* **139**, 140–145.
83. Ross, S. A. and ElSohly, M. A. (1996) The volatile oil composition of fresh and air-dried buds of Cannabis sativa. *J. Nat. Prod.* **59**, 49–51.
84. Barni Comparini, I. and Centini, F. (1983) Packed column chromatography, high-resolution gas-chromatography and high pressure liquid chromatography in comparison for the analysis of cannabis constituents. *Forens. Sci. Int.* **21**, 129–137.
85. Harvey, D. J. (1990) Stability of cannabinoids in dried samples of cannabis dating from around 1896–1905. *J. Ethnopharmacol.* **28**, 117–128.
86. Turner, C. E., Bouwsma, O. J., Billets, S., and Elsohly, M. A. (1980) Constituents of Cannabis sativa L. XVIII—Electron voltage selected ion monitoring study of cannabinoids. *Biomed. Mass Spectrom.* **7**, 247–256.
87. Brenneisen, R. and ElSohly, M. A. (1988) Chromatographic and spectroscopic profiles of Cannabis of different origins: Part I. *J. Forens. Sci.* **33**, 1385–1404.
88. Bosy, T. Z. and Cole, K. A. (2000) Consumption and quantitation of delta-9-tetrahydrocannabinol in commercially available hemp seed oil products. *J. Anal. Toxicol.* **24**, 562–566.
89. Lercker, G., Bocci, F., Frega, N., and Bortolomeazzi, R. (1992) Cannabinoid acids analysis. *Farmaco* **47**, 367–378.
90. Vree, T. B. (1977) Mass spectrometry of cannabinoids. *J. Pharm. Sci.* **66**, 1444–1450.
91. Novotny, M., Lee, M. L., Low, C. E., and Raymond, A. (1976) Analysis of marijuana samples from different origins by high-resolution gas-liquid chromatography for forensic application. *Anal. Chem.* **48**, 24–29.
92. Raharjo, T. J. and Verpoorte, R. (2004) Methods for the analysis of cannabinoids in biological materials: a review. *Phytochem. Anal.* **15**, 79–94.
93. Lehmann, T. and Brenneisen, R. (1995) High performance liquid chromatographic profiling of Cannabis products. *J. Liq. Chromatogr.* **18**, 689–700.
94. Barni Comparini, I. and Centini, F. (1983) Packed column chromatography, high-resolution gas-chromatography and high pressure liquid chromatography in comparison for the analysis of cannabis constituents. *Forens. Sci. Int.* **21**, 129–37.
95. Zoller, O., Rhyn, P., and Zimmerli, B. (2000) High-performance liquid chromatographic determination of delta9-tetrahydrocannabinol and the corresponding acid in hemp containing foods with special regard to the fluorescence properties of delta9-tetrahydrocannabinol. *J. Chromatogr. A* **872**, 101–110.

96. Baker, P. B., Gough, T. A., and Wagstaffe, P. J. (1983) Determination of the distribution of cannabinoids in cannabis resin from Morocco using high-performance liquid chromatography. Part II. *J. Anal. Toxicol.* **7**, 7–10.
97. Baker, P. B., Taylor, B. J., and Gough, T. A. (1981) The tetrahydrocannabinol and tetrahydrocannabinolic acid content of cannabis products. *J. Pharm. Pharmacol.* **33**, 369–372.
98. McDonald, P. A. and Gough, T. A. (1984) Determination of the distribution of cannabinoids in cannabis resin from the Lebanon using HPLC. Part III. *J. Chromatogr. Sci.* **22**, 282–284.
99. Brenneisen, R. (1984) Psychotropic drugs. II. Determination of cannabinoids in Cannabis sativa L. and in cannabis products with high pressure liquid chromatography (HPLC). *Pharm. Acta Helv.* **59**, 247–259.
100. Rustichelli, C., Ferioli, V., Baraldi, M., Zanoli, P., and Gamberini, G. (1998) Analysis of cannabinoids in fiber hemp plant varieties (Cannabis sativa) by high-performance liquid chromatography. *Chromatographia* **48**, 215–222.
101. Baker, P. B., Fowler, R., Bagon, K. R., and Gough, T. A. (1980) Determination of the distribution of cannabinoids in cannabis resin using high performance liquid chromatography. *J. Anal. Toxicol.* **4**, 145–152.
102. Nakahara, Y. and Tanaka, K. (1988) Studies on discrimination of confiscated cannabis products by high performance liquid chromatography with electrochemical detector. *Eisei Shikenjo Hokoku*, Bulletin of National Institute of Hygenic Sciences, pp.11–18.
103. Rustichelli, C., Ferioli, V., Vezzalini, F., Rossi, M. C., and Gamberini, G. (1996) Simultaneous separation and identification of hashish constituents by coupled liquid chromatography-mass spectrometry (HPLC-MS). *Chromatographia* **43**, 129–134.
104. Lurie, I. S., Meyers, R. P., and Conver, T. S. (1998) Capillary electrochromatography of cannabinoids. *Anal. Chem.* **70**, 3255–3260.
105. Backstrom, B., Cole, M. D., Carrott, M. J., Jones, D. C., Davidson, G., and Coleman, K. (1997) A preliminary study of the analysis of Cannabis by supercritical fluid chromatography with atmospheric pressure chemical ionisation mass spectroscopic detection. *Sci. Justice* **37**, 91–97.
106. Miller Coyle, H., Ladd, C., Palmbach, T., and Lee, H. C. (2001) The green revolution: botanical contributions to forensics and drug enforcement. *Croat. Med. J.* **42**, 340–345.
107. Miller Coyle, H., Palmbach, T., Juliano, N., Ladd, C., and Lee, H. C. (2003) An overview of DNA methods for the identification and individualization of marijuana. *Croat. Med. J.* **44**, 315–321.
108. Cole, M. D. and Linacre, A. M. T. (2002) The identification of controlled plant drugs using phytochemistry and DNA. *Curr. Topics Phytochem.* **5**, 129–140.
109. Linacre, A. and Thorpe, J. (1998) Detection and identification of cannabis by DNA. *Forens. Sci. Int.* **91**, 71–76.
110. Siniscalco Gigliano, G., Caputo, P., and Cozzolino, S. (1997) Ribosomal DNA analysis as a tool for the identification of Cannabis sativa L. specimens of forensic interest. *Sci. Justice* **37**, 171–174.
111. Gillan, R., Cole, M., Linacre, A., Thorpe, J. W., and Watson, N. D. (1995) Comparison of Cannabis sativa by random amplification of polymorphic DNA (RAPD) and HPLC of cannabinoids: a preliminary study. *Sci. Justice* **35**, 169–177.
112. Miller Coyle, H., Sutler, G., Abrams, S., et al. (2003) A simple DNA extraction method for Marijuana samples used in amplified fragment length polymorphism (AFLP) analysis. *J. Forens. Sci.* **48**, 343–347.
113. Hsieh, H. M., Hou, R. J., Tsai, L. C., et al. (2003) A highly polymorphic STR locus in Cannabis sativa. *Forens. Sci. Int.* **131**, 53–58.

114. Gilmore, S., Peakall, R., and Robertson, J. (2003) Short tandem repeat (STR) DNA markers are hypervariable and informative in Cannabis sativa: implications for forensic investigations. *Forens. Sci. Int.* **131**, 65–74.
115. Kojoma, M., Iida, O., Makino, Y., Sekita, S., and Satake, M. (2002) DNA fingerprinting of Cannabis sativa using inter-simple sequence repeat (ISSR) amplification. *Planta Med.* **68**, 60–63.
116. Gigliano, G. (1998) Identification of Cannabis sativa L. (Cannabaceae) using restriction profiles of the Internal Transcribed Spacer II (ITS2). *Sci. Justice* **38**, 225–230.
117. Alghanim, H. J. and Almirall, J. R. (2003) Development of microsatellite markers in Cannabis sativa for DNA typing and genetic relatedness analyses. *Anal. Bioanal. Chem.* **376**, 1225–1233.

Chapter 3

Chemical Fingerprinting of Cannabis *as a Means of Source Identification*

Mahmoud A. ElSohly, Donald F. Stanford, and Timothy P. Murphy

1. Introduction

Marijuana is the most widely abused and readily available illicit drug in the United States, with an estimated 11.5 million current users annually purchasing more than $10 billion of the drug *(1)*. Drug enforcement agencies are therefore keenly interested in trafficking routes of both foreign and domestically grown supplies of marijuana. From confidential sources to satellites, these agencies employ a multitude of methods to gather intelligence to direct resources, plan control operations, and develop policies. A practical means to recognize the source of seized marijuana would be a valuable tool for those purposes. Based on findings from 1990 to 1992 and described here, one way to determine origin is by using a chemical fingerprint system, a method that has shown promise as an effective intelligence tool to ascertain the geographic origin of confiscated marijuana samples. Of the many factors that affect the chemical constituents of marijuana, it is apparent that environmental factors consistently induce profiles unique to each environ. An "environ of origin" as broad as a continent or as small as an indoor garden may be differentiated based on the chemical fingerprint, or "signature," of marijuana cultivated there—if a statistically significant number of samples grown in that environ are available for comparison. However, because all environs are not unique, the chemical fingerprint of cannabis is not considered to be an ultimate tool for forensic applications, although the technique may effectively sup-

From: *Forensic Science and Medicine: Marijuana and the Cannabinoids*
Edited by: M. A. ElSohly © Humana Press Inc., Totowa, New Jersey

port other types of evidence and is certainly of particular value in intelligence operations.

Scientists have developed sophisticated techniques to study the unique patterns of the infinite combinations of chemical compounds making up specific materials and have applied those techniques to various disciplines.

Over some 35 years, a number of researchers have examined the chemical compounds unique to the *Cannabis* plant and have consistently reported that the "cannabinoids" are indicative of the country of origin and that environmental factors affect cannabinoid profiles. During the 1970s a number of publications appeared that used gas chromatography (GC), thin-layer chromatography, and high-performance liquid chromatography techniques to compare cannabinoid concentrations of marijuana grown in various regions of the world *(2–10)*. In the 1980s and 1990s those technologies advanced greatly, and researchers continued to reach similar conclusions *(11–19)*. Marijuana from different geographical regions has also been compared using other analytical techniques, including elemental analysis *(20,21)*, GC analysis of headspace volatiles (22), analysis of free sugars in the plants (23), microscopic examination of pollen *(24)*, and even comparison of insect species found in confiscated materials *(25,26)*.

Nearing the 21st century, as technologies further advanced, scientists turned their attention to genetic analyses of marijuana and developed techniques very suitable for forensic purposes *(27–30)*. Examination of the DNA of marijuana plants now allows forensic investigators to identify even minute particles as *Cannabis* and to determine whether a sample is from the drug or the fiber type of the plant. Just as human DNA testing has revolutionized criminology, so has the genetic testing of marijuana given prosecutors a reliable means to assert that the stash in a defendant's pocket was harvested from the plant found under a grow light in his basement. However, DNA testing can be expensive and time-consuming and only reflects a plant's lineage, not the environment in which it was grown.

The primary mission of the US Drug Enforcement Administration (DEA) is to enforce the US statutes and regulations concerning controlled substances. One part of that mission is to manage a national drug intelligence program. To collect, analyze, and disseminate intelligence information at federal, state, local, and foreign levels, the DEA uses scientific technologies to help gather the pieces of the worldwide puzzle of drug trafficking. In 1977, the DEA initiated the Heroin Signature Program to enhance the agency's ability to identify the source of heroin seized or purchased within the United States. Following the success of that program, a similar program for cocaine profiling was set up in 1997, and a methamphetamine profiling program in 1999. In the mid-1980s, realizing the potential value of a fully integrated "cannabis fingerprint system" including standardized equipment and methods, a database for reference, and an automated means to interpret data, officials turned to the scientific community for assistance.

In 1987, the National Institute of Drug Abuse (NIDA) funded a Small Business Innovative Research grant submitted by ElSohly Laboratories, Inc. (ELI), to develop analytical methodologies that could be used to compare complete chemical fingerprints of *Cannabis* samples of different geographical origins. At that time, the DEA also provided funds to conduct a feasibility study to demonstrate if a practical chemical fingerprint system could be developed. In 1988, ELI reported positive results and as a result the DEA funded a phase II study (beginning in 1990) to develop a fully operational *Cannabis* fingerprint system and to establish an initial database of marijuana fingerprints from major production regions. The results of the phase II study were reported to DEA in 1992 and are summarized in this chapter.

2. CHEMOMETRICS

Having had many years of experience in analyzing marijuana and considering the scientific precedents of others' work on a portion of the chemical fingerprint, we determined that GC/mass spectrometry (MS) would be the most appropriate methodology to collect test data. GC/MS instrumentation would provide not only a chemical fingerprint of a marijuana sample, but also spectral data, which would aid in the identification of each of those components. Law enforcement agencies agreed to provide marijuana samples of presumed authenticity specifically chosen to build a useful database of major production areas. To avoid bias, statistical software was used to analyze the data.

At the time of the phase I study, the science of chemometrics—the application of statistics and mathematical methods to chemical data—was a burgeoning field within the computer science and analytical chemistry communities. Although standardized pattern-matching software was just beginning to become available, an in-house program was developed by ELI personnel to analyze the data. At the conclusion of the study an independent chemometrics company, InfoMetrix, was enlisted to evaluate the data using various pattern recognition and statistical methods to further validate the concept of a turnkey system. Their report in March 1989 stated that, based on studies using their own statistical software, the concept was indeed viable, that every sample of foreign origin had been correctly classified by country of origin, and that every sample of domestic origin had been correctly classified by state of origin.

For data analysis in the phase II study, we used a commercial version of InfoMetrix software—Pirouette®. At this writing, the latest version of Pirouette is marketed as their most comprehensive chemometrics software used to discover associations of patterns in data and to prepare and use multivariate classification models. Pirouette, like all commercial software, has dramatically evolved in the past 15 years, but the early version used in the phase II study perfectly suited the requirements at the time, including the capability for interlaboratory data sharing. Its graphical interface allowed us to view a three dimensional representation of an unknown sample compared to a model and to rotate the image in order to actually see the relationships of the principal chemical components.

Mathematical algorithms such as principal component analysis and hierarchical cluster analysis were used to reduce the large complex data sets into comprehensible forms *(31)*. The graphic views emphasized the natural groupings in the data and showed which variables most strongly influenced those patterns. The basis of the project was to first construct a "model," that is, a set of data that represented the chemical fingerprint of a plant typical of the "class" to which it is assigned, in this case a country, a state, or any other environ to be studied. How well a model actually represented the real world was a matter of the quality of the data, which was in turn dependent on the quality (authenticity) of the marijuana samples and of the GC/MS analyses. The success of the study hinged on how well the models could be built—a daunting task.

To validate proposed multivariate models, "training sets" of data known to be representative of the various classes were processed. Once Pirouette was trained to recognize classes using a K-nearest-neighbor modeling technique *(32)*, data from samples of unknown origin could be tested and shown to be either in or not in a certain class or perhaps overlapping two or more classes. Based on the amount of variance in the model, Pirouette also provided a measure of the probability of the accuracy of the results, i.e., a "confidence" value *(32)*.

3. Chemical Constituents of *Cannabis*

Many of the chemical constituents of *Cannabis* are common to other plants; however, cannabinoids are unique to their namesake *(33)*. Of the hundreds of chemicals found in *Cannabis*—and described at length in this book—175 were used to develop the chemical fingerprint system. Of those compounds readily detectable by the methods developed in phase I, 46 were positively identified, including 22 monoterpenes or sesquiterpenes, 16 cannabinoids, two noncannabinoid phenols, two hydrocarbons, three fatty acid esters, and one miscellaneous aromatic compound (*see* Table 1). The remaining 129 compounds were necessarily included because all of the chemical compounds contribute to the fingerprint, and only the multivariate data analysis software could sort out which ones were important to establish relationships and differentiate between the classes.

For the fingerprint system to be of practical use in all laboratories, the methods needed to be reproducible and cost-effective, so simple methods using common laboratory equipment were developed. The methods used in this study have not been validated for reproducibility between different laboratories, but because of the simple analytical techniques employed we assumed that the methods would be robust and that different laboratories could generate similar data in house. Because the fingerprint chromatograms are so complex, however, it may be difficult to compare data generated at different laboratories. Interlaboratory variation in signature analysis is a common and vexing problem in this field; for this reason, the DEA has centralized its signature programs at a single, specialized laboratory.

To prepare a sample for GC/MS analysis, the dried plant material was extracted with solvent, and then a portion of the extract was diluted with additional solvent to produce a test sample ready to be injected into the instrument. Of the compounds extractable using that method, only a portion of those were detectable under the particular GC/MS conditions used in the study. Although all of the 175 compounds making up the standardized fingerprints could not be specifically identified (even though the spectral evidence suggested some possibilities), each was numbered for reference.

For the study to be complete, however, it was necessary to identify as many of the compounds as possible to better grasp the relationships of the chemical fingerprints to their environs. Several techniques were employed in order to understand the makeup of the chemical fingerprints.

Table 1
Chemical Compounds Identified in a Phase II Study

Compound	Peak	Compound	Peak
Terpenes		**Cannabinoids**	
Allo-aromadenrene	61	Cannabichromene	17
α-*cis*-Bergamotene	3	Cannabicitran	48
α-*trans*-Bergamotene	5	Cannabicumaronone	41
α-Bisabalol	77	Cannabicyclol	15
β-Caryophyllene	4	Cannabidiol	16
Caryophyllene oxide	23	Cannabielsoin	97
α-Cedrene	84	Cannabifuran	44
Curcumene	153	Cannabigerol	32
γ-Eudesmol	101	Cannabinol	19
Eupatorio chromene	112	Cannabiviran	167
α-Quaine	85	Dehydrocannabifuran	168
Guaiol	100	Δ^8-Tetrahydrocannabinol	31
α-Humulene	6	Δ^9-Tetrahydrocannabinol	18
Isoledene	132	Tetrahydrocannabinol-C_4	51
Longifolene	2	Tetrahydrocannabiorocal	105
cis-Nerolidol	92	Tetrahydrocannabiviran	14
trans-Nerolidol	69		
Sativene	83	**Noncannabinoid phenols**	
α-Selinnene	66	Cannabispiran	30
α-Terpineol	107	Dehydrocannabispiran	58
Valencene	152		
α-Zingeberene	73	**Fatty acid esters**	
		Palmitic acid methyl ester	38
Hydrocarbons		Oleicacid methyl ester	56
Heptacosane	57	Linoleic acid methyl ester	140
Nonacosane	21		
		Aromatic compounds	
		Butylated hydroxytoluene	130

A 1988 study provided information to identify most of the cannabinoids based on retention time and mass spectra *(34)*, but other components were more elusive. Because many of the compounds have almost identical mass spectra and can only be positively identified by GC/MS using a pure reference standard of that compound to establish the retention time on a particular instrument, as many reference standards as could be obtained within the scope of the study were analyzed.

The terpenes were of great interest because their production by plants was likely to consistently reflect the immediate environment, whereas the cannabinoids would tend to reveal genetic relationships. A commercial GC/MS data library *(35)* was available in both digital and print formats to help identify many of the terpene compounds.

4. Experimental Design

The specific goal of the study was to develop a fully operational fingerprint system that could be used to determine the probability that a particular marijuana sample of unknown origin had been grown in one of the target foreign countries or domestic states or other environs in the database. The top priority for the experimental design was to be able to distinguish between foreign and domestically produced marijuana in order to determine the prevalence of foreign material entering the country vs domestic material being trafficked. The second objective was to accurately determine the country of origin. The third goal was to provide a method to accurately estimate the ratio of indoor vs outdoor domestic production. Determination of the state of origin of plants grown outdoors in the United States was of lower priority.

Specimens, or "exhibits," from the various regions known to be major contributors to the illicit marijuana market in the United States were submitted by law enforcement agencies. To ensure the validity of the origins of the specimens, they were shipped directly from the areas of collection and were therefore presumed to represent true authentics. Both marijuana and hashish specimens were made available for the study. Additional specimens cultivated under experimental conditions were produced at the NIDA Marijuana Project garden at the University of Mississippi (UM). To maintain the integrity of specimens over the length of the study, all were stored in a freezer (–20°C) before analysis. Samples were usually analyzed within 4 weeks of preparation.

Of the 202 marijuana exhibits representing six regions, 157 passed the initial quality control (QC) requirements of specimen integrity designed to ensure representative fingerprints. To ensure consistency, only mature female plants were included in the study. Specimens that could not be determined to be from mature plants (no buds or seeds), those in poor condition (molded or decayed), those contaminated with soil, and those composed of mostly seeds, stems, and roots but lacking suitable leaf material were rejected. The exhibits from regions included in the phase II database included 26 Colombian, 35 Jamaican, 20 Mexican, 30 Thai, 25 Californian, and 21 Hawaiian samples. Of course, Hawaiian marijuana was expected to have a fingerprint with foreign traits.

The original study also included 17 exhibits from Tennessee that were not definitely mature but were included in the study to provide data from the eastern United States. We have chosen to exclude those data here because the profiles of the Tennessee exhibits were shown to be unreliable, which could be related to their stage of maturity. The exclusion of these data had no effect on the conclusions of the study.

Because marijuana grown under controlled conditions was necessary to support the fingerprint studies, several growing experiments were carried out at the UM marijuana garden during both phase I and II periods. Second-generation daughter plants were grown from seeds collected from 38 phase I exhibits to compare the fingerprints of genetically equivalent plants grown outside the country of origin.

Two experiments were conducted to compare the fingerprints of plants grown indoors to those grown outdoors. Twenty cuttings from a Jamaican female plant obtained from the US Department of Agriculture Laboratory in Beltsville, MD, were grown under three conditions: outdoors in the ground, outdoors in pots, and in pots indoors under artificial lighting. For the second indoor/outdoor experiment, 10 plants of a single high-tetrahydrocannabinol-potency variety were grown both indoors in pots using commercial potting soil and outdoors in the ground of the University of Mississippi marijuana garden.

To study how the chemical fingerprints of both sexes of marijuana plants vary at different stages of plant maturity, leaf samples were collected at regular intervals from plants of Mexican origin grown outdoors. Specimens from five male and five female plants were analyzed to study how their fingerprints developed at 8, 12, 16, 20, and 25 weeks of age.

Because many chemical compounds readily decompose, given time, and because the decomposition generally occurs more rapidly at elevated temperatures, a study was initiated to determine how fingerprints change during the time between the collection of exhibits and their transfer to a freezer. For this experiment, 80 specimens from the UM garden were stored in paper bags both at room temperature and at an elevated temperature and then transferred to a freezer after 30- and 90-day intervals.

Because of the inherent nature of hashish, a refined product made from the resin of *Cannabis* and intended for commerce, all of the available exhibits were suitable for chemical analysis, except that several localities were not represented with a statistically significant number of specimens. Of the 73 hashish exhibits from nine countries, 68 were included in the database: 8 from Afghanistan, 6 from Colombia, 18 from India, 10 from Lebanon, and 26 from Pakistan. A recent report indicated lack of homogeneity in bars of compressed *Cannabis* resin (hashish; ref. *36*). However, because the amount of material received from each sample was small (~5 g), homogenicity of each sample was presumed.

5. Methodology

5.1. Extraction

Each marijuana sample was first manicured so that the material became a homogeneous mixture of leaf particles with no seeds or stems. A 100.0 mg portion of the sample was transferred to a test tube, and to that tube was added 1.0 mL of the extraction solution. The extraction solution was methanol and chloroform mixed in a ratio of 9:1, in which was dissolved phenanthrene at a concentration of 0.2 mg/mL. Phenanthrene served as an internal standard, a chemical not naturally present in cannabis but appearing as an isolated peak in the chromatograms for use as both a retention time marker and a reference for the calculation of the quantities of the peaks of interest. The tube containing the sample and extraction solution was placed in an ultrasonic water bath for 15 minutes to break the plant tissue and allow soluble chemicals of *Cannabis* to be dissolved in the extraction solution. The tube was then spun in a centrifuge to force the plant particles to the bottom so that the resulting clear green solution could then be transferred to a screw-capped vial without disturbing the sediment. Our experience indicated that extracts would remain stable at low temperature, so extracts were stored in a freezer (–20°C) until time for GC/MS analysis.

Hashish samples were prepared very similarly, with the exception that a 50.0-mg portion of each sample was extracted. Because hashish in such small quantities was presumed to be homogeneous, the analytical sample was separated from the bulk sample using a razor blade to slice from the inner portion while avoiding the outer part, which could have been contaminated or excessively oxidized.To prepare a sample test solution suitable for injection into the GC/MS, an extract was removed from the freezer and a 0.1-mL aliquot was transferred to another vial, to which was added 0.9 mL of methanol.

5.2. GC/MS Analysis

The GC/MS system consisted of a Varian 3300 gas chromatograph interfaced to a Finnigan 700 ion trap detector mass spectrometer. A 30-m DB-1 fused silica capillary column (J&W Scientific, Inc.), 0.25 mm OD, 0.25 μm film was used.

For each run, the column was initially held at 70°C for 1 minute; the temperature was then increased to 250°C at the rate of 5°C per minute, then held 25 minutes at the final temperature for a total run time of 62 minutes. The injection port was heated to 200°C and used in the splitless mode with the split valve delayed 30 seconds before opening. The interface between the GC and the MS was heated to 250°C.

The data system used to control the GC/MS and quantitate the peaks in the chromatograms was a desktop PC using Finnigan ITDS 4.10 software. Mass spectral data was acquired within the range of 55–450 amu at a rate of 0.5 seconds per scan. After a sample was injected, data acquisition automatically started after 5 minutes to allow the solvent to pass before peaks of interest began to elute. Although the GC oven cycled back to the starting temperature after 62 minutes, data acquisition ended 54 minutes into the run after the last peak was recorded.

To ensure that the instrument was operating properly, a QC solution was injected after every nine test samples, and the QC chromatogram was examined for integrity. A mixture of terpenes, cannabinoids, hydrocarbons, and the internal standard was selected for QC to provide a reference of known peaks throughout the entire time of the run. The QC sample consisted of a methanolic solution of α-terpineol (21 μg/mL), α-terpinene (21 μg/mL), β-caryophylene (21 μg/mL), allo-aromadendrene (21 μg/mL), nonacosane (83 μg/mL), cannabidiol (123 μg/mL), cannabinol (124 μg/mL), Δ^9-tetrahydrocannabinol (THC; 41 μg/mL), and phenanthrene (25 μg/mL). Injector and column maintenance was performed on a routine schedule to prevent any "memory effect" resulting from repeated injections, but no blanks were run between samples.

Each test sample chromatogram was evaluated for acceptability before data analysis. If the chromatogram exhibited an unusual baseline or low sensitivity, the injection was repeated. The area under each peak was measured using ITDS software in the manual mode rather than the automatic mode so that the operator could evaluate each of the 175 peaks (plus the internal standard peak) for proper peak shape and to ensure correct identity assignments as well. Quantitative values of each peak were automatically calculated by determining the ratio of the area of the peak to that of the internal standard within the same chromatogram and comparing that ratio to that of a standardized calibration file.

5.3. Multivariate Data Analysis

Quantitation files created by ITDS software were converted to ASCII files containing only the peak numbers (identity assignments) and the quantitative values of each. The ASCII files were downloaded to the Pirouette program (InfoMetrix, Incorporated, Woodinvil, WA) and saved as a compatible file format.

To analyze the data using the power of Pirouette, first the database of all marijuana exhibits from the four countries and two states was used to construct a model of the six classes of fingerprints. The data within the model were examined to ascertain similarities and differences of the location classes. Then other models containing only 80% of the database were constructed, leaving 20% of the samples to be tested against the models. Having appropriate models for comparison, the remainder of the proposed data analysis experiments were conducted, constructing additional models as necessary. All results were based on the a K-nearest-neighbor classification method *(31)*.

6. Results of the Phase II Study

6.1. Similarities Within the Model

Within the comparison of the broad classes of domestic vs foreign, all foreign exhibits were correctly classified. Only one domestic exhibit, a Hawaiian specimen, was misclassified.

When the domestic exhibits were compared with the four foreign countries, the single exhibit discrepant in the domestic vs foreign test was again misclassified, being indicated to be from Jamaica. All Jamaican and Mexican exhibits were correctly classified, as were 93% of the Thai exhibits and 92% of the Colombian.

The number of misclassifications increased when the exhibits representing individual states were tested within a six-region model. Of the Hawaiian exhibits, 78% were correctly located. The majority of misclassified Hawaiian specimens again looked Jamaican. All Californian exhibits were correctly identified.

6.2. Identification of Unknowns

Satisfied that the phase II fingerprint data were valid when samples included in the model were tested, the system was challenged with specimens not included in the model. The random removal of 20% of specimens from the database redefined the model and provided "unknowns" for the definitive test of the system. This evaluation was repeated five times, each time removing different exhibits and testing those against each new model. The results are summarized in Table 2, which shows correct classifications vs total unknowns for each of the five rounds of evaluation and the totals of the individual rounds.

Although the results certainly ascertained the viability of the fingerprint system, we were still concerned about the source of the errors. To investigate the causes of the erroneous predictions, we closely examined the data from a different viewpoint. Presented in Table 3 is a matrix chart of the misclassified exhibits showing which locations fit the fingerprint more closely than the model of its actual origin. It was evident that exhibits within certain regions tended to be misclassified more often than those from other locations, but those trends would likely be tempered in a database composed of more exhibits. Although the distinctive fingerprints of the Hawaiian marijuana improved the classification rates of those exhibits, those differences also weakened the domestic model. The majority of California exhibits were known to have been grown in the northern part of the state, but the single exhibit from southern

Table 2
Correct Classifications of Unknowns

Location	Round 1	Round 2	Round 3	Round 4	Round 5	Total	Correct (%)
California	3/5	4/5	5/5	5/5	5/5	22/25	88
Hawaii	4/4	2/4	4/4	3/4	4/5	17/21	81
Colombia	6/6	5/5	5/5	5/5	4/5	25/26	96
Jamaica	7/7	7/7	7/7	7/7	7/7	35/35	100
Mexico	4/4	4/4	3/4	4/4	4/4	19/20	95
Thailand	4/6	6/6	5/6	5/6	6/6	26/30	87
Foreign	—	—	—	—	—	105/111	95
Domestic	—	—	—	—	—	39/46	85
Total	—	—	—	—	—	144/157	92

Table 3
Misclassification Matrix

Origin	Number tested	Number of exhibits misclassified as: CA	HI	COL	JAM	MEX	THAI	Total
California	25	—	0	0	0	2	1	3
Hawaii	21	1	—	0	2	0	0	3
Colombia	26	0	0	—	0	1	0	1
Jamaica	35	0	0	0	—	0	0	0
Mexico	20	1	0	0	0	—	0	1
Thailand	30	1	0	0	1	2	—	4
Total	157	3	2	0	7	7	1	12

California had a fingerprint very similar to Mexican marijuana, a not-so-surprising misclassification.

6.3. Indoor vs Outdoor

For year-round production and to avoid routine surveillance, marijuana growers in the United States increasingly prefer to nurture their plants indoors out of sight. An added benefit of indoor horticulture is that the grower, rather than Mother Nature, controls the environment and can provide ideal lighting and temperature conditions as well as exact levels of water and nutrients. Not surprisingly, therefore, the fingerprints of plants grown indoors are significantly dissimilar to those of outdoor plants.

A model consisting of three classes—outdoors in the ground, outdoors in pots (commercial potting soil), and indoors (commercial potting soil)—was constructed from fingerprints of Jamaican plants grown in the UM facilities. All of those specimens were then tested against that model. It was found that the fingerprints of the indoor plants could be differentiated from their outdoor brethren with 100% accuracy. The only misclassifications were within the outdoor group, as those plants with roots in the earth were sometimes confused with those in pots, a trend that indicates that light and temperature may influence the chemical profiles more than soil conditions.

A second indoor/outdoor experiment, which involved high-potency plants, supported the previous results, as all of those plants were correctly classified.

6.4. Daughter Plants Grown in a Different Region

A most interesting experiment was the test to see how the fingerprints of plants from foreign seeds cultivated in Mississippi would fare in the system. Seeds from exhibits from Colombia, Jamaica, Mexico, Thailand, and Hawaii were planted outdoors at the UM garden. Fingerprints of the resulting plants were tested against the model constructed from all of the phase II exhibits.

Of all the Hawaiian daughter plants, 60% were matched to their home state, whereas only 14% of the Thai daughters were recognized. The majority of daughter plants (56%) were classified as domestically grown. The high rate of misclassification supported original predictions that, although genetic relationships are reflected in the fingerprints, the environment has a greater effect on the chemical profiles.

6.5. Age and Sex

The original experimental design of the fingerprint study required that all specimens included in the database be from mature female plants, the type of marijuana commonly trafficked in the illicit market. To determine if those criteria were actually necessary was the intention of the exercise based on the age and sex of plants. Experimentally grown specimens of 8 and 12 weeks of age were considered immature, whereas those 16, 20, and 25 weeks of age were included in the mature class. An equal number of both sexes were included.

Analysis of the data showed a high rate of correct classification (94%); all the misses were among the immature group. Results from the model based on sex misclassified 30% of the males but only 8% of the females.

It appears from these data that the sex of the plant did not contribute as much to the fingerprint as did the age of the plant. The maturity of the plants, although not of great interest to the intelligence community, was definitely a factor in the accuracy of the fingerprint system. Our experience analyzing confiscated marijuana for more than 30 years shows that the majority of the samples were from mature plants (based on the physical examination of the samples). The only exception is those samples seized at the growing locations before time to harvest.

6.6. Storage Conditions

To determine the effect of storage conditions on chemical fingerprints, sets of data were compiled into four models, each having one constant condition and one variant condition of the two factors: time and temperature. Samples stored at the two temperature levels (80 and 120°F) for the two time intervals (30 and 90 days) were tested within those models.

Samples stored at 80°F were distinct from those stored at 120°F, indicating that temperature has a significant effect on the chemical profiles. Those stored at 80°F had similar profiles over the two periods, indicating that at the lower temperature the profiles do not change over a period of at least 3 months. Samples stored at 120°F for 30 days, however, could easily be differentiated from those stored for 90 days.

6.7. Application of the Marijuana Fingerprint System to Analysis of Hashish Samples

The fingerprints of hashish exhibits are expected to differ greatly from those of marijuana because hashish is a product of *Cannabis* processed to concentrate the cannabinoids, primarily THC. For this study the GC/MS data of the hashish samples were obtained using the same fingerprint template developed for marijuana, not a new set of chromatographic peaks specific to the typical hashish profile.

Five countries were represented in the 68 hashish exhibits provided for the study, but only three broad regions: South America (Colombia), the Middle East (Lebanon), and Southwest Asia (Afghanistan, India, and Pakistan). A model based on the five countries produced correct classifications at rates of 67% Colombia, 100% Lebanon, 50% Afghanistan, 67% India, and 73% Pakistan. Because it was noted that the misclassified Afghan, Indian, and Pakistani exhibits all fell in the other Asian classes, those countries were combined, and a second model was created with South America, Middle East, and Southwest Asia as the classes. In the second model, Southwest Asia had 98% correct hits, whereas Colombia and Lebanon were 67 and 100%, respectively, leading us to postulate that the manufacturing methods particular to a region may induce distinct differences in the chemical profiles of hashish. The anomalies in the Colombian samples were attributed to the small number of available exhibits.

Although the *Cannabis* fingerprint system as designed for marijuana reliably determined the origins of hashish samples, a fingerprint based on the actual peaks found in hashish chromatograms would undoubtedly improve the accuracy. Additionally, a study of a marijuana profile compared with the profile of hashish made from that same marijuana could offer insight into the design of a hashish database.

6.8. Examination of Chemical Profiles for Distinguishing Peaks Characteristic of Specific Regions

To determine if certain chemical "marker" compounds could be present in marijuana plants from one region, but absent in plants from another region, data were again crunched, and Pirouette offered some likely candidates to test this so-called silver bullet theory.

Three sesquiterpenes—peak 70, peak 92, and peak 63—were predominantly found in domestic fingerprints. Peak 70 was present in 54% of the domestic specimens and absent in the foreign ones, peak 92 in 90% of the domestic and 13% of the foreign, and peak 63 in 93% domestic and 14% foreign specimens. Peak 92 was identified as *cis*-nerolidol, but the others were only tentatively identified because reference standards for those compounds could not be obtained. Mass spectral evidence suggested that peak 63 was γ-elmene and peak 70 either α- or γ-gurjunene.

Peak 130, identified as butylated hydroxytoluene, was detected only in foreign specimens, particularly Jamaican, but never in domestic ones. A sesquiterpene, peak 86, possibly γ-cadinene or β-farnesene, was totally absent from Colombian, Jamaican, and Mexican fingerprints but was detected in more than 50% of the Thai and some domestic profiles. Peak 100, a sesquiterpene identified as guaiol, was detected in only a few Californian, Hawaiian, and Mexican specimens.

Table 4
Possible Marker Compounds

Compound	Presence indicates
cis-Nerolidol	Domestic
γ-Elemene[a]	Domestic
α- or γ-Gurjunene[a]	Domestic
Butylated hydroxytoluene	Foreign (likely Jamaica)
γ-Cadinene or β-farnesene[a]	Thailand (or possibly domestic)
Guaiol	California, Hawaii, or Mexico

[a]Tentative identification.

Individual compounds that could possibly be used as markers for indication of origin are summarized in Table 4.

7. Conclusions

It is concluded from this work that chemical profiles of *Cannabis* samples could be used to determine the geographic origin of the samples provided that a database is available that has been established with profiles of samples of known origin. The predictions that specimens from mature female plants would yield the most consistent data and that specimens should be protected from elevated temperatures were confirmed, as was the likelihood that certain chemical compounds, particularly terpenes, contributed the most evidence of geographic origin.

Having in hand a fully functional *Cannabis* fingerprint system that could readily be utilized to gather trafficking data, the goals of the study were realized. The system provided a means to distinguish foreign grown marijuana from that grown domestically as well as to distinguish plants grown indoors from those grown outdoors. The system could also reliably determine the foreign sources of seizures of both marijuana and hashish.

The reliability of the system and its utility is expected to be more in the area of intelligence than for forensic purposes. The techniques developed for the fingerprint system could, however, be applied in certain forensic situations, where the analysis of the multiple constituents of a marijuana sample could rule out the possible sources of origin, but not to definitively determine a specific source.

Although the system did not correctly classify every single specimen, it did show the possibility that one could confidently reveal trends of both worldwide and domestic drug sources. For the system to remain useful over time, the database would need to be updated at regular intervals with high-quality authentic samples that reflect current trends in marijuana production.

Following the phase II studies, agencies in the United States and abroad expressed interest in a *Cannabis* fingerprint system. In 1998, UM licensed the *Cannabis* fingerprint methodologies to the Kentucky State Police in support of their Marijuana Signature Laboratory, part of intelligence operations focused on certain trafficking areas in Kentucky, Tennessee, and West Virginia known as the Appalachia HIDTA (high-intensity drug trafficking areas).

Since the completion of this work, others have reported on the use of other techniques for chromatographic profiling of *Cannabis* and hashish to a very limited extent *(37,38)*. Interest in the fingerprint system continues today. For example, colleagues at the University of Bern, Switzerland, have recently completed a project to use Pirouette software to determine any geographical correlations in *Cannabis* fingerprints of various origins. In a report to the Swiss Federal Office of Public Health in 2004, they concluded that a *Cannabis* fingerprint system could effectively determine the source of marijuana found within Switzerland *(39)*.

Acknowledgments

The authors wish to acknowledge Dr. P. Tobin Maginnis, Associate Professor of Computer and Information Science at the University of Mississippi, who orchestrated our data analysis systems. We also wish to thank the Drug Enforcement Administration and the National Institute on Drug Abuse, which provided both the impetus and the funding for these studies.

References

1. Marnell, T. (ed.) (2001) *Drug Identification Bible.* Amera-Chem, Grand Junction, CO.
2. Holley, J. H., Hadley, K. W., and Turner, C. E. (1975) Constituents of Cannabis sativa L. XI. Cannabindiol and cannabichromene in samples of known geographic origin. *J. Pharm. Sci.* **64(5)**, 892–895.
3. Small, E., Beckstead, H. D., and Chan, A. (1975) The evolution of cannabinoid phenotype in cannabis. *Econ. Bot.* **29(3)**, 219–232.
4. Steinberg, S., Offermeier, J., Field, B. I., and Jansen Van Ryssen, F. W. (1975) Investigation of the influence of soil types, environmental conditions, age and morphological plant parts on the chemical composition of *Cannabis sativa* (dagga) plants. *S. Afr. Med. J.* **49**, 279.
5. De Faubert Maunder, J. G. (1970) A comparative evaluation of the delta-9-tetrahydrocannabinol content of cannabis plants. *J. Assoc. Pub. Anal.* **8**, 42–47.
6. Jenkins, R. W. and Patterson, D. A. (1973) Relation between chemical composition and geographical origin of cannabis. *Forensic Sci.* **2(1)**, 59–66.
7. Novotny, M., Lee, M. L., and Low, C. E. (1976) Analysis of marihuana samples from different origins by high resolution gas chromatography for forensic application. *Anal. Chem.* **48(1)**, 24–29.
8. Wheals, B. B. (1976) Forensic applications of high pressure liquid chromatography. *Chromatography* **122**, 85–105.
9. Baker, P. B. and Fowler, R. (1978) Analytical aspects of the chemistry of cannabis. *Proc. Anal. Div. Chem. Soc.* **15(12)**, 347–349.
10. Tucker, R. B. and Graham, B. F. (1979) Cannabinoid content of a stand of cannabis grown clandestinely in Nova Scotia. *J. Can. Soc. Forensic Sci.* **12(4)**, 163–172.
11. Baker, P. B., Fowler, R., Bagon, K. R., and Gough, T. A. (1980) Determination of the distribution of cannabinoids in cannabis resin using high performance liquid chromatography. *J. Anal. Toxicol.* **4(3)**, 145–152.
12. Baker, P. B., Gough, T. A., and Taylor, B. J. (1980) Illicitly imported cannabis products: some physical and chemical features indicative of their origin. *Bull. Narc.* **32(2)**, 31–40.
13. Baker, P. B., Bagon, K. R., and Gough, T. A. (1980) Variation in the THC content of illicitly imported cannabis products. *Bull. Narc.* **32(4)**, 47–54.

14. Hemphill, J. K., Turner, J. C., and Mahlberg, P. G. (1980) Cannabinoid content of individual plant organs from different geographical strains of *Cannabis sativa*, L. *J. Nat. Prod.* **43(1)**, 112–122.
15. Baker, P. B., Gough, T. A., and Taylor, B. J. (1982) The physical and chemical features of cannabis plants grown in the United Kingdom of Great Britain and Northern Ireland from seeds of known origin. *Bull. Narc.* **34(1)**, 27–36.
16. Idilbi, M. M., Huvenne, J. P., Fleury, G., Tran Van Ky, P., Muller, P. H., and Moschetto, Y. (1985) Hashish analysis using gas chromatography coupled to fourier transform infrared spectroscopy. II. Tetrahyrocannabinol determiniation. *Bull. Soc. Pharm. Lille* **41(4)**, 33–35.
17. Nakahara, Y. and Tanak, K. (1988) Studies on discrimination of confiscated cannabis products by high performance liquid chromatography with electrochemical detector. *Bull. Natl. Inst. Hyg. Sci.* **106**, 11–88.
18. Gough, T. A. (1991) The examination of drugs in smuggling offences, in *The Analysis of Drugs of Abuse* (Gough, T. A., ed.), John Wiley & Sons, Hoboken, NJ, pp. 511–565.
19. Pitts, J. E., Neal, J. D. and Gough, T. A. (1992) Some features of cannabis plants grown in the United Kingdom from seeds of known origin. *J. Pharm. Pharmacol.* **44(12)**, 947–951.
20. Fagioli, F., Locatelli, C., Scanavini, L., Landi, S., and Donini, G. B. (1986) Characterization of narcotics of vegetal origin by their content of various elements determined by atomic adsorption spectrophotometry with sampling in carbonaceous slurry. *Anal. Sci.* **2(3)**, 239–242.
21. Watling, R. J. (1998) Sourcing the provenance of cannabis crops using inter-element association patterns "fingerprinting" and laser ablation inductively coupled plasma mass spectrometry. J. Anal. Atomic Spectrometry **19(9)**, 917–926.
22. Hood, L. V. S. and Barry, G. T. (1978) Headspace volatiles of marihuana and hashish: gas chromatographic analysis of samples of different geographic origin. *J. Chromatogr.* **166(2)**, 499–506.
23. Krishnamurty, H. G. and Kaushal, R. (1976) Free sugars and cyclitols of Indian marijuana (*Cannabis sativa*, L.). *J. Chem.* **14B(8)**, 639–640.
24. Bryant, V. M., Jones, J. G., and Midenhall, D. C. (1990) Forensic palynology in the United States of America. *Palynology* **14**, 193–208.
25. Crosby, T. K., Watt, J. C., Kistemaker, A. C., and Nelson, P. E. (1986) Entomological identification of the origin of imported cannabis. *J. Forensic Sci. Soc.* **26(1)**, 35–44.
26. Smith, K. G. V. (ed.) (1986) Cannabis insects, in *A Manual of Forensic Entomology*, Cornell University Press, Ithaca, NY, pp. 169–173.
27. Gilmore, S., Peakall, R., and Robertson, J. (2003) Short tandem repeat (STR) DNA markers are hypervariable and informative in Cannabis sativa: implications for forensic investigations. *Forensic Sci. Int.* **131(1)**, 65–74.
28. Miller, C. H., Palmbach, T., Juliano, N., Ladd, C., and Lee, H. C. (2003) An overview of DNA methods for the identification and individualizion of marijuana. *Croat. Med. J.* **44(3)**, 315–321.
29. Hsieh, H. M., Hou, R. J., Chen, K. F., et al. (2004) Establishing the rDNA IGS signature of *Cannabis sativa*. *J. Forensic Sci.* **49(3)**, 477–480.
30. Gigliano, G. S. and Finizio, A. D. (1997/1998) The Cannabis *sativa* L. fingerprint as a tool in forensic investigations. *Bull. Narc.* **XLIX & L(1 & 2)**, 129–137.
31. Adelmonem, A., Clark, V. A., and May, S. (2004) *Computer Aided Multivariate Analysis*, Chapman & Hall/CRC Press, Boca Raton, FL.
32. Everitt, B. S. and Dunn, G. (2001) *Applied Multivariate Data Analysis*, Oxford University Press, New York.
33. Turner, C. E., ElSohly, M. A., and Boeren, E. G. (1980) Constituents of *Cannabis sativa* L, XVII: a review of the natural constituents. *J. Nat. Prod.* **43(2)**, 169–234.

34. Brenneisen, R. and ElSohly, M. A. (1988) Chromatographic and spectroscopic profiles of *Cannabis* of different origins: Part I. *J. Forensic Sci.* **33(6)**, 1385–1404.
35. Adams, R. P. (1989) *Identification of Essential Oils by Ion Trap Mass Spectroscopy*, Academic Press, San Diego, CA.
36. Lewis, R., Ward, S., Johnson, R., and Thorburn Burns, D. (2005) Distribution of the principal cannabinoids within bars of compressed cannabis resin. *Anal. Chim. Acta* **538**, 399–405.
37. Lehmann, T. and Brenneisen, R. (1995) High performance liquid chromatographic profiling of cannabis products. *J. Liq. Chromatogr.* **18(4)**, 689–700.
38. Hida, M., Mitsui, T., Minami, Y., and Fujimura, Y. (1995) Classification of hashish by pyrolysis-gas chromatography. *J. Anal. Appl. Pyrolysis* **32**, 197–204.
39. Brenneisen, R. and Meyer, P. (2004) Chemical profiling of cannabis produced in Switzerland. *Final Report to Swiss Federal Office of Public Health*, University of Bern, Switzerland.

Chapter 4

Marijuana Smoke Condensate

Chemistry and Pharmacology

Hala N. ElSohly and Mahmoud A. ElSohly

1. Introduction

Cannabis sativa is one of the oldest plants known to medicine and one of the most thoroughly studied plants today. Much knowledge has been gained about the chemistry, pharmacology, metabolism, and pharmacokinetics of pure compounds from *Cannabis*, as well as the chemical and biological analysis of marijuana smoke condensate (MSC). In this chapter, we review data related to the preparation of MSC, the composition and analysis of MSC, and the pharmacological and toxicological effects of MSC.

2. Preparation of Marijuana Smoke Condensate

Patel and Gori *(1)* described the preparation of marijuana cigarettes and the production of MSC. Various analytical parameters of blended marijuana (i.e., ash, hexane solubles, nitrate, reducing sugars, citric acid, malic acid, oxalic acid, potassium, sodium, calcium, magnesium, cadmium, chromium, and Δ^9-tetrahydrocannabinol [THC]) and marijuana cigarettes (average weight, average moisture content, static burning rate, fire zone temperature at 15- and 55-mm marks) were determined.

2.1. Production of Smoke Condensate

The cigarettes to be smoked were first conditioned at 24 ± 1°C and 60 ± 5% relative humidity. The average weight of a marijuana cigarette was 1.1 g. The smoking machine used was designed to automatically load, light, smoke, and eject approx 2000 cigarettes per hour and take a maximum of 10 puffs per cigarette at the rate of

From: *Forensic Science and Medicine: Marijuana and the Cannabinoids*
Edited by: M. A. ElSohly © Humana Press Inc., Totowa, New Jersey

one puff per minute. The smoke condensate-trapping system consisted of four 3-L Pyrex reaction flasks with Teflon® covers, glass and Teflon interconnecting piping, and a leak-tight stainless steel tank with metal support for flasks. The assembled traps were housed in a refrigerated cabinet capable of sustained operation down to –30°F. The traps were further cooled down to –90°F by immersion in a slurry of dry ice and isopropanol. The condensate from the trapping system was extracted with acetone and concentrated *in vacuo* (<40°C) to yield a smoke condensate sample with less than 5% water. The mean dry smoke condensate yield was 9.37 ± 1.05 (mg/cigarette). Analysis of cannabinoids in the smoke condensate was carried out by gas chromatography/flame ionization detection (GC/FID) *(2)* using a packed column (6 ft × 2 mm, 3% OV-17 on 180-120 mesh Gas-Chrom Q). The mean percentage ($n = 8$) of Δ^9-THC, cannabidiol, and cannabinol in the smoke condensate was 3.63 ± 0.15, 1.95 ± 0.13, and 1.87 ± 0.08, respectively.

Sparacino et al. *(3)* prepared cigarettes from Mexican marijuana containing 1.3% Δ^9-THC (labeled as low dose) and 4.4% Δ^9-THC (labeled as high dose) using low-porosity "street" cigarette papers. Standard research tobacco cigarettes were also prepared. Marijuana and tobacco cigarettes were used to generate smoke condensates under constant draft or intermittent puff smoking modes. The evaluation of smoke condensates from these two systems would provide a qualitative and quantitative range within which the various components of the marijuana smoke actually experienced by human smokers might be found. The cigarette smoking was conducted at flow rates of 1200 mL per minute for all constant draft combustion runs, 40 mL per 2-second puff (one puff per minute) for puff mode combustion runs with marijuana, and 35 mL per 2-second puff (one puff per minute) for puff mode combustion runs with tobacco cigarettes. Six smoke condensates were generated: MSC—low potency by puff and constant draft mode; MSC—high potency by puff and by constant draft; and tobacco smoke condensate by puff and by constant draft.

3. Fractionation and Analysis of Marijuana Smoke Condensate

MSC is a highly complex matrix containing several thousand compounds that may vary over several orders of magnitude *(4)*. A liquid–liquid fractionation scheme *(5,6)* allowed the separation of these components into different classes of compounds (i.e., acidic, basic, and neutral: nonpolar, polar, and polyaromatic hydrocarbons; *see* Fig. 1).

In 1975, Jones and Foote *(7)* reported acids, phenols, and bases that were chemically separated from the smoke condensate of 2638 marijuana cigarettes and semi-quantitatively analyzed by GC and GC/mass spectrometry (MS). The analysis of the basic fraction (1.47 g, 4.8% of total MSC hydrochlorides) was carried out by GC/FID using a packed column (10 ft. × $^1/_8$ in., 28% Pennwalt 223 + 4% KOH on chromosorb R, 80-100 mesh). While no fore-column was used for the GC/MS analysis, a glass fore-column was used for GC/MS analysis with the first 2 in. packed with powdered soda lime to liberate the amines and the remaining 5 in. packed with ascarite to absorb water. The phenolic fraction (0.96 g, 4.6% of total MSC) was analyzed as the TMS derivative by GC/thermal conductivity detector using a packed column (5% OV-17 on Diatoport S, 60-80 mesh). The acidic fraction (1.57g, 7.5% of total MSC) was esteri-

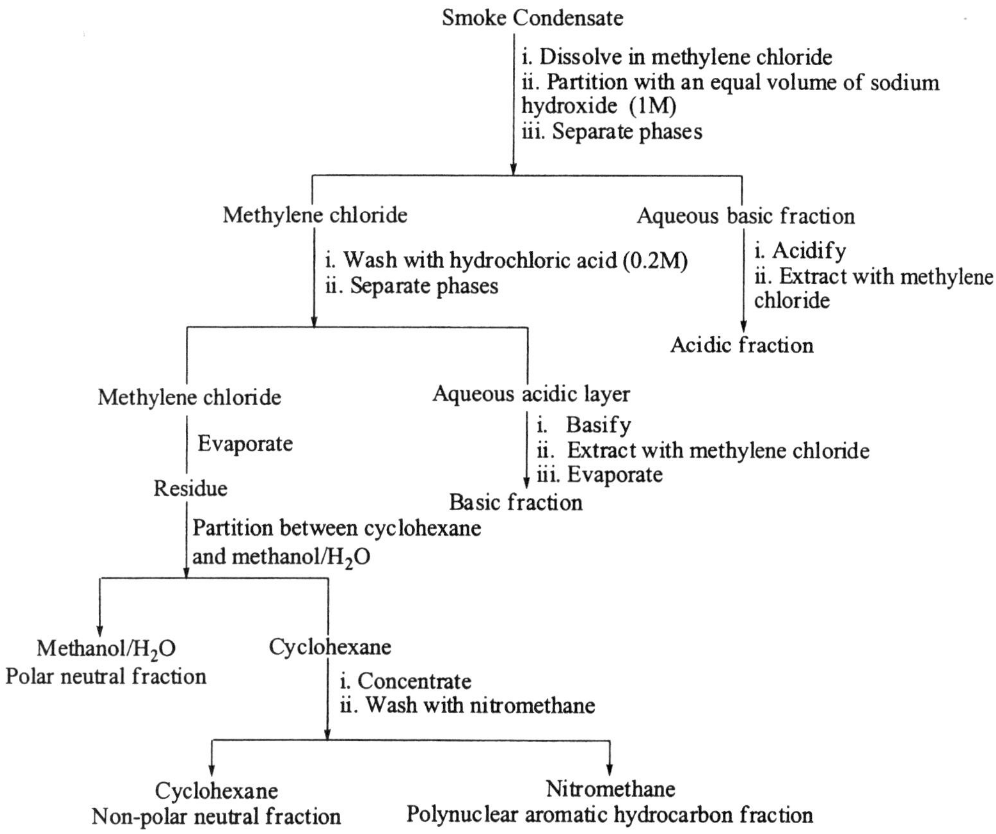

Fig. 1. Fractionation scheme for marijuana smoke condensate.

fied with boron trifluoride-methanol (BF_3-MeOH, 14%, V/V) to the corresponding methyl esters and analyzed by GC/FID using a packed column (2% OV-17 on Gas-Chrom Q, 80-100 mesh). The neutral fraction (17.4 g, 83.1% of the total MSC) was not analyzed.

Van Den Bosch et al. *(8)* reported on the constituents of MSC generated from 640 cigarettes hand-rolled from Mexican marijuana (Δ^9-THC content 1.29%). The condensate was fractionated into basic (0.3 g), phenolic (1.6 g), acidic (0.3 g), and neutral (6.9 g) fractions. The neutral fraction was further purified by column chromatography using silica gel and a step-gradient mobile phase consisting of *n*-hexane, *n*-hexane-benzene, benzene, ether, and methanol. The different fractions were analyzed by GC and GC/MS using a glass column (200 × 3 mm id) packed with 3% OV-17 on chrompak SA (80-100 mesh) or a glass capillary column containing OV-101.

Zamir-ul Haq et al. *(9)* identified and quantitatively determined the *N*-heterocyclic carbazole, indole, and skatole in MSC using GC, MS, and liquid scintillation spectrometry. The dry condensate was partitioned between hexane and methanol/water. The hexane fraction was subjected to column chromatography to yield a fraction enriched in the above-mentioned compounds. Qualitative analysis was carried out by GC/FID/MS using a glass column (6 ft × 2 mm) packed with 3% Silar 5CP on Gas

Chrom Q. For the quantitative analysis, separate experiments were done using individual radiolabeled carbazole, indole, and skatole as internal standards. The operational losses of carbazole, indole, and skatole were quite different from each other, and thus none of the internal standards could be used for the quantitation of the other components. The average amounts of carbazole, indole, and skatole were 89 ± 3, 826 ± 4, and 597 ± 7 μg/g of fresh condensate, respectively. The effect of aging of the condensate was studied by analysis of a composite of all samples collected every 8 weeks for 2 years. The data showed a decrease in the levels of carbazole and indole, whereas levels of skatole increased on standing.

The previously described solvent partition method (Fig. 1; ref. *6*) was used by Merli et al. *(10)* to separate the basic fraction of Mexican MSC. Enrichment of some trace components was accomplished with high-performance liquid chromatography on an aminosilane-bonded Porasil C *(11)*. The analysis of this fraction was carried out by capillary GC/MS using a glass capillary column (50 m × 0.25 mm id) etched with gaseous HCl at 400°C and statically coated with UCON 50-HB-2000 stationary phase. Kalignost or benzyltriphenyl phosphonium chloride was added directly to the stationary phase solution in order to form a 10% addition to the amount of polymer phase used. The method allowed the identification of more than 300 nitrogen-containing compounds. The authors pointed to the fact that certain compounds of the hydrogen-donor nature, e.g., indole and carbazole derivatives, may end up in the polar neutral fraction *(12)* while using this solvent partitioning scheme. In addition, the comparison of MSC with that of tobacco (prepared and characterized by the same methodology) revealed that there are both qualitative and quantitative differences between the two condensates.

Further analysis of the basic fraction of marijuana and tobacco smoke condensates was carried out by Novotny et al. *(13)* using capillary GC/MS. The use of thermostable Superox-coated glass capillary column (Superox-4, 15 m × 0.25 mm id) allowed for the elution of relatively large nitrogen-containing compounds. The use of short columns allowed the elution of larger nitrogen-containing molecules in a reasonable time without sacrificing the peak resolution needed for the subsequent mass spectral investigations. Marijuana and tobacco smoke condensates showed qualitative similarities with a number of alkylated pyridine and quinoline derivatives, aza-indoles, and aza-carbazoles; however, quantities of these components in both condensates were quite different.

Sparicino et al. *(3)* analyzed the strongly mutagenic fraction of MSC, produced from high-dose marijuana (Δ^9-THC, 4.4%) under constant draft mode, by GC/MS. A capillary column (60 m, packed with DB-1701) was used. Approximately 200 compounds were identified. About half of this total were amines; with about half of these being aromatic amines. Pyrazines, pyrimidines, pyrroles, pyridines, and isoxazoles were the predominant compound classes. Some alkylated pyrazoles and pyrazines, as well as an alkylated benzimidazole, were detected in very large amounts.

Chemical ionization/MS was used to quantify noncannabinoid phenols in MSC *(14)*. The methylene chloride-soluble material of the smoke condensate generated from 100 cigarettes prepared from female Mexican marijuana was fractionated between saturated aqueous sodium bicarbonate and then with 0.1 *N* aqueous sodium hydroxide solution. The aqueous sodium bicarbonate and sodium hydroxide solutions were acidified, extracted with ether, and analyzed as their TMS derivatives. A stainless steel column (3 m, 1% OV-17 on 100/120 mesh Gas-Chrom Q) and FID were used.

A capillary GC/MS method was developed by Maskarinec et al. *(15)* for the analysis of organic acids and phenols in MSC. The methodology used consisted of solvent partitioning *(6)*, selective fraction enrichment by gel chromatography, followed by conversion of sample components to volatile methyl ester/ether derivatives for GC. A glass capillary column (20 m × 0.25 mm id) coated with free fatty acid phase was used, and it provided adequate resolution required for the MS investigation of the sample components. GC profiles of the acidic fractions obtained from Mexican (100 cigarettes, Δ^9-THC, 2.8%; 6.25 mg acid/cigarette) and Turkish marijuana (100 cigarettes, Δ^9-THC, 0.3%) and standard tobacco (prepared from equal weight, 2.05 mg acid/cigarette) smoke condensates were compared and indicated both qualitative and quantitative changes in the constituents of chromatographic profiles. Forty-nine components were identified in the acidic fraction of Mexican MSC.

Analysis of the polynuclear aromatic hydrocarbon fraction (*see* Fig. 1; ref. *6*) of marijuana and tobacco smoke condensates was carried out with a combination of chromatographic and spectral methods *(16)*. Selective enriched extracts were further purified by liquid chromatographic methods and analyzed by capillary GC/MS using a capillary column (11 m × 0.26 mm id) coated with SE-52 methyl phenyl silicone as a stationary phase. Approximately 150 polynuclear compounds in each smoke material type were quantitated and tentatively identified as to parent ring structures and type of alkyl substituents. Further identification of methyl derivatives of polynuclear aromatic hydrocarbons in air particulates, tobacco, and MSCs was accomplished by chromatographic separation into fractions of similar ring types and analysis using nuclear magnetic resonance *(17)*. The positions of substitution in the rings were identified from the methyl chemical shifts. For the lower relative molecular mass fractions of anthracene-phenanthrene and fluoranthene-pyrene, the smaller number of methyl derivatives made identification possible from nuclear magnetic resonance alone. For mixtures containing benz[*a*]anthracene and chrysene derivatives, additional GC/MS was required. Overnight accumulation of Fourier transform spectra allowed approx 20-μg amounts of single constituents to be measured in 0.5- to 1.5-mg fractions.

The analysis of the neutral constituents (polar and nonpolar) of the smoke condensates of Mexican marijuana and standard tobacco (obtained according to Fig. 1) was carried out using GC/MS *(18)*. Because the constituents of the polar neutral fraction were mostly nonvolatile, silylation facilitated a partial characterization of this fraction. A glass capillary column (50 m × 0.25 mm id) coated with OV-101 methyl silicone fluid was used. In total, more than 130 neutral smoke components were characterized. It is to be pointed out that the comparison of the chromatographic profiles of the nonpolar fractions for marijuana and tobacco indicated some similarities, but also qualitative and quantitative differences in their terpenic compositions. The authors noted that peaks eluting in the temperature range of 120–160°C represent fairly unique components of marijuana smoke. Terpenes of these and similar structures have previously been found in the unburned marijuana samples *(19)* and are believed to be responsible for the characteristic odor of marijuana and its smoke. The components of the polar neutral fraction of both marijuana and tobacco smoke condensates revealed considerable similarity between the two materials. The only notable differences are the expected presence of nicotine and main cannabinoids in tobacco and marijuana smoke, respectively. The profiles of phenolic substances in tobacco and marijuana were qualitatively and quantitatively similar. A summary of the acidic, phenolic, non-polar neutral, polar neutral and polynuclear aromatic hydrocarbons is presented in Table 1.

4. Pharmacological and Toxicological Activities

4.1. Behavioral Activity

Whole smoke condensate from female Mexican marijuana was solvent-fractionated into four fractions using pentane, ether, methylene chloride, and ethanol. These fractions were tested in the rat (iv via leg or tail veins) for spontaneous posture, catatonic, locomotion, and coordination as well as evoked responses of arousal, startle, vocalization, and biting. The smoke condensate of marijuana (6 mg/mL, 0.44 mg/mL of Δ^9-THC) and the pentane fraction (3 mg/mL, 0.5 mg/mL of Δ^9-THC) had less behavioral effects in the rat than the corresponding amounts of Δ^9-THC contained in those extracts. The EtOH extract (2 mg/mL, $\leq$0.04 mg/mL Δ^9-THC) had behavioral effects in two or three depressant parameters, and these effects were enhanced by the addition of Δ^9-THC. The methylene chloride (2 mg/mL, $\leq$0.04 mg/mL Δ^9-THC) showed no behavioral activity when given alone, but produced with added Δ^9-THC an enhanced catatonic effect and decreased the provoked bite effect that Δ^9-THC produces. It was concluded *(21)* that the various fractions of MSC produced behavioral effects in the absence of Δ^9-THC. Subsequently, a study *(22)* was carried out on the pharmacological activity of the acidic, basic, and polar-neutral fractions of marijuana whole smoke condensate alone and in combination with Δ^9-THC. Male Swiss-Webster mice were used for all studies, and all administrations were via the tail vein. The acidic fraction was essentially inactive in a general activity screen at doses of 5 and 25 mg/kg. A dose of 125 mg/kg caused a nonspecific depression of behavioral and neurological parameters with little effect on autonomic function. The basic fraction also showed little activity in a general pharmacological screen at doses of 5, 10, and 20 mg/kg. Incidence of defecation and urination was also reduced at doses of 17 and 29 mg/kg. The polar-neutral fraction lowered body position, impaired motor coordination, and induced hypothermia at 30 and 60 minutes postinjection at a dose of 200 mg/kg. Both the acidic and polar-neutral fractions altered the activity of Δ^9-THC when administered with that compound. Doses of 5.6 mg/kg acidic fraction and 7.4 mg/kg polar-neutral fraction prolonged the hypothermia induced by 1 mg/kg Δ^9-THC, while not affecting body temperature when administered alone. The basic fraction, however, did not alter body temperature when given alone or in combination with Δ^9-THC. A subsequent study on the basic fraction of MSC obtained from Mexican marijuana (0.8% Δ^9-THC) was evaluated in mice *(23)* looking at behavioral, neurological, and autonomic effects. This fraction administered by intravenous route (tail vein) at doses of 5, 10, and 20 mg/kg caused impairment of visual placing, increase in tail pinch response, decrease in tail evaluation, and induction of piloerection. These effects, although statistically significant, were slight and not consistently dose dependent. In doses rang-

Table 1
Basic, Acidic, Phenolic, Nonpolar Neutral, Polar Neutral and Polynuclear Aromatic Hydrocarbons Present in Marijuana Smoke Condensate

Class of compounds	Amount	Ref.	Present in tobacco smoke?
Basic			
Dimethylamine	4%	*7*	No
Piperidine	2%	*7*	No
Pyridine	43%	*7,10*	Yes
2-Methylpyridine	16%	*7,10*	Yes
Pyrrole	2%	*7*	
3-(and/or 4-)Methylpyridine + dimethylpyridine	18%	*7*	
Two dimethyl- or ethylpyridines		*8,10*	
One trimethyl-, methyl ethyl-, or propylpyridine		*8,13*	
Quinoline		*8,13*	No
Methylpyrazine		*3,8,10*	No
2,5-Dimethylpyrazine		*8*	
2,6-Dimethylpyrazine		*8*	
Methyl ethyl pyrazine		*3,8,10*	
One dimethyl-, diethyl-, methylpropyl-, or butylpyrazine		*3,8*	
Norharman		*8*	
Harman		*8*	
Carbazole	89 ± 3 μg/g of fresh condensate	*9,16*	
Indole[a]	826 ± 4 μg/g of fresh condensate	*9,18*	
Skatole	597 ± 7 μg/g of fresh condensate	*9*	
Dimethylamino acetonitrile		*10*	Yes
Methylpyrimidine		*3,10*	No
2,6-Dimethylpyridine		*10*	Yes
3-Methylpyridine		*10*	Yes
Dimethyl- or ethylthiazole or -isothiazole (2 isomers)		*10*	Yes
4-Methylpyridine		*10*	Yes
2-Ethylpyridine		*10*	Yes
Dimethyl-, ethylpyrazine or -pyrimidine (3 isomers)		*10*	No
Trimethyl-, ethyl methyl-, or propyl pyridine (20 isomers)		*10,13*	Yes
2,5-Dimethyl pyridine		*10*	Yes

(continued)

Table 1 *(continued)*

Class of compounds	Amount	Ref.	Present in tobacco smoke?
2,4-Dimethyl pyridine		*10*	Yes
2,3-Dimethyl pyridine		*10*	Yes
3-Ethyl pyridine		*10*	Yes
2-Vinyl pyridine		*3,10*	Yes
4-Ethyl pyridine		*10*	Yes
Trimethyl- or methylethylthiazole or isothiazole		*10*	No
Trimethyl or methyl ethyl pyrazine or pyrimidines (4 isomers)		*10*	Yes
Trimethyl pyrimidines		*10*	Yes
Methyl ethyl pyrimidines		*10*	Yes
Butyl-, methyl propyl-, diethyl-, ethyldimethyl-, or tetramethylpyridine (33 isomers)		*10*	Yes
3,5-Dimethylpyridine		*10*	Yes
Propyl-, methyl ethyl-, or trimethylpyrazole or -imidaole (15 isomers)		*3,10,13*	Yes
3-Vinyl pyridine		*10,13*	Yes
3,4-Dimethylpyridine		*7,10*	Yes
Methyl vinyl- or propenyl pyridine, or azaindan		*10,13*	Yes
Butyl-, methyl propyl-, diethyl-, diethylmethyl-, or tetramethylpyridine or -pyrazine (5 isomers)		*10*	Yes
Alkylpyridine with five or more carbon atoms in saturated side chains (45 isomers)		*10*	Yes
Butyl-, methyl propyl-, diethyl-, dimethylethyl-, or tetramethylpyrazole or -imidazole (16 isomers)		*3,10*	No
3-Methoxypyridine		*10*	Yes
2-Acetylpyridine		*3,10*	Yes
N-Furfurylpyrrolidine (?)		*10*	Yes
Methylmethoxypyridine		*10*	No
4-Methylthio-2-butanone (?)		*10*	No
Methylacetylpyridine (4 isomers)		*10,13*	Yes
1-Methylimidazole		*3,10*	No
Furfuryl alcohol		*10,13*	Yes
Ethylvinyl-, dimethylvinyl-, methylpropenyl-, or methyl azaindan or tetrahydronaphthalene (35 isomers)		*10,13*	Yes

(continued)

Table 1 *(continued)*

Class of compounds	Amount	Ref.	Present in tobacco smoke?
Ethyl- or dimethylpyrazole or imidazole (5 isomers)		*3,10*	Yes
Benzoxazole		*10*	No
3-Acetylpyridine		*10*	Yes
Methylamino- or aminomethylpyridine (15 isomers)		*10*	Yes
Pyridine with five or more carbons in side chains including one double bond, or forming one ring (41 isomers)		*10*	Yes
Methylfurfurylpyrrolidine (?)		*10*	Yes
2-Propionylpyridine		*10*	No
4-Acetylpyridine		*10*	No
Dimethyl- or ethylacetylpyridine (2 isomers)		*10,13*	Yes
2-Aminopyridine		*10*	Yes
Alkylpyrazole or -imidazole with five or more carbon atoms in saturated side chain(s) (42 isomers)		*3,10*	No
Methylamino- or amino methylpyrazine or -pyrimidine or dimethylaminopyridine (4 isomers)		*10*	No
Aminoethyl-, ethylamino-, aminodimethyl amino-, or methylaminomethylpyridine (13 isomers)		*10*	Yes
Divinylpyridine, azadihydronaphthaline or methyl azaindine (2 isomers)		*10*	Yes
Quinoline		*3,10,13*	No
Nicotine		*3,10,13*	Yes
Diazanaphthalene (2 isomers)		*10*	Yes
Methoxyaminopyridine (?)		*10*	No
Isoquinoline		*10,13*	No
Indazole or pyrrolopyridine (3 isomers)		*10*	Yes
Aminoethyl-, ethylamino-, aminodimethyl dimethylamino-, methylaminomethylpyrazine or pyrimidine or methyldiaminopyridine (5 isomers)		*10*	Yes
8-Methylquinoline		*10*	No

(continued)

Table 1 *(continued)*

Class of compounds	Amount	Ref.	Present in tobacco smoke?
2-Methylquinoline		*10*	No
7-Methylquinoline		*10*	No
4-Methylquinoline		*10*	No
Other methylquinolines and -isoquinolines (10 isomers, 14 in all)		*10*	Yes
Methylindazole, -benzimidazole, or -pyrrolopyridine (12 isomers)		*3,10*	Yes
Pyridine with five or more carbon atoms in side chains including two double bonds or containing one ring and one double bond (11 isomers)		*10,13*	Yes
2-*tert*-Butylphenol		*10*	No
2,4-Dimethylquinoline		*10*	No
Other dimethyl- or ethylquinolines or -isoquinolines (19 isomers, 20 in all)		*10*	Yes
Methyldiazanaphthalene (3 isomers)		*10*	Yes
Dimethyl- or ethylindazole, benzimidazole, or pyrrolopyridine (23 isomers)		*3,10*	Yes
Aminopyrazine or -pyrimidine with three carbon atoms in saturated side chain(s) or a dimethyl- or ethyldiaminopyridine		*10*	Yes
Vinylquinoline or phenylpyridine (3 isomers)		*10*	Yes
Methylvinylquinoline or methylphenylpyridine (6 isomers)		*10*	Yes
2-Pyridine carboxamide		*10,13*	Yes
Aminopyridine with four carbon atoms in saturated side chain(s) (3 isomers)		*10*	No
Azaindanone (?)		*10*	No
Methylpyridine carboxamide		*10,13*	No
Methylpyrrolopyrimidine or -pyrazine (?) (2 isomers)		*10*	No
Dimethyl- or ethylpyrrolopyrimidine or -pyrazine (?)		*10*	No
Propyl-, methyl ethyl-, trimethylquinoline or -isoquinoline (4 isomers)		*10*	Yes

(continued)

Table 1 *(continued)*

Class of compounds	Amount	Ref.	Present in tobacco smoke?
Quinoline or isoquinoline with four or more carbon atoms in saturated side chain(s) (2 compounds)		*10*	No
Methylazanaphthalene (7 isomers)		*13*	Yes
Methylazaindole (6 isomers)		*13*	Yes
C_2 Azanaphthalene (9 isomers)		*13*	Yes
C_3 Azanaphthalene (2 isomers)		*13*	No
An allylquinoline (?)		*13*	No
An azaindole		*13*	No
C_2 Azaindole (9 isomers)		*13*	Yes[b]
Vinylazanaphthalene (2 isomers)		*13*	Yes[b]
C_3 Azaindole (3 isomers)		*13*	No
Alkyldiazole (6 isomers)		*13*	No
N-Methylazacarbazole		*13*	Yes
A hexenylazaindole (?)		*13*	No
A C_6 diazanaphthalene (?)		*13*	No
A dimethylazacarbazole		*13*	No
An ethylazacarbazole		*13*	No
Methylazacarbazole (4 isomers)		*13*	Yes[c]
C_3 azacarbazole (2 isomers)		*13*	No
Azacarbazole (2 isomers)		*13*	Yes[b]
A C_4 azacarbazole		*13*	No
A C_2 diazole		*13*	Yes
C_3 Pyridine (3 isomers)		*13*	No
C_4 Pyridine (3 isomers)		*13*	Yes
C_5 Pyridine (5 isomers)		*13*	No
C_2 Vinylpyridine (6 isomers)		*13*	No
Acetylpyridine		*13*	No
C_3 Vinylpyridine (3 isomers)		*13*	No
C_4 Azaindole[d]		*13*	Yes
Myosmine[d]		*13*	Yes
Bipyridyl[d] (3 isomers)		*13*	Yes
C_2 bipyridyl[d] (4 isomers)		*13*	Yes
C_3 bipyridyl[d]		*13*	Yes
Methylbipyrdiyl[d]		*13*	Yes
N-Mcthylanatabine[d]		*13*	Yes
Nicotine[d]		*13*	Yes
Anatabine[d]		*13*	Yes
Methylbipyridyl[d] (3 isomers)		*13*	Yes
N-Furfurylnornicotine[d]		*13*	Yes
N-Furfurylanabasine[d]		*13*	Yes
Cotinine[d]		*13*	Yes
Aminoquinoline[d]		*13*	Yes
N-Formylnornicotine[d]		*13*	Yes

(continued)

Table 1 *(continued)*

Class of compounds	Amount	Ref.	Present in tobacco smoke?
N-Acetylanatabine[d] (?)		*13*	Yes
N-Formylanatabine[d] (?)		*13*	Yes
Methylpyridoyl pyrrolidine[d] (?)		*13*	Yes
N-Ethylnornicotine[d] (?)		*13*	Yes
N-Methylanabasine[d] (?)		*13*	Yes
Methylnicotine[d] (?)		*13*	Yes
N-Propylnornicotine[d] or *N*-ethylanabasine[d]		*13*	Yes
A chloro-C_2-diazanaphthalene[d] (?)		*13*	Yes
A methylpyridylmethyldiazole[d] (?)		*13*	Yes
A C_2 pyridylmethyldiazole[d] (?)		*13*	Yes
A pyridyl-C_4 diazole[d] (?)		*13*	Yes
N-Methyl-3-pyridine carboxamide[d] (?)		*13*	Yes
Propionamide		*3*	
Butyroamide		*3*	
Cyclopentadiene		*3*	
Dimethyltrisulfide		*3*	
3,3-Dimethyloxetase		*3*	
3,3-Dimethylcyclobutanecarbonitrile		*3*	
Methylethylpyrrole		*3*	
Dimethylpiperazine		*3*	
N-Methyl-2-pyridinamine		*3*	
Dimethylethylpyrrole		*3*	
Valeramide		*3*	
2-Methoxy-3-Methylpyrazine		*3*	
Dimethylethanamine imidazole		*3*	
Tropolone		*3*	
Nitropicoline		*3*	
C_7-Alkylamine		*3*	
C_3-Alkylpyrazole		*3,18*	
Dimethylethylpyrimidone		*3*	
Methyl acetyl pyrrole		*3*	
1,4-Benzoquinone		*3*	
Alkylamide		*3*	
m-Aminophenol		*3*	
1-Butoxy-2-propanol		*3*	
Methylpropionylfuran			
3-Methyl-5-triazolo(4,3-a)pyrazine		*3*	
N-(a-picolidene)-*n*-propylamine		*3*	
5-Hydroxyindole		*3*	
C_8-Alkylamine		*3*	
Dimethyltetrazine		*3*	
C_4-Alkylpyrazole isomer		*3,18*	
C_9-Alkylamine		*3*	

(continued)

Table 1 *(continued)*

Class of compounds	Amount	Ref.	Present in tobacco smoke?
C_5-Alkylpyrazole isomer		*3*	
3-Methyl-4-ethylpyrrole		*3*	
$C_9H_{12}O$		*3*	
$C_9H_{14}O$		*3*	
$C_{10}H_{14}O$		*3*	
$C_8H_{12}O$		*3*	
Phenoxyethanol		*3*	
Aminobenzamide		*3*	
Phenylurea		*3*	
Methylthiopyridine		*3*	
Methylquinoline		*3*	
C_6-Alkylpyrazole		*3*	
Methoxybenzaldehyde		*3*	
4-Methyl carbostyril		*3*	
C_4-Alkyl pyrazine		*3*	
Propylmethoxyphenol isomer		*3*	
3-Methyl-1,8-naphthyridine isomer		*3*	
Pyridine carboxylic acid, methyl		*3*	
Benzoic acid, 3-methyl		*3*	
Phenyl pyrazoline		*3*	
3,4-Dimethylbenzoic acid		*3*	
Benzylacetate		*3*	
1,2-Dihydro-3-isobutyl-1-methylpyrazin-2-one		*3*	
Ethyl hydroxyacetophenone		*3*	
2,4-Dimethylquinazoline		*3*	
Phenyl methyl urea		*3*	
Phenyl pyridine		*3*	
Propylbenzimidazole		*3*	
Aminoquinoline or $C_9H_8N_2$		*3*	
Dimethylnaphthyridine		*3*	
N-Phenylacrylamide		*3*	
Methoxypropylpyrazine		*3*	
Phenyl alcohol		*3*	
Ethoxybenzaldehyde		*3*	
Tolyl azide		*3*	
Phenylmethylguanidine		*3*	
C_6-Alkylphenol		*3*	
C_3-Alkylbenzimidazole		*3*	
1-Decanol		*3*	
C_5-Alkylpyrazine		*3*	
Alkylamide		*3*	
Dimethyl benzimidazone isomer		*3*	
Trimethyl-2-oxo-1,2,3,4-tetrahydropyrimidine		*3*	

(continued)

Table 1 *(continued)*

Class of compounds	Amount	Ref.	Present in tobacco smoke?
Dimethoxybenzene isomer		*3*	
Aminodimethylpyrimidine		*3*	
Hydroxymethylquinoline		*3*	
Methylbenzoxazole		*3*	
tert-Butyl-hydroxybenzoate		*3*	
$C_{10}H_{12}O_2$ (ester)		*3*	
Methyl-*n*(pyrid-2-yl)dihydropyrrole		*3*	
$C_{12}H_{18}O$		*3*	
Methylaminonaphthyridine		*3*	
Diphenylamine		*3*	
$C_9H_{10}O_3$		*3*	
Ethoxyquinazoline or isomer		*3*	
Diethylphenylene diamine		*3*	
$C_5H_5N_5$ isomer		*3*	
N,N-Dimethyl-*N*-(*p*-methoxyphenyl)formamide		*3*	
Nitroacetamide		*3*	
2,2,4-Trimethylpenta-1,3-diol di-isobutyrate		*3*	
$C_{11}H_6O$ (alcohol)		*3*	
N,N'-Dimethyl-*N,N'*-diethyl-*p*-phenylene diamine		*3*	
Dimethylbenzimidazole		*3*	
Diethyl biphenyl		*3*	
N-Benzyl-4-aminobutyronitrile		*3*	
N-Methyl diphenylamine		*3*	
1-Undecanol		*3*	
Dimethylnaphthyridine or $C_{10}H_{10}N_2$ isomer		*3*	
Trimethylnaphthyridine or $C_{11}H_{12}N_2$ isomer		*3*	
Alkylamide		*3*	
Hexanenitrile 3(pyrrolidinylmethylene) or ($C_{11}H_{18}N_2$) isomers		*3*	
Aminodiphenylene oxide		*3*	
Methylpteridinone isomer		*3*	
Alkyl nitrile		*3*	
2-(Propylamino)benzothiazole		*3*	
$C_{13}H_{22}N_2$ isomer		*3*	
Phenylbenzothiazole		*3*	
Aminomethylquinoline		*3*	
Tetramethylcyclopentanedione		*3*	
1-Methyl-dihydro-β-carboline		*3*	
Alkylamine		*3*	
Alkylthiopyridine		*3*	

(continued)

Table 1 *(continued)*

Class of compounds	Amount	Ref.	Present in tobacco smoke?
Lystrin		*3*	
N,N-Dicyano-4-methylphenylene diamine		*3*	
Alkyl thiopyridine		*3*	
7,8-Benzoquinoline		*3*	
5,5-Diphenylimidazolid-4-one		*3*	
1-Methylphenazine		*3*	
n-Dodecanol		*3*	
Alkyl amide		*3*	
Alkyl amine		*3*	
Methyl palmitate		*3*	
Dimethylnaphtho (2,3,6-) thiophene		*3*	
Homologous aliphatic alcohol (*n*-tridecanol)		*3*	
1-Methyl-β-carboline		*3*	
n-$C_{28}H_{58}$ (octacosane)		*3*	
n-$C_{29}H_{60}$ (nonacosane		*3*	
Alkyl phthalate		*3*	
n-$C_{30}H_{62}$		*3*	
β-carboline		*3*	
p-Cumylphenol		*3*	
Dibutylphthalate		*3*	
Benzyl acetophenone		*3*	
n-Tetradecanol		*3*	
Diphenylpyridine isomer		*3*	
Alkyl ester		*3*	
Dihydroxymethyl phenyl quinazoline		*3*	
Ditolylethane		*3*	
1-Azido naphthalene		*3*	
1-Phenyl decane		*3*	
Dimethyl-β-carboline isomer		*3*	
Alkylamide		*3*	
Phenylbenzimidazole		*3*	
2,6-Diterbutylnaphthalene or isomer		*3*	
$C_{14}H_8O_3$ isomer		*3*	
Methylthiazolopyrimidine		*3*	
8-Acetoxy-pyrazolobenzo-as triazine or $C_{11}H_8N_2O_4$		*3*	
Methyl stearate		*3*	
Methyl phenylcinnoline or $C_{15}H_{12}N_2$ isomer		*3*	
2-Thiocyanatodiphenylamine		*3*	
Methylpyriloindole		*3*	
Alcohol (*n*-pentadecanol ?)		*3*	
Naphtho-sydinone		*3*	

(continued)

Table 1 *(continued)*

Class of compounds	Amount	Ref.	Present in tobacco smoke?
n-Hexadecanol		*3*	
n-$C_{22}H_{46}$ (Docosane)		*3*	
Alkylamine		*3*	
$C_{12}H_{10}N_2O_4$ isomer		*3*	
n-$C_{23}H_{48}$, tricosane		*3*	
Homologous aliphatic alcohol (*n*-heptadecanol ?)		*3*	
n-$C_{24}H_{50}$ (Tetrosane)		*3*	
DL-Cannabichrome		*3*	
n-$C_{25}H_{52}$ (Pentacosane)		*3*	
3-*n*-Pentyl-delta-9-tetrahydrocannabinol		*3*	
Dioctyl phthalate		*3*	
n-$C_{26}H_{54}$ (Hexacosane)		*3*	
3-*n*-Pentyl cannabinol		*3*	
n-$C_{27}H_{56}$ (Heptacosane)		*3*	
Alkylamide		*3*	
n-$C_{28}H_{58}$ (Octacosane)		*3*	
Saturated hydrocarbon		*3*	
n-$C_{29}H_{60}$ (Nonacosane)		*3*	
Alkylphthalate		*3*	
Saturated hydrocarbons		*3*	
n-$C_{30}H_{62}$		*3*	
Acidic			
Hexanoic acid	6%	*7,14,15*	
Heptanoic acid	9%	*7,14*	
Octanoic acid	13%	*7,14*	
Benzoic acid	23%, 9.3%	*7,14,15*	
Salicylic acid	5%	*7*	
Hexadecanoic acid	0.2%	*7*	
Heptadecanoic acid	0.3%	*7*	
Octadecanoic acid	0.2%	*7*	
Phenylacetic acid		*8,15*	
β-Phenylpropionic acid		*8*	
p-Hydroxybenzaldehyde		*8*	
Vanillin		*8*	
2-Hydroxy-3-methyl-2-cyclopenten-1-one		*8*	
Myristic acid	4.6%	*14*	
Palmitic acid	35.2%	*14,15*	
Stearic acid	10.8%	*14,15*	
Linolenic acid	4.9%	*14,15*	
Furoic acid	3.1%	*14,15,18*[a]	
Nonanoic acid		*15*	
Decanoic acid		*15*	

(continued)

Table 1 *(continued)*

Class of compounds	Amount	Ref.	Present in tobacco smoke?
Glutaric acid		*15*	
Dodecanoic acid		*15*	
Phenylisopropionic acid		*15*	
Tetradecanoic acid		*15*	
Palmitoleic acid		*15*	
Palmitolenic acid		*15*	
Oleic acid		*15*	
Lenoleic acid		*15*	
Arachidic acid		*15*	
Eicosanoic acid		*15*	
Eicosadienoic acid		*15*	
Behenic acid		*15*	
Erucic acid		*15*	
Tricosanoic acid		*15*	
2-Ethyl-3-hydroxy-5-pentylbenzoic acid		*15*	
Lignoceric acid		*15*	
Tetracosatetraenoic acid		*15*	
Hexacosanoic acid		*15*	
Hexacosadienoic acid		*15*	
Octacosanoic acid		*15*	
2-Methyl butanoic acid		*15*	
3-Methyl butanoic acid		*15*	
4-Pentenoic acid		*15*	
Phenolic			
Phenol	0.6%, 7.6%	*3,7,14,15,18*[a]	
Cresols	1.2%	*7*	
Guaicol	0.5%	*7*	
Catechol	3.1%	*7*	
Hydroquinone	0.6%	*7*	
p-Hydroxyacetophenone	3.7%, 2.6%	*7,14*	
α-Dimethylphenol		*3,8,18*[a]	
β-Naphthol		*8*	
4-Methylguaicol		*8*	
o-Cresol		*14,15,18*[a]	
p-Cresol	9.2%	*14,15,18*[a]	
p-Ethylphenol	1.9%	*14,18*[a]	
p-Vinylphenol	2.1%	*14,18*[a]	
Catechol	12.1%	*14,15,18*	
m-Cresol		*15*	
o,p-Divinyl phenol		*15*	
o-Isopropenylphenol		*15*	
4-Hydroxy-3-methoxystyrene		*14*	
m-Hydroxy-*p*-methoxystyrene		*15*	

(continued)

Table 1 *(continued)*

Class of compounds	Amount	Ref.	Present in tobacco smoke?
2,4-Dihydroxyanisole		*15*	
p-Hydroxybenzaldehyde		*8*	
o-Hydroxybenzaldehyde		*15*	
o-Hydroxyacetophenone		*15*	
Olivetol		*15,18*	
3-Isopropyl-5-hydroxybenzaldehyde		*15*	
2,4-Dihydroxybenzaldehyde		*15*	
p-Hydroxybenzyl-2-butenyl ketone		*15*	
Neutral			
(A) Nonpolar neutral			
Benzaldehyde		*8,10*	
Acetophenone		*8*	
Propiophenone		*8*	
Benzonitrile		*8*	
Tolunitrile		*8*	
Benzylcyanide		*8*	
β-Phenylethylcyanide		*8*	
Three dimethyl or ethyl indoles		*8,20*	
One trimethyl-methylethyl- or propylindole		*8,20*	
Three methyl carbazoles		*8,20*	
One dimethyl or ethylcarbazole		*8,20*	
Furfural		*8*	
5-Methylfurfural		*8*	
2-Acetylfuran		*8*	
5-Methyl-2-acetylfuran		*8*	
4-Hydroxy-6-*n*-pentylbenzofuran		*8*	
5-Hydroxy-7-*n*-pentyl-2H-methyl-6-*n*-Pentylbenzofuran		*8*	
2,2-Dimethyl-5-hydroxy-7-*n*-pentylchromene		*8*	
Cannabifuran		*8,20*	
2-Oxo-$\Delta^{3(4)}$-tetrahydrocannabinol		*8,20*	
Cannabichromanone		*8,18,20*	
$\Delta^{1(2)}$-Tetrahydrocannabinol methyl ether		*8*	
Dehydrocannabifuran		*8,20*	
Cannabinol methyl ether		*8*	
Ethyl methyl benzene (2 isomers)		*18*	Yes
C_2-Ethylbenzene		*18*	No
Limonene		*18*	Yes
C_2-Styrene		*18*	Yes
Undecene		*18*	Yes
Undecane		*18*	Yes

(continued)

Table 1 *(continued)*

Class of compounds	Amount	Ref.	Present in tobacco smoke?
Methylindene or dihydro-naphthalene (2 isomers)		*18*	Yes
Naphthalene		*18*	No
Dodecane		*18*	Yes
An isomer of tridecane		*18*	No
2-Methylnaphthalene		*18*	Yes
1-Methylnaphthalene		*18*	Yes
An ethylnaphthalene		*18*	No
An ethylnaphthalene		*18*	No
A sesquiterpene		*18*	No
A tetradecene		*18*	Yes
β-Caryophyllene		*18*	No
α-Bergamotene		*18*	No
Humulene		*18*	No
A sesquiterpene		*18*	No
β-Farnesene		*18*	Yes
A sesquiterpene		*18*	No
A sesquiterpene		*18*	No
A sesquiterpene		*18*	No
A sesquiterpene		*18*	No
Bisabolene		*18*	No
Pentadecane		*18*	Yes
A C_3 naphthalene		*18*	No
A sesquiterpene		*18*	No
A dehydrosesquiterpene		*18*	No
A sesquiterpene alcohol		*18*	No
Norphytene		*18*	Yes
An octadecene		*18*	No
Neophytadiene		*18*	Yes
A nonadecene		*18*	Yes
An eicosadiene		*18*	Yes
An eicosadiene		*18*	No
Cannabicitran		*18*	No
Tetrahydrocannabidivarol		*18*	No
Isotetrahyrocannabinol		*18*	No
Cannabidiol monomethylether		*18*	No
Cannabichromene monomethylether		*18*	No
Cannabicyclol		*18*	No
Cannabidiol		*18*	No
Cannabichromene		*18*	No
Δ^9-Tetrahydrocannabinol		*18*	No
A dihydrocannabinol		*18*	No
Cannabinol		*18*	No
Heptacosane		*18*	Yes

(continued)

Table 1 *(continued)*

Class of compounds	Amount	Ref.	Present in tobacco smoke?
Octacosane		*18*	Yes
Nonacosane		*18*	Yes
An isomer of triacontane		*18*	Yes
Triacontane		*18*	Yes
Myrcene[d]		*18*	
An acyclic diene[d]		*18*	
Decane[d]		*18*	
A dihydrolimonene[d]		*18*	
A C_4-benzene		*18*	
Tridecene[d] (2 isomers)		*18*	
Nocotine[d]		*18*	
Solanone[d]		*18*	
A tetradecene[d]		*18*	
A dihydrosesquiterpene[d]		*18*	
An isomer of pentadecane[d]		*18*	
A hexadacene[d]		*18*	
Eicosatetraene[d] (2 isomers)		*18*	
Androstadienone[d] (2 isomers)		*18*	
An eicosadiene[d]		*18*	
Eicosatriene[d] (2 isomers)		*18*	
Dihydrosesquiterpene[d] (2 isomers)		*18*	
Pentacosane[d]		*18*	
Squalene[d]		*18*	
An isomer of squalene[d]		*18*	
An isomer of nonacosane[d]		*18*	
An isomer of hentriacontane[d]		*18*	
Hentriacontane[d]		*18*	
(B) Polar neutal			
2-Methylphenol (2 isomers)		*18*	
Dimethylphenol (3 isomers)		*18*	
C_3-Phenol (2 isomers)		*18*	
Methoxymethylphenol[d]		*18*	
Hydroxyfuroic acid (2 isomers)		*18*	
Methylbenzenediol (2 isomers)		*18*	
A vinylmethoxyphenol (e.g., isoeugenol)		*18*	
C_2-Benzenediol (5 isomers)		*18*	
A methylhydroxyfuroic acid		*18*	
A methyl indole		*18*	
A hydroxyacenaphthalene		*18*	
A styrenediol (2 isomers)		*18*	
A pentenylphenol		*18*	
A C_4 Methoxyphenol		*18*	
A methylstyrene diol		*18*	
A methoxymethylbenzenediol		*18*	
A dichlorobenzenediol[d]		*18*	

(continued)

Table 1 *(continued)*

Class of compounds	Amount	Ref.	Present in tobacco smoke?
A styrenetriol		*18*	
A methoxynaphthol[d]		*18*	
A methoxydihydroxybenzofuran		*18*	
(C) **Polynuclear aromatic hydrocarbons**			
Methylindole	6.3[e]	*16*	0.3[e]
Ethylindole	3.2[e]	*16*	No
Dibenzofuran	1.0[e]	*16*	No
Methylacenaphthalene	1.4[e]	*16*	0.5[e]
2-Methylfluorene	0.8[e]	*16*	0.3[e]
1-Methylfluorene	1.4[e]	*16*	0.3[e]
Phenanthrene	8.9[e]	*16*	8.5[e]
Anthracene	3.3[e]	*16*	2.3[e]
Ethylmethylbiphenyl[f]	0.4[e]	*16*	0.1[e]
Methylcarbazole	3.4[e]	*16*	No
3-Methylphenanthrene	2.6[e]	*16*	2.0[e]
2-Methylphenanthrene	5.3[e]	*16*	5.6[e]
2-Methylanthracene	3.2[e]	*16*	2.4[e]
4*H*-Cyclopenta[*d e f*] phenanthrene	3.2[e]	*16*	2.4[e]
9-Methylphenanthrene	2.9[e]	*16*	2.7[e]
1-Methylphenanthrene	4.2[e]	*16*	3.2[e]
Methylcarbazole	3.6[e]	*16*	No
Methylcarbazole	5.1[e]	*16*	No
Methyl-4*H*-cyclopenta[*d e f*] phenanthrene	3.1[e]	*16*	1.6[e]
Methylcarbazole	3.0[e]	*16*	No
Ethylphenanthrene or ethylanthracene[g]	0.3[e]	*16*	0.4[e]
Ethylphenanthrene or ethylanthracene[g]	0.7[e]	*16*	0.6[e]
Ethylphenanthrene or ethylanthracene[g]	0.6[e]	*16*	0.5[e]
Ethylphenanthrene or ethylanthracene[g]	0.7[e]	*16*	0.5[e]
Ethylphenanthrene or ethylanthracene[g]	1.5[e]	*16*	0.8[e]
Ethylphenanthrene or ethylanthracene[g]	0.7[e]	*16*	0.6[e]
Ethylphenanthrene or ethylanthracene[g]	0.6[e]	*16*	0.7[e]
Ethylphenanthrene or ethylanthracene[g]	3.0[e]	*16*	1.6[e]
Ethylphenanthrene or ethylanthracene[g]	4.3[e]	*16*	1.8[e]

(continued)

Table 1 *(continued)*

Class of compounds	Amount	Ref.	Present in tobacco smoke?
Ethylphenanthrene or ethylanthracene[g]	2.5[e]	*16*	1.9[e]
Fluoranthene	8.9[e]	*16*	8.3
Ethylphenanthrene or ethylanthracene	0.6[e]	*16*	1.6[e]
Benzacenaphthalene	2.9[e]	*16*	1.2[e]
Ethylphenanthrene or ethylanthracene[g]	4.9[e]	*16*	3.4[e]
Pyrene	6.6[e]	*16*	6.8
Ethyl-4-*H*-cyclopenta[*d e f*] phenanthrene[g]	1.9[e]	*16*	0.7[e]
Ethyl-4-*H*-cyclopenta[*d e f*] phenanthrene[g]	2.2[e]	*16*	0.7[e]
Ethyl-4-*H*-cyclopenta[*d e f*] phenanthrene[g]	1.3[e]	*16*	1.4[e]
Ethyl-4-*H*-cyclopenta[*d e f*] phenanthrene[g]	1.9[e]	*16*	0.8[e]
Ethylmethylphenanthrene or ethylmethyl anthracene[f]	0.6[e]	*16*	0.5[e]
Ethylmethylphenanthrene or ethylmethyl anthracene[f]	1.4[e]	*16*	0.7[e]
Ethyl-4*H*-cyclopenta[*d e f*] phenanthrene[g]	2.4[e]	*16*	1.6[e]
Methylfluoranthene	4.0[e]	*16*	4.6[e]
Methylfluoranthene	1.8[e]	*16*	1.8[e]
Methylfluoranthene	3.8[e]	*16*	3.6[e]
Benzo[*c*] fluorene	4.2[e]	*16*	4.9[e]
2-Methylpyrene and benzo[*b*] fluorene	5.4[e]	*16*	5.5[e]
Ethylmethylphenanthrene or ethylmethyl anthracene[f]	2.5[e]	*16*	1.2[e]
4-Methylpyrene	4.1[e]	*16*	4.4[e]
1-Methylpyrene	4.8[e]	*16*	5.6[e]
Methylfluoranthene	0.8[e]	*16*	0.9[e]
Methylfluoranthene	0.6[e]	*16*	0.3[e]
Ethylfluoranthene or ethylpyrene[g]	1.1[e]	*16*	1.5[e]
Ethylfluoranthene or ethylpyrene[g]	0.3[e]	*16*	0.5[e]
Ethylfluoranthene or ethylpyrene[g]	0.5[e]	*16*	0.9[e]
Ethylfluoranthene or ethylpyrene[g]	1.1[e]	*16*	1.0[e]
Ethylfluoranthene or ethylpyrene[g]	2.1[e]	*16*	2.4[e]

(continued)

Table 1 *(continued)*

Class of compounds	Amount	Ref.	Present in tobacco smoke?
Ethylfluoranthene or ethylpyrene[g]	2.1[e]	*16*	2.4[e]
Ethylfluoranthene or ethylpyrene[g]	2.5[e]	*16*	2.7[e]
Ethylfluoranthene or ethylpyrene[g]	1.4[e]	*16*	1.8[e]
Ethylfluoranthene or ethylpyrene[g] + acefluoranthene	1.7[e]	*16*	1.6[e]
Ethylfluoranthene or ethylpyrene[g]	2.4[e]	*16*	3.0[e]
Ethylfluoranthene or ethylpyrene[g] + acepyrelene	2.3[e]	*16*	2.6[e]
Ethylfluoranthene or ethylpyrene[g]	1.2[e]	*16*	1.4[e]
Ethylfluoranthene or ethylpyrene[g]	1.6[e]	*16*	1.7[e]
Ethylfluoranthene or ethylpyrene[g]	1.4[e]	*16*	1.3[e]
Benzo[*g h i*]fluoranthene, ethylpyrene or ethylfluoranthene[g]	0.4[e]	*16*	0.4[e]
Benz [*a*] anthracene	3.3[e]	*16*	2.6[e]
Chrysene	5.5[e]	*16*	5.1[e]
Ethylmethylfluoranthene or ethylmethylpyrene[f]	0.9[e]	*16*	0.8[e]
Ethylmethylfluoranthene or ethylmethylpyrene[f]	0.7[e]	*16*	0.6[e]
Ethylmethylfluoranthene or ethylmethylpyrene[f]	0.9[e]	*16*	0.6[e]
Ethylmethylfluoranthene or ethylmethylpyrene[f]	1.0[e]	*16*	0.7[e]
Ethylmethylfluoranthene or ethylmethylpyrene[f]	0.8[e]	*16*	0.6[e]
Ethylmethylfluoranthene or ethylmethylpyrene[f]	1.0[e]	*16*	0.7[e]
Ethylmethylfluoranthene or ethylmethylpyrene[f]	0.7[e]	*16*	0.7[e]
Methylchrysene or methylbenz[*a*]anthracene	1.0[e]	*16*	0.6[e]
Methylchrysene or methylbenz[*a*]anthracene	1.0[e]	*16*	0.5[e]
Methylchrysene or methylbenz[*a*]anthracene	2.7[e]	*16*	2.2[e]
Methylchrysene or methylbenz[*a*]anthracene	2.1[e]	*16*	2.2[e]

(continued)

Table 1 *(continued)*

Class of compounds	Amount	Ref.	Present in tobacco smoke?
Methylchrysene or methylbenz[*a*]anthracene	1.0[e]	*16*	1.1[e]
Methylchrysene or methylbenz[*a*]anthracene	0.9[e]	*16*	0.7[e]
Methylchrysene or methylbenz[*a*]anthracene	2.2[e]	*16*	1.9[e]
Methylchrysene or methylbenz[*a*]anthracene	2.7[e]	*16*	2.9[e]
Binaphthyl	0.5[e]	*16*	0.5[e]
Binaphthyl	0.5[e]	*16*	0.3[e]
Ethylchrysene or ethylbenz[*a*]anthracene[g]	0.8[e]	*16*	0.7[e]
Ethylchrysene or ethylbenz[*a*]anthracene[g]	0.6[e]	*16*	0.6[e]
Ethylchrysene or ethylbenz[*a*]anthracene[g]	1.0[e]	*16*	0.7[e]
Ethylchrysene or ethylbenz[*a*]anthracene[g]	0.5[e]	*16*	0.6[e]
Ethylchrysene or ethylbenz[*a*]anthracene[g]	1.5[e]	*16*	0.7[e]
Ethylchrysene or ethylbenz[*a*]anthracene[g]	0.7[e]	*16*	0.7[e]
Ethylchrysene or ethylbenz[*a*]anthracene[g]	0.4[e]	*16*	0.3[e]
Ethylchrysene or ethylbenz[*a*]anthracene[g]	0.7[e]	*16*	0.7[e]
Methylbinaphthyl	0.6[e]	*16*	0.6[e]
Methylbinaphthyl	0.4[e]	*16*	0.4[e]
Methylbinaphthyl	0.4[e]	*16*	0.3[e]
Methylbinaphthyl	0.6[e]	*16*	0.3[e]
Methylbinaphthyl	0.3[e]	*16*	0.3[e]
Ethylmethylchrysene or ethylmethylbenz[*a*] anthracene[f]	0.3[e]	*16*	0.6[e]
Ethylmethylchrysene or ethylmethylbenz[*a*] anthracene[f]	0.3[e]	*16*	0.4[e]
Ethylbinaphthyl[g]	0.4[e]	*16*	0.4[e]
Ethylbinaphthyl[g]	0.3[e]	*16*	0.3[e]
Benzo [*j*] fluoranthene	3.0[e]	*16*	2.1[e]
Benzo [*k*] fluoranthene	1.1[e]	*16*	1.2[e]
Benzofluoranthene	1.1[e]	*16*	0.7[e]
Benzofluoranthene	0.7[e]	*16*	0.5[e]
Benzo [*e*] pyrene	1.8[e]	*16*	1.3[e]
Benzo [*a*] pyrene	2.9[e]	*16*	1.7[e]

(continued)

Table 1 *(continued)*

Class of compounds	Amount	Ref.	Present in tobacco smoke?
Perylene	0.9[e]	*16*	No
Methylbenzopyrene or methylbenzofluoranthene	0.3[e]	*16*	0.2[e]
Methylbenzopyrene or methylbenzofluoranthene	0.8[e]	*16*	0.6[e]
Methylbenzopyrene or methylbenzofluoranthene	0.5[e]	*16*	0.5[e]
Methylbenzopyrene or methylbenzofluoranthene	0.6[e]	*16*	0.6[e]
Methylbenzopyrene or methylbenzofluoranthene	0.6[e]	*16*	0.6[e]
Methylbenzopyrene or methylbenzofluoranthene	1.2[e]	*16*	0.6[e]
Methylbenzopyrene or methylbenzofluoranthene	0.9[e]	*16*	0.7[e]
Methylbenzopyrene or methylbenzofluoranthene	No	*16*	0.6[e]
Methylbenzopyrene or methylbenzofluoranthene	0.7[e]	*16*	0.5[e]
Methylbenzopyrene or methylbenzofluoranthene	0.5[e]	*16*	0.5[e]
Methylbenzopyrene or methylbenzofluoranthene	0.5[e]	*16*	0.3[e]
Methylbenzopyrene or methylbenzofluoranthene	No	*16*	0.2[e]
Methylbenzopyrene, ethylbenzopyrene, or ethylbenzofluoranthene[g]	0.3[e]	*16*	0.4[e]
Ethylbenzopyrene or ethylbenzofluoranthene[g]	0.4[e]	*16*	0.5[e]
Ethylbenzopyrene or ethylbenzofluoranthene[g]	0.3[e]	*16*	0.3[e]
[h]	0.3[e]	*16*	No
[h], Dibenz[*a*,*i*]anthracene	0.3[e]	*16*	No
[h]	0.6[e]	*16*	No
[h]	1.0[e]	*16*	0.3[e]
[h]	0.3[e]	*16*	No
Dibenz[*a*,*h*]anthracene or dibenz[*a*,*c*]anthracene	0.3[e]	*16*	0.6[e]
[h]	0.4[e]	*16*	0.2[e]
Benzo[*g h i*]perylene	0.7[e]	*16*	0.3[e]
[h]	0.4[e]	*16*	No
Anthracene	0.5[e]	*16*	No
[i]	0.5[e]	*16*	No
[i]	0.2[e]	*16*	No

(continued)

Table 1 *(continued)*

Class of compounds	Amount	Ref.	Present in tobacco smoke?
[i]	0.4[e]	*16*	No
[i]	0.5[e]	*16*	No
[i]	0.4[e]	*16*	No
[i], Dibenzopyrene	0.5[e]	*16*	No
[i], Dibenzopyrene	0.3[e]	*16*	No
[i]	0.4[e]	*16*	No
Diphenylacenaphthalene	0.3[e]	*16*	No
Quarterphenyl	1.2[e]	*16*	No

[a]Denotes its presence also in the polar neutral fraction.
[b]One isomer.
[c]Two isomers.
[d]Present only in tobacco.
[e]µg/100 g cigarettes.
[f]Could also be trimethyl or propyl.
[g]Could also be dimethyl.
[h]Compounds with molecular weight 276 can be any of the following: indeno[1,2,3-*c d*]pyrene; indeno[1,2,3,-*c d*] fluoranthene; aceperylene; phenanthro[10,1,2,3-*c d e f*] fluorene; acenaphth[1,2-α]acenaphthylene; dibenzo[*b, m n o*] fluoranthene. Further possibilities are the benzo derivatives of acepyrylene and acefluoranthene.
[i]Compounds with molecular weight 290 are methyl derivatives of those with molecular weight 276.

ing from 10 to 29 mg/kg, the basic fraction caused a decrease in spatial locomotion, rearing behavior, and urination incidence. The authors concluded from these results that although the basic fraction of marijuana whole smoke condensate has pharmacological activity in mice, it offers little evidence for the presence of highly active compounds.

4.2. Mutagenicity

A study by Novotny et al. *(24)* has shown a possible chemical basis for the higher mutagenicity of marijuana smoke as compared to tobacco smoke. The total weights of polynuclear aromatic fractions containing three rings or more were significantly higher in MSC than in high-tar cigarette smoke condensate. The well known carcinogen benzo[*a*]pyrene was present in MSC by a 70% higher amount than in TSC. It was suggested that the pyrolysis products of Δ^9-THC and other cannabinoids are major contributors to the formation of polynuclear aromatic hydrocarbons. MSC was shown to be mutagenic in strain TA 98 of the Ames Salmonella/microsome test *(25)*, a short-term bioassay that estimates the mutagenic potential of some chemicals. The mutagens in MSCs required liver enzymes to be activated. The authors concluded that the basic fraction accounted for 76% of the recovered mutagenic activity. Further work on the mutagenic activity of extracts and smoke condensates of marijuana, Transkei home-grown tobacco, and commercial cigarette tobaccos was carried out *(26)* using *Salmonella typhimurium* strains TA 98, TA 100, TA 1535, TA 1537, and TA 1538, both with and without metabolic activation. No mutagenic activity was detected in the methylene chloride extracts of marijuana and tobacco, but all the smoke condensates exhibited mutagenicity with metabolic activation. The only strain not mutated by any of the pyrolyzates was TA 1535. Transkei tobacco pyrolyzate was most mutagenic, followed by marijuana, pipe, and cigarette tobacco. Mutagenicity was associated with the nitrogen content of the various products.

The yield of MSC was 50% higher than that of cigarette and pipe tobacco, indicating a high carcinogenic risk associated with marijuana smoking. Bioassay results *(3)* showed that the acidic fractions were not significantly mutagenic, the neutral fractions were weakly mutagenic, but the basic fractions were significantly mutagenic. The constant draft base fractions were more mutagenic than puff mode basic fractions for both marijuana and tobacco, and the more polar subfractions (numbers 4–7) of the base fraction were more mutagenic than the less polar subfractions.

4.3. Pulmonary Hazards

The pulmonary effects associated with smoking marijuana and tobacco were examined in men (mean age 31.5 ± 7.1 years) by quantification of the relative burden to the lung of insoluble particulates (tar) and carbon monoxide from the smoke of similar quantities of marijuana and tobacco *(27)*. Fifteen subjects who had smoked both marijuana and tobacco habitually for the previous 5 years were included in this study. Each subject's blood carboxyhemoglobin level before and after smoking and the amount of tar inhaled and deposited in the respiratory tract from the smoke of a single filter-tipped tobacco cigarette (900–1200 mg) and marijuana cigarettes (741–985 mg) containing 0.004% or 1.24% Δ^9-THC were measured. Compared with smoking tobacco, smoking marijuana was associated with a nearly fivefold increment in the blood carboxyhemoglobin level, an approximate threefold increase in the amount of tar inhaled, and retention in the respiratory tract of one third more inhaled tar ($p < 0.001$). Significant differences were also noted in the dynamics of smoking marijuana and tobacco, among them an approximately two-thirds larger puff volume, a one-third greater depth of inhalation, and a fourfold longer breath-holding time with marijuana than with tobacco ($p < 0.001$). These results may account for previous findings that smoking only a few marijuana cigarettes a day (without tobacco) has the same effect on the prevalence and chronic respiratory symptoms *(28)* and the extent of tracheobronchial epithelial histopathology *(29)* as smoking more than 20 tobacco cigarettes a day (without marijuana). These observations justify concern about the potential adverse pulmonary effects resulting from the long-term smoking of only a few marijuana cigarettes a day.

4.4. Interaction With Estrogen Receptor

Intraperitoneal administration of marijuana resin and smoke condensate to rat in doses of 10 and 20 mg/kg (in maize oil) affected their estrous cycle *(30)*. Estrous was shortened with doses of both the resin and the smoke condensate, whereas diestrous was lengthened with the 20 mg/kg dose of the resin and both the 10 and 20 mg/kg doses of the smoke condensate. In addition, the administration of 20 mg/kg of either the resin or the smoke condensate resulted in a lengthening of the postestrous cycle.

Sauer et al. *(31)* showed that crude marijuana extract at a concentration of 2.4×10^5 *M* Δ^9-THC ($n = 6$) competed with estradiol for binding to the estrogen receptor of rat uterine cytosol. MSC at an equivalent Δ^9-THC concentration ($n = 3$) also competed with estradiol for its receptor. Pure Δ^9-THC and 10 Δ^9-THC metabolites failed to compete with estradiol for its receptor. Of several other cannabinoids tested, only cannabidiol showed receptor-binding activity at very high concentrations (5.6×10^6 M; $n = 2$).

Apigenin, a flavone present in marijuana, displayed high affinity for the estrogen receptor at a concentration ranging from 5 to 50×10^{-7} M ($n = 6$). In vivo measurement of estrogen activity using uterine growth bioassay (immature rats) and crude marijuana extract administered subcutaneously in a dose containing 6.3–15.2 mg per day Δ^9-THC failed to exhibit estrogenic or antiestrogenic effects. In conclusion, direct estrogenic activity of *Cannabis* extract could not be demonstrated in vivo.

4.5. Inhibition of Dihydrotestosterone Binding to the Androgen Receptor

MSC and two constituents of *Cannabis*, Δ^9-THC and cannabinol, were tested for their ability to interact with the androgen receptor in rat prostate cytosol *(32)*. The above-mentioned materials competitively inhibited the specific binding of dihydrotestosterone to the androgen receptor with a dissociation constant (Ki) of 2.1×10^{-7} M for CBN, 2.6×10^{-7} M for Δ^9-THC, and 5.8×10^{-7} M for MSC. The data indicate that the antiandrogenic effects associated with marijuana use result, at least in part, from inhibition of androgen action at the receptor level.

References

1. Patel, A. R. and Gori, G. B. (1975) Preparation and monitoring of marijuana smoke condensate samples. *Bull. Narc.* **27**, 47–54.
2. Lerner, M. and Zeffert, J. T. (1968) Determination of tetrahydrocannabinol isomers in marihuana and hashish. *Bull. Narc.* **20**, 53–54.
3. Sparacino, C. M., Hyldburg, P. A., and Hughes, T. J. (1990) Chemical and biological analysis of marijuana smoke condensate. NIDA Research Monograph **99**, 121–140.
4. Gudzinowicz, B. and Gudzinowicz, M. (1980) *Analysis of Drugs and Metabolites by Gas Chromatography/Mass Spectrometry. Vol. 7. Natural, Pyrolytic and Metabolic Products of Tobacco and Marihuana,* Marcel Dekker, New York.
5. Schmeltz, I., Dooley, C. J., Stedman, R. L., and Chamberlain, W. J. (1967) Composition studies of tobacco. XXII. The nitromethane soluble, neutral fraction of cigarette smoke. *Phytochemistry* **6**, 33–38.
6. Novotny, M., Lee, M. L., and Bartle, K. D. (1974) The methods for fractionation, analytical separation and identification of polynuclear aromatic hydrocarbons in complex mixtures. *J. Chromatogr. Sci.* **12**, 606–612.
7. Jones, L. A. and Foote, R. S. (1975) Identification of some acids, bases and phenols. *J. Agric. Food Chem.* **23**, 1129–1131.
8. Kettenes-Van Den Bosch, J. J. and Salemink, C. A. (1977) Cannabis XVI. Constituents of marihuana smoke condensate. *J. Chromatogr.* **131**, 422–424.
9. Zamir-ul Haq, M., Rose, S. J., Deiderich, L. R., and Patel, A. R. (1974) Identification and quantitative measurement of some N-heterocyclics in marijuana smoke condensates. *Anal. Chem.* **46**, 1781–1785.
10. Merli, F., Wiesler, D., Maskarinec, M. P., and Novotny, M. (1981) Characterization of the basic fraction of marijuana smoke condensate by capillary gas chromatography/mass spectrometry. *Anal. Chem.* **53**, 1929–1935.
11. Merli, F., Novotny, M., and Lee, M.L. (1980) Fractionation and gas chromatographic analysis of aza-arenes in complex mixtures. *J. Chromatogr.* **199**, 371–378.

12. Novotny, M., Strand, J. W., Smith, S. L., Wiesler, D., and Schwende, F. J. (1981) Compositional studies of coal tar by capillary gas chromatography/mass spectrometry. *Fuel* **60**, 213–230.
13. Novotny, M., Merli, F., Wiesler, D., and Saeed, T. (1982) Composition of the basic fraction of marijuana and tobacco condensates: a comparative study by capillary GC/MS. *Chromatographia* **15,** 564–568.
14. Fentiman, Jr., A. F., Foltz, R. L., and Kinser, G. W. (1973) Identification of noncannabinoid phenols in marihuana smoke condensate using chemical ionization/mass spectrometry. *Anal. Chem.* **45**, 580–582.
15. Maskarinec, M. P., Alexander, G., and Novotny, M. (1976) Analysis of the acidic fraction of marijuana smoke condensate by capillary gas chromatography-mass spectrometry. *J. Chromatogr.* **126**, 559–568.
16. Lee, M. L., Novotny, M., and Bartle, K. D. (1976) GC / Mass and nuclear magnetic resonance spectrometric studies of carcinogenic polynuclear aromatic hydrocarbons in tobacco and marijuana smoke condensates. *Anal. Chem.* **48**, 405–416.
17. Bartle, K. D., Lee, M. L., and Novotny, M. (1977) Identification of environmental polynuclear aromatic hydrocarbons by pulse Fourier-transform proton nuclear magnetic resonance spectroscopy. *Analyst* **102**, 731–738.
18. Novotny, M., Merli, F., Wiesler, D., Fencl, M., and Saeed, T. (1982) Fractionation and capillary gas chromatographic-mass spectrometric characterization of the neutral components in marijuana and tobacco smoke condensates. *J. Chromatogr.* **238**, 141–150.
19. Hood, L. V., Dames, M. E., and Barry, G. T. (1973) Headspace volatiles of marijuana. *Nature* (London) **242**, 402–403.
20. Friedrich-Fiechtl, J. and Spitetller, G. (1975) New cannabinoids. *Tetrahedron* **31**, 479–487.
21. Truitt, E. B. Jr., Kinser, G. W., and Berlo, J .M. (1976) Behavioral activity in various fractions of marihuana smoke condensate in the rat, in *Pharmacology of Marijuana* (Braude, M. C. and Szara, S., eds.), Raven, New York, pp. 2, 463–474.
22. Johnson, J. M. (1981) The pharmacological activity of the acidic, basic, and polar-neutral fractions of marihuana whole smoke condensate alone, and in combination with Δ^9-tetrahydrocannabinol. Indiana University, Bloomington, IN, dissertation abstract **42(3)**, 983.
23. Johnson, J. M., Lemberger, L., Novotny, M., Forney, R. B., Dalton, W. S., and Maskarinec, M. P. (1984) Pharmacological activity of the basic fraction of marijuana whole smoke condensate alone and in combination with Δ^9-tetrahydrocannabinol in mice. *Tox. Appl. Pharm.* **72**, 440–448.
24. Novotny, M., Lee, M. L., and Bartle, K. D. (1976) A possible chemical basis for the higher mutagenicity of marihuana smoke as compared to tobacco smoke. *Experientia* **32,** 280–282.
25. Busch, F. W., Seid, D. A., and Wei, E. T. (1979) Mutagenic activity of marihuana smoke condensates. *Cancer Lett.* **6**, 319–324.
26. Wehner, F. C., Van Rensburg, S. J., and Theil, P. G. (1980) Mutagenic activity of marihuana and Transkei tobacco smoke condensates in the Samonella / microsome assay. *Mutat. Res.* **77**, 135–142.
27. Wu, T. C., Tashkin, D. P., Djahed, B., and Rose, J. E. (1988) Pulmonary hazards of smoking marijuana as compared with tobacco. *N. Engl. J. Med.* **318**, 347–351.
28. Tashkin, D. P., Coulson, A. H., and Clark, V. A. (1987) Respiratory and lung function in habitual heavy smokers of marijuana alone, smokers of marijuana and tobacco, smokers of tobacco alone, and non-smokers. *Am. Rev. Respir. Dis.* **135**, 209–216.
29. Gong, H., Fliegel, S., Tashkin, D. P., and Barbers, R. G. (1987) Tracheobronchial changes in habitual, heavy smokers of marijuana with and without tobacco. *Am. Rev. Respir. Dis.* **136**, 142–149.

30. Lares, A., Ochoa, Y., Bolanos, A., Aponte, N., and Montenegro, M. (1981) Effects of the resin and smoke condensate of *Cannabis sativa* on the oestrous cycle of the rat. *Bull. Narc.* **33**, 55–61.
31. Sauer, M. A., Rifka, S. M., Hawks, R. L., Cutler, G. B., Jr., and Loriaux, D. L. (1983) Marijuana: interaction with the estrogen receptor. *J. Pharmacol. Exp. Ther.* **224**, 404–407.
32. Purohit, V., Ahluwahlia, B. S., and Vigersky, R. A. (1980) Marihuana inhibits dihydrotestosterone binding to the androgen receptor. *Endocrinology* **107**, 848–850.

Chapter 5

Pharmacology of Cannabinoids

Lionel P. Raymon and H. Chip Walls

1. Introduction

Ever since the cloning of two distinct cannabinoid receptors and the discovery of lipids derived from arachidonic acid as endogenous ligands, cannabinoid pharmacology has received increased attention and yielded new insights in the understanding of the complex effects of smoking marijuana. Novel receptors offer the prospect of new therapeutics, and after decades of sparse research cannabinoid pharmacology is once again on the forefront of medical news. The use of molecular biology techniques, such as knockout mice, and the development of antagonists and agonists of the cannabinoid receptors are slowly unraveling a network of intricate physiological and neurological effects.

1.1. Endogenous Ligands

A family of lipids has been identified as the endogenous ligands to the cannabinoid receptors. Two arachidonic acid derivatives were first isolated: an amide, arachidonoyl ethanolamide, or anandamide *(1)* and an ester, 2-arachidonoyl glycerol (2-AG) *(2–4)*. Recently, a third derivative was isolated, an ether, 2-arachidonyl glyceryl ether, also known as noladin ether *(5)*. These lipid compounds differ totally in structure from Δ^9-tetrahydrocannabinol (THC), the main exogenous cannabinoid. Except for the notable absence of a nitrogen atom in THC, there is little to remind us of the eicosanoid- or prostaglandin-like structure of the anandamide family.

Endocannabinoids are considered either neurotransmitters or neuromodulators: they have distinct synthetic pathways, are released from cells upon depolarization and calcium entry, and their synaptic action is rapidly terminated by reuptake and intracellular enzymatic degradation (Fig. 1). These requirements are met for anandamide and,

From: *Forensic Science and Medicine: Marijuana and the Cannabinoids*
Edited by: M. A. ElSohly © Humana Press Inc., Totowa, New Jersey

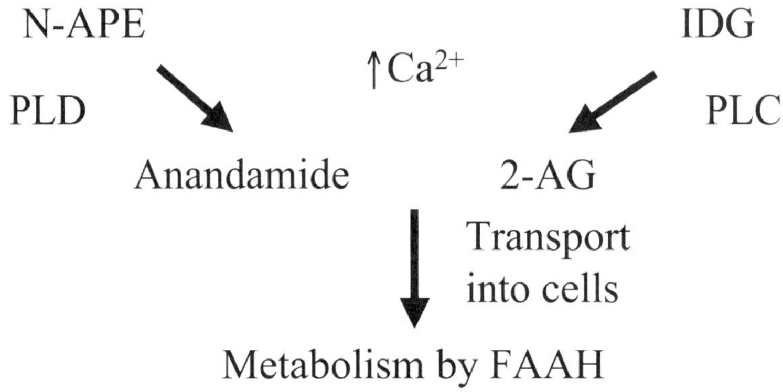

Fig. 1. Metabolism of endogenous cannabinoids. N-APE, *N*-arachidonyl phosphatidyl ethanolamine; PLD, phospholipase D; IDG, inositol-1,2-diacylglycerol; PLC, phospholipase C; 2-AG, 2-arachidonoyl glycerol; FAAH, fatty acid amide hydrolase.

to a certain extent, 2-AG, but are still unclear for noladin ether. Anandamide and 2-AG are produced from cleavage of two different phospholipid precursors present in the cell membranes of neurons and immune cells in particular. Anandamide is synthesized from the membrane phospholipid *N*-arachidonyl phosphatidylethanolamine by a phosphodiesterase called phospholipase D, an enzyme stimulated by depolarization-induced increase in intracellular Ca^{2+} *(5,6)*. The synthetic pathway is also indirectly stimulated by cyclic adenosine monophosphate (cAMP)/protein kinase A, indicating possible receptor-mediated mechanisms *(7,8)*. Anandamide amounts of 10–50 pmol/g of brain tissue have been reported *(6)*. 2-AG is mainly the product of phospholipase C digestion of inositol-1, 2-diacylglycerol and, interestingly, is much more abundant than anandamide, with amounts ranging from 2 to 10 nmol/g of tissue *(9)*. The synthesis of 2-AG is also calcium-dependent *(4)*. An interesting feature of anandamide and 2-AG is the "on-demand" synthesis and release of these lipids, possibly not from vesicles, differentiating the endocannabinoids from classical neurotransmitters—hence the term "modulator" *(10)*. Anandamide is then known to be transported into cells by carrier-mediated uptake, which does not depend on sodium or adenosine-5'-triphosphate (ATP), another difference from classical neurotransmitters, but similar to the structurally related prostaglandin E_2 *(11)*. This transporter participates in the inactivation of anandamide. Both anandamide and 2-AG are known to be rapidly hydrolyzed by the intracellular enzyme fatty acid amide hydrolase (FAAH) *(6,12,13)*.

Endocannabinoids may function physiologically as retrograde synaptic messengers (Fig. 2) *(14,15)*. When a postsynaptic neuron is strongly depolarized, it synthesizes and releases endocannabinoids through a nonvesicular mechanism. These molecules, in turn, bind the presynaptic neuron at CB_1 receptors and inhibit its neurotransmitter release. It is a form of negative feedback. The chemical nature of the presynaptic neuron is important. If the release of an inhibitory transmitter like γ-aminobutyric acid (GABA) is decreased, it is called in electrophysiology depolarization-induced suppression of inhibition (DSI) and would result in exacerbation of postsynaptic transmission. If the release of an excitatory neurotransmitter like glutamate

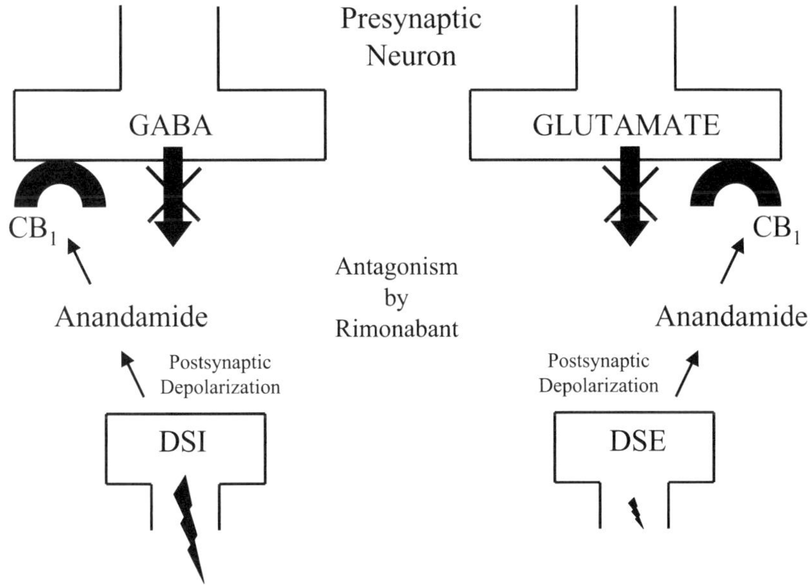

Fig. 2. Cannabinoid synapse: endocannabinoids are retrograde synaptic messengers through CB_1 receptors. GABA, γ-aminobutyric acid; DSI, depolarization-induced suppression of inhibition; DSE, depolarization-induced suppression of excitation.

is decreased, it is referred to as depolarization-induced suppression of excitation (DSE), and would diminish postsynaptic transmission. Several studies argue in favor of this physiological role of anandamide and other endogenous cannabinoids *(16–18)*. Both DSI and DSE depend on rises in calcium and on G_i proteins, which are also necessary for the synthesis and release of endogenous cannabinoids and a feature of their receptors. DSI and DSE are antagonized by rimonabant, a selective CB_1 receptor antagonist. And finally, CB_1 stimulation inhibits GABA release from hippocampal interneurons (which synapse with the important pyramidal neurons) and glutamate from cerebellar basket cells (which synapse with Purkinje neurons).

1.2. Cannabinoid Receptors

Two cannabinoid receptors, CB_1 and CB_2, have been cloned from various animal species, including humans *(19–21)*. There is a shorter-isoform splice variant of CB_1, CB_{1A}, with no known function, and recent reports indicate other types of receptors yet to be cloned. Cannabinoid receptors belong to the superfamily of G protein-linked receptors *(14,15,22)*. These receptors are characterized by 7-transmembrane domains, an extracellular NH_2 terminus, and an intracellular COOH terminus. Once bound, G protein-linked receptors activate a G protein. A G protein is a trimeric protein (α- and βγ-subunits), which uses guanosine triphosphate as a source of energy to "do its job," i.e., change the activity of enzymes downstream in the signal transduction pathway (Fig. 3). It therefore allows signal transduction from the outside of the cell, where the ligand binds to the receptor, to the inside of the cell, where molecular changes in key target proteins will result in a biological response. Cannabinoid receptors are said to

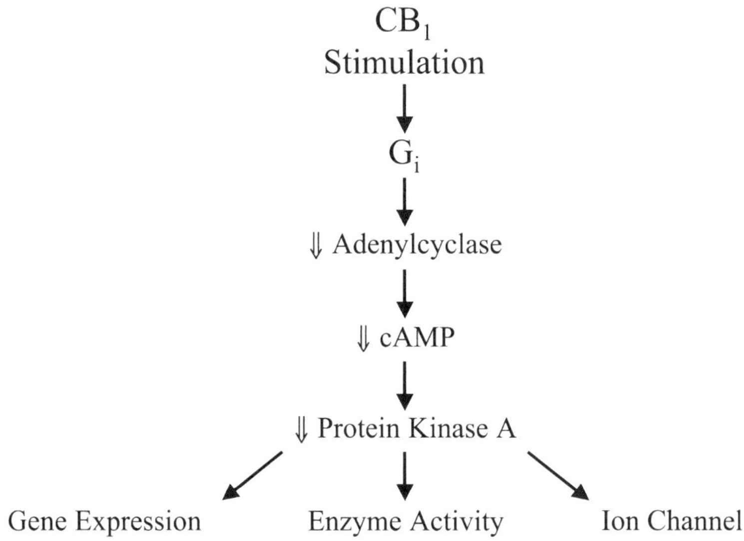

Fig. 3. CB_1 receptors are G_i-coupled: an inhibitory effect on cellular function is expected from receptor stimulation.

be G_i coupled: a G_i protein, when activated, inhibits the enzyme adenylate cyclase. It is the α subunit that interferes with adenylate cyclase. The $\beta\gamma$ dimer can regulate other enzymes such as mitogen-activated protein kinase (MAPK) and phosphatidylinositol-3-kinase (PI3K) or directly modify the activity of ion channels. Adenylate cyclase in turn no longer breaks ATP to form the second messenger cAMP. The result of cannabinoid receptor stimulation is therefore a decreased concentration of intracellular cAMP. cAMP is referred to as the second messenger (the drug/endogenous ligand binding to the receptor being the first messenger). cAMP plays major roles inside a cell: through protein kinase A it can phosphorylate a number of proteins, and phosphorylation of proteins changes their activity. An enzyme may be turned on or off by phosphorylation, altering metabolic pathways; an ion channel may open or close, changing the membrane potential status of an electrical cell; importantly, transcription factors (proteins that control gene expression such as cAMP response element-binding protein) may be activated and modify the proteins actually expressed by the cell. Whereas changes in gene expression might take days to fully take place, opening or closing an ion channel would have immediate effects (seconds or less).

Overall, the decreased cAMP in the cells expressing CB_1 or CB_2 receptors would tend to result in an inhibition of function. A rapid effect of CB_1 stimulation seems to be mediated through a decreased phosphorylation of A-type potassium channels, resulting in their opening *(23)*. When a potassium channel is opened, the net force (electrical and concentration gradient) results in an efflux of potassium, and the loss of positive charges from the cell renders the cell less excitable (hyperpolarized). A number of calcium channels are closed by the same mechanism, particularly neuronal N-type, resulting in a decreased excitability also *(24)*. Most CB_1 receptors are found presynaptically and can modulate neurotransmitter release through presynaptic inhibition. Decreased release of glutamate, GABA, norepinephrine, dopamine, serotonin, and acetylcholine in slices of hippocampus, cerebellum, and neocortex has been reported either from direct observation or indirectly, through electrophysiological methods *(25)*. Other key proteins are regulated through signal transduction from cannabinoid receptors. They include focal adhesion kinase, which is phosphorylated on tyrosine residues and plays a role in synaptic plasticity *(26)*, and PI3K activation by βγ-subunits of G_i, resulting in phosphorylation of Raf-1 and then phosphorylation of MAPK to activate it. In turn, MAPK can activate phospholipase A_2 and trigger the arachidonic acid cascade and production of prostaglandins *(27)*, and can decrease growth factor receptor synthesis in certain tissue, a basis for antiproliferative action of cannabinoids *(28)*. PI3K is also biochemically associated with mediation of insulin-like effects with upregulation of glucose transporter 4 (insulin-dependent glucose uptake in skeletal muscle and adipose tissue), stimulation of glycogen synthesis, and glycolysis (liver cells). These latter effects would require the presence of receptors to anandamide on the appropriate target cells.

Distribution of receptors and the role of the cells affected can give insight into the pharmacology of agonists and antagonists of these receptors, and correlation between observed effects and expected effects can be theorized. CB_1 has been mapped mainly to the central nervous system (CNS) and peripherally to sensory neurons and the autonomic nervous system. CB_2 receptors are strictly peripheral and are found particularly on mature B cells and macrophages and on immune-related tissues such as tonsils and spleen. In the CNS, CB_1 receptors have been mapped in various animal species and in humans using autoradiography and immunohistochemical mapping techniques *(29–31)*. Whereas CB_1 receptors correlate poorly with anandamide distribution, they are found in brain regions rich in the degradative enzyme FAAH. Interestingly, FAAH is found postsynaptically and CB_1 receptors are found presynaptically, an anatomical arrangement that correlates well with the role of endogenous cannabinoids as retrograde synaptic messengers *(32)*. The highest densities are found in the cerebral cortex, particularly the association cortex, in the basal ganglia and cerebellum, and in the limbic forebrain (particularly hypothalamus, hippocampus, and anterior cingulate cortex). They are relatively absent from brainstem nuclei.

Cannabinoids affect cognitive and motor functions. Their subjective effects are well documented by chronic users and include enhancement of senses, errors in time and space judgment, emotional instability, irresistible impulses, illusions, and even hallucinations. Objective effects have been measured and studied, and decreased psychomotor performance, interference with attention span, and loss of efficiency in short-term memory are classically reported in the literature. Cannabinoids also have a number of peripheral effects, notably vasodilatation, tachycardia, and immunosuppressant properties. This chapter explains the neurophysiological and anatomical bases of these disorders and correlate them with what is known of the cannabinoid receptors.

2. Effects of Cannabinoids on Motor Coordination

2.1. Cortical Areas

Complex brain functions such as cognition, language, sexuality, sleep/wakefulness, emotions, and memory require constant information processing. Of the human cortex, 75% is association cortex (Fig. 4). The ability to attend, identify, and plan a

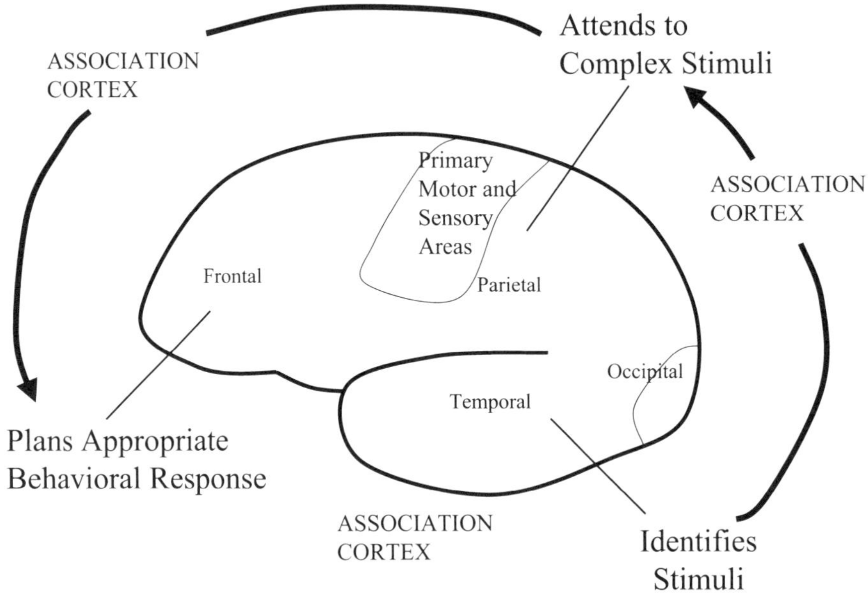

Fig. 4. Role of brain cortical areas: after identification of a stimulus by temporal regions, parietal areas attend to the stimulus, and frontal areas plan the appropriate behavioral responses. CB_1 receptors are dense in all cortical areas.

meaningful response to external or internal stimuli depends to a large extent on that association cortex, and one could define cognition as the processes by which we come to know and understand the world. Most inputs to the association cortex come from other cortical areas (hence the name "association"), either on the same hemisphere or the opposite one. Classically, three big areas are described. Imagine a driver and the sound of a horn—the temporal association cortex identifies the stimulus. The information is then relayed to the parietal association cortex, which decides whether to attend to the stimulus or not. In turn, the processed information is sent to the frontal association cortex for planning of appropriate behavioral response. The remainder (25%) of the cortical areas is subdivided into the primary sensory cortex, which receives inputs from the periphery by the intermediate of the thalamus, and the motor cortex, which receives inputs from the basal ganglia and the cerebellum, also through the thalamus. Two structures, the corpus callosum and the anterior commissure, allow communication from one side of the brain to the other.

Much of our understanding of brain regional neurophysiology comes from pathological lesions and their observation. Often, a drug, by altering physiological systems, can mimic in part what the pathology describes. For example, lesions of the temporal lobes result in recognition deficits. The patient has difficulty recognizing, identifying, or naming familiar objects. Syndromes of temporal lobe lesions are called agnosias, such as prosopagnosia, in which the patient cannot name things. Lesions of the parietal lobes lead to attention and perception deficits, often referred to as contralateral neglects—the patient fails to report, respond, or orient to a stimulus presented to the

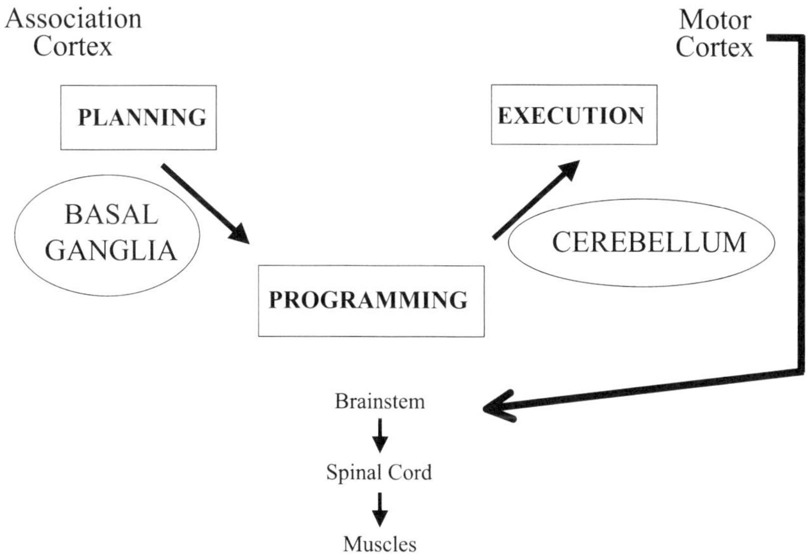

Fig. 5. Role of basal ganglia and cerebellum in the programmation of movements: whereas the basal ganglia allows the initiation of movement, the cerebellum controls the ongoing aspects of it. CB_1 receptors are highly expressed in the basal ganglia and cerebellum.

side of the body or visual space opposite the brain lesion. Finally, lesions of the frontal lobes alter the individual's personality, the ability to plan a behavior in relationship to the environment, and to use memories as a guide to appropriateness of behavior in various situations.

CB_1 receptors are particularly dense in all cortical areas *(31)*, particularly the cingulate cortex (*see* Section 3), and inhibition of evoked release of a number of neurotransmitters would result in cognitive impairment such as perception, attention, and behavioral deficits. It is difficult to ascribe specific deficits because of the complexity of the neural wiring in cortical regions.

2.2. Basal Ganglia and Cerebellum

The basal ganglia and the cerebellum interact with the cortex through a series of feedback circuits. The basal ganglia, a group of midbrain nuclei, are involved mainly with the initiation and execution of a movement, whereas the cerebellum tends to modulate ongoing movement (Fig. 5). Again, pathology clearly describes the role played by these structures in motor coordination. The most relevant disorders are the dyskinesias, or abnormal movements. Basal ganglia degeneration results in movement disorders such as Parkinson's disease (selective destruction of dopamine-containing neurons) and Huntington's disease (selective destruction of GABA interneurons). Parkinson's disease is classically associated with the triad of resting tremors, muscle rigidity (cogwheel-like), and slowness of movement (bradykinesia, with a festinating gait). Huntington's dyskinesias tend to be the opposite of Parkinson's, with excessive initiation of unwanted movements. Cerebellar degeneration is associated with asynergy, the inability to achieve a properly timed and balanced activation of the muscles during movement. Asynergy causes a decomposition of movements, resulting in the move going too far or falling short (dysmetria—the error is overcompensated). The gait becomes uncertain in cerebellar damage, with the feet placed far apart and the steps overshooting (ataxia), and it is no longer possible to make movements in rapid succession (dysdiadochokinesia). There are corresponding disturbances of speech and vision. In cerebellar injuries, the tremors do not appear at rest, but rather occur during movement (intention tremors), and the muscle tone tends to be low, with weak muscles that become tired easily. These are the kind of disturbances often seen at the roadside in field sobriety exercises such as one-leg-stand, walk-and-turn, and the finger-to-nose test when a driver is under the influence of drugs such as marijuana.

CB_1 receptors are highly expressed in the basal ganglia and the cerebellum. To understand the possible effect of THC binding to these receptors, some well-established neuronal connections between these structures are relevant to review prior to correlation with CB_1 receptor distribution. The basal ganglia illustrates well the concept of disinhibition at the neuronal level. Two key pathways are described: the direct and the indirect pathways (Figs. 6 and 7).

The association cortex and substantia nigra send excitatory impulses to the caudate putamen. The excitation comes from the neurotransmitter released at these synapses, glutamate, which is the major excitatory amino acid transmitter in the human brain. This in turn activates a GABA interneuron, GABA being the major inhibitory neurotransmitter in the human brain. The release of GABA occurs in the globus pallidus (internal segment) and at the synapse of another GABA neuron. This latter neuron is called a tonic neuron. It is always active, releasing GABA in motor nuclei of the thalamus (ventral lateral and anterior), resulting in inhibition of the thalamic excitatory outflow to the premotor cortex. The stimulation of the GABA interneuron turns off (inhibits) the tonic GABA neuron, resulting in disinhibition of the excitatory thalamic outflow to the premotor cortex: as a result, movement is initiated. Electrophysiology has shown that electrical activity in the tonic GABA neuron ceases before execution of a complex movement and resumes once the movement is underway.

The indirect pathway is more complex than the direct pathway. The tonic GABA neuron from the internal segment of globus pallidus is also under excitatory control from a glutamate excitatory interneuron from the subthalamic nucleus. Under normal conditions, this glutamate interneuron is inhibited by a tonic GABA neuron that arises from the globus pallidus external segment. In the indirect pathway, excitatory inputs from the associative cortex turn on a GABA interneuron from the caudate-putamen. This prevents the tonic GABA neuron from the globus pallidus from firing and disinhibits the glutamate interneuron from the subthalamic nucleus. The firing of the glutamate interneuron results in stronger inhibitory tone from the tonic GABA neuron projecting to the thalamus and prevents movement from being initiated. An alternative with the opposite effects arises from dopamine-containing inhibitory neurons from substantia nigra impacting the same GABA interneuron as the cortical excitatory input. The indirect pathway antagonizes the direct pathway and therefore allows fine control of the excitatory outputs to motor and premotor cortices, allowing coordinated movements to occur.

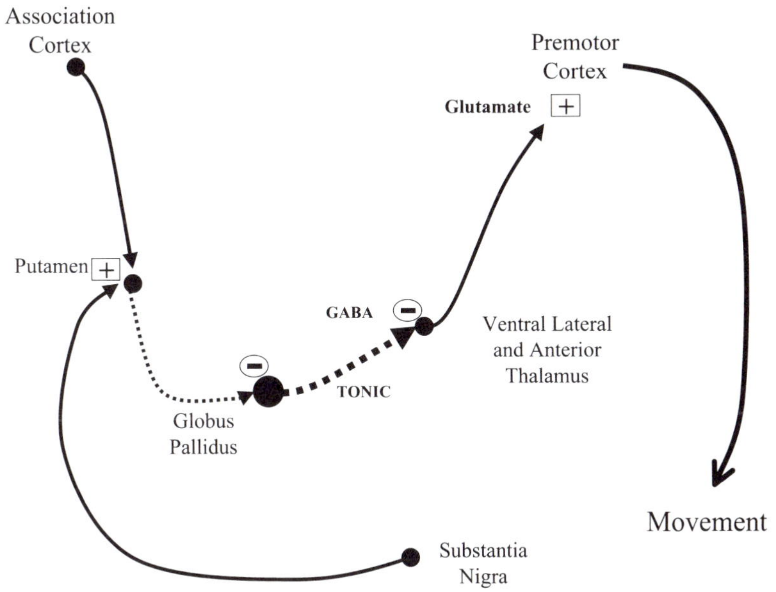

Fig. 6. Initiation of movement: the direct pathway. Neurons in dashed line are inhibitory, containing principally γ-aminobutyric acid (GABA); neurons in solid line are excitatory, containing principally glutamate. A tonic neuron is a neuron that always fires. CB_1 receptors are found on GABA interneurons and glutamate projection neurons, leading to complex motor effects.

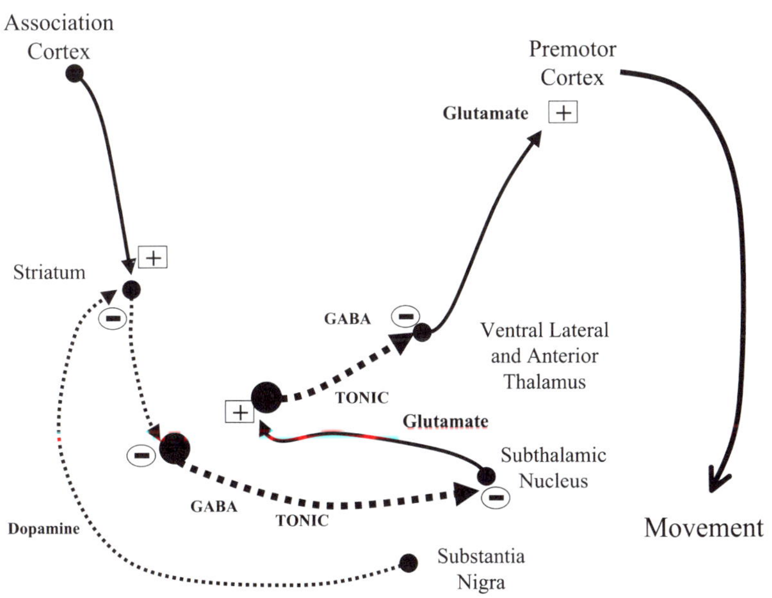

Fig. 7. Initiation of movement: the indirect pathway. Neurons in dashed line are inhibitory, containing principally γ-aminobutyric acid (GABA); neurons in solid line are excitatory, containing principally glutamate. A tonic neuron is a neuron that always fires. The indirect pathway opposes itself to the direct pathway, allowing coordination of movements. Notice the role of nigral dopamine in movement initiation.

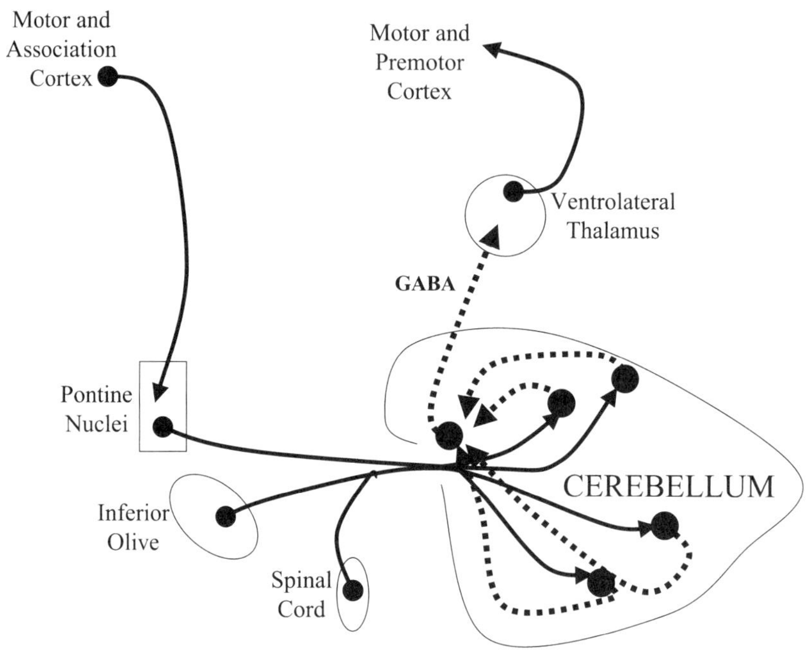

Fig. 8. Cerebellar pathways: CB_1 receptors are found on virtually all principal glutamate or γ-aminobutyric acid inputs to cerebellar Purkinje cells.

In the basal ganglia, CB_1 receptors are found on GABA medium spiny projection neurons (interneurons), particularly at the axon terminal. CB_1 receptors are also found on glutamate projection neurons, and whereas GABA interneurons are inhibitory, glutamate neurons are excitatory. The effect on movement initiation is therefore complex, depending on which system is inhibited by CB_1 receptor stimulation. Basal motor activity is regulated in part by CB_1 receptors, and a general inhibition of movement and tremors has been reported in animal experiments and human observations. Decreased glutamate release from the subthalamic neurons (indirect pathway) would result in this inhibition, as well as a decreased release of GABA from interneurons of the direct pathway or from the GABA tonic neurons of the globus pallidus projecting to the subthalamic nucleus (indirect pathway).

The wiring to and from the cerebellum is analogous to the ones in the basal ganglia (Fig. 8). The cerebellum receives three kinds of information: from the cortex, from vestibular nuclei in the brainstem, and from the spinal cord. The impulses come through excitatory climbing and mossy fibers. Climbing fibers are important because they adjust the flow of information that reaches the Purkinje cells and influence motor learning by inducing plastic changes in the synaptic activity of Purkinje neurons. The cerebellum has a unique output, the Purkinje neurons, which are GABA-containing neurons. They send information through inhibitory control of deep cerebellar relay nuclei, which in turn inform the thalamus and then the cortex, giving the cerebellum access to corticospinal projection neurons. This allows the cerebellum to organize the sequence of muscular contractions in complex ongoing movements and finely regulate them.

CB_1 receptors are found on virtually all the principal glutamate and GABA inputs to cerebellar Purkinje cells and, through inhibition of glutamate or GABA release, can exert complex motor effects.

Rodriguez de Fonseca et al. *(33)* have reviewed the literature related to motor effects of *Cannabis* on animals and humans. Studies of locomotor activities (LMA) in mice have showed dose-dependent effects of THC, with a decreased LMA at doses of 0.2 mg/kg and increased LMA at doses of 1–2 mg/kg and eventually catalepsy at doses in excess of 2.5 mg/kg. These changes could relate to differential sensitivities of neuron populations to CB_1 stimulation, resulting in different levels of inhibition of excitatory glutamate or inhibitory GABA release. Human studies have corroborated these results: impaired balance *(34)* and problems with tracking and pursuit of a moving point of light *(35)*. Importantly, often unpublished Drug Recognition Officer reports filled out by law-enforcement experts and collected in a number of forensic toxicology laboratories anecdotally support the impaired locomotor functions of humans under the influence of *Cannabis*. Some interesting new studies have used knockout mice models. A knockout mouse is an animal model in which a fertilized ovum from a pregnant female mouse (rat) has been genetically altered in a way to delete a specific gene and is then reimplanted to allow the pregnancy to continue. The offspring is then referred to as a knockout animal because in every nucleated cell a specific gene is missing. The lack of expression of the protein encoded by the missing gene results in symptoms that can be carefully correlated with the role of this protein in the wild animal. However, it is impossible to predict any effects from compensatory changes in expression of other genes as a result of the deletion. CB_1 knockout mice have been developed *(36)* and have been extensively studied. But conflicting results have been reported: a decreased basal activity in these animals suggests that tonic activation of CB_1 receptors actually promote movements. On the other hand, Ledent et al. *(37)* showed increased locomotor activity in a different strain of knockout mice (CD1 vs C57BL/6J). The availability of a selective antagonist of CB1 receptors, rimonabant (SR141716A), also contributed some information on the effects of THC on psychomotor movement, with an increased LMA noted in mice treated with the antagonist *(38)*.

3. Effects of Cannabinoids on the Limbic System

A major function of the CNS is to keep the internal environment stable and constant (homeostasis). The limbic system in general and the hypothalamus in particular are vital for this through three major, closely related processes: the secretion of hormones, the central control of the autonomic nervous system, and the development of emotional and motivational states. The limbic system is the primitive brain ("reptilian" brain) and consists of deeply seated brain structures: the hippocampus, communicating through the fornix with mamillary bodies (close to the hypothalamus), themselves linked to the anterior thalamus and feeding and receiving information from association areas and frontal cortex, critical in memory making and retrieving; the olfactory bulbs and the amygdala, instrumental in behavior and receiving highly processed sensory information; and the limbic system, with its own cortex, the cingulate cortex, wrapped around these structures and very much involved in behavior. The limbic sys-

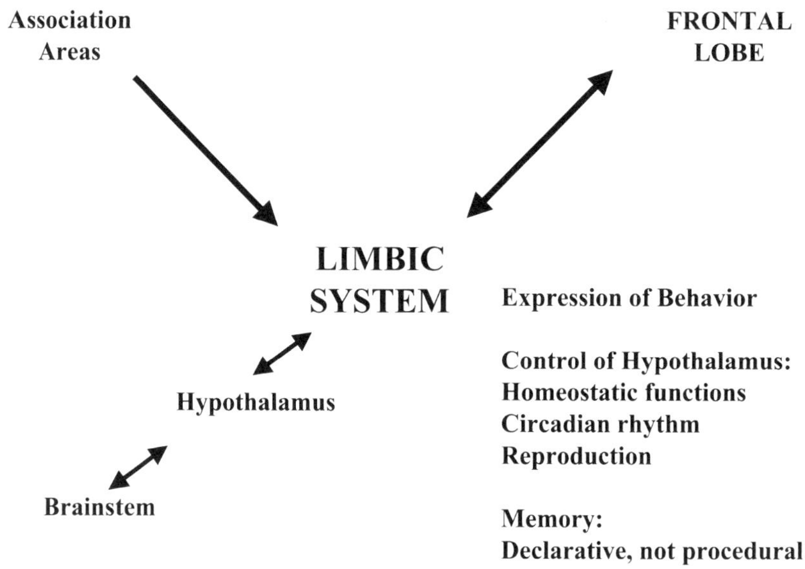

Fig. 9. The limbic system and its connections.

tem receives information from all association cortex areas of the brain and communicates with the frontal lobe, the hypothalamus, and the brainstem. Hypothalamic and limbic neurons interact with the reticular formation and the neocortex for maintenance of a general state of awareness (arousal). The roles of the limbic system can be simplified to three major tasks: the expression of behavior; the control of the hypothalamus (homeostatic functions, circadian rhythm, and reproductive behavior and control); and memory (Fig. 9).

3.1. Hippocampus and Memory Impairment

Classically, memory is associated with the hippocampus. But in reality, the basal ganglia and the cerebellum are also involved in formulating and retrieving memories. There are two different types of memories, referred to as declarative and procedural. Declarative memory is the storage and retrieval of material available to the conscious mind. It is encoded in symbols and can be expressed as language (hence, declarative), for example, remembering someone's name, a phone number, or an appointment date. The hippocampus and association cortex are critical in declarative memory. Procedural memory is not available to the conscious mind. It is about things we do not think of. Such memory involves skills and associations that are occurring unconsciously, for example, riding a bicycle, driving a car, or playing a piece of piano music. When we perform a complex action, we do not need to be conscious of a particular memory, and even thinking about it may actually inhibit the ability to perform this complex action smoothly. Procedural memory involves the basal ganglia, the cerebellum, and the motor cortex.

Another way to classify memory is based on a temporal scale: short-term memory occurs in hippocampal and related structures of the limbic system; long-term memory storage is not clearly located in a specific structure, but rather seems to involve cortical areas, such as the temporal cortex for the memory of faces or Wernicke's area for the memory of words. Pathology again has revealed a great deal about the importance of the hippocampus and memory formation: in medical history, an epileptic patient had the tips of both temporal lobes removed by surgery and as a result was incapable of remembering anything new, but had no change in intelligence and could remember things that occurred prior to the operation (anterograde amnesia).

Cannabis use in humans has long been known to impair short-term memory in humans *(39,40)*. Most of the tests used in humans have shown deficits in declarative memory. In animals, deficits in short-term memory have also been described, particularly in procedural memory (spatial learning tasks; ref. *41*). Both THC and anandamide cause these effects, and they are reversed by the antagonist rimonabant, suggesting the involvement of CB_1 receptors *(42,43)*. At the cellular level, the hippocampus has clearly defined pyramidal cells, which contain glutamate and communicate extensively with basket cell interneurons, which contain GABA. CB_1 receptor distribution is high in the hippocampus on both types of neuron *(44)*. THC and other CB_1 agonists likely decrease the release of GABA and glutamate at hippocampal synapses, interfering with the phenomenon of long-term potentiation, a critical synaptic event associated with engraving recent event in short-term memory. Supporting this are results from the study of CB_1 knockout mice: the absence of CB_1 receptors resulted in increased long-term potentiation *(45)* and increased memory *(46)*. Further, rimonabant was shown to improve memory in rodents *(47)*. These data suggest that CB_1 receptor stimulation inhibits the mechanisms by which short-term memorization occurs.

3.2. Amygdala and Behavioral Effects

The amygdaloid complex comprises basolateral and corticomedial nuclei. They are intrinsically connected. Afferents come from virtually all brain areas, as do efferents. Damage to the amygdala in humans is called the Kluver–Bucy syndrome: the patient can no longer recognize objects by sight, touch, or hearing (visual, tactile, and auditory agnosia) and is docile, eats excessively (sometimes objects that are not food), and has inappropriate behavior, particularly hypersexuality. Stimulation of the amygdala in animals results in aggressive or defensive behavior. CB_1 receptors are found on GABA neurons of the amygdala *(48)*. If the effects of GABA at the level of the amygdala are to decrease the excitability of efferent neurons, CB_1 stimulation at this level may well result in aggressive behaviors. Interestingly, *Cannabis* psychosis has been reported in the literature *(49,50)*, and *cannabis* users have sometimes been hospitalized and met the criteria for schizophrenia.

3.3. Hypothalamus and Neuroendocrine Effects

The hypothalamus is the principal brain region controlling feeding and regulation of body weight. Several neurotransmitters are involved in the control of food intake. Serotonin and norepinephrine tend to inhibit feeding; peptides such as NPY and orexins A and B tend to stimulate eating behaviors, whereas cocaine- and amphetamine-regulated transcripts and proopiomelanocortin-derived peptides are anorectic; hormones such as insulin and leptin also play a role, with leptin preventing body weight gain and insulin increasing body weight. Endogenous cannabinoids participate in the control of food intake, in part through interaction with leptin. Animals with defective leptin signaling are obese and have been found to have more anandamide and 2-AG than normal animals *(51)*. Giving leptin to normal rats results in decreased levels of endogenous cannabinoids. Further, rimonabant reduces food intake and causes weight loss, and CB_1 knockout mice eat less than wild-type mice. *Cannabis* use in humans is associated with the stimulation of appetite. Dronabinol, a US Food and Drug Administration-approved oral formulation of THC, has been successfully used in the treatment of AIDS wasting syndrome. Animals who are receiving THC or anandamide also eat more, and this effect is blocked by rimonabant, which is currently being investigated as an appetite suppressant *(51–53)*. Although there are relatively low densities of CB_1 receptors in the hypothalamus, all nuclei seem to show binding by autoradiography, particularly in the medial preoptic area and in the arcuate nucleus *(54)*. Besides central effects of cannabinoids on food intake, there is also evidence of a peripheral metabolic action of CB_1 receptors. Rimonabant was shown to decrease hyperinsulinemia in obese rats and increase the gene expression of adiponectin (adipocyte complement-related protein, or Acrp30; ref. *55*). Adiponectin is expressed in the adipose tissue, induces fatty acid oxidation, and causes weight reduction and increased insulin responses. If rimonabant is truly an antagonist, this suggests a metabolic role for elusive peripheral CB_1 receptors.

THC influences many other hypothalamic controlled neuroendocrine responses. Through decreased norepinephrine release, CB_1 stimulation results in decreased gonadotropin-releasing hormone and suppression of luteinizing hormone and follicle-stimulating hormone release by the pituitary as a result *(56)*. There are also reports of decreased growth hormone release and decreased prolactin release *(57)*, probably resulting from decreased dopamine release and effects on other anterior pituitary hormones under hypothalamic control.

A related central effect is the antiemetic effects of THC and analogs. Nabilone is a synthetic cannabinoid Food and Drug Administration-approved for chemotherapy-induced nausea and vomiting (like dronabinol), but its use has long been supplanted by the serotonin $5HT_3$ receptor antagonist family of drugs. Interestingly, there are CB_1 receptors in the area postrema, part of the nucleus tractus solitarius, which represents the "vomiting" center in the medulla *(54)*. Neurons in the area postrema are serotonergic and dopaminergic, with stimulation of D_2-like receptors or $5HT_3$ receptors resulting in vomiting. It is possible that CB_1 stimulation results in decreased release of dopamine or, as suggested in rat studies, of serotonin *(58)*.

4. Cannabinoids and Analgesia

Pain pathways are described at three levels: in the periphery, where it originates; at the level of the spinal cord, where some control "gating" the transmission of pain exists; and in the CNS, particularly at the level of the periaqueductal gray. CB_1 receptors are found on peripheral nerves *(59)*, and injection of anandamide into tissues swollen from carageenan-induced inflammation has been shown to reduce pain in rats *(60)*. But there is much more evidence for a spinal and a central site of action of cannabinoids. To understand better some of the sites and mechanisms of action of cannabinoids, a simplified pain pathway model is presented in Figs. 10 and 11.

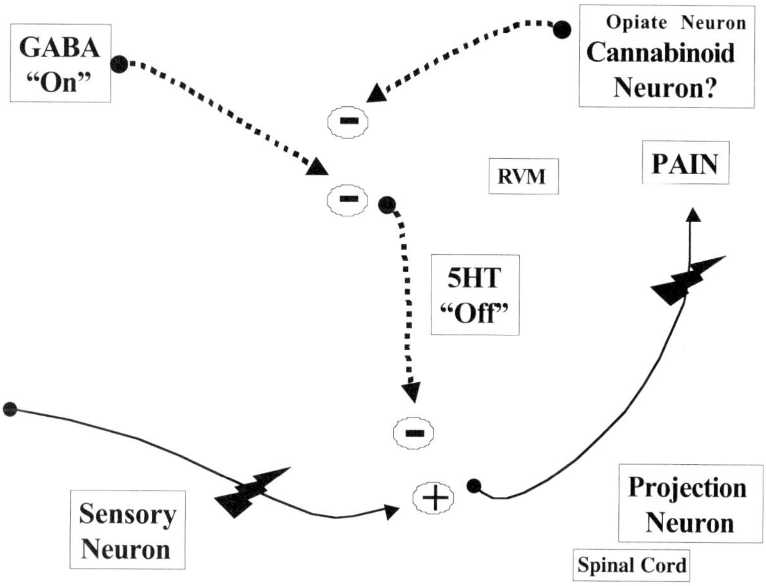

Fig. 10. Neurotransmitters and spinal modulation of pain: whereas serotonin (5HT) abolishes pain transmission, γ-aminobutyric acid (GABA) increases it by inhibition of the 5HT neuron. Cannabinoids may modulate pain transmission by inhibiting the firing of this GABA neuron, in a way similar to opiates. RVM, rostral ventrolateral medulla.

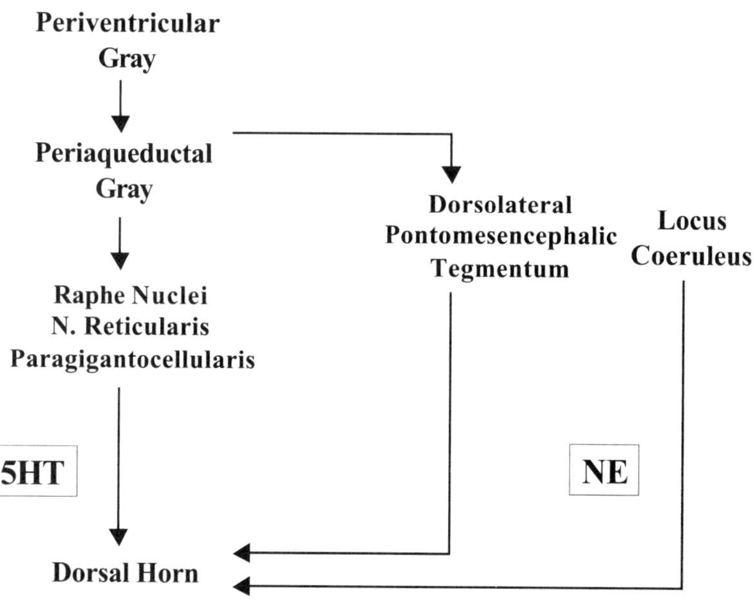

Fig. 11. Modulation of pain by descending pathways. Whereas serotonin (5HT) inhibits pain transmission, norepinephrine (NE) stimulates it. An inhibition of NE release through CB_1 receptors could also explain some of the analgesic effects of cannabinoids.

Pain transmission ascends through the spinal cord to the thalamus and then to somatosensory cortical areas and prefrontal cortex. The main pathway carrying nociceptive stimuli to the brain is the prominent spinothalamic tract. Figure 11 shows that the synapse between the peripheral sensory neuron (first-order neuron) and the secondary projection neuron is under the control of a serotonin-descending neuron, which abolishes the transmission of pain to higher centers. The serotonin neuron is itself under the inhibitory control of a GABA interneuron. When GABA is released, the serotonin neuron is turned off, and pain transmission occurs. Interneurons communicate the ascending information to the reticular formation of the medulla, the periaqueductal gray (PAG) of the midbrain, and the periventricular nucleus of the hypothalamus. These structures in turn modulate pain transmission through descending pathways, synapsing with all the above structures. These pathways have been extensively studied as a site for opiate action and are now relevant as a site of action of cannabinoids as well. For example, the PAG stimulates directly raphe nuclei, where serotonin-containing neurons can inhibit pain transmission (Fig. 12). The PAG also sends signals to the dorsolateral pontomesencephalic tegmentum (DLPMT) and the periventricular nucleus of the hypothalamus. The DLPMT is the beginning of the second major descending pathway, which involves norepinephrine and locus coeruleus neurons. But unlike serotonin, norepinephrine is a nociceptive substance in this modulatory pathway: it causes pain.

Any stimulation of the serotonin-descending pathway, such as through GABA release inhibition, or any inhibition of the noradrenergic-descending pathway, such as through decreased synaptic release of norepinephrine, would result in analgesia.

Evidence shows that THC and cannabinoids prevent pain transmission when injected directly into the spinal cord, the brainstem, or even the thalamus *(61)*. CB_1 receptors are very dense in specific layers of the dorsal horn of the spinal cord, where peripheral sensory afferents synapse with second-order neurons to transmit pain to higher centers *(62,63)*. Further, pain itself causes the release of anandamide in the PAG, suggesting that endogenous cannabinoids physiologically play a role in the modulation of pain signaling *(64)*. Because these pathways are generally associated with opiate pharmacology, it was important to investigate if opiate receptors were involved. Results suggest a parallel but distinct neural pathway for cannabinoids and opiates. For example, if morphine and THC were given together, an additive or synergistic effect would be expected. Both rimonabant and naloxone could block this effect, indicating the participation of CB_1 and opiate receptors, respectively *(65)*. Opiates are known to decrease GABA release at the level of the serotonergic neuron, resulting in inhibition of an ascending pain pathway. It is possible that cannabinoids may decrease GABA release at the same level, but through a distinct CB_1 receptor effect. Some studies suggest an effect on norepinephrine release because intrathecal injection of yohimbine, an α_2 antagonist that would increase the synthesis and release of norepinephrine at the synaptic cleft, blocks THC-induced analgesia *(66)*. It is interesting to note that CB_1 and α_2 receptors are negatively coupled to cAMP production through G_i proteins.

CB_1 knockout mice bring an interesting development in understanding the complexity of pain modulation by THC and endogenous cannabinoids: anandamide continues to cause analgesia in these animals in spite of the absence of CB_1 receptor expression, whereas THC does not *(67)*. The discrepancy may be explained by a novel cannabinoid receptor or through anandamide's binding to the vanilloid receptor VR_1, which is present in primary afferent sensory neurons *(68,69)*. VR_1 is a capsaicin-sensitive cationic channel (Na^+, Ca^{2+}, K^+), and anandamide is proposed to be the endogenous ligand *(70)*. Other stimuli for the channel are heat and protons, and VR_1 plays a role in the modulation of intracellular calcium, which in turn regulates neurotransmitter release. This new pharmacology is at the center of a debate regarding legalization and the use of *Cannabis* products in the management of pain as well as in a number of inflammatory disorders.

5. Cannabinoids and Addiction

Cannabis remains the most commonly used illicit drug of abuse in the United States and probably in the world. A typical *Cannabis* high starts with tingling of the body and head, progresses to dizziness and a quickening of mental associations with sharpened senses, heightened perception, increased appetite, and a distortion of the sense of time, causing it to go faster, and ends with calm, drowsiness, and eventually sleep *(15)*. CB_1 receptors are central to the intoxicating effects, as evidenced by the blockade of those effects by rimonabant *(71)*. Dopamine plays a major role in reward, and most drugs abused directly increase dopamine levels in the mesocorticolimbic pathways involved with reinforcement and pleasure *(72)*. The neural substrates of reward involve the medial forebrain bundle (MFB) and its connected structures, including most of the brain monoamine systems. The ventral tegmental area (VTA), basal forebrain, and MFB support intracranial self-stimulation in animal experiments. The basal forebrain, nucleus accumbens, olfactory tubercles, frontal cortex, and amygdala are all connected to the VTA through dopaminergic projections within the MFB. Other neurotransmitters playing a role in these pathways are opioids, GABA, glutamate, and serotonin.

Interaction with opioid and dopaminergic neurons seems to underlie the rewarding effects of THC (Fig. 12). THC has been shown to stimulate dopaminergic neurons from the VTA *(73)* and to increase the release of dopamine at one of the output, the shell of the nucleus accumbens *(74)*. Naloxonazine, a μ_1 receptor antagonist, reversed this effect, suggesting that the increased dopamine release by THC was indirectly mediated by an opioid interneuron relieving an inhibitory tone on dopaminergic pathways. Other findings suggesting an opiate mechanism to the reinforcing effects of *Cannabis* include opioid-dependent rats in which rimonabant injection precipitates withdrawal *(75)*. Furthermore, cannabinoids can induce the synthesis and release of endogenous opioid peptides *(76)*. However, it is important to note that in humans naloxone fails to significantly change the subjective and physiological effects of smoked marijuana *(77)*.

Addiction to *Cannabis* exhibits tolerance and dependence, as proven by the existence of a withdrawal syndrome characterized by craving for *Cannabis* (psychological dependence), decreased appetite, insomnia and nightmares, and some degree of agitation, restlessness, or irritability *(78)*. The dependence and withdrawal are not

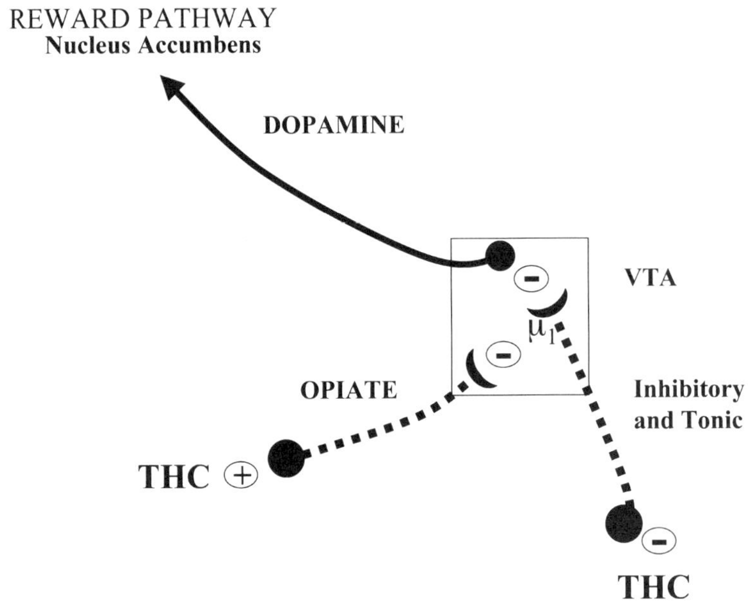

Fig. 12. The reward pathway: possible site of action of *Cannabis*. Δ^9-Tetrahydrocannabinol may reinforce the effects of opiates and increase the firing of dopamine neurons from the ventral tegmental area. Neurons in the dashed line are inhibitory; neurons in the solid line are excitatory.

likely to be severe in the case of THC use because THC is highly lipophilic and slow release from the fat tissues in chronic users should result in a tapering of the effects of *Cannabis* over time. Nevertheless, rimonabant can precipitate withdrawal in animals, indicating the involvement of CB_1 receptors in tolerance and dependence to THC *(79)*. When agonists are chronically used, receptors desensitize or downregulate. CB_1 receptors are downregulated after chronic exposure to THC *(80)*, and chronic exposure to an anandamide derivative, methanandamide, causes internalization of G protein-linked receptors from the plasma membrane of hippocampal neurons, an effect blocked by rimonabant *(81)*. These findings would result in an expected reduction of effects of cannabinoids when administered chronically. Not all effects of a drug show the same degree of tolerance. In animals, tolerance to the hypothermic, locomotor, analgesic, and immune-suppressant effects of cannabinoids in mice was studied *(82,83)*. But there is a notable absence of tolerance to cognition defects induced by THC in animals, suggesting that impairing effects of *Cannabis* on learning and memory would persist in chronic marijuana users *(84)*. The same is true of the increased dopamine firing in the VTA of rats, suggesting a lack of tolerance to the pleasurable effects of *Cannabis* use in humans *(83)*.

6. Cannabinoids and Cardiovascular Effects

Most of the research on cannabinoids has focused on the CNS, yet there are very well-described effects of synthetic and endogenous cannabinoids in the periphery,

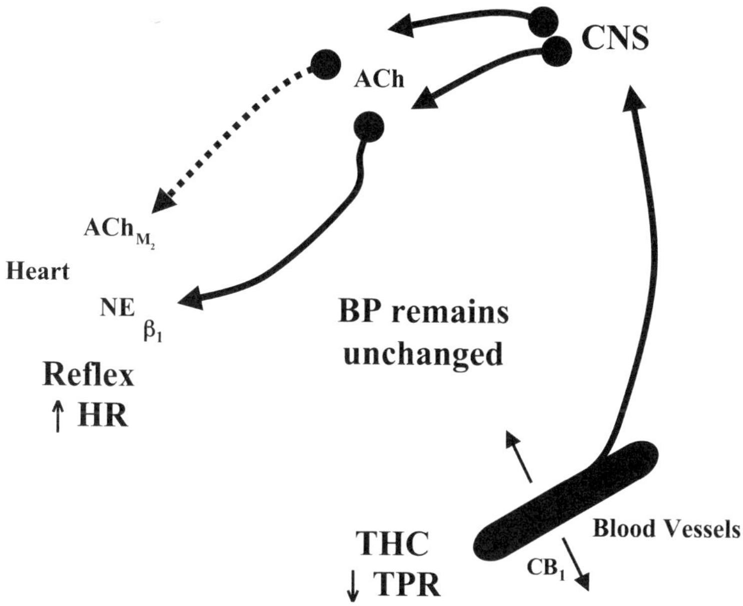

Fig. 13. Control of blood pressure by baroreceptor reflexes: Δ^9-tetrahydrocannabinol causes reflex tachycardia through CB_1-mediated vasodilatation. ACh, acetylcholine; NE, norepinephrine; BP, blood pressure; TPR, total peripheral resistance; HR, heart rate; CNS, central nervous system.

particularly at the level of vascular tone, resulting in complex blood pressure and cardiac responses. In humans, the acute administration of cannabinoids causes marked tachycardia and a small increase in blood pressure, whereas in chronic users, hypotension and bradycardia are generally noted *(85,86)*. Blood vessel tone and heart contractility act in concert to regulate blood pressure thanks to what is known as baroreceptor reflexes, which involve the autonomic nervous system. Principles of hemodynamics illustrate how blood pressure is directly proportional to the total peripheral resistance (how constricted blood vessels are) and to the cardiac output (how much blood is forced by the pump in the vasculature, the "plumbing"). Cardiac output is itself controlled by heart rate (how fast the pump is working) and stroke volume (how much blood is ejected at each contraction of the heart).

Total peripheral resistance is the main determinant of blood pressure, and the vasculature is mainly under sympathetic innervation control. Any vasoconstriction (increased resistance) results in increased blood pressure and the firing of receptors situated in the carotid sinuses and the aortic arch. These receptors in turn inform cardiovascular centers of the brainstem (in the rostral ventrolateral medulla and the nucleus of tractus solitarius), which adapt the autonomic balance between sympathetic and parasympathetic outflow to the cardiovascular system in order to restore the blood pressure to lower levels (*see* Fig. 13). The net effect of increased blood pressure is increased parasympathetic activity to decrease the heart rate and contractility and decreased sympathetic outflow to decrease peripheral resistance of the vasculature.

The effects of cannabinoids could therefore be mediated centrally; CB_1 receptors are found in these cardiovascular centers *(87)*, and intravenous injection of CB_1 agonists decreases sympathetic outflow centrally (probably through presynaptic inhibition), leading to vasodilatation and hypotension *(88)*. The responses, being absent in CB_1 knockout mice, suggest that the hypotension and bradycardia resulting from increased parasympathetic and decreased sympathetic outflows are CB_1 mediated *(37)*. These effects observed in animals would explain the chronic findings in humans using *Cannabis*, but not the marked tachycardia associated with acute use of the drug. The marked tachycardia would require a decreased parasympathetic and increased sympathetic activity, as would occur centrally if inhibition of parasympathetic outflow was occurring or peripherally if a marked vasodilatation was induced by cannabinoids. Interestingly, Glass et al. *(31)* showed a high density of CB_1 receptors in the dorsal motor nucleus of the vagus in the brainstem (parasympathetic centers), and inhibition of this center through CB_1 would result in decreased parasympathetic outflow. It could also explain other measured effects of THC in humans besides tachycardia, such as a degree of mydriasis and an antiemetic effect.

To confuse the issue of the cardiovascular effects of cannabinoids further, anandamide is a vasodilator in vitro in selective isolated vessel preparations and not others, pointing at a direct effect on smooth muscle tone of the vasculature *(89)*. Subsequent studies have suggested that anandamide acts through inhibition of calcium release in smooth muscle cells *(90)*. Recently, anandamide has been implicated as a natural ligand of the vanilloid receptor VR_1 *(91)*. VR_1 receptors are found on sensory nerves, and stimulation results in calcium entry and release by the nerve of a number of transmitters, which could be associated with vasodilatation, such as nitric oxide, substance P, neurokinins, ATP, and calcitonin gene-related peptide. For example, nitric oxide diffuses to the smooth muscle and increases cGMP as a mode of vasodilatation, and calcitonin gene-related peptide binds to G protein-linked receptors, which increase cAMP, another way of causing relaxation of vascular smooth muscle.

It is important to note that at this point in time, no precise molecular action of cannabinoids has been found, and every mechanism proposed has been confirmed and refuted by research. Methodology issues, in vitro versus in vivo effects, and species differences may be explanatory. Most recently, Offertaler et al. *(92)* suggested the existence of a non-CB_1, non-CB_2, non-VR_1 endothelial anandamide receptor. This receptor would be G protein-coupled and result in MAPK activation. Could the tachycardia from *Cannabis* use in humans be simply a result of a direct vasodilatory effect resulting in sympathetically mediated baroreceptor reflexes?

7. Cannabinoids and Immunomodulation

Immune/inflammatory responses are at the basis of a number of pathological conditions. CB_1 are mainly found centrally and mediate analgesic effects of cannabinoids. CB_2 receptors are mainly found on cells of the immune system, such as macrophages, T-lymphocytes, and natural killer cells *(93)*. High doses of cannabinoids suppress immune responses, whereas low doses cause metabolic stimulation of lymphocytes *(94,95)*. The mechanism of immunomodulation by cannabinoids is still unclear, but evidence suggests that CB_2 receptors mediate most of these effects, with downregulation of mast cells and granulocytes and reduced cytokine release, although VR_1 receptors may be implicated *(96)*.

The immunomodulatory effects of THC have been tested in a laboratory model of multiple sclerosis, experimental autoimmune encephalomyelitis. Placebo-treated animals died, whereas THC-treated animals survived and had no or minimal signs *(97)* and notably reduced inflammatory response. These results were reproduced with various THC-like drugs, and anecdotal reports from multiple sclerosis patients that marijuana would decrease spasticity and symptoms of the disease indicated a possible use of *Cannabis* in the management of this debilitating demyelinating disorder (for a review, *see* ref. *98*). However, these effects required high doses of cannabinoids, which may not be tolerated in humans or certainly have central effects. Recently, Killestein et al. *(99)* concluded a clinical trial with smaller oral doses of THC and measured signs of pro-inflammatory actions in multiple sclerosis patients, which may cause actual worsening of the symptoms. More knowledge of CB_2 pharmacology and the development of non-CB_1 agonists might help in the development of significant anti-inflammatory cannabinoids with therapeutic potential in humans. For example, ajulemic acid, a derivative of the main inactive metabolite of THC, carboxy-THC, has promising anti-inflammatory action, and a mechanism of action for its effects was recently discovered *(100)*. Ajulemic acid binds peroxisome proliferator-activated receptor gamma (PPARγ), causing an inhibition of cytokine expression. PPARγ is an important transcription factor, which is also involved in lipid metabolism, glucose homeostasis, and adipocyte differentiation (drugs are available interfering with this target in the treatment of diabetes and hyperlipidemia). Other transcription factors involved in inflammatory/immune responses are targeted by cannabinoids, notably inhibition of activator protein-1, nuclear factor κB, and signal transducer and activator of transcription *(101–103)*. These data point to a mechanism involving changes in gene expression, probably mediated through complex signal transduction changes, which may or may not involve classic cannabinoid receptors on the surface of the cell because cannabinoids are lipophilic and may access transcription factors intracellularly.

8. Conclusions

The complex pharmacology of cannabinoids, whether exogenous or endogenous, exists only in its infancy. From the discovery of specific cannabinoid receptors and other targets to that of endogenous ligands and a biochemical pathway of synthesis, degradation and reuptake, the therapeutic potential of cannabinoids is only emerging. Central actions on motor regulatory pathway may give rise to drugs useful in dyskinesias such as Huntington's or Parkinson's disease. Central effects on glutamate release may yield medications aimed at decreasing the pathological consequences of strokes. The analgesic effects of cannabinoids already see some application in neuropathic pain *(104)*. Could an antagonist help in increasing memory in Alzheimer's disease patients? Already, central effects such as appetite stimulation and antiemetic properties are clinically used. Peripheral effects on the cardiovascular system could help in the development of novel antihypertensive medications. The peripheral pharmacology of cannabinoids may also lead to drugs modifying immune or inflammatory function, such as multiple sclerosis, as well as asthma or autoimmune disorders. The future will shed light on the place of cannabinoid pharmacology in our medical arsenal to fight diseases, and developing research will undoubtedly enhance our understanding of existing and yet unknown molecular pathways cells use to appropriately respond to internal and external stimuli.

References

1. Devane, W. A., Hanus, L., Breuer, A., et al. (1992) Isolation and structure of a brain constituent that binds to the cannabinoid receptor. *Science* **258**, 1946–1949.
2. Mechoulam, R., Ben-Shabat, S., Hanus, L., et al. (1995) Identification of an endogenous 2-monoglyceride, present in canine gut, that binds to cannabinoid receptors. *Biochem. Pharmacol.* **50**, 83–90.
3. Sugiura, T., Kondo, S., Sukagawa, A., et al. (1995) 2-Arachidonoylglycerol: a possible endogenous cannabinoid receptor ligand in brain. *Biochem. Biophys. Res. Commun.* **215(1)**, 89–97.
4. Stella, N., Schweitzer, P., and Piomelli, D. (1997) A second endogenous cannabinoid that modulates long-term potentiation. *Nature* **388**, 773–778.
5. Hanus, L., Abu-Lafi, S., Fride, E., et al. (2001) 2-Arachidonyl glyceryl ether, an endogenous agonist of the cannabinoid CB_1 receptor. *Proc. Natl. Acad. Sci. USA* **98(7)**, 3662–3665.
6. Di Marzo, V., Fontana, A., Cadas, H., et al. (1994) Formation and inactivation of endogenous cannabinoid anandamide in central neurons. *Nature* **372**, 686–691.
7. Sugiura, T., Kondo, S., Sukagawa, A., et al. (1996) Enzymatic synthesis of anandamide, an endogenous cannabinoid receptor ligand, through N-acylphosphatidylethanolamine pathway in testis: involvement of Ca^{2+}-dependent transacylase and phosphodiesterase activities. *Biochem. Biophys. Res. Commun.* **218**, 113–117.
8. Cadas, H., Gaillet, S., Beltramo, M., Venance, L., and Piomelli, D. (1996) Biosynthesis of an endogenous cannabinoid precursor in neurons and its control by calcium and cAMP. *J. Neurosci.* **16**, 3934-3942.
9. Cadas, H., di Tomaso, E., and Piomelli, D. (1997) Occurrence and biosynthesis of endogenous cannabinoid precursor, N-arachidonoyl phosphatidylethanolamine in rat brain. *J. Neurosci.* **17**, 1226–1242.
10. Piomelli, D., Beltramo, M., Giuffrida, A., and Stella, N. (1998) Endogenous cannabinoid signaling. *Neurobiol. Dis.* **5**, 462–473.
11. Hillard, C. J. and Jarrahian, A. (2000) The movement of N-arachidonoylethanolamine (anandamide) across cellular membranes. *Chem. Phys. Lipids* **108**, 123–134.
12. Giuffrida, A., Beltramo, M., and Piomelli, D. (2001) Mechanisms of endocannabinoid inactivation: biochemistry and pharmacology. *J. Pharmacol. Exp. Ther.* **298**, 7–14.
13. Ueda, N., Puffenbarger, R. A., Yamamoto, S., and Deutsch, D. G. (2000) The fatty acid amide hydrolase (FAAH). *Chem. Phys. Lipids* **108**, 107–121.
14. Pertwee, R. G. and Ross, R. A. (2002) Cannabinoid receptors and their ligands. *Prostaglandins Leukot. Essent. Fatty Acids* **66(2, 3)**, 101–121.
15. Iversen, L. (2003) Cannabis and the brain. *Brain* **126**, 1252–1270.
16. Wilson, R. I. and Nicoll, R. A. (2001) Endogenous cannabinoids mediate retrograde signaling at hippocampal synapses. *Nature* **410**, 588–592.
17. Kreitzer, A. C. and Regehr, W. G. (2001) Retrograde inhibition of presynaptic calcium influx by endogenous cannabinoids at excitatory synapses onto Purkinje cells. *Neuron* **29**, 717–727.
18. Ohno-Shosaku, T., Maejima, T., and Kano, M. (2001) Endogenous cannabinoids mediate retrograde signals from depolarized postsynaptic neurons to presynaptic terminals. *Neuron* **29**, 729–738.

19. Matsuda, L. A., Lolait, S. J., Brownstein, M. J., Young, A. C., and Bonner, T .I. (1990) Structure of a cannabinoid receptor and functional expression the cloned cDNA. *Nature* **346**, 561–564.
20. Gerard, C.M., Mollereau, C., Vassart, G., and Parmentier, M. (1991) Molecular cloning of a human cannabinoid receptor which is also expressed in testis. *Biochem. J.* **279**, 129–134.
21. Munro, S., Thomas, K. L., and Abu-Shaar, M. (1993) Molecular characterization of a peripheral receptor for cannabinoids. *Nature* **365**, 61–65.
22. Howlett, A. C., Barth, F., Bonner, T. I., et al. (2002) International union of pharmacology. XXVII. Classification of cannabinoid receptors. *Pharmacol. Rev.* **54**, 161–202.
23. Childers, S. R. and Deadwyler, S. A. (1996) Role of cyclic AMP in the actions of cannabinoid receptors. *Biochem. Pharmacol.* **52**, 819–827.
24. Caulfield, M. P. and Brown, D. A. (1992) Cannabinoid receptor agonists inhibit Ca^{2+} current in NG108-15 neuroblastoma cells via a pertussis toxin-sensitive mechanism. *Br. J. Pharmacol.* **106**, 231–232.
25. Schlicker, E. and Kathmann, M. (2001) Modulation of transmitter release via presynaptic cannabinoid receptors. *Trends Pharmacol. Sci.* **22**, 565–572.
26. Derkinderen, P., Toutant, M., Burgaya, F., et al. (1996) Regulation of a neuronal form of focal adhesion kinase by anandamide. *Science* **273**, 1719–1722.
27. Wartmann, M., Campbell, D., Subramanian, A., Burstein, S. H., and Davis, R. J. (1995) The MAP kinase signal transduction pathway is activated by the endogenous cannabinoid anandamide. *FEBS Lett.* **359**, 133–136.
28. De Petrocellis, L., Melck, D., Palmisano, A., et al. (1998) The endogenous cannabinoid anandamide inhibits human breast cancer cell proliferation. *Proc. Natl. Acad. Sci. USA* **95**, 8375–8380.
29. Herkenham, M., Lynn, A. B., Little, M. D., et al. (1990) Cannabinoid receptor localization in brain. *Proc. Natl. Acad. Sci. USA* **87**, 1932–1936.
30. Ergotova, M. and Elphick, M. R. (2000) Localisation of cannabinoid receptors in the rat brain using antibodies to the intracellular C-terminal tail of CB_1. *J. Comp. Neurol.* **422**, 159–171.
31. Glass, M., Dragunow, M., and Faull, R. L. M. (1997) Cannabinoid receptors in the human brain: a detailed anatomical and quantitative autoradiographic study in the fetal, neonatal and adult human brain. *Neuroscience* **77**, 299–318.
32. Elphick, M. R. and Egertova, M. (2001) The neurobiology and evolution of cannabinoid signalling. *Philos. Trans. R. Soc. Lond. B Biol. Sci.* **356**, 381–408.
33. Rodriguez de Fonseca, F., Del Arco, I., Martin-Calderon, J. L., Gorriti, M.A., and Navarro, M. (1998) Role of the endogenous cannabinoid system in the regulation of motor activity. *Neurobiol. Dis.* **5**, 483–501.
34. Greenberg, H. S., Werness, S. A., Pugh, J. E., Andrus, R. O., Anderson, D. J., and Domino, E. F. (1994) Short-term effects of smoking marijuana on balance in patients with multiple sclerosis and normal volunteers. *Clin. Pharmacol. Ther.* **55**, 324–328.
35. Manno, J. E., Kiplinger, G.F., Haine, S. E., Bennett, I.F., and Forney, R. B. (1970) Comparative effects of smoking marihuana or placebo on human motor and mental performance. *Clin. Pharmacol. Ther.* **11(6)**, 808–15.
36. Zimmer, A., Zimmer, A. M., Hohmann, A. G., Herkenham, M., and Bonner, T. I. (1999) Increased mortality, hypoactivity and hypoalgesia in cannabinoid CB_1 receptor knockout mice. *Proc. Natl. Acad. Sci. USA* **96**, 5780–5785.
37. Ledent, C., Valverde, O., Cossu, G., et al. (1999) Unresponsiveness to cannabinoids and reduced addictive effects of opiates in CB_1 receptor knockout mice. *Science* **283**, 401–404.
38. Compton, D. R., Aceto, M. D., Lowe, J., and Martin, B. R. (1996) In vivo characterization of a specific cannabinoid receptor antagonist (SR141716A): inhibition of Δ^9-tetrahy-

drocannabinol-induced responses and apparent agonist activity. *J. Pharmacol. Exp. Ther.* **277**, 586–594.
39. Jones, R. T. (1978) Marihuana: human effects, in *Handbook of Psychopharmacology*, Vol. 12 (Iversen, S. D. and Snyder, S. H., eds.), Plenum Press, New York, pp. 373–412.
40. Mendelson, J. H., Babor, T. F., Kuehnle, J. C., et al. (1976) Behavioral and biologic aspects of marijuana use. *Ann. NY Acad. Sci.* **282**, 186–210.
41. Hampson, R. E. and Deadwyler, S. A. (1999) Cannabinoids, hippocampal function and memory. *Life Sci.* **65**, 715–723.
42. Lichtman, A. H. and Martin, B. R. (1996) Δ^9-Tetrahydrocannabinol impairs spatial memory through a cannabinoid receptor mechanism. *Psychopharmacology* **126**, 125–131.
43. Mallet, P. E. and Beninger, R. J. (1998) The cannabinoid CB_1 receptor antagonist SR141716A attenuates the memory impairment produced by Δ^9-tetrahydrocannabinol or anandamide. *Psychopharmacology* **140**, 11–19.
44. Katona, I., Sperlagh, B., Magloczky, Z., et al. (2000) GABAergic interneurons are the targets of cannabinoid actions in the human hippocampus. *Neuroscience* **100(4)**, 797–804.
45. Bohme, G. A., La Ville, M., Ledent, C., Parmentier, M., and Imperato, A. (2000) Enhanced long term potentiation in mice lacking cannabinoid CB_1 receptors. *Neuroscience* **95(1)**, 5–7.
46. Reibaud, M., Obinu, M. C., Ledent, C., Parmentier, M., Bohme, G. A., and Imperato, A. (1999) Enhancement of memory in cannabinoid CB_1 receptor knockout mice. *Eur. J. Pharmacol.* **379**, R1–R2.
47. Terranova, J. P., Storme, J. J., Lafon, N., et al. (1996) Improvement of memory in rodents by the selective CB_1 cannabinoid receptor antagonist, SR 141716. *Psychopharmacology* **126**,165–72.
48. Katona, I., Rancz, E. A., Acsady, L., et al. (2001) Distribution of CB_1 receptors in the amygdala and their role in the control of GABAergic transmission. *J. Neurosci.* **21(23)**, 9506–9518.
49. Hall, W. and Degenhardt, L. (2000) Cannabis use and psychosis: a review of clinical and epidemiological evidence. *Aust. NZ J. Psychiatry* **34**, 26–34.
50. Johns, A. (2001) Psychiatric effects of cannabis. *Br. J. Psychiatry* **178**, 116–122.
51. Di Marzo, V., Goparaju, S. K., Wang, L., et al. (2001) Leptin-regulated endocannabinoids are involved in maintaining food intake. *Nature* **410**, 822–825.
52. Beal, J. E., Olson, R., Laubenstein, L., et al. (1995) Dronabinol as a treatment for anorexia associated with weight loss in patients with AIDS. *J. Pain Symptom Manage.* **10(2)**, 89–97.
53. Colombo, G., Agabio R., Diaz, G., Lobina, C., Reali, R., and Gessa, G.L. (1998) Appetite suppression and weight loss after the cannabinoid antagonist SR141716A. *Life Sci.* **63**, PL113–117.
54. Herkenham, M., Lynn, A. B., Johnson, M. R., Melvin, L. S., de Costa, B. R., and Rice, K. C. (1991) Characterization and localization of cannabinoid receptors in rat brain: a quantitative in vitro autoradiographic study. *J. Neurosci.* **11**, 563–583.
55. Bensaid, M., Gary-Bobo, M., Esclangon, A., et al. (2003) The cannabinoid CB_1 receptor antagonist SR141716 increases Acrp30 mRNA expression in adipose tissue of obese fa/fa rats and in cultured adipocyte cells. *Mol. Pharmacol.* **63(4)**, 908–914.
56. Murphy, L. L., Steger, R. W., Smith, M. S., and Bartke, A. (1990) Effects of delta-9 tetrahydrocannabinol, cannabinol and cannabidiol, alone and in combinations, on luteinizing hormone and prolactin release and on hypothalamic neurotransmitters in the male rat. *Neuroendocrinology* **52**, 316–321.

57. Rettori, V., Wenger, T., Snyder, G., Dalterio, S., and McCann, S. M. (1988) Hypothalamic action of delta-9-tetrahydrocannabinol to inhibit the release of prolactin and growth hormone in the rat. *Neuroendocrinology* **47**, 498–503.
58. Fan, P. (1995) Cannabinoid agonists inhibit the activation of $5HT_3$ receptors in rat nodose ganglion neurons. *J. Neurophysiol.* **73**, 907–910.
59. Hohmann, A. G. and Herkenham, M. (1999) Cannabinoid receptors undergo axonal flow in sensory nerves. *Neuroscience* **92(4)**, 1171–1175.
60. Richardson, J. D., Kilo, S., and Hargreaves, K. M. (1998) Cannabinoids reduce hyperalgesia and inflammation via interaction with peripheral CB_1 receptors. *Pain* **75**, 111–119.
61. Pertwee, R. G. (2001) Cannabinoid receptors and pain. *Prog. Neurobiol.* **63**, 569–611.
62. Drew, L. J., Harris, J., Millns, P. J., Kendall, D. A., and Chapman, V. (2000) Activation of spinal cannabinoid $_1$ receptors inhibits C-fibre driven hyperexcitable neuronal responses and increases [^{35}S]GTPγS binding in the dorsal horn of the spinal cord of noninflamed and inflamed rats. *Eur. J. Neurosci.* **12**, 2079–2086.
63. Hohmann, A. G. and Herkenham, M. (1998) Regulation of cannabinoid and mu opioid receptors in rat lumbar spinal cord following neonatal capsaicin treatment. *Neurosci. Lett.* **252**, 13–16.
64. Walker, J. M. and Huang, S. M. (2002) Cannabinoid analgesia. *Pharmacol. Ther.* **95**, 127–135.
65. Fuentes, J. A., Ruiz-Gayo, M., Manzanares, J., Vela, G., Reche, I., and Corchero, J. (1999) Cannabinoids as potential new analgesics. *Life Sci.* **65(6–7)**, 675–685.
66. Lichtman, A. H. and Martin, B. R. (1991) Spinal and supraspinal components of cannabinoid-induced antinociception. *J. Pharmacol. Exp. Ther.* **258**, 517–523.
67. Di Marzo, V., Breivogel, C. S., Tao, Q., et al. (2000) Levels, metabolism, and pharmacological activity of anandamide in CB_1 cannabinoid receptor knockout mice: evidence for non-CB_1, non-CB_2 receptor-mediated actions of anandamide in mouse brain. *J. Neurochem.* **75(6)**, 2434–2444.
68. Di Marzo, V., Bisogno, T., and De Petrocellis, L. (2001) Anandamide: some like it hot. *Trends Pharmacol. Sci.* **22(7)**, 346–349.
69. Breivogel, C. S., Griffin, G., Di Marzo, V., and Martin, B. R. (2001) Evidence for a new G protein-coupled cannabinoid receptor in mouse brain. *Molec. Pharmacol.* **60(1)**, 155–163.
70. Benham, C. D., Davis, J. B., and Randall, A. D. (2002) Vanilloid and TRP channels: a family of lipid-gated cation channels. *Neuropharmacology* **42**, 873–888.
71. Huestis, M. A., Gorelick, D. A., Heishman, S. J., et al. (2001) Blockade of effects of smoked marijuana by the CB_1-selective cannabinoid receptor antagonist SR141716. *Arch. Gen. Psychiatry* **58**, 322–328.
72. Wise, R. A. (1987) The role of reward pathways in the development of drug dependence. *Pharmacol. Ther.* **35**, 227–263.
73. French, E. D., Dillon, K., and Wu, X. (1997) Cannabinoids excite dopamine neurons in the ventral tegmentum and substantia nigra. *Neuroreport* **8**, 649–652.
74. Tanda, G., Pontieri, F. E., and Di Chiara, G. (1997) Cannabinoid and heroin activation of mesolimbic dopamine transmission by a common μ_1 opioid receptor mechanism. *Science* **276**, 2048–2050.
75. Navarro, M., Chowen, J., Carrera, M., et al. (1998) CB_1 cannabinoid receptor antagonist-induced opiate withdrawal in morphine-dependent rats. *Neuroreport* **9**, 3397–3402.
76. Manzanares, J., Corchero, J., Romero, J., Fernandez-Ruiz, J. J., Ramos, J. A., and Fuentes, J. A. (1999) Pharmacological and biochemical interactions between opioids and cannabinoids. *Trends Pharmacol. Sci.* **20**, 287–294.
77. Wachtel, S. R. and De Wit, H. (2000) Naltrexone does not block the subjective effects of oral Δ^9-tetrahydrocannabinol in humans. *Drug Alcohol Depend.* **59**, 251–260.

78. Budney, A. J., Hughes, J. R., Moore, B. A., and Novy, P. L. (2001) Marijuana abstinence effects in marijuana smokers maintained in their home environment. *Arch. Gen. Psychiatry* **58**, 917–924.
79. Aceto, M. D., Scates, S. M., Lowe, J. A., and Martin, B. R. (1996) Dependence on delta-9-tetrahydrocannabinol: studies on precipitated and abrupt withdrawal. *J. Pharmacol. Exp. Ther.* **278**, 1290–1295.
80. Oviedo, A., Glowa, J., and Herkenham, M. (1993) Chronic cannabinoid administration alters cannabinoid receptor binding in rat brain: a quantitative autoradiographic study. *Brain Res.* 616, 293–302.
81. Coutts, A. A., Anavi-Goffer, S., Ross, R. A., et al. (2001) Agonist-induced internalization and trafficking of cannabinoid CB_1 receptors in hippocampal neurons. *J. Neurosci.* **21(7)**, 2425–2433.
82. Bass, C. E. and Martin, B. R. (2000) Time course for the induction and maintenance of tolerance to Δ^9-tetrahydrocannabinol in mice. *Drug Alcohol Depend.* **60**, 113–119.
83. Wu, X. and French, E. D. (2000) Effects of chronic Δ^9-tetrahydrocannabinol on rat midbrain dopamine neurons: an electrophysiological assessment. *Neuropharmacology* **39**, 391–398.
84. Pope, H. G. Jr., Gruber, A. J., Hudson, J. I., Huestis, M. A., and Yurgelun-Todd, D. (2001) Neuropsychological performance in long term cannabis users. *Arch. Gen. Psychiatry* **58**, 909–915.
85. Benowitz, N. L. and Jones, R. T. (1975) Cardiovascular effects of prolonged delta-9-tetrahydrocannabinol ingestion. *Clin. Pharmacol. Ther.* **18**, 287–297.
86. Benowitz, N. L., Rosenberg, J., Rogers, W., Bachman, J., and Jones, R. T. (1979) Cardiovascular effects of intravenous delta-9-tetrahydrocannabinol: autonomic nervous mechanisms. *Clin. Pharmacol. Ther.* **25**, 440–446.
87. Tsou, K., Brown, S., Sanudo-Pena, M.C., Mackie, K., and Walker, J.M (1998) Immunohistochemical distribution of cannabinoid CB_1 receptors in the rat central nervous system. *Neurosci.* **83(2)**, 393–411.
88. Niederhoffer, N. and Szabo, B. (1999) Effect of the cannabinoid receptor agonist WIN 55212-2 on sympathetic cardiovascular regulation. *Br. J. Pharmacol.* **126**, 457–466.
89. Ellis, E. F., Moore, S. F., and Willoughby, K. A. (1995) Anandamide and delta 9-THC dilation of cerebral arterioles is blocked by indomethacin. *Am. J. Physiol. (Heart Circul.)* **269**, H1859–H1864.
90. White, R. and Hiley, C. R. (1998) The actions of some cannabinoid receptor ligands in the rat isolated mesenteric artery. *Br. J. Pharmacol.* **125**, 533–541.
91. Zygmunt, P. M., Petersson, J., Andersson, D. A., et al. (1999) Vanilloid receptors on sensory nerves mediate the vasodilator action of anandamide. *Nature* **400**, 452–457.
92. Offertaler, L., Mo, F. M., Batkai, S., et al. (2003) Selective ligands and cellular effectors of a G-protein coupled endothelial cannabinoid receptor. *Mol. Pharmacol.* **63(3)**, 699–705.
93. Klein, T. W., Newton, C., and Friedman, H. (1998) Cannabinoid receptors and immunity. *Immunol. Today* **19(8)**, 373–381.
94. Berdyshev, E.V., Boichot, E., Germain, N., Allain, N., Anger, J. P., and Lagente, V. (1997) Influence of fatty acid ethanolamides and Δ^9-tetrahydrocannabinol on cytokine and arachidonate release by mononuclear cells. *Eur. J. Pharmacol.* **330**, 231–240.
95. Zhu, L. X., Sharma, S., Stolina, M., et al. (2000) Δ^9-Tetrahydrocannabinol inhibits antitumor immunity by a CB_2 receptor-mediated, cytokine-dependent pathway. *J. Immunol.* **165**, 373–380.
96. Hwang, S. W. and Oh, U. (2002) Hot channels in airways: pharmacology of the vanilloid receptor. *Curr. Opin. Pharmacol.* **2**, 235–242.

97. Lyman, W. D., Sonett, J. R., Brosnan, C. F., Elkin, R., and Bornstein, M. B. (1989) Delta-9-tetrahydrocannabinol: a novel treatment for experimental autoimmune encephalomyelitis. *J. Neuroimmunol.* **23(1)**, 73–81.
98. Pertwee, R. G. (2002) Cannabinoids and multiple sclerosis. *Pharmacol. Ther.* **95**, 165–174.
99. Killestein, J., Hoogervorst, E. L., Reif, M., et al. (2003) Immunomodulatory effects of orally administered cannabinoids in multiple sclerosis. *J. Neuroimmunol.* **137**, 140–143.
100. Liu, J., Li, H., Burstein, S. H., Zurier, R. B., and Chen, J. D. (2003) Activation and binding of peroxisome proliferator-activated receptor γ by synthetic cannabinoid ajulemic acid. *Mol. Pharmacol.* **63(5)**, 983–992.
101. Faubert, B. L. and Kaminski, N. E. (2000) AP-1 activity is negatively regulated by cannabinol through inhibition of its protein components, c-fos and c-jun. *J. Leukoc. Biol.* **67**, 259–266.
102. Sancho, R., Calzado, M. A., Di Marzo, V., Appendino, G., and Munoz, E. (2003) Anandamide inhibits nuclear factor kB activation through a cannabinoid receptor-independent pathway. *Mol. Pharmacol.* **63(2)**, 429–438.
103. Zheng, Z. M. and Specter, S. (1996) Delta-9-tetrahydrocannabinol: an inhibitor of STAT1α protein tyrosine phosphorylation. *Biochem. Pharmacol.* **51**, 967–973.
104. Clermont-Gnamien, S., Atlani, S., Attal, N., Le Mercier, F., Guirimand, F., and Brasseur, L. (2002) The therapeutic use of Δ^9-tetrahydrocannabinol (dronabinol) in refractory neuropathic pain. [French]. *Presse Med.* **31**, 1840–1845.

Chapter 6

The Endocannabinoid System and the Therapeutic Potential of Cannabinoids

Billy R. Martin

1. Introduction

Much has been written about the history of the medical uses of cannabis *(1)*. In the past two centuries, there have been numerous references to the use of cannabis extracts for a wide range of disorders *(2)*. In the early part of the 20th century, a standardized cannabis elixir was marketed in the United States. Following the introduction of synthetic drugs such as barbiturates and opioids into medicine, interest in cannabis elixir declined. The discovery of the primary active constitutent in marijuana, Δ^9-tetrahydrocannabinol (THC), in 1964 *(3)* rekindled interest in the area. However, the emphasis shifted to synthetic cannabinoids rather than the plant or plant extracts. For example, in the 1970s, clinical studies were conducted in an effort to determine the efficacy of THC as an analgesic *(4)*, antiemetic (5), antidepressant *(6,7)*, appetite stimulant *(7)*, and for treatment of glaucoma *(8)*. These efforts resulted in the approval of THC (dronabinol, Marinol™) for treatment of chemotherapy-induced nausea and vomiting in 1985 and for appetite stimulation in 1992.

There have been several attempts to develop THC derivatives for medical uses. Nabilone was found to have anxiolytic *(9)* and antiemetic properties *(10)* and is presently marketed as Cesamet™. Levonantradol was evaluated as an antiemetic *(11)* and analgesic *(12)* but was never approved for clinical use. Nabitan was studied clinically as an analgesic in cancer pain *(13)* but, like levonantradol, was never approved for use. However, the emphasis shifted back to cannabis in the early 1990s following the HIV epidemic. The lack of effective treatments for HIV led the advocacy community

From: *Forensic Science and Medicine: Marijuana and the Cannabinoids*
Edited by: M. A. ElSohly © Humana Press Inc., Totowa, New Jersey

to demand more effective treatments and greater access to any material that might be beneficial for symptoms management. Hence, there has been increased attention to smoked marijuana not only for HIV patients, but also for a wide range of diseases. During this same period it became obvious that THC and marijuana were producing their effects through a newly discovered endocannabinoid system. The discovery of this biological system has provided opportunities for developing new medications that were not possible previously.

2. Endocannabinoid System

Although early structure–activity relationship *(14)* and initial receptor-binding studies *(15)* suggested the existence of cannabinoid receptors, it was not until the late 1980s that compelling evidence for a cannabinoid receptor emerged. Devane et al. *(16)* characterized a binding site that had all of the properties of a cannabinoid receptor. Shortly thereafter, the cannabinoid receptor was cloned, thereby verifying the existence of a specific target for cannabinoids *(17)*. Compton et al. *(18)* extended these characterizations by showing a strong correlation between binding affinity for this site and cannabinoid potency for a large number of cannabinoid analogs. This receptor is referred to as the CB_1 cannabinoid receptor. The cannabinoid receptor, while uniquely recognized by cannabinoids, is a member of a large family of receptors that are coupled to G proteins. CB_1 receptors are also found in brain and peripheral tissues that include sensory nerve fibers, the autonomic nervous system, testis, and immune cells *(19)*. Surprisingly, the CB_1 cannabinoid receptor was found to be present in very high quantities in the central nervous system, exceeding the levels of almost all neurotransmitter receptors. Although the CB_1 receptor is present throughout brain, the highest levels are found in brain structures associated with neurophysiological functions altered by cannabinoids *(20)*. The densest binding occurs in the basal ganglia (substantia nigra pars reticulata, globus pallidus, entropeduncular nucleus, and lateral caudate putamen) and the molecular layer of the cerebellum. Receptors in these regions are consistent with cannabinoid interference with movement. Intermediate levels of receptor binding are present in the CA pyramidal cell layers of the hippocampus, the dentate gryus, and layers I and VI of the cortex. The presence of CB_1 receptors in these regions is expected given the effects of cannabinoids on cognitive processes. The hippocampus stores memory and codes sensory information. The presence of cannabinoid receptors in regions associated with mediating brain reward (ventromedial striatum and nucleus accumbens) is consistent with the role that cannabinoids play in the neurobiology of reward *(21)*. Lower levels are found in the brainstem, hypothalamus, corpus callosum, and the deep cerebellum nuclei. At the cellular level, the CB_1 receptors are located predominantly on presynaptic terminals of γ-aminobutyric acid (GABA) and glutamate neurons. In the striatum they are present on glutamatergic terminals emanating from the cortex *(22)*, GABA interneurons *(23)*, and axon terminals of GABA-associated medium spiny neurons *(24)*. Cerebellar CB_1 receptors are present on excitatory terminals and GABA interneurons *(25)*.

A second receptor subtype has been identified and is termed the CB_2 cannabinoid receptor *(26)*. The CB_2 receptor is present primarily in tissues that are associated with immune function, including spleen, thymus, tonsils, bone marrow, pancreas, splenic macrophages/monocytes, mast cells, and peripheral blood leukocytes *(19)*. The messenger RNA for the CB_2 receptor varies considerably among various human blood cell populations, with B-lymphocytes > natural killer cells >> monocytes > polymorphonuclear neutrophils > T8-lymphocytes > T4-lymphocytes *(27)*. There is no evidence that this receptor subtype is associated with neuronal tissue. However, there is evidence that CB_2 receptors can be induced in microglia, a cell of macrophage lineage that is present in brain *(28)*. CB_1 and CB_2 receptors are activated by THC.

Several cannabinoid receptor signaling pathways have also been identified. Both cannabinoid receptor subtypes have the molecular signature of G protein-coupled receptors. Actually, evidence for a G protein-coupled cannabinoid receptor preceded the cloning of the CB_1 receptor *(29)*. There is strong evidence for CB_1 receptor coupling to multiple $G_{i/o}$ proteins *(30)*. The predominant effects of cannabinoids occur through inhibitory G protein function, including inhibition of adenylyl cylase, inhibition of calcium channels (N and Q types), as well as activation of inwardly rectifying potassium channels *(31,32)*. These actions are highly relevant to neurotransmitter release, as will be discussed later.

Although evidence of cannabinoid receptors and their signaling pathways was sufficient to establish biological relevance, identification of the natural ligands was essential for functional relevance. Three distinct arachidonoyl derivatives have been identified as natural ligands for the cannabinoid receptors. The amide anandamide *(33)*, the ester 2-arachidonoyl-glycerol *(34,35)*, and the 2-arachidonoyl glyceryl ether *(36)* have been identified thus far as endocannabinoids. These endogenous substances are considered endocannabinoids because they activate CB_1 cannabinoid receptors and produce effects that are consistent with CB_1 cannabinoid receptor activation. Moreover, the synthetic and degradative pathways for anandamide and 2-arachidonoylglycerol have been identified in relevant tissues.

There is substantial evidence that a calcium-dependent, energy-independent transacylase transfers arachidonic acid from the *sn*-1 position of phosphatidylcholine to the amino group in phosphatidylethanolamine to form *N*-arachidonoyl-phosphatidylethanolamine, with subsequent hydrolysis by a phospholipase D-type enzyme to form anandamide *(37)*. Inactivation of anandamide occurs primarily via fatty acid amide hydrolase, an enzyme that has been cloned (38). Blockade or deletion of this enzyme in mice greatly potentiates the actions of exogenously administered anandamide *(39)*. Diacylglycerol lipase synthesizes 2-arachidonoylglycerol *(40)*. This enzyme is required for axonal growth during development and for retrograde synaptic signaling at mature synapses. The inactivation of 2-arachidonoylglycerol occurs by a monoglyceride lipase *(41)*. Both of these synthetic and degradative 2-arachidonoylglycerol enzymes have been cloned.

The discovery that the endogenous cannabinoid system consists of two receptor subtypes, signaling pathways, endogenous ligands, and synthetic and metabolic pathways for these ligands provided unique opportunities to understand the mechanisms through which cannabinoids produce their effects. More importantly, the endogenous cannabinoid system provides a means for verifying whether cannabinoids are acting directly or indirectly to produce their wide range of pharmacological effects. At the same time, the functional role of the endogenous cannabinoid system in normal physiological processes, as well as in disease states, is beginning to emerge. This chapter is confined to appetite, emesis, pain, and drug dependence.

3. Appetite

The desire to consume food represents one of the fundamental physiological processes essential for survival. It is therefore not surprising that appetite is regulated by a highly complex integration of hormonal and neuronal systems to maintain homeostasis. Disruptions of these homeostatic mechanisms can result in either food deprivation or excess eating. Appetite is also easily disrupted in many disease states, such as cancer and HIV infection.

There is ample evidence that the endogenous cannabinoid system plays a role in appetite homeostasis. Although both marijuana and THC have been shown to stimulate appetite, direct evidence for the involvement of cannabinoid receptors was provided by a study in which CB_1 receptor knockout mice ate less than wild-type mice following food restriction *(42)*. The selective antagonist, rimonabant (SR 141716), provided additional support for CB_1 receptor involvement in that this compound reduced food intake in wild-type but not CB_1 knockout mice *(42)*. There are several lines of evidence indicating that the brain is a prominent site for cannabinoid regulation of appetite. For example, the hypothalamus contains both CB_1 receptors and the endocannabinoids anandamide and 2-arachidonoylglycerol. Direct injections of anandamide into the hypothalamus of rats induced hyperphagia, an effect that was blocked by the CB_1 receptor antagonist rimonabant *(43)*. In addition, there is evidence of an interrelationship between the endocannabinoids and leptin, a key anorexigenic agent that is secreted by adipose tissue and acts within the hypothalamus at the arcuate nucleus to suppress appetite-stimulating peptides and stimulate the activity of appetite-reducing peptides. Di Marzo et al. *(42)* demonstrated that acute treatment with leptin reduces the levels of anandamide and 2-arachidonoyl glycerol in the hypothalamus of normal rats. On the other hand, these endocannabinoids were elevated in obese leptin-deficient *ob/ob* and obese leptin-receptor-deficient *db/db* mice.

A second central component of cannabinoid-mediated food intake likely involves reward pathways and the hedonic aspect of eating. Higgs et al. *(44)* recently demonstrated that both THC and anandamide increased sucrose intake in rats, whereas rimonabant decreased it. Fasting increases levels of anadamide and 2-arachidonoylglycerol in the nucleus accumbens, a brain structure crucial for reward *(45)*. Levels of endocannabinoids were not changed in satiated rats. In diet-induced obese rats there was a significant decrease in CB_1 receptor density in hippocampus, cortex, nucleus accumbens, and entopeduncular nucleus, but not in hypothalamus *(46)*. Collectively, these data strongly implicate a central mechanism for endocannabinoid influence on diet.

There are also several suggestions that endocannabinoids act peripherally to regulate metabolism. Cota et al. *(47)* found CB_1 receptors in adipocytes, thereby raising the possibility of a direct peripheral lipogenic mechanism. Furthermore, rimonabant stimulated Acrp30 (adiponectin) messenger RNA expression in adipose tissue and reduced hyperinsulinemia in obese (*fa/fa*) rats *(48)*. At present, there is no evidence that CB_1 receptor agonists produce opposing effects. Nevertheless, these findings suggest that the endocannabinoid system may have a direct effect on energy balance and lipid metabolism.

Based on the above findings, it seems logical that the endocannabinoid system could be manipulated for the purpose of treating either weight loss or obesity *(49)*. Indeed, one of the most consistent effects of smoking marijuana is an increase in appetite. A recent study compared marijuana smoking with oral THC, and both treatments increased food intake *(50)*. However, the results in patient populations have been less definitive. Beal et al. *(51)* examined the effects of THC on appetite and weight in patients with AIDS-related anorexia. They reported modest improvement in appetite and mood along with stabilization in weight. Several early investigations showed that THC increased appetite in cancer patients *(52,53)*. More recently, Jatoi et al. *(54)* compared megestrol acetate with THC for palliating cancer-associated anorexia. They found that megestrol acetate provided superior anorexia palliation among advance cancer patients. On the other hand, Nelson et al. *(55)* evaluated the effects of THC on appetite in advanced cancer patients suffering from anorexia. Most patients completed the 28-day study and experienced improved appetite. With regard to the CB_1 receptor antagonist rimonabant, it has been shown to be effective in reducing food intake in both laboratory animals (described earlier) and in promoting weight loss in humans during recent phase III clinical trials.

4. Emesis

Although emesis has a dramatic impact on appetite, the mechanisms underlying emesis trials and nausea/vomiting are quite distinct. In contrast to the predominant role of the hypothalamus in appetite, the postrema-nucleus tractus solatarius in the brainstem plays an essential role in emesis. Additionally, the dopaminergic, cholinergic, and serotonergic systems in the gastrointestinal tract can contribute to emesis. Several animal studies indicate a direct role for endocannabinoid modulation of emesis. Darmani et al. *(56)* showed that CB_1 receptor agonists reduced cisplatin-induced emesis in the least shrew, whereas the antagonist rimonabant produced the opposite effects. Similar findings were reported with cannabinoid agonists that attenuated lithium-induced vomiting in the musk shrew *(57,58)*. In addition, combinations of inactive doses of THC and ondansetron were effective in blocking vomiting in the musk shrew *(58)*. The musk shrew has also been used to study conditioned retching, an animal model of anticipatory nausea and vomiting. THC completely suppressed conditioned retching in this model *(59)*. In addition, cannabinoid agonists suppressed lithium-induced conditioned rejection, a model of nausea in rats *(60)*. Opioids are known to be powerful emetogenic agents. Activation of the cannabinoid system was also effective in blocking opioid-induced vomiting in ferrets *(61)*. CB_1 cannabinoid receptors were strongly implicated in that rimonabant blocked the action of cannabinoid agonists in this model. Importantly, Darmani et al. *(62)* found prominent CB_1 receptor binding in the nucleus tractus solartius of the shrew. The exact nature of the role played by endocannabinoids is unclear at this time. A metabolically stable analog of anandamide blocked vomiting, whereas another endocannabinoid, 2-arachidonoylglycerol, was emetogenic *(62)*.

As for clinical evidence, anecdotal reports of patients smoking marijuana to control chemotherapy-induced nausea and vomiting provided the initial clues. These reports led to clinical studies with THC in which it was found to be useful in patients whose chemotherapy-induced nausea and vomiting were refractory to other standard antiemetics available at that time *(63)*. Plasse et al. *(53)* reported that combinations of THC and prochlorperazine resulted in enhancement of efficacy as measured by duration of episodes of nausea and vomiting and by severity of nausea. In addition, the incidence of psychotropic effects from THC appeared to be decreased by concomitant administration of prochlorperazine. The combination was significantly more effective than was either single agent in controlling chemotherapy-induced nausea and vomiting *(64)*. Nabilone, a synthetic derivative of THC, was also reported to be an effective oral antiemetic drug for moderately toxic chemotherapy *(65)*. Cannabinoids have also been found to be effective in treating nausea and vomiting in children undergoing chemotherapy *(66,67)*. As for the current status of antiemetics, serotonergic anatagonists such as ondansetron have become the standards for managing emesis. These agents have proven to be effective in preventing chemotherapy-induced nausea and vomiting in most patients. However, delayed nausea and vomiting are less well controlled. Therefore, the search for more effective agents continues. Combination therapy with ondansetron and THC has not been fully explored. In addition, there is a need for a higher-efficacy CB_1 receptor agonist with fewer side effects.

5. Pain

Animal studies have firmly established cannabinoid-induced analgesia in a wide array of acute and chronic pain models *(68)*. Most of this evidence is based on CB_1 receptor agonists such as THC and related synthetic derivatives. It has been firmly established that these effects are being mediated through the endocannabinoid system. First, there is an excellent correlation between cannabinoid analgesics and their affinity for the CB_1 receptor *(69)*. Second, the CB_1 receptor antagonist rimonabant is effective in blocking the analgesic effects of cannabinoid agonists *(70,71)*. As expected, the endogenous ligands anandamide and 2-arachidonoylglycerol exhibit analgesic properties when administered to laboratory animals *(34,72)*. Mice with genetic deletion of fatty acid amidohydrolase, the enzyme that hydrolyzes anandamide, exhibit enhanced analgesic activity with exogenously administered anandamide *(39)*. More importantly, these animals have elevated endogenous anandamide levels as well as an increased pain threshold, evidence that supports a physiological role for endocannabinoids in pain perception. Additional evidence for endocannabinoid pain modulation includes cannabinoid suppression of spinal and thalamic nociceptive neurons, identification of spinal, supraspinal, and peripheral sites of action, as well as evidence that endocannabinoids are released upon electrical stimulation of the periaqueductal gray and following inflammation in the periphery *(73,74)*.

Although nociceptive events will stimulate the release of endocannabinoids, the exact nature of their actions on pain neurotransmission remains to be fully established. CB_1 receptors are located predominantly on presynaptic terminals, and their activation results in the inhibition of the neurotransmitter released at this site. Hohman et al.

examined the distribution of CB_1 receptors in rat dorsal root ganglion and found them present in only a subset of neurons containing substance P and calcitonin gene-related peptide *(75)*. There is evidence for localization of CB_1 receptors on neurons containing endogenous opioids. Welch and Stevens *(76)* demonstrated that cannabinoid agonists potentiated morphine analgesia in laboratory animals. This laboratory later demonstrated that THC, but not anandamide, stimulates the release of dynorphin A *(77)*. While there is an abundance of data illustrating interactions between the opioid and cannabinoid systems, the exact nature of these interactions remains to be elucidated.

Although there is strong evidence that the endocannabinoid system regulates pain pathways, the effectiveness of CB_1 agonists as analgesics has been equivocal. Despite intense efforts to develop cannabinoid analgesics, there has been little success in devising a CB_1 receptor agonist that is devoid of behavioral effects. For example, Noyes et al. *(78)* found that oral THC was as efficacious as codeine in producing analgesia in a patient population, but its behavioral side effects precluded the use of higher doses. As for synthetic cannabinoid derivatives that might be useful as analgesics, nabitan is one such analog that was evaluated in at least two studies. Jochimsen et al. *(79)* failed to observe pain relief in cancer patients, and there was some evidence for increased pain sensitivity. On the other hand, another research group *(13)* reported analgesia comparable to that of codeine in cancer patients. Levonantradol, another cannabinoid derivative, elicited some benefit for postoperative surgical pain but only at doses that produced significant behavioral disturbances *(80)*. Several recent clinical studies have found THC to lack sufficient efficacy in postoperative pain *(81)*, neuropathic pain *(82)*, and refractory neuropathic pain *(83)*. On the other hand, THC was found to exert some benefit in treating intractable neuropathic pain in two adolescents *(84)*. A review of clinical studies regarding cannabinoid agonist treatment of cancer pain led the author to conclude that the present studies do not justify the use of cannabinoid agonists for pain management *(85)*.

The evidence suggests that the CB_1 receptor agonists that have been developed thus far are unlikely to be highly efficacious in controlling high-intensity pain. However, the possibility remains that they might be useful in more moderate pain, particularly in case in which some of the typical cannabinoid side effects (sedation, dizziness, etc.) might be more tolerated. Theoretically, CB_1 receptor agonists should be effective as adjuvants to other analgesics. Numerous preclinical studies have shown that THC will enhance opioid analgesia. However, in a recent study in human experimental pain models, THC offered relatively small additive analgesic effects when combined with morphine *(86)*. It remains to be determined whether similar results would occur in pain patients.

There are several possible explanations for the discrepancy between the analgesic effects of CB_1 receptor agonists in laboratory animals and humans. Certainly, higher doses can be administered to laboratory animals, and hence greater analgesic effects achieved, than in humans. Pharmacokinetics may also play a very important part. The studies that have been carried out thus far have relied on oral administration of THC, a route that does not allow for easy optimization of treatment. Efforts are underway to develop alternative formulations of THC to allow for other routes of administration.

Rectal suppositories of THC hemisuccinate have been found to be effective in treating spasticity and pain *(87)*. A water-soluble analog of THC has been developed that may be appropriate for intravenous use *(88)*. There have been recent studies demonstrating that topical administration of cannabinoids produce analgesic effects *(89)*. Moreover, topical administration produced a synergistic interaction with spinally administered cannabinoids. A separate group of investigators reported an analgesic interaction between topical opioids and cannabinoids administered either topically or spinally *(90)*. These observations reinforce the notion that treatment regimens of opioid and cannabinoids combinations have yet to be optimized clinically. Unfortunately, a topical preparation of THC or related cannabinoid is not yet available for clinical use. Another attractive approach is the inhalation route. An inhalation formulation of THC was developed years ago, but unfortunately it produced bronchial irritation *(91)*. The recent develop of a THC aerosol delivered through a metered-dose inhaler holds promise *(92)*.

The discussion so far has been devoted to nonselective CB_1 and CB_2 agonists, such as THC, because most of the analgesic literature has been generated with these compounds. The discovery of the CB_2 receptor in nonneuronal tissues such as immune cells attracted interest in its potential modulation of immune function. However, there are now numerous reports that CB_2 selective agonists have analgesic properties. One such CB_2 selective agonist is AM 1241, which was shown to be highly active in a thermal pain model in rats *(93)*. It was also shown to suppress capsaicin-induced hyperalgesia *(94)*. HU 308 is another CB_2 selective agonist that has been reported to produce analgesic effects in rodents *(95)*. The advantage of these compounds is that they are devoid of the behavioral effects produced by CB_1 selective agonists. At present there are no reports of clinical efficacy of CB_2 selective agonists.

6. Drug Dependence

Marijuana dependence has long been a controversial issue, in part as a result of the lack of understanding of drug dependence. It is clear that a major physical withdrawal syndrome does not occur upon abrupt cessation of marijuana use. Certainly, dependence on many substances occurs without a prominent physical aspect of the syndrome. What is clear is that continual use of marijuana can lead to dependence as defined by the *Diagnostic and Statistical Manual of Mental Disorders*, 4th ed. criteria, or essentially the inability to the user to exert control over their use. In actual fact, an abrupt cannabinoid withdrawal syndrome was described in humans following discontinuation of a rather rigorous treatment regimen of THC *(96,97)*. Studies in more recent times have used treatment regimens that more closely reflect typical marijuana use patterns and have also demonstrated an abstinence symptom that included subjective effects of anxiety, irritability, and stomach pain, as well as decreases in food intake, following abrupt withdrawal from continued administration of either oral THC *(98)* or marijuana smoke inhalation *(99)*. There have been several efforts to devise strategies for treating marijuana dependence. Haney et al. *(100)* found that bupropion worsened mood during marijuana withdrawal. The antidepressant nefazodone provided partial relief *(101)*. They also demonstrated that oral THC decreased marijuana craving and withdrawal signs during abstinence *(102)*.

Demonstrating a well-defined abstinence withdrawal syndrome following prolonged cannabinoid administration in laboratory animals also presented challenges. Several unconditional behavioral effects, including hyperirritability, tremors, and anorexia, were reported to occur during THC abstinence *(103)*, while other studies failed to observe abrupt withdrawal effects following chronic THC administration in dogs *(104)* or rats *(105,106)*. Abrupt withdrawal from chronic THC has been reported in rhesus monkeys *(107)*. The fact that readministration of THC reversed the withdrawal effects suggested that the animals were cannabinoid-dependent. The development of rimonabant *(70)*, a selective CB_1 receptor cannabinoid antagonist, represented the first opportunity to determine whether a physical withdrawal syndrome could be precipitated with an antagonist challenge. Antagonist-precipitated withdrawal is much easier and more reliable to quantitate than withdrawal following abrupt cessation of the dependence-producing drug. Indeed, a robust withdrawal syndrome was observed in THC-treated rats that were challenged with rimonabant *(108,109)*. Subsequent studies verified precipitated withdrawal in both mice *(110)* and dogs *(111)*. Another contribution of rimonabant was that it enabled investigators to carefully document the symptoms of withdrawal as well as the time course, both of which are critical for assessing abrupt withdrawal. Subsequently, Aceto et al. *(112)* were able to document abrupt withdrawal following cessation of infusion with the synthetic CB_1 receptor agonist WIN 55,212.

Although it was important to demonstrate that abrupt and precipitated withdrawal can be documented, most dependence-producing agents will also be self-administered by laboratory animals. Unfortunately, THC is not readily self-administered by animals. There was an early report that rats would self-administer THC *(113)*. However, it has not been an easy task to get rats to self-administer cannabinoids *(114)*. It has now been shown that THC can be reliably self-administered in squirrel monkeys *(115,116)*.

There is now increasing knowledge that the endocannabinoid system participates in dependence on drugs other than THC. There has always been considerable interest in the interactions of cannabinoids and opioids as it relates to dependence. Naloxone has been reported to precipitate withdrawal effects in rats treated chronically with THC *(117,118)*. Conversely, naloxone was ineffective in precipitating withdrawal in THC-dependent monkeys *(107)*, pigeons *(104)*, or mice *(119)*. It has long been known that THC produces a moderate attenuation of naloxone-precipitated withdrawal in morphine-dependent mice *(120,121)* and rats *(122,123)*. The endogenous cannabinoids anandamide *(124)* and 2-arachidonoylglycerol *(125)* have both been reported to decrease naloxone-induced morphine withdrawal.

Actually, the availability of mice lacking either μ-opioid or CB_1 receptors has greatly advanced our understanding of the interrelationship between the opioid and endocannabinoid systems. CB_1 receptor knockout mice exhibited substantial decreases in both morphine self-administration and naloxone-precipitated morphine withdrawal *(126)*. In addition, rimonabant reduced the rewarding responses of morphine in the conditioned place preference paradigm *(127)*. Co-administration of rimonabant and morphine led to decreases in naloxone-precipitated wet dog shakes and jumping but had no effects on other indices of opioid withdrawal, including paw tremors, ptosis, sniffing, and body tremors *(127)*. Repeated administration of rimonabant in rats implanted with morphine pellets reduced some, but not all, naloxone precipitated withdrawal effects *(128)*.

The converse also appears to be true, in that opioid receptors may play a modulatory role on cannabinoid dependence. Rimonabant-precipitated THC withdrawal symptoms were significantly diminished in pre-proenkephalin-deficient mice compared to the wild-type mice *(129)*. Similarly, mice lacking the μ-opioid receptor exhibited significant attenuation of rimonabant-precipitated withdrawal signs compared with the wild-type controls. These findings implicate a role for opioid system in the modulation of cannabinoid dependence.

The finding that modulation of the endocannabinoid system is capable of influencing opioid dependence—and vice versa—raises the possibility that the CB_1 receptor antagonist might influence opioid dependence. Indeed, Navarro et al. *(130)* found that rimonabant was capable of blocking heroin self-administration in rats. Several other laboratories evaluated CB_1 receptor agonists and antagonists for their ability to influence reinstatement of heroin self-administration *(131,132)*. They found that several CB_1 receptor agonists restored heroin-seeking behavior, whereas rimonabant prevented reinstatement.

The question arises as to whether the endocannabinoid system is involved in dependence to drugs other than opioids. De Vries et al. *(133)* reported that the potent CB_1 receptor agonist HU210 provoked relapse to cocaine seeking after prolonged withdrawal periods. In addition, rimonabant attenuated relapse induced by re-exposure to cocaine-associated cues or cocaine itself, but not relapse induced by exposure to stress. On the other hand, another laboratory reported that a CB_1 receptor agonist attenuated the effects of cocaine on brain self-stimulation thresholds, whereas rimonabant did not alter cocaine's effects *(134)*. These findings suggest that the endocannabinoid system plays a greater role in relapse to cocaine use than in maintaining cocaine self-administration.

Another drug that is frequently used in conjunction with marijuana is alcohol. There are several indications that the endocannabinoid system may influence alcohol intake. It has been shown that rimonabant will decrease alcohol self-administration in laboratory animals *(135)* and that alcohol preference is reduced by rimonabant *(136)*. Also, alcohol withdrawal symptoms are absent in CB_1 receptor knockout mice, which provides further support for a role of the endocannabinoid system in alcohol dependence. Rimonabant has also been evaluated for its potential effects on the motivational effects of nicotine in the rat *(137)*. Rimonabant decreased nicotine self-administration but did not substitute for nicotine nor antagonize the nicotine cue in a nicotine-discrimination procedure. It also blocked nicotine-induced dopamine release in the shell of the nucleus accumbens and the bed nucleus of the stria terminalis *(137)*. Dopamine release induced by ethanol in the nucleus accumbens was also reduced by rimonabant.

The fact that the endocannabinoid system is an active participant in the dependence on a wide range of drugs argues that it may play a fundamental role in the perturbation of reward pathways that underlie drug dependence. These results suggest that activation of the endogenous cannabinoid system may participate in the motivational and dopamine-releasing effects of nicotine and ethanol as well as possibly other drugs of abuse. Thus, CB_1 receptor antagonists may be effective in treating drug dependence induced by opioids, psychomotor stimulants, nicotine, and ethanol, in addition to marijuana.

7. Summary

Because the endocannabinoid system represents an important target for addressing symptoms arising from numerous disease states, the ability to manipulate this system becomes of paramount importance. At present, the only means of activating the endocannabinoid system is with CB_1 and CB_2 receptor agonists. The disadvantage of CB_1 receptor agonists is that they have a broad pharmacological spectrum of action that limits their clinical utility. Attempts to develop CB_1 receptor agonists that have improved the therapeutic-to-adverse effect ratio have met with limited success. However, the new evidence that is emerging regarding the multiple signaling pathways activated by the CB_1 receptor provides encouragement that development of agonists with improved pharmacological profile is possible. Moreover, structure–activity relationship studies continually provide new chemical templates for agents that activate the CB_1 receptor. In the near term, the most likely success will come from new formulations of current CB_1 receptor agonists that are already approved for clinical use.

As for selective CB_2 receptor agonists, there is intense interest in these compounds as potential therapeutic agents because they will be devoid of the behavioral effects that currently plague the CB_1 receptor agonists. The fact that selective CB_2 receptor agonists have been found to be effective in some animal models of pain provides an exciting possibility for development of new analgesics.

Efforts are also underway to develop inhibitors of the enzymes that degrade anandamide. Indeed, deletion of this enzyme in mice through genetic engineering resulted in elevated anandamide levels and increased resistance to pain *(39)*. Highly potent inhibitors of this enzyme have also been synthesized *(138)*. By elevating anandamide levels, these inhibitors represent an entirely new strategy for activating the endocannabinoid system. Elevation of 2-arachidonoylglycerol levels could occur through the blockade of monoglyceride lipase, the enzyme that metabolizes this endocannabinoid *(41)*. There are at present no selective inhibitors of this enzyme.

It is also abundantly clear that attenuating the endocannabinoid system has important therapeutic uses. The CB_1 receptor antagonist rimonabant has been shown to be effective in both animal models and clinical trials for treatment of decreased appetite and increased weight loss. Moreover, it has been shown to alter alcohol, cocaine, heroin, and nicotine dependence. Another potential means of attenuating the endocannabinoid system is through inhibition of the synthesis of anandamide and 2-arachidonolylglycerol. Although these enzymes have been identified, there are at present no inhibitors shown to have potential as therapeutic agents in, for example, obesity or drug dependence.

References

1. Mechoulam, R. and Hanus, L. (2000) A historical overview of chemical research on cannabinoids. *Chem. Phys. Lipids* **108**, 1–13.

2. Grinspoon, L. and Bakalar, J. B. (1993) *Marihuana: The Forbidden Medicine.* (eds.), Yale University Press, New Haven, CT, p. 184.
3. Gaoni, Y. and Mechoulam, R. (1964) Hashish. III. Isolation, structure, and partial synthesis of an active constituent of hashish. *J. Am. Chem. Soc.* **86**, 1646–1647.
4. Noyes, R. Jr., Brunk, S. F., Baram, D. A., and Canter, A. (1975) Analgesic effect of delta-9-tetrahydrocannabinol. *J. Clin. Pharmacol.* **15**, 139–143.
5. Sallan, S. E., Zinberg, N. E., and Frei, E., 3rd (1975) Antiemetic effect of delta-9-tetrahydrocannabinol in patients receiving cancer chemotherapy. *N. Engl. J. Med.* **293**, 795–797.
6. Noyes, R. Jr., Brunks, S. F., Avery, D. H., and Canter, A. (1976) Psychologic effects of oral delta-9-tetrahydrocannabinol in advanced cancer patients. *Comp. Psychiatry* **17**, 641–646.
7. Regelson, W., Bulter, J. R., Schulz, J., et al. (1976) Δ^9-Tetrahydrocannabinol as an effective antidepressant and appetite-stimulating agent in advanced cancer patients, in *The Pharmacology of Marihuana* (Braude, M. C. and Szara, S., eds.), Raven Press, New York, pp. 763–776.
8. Green, K., Kim, K., and Bowman, K. (1976) Ocular effects of Δ^9-tetrahydrocannabinol, in *The Therapeutic Potential of Marihuana* (Cohen, S. and Stillman, R., eds.), Plenum Medical Book, New York, pp. 49–62.
9. Fabre, L. F., McLendon, D. M., and Stark, P. (1978) Nabilone, a cannabinoid, in the treatment of anxiety: an open-label and double-blind study. *Curr. Ther. Res.* **24**, 161–169.
10. Cunningham, D., Bradley, C. J., Forrest, G. J., et al. (1988) A randomized trial of oral nabilone and prochlorperazine compared to intravenous metoclopramide and dexamethasone in the treatment of nausea and vomiting induced by chemotherapy regimens containing cisplatin or cisplatin analogues. *Eur. J. Cancer Clin. Oncol.* **24**, 685–689.
11. Cronin, C. M., Sallan, S. E., Gelber, R., Lucas, V. S., and Lazlo, J. (1981) Antiemetic effect of intramuscular levonantradol in patients receiving anticancer chemotherapy. *J. Clin. Pharmacol.* **21**, 43S–50S.
12. Koe, B. K. (1981) Levonantradol, a potent cannabinoid-related analgesic, antagonizes haloperidol-induced activation of striatal dopamine synthesis. *Eur. J. Pharmacol.* **70**, 231–235.
13. Staquet, M., Gantt, C., and Machin, D. (1978) Effect of a nitrogen analog of tetrahydrocannabinol on cancer pain. *Clin. Pharmacol. Ther.* **23**, 397–401.
14. Razdan, R. K. (1986) Structure-activity relationships in cannabinoids. *Pharmacol. Rev.* **38**, 75–149.
15. Harris, L. S., Carchman, R. A., and Martin, B. R. (1978) Evidence for the existence of specific cannabinoid binding sites. *Life Sci.* **22**, 1131–1137.
16. Devane, W. A., Dysarz, F. A. III, Johnson, M. R., Melvin, L. S., and Howlett, A. C. (1988) Determination and characterization of a cannabinoid receptor in rat brain. *Mol. Pharmacol.* **34**, 605–613.
17. Matsuda, L. A., Lolait S. J., Brownstein, M. J., Young, A. C., and Bonner, T. I. (1990) Structure of a cannabinoid receptor and functional expression of the cloned cDNA. *Nature* **346**, 561–564.
18. Compton, D. R., Johnson, M. R., Melvin, L.S., and Martin, B. R. (1992) Pharmacological profile of a series of bicyclic cannabinoid analogs: classification as cannabimimetic agents. *J. Pharmacol. Exp. Ther.* **260**, 201–209.
19. Howlett, A. C., Barth, F., Bonner, T. I., et al. (2002) International Union of Pharmacology. XXVII. Classification of cannabinoid receptors. *Pharmacol. Rev.* **54**, 161–202.
20. Herkenham, M., Lynn, A. B., Johnson, M. R., Melvin, L. S., De Costa, B. R., and Rice, K. C. (1991) Characterization and localization of cannabinoid receptors in rat brain: a quantitative in vitro autoradiographic study. *J. Neurosci.* **11**, 563–583.

21. Gardner, E. L. (2002) Addictive potential of cannabinoids: the underlying neurobiology. *Chem. Phys. Lipids* **121**, 267–290.
22. Gerdeman, G. and Lovinger, D. M. (2001) CB1 cannabinoid receptor inhibits synaptic release of glutamate in rat dorsolateral striatum. *J. Neurophysiol.* **85**, 468–471.
23. Hohmann, A. G. and Herkenham, M. (2000) Localization of cannabinoid CB(1) receptor mRNA in neuronal subpopulations of rat striatum: a double-label in situ hybridization study. *Synapse* **37**, 71–80.
24. Herkenham, M., Lynn, A. B., De Costa, B. R., and Richfield, E. K. (1991) Neuronal localization of cannabinoid receptors in the basal ganglia of the rat. *Brain Res.* **547**, 267–274.
25. Tsou, K., Brown, S., Sanudo-Pena, M. C., Mackie, K., and Walker, J. M. (1998) Immunohistochemical distribution of cannabinoid CB1 receptors in the rat central nervous system. *Neuroscience* **83**, 393–411.
26. Munro, S., Thomas, K. L., and Abu-Shaar, M. (1993) Molecular characterization of a peripheral receptor for cannabinoids. *Nature* **365**, 61–65.
27. Galiegue, S., Mary, S., Marchand, J., et al. (1995) Expression of central and peripheral cannabinoid receptors in human immune tissues and leukocyte subpopulations. *Eur. J. Biochem.* **232**, 54–61.
28. Carlisle, S. J., Marciano-Cabral, F., Staab, A., Ludwick, C., and Cabral, G. A. (2002) Differential expression of the CB2 cannabinoid receptor by rodent macrophages and macrophage-like cells in relation to cell activation. *Int. Immunopharmacol.* **2**, 69–82.
29. Howlett, A. C. and Fleming, R. M. (1984) Cannabinoid inhibition of adenylate cyclase. Pharmacology of the response in neuroblastoma cell membranes. *Mol. Pharmacol.* **26**, 532–538.
30. Prather, P. L., Martin, N. A., Breivogel, C. S., and Childers, S. R. (2000) Activation of cannabinoid receptors in rat brain by WIN 55212-2 produces coupling to multiple G protein alpha-subunits with different potencies. *Mol. Pharmacol.* **57**, 1000–1010.
31. Mackie, K. and Hille, B. (1992) Cannabinoids inhibit N-type calcium channels in neurobalstoma-glioma cells. *Proc. Natl. Acad. Sci. USA* **89**, 3825–3829.
32. Mackie, K., Lai, Y., Westenbroek, R., and Mitchell, R. (1995) Cannabinoids activate an inwardly rectifying potassium conductance and inhibit Q-type calcium currents in AtT20 cells transfected with rat brain cannabinoid receptor. *J. Neurosci.* **15**, 6552–6561.
33. Devane, W. A., Hanus, L., Breuer, A., et al. (1992) Isolation and structure of a brain constituent that binds to the cannabinoid receptor. *Science* **258**, 1946–1949.
34. Mechoulam, R., Ben-Shabat, S., Hanus, L., et al. (1995) Identification of an endogenous 2-monoglyceride, present in canine gut, that binds to cannabinoid receptors. *Biochem. Pharmacol.* **50**, 83–90.
35. Sugiura, T., Kondo, S., Sukagawa, A., et al. (1995) 2-Arachidonoyglycerol: a possible endogenous cannabinoid receptor ligand in brain. *Biochem. Biophys. Res. Comm.* **215**, 89–97.
36. Hanus, L., Abu-Lafi, S., Fride, E., et al. (2001) 2-Arachidonyl glyceryl ether, an endogenous agonist of the cannabinoid CB1 receptor. *Proc. Natl. Acad. Sci. USA* **98**, 3662–3665.
37. Schmid, H. H. (2000) Pathways and mechanisms of N-acylethanolamine biosynthesis: can anandamide be generated selectively? *Chem. Phys. Lipids* **108**, 71–87.
38. Patricelli, M. P., Lashuel, H. A., Giang, D. K., Kelly, J. W., and Cravatt, B. F. (1998) Comparative characterization of a wild type and transmembrane domain-deleted fatty acid amide hydrolase: identification of the transmembrane domain as a site for oligomerization. *Biochemistry* **37**, 15177–15187.
39. Cravatt, B. F., Demarest, K., Patricelli, M. P., et al. (2001) Supersensitivity to anandamide and enhanced endogenous cannabinoid signaling in mice lacking fatty acid amide hydrolase. *Proc. Natl. Acad. Sci. USA* **98**, 9371–9376.

40. Bisogno, T., Howell, F., Williams, G., et al. (2003) Cloning of the first sn1-DAG lipases points to the spatial and temporal regulation of endocannabinoid signaling in the brain. *J. Cell. Biol.* **163**, 463–468.
41. Dinh, T. P., Carpenter, D., Leslie, F.M., et al. (2002) Brain monoglyceride lipase participating in endocannabinoid inactivation. *Proc. Natl. Acad. Sci. USA* **99**, 10819–10824.
42. Di Marzo, V., Goparaju, S. K., Wang, L., et al. (2001) Leptin-regulated endocannabinoids are involved in maintaining food intake. *Nature* **410**, 822–825.
43. Jamshidi, N. and Taylor, D. A. (2001) Anandamide administration into the ventromedial hypothalamus stimulates appetite in rats. *Br. J. Pharmacol.* **134**, 1151–1154.
44. Higgs, S., Williams, C. M., and Kirkham, T. C. (2003) Cannabinoid influences on palatability: microstructural analysis of sucrose drinking after delta(9)-tetrahydrocannabinol, anandamide, 2-arachidonoyl glycerol and SR141716. *Psychopharmacology (Berl)* **165**, 370–377.
45. Kirkham, T. C., Williams, C. M., Fezza, F., and Di Marzo, V. (2002) Endocannabinoid levels in rat limbic forebrain and hypothalamus in relation to fasting, feeding and satiation: stimulation of eating by 2-arachidonoyl glycerol. *Br. J. Pharmacol.* **136**, 550–557.
46. Harrold, J. A., Elliott, J. C., King, P. J., Widdowson, P. S., and Williams, G. (2002) Down-regulation of cannabinoid-1 (CB-1) receptors in specific extrahypothalamic regions of rats with dietary obesity: a role for endogenous cannabinoids in driving appetite for palatable food? *Brain Res.* **952**, 232–238.
47. Cota, D., Marsicano, G., Tschoep, M., et al. (2003) The endogenous cannabinoid system affects energy balance via central orexigenic drive and peripheral lipogenesis. *J. Clin. Invest.* **112**, 423–431.
48. Bensaid, M., Gary-Bobo, M., Esclangon, A., et al. (2003) The cannabinoid CB1 receptor antagonist SR141716 increases Acrp30 mRNA expression in adipose tissue of obese fa/fa rats and in cultured adipocyte cells. *Mol. Pharmacol.* **63**, 908–914.
49. Harrold, J. A. and Williams, G. (2003) The cannabinoid system: a role in both the homeostatic and hedonic control of eating? *Br. J. Nutr.* **90**, 729–734.
50. Hart, C. L., Ward, A. S., Haney, M., Comer, S. D., Foltin, R. W., and Fischman, M. W. (2002) Comparison of smoked marijuana and oral delta(9)-tetrahydrocannabinol in humans. *Psychopharmacology (Berl)* **164**, 407–415.
51. Beal, J. E., Olson, R., Laubenstein, L., et al. (1995) Dronabinol as a treatment for anorexia associated with weight loss in patients with AIDS. *J. Pain Symptom Manage.* **10**, 89–97.
52. Sallan, S. E., Cronin, C., Zelen, M., and Zinberg, N. E. (1980) Antiemetics in patients receiving chemotherapy for cancer - a randomized comparison of delta-9-tetrahydrocannabinol and prochlorperazine. *N. Engl. J. Med.* **302**, 135–138.
53. Plasse, T. F., Gorter, R. W., Krasnow, S. H., Lane, M., Shepard, K. V., and Wadleigh, R. G. (1991) Recent clinical experience with dronabinol. *Pharmacol. Biochem. Behav.* **40**, 695–700.
54. Jatoi, A., Windschitl, H. E., Loprinzi, C. L., et al. (2002) Dronabinol versus megestrol acetate versus combination therapy for cancer-associated anorexia: a North Central Cancer Treatment Group study. *J. Clin. Oncol.* **20**, 567–573.
55. Nelson, K., Walsh, D., Deeter, P., and Sheehan, F. (1994) A phase II study of delta-9-tetrahydrocannabinol for appetite stimulation in cancer-associated anorexia. *J. Palliat. Care* **10**, 14–18.
56. Darmani, N. A. (2001) Delta(9)-tetrahydrocannabinol and synthetic cannabinoids prevent emesis produced by the cannabinoid CB(1) receptor antagonist/inverse agonist SR 141716A. *Neuropsychopharmacology* **24**, 198–203.
57. Parker, L. A., Kwiatkowska, M., Burton, P., and Mechoulam, R. (2004) Effect of cannabinoids on lithium-induced vomiting in the Suncus murinus (house musk shrew). *Psychopharmacology* **171**, 156–161.

58. Kwiatkowska, M., Parker, L. A., Burton, P., and Mechoulam, R. (2004) A comparative analysis of the potential of cannabinoids and ondansetron to suppress cisplatin-induced emesis in the Suncus murinus (house musk shrew). *Psychopharmacology (Berl)* 174, 254–259.
59. Parker, L. A. and Kemp, S. W. (2001) Tetrahydrocannabinol (THC) interferes with conditioned retching in Suncus murinus: an animal model of anticipatory nausea and vomiting (ANV). *Neuroreport* **12**, 749–751.
60. Parker, L. A., Mechoulam, R., Schlievert, C., Abbott, L., Fudge, M. L., and Burton, P. (2003) Effects of cannabinoids on lithium-induced conditioned rejection reactions in a rat model of nausea. *Psychopharmacology (Berl)* **166**, 156–162.
61. Simoneau, I. I., Hamza, M. S., Mata, H. P., et al. (2001) The cannabinoid agonist WIN55,212-2 suppresses opioid-induced emesis in ferrets. *Anesthesiology* **94**, 882–887.
62. Darmani, N. A., Sim-Selley, L. J., Martin, B. R., et al. (2003) Antiemetic and motor-depressive actions of CP55,940: cannabinoid CB1 receptor characterization, distribution, and G-protein activation. *Eur. J. Pharmacol.* **459**, 83–95.
63. McCabe, M., Smith, F. P., Macdonald, J. S., Woolley, P. V., Goldberg, D., and Schein, P. S. (1988) Efficacy of tetrahydrocannabinol in patients refractory to standard antiemetic therapy. *Invest. New Drugs* **6**, 243–246.
64. Lane, M., Vogel, C. L., Ferguson, J., et al. (1991) Dronabinol and prochlorperazine in combination for treatment of cancer chemotherapy-induced nausea and vomiting. *J. Pain Symptom Manage.* **6**, 352–359.
65. Ahmedzai, S., Carlyle, D. L., Calder, I. T., and Moran, F. (1983) Anti-emetic efficacy and toxicity of nabilone, a synthetic cannabinoid, in lung cancer chemotherapy. *Br. J. Cancer.* **48**, 657–663.
66. Abrahamov, A., Abrahamov, A., and Mechoulam, R. (1995) An efficient new cannabinoid antiemetic in pediatric oncology. *Life Sci.* **56**, 2097–2102.
67. Chan, H. S., Correia, J. A., and MacLeod, S. M. (1987) Nabilone versus prochlorperazine for control of cancer chemotherapy-induced emesis in children: a double-blind, crossover trial. *Pediatrics* **79**, 946–952.
68. Martin, B. R. and Lichtman, A. H. (1998) Cannabinoid transmission and pain perception. *Neurobiol. Dis.* **5**, 447–461.
69. Compton, D. R., Rice, K. C., De Costa, B. R., Razdan, R. K., and Melvin, L. S. (1993) Cannabinoid structure-activity relationships: Correlation of receptor binding and in vivo activities. *J. Pharmacol. Exp. Ther.* **265**, 218–226.
70. Rinaldi-Carmona, M., Barth, F., Heaulme, M., et al. (1994) SR141716A, a potent and selective antagonist of the brain cannabinoid receptor. *FEBS Lett.* **350**, 240–244.
71. Compton, D. R., Aceto, M. D., Lowe, J., and Martin, B. R. (1996) In vivo characterization of a specific cannabinoid receptor antagonist (SR141716A): Inhibition of delta-9-tetrahydrocannabinol-induced responses and apparent agonist activity. *J. Pharmacol. Exp. Ther.* **277**, 586–594.
72. Smith, P. B., Compton, D. R., Welch, S. P., Razdan, R. K., Mechoulam, R., and Martin, B. R. (1994) The pharmacological activity of anandamide, a putative endogenous cannabinoid, in mice. *J. Pharmacol. Exp. Ther.* **270**, 219–227.
73. Walker, J. M., Krey, J. F., Chu, C. J., and Huang, S. M. (2002) Endocannabinoids and related fatty acid derivatives in pain modulation. *Chem. Phys. Lipids* **121**, 159–172.
74. Walker, J. M., Strangman, N. M., and Huang, S. M. (2001) Cannabinoids and pain. *Pain Res. Manag.* **6**, 74–79.
75. Hohmann, A. G. and Herkenham, M. (1999) Localization of central cannabinoid CB1 receptor messenger RNA in neuronal subpopulations of rat dorsal root ganglia: a double-label in situ hybridization study. *Neurosci.* **90**, 923–931.

76. Welch, S. P. and Stevens, D. L. (1992) Antinociceptive activity of intrathecally administered cannabinoids alone, and in combination with morphine, in mice. *J. Pharmacol. Exp. Ther.* **262**, 10–18.
77. Houser, S. J., Eads, M., Embrey, J. P., and Welch, S. P. (2000) Dynorphin B and spinal analgesia: induction of antinociception by the cannabinoids CP55,940, delta(9)-THC and anandamide. *Brain Res.* **857**, 337–342.
78. Noyes, R. Jr., Brunk, S. F., Avery, D. A., and Canter, A. C. (1975) The analgesic properties of delta-9-tetrahydrocannabinol and codeine. *Clin. Pharmacol. Ther.* **18**, 84–89.
79. Jochimsen, P. R., Lawton, R. L., VerSteeg, K., and Noyes, R. Jr. (1978) Effect of benzopyranoperidine, a Δ^9-THC congener, on pain. *Clin. Pharmacol. Ther.* **24**, 223–227.
80. Jain, A. K., Ryan, J. R., McMahon, F. G., and Smith, G. (1981) Evaluation of intramuscular levonantradol and placebo in acute post-operative pain. *J. Clin. Pharmacol.* **21**, 3205–3265.
81. Buggy, D. J., Toogood, L., Maric, S., Sharpe, P., Lambert, D. G., and Rowbotham, D. J. (2003) Lack of analgesic efficacy of oral delta-9-tetrahydrocannabinol in postoperative pain. *Pain* **106**, 169–172.
82. Attal, N., Brasseur, L., Guirimand, D., Clermond-Gnamien, S., Atlami, S., and Bouhassira, D. (2004) Are oral cannabinoids safe and effective in refractory neuropathic pain? *Eur. J. Pain* **8**, 173–177.
83. Clermont-Gnamien, S., Atlani, S., Attal, N., Le Mercier, F., Guirimand, F., and Brasseur, L. (2002) The therapeutic use of Δ^9-tetrahydrocannabinol (dronabinol) in refractory neuropathic pain. *Presse Med.* **31**, 1840–1845.
84. Rudich, Z., Stinson, J., Jeavons, M., and Brown, S.C. (2003) Treatment of chronic intractable neuropathic pain with dronabinol: case report of two adolescents. *Pain Res. Manag.* **8**, 221–224.
85. Campbell, F. A., Tramer, M. R., Carroll, D., et al. (2001) Are cannabinoids an effective and safe treatment option in the management of pain? A qualitative systematic review. *BMJ* **323**, 13–16.
86. Naef, M., Curatolo, M., Petersen-Felix, S., Arendt-Nielsen, L., Zbinden, A., and Brenneisen, R. (2003) The analgesic effect of oral delta-9-tetrahydrocannabinol (THC), morphine, and a THC-morphine combination in healthy subjects under experimental pain conditions. *Pain* **105**, 79–88.
87. Brenneisen, R., Egli, A., ElSohly, M. A., Henn, V., and Spiess, Y. (1996) The effect of orally and rectally administered delta 9-tetrahydrocannabinol on spasticity: a pilot study with 2 patients. *Int. J. Clin. Pharmacol. Ther.* **34**, 446–452.
88. Pertwee, R. G., Gibson, T. M., Stevenson, L. A., et al. (2000) O-1057, a potent water-soluble cannabinoid receptor agonist with antinociceptive properties. *Br. J. Pharmacol.* **129**, 1577–1584.
89. Dogrul, A., Gul, H., Akar, A., Yildiz, O., Bilgin, F., and Guzeldemir, E. (2003) Topical cannabinoid antinociception: synergy with spinal sites. *Pain* **105**, 11–16.
90. Yesilyurt, O., Dogrul, A., Gul, H., et al. (2003) Topical cannabinoid enhances topical morphine antinociception. *Pain* **105**, 303–308.
91. Olsen, J. L., Lodge, J. W., Shapiro, B. J., and Tashkin, D. P. (1976) An inhalation aerosol of delta-9-Tetrahydrocannabinol. *J. Pharm. Pharmacol.* **28**, 86–86.
92. Wilson, D. M., Peart, J., Martin, B. R., Bridgen, D. T., Byron, P. R., and Lichtman, A. H. (2002) Physiochemical and pharmacological characterization of a delta(9)-THC aerosol generated by a metered dose inhaler. *Drug Alcohol Depend.* **67**, 259–267.
93. Malan, T. P. Jr., Ibrahim, M. M., Deng, H., et al. (2001) CB2 cannabinoid receptor-mediated peripheral antinociception. *Pain* **93**, 239–245.
94. Hohmann, A. G., Farthing, J. N., Zvonok, A. M., and Makriyannis, A. (2004) Selective activation of cannabinoid CB2 receptors suppresses hyperalgesia evoked by intradermal capsaicin. *J. Pharmacol. Exp. Ther.* **308**, 446–453.

95. Hanus, L., Breuer, A., Tchilibon, S., et al. (1999) HU-308: a specific agonist for CB(2), a peripheral cannabinoid receptor. *Proc. Natl. Acad. Sci. USA* **96**, 14228–14233.
96. Jones, R. T., Benowitz, N., and Bachman, J. (1976) Clinical studies of cannabis tolerance and dependence. *Ann. NY Acad. Sci.* **282**, 221–239.
97. Jones, R. T. and Benowitz, N. (1976) The 30-day trip—clinical studies of cannabis tolerance and dependence, in *Pharmacology of Marihuana* (Braude, M. C. and Szara, S., eds.), Raven Press, New York, pp. 627–642.
98. Haney, M., Ward, A. S., Comer, S. D., Foltin, R. W., and Fischman, M. W. (1999) Abstinence symptoms following oral THC administration to humans. *Psychopharmacology (Berl)* **141**, 385–394.
99. Haney, M., Ward, A. S., Comer, S. D., Foltin, R. W., and Fischman, M. W. (1999) Abstinence symptoms following smoked marijuana in humans. *Psychopharmacology (Berl)* **141**, 395–404.
100. Haney, M., Ward, A. S., Comer, S. D., Hart, C. L., Foltin, R. W., and Fischman, M. W. (2001) Bupropion SR worsens mood during marijuana withdrawal in humans. *Psychopharmacology (Berl)* **155**, 171–179.
101. Haney, M., Hart, C. L., Ward, A. S., and Foltin, R. W. (2003) Nefazodone decreases anxiety during marijuana withdrawal in humans. *Psychopharmacology (Berl)* **165**, 157–165.
102. Haney, M., Hart, C. L., Vosburg, S. K., et al. (2004) Marijuana withdrawal in humans: effects of oral THC or divalproex. *Neuropsychopharmacology* **29**, 158–170.
103. Kaymakcalan, S. and Deneau, G. A. (1972) Some pharmacologic properties of synthetic Δ^9-tetrahydrocannabinol. *Acta Med. Turc.* **Suppl. 1**, 27.
104. McMillan, D. E., Dewey, W. L., and Harris, L. S. (1971) Characteristics of tetrahydrocannabinol tolerance. *Ann. NY Acad. Sci.* **191**, 83–99.
105. Leite, J. R. and Carlini, E. A. (1974) Failure to obtain "cannabis-directed behavior" and abstinence syndrome in rats chronically treated with cannabis sativa extracts. *Psychopharmacologia* **36**, 133–145.
106. Aceto, M.D., Scates, S.M., Lowe, J.A., and Martin, B.R. (1996) Dependence on Δ^9-tetrahydrocannabinol: studies on precipitated and abrupt withdrawal. *J. Pharmacol. Exp. Ther.* **278**, 1290–1295.
107. Beardsley, P. M., Balster, R. L., and Harris, L. S. (1986) Dependence on tetrahydrocannabinol in rhesus monkeys. *J. Pharmacol. Exp. Ther.* **239**, 311–319.
108. Tsou, K., Patrick, S. L., and Walker, J. M. (1995) Physical withdrawal in rats tolerant to delta-9-tetrahydrocannabinol precipitated by a cannabinoid receptor antagonist. *Eur. J. Pharmacol.* **280**, R13–R15.
109. Aceto, M. D., Scates, S. M., Lowe, J. A., and Martin, B. R. (1995) Cannabinoid precipitated withdrawal by the selective cannabinoid receptor antagonist, SR 141716A. *Eur. J. Pharmacol.* **282**, R3–R4.
110. Cook, S. A., Lowe, J. A., and Martin, B. R. (1998) CB1 receptor antagonist precipitates withdrawal in mice exposed to Δ9-tetrahydrocannabinol. *J. Pharmacol. Exp. Ther.* **285**, 1150–1156.
111. Lichtman, A. H., Wiley, J. L., LaVecchia, K. L., et al. (1998) Effects of SR141716A after acute or chronic cannabinoid administration in dogs. *Eur. J. Pharmacol.* **357**, 139–148.
112. Aceto, M. D., Scates, S. M., and Martin, B. R. (2001) Spontaneous and precipitated withdrawal with a synthetic cannabinoid, WIN 55212-2. *Eur. J. Pharmacol.* **416**, 75–81.
113. Takahashi, R. N. and Singer, G. (1979) Self-administration of Δ^9-tetrahydrocannabinol by rats. *Pharmacol. Biochem. Behav.* **11**, 737–740.
114. Mansbach, R. S., Nicholson, K. L., Martin, B. R., and Balster, R. L. (1994) Failure of delta-9-tetrahydrocannabinol and CP 55,940 to maintain intravenous self-administration under a fixed-interval schedule in rhesus monkeys. *Behav. Pharmacol.* **5**, 219–225.
115. Tanda, G., Munzar, P., and Goldberg, S. R. (2000) Self-administration behavior is maintained by the psychoactive ingredient of marijuana in squirrel monkeys. *Nature Neurosci.* **3**, 1073–1074.

116. Justinova, Z., Tanda, G., Redhi, G. H., and Goldberg, S. R. (2003) Self-administration of delta-9-tetrahydrocannabinol (THC) by drug naive squirrel monkeys. *Psychopharmacology (Berl)* **169**, 135–140.
117. Kaymakcalan, S., Ayhan, I. H., and Tulunay, F. C. (1977) Naloxone-induced or postwithdrawal abstinence signs in delta-9-tetrahydrocannabinol-tolerant rats. *Psychopharmacology* **55**, 243–249.
118. Hirschhorn, I. D. and Rosecrans, J. A. (1974) Morphine and delta-9-tetrahydrocannabinol: Tolerance to the stimulus effects. *Psychopharmacology* **36**, 243–253.
119. Lichtman, A. H., Sheikh, S. M., Loh, H. H., and Martin, B. R. (2001) Opioid and cannabinoid modulation of precipitated withdrawal in Δ(9)-tetrahydrocannabinol and morphine-dependent mice. *J. Pharmacol. Exp. Ther.* **298**, 1007–1014.
120. Bhargava, H. N. (1976) Effect of some cannabinoids on naloxone-precipitated abstinence in morphine-dependent mice. *Psychopharmacology* **49**, 267–270.
121. Bhargava, H. N. (1978) Time course of the effects of naturally occurring cannabinoids on morphine abstinence syndrome. *Pharmacol. Biochem. Behav.* **8**, 7–11.
122. Frederickson, R. C. A., Hewes, C. R., and Aiken, J. W. (1976) Correlation between the in vivo and an in vitro expression of opiate withdrawal precipitated by naloxone: their antagonism by l-(-)-Δ^9-tetrahydrocannabinol. *J. Pharmacol. Exp. Ther.* **199**, 375–384.
123. Hine, B., Friedman, E., Torrelio, M., and Gershon, S. (1975) Morphine-dependent rats: blockade of precipitated abstinence by tetrahydrocannabinol. *Science* **187**, 443–445.
124. Vela, G., Ruiz-Gayo, M., and Fuentes, J.A. (1995) Anandamide decreases naloxone-precipitated withdrawal signs in mice chronically treated with morphine. *Neuropharmacology* **34**, 665–668.
125. Yamaguchi, T., Hagiwara, Y., Tanaka, H., et al. (2001) Endogenous cannabinoid, 2-arachidonoylglycerol, attenuates naloxone-precipitated withdrawal signs in morphine-dependent mice. *Brain Res.* **909**, 121–126.
126. Ledent, C., Valverdej, O., Cossu, G., et al. (1999) Unresponsiveness to cannabinoids and reduced addictive effects of opiates in CB1 receptor knockout mice. *Science* **283**, 401–404.
127. Mas-Nieto, M., Pommier, B., Tzavara, E. T., et al. (2001) Reduction of opioid dependence by the CB(1) antagonist SR141716A in mice: evaluation of the interest in pharmacotherapy of opioid addiction. *Br. J. Pharmacol.* **132**, 1809–1816.
128. Rubino, T., Massi, P., Vigano, D., Fuzio, D., and Parolaro, D. (2000) Long-term treatment with SR141716A, the CB1 receptor antagonist, influences morphine withdrawal syndrome. *Life Sci.* **66**, 2213–2219.
129. Valverde, O., Maldonado, R., Valjent, E., Zimmer, A. M., and Zimmer, A. (2000) Cannabinoid withdrawal syndrome is reduced in pre-proenkephalin knock-out mice. *J. Neurosci.* **20**, 9284–9289.
130. Navarro, M., Carrera, M. R. A., Fratta, W., et al. (2001) Functional interaction between opioid and cannabinoid receptors in drug self-administration. *J. Neurosci.* **21**, 5344–5350.
131. Fattore, L., Spano, M. S., Cossu, G., Deiana, S., and Fratta, W. (2003) Cannabinoid mechanism in reinstatement of heroin-seeking after a long period of abstinence in rats. *Eur. J. Neurosci.* **17**, 1723–1726.
132. De Vries, T. J., Homberg, J. R., Binnekade, R., Raaso, H., and Schoffelmeer, A. N. M. (2003) Cannabinoid modulation of the reinforcing and motivational properties of heroin and heroin-associated cues in rats. *Psychopharmacology (Berl)* **168**, 164–169.
133. De Vries, T. J., Shaham, Y., Homberg, J. R., et al. (2001) A cannabinoid mechanism in relapse to cocaine seeking. *Nat. Med.* **7**, 1151–1154.
134. Vlachou, S., Nomikos, G. G., and Panagis, G. (2003) WIN 55,212-2 decreases the reinforcing actions of cocaine through CB1 cannabinoid receptor stimulation. *Behav. Brain Res.* **141**, 215–222.

135. Freedland, C. S., Sharpe, A. L., Samson, H. H., and Porrino, L. J. (2001) Effects of SR141716A on ethanol and sucrose self-administration. *Alcohol Clin. Exp. Res.* **25**, 277–282.
136. Wang, L., Lui, J., Harvey-White, J., Zimmer, A., and Kunos, G. (2003) Endocannabinoid signaling via cannabinoid receptor 1 is involved in ethanol preference and its age-dependent decline in mice. *Proc. Natl. Acad. Sci. USA* **100**, 1393–1398.
137. Cohen, C., Perrault, G., Voltz, C., Steinberg, R., and Soubrie, P. (2002) SR141716, a central cannabinoid (CB1) receptor antagonist, blocks the motivational and dopamine-releasing effects of nicotine in rats. *Behav. Pharmacol.* **13**, 451–463.
138. Boger, D. L., Sato, H., Lerner, A. E., et al. (2000) Exceptionally potent inhibitors of fatty acid amide hydrolase: the enzyme responsible for degradation of endogenous oleamide and anandamide. *Proc. Natl. Acad. Sci. USA* **97**, 5044–5049.

Chapter 7

Immunoassays for the Detection of Cannabis *Abuse*

Technologies, Development Strategies, and Multilevel Applications

Jane S-C. Tsai

1. Introduction

The power of molecular recognition and effective interaction of specific binding partners have been exploited to develop assay technologies for diverse biochemical analysis. The unique features of immunoglobulins and technological advancement in antibody engineering and manipulation have made antibodies the most versatile binding reagents for detecting analytes of interest in a variety of matrices. The term *immunoassay* is customarily used to denote antibody-mediated analytical procedures; however, there are assortments of nomenclature for various immunoassay techniques that usually are named after the reaction principle of the particular immunoassay format.

A number of immunoassay technologies have been applied to the development of assays for small molecules such as drug compounds and their metabolites. To date, these immunoassays have been widely utilized as cost-effective initial tests to efficiently screen out the negative specimens from further analysis in the two-stage drugs-of-abuse testing (DAT) programs. Subsequently, the non-negative or presumptive positive specimens are subjected to confirmatory testing with an alternative chemical principle such as gas (or liquid) chromatography/mass spectrometry (GC/MS or LC/MS).

Proper utilization of DAT technologies requires familiarity with the characteristics of the analytical methodologies employed. Each of the abused drugs has specific

From: *Forensic Science and Medicine: Marijuana and the Cannabinoids*
Edited by: M. A. ElSohly © Humana Press Inc., Totowa, New Jersey

requirements and challenges for immunoassay performance. Among the more prominent challenges for a DAT immunoassay is the ability to react with a desired panel of structurally related compounds with ideal levels of affinity while excluding the reaction with other similarly related structures. In certain cases, the desirable cross-reactivity characteristics may vary depending on the market segments, regulatory implications, and the goals of the DAT programs. Additionally, each of the biological sample matrices has unique requirements and challenges for developing a suitable DAT immunoassay. Good knowledge of the chemistry, metabolism, and cross-reactivity of the relevant substances is important for the apposite interpretation of the drug screening assays. These issues are of particular interest when evaluating immunoassays for detecting cannabis abuse due to the complexity of cannabinoid chemistry and metabolism. Moreover, the performance and improvement in the gold standard GC/MS reference methodologies can influence the overall assessment of cannabinoids immunoassays.

The main objective of this chapter is to provide an overview of the design strategy, development, and applications of commonly used DAT immunoassays for cannabinoid analysis. The factors that impact the performance and result interpretations of these immunoassays in cannabinoid screening are discussed. Examples of comparative evaluations of cannabinoid immunoassays will also be reviewed. It has long been recognized that *Cannabis*-derived substances are the most frequently abused drugs worldwide *(1–3)*. Likewise, cannabinoids continue to be the most widely investigated and extensively published illicit drugs.

2. Commonly Used Immunoassays for Drugs-of-Abuse Screening

All currently used immunoassay techniques for DAT screening have been developed and refined over the past few decades. The reaction principles of these immunoassays have been described in a number of publications and commercial product information documents. Therefore, this section will provide only a brief overview of the commonly used drugs-of-abuse screening techniques.

The majority of DAT immunoassays are based on the competition of drug molecules in the specimen and drug derivatives in the assay reagent for binding to a prespecified antibody reagent. The discriminatory power of the antibody-binding site gives the assay specificity, even though the cross-reactivity profile can be influenced by factors beyond the binding interaction alone.

The immunoassay indicator for monitoring the binding interactions can be labeled drug-derivative, antibody, or an independently labeled molecule that can specifically bind to the antigen or antibody. The labels convey a measurable property to meet the performance requirements of the specific immunoassay.

In general, the heterogeneous type of immunoassay contains excess labeled-binding reagent in the reaction mixture, and the reaction outcome is determined by the relative fractions or activities of the "bound" (e.g., solid phase bound) labels. Thus, heterogeneous competitive immunoassays involve sequential incubation and separation or washing steps but can generally achieve lower detection limits and wider dynamic ranges.

In contrast, the antibody-antigen reactions in the homogeneous immunoassay systems can modulate the physical properties or activities of the labels in solution or in a homogeneous suspension of particles. Such features allow the direct detection of the reaction outcome in the original reaction mixture. Therefore, the homogeneous immunoassays can be more readily adapted to screening large amounts of samples using automatic analyzers. During the design, development, and validation of an immunoassay, the labeled reagent, the specific binding partner, and the reaction modulators are prepared in specified and stabilized reagent formulations. In an actual testing, sample and reagents are processed according to the parameters optimized for the application of the immunoassay on the specific analyzer system.

2.1. Homogeneous Competitive Immunoassays

In recent years, routine laboratory screening of drugs of abuse in urine has mainly been carried out by homogeneous competitive immunoassays. The most widely used homogeneous drug-testing immunoassay technologies include enzyme-multiplied immunoassay technique (EMIT), fluorescence polarization immunoassay (FPIA), kinetic interaction of microparticles in solution (KIMS), and cloned enzyme donor immunoassay (CEDIA). The major assay labels and the technologies are implied in the respective immunoassay nomenclature.

The assay principle of EMIT is based on the modulation of enzyme activities by the binding of specific antibodies to the enzyme-labeled drug derivatives *(4–6)*. Currently, EMIT-based DAT immunoassays can be purchased from several companies, and a common enzyme of choice is the genetically modified glucose-6-phosphate dehydrogenase (rG6PDH). The oxidation of enzyme substrate G6P to form glucuronolactone-6-phosphate is coupled with the reduction of the cofactor nicotinamide adenine dinucleotide (NAD) to NADH. In the absence of drugs in the sample, the antibodies bind to the enzyme-labeled drugs and inhibit the enzymatic activity. Free drugs in the specimen compete for antibody binding, so fewer antibodies are available for binding to the drug–enzyme conjugates and enzymatic activity is less inhibited. The rate of NADH production, as reflected by the change in absorbance at 340 nm, is directly related to the G6PDH enzyme activity. Therefore, the change of absorbance can be plotted vs the corresponding calibrator concentration to construct a calibration curve for running a semi-quantitative assay. The assay can also be run qualitatively by comparing the sample rate to the calibrated cutoff rate.

The measurement of FPIA relies on detecting the degree of polarization of the emitted fluorescent light when the fluorophore label is excited with plane-polarized light *(7,8)*. FPIA requires a specific FP photometer *(9,10)*. A polarization filter (rotational) and an emission filter (stationary) enables the photomultiplier tube to read emitted parallel and perpendicular polarized light. The degree of polarization is dependent on the rate of rotation of the drug–fluorophore conjugate (tracer) in solution. Small molecules such as tracers can rotate rapidly before light emission occurs, resulting in depolarization of the emitted light. When bound to the antibody, the tracer rotates more slowly and the level of fluorescence polarization is higher. An optimized amount of the tracer competes with free drugs in the sample for binding to a limited amount of antibodies. Hence the drug concentration is inversely related to the degree of polarization. Calibrators containing known amounts of drugs interact with the tracers and antibodies to produce a calibration curve relating drug concentrations to arbitrary "milliPolarization" units (mP). The interactions of the drugs in the specimen, the tracers, and the antibodies under the same condition controlled by the analyzer yield mP units that can be correlated with the drug level in the specimen by making a comparison with the calibration curve.

The principle of microparticle agglutination–inhibition tests has been applied to various drug screening assay formats *(11–15)*. One KIMS DAT format is based on the competition of microparticle-labeled drug derivatives and the free drugs in the specimen for binding to a limited amount of free antibodies in solution *(14,15)*. The drug conjugates are labeled with microparticles through covalent coupling. These drug conjugates react with free antibodies and form particle aggregates that scatter transmitted light. The KIMS-II format contains soluble polymer drug derivative conjugates and microparticle-labeled antibodies *(16)*. The binding of the conjugates to the antibodies promotes the aggregation and leads to subsequent particle lattice formation. In both cases, the aggregation reaction in solution results in a kinetic increase in absorbance values. Free drugs in the sample compete for antibody binding and inhibit the particle aggregation. The absorbance difference between a defined initial reading and final reading decreases with increasing drug concentration, and the signal generated can be monitored spectrophotometrically. The assay can be run qualitatively in comparison with the cutoff calibrator. The assay can also be run semi-quantitatively using four or five levels of calibrators to construct a calibration curve via a logit/log fitting function.

The measurement of CEDIA is based on the antibody modulation of the complementation of two inactive polypeptide fragments to associate in solution to form an active enzyme. The fragments of the recombinant microbial β-galactosidase are called the the enzyme donor (ED) and enzyme acceptor (EA). The binding of antibodies to the drug–ED conjugates can inhibit the spontaneous assembly of active enzymes *(17,18)*. The CEDIA reagent composition includes the lyophilized EA and ED reagents and their respective reconstitution buffer solutions. The antibody binding to drug–ED conjugates in the analyzer reaction cuvet prevents the formation of active enzymes in the cuvet. Conversely, free drugs in the specimen compete for antibody binding and allow the drug–ED conjugates to reassociate with the EA fragments. Therefore, the drug concentration is proportional to the amount of active enzyme formed. The enzyme catalyzes the hydrolysis of selected substrate such as chlorophenol red-β-D-galactopyranoside, and the resulting absorbance rate change is measured as a function of time (mA/min). CEDIA assays can be run either qualitatively or semi-quantitatively based on an appropriate calibration curve.

2.2. Heterogeneous Competitive Immunoassays

A variety of heterogeneous immunoassay formats have been explored and developed; among those broadly used for DAT are the radioimmunoassay (RIA) and the enzyme-linked immunosorbent assay (ELISA). Again, the assay labels and principles of these technologies are implied in their respective immunoassay nomenclature.

Different formulations of RIA have been developed and evaluated for the detection and quantification of abused drugs in a myriad of biological matrices, including urine, blood, serum, plasma, saliva/oral fluids, meconium, hair, and fingernails *(6,14,15,18–23)*. The most commonly used radiolabel is ^{125}I. Several methods, such as the double-antibody approach and the coated-tube technique, were developed to facilitate the effective separation of free, radiolabeled drug derivatives from the bound complex. The double-antibody approach employs a second antibody to bind the primary antibody and precipitate the complex formed by primary antibodies and ^{125}I-drug derivatives. The coat-a-count technique utilizes precoated primary antibodies in the reaction tube to allow the removal of the free radiolabeled drug derivatives in the supernatant. The radioactivity from the bound ^{125}I-labeled drugs in the precipitated complex, or the bound solid phase, is inversely proportional to the amount of drug in the sample. Thus, the drug concentration in the sample can be determined by mathematically comparing average counts per minute (CPM) obtained from the sample with the CPM obtained from the positive reference standard. For quantification, a dose–response curve can be established by plotting standard concentrations against corresponding B/B_0 (B_0 = CPM obtained from the zero-dose control). Alternatively, a standard curve can be constructed by plotting logit of $[B/B_0]$ vs corresponding values of $\log_e$ [drug concentration].

Various commercial or esoteric ELISA methodologies have been utilized for DAT in forensic, clinical, and toxicological laboratories. Currently, there are approximately a dozen companies that offer an array of ELISA kits for an extended menu of drug analysis. Commercial ELISA kits can be applied to test forensic matrices such as urine, blood, serum, oral fluid, sweat, meconium, bile, vitreous humor, and tissue extracts *(24–29)*. In recent years, the highest volume of laboratory-based oral fluid DAT has been performed with qualitative microplate enzyme immunoassays *(27)*. Most of the ELISA kits use high-affinity capture antibody-coated microtiter plates (or 12- × 8-well strips) and enzyme-labeled drug derivatives. One commonly used enzyme is horseradish peroxidase, which catalyzes the reduction of peroxide and the oxidation of the substrate tetramethylbenzidine. The reaction is stopped by diluted acid, and the resulting color can be measured by absorbance at 450 nm. A few ELISA tests offer the option to qualitatively determine the absence or presence of drugs by visually comparing the sample well reaction color to that of the cutoff calibrator and appropriate negative and positive controls. The drug concentration is inversely proportional to the amount of signal produced. Various instrument platforms for ELISA are available with optional data management software.

Immunoassays with chemiluminescence detection techniques have the advantages of lower detection limits, and the signals can be further amplified if coupled with an enzyme label *(30)*. An example of commercial enzyme-enhanced chemiluminescence assay for DAT is the IMMULITE® cannabinoid assay. The chemiluminescent substrate (1,2-dioxetane) is destabilized by the enzyme (alkaline phosphatase), and the unstable dioxetane intermediate will emit light upon decay back to the ground state. Although this is a heterogeneous immunoassay in principle, the analyzer for Immulite assay utilizes a test unit that contains polystyrene beads to capture antibody and hence separate the reaction components within the unit. The tube is the reaction vessel for incubations, washes, and signal development. The photon count is mathematically converted to analyte concentration by the external computer.

2.3. Point-of-Collection Drug Immunoassays

In the early phases of drug-testing program implementation, the majority of on-site, point-of-care, or point-of-collection (POC) DAT programs employed instrument-based immunoassays that were performed at "on-site, initial screening only testing facilities" *(31–33)*. Pioneers of noninstrumented DAT on-site testing have been available since the early 1980s, yet the markets for single-use DAT devices only became mature in the 1990s *(12,13,34–45)*. In recent years, there has been an increase in the numbers, and especially in the distributors, of on-site drug testing products. The more extensive list of the commercial POC drug testing (POCT) products can be found in reports that include the initial evaluation or inventory of the contemporary on-site testing products in their study protocols *(35–37)*.

In general, there are three major categories of POCT products. One type consists of the microparticle agglutination–inhibition based assays with ready-to-dispense liquid reagents *(13,37)*. Another category of POCT product contains both liquid reagent and membrane-immobilized reagent, such as membrane enzyme immunoassay or the ASCEND® multi-immunoassay *(37,38)*. The most widely commercialized and commonly employed immunoassay for on-site DAT is the membrane-based, dry chemistry, one-step lateral-flow immunochromatography *(37,39–45)*. The lateral flow test strip configurations include the colloidal gold-based test strip configuration *(40,41,46)* and latex-enhanced immunochromatography *(39,47)*. A number of readers have also been marketed to assist in interpreting and/or recording the results of the POC test strips. In addition, a few nonconventional immunoassay technologies have been explored to utilize small instruments with quantitative ability for on-site drug testing or monitoring *(48–50)*.

The advantages generally cited for using POCT products include the speed in obtaining a qualitative determination and the ease of use. Many of the POCT devices are self-contained, panel-testing devices that can be stored at room temperature. The ready-to-use devices depend on precalibration during manufacturing. Although the devices generally have less clear differentiation in near-cutoff result reading, these assays in routine use have been shown to provide comparable performance with conventional immunoassays in most drug-screening settings that demand a rapid turnaround time.

3. Cannabinoid Immunoassays

3.1. Cannabinoid Test System

Cannabis is by far the most widely cultivated, trafficked, and abused illicit drug in the world *(1–3)*. According to the recent Drug Abuse Warning Network update *(51)*, the rate of drug abuse-related emergency department visits involving marijuana rose 139% nationally from 1995 to 2002. As reported in the Drug Testing Index series published by Quest Diagnostics *(52)*, cannabinoid analysis has always had the highest "drug positivity rate by drug category" among all of the abused drugs tested in workplace drug-testing programs. Likewise, cannabinoid assays are among the most frequently performed tests in society drug testing, behavior toxicology, and criminal justice testing.

Cannabinoid is a term originally used to denote the unique C_{21} compounds found in the plant *Cannabis sativa* L. *(53,54)*. Recent progress in cannabinoid research has been extended to various ligands of the cannabinoid receptors and related compounds, including the transformation products of cannabinoids, synthetic cannabinoid analogs, and the endocannabinoids, namely, the endogenous ligands of the cannabinoid receptors *(55–58)*. As reflected by the profuse publications in cannabinoid chemistry, tremendous efforts have been invested in the isolation of the chemical constituents and the investigation of the structure–activity relationships of the cannabinoids.

The *Cannabis* plant contains more than 400 chemical compounds belonging to 18 different classes, including more than 60 phytocannabinoids that contain a typical C_{21} structure with pyran and phenolic rings *(53–60)*. Most of the phytocannabinoids belong to several subclass types, including the tetrahydrocannabinol (Δ^9-THC and Δ^8-THC), cannabinol (CBN), cannabidiol (CBD), cannabichromene (CBC), and cannabigerol types (Fig. 1). The main active constituent of cannabis, and the primary psychoactive cannabinoid is Δ^9-THC *(55–59)*. The nomenclature Δ^9-THC is based on the dibenzopyran numbering system; the same compound can also be called Δ^1-THC according to the monoterpene numbering system *(54)*. Immunoassays for detecting cannabis abuse in urine have been designed to detect THC metabolites and are generally referred to as the cannabinoid assay or THC assay.

In *The Federal Register* (21 CFR 862.3870), the cannabinoid test system is identified as "a device intended to measure any of the cannabinoids, hallucinogenic compounds endogenous to marihuana, in serum, plasma, saliva, and urine. Cannabinoid compounds include Δ^9-THC, CBD, CBN, and CBC. Measurements obtained by this device are used in the diagnosis and treatment of cannabinoid use or abuse and in monitoring levels of cannabinoids during clinical investigational use." Quantitatively, the most important cannabinoids present in the cannabis plant are THC and the much less prominent constituents CBD, CBN, and CBC *(58–60)*. Immunoassays developed to detect THC metabolites usually have certain degrees of cross-reactivity with CBN but have minimal or no detectable level of cross-reactivity with the ring-opened compounds such as CBD, CBC, and cannabigerol.

In analyzing 35,312 cannabis preparations confiscated in the United States between 1980 and 1997 *(59)*, ElSohly et al. reported that the average concentrations for THC were 3.1% in marijuana (herbal cannabis), 5.2% in hashish (cannabis resin), 15.0% in hash oil (liquid cannabis), and 8.0% in sinsemilla (unfertilized flowering tops from the female *Cannabis* plant). The average THC content of these cannabis preparations all showed significant increase over the years. The outcome of a cannabinoid test can be affected not only by the analytical performance but also by drug-administration factors such as the potency (%THC) of the drug consumed, the route of administration, the methods, vehicles, and frequency of drug intake, the timing of drug use and sample collection, the type of samples tested, and the pharmacokinetics and pharmacodynamics of cannabinoids *(23,61–73)*.

3.2. Cannabinoids: Pharmacokinetics and Drug Analysis

Cannabinoids immunoassays for each type of biological matrix have to be designed and interpreted in the context of Δ^9-THC absorption and metabolism. The

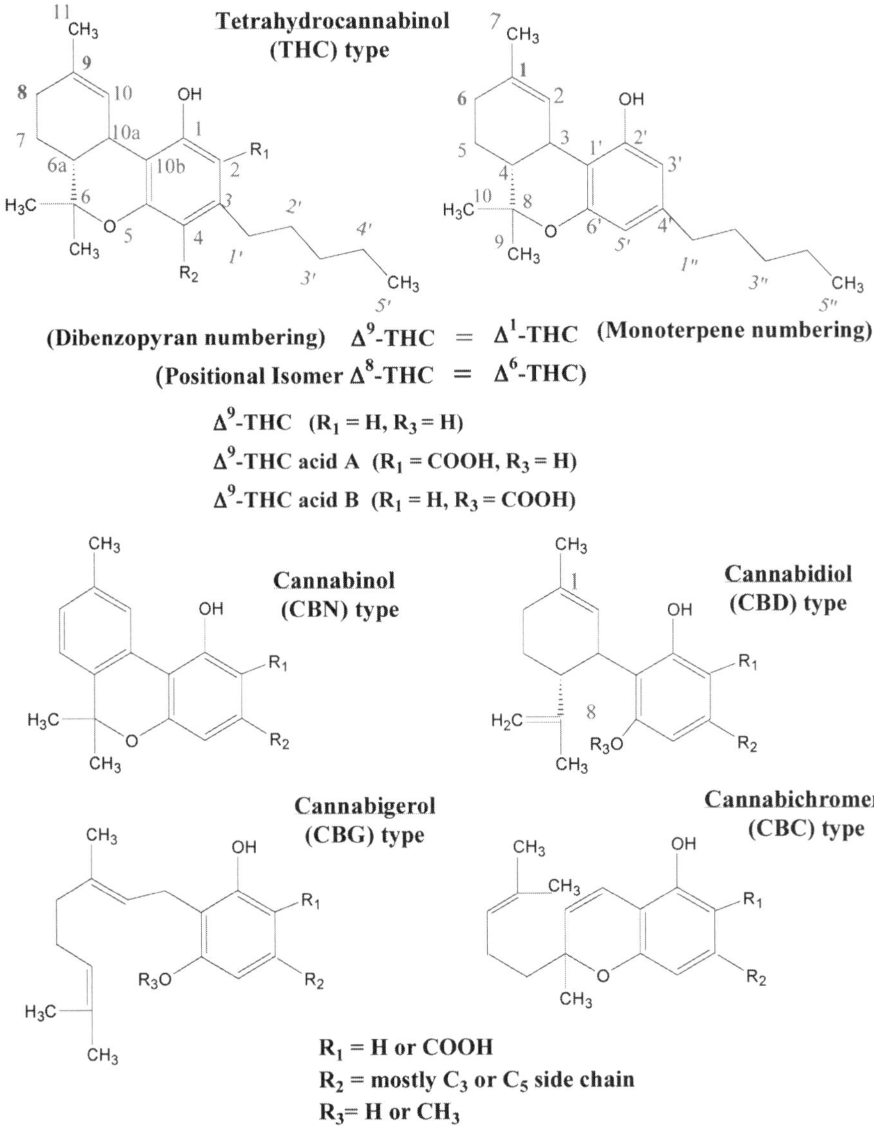

Fig. 1. Chemical structure of naturally occurring cannabinoids. 21 CFR 862.3870 defines a "cannabinoid test system" as "a device intended to measure any of the cannabinoids, hallucinogenic compounds endogenous to marihuana, in serum, plasma, saliva, and urine. Cannabinoid compounds include Δ^9-tetrahydrocannabinol, cannabidiol, cannabinol, and cannabichromene. Measurements obtained by this device are used in the diagnosis and treatment of cannabinoid use or abuse and in monitoring levels of cannabinoids during clinical investigational use."

pharmacokinetics, metabolism, and excretion profiles of cannabinoids have been comprehensively studied and reported *(20,21,23,54–58,61–76)*. THC is known to be extensively metabolized to a large number of compounds, even though most of the compounds are inactive *(73–77)*. As shown in Fig. 2, Δ^9-THC is mainly hydroxylated

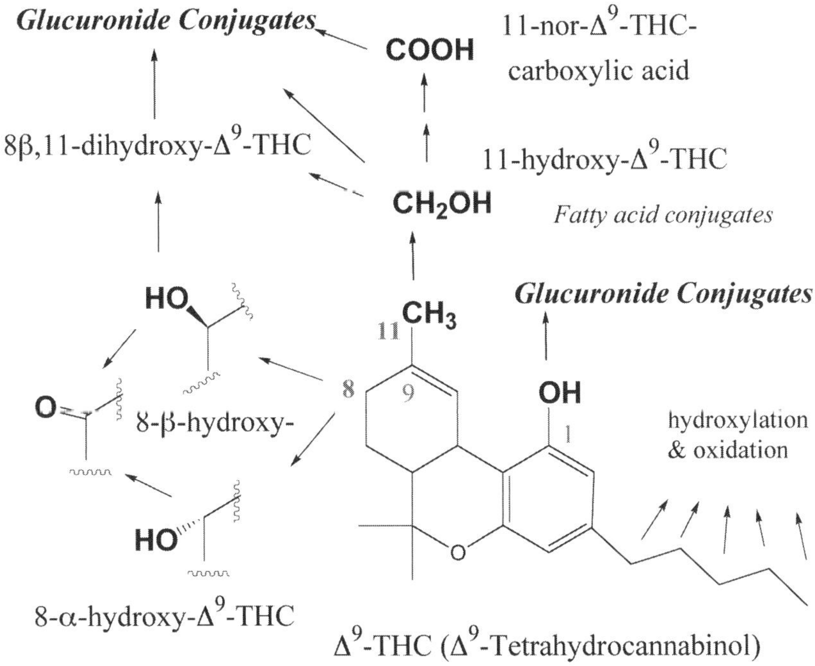

Fig. 2. Metabolic transformation of Δ^9-tetrahydrocannabinol (THC). (Note: Analogous pathways exist for Δ^8-THC and cannabichromanon.)

at the allylic positions (C-11 and C-8) and further oxidized. Oxidation also occurs at the pentyl side chains. Similar biotransformation pathways exist for Δ^8-THC (C-7 and C-11) and other cannabinoids. Smaller quantities of other metabolites are produced by minor metabolic pathways.

It has been well established that the oxidative metabolism of aliphatic, benzyl, phenylethyl, and allylic alcohols to the corresponding carbonyl compounds is catalyzed by numerous cytochrome P450 (CYP) enzymes with overlapping substrate specificity *(74–77)*. In human liver microsomes, the C-11 position of THC is metabolized by CYP2C subfamilies, and the C-7 and C-8 positions are metabolized by the CYP3A isoforms. Pharmacogenetic studies have demonstrated the significant interindividual variations in CYP-catalyzed metabolism. Metabolite composition varies with specimen source and experimental conditions. The presence of various amounts of metabolites in a given biological matrix and their relative binding affinity to the given antibodies may both contribute to different degrees of cumulative total binding activities for different immunoassays.

Initial metabolism following inhalation takes place in the lungs and liver to 11-hydroxy-Δ^9-THC (11-OH-THC), which is subsequently oxidized in the liver through 11-oxo-THC as an intermediate to 11-nor-Δ^9-tetrahydrocannabinol-9-carboxylic acid (THC-COOH) and other inactive metabolites. The major THC metabolite in plasma and urine following smoking is THC-COOH, whereas a higher level of 11-OH-THC is present in blood after oral ingestion *(61–70)*. In frequent smokers, residual levels of THC and THC-COOH have been detected for an extended period of time after cessation of drug use. Most commercial cannabinoid immunoassays are calibrated with the major metabolite, THC-COOH, but also have to meet the product design specifications for the antibody cross-reactivities with THC drug and other THC metabolites (e.g., 8-α-hydroxy-Δ^9-THC, 8-β-hydroxy-Δ^9-THC, 8-β,11-di-hydroxy-Δ^9-THC, and 11-OH-THC). Although immunoassays developed for urinalysis can be adapted for alternative specimen testing, the cross-reactivity characteristics selected for urine drug screening may not be optimal for other biological matrices. The antibody reactivity with the parent Δ^9-THC is especially important for oral fluid testing.

Glucuronic acid conjugation with Δ^9-THC and its hydroxylated and carboxylated metabolites generates water-soluble compounds; thus THC-COOH and other metabolites are mainly excreted as their glucuronide conjugates in urine and meconium *(78–86)*. In routine cannabinoid urinalysis, presumptive positive samples are confirmed by GC/MS detection of free THC-COOH, which was liberated from its glucuronide by chemical or enzymatic hydrolysis prior to sample extraction. Kemp et al. *(83)* evaluated different hydrolysis methods in the quantification of Δ^9-THC and its major metabolites in urine and demonstrated the inefficiencies of base hydrolysis on the hydroxylated compounds. There is a species-dependent glucuronidase activity; hydrolysis with *Escherichia coli* glucuronidase greatly increased the concentration of free Δ^9-THC and free 11-OH-THC in urine collected following marijuana smoking. The concentration of free THC-COOH was not significantly affected by hydrolysis method.

Gustafson et al. *(81)* analyzed plasma samples collected in a controlled oral Δ^9-THC administration study and found increases of 40% for 11-OH-THC and 42% for THC-COOH concentration between hydrolyzed and nonhydrolyzed results. ElSohly and Feng *(79)* compared the effect of hydrolysis on the detection of Δ^9-THC metabolites in meconium and demonstrated significant levels of 11-OH-THC and 8-β,11-diOH-Δ^9-THC after hydrolysis but none without hydrolysis. Among the samples examined, one showed an almost 50% increase in THC-COOH concentration as a result of enzymatic hydrolysis. Analysis of several meconium specimens that "screened positive for cannabinoids but failed to confirm for THC-COOH" showed significant amounts of 11-OH-THC and 8-β,11-diOH-Δ^9-THC. Hence, the authors suggested that GC/MS confirmation of cannabinoids in meconium should include analysis for these metabolites in addition to THC-COOH.

The ratio of glucuronidated vs free THC-COOH in the sample at the time of immunoassay analysis may influence the comparative immunoassay evaluation. Employing LC/MS/MS with and without enzyme hydrolysis, Weinmann et al. *(86)* determined that the molar concentration ratio of glucuronidated vs free THC-COOH in urine samples of cannabis users was between 1.3 and 4.5. In studying the profiles of THC metabolites in urine, Alburges et al. *(78)* observed that all of the THC-COOH excreted in the first 8 hours from an infrequent user was in conjugated form, whereas free THC-COOH could be detected in urine from a frequent user for at least 24 hours. Skopp et al. *(84,85)* investigated the dynamic changes of free vs conjugated THC-COOH in urine and found that free THC-COOH was not detected in 20 out of 38 fresh, authentic samples. At the end of the observation period, 5–81 ng/mL of THC-COOH was detectable in 11 samples that initially tested negative. The results showed that THC-COOH and THC-COOglu, as well as total THC-COOH concentrations, might undergo dynamic changes in urine samples depending on pH and storage conditions *(85)*. THC-COOH is the primary urinary cannabinoid analyte quantified by GC/MS after hydrolysis and extraction. In contrast, immunoassays are calibrated for THC-COOH detection, and the antibodies generally have variable degrees of cross-reactivity towards the glucuronidated metabolites.

By and large, the immunoassay result is based on the sum of various levels of antibody immunoreactivities in the sample matrix tested. The overall reactivity (as expressed in apparent THC-COOH concentration or calibrator-equivalent unit) can be affected by various factors. Among the pivotal factors is the design of the chemical structures for both the drug derivatives for reagent conjugation and the immunogens used for antibody generation.

3.3. Immunogen Strategies for Antibody Generation

The overall analytical sensitivity and specificity of an immunoassay is, to a significant extent, related to the characteristics of the antibody used in the assay. Because drugs such as cannabinoids are small molecular weight haptens, a carrier protein is needed to produce an effective Immunogen. The site of linkage on the drug molecule to the protein carrier can determine the reactivity of the resulting antibodies. The specificity of an antibody is usually directed toward those structures on the hapten that are distal to the linkage group. Thus, the linkage site allows haptens to be coupled to the carrier in such a way that characteristic functional groups are exposed for antibody generation *(20,21,87–89)*.

Figure 3 shows the published linkage sites for coupling cannabinoid haptens to a carrier protein. These linker groups include those out of the C1-position, the C2-position, the C9-position, and the C5'-position of the THC-COOH compound or a very closely related compound. Various immunogen design structures were described in the National Institute on Drug Abuse Research Monographs 7 and 42 *(20,21)*. Most of these antibodies were used for the development of RIAs with the exceptions of immunogen structures depicted for developing EMIT assay with the enzyme "pig heart malate dehydrogenase." There are a few major families of US/European/World patents for cannabinoid immunoassays along with claims for the structures of drug derivatives and/or immunogens. The patent families include those for Abbott's FPIA and those for Roche's RIA, enzyme immunoassay, FPIA, and KIMS cannabinoid assays *(88,89)*.

Salamone et al. *(87)* comprehensively reviewed the selectivity of different immunogen structures and also described an approach to generate antibodies with a broader spectrum of cross-reactivities towards THC metabolites by "sequential immunization" and by designing a noncannabinoid, benzpyran core, immunogen. Taken together, the antibody generation approaches can be summarized as follows:

1. In general, antibodies generated from immunogens with the linkage position out of the C1-, C2-, or C5'-positions are more selective for the cyclohexyl ring, hence they usually display high selectivity for the unconjugated form of THC-COOH. The cross-reactivities for the 8-, 9-, and 11-substituted metabolites is lower because of the high recognition of the antibodies for this part of the molecule. Likewise, the cross-reactivities with the glucuronidated compounds are lower because the ether bond forms between

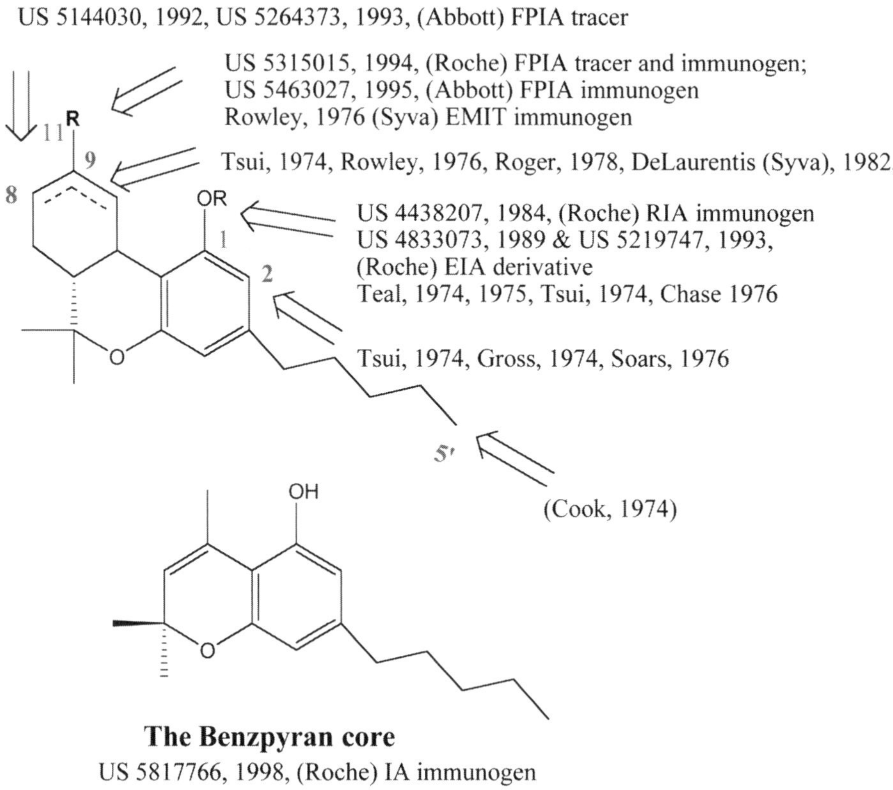

Fig. 3. Immunogen strategies for the generation of anticannabinoid antibodies: common sites of linkage of cannabinoid haptens to a carrier protein. (From refs. *4,19,20,83–85*.)

glucuronic acid and the hydroxyl moiety at C-11 for 11-OH-THC, and the ester bond forms between the glucuronide and the carboxyl moiety at C-11 for THC-COOH.

2. On the other hand, antibodies generated by immunogens with the C-9 position linkage are less selective for the cyclohexyl ring. Nevertheless, these antibodies typically show better binding to the 8-, 9-, and 11-substituted metabolites, as well as improved binding to their corresponding glucuronides. The antibodies also exhibit some selectivity for the cannabinoid nucleus in this region. These types of antibodies can be selected for high cross-reactivities for some, but not all, of the 8-, 9-, and 11-hydroxylated metabolites.
3. To increase the spectrum and degree of cross-reactivities for THC metabolites, a noncannabinoid immunogen was designed not to hold the antigenic determinants of the cyclohexyl ring, and hence the resulting antibodies will be indifferent to the cyclohexyl portion of the cannabinoid nucleus. Such a bicyclic immunogen contained only the structure of the benzpyran core. By eliminating the portion of the molecule that undergoes extensive metabolism from the immunogen and by preserving the core structure, antibodies with higher cross-reactive values with positive clinical samples can be generated. The resulting antibodies from the benzpyran core immunogens all showed broader cross-reactivities towards the 8-, 9-, and 11-hydroxylated metabolites.

The broad-spectrum antibodies can be utilized beyond the development of immunoassays. Feng et al. *(80)* immobilized THC antibody that was generated from the benzpyran core immunogen to prepare immunoaffinity chromatography for developing a simpler extraction procedure for Δ^9-THC and its metabolites from various biological specimens. Good recovery was achieved by simultaneous extraction of Δ^9-THC and its major metabolites, including THC-COOH, 11-OH-THC, and 8-β,11-diOH-Δ^9-THC, from plasma or urine after enzyme hydrolysis. A similar approach was also used for meconium analysis and confirmed that 11-OH-THC *(80)* is indeed an important metabolite in meconium.

The evolution of assay specificity can also be observed from the review of three decades of publications regarding cannabinoid immunoassays. In the earlier stages of drug immunoassay development, immunogens were used to produce polyclonal antibodies from selected animals. Naturally, polyclonal antibodies have broader cross-reactivities that are collectively contributed by a range of antibody affinity, avidity, and binding characteristics. The overall cross-reactivity manifestation can vary a bit from animal to animal and may change slightly over different time periods. Thus, it is not unusual for large pools of polyclonal antibodies to be validated and sequestered. Most current DAT immunoassays use monoclonal antibodies that are much more selective and specific and possess consistent quality. High specificity toward the target THC-COOH may increase overall immunoassay specificity at the expense of sensitivity. Thus, high antibody specificity may have the disadvantage of lower detection rate for clinical samples that contain THC-COOH near the screen cutoff concentration. Broad-spectrum monoclonal antibodies can possess the advantages of both monoclonal antibody consistency and the broader cross-reactivity profile. Nevertheless, the increased immunoassay sensitivity resulting from the higher values of THC-COOH equivalents might have the disadvantage of producing unconfirmed positives and might need a lower GC/MS cutoff *(87)*.

Bearing in mind the variations in the relative percentages and forms of Δ^9-THC metabolites present in the testing samples, both the detection and confirmation rates can have trade-offs, especially for near-cutoff samples. The ultimate goal for a cannabinoid immunoassay design is to balance the assay sensitivity and specificity for its comparative performance to the GC/MS analysis according to their respective cutoff guidelines and regulations.

3.4. Regulations and Guidelines

Globally, various guidelines for substance abuse management have been developed by government agencies, forensic societies, and clinical organizations. Some of the guidelines include more detailed technical and procedural recommendations for specimen collection and processing, initial drug screening, confirmation analysis, quality control and assurance, and documentation and result-reporting requirements.

In the United States, the federally regulated drug-testing programs are implemented and administered by the Substance Abuse and Mental Health Services Administration (SAMHSA, formerly National Institute of Drug Abuse) and Department of Health and Human Services. The 1994 SAMHSA Mandatory Guidelines for Federal Workplace Drug Testing Programs *(90)* define initial test or screening test as "an immunoassay test to eliminate negative urine specimens from further consideration and to identify the presumptively positive specimens that require confirmation or further testing." The guidelines mandate that the initial test "shall use an immunoassay which meets the requirements of the Food and Drug Administration (FDA) for commercial distribution." The guidelines also permit multiple initial tests (or rescreening) to be performed utilizing different immunoassays for the same drug or drug class under the stipulation that "all tests meet all Guideline cutoffs and quality control requirements."

The regulated approach to initial screening "permits rapid identification of presumptive positives within a framework of extensive quality control and offers a defined reference if the next step confirmation is required." This allows a process with a set "administrative cutoff" for uniform comparison across different assay principles and various volumes of screening. The specified cutoff levels for cannabinoids testing were set at 100 ng/mL for immunoassays and 15 ng/mL for GC/MS in the first Mandatory Guidelines (53 FR 11970, 1988). The cutoff for immunoassay was lowered to 50 ng/mL in the subsequent version of the federal guidelines *(91)*. In case a retest is required for a specimen or for the testing of Bottle B of a split specimen, the federal guidelines state that the retest quantification is not subject to a cutoff requirement. However, the retest "must provide data sufficient to confirm the presence of the drug or metabolite" *(90)*.

The proposed revisions for the next version of the Mandatory Guidelines *(91,92)* will include regulations on specimen validity testing, POCT, and alternative specimen testing. Additionally, the new guidelines will expand the authorized confirmation method from only GC/MS to allow the use of additional confirmation technologies such as LC/MS. However, the new guidelines draft does not change the cutoff requirements for cannabinoid testing. Other civilian drug-testing programs, such as the College of American Pathologists Forensic Urine Drug Testing laboratory accreditation program, allow the cutoff determinations be made according to the need of the laboratory or to the intent of its clients' drug-testing programs. Generally speaking, even in nonregulated sectors, many drug-testing programs follow the cutoff defined by the federal guidelines and require reporting positive results if both the initial immunoassay results and the GC/MS analysis are at or above their respective cutoff concentration.

The provisions of the rules that affect US corporations may be imposed on their global employees. In contrast, countries in the European Union, Asia, and Australia differ in their concerns and strategies in relation to substance abuse problems. Surveys of DAT in European Union laboratories in the late 1990s indicated that a high percentage of laboratories did not use or report cutoff *(93–95)*. A few work groups in Europe have proposed consensus or country-specific guidelines and cutoffs, including drug-testing application-specific cutoffs, for DAT (*see*, e.g., refs. *96–98*). The European Laboratory Guidelines for Legally Defensible Workplace Drug Testing were developed by the European Workplace Drug Testing Society with an aim to "establish best practice" for laboratories within Europe "whilst allowing individual countries to operate within the requirements of national customs and legislation" *(98)*. For urine drug testing, the maximum cutoff for screening test and the confirmation cutoff recommended by the European Workplace Drug Testing Society for cannabis metabolites are the same as those mandated by the current SAMHSA guidelines.

3.5. Comparative Evaluation of Cannabinoid Immunoassays

3.5.1. General Evaluations

Immunoassays for commercial applications have to be developed and manufactured in compliance with a number of regulations and quality-management requirements. Currently, all projects for immunoassay research, development, and commercialization are required to follow the FDA Design Controls and Quality System Regulations. The overall assay performance characteristics have to meet an array of predefined specifications with robust assurances at each of the design control milestone reviews in order to receive approval for proceeding to the next milestone. The manufacturers then submit data and statistical analyses in support of claimed performance parameters for the assay/device/instrument application to FDA for 510K review and approval for premarket clearance. Likewise, the manufacturers have to declare conformity and submit required data and documentations to the European In Vitro Diagnostic Directive for the immunoassays to be registered for the "CE mark." There are also country-specific processes for registration and approval for commercialization in countries such as Japan and Canada. Additionally, many companies require external clinical trials during product development to simulate the performance in the field as well as to anticipate any potential findings or cross-reactivity issues not observed during the in-house development. To date, the majority of published evaluations of different immunoassay products have involved authentic clinical samples from either controlled drug-administration study or specimens collected for routine laboratory drug testing (*see*, e.g., refs. *14, 15, 18, 35, 36,* and *99–105*).

3.5.2. Cutoff Concentrations and Immunoassay Evaluations

Because a cutoff is the concentration of drug below which all specimens are considered to be negative, the cutoff decision has a direct impact on the detection time window and the positive rate. The most commonly used method for immunoassay performance comparisons is to evaluate the so-called true-positive (TP), true-negative (TN), false-positive (FP), and false-negative (FN) of the assay. These results can then be used to calculate the specificity [TN / (TN + FP)] × 100%, sensitivity [TP / (TP + FN)] × 100%, efficiency [(TP + TN) / (TN + FP + TP + FN)] × 100%, or positive or negative predictive values of the assay. Because the criteria for either true or false are based on the comparison of immunoassay and GC/MS interpretation at their respective screening and confirmation cutoff levels, the goals and strategies for balancing the relative performance around the selected cutoff concentrations are among the important considerations for designing an immunoassay for cannabinoid testing.

Traditionally, the cutoff decision can be made by considering the assay limit of detection or a predefined, higher concentration. Although not generally inferred in the context of drug testing, cutoff sometimes is used to refer to the analyte concentration at which repeated tests on the same sample yield positive results 50% of the time and negative results for the other 50%. In a near-cutoff zone as concentrations close to the cutoff value, some results may be positive or negative for different analytical methodologies or for repeated testings using the same method. For most drug-testing programs, the "administrative cutoffs" were chosen with the consideration that the cutoff is sufficiently above the assay limit of detection, yet low enough to allow the detection of drug use within a reasonable time frame *(90,91)*. One of the earlier concerns in setting the immunoassay cutoff for cannabinoids was the risk of falsely identifying urine samples as positive for individuals exposed to passive marijuana smoke. Nonetheless, further studies on passive inhalation have led to the conclusion that the levels of cannabinoids in the body from passive inhalation would not be enough to cause urine specimens from a non-marijuana user to test positive using a screen cutoff concentration of 50 ng/mL *(72,106,107)*.

Several studies have since demonstrated that higher positive rates for marijuana detection were achieved by lowering the initial testing cutoff in urine *(100–105)*. The sensitivity vs specificity tradeoff also reflects the fact that the target analyte specificity is related to the detection rate of cannabinoid immunoassays, especially for samples that contain THC-COOH concentrations between the mandated GC/MS cutoff and the mandated (or chosen) immunoassay cutoff levels *(100–105,108–110)*.

Luzzi et al. *(111)* investigated analytical performance of drug detection below the SAMHSA cutoffs and showed that the accuracy of urine drug-screening results between the SAMHSA-specified cutoffs and the precision-based cutoffs was less than the accuracy for specimens above the SAMHSA cutoffs. The use of the precision-based cutoff for clinical drug testing increased both the number of screen-positive specimens and the detection of specimens that yielded positive results on confirmatory testing. However, the confirmatory rates for subcutoff-positive specimens were lower than for specimens screened positive at cutoff. When choosing 35 ng/mL as the subcutoff for EMIT screening, 90% of the subcutoff-positive THC specimens contained THC-COOH by GC/MS analysis. Similarly, Hattab et al. *(112)* stated that the immunoassay cutoff could be further lowered for detecting maternal and neonatal drug exposure. Using the lower thresholds, drugs were detected in 4–5% of the subjects that had screened negative at the conventional threshold concentrations. GC/MS analysis confirmed the presence of cannabinoids in 74% of urine specimens that rescreened positive at a lower cutoff.

The target ranges of cutoff concentrations for alternative specimen testing are significantly lower than those for urine drug testing. The application of alternative specimens for drug testing is still an evolving field, and there have been ongoing discussions and studies over recent years *(23,27–29,42,45,113–122)*. In a prevalence study that compared positivity rates of oral fluid test results with urine test results for different drugs, the screening and confirmation cutoff concentrations selected for oral fluid cannabinoids testing were 3 and 1.5 ng/mL, respectively *(27)*. The overall confirmed-positive prevalence rate for oral fluid testing at these cutoff concentrations was 3.2%. In comparison, the confirmed-positive prevalence rates for urine testing using 50 and 15 ng/mL as the respective screening and confirmation cutoffs were 1.7% for federally mandated urine testing and 3.2% for private sector workplace testing.

With the low cutoff concentrations for oral fluid cannabinoid screening and confirmation, oral fluid testing also has the potential to produce positive results from passive cannabis smoke exposure. In a controlled dosing study, Niedbala et al. reported that two individuals who were passively exposed to the smoke from 10 cannabis cigarettes produced positive screening results, which failed to test positive by GC/MS/MS

(27). In a subsequent study with five cannabis smokers and four passive subjects, the authors observed a biphasic pattern of decline for THC in oral fluid specimens collected from active smokers, whereas the pattern of THC decline was linear in specimens collected from passive subjects *(28)*. The authors concluded that the risk of positive oral fluid tests from passive inhalation is limited to a period of approx 30 minutes following smoke exposure.

In the latest version of the Proposed SAMHSA Guidelines *(91)*, the following cutoff concentrations are recommended for detecting cannabis abuse:

1. Initial tests:
   a. 1 pg marijuana metabolite/mg hair sample.
   b. 4 ng marijuana metabolite/sweat patch.
   c. 4 ng "THC parent drug and metabolites"/mL oral fluid specimen.
   d. 50 ng "THC metabolites"/mL urine specimen.
2. Confirmation:
   a. 0.05 pg THC-COOH/mg hair sample.
   b. 1 ng THC parent drug/sweat patch.
   c. 2 ng THC parent drug/mL oral fluid specimen.
   d. 15 ng THC-COOH/ mL urine specimen.

3.5.3. Correlation of Results From Cannabinoid Immunoassay and GC/MS Analysis

A number of studies have been conducted to investigate how well results from cannabinoid immunoassays can correlate to GC/MS analysis and/or to select an appropriate cutoff value for each of the initial test methods *(99–105)*. In all cases the general correlations exist, yet the data points could be rather scattered. Generally speaking, the correlation coefficients are more sensitive to the change of sample groups, in which the distributions in the relative concentrations of THC-COOH and other cross-reacting compounds varies.

The relative concentrations of THC metabolites in plasma and urine have been studied to determine if a temporal relationship could be estimated between marijuana use and metabolite excretion *(65,69)*. With the addition of the β-glucuronidase hydrolysis step in the extraction protocol, the presence of significant quantities of THC and 11-OH-THC in urine could be demonstrated *(69)*. The relative concentrations of THC-COOH and 11-OH-THC can be shown in a scatter plot when all data for urinary THC-COOH and 11-OH-THC concentrations published in the article by Manno et al. *(69)* were used to create the plot shown in Fig. 4. For samples with THC-COOH levels closely surrounding the 15 ng/mL cutoff, the relative cross-reactivities of an immunoassay with 11-OH-THC, THC-COOH, and their relative abundance may contribute to the immunoassay outcome by rendering the results false positive or false negative when compared to a fixed GC/MS value of THC-COOH.

In addition to the interindividual metabolism and metabolite variability, the correlation of immunoassay and GC/MS results can also be influenced by the total performance characteristics of not only the screening but also confirming techniques used *(123–127)*. Because all analytical techniques have an acceptable range of imprecision, it is essential to note that a value generated from immunoassay or GC/MS analysis is

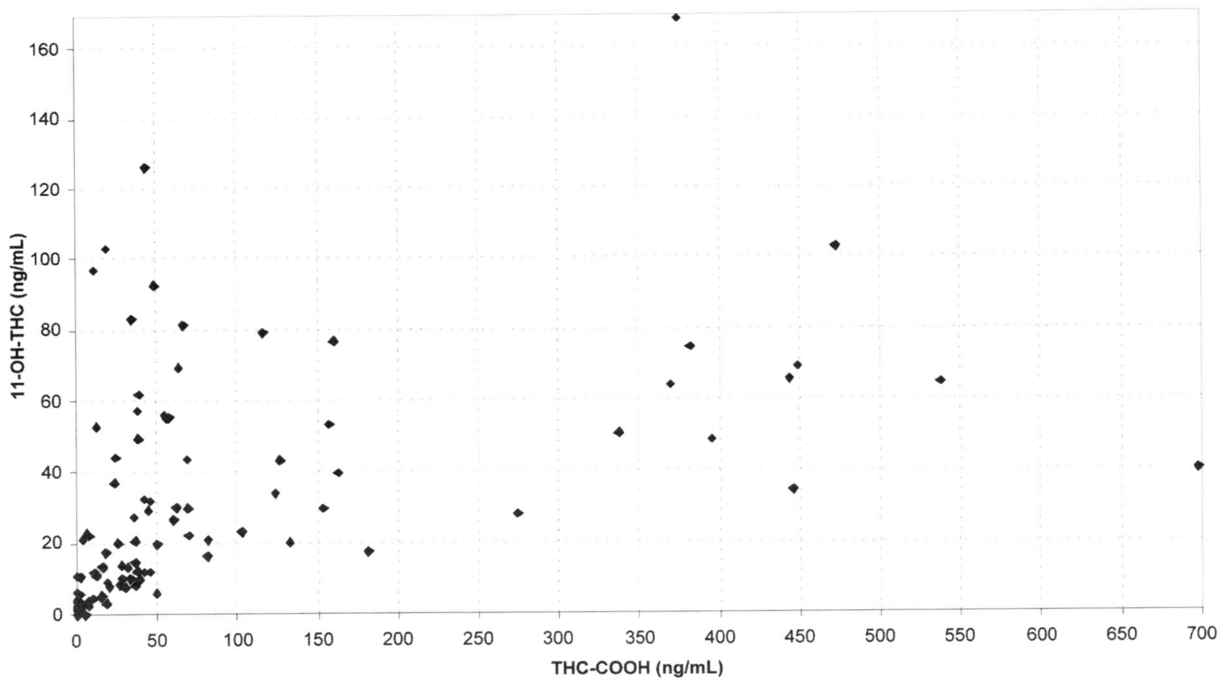

Fig. 4. Relative concentrations of THC-CODH and 11-OH-TCH in cannabinoids containing urine samples. (Adapted from data from ref. *65*.)

Table 1
Examples of the AACC/CAP Forensic Urine Drug Testing (Confirmatory) Survey Results

Survey	No. labs	Mean (ng/mL)	Coefficient of variation (%)	Low value (ng/mL)	High value (ng/mL)
UDC-1, 2003	128	514.61	16.9	247.3	718.8
	112	77.18	10.9	53.9	101.0
	111	10.6	12.1	7.4	14.3
UDC, 2002	113	91	13.7		
(year-end	127	591	15.0		
critique)	118	97	12.4		
	122	95	11.2		
	109	36	12.7		
	126	14	12.7		
	145	13	13.8		

Data were obtained with permission from American Association for Clinical Chemistry/College of American Pathologists (AACC/CAP) forensic urine drug testing (confirmatory) Survey UDC-A of 2003 and Survey 2002 year-end critique for Δ^9-THC-COOH.

not an absolutely fixed number. These analytical techniques all have to be validated and meet a host of quality-control and quality-assurance requirements. Similar to the requirements for proper utilization of immunoassays, knowledge of the advantages and potential pitfalls of different GC/MS systems as well as ionization and detection modes would facilitate proper optimization for the accuracy of compound quantification and identification *(124)*.

Because GC/MS involves multiple steps of extraction, derivatization, and quantitative analysis, the laboratory has to determine the acceptable criteria for replicate analysis. Generally, the repeatability and reproducibility of GC/MS in a certified laboratory are excellent, even though there are interlaboratory variabilities among the certified laboratories. For years, the College of American Pathologists and American Association for Clinical Chemistry have been conducting quarterly surveys and year-end critiques for all certified laboratories. The survey results of THC-COOH analysis for year-end 2002 and the first quarter of 2003 are listed in Table 1. The results are fairly consistent over the years, and the interlaboratory coefficient of variation has been approx 10–15%. Statistically, the variations may not significantly affect the confirmation of presumptive positives, even though the confirmation rate for near-cutoff samples can be more readily affected.

A semi-quantitative immunoassay produces a numerical concentration that approximates the total amount of THC-COOH along with associated metabolites in the specimen, namely, a value for apparent THC-COOH equivalent. The results of unknown clinical samples are calculated by the automatic analyzers based on a calibration curve. The calibration curve is calculated from prevalidated equations for the best-fit curve. The claimed concentrations of calibrators must be established by repeated

GC/MS analysis to ensure that the THC-COOH concentration in the calibrators stays within the acceptable range of GC/MS values for the entire duration of its shelf life.

Table 2 shows a collection of analytical recovery data or imprecision data from various package inserts of commercial immunoassays. The nominal THC-COOH concentration is the amount of THC-COOH compound spiked into urine for running the immunoassays, and the numerical value of apparent THC-COOH concentration is the average of replicate results obtained from the immunoassays.

In general, the results of semi-quantitative immunoassays provide an indication of the levels of THC metabolites to assist in making dilutions for GC/MS analysis. How closely a semi-quantitative immunoassay result can match the nominal value is affected by a number of factors, including the quantitative accuracy of calibrators, the quantitative accuracy of the spiked samples for evaluation, the constituents of the specimens, the assay precision for the lot of reagents used, and the assay dynamic range. The results may no longer be semi-quantitative in that the absorbance changes of the immunoassay flatten out or reach the plateau *(128)*. Commonly used commercial immunoassays offer applications for multiple cutoff choices to meet the requirement of different drug-testing programs. Depending on the drug-testing program goals and preferences, the more frequently used cutoff concentrations for urinary cannabinoid immunoassays are 20, 25, 50, and 100 ng/mL.

In a study designed to understand the relationship of THC concentrations in oral fluid and plasma after controlled administration of smoked cannabis, Heustis and Cone observed that results from an RIA selective for THC were higher than those obtained from GC/MS. The mean ± standard deviation ratio of RIA to GC/MS concentration was 3.35 ± 2.16, with a range of 1.1–8.8 *(23)*. The higher estimated THC concentrations in oral fluid by the RIA screen method were attributed to cross-reactivities of the THC RIA antibody to other cannabis constituents. In this study, THC RIA concentrations at 0.2 hour were generally 20-fold or more than those measured at 0.27 hour. With a 1.0 ng/mL screening cutoff concentration, the mean detection times by RIA for the 1.75% and 3.55% doses were 5.7± 0.8 and 8.8 ± 8.3 hours, respectively. The authors also compared the excretion rates in three biological specimens from the same subject by GC/MS analysis of THC (for oral fluid and plasma) and THC-COOH (for urine) and reported half-life estimates of 0.8 hour for oral fluid, 0.9 hour for plasma, and 16.9 hours for urinary specimens.

3.5.4. Stability of Cannabinoids in Biological Matrices

Different stability studies have been conducted to investigate the stability of THC-COOH in urine or the stability of THC and THC-COOH in blood *(84,85,129–134)*. The hydrophobic nature of cannabinoid molecules may lead to the loss of drugs in the specimen caused by surface adsorption to the specimen-handling and storage devices and containers. The loss of analyte from calibrator solutions can lead to inaccuracy of the analytical system *(129)*. The stability of cannabinoids in immunoassay calibrator solutions and in urine samples has been extensively evaluated in various container materials at different temperatures *(129–134)*. In addition to potential analyte loss to surface adsorption, the temperature and storage conditions can affect the stability of cannabinoids in specimens. Drug partition into strata when frozen in urine was observed and postulated to be due to the thermodynamics of the freezing process *(131)*.

Table 2
Analytical Recovery of Semi-quantitative Cannbinoid Immunoassays at Different Cutoff Concentrations[a]

	Nominal THC-COOH (ng/mL) vs average "apparent THC-COOH concentration" (ng/mL) at different cutoff levels																				
Assay cutoff[b]	15	18	20	22	25	30	37.5	40	45	50	55	62.5	60	75	80	90	100	125	135	150	180
EMIT-100[c]	12							36	36	41				62		74	95	110		153	192
EMIT-50[c]					30	33	39	42	42	45	48			65				130		163	179
EMIT-20[c]	16	18		20	21	24					51										
FPIA[d]					21			34		45			54		78		98		135		
KIMS II-100/50/20[e]	16		20		23		39			49		69		79			96	140			

[a]Average THC-COOH concentration reported in the packiage inserts for either "accuracy by recovery" or "impression studies" of the immunoassay products. The "nominal THC-COOH concentration" is the amount of THC-COOH compound spiked for running the immunoassays and the "apparent THC-COOH concentration" is the average result obtained from the immunoassays.

[b]The products are indicated the "immunoassay technology-cutoff level;" the information is not shown on CEDIA package inserts.

[c]Package inserts of Emit II Plus Cannabinoids assay, Dade Behring, Inc., June 2001. Three cutoff levels: 100, 50, and 20 ng/mL.

[d]Package inserts of AxSYM Cannabinoids assay, Abbott Laboratories, 1997.

[e]Package inserts on ONLINE DAT Cannabinoids II assay, Roche Diagnositcs, 2003. The assays were run at three concentrations for each of the three cutoff levels: 100, 50, and 20 ng/mL.

Recently, Skopp and colleagues *(84,85)* published several studies investigating the stability of free and glucuronidated THC metabolites in plasma and authentic urine specimens. Formation of free THC-COOH increased with increasing storage temperature in both plasma and urine. In urine samples, THC-COOH exists primarily as the glucuronide, and free THC-COOH is present in minute amounts. During storage, THC-COOH was liberated from its glucuronide in a time- and temperature-dependent manner *(84)*. The authors reported that the dynamic change in the breakdown of the glucuronide is of considerable importance for the broad and highly variable changes observed during storage of authentic samples. The authors also investigated the stability of cannabinoids in hair samples exposed to sunlight *(135)*. The stability of THC in oral fluid is also an issue of concern, although commercially available collection devices generally contain preservative chemicals. In the near future, it is expected that more studies will be carried out to investigate the stability of cannabinoids in various alternative specimens.

3.5.5. Hemp Seed/Oil Products, Synthetic THC Medication, and Drug Testing

The question of whether the consumption of cannabinoid-containing foodstuffs or cannabinoid-based therapeutics could be used to justify the presence of urinary THC-COOH has been extensively investigated and reported in the literature *(70,110,136–144)*. A number of studies in 1997 clearly showed that ingestion of what were commercially available hemp seed oils could produce positive cannabinoid immunoassay results for several days *(137–140)*. These screen-positive specimens were shown to contain THC-COOH by GC/MS in most of the studies *(137–139)*. Later studies indicated that there has been a significant reduction in the THC concentration of hemp food products. These studies observed only occasional screen-positive samples and showed decreased levels of urinary THC-COOH with shortened detection time *(141,142)*. In addition, the Drug Enforcement Agency (DEA) and Justice Department added an interpretive rule to 21 CFR Part 1308. DEA interprets the Controlled Substances Act and DEA regulations to declare any product that contains any amount of THC to be a schedule I controlled substance, even if such product is made from portions of the *Cannabis* plant that are excluded from the Controlled Substances Act definition of "marihuana" *(145)*. However, a number of sources still exist globally that may provide hemp oils with considerable THC concentration.

Oral ingestion of prescribed synthetic THC medication (dronabinol [Marinol®]) can also produce positive results for cannabinoid testing. Immunoassays alone cannot determine if a positive result could be solely a result of the use of synthetic THC. Importantly, ElSohly et al. *(140,141)* demonstrated that Δ^9-tetrahydrocannabivarin (THCV), the C3 homolog of Δ^9-THC, is a marker for the ingestion of marijuana or a related product. THCV is a natural product that exists only in *Cannabis* plants with THC. Thus, the detection of THCV-COOH in plasma and urine specimens would indicate the use or ingestion of cannabis-related products and would not support claims of the sole use of Marinol *(143,144)*.

Recently, Gustafson et al. *(70)* studied urinary pharmacokinetics of THC-COOH after controlled clinical study of multiple-dose oral THC administration. Varying THC doses were administered through gelatin capsule and liquid hemp oil, along with THC in sesame oil, to examine effects of dose, vehicle type, and form. The maximum THC-COOH concentration ranges in urine samples were 7.3–38.2, 5.4–31, 26–436, and 19–264 ng/mL for THC daily doses of 0.39, 0.47, 7.5, and 14.8 mg, respectively. Following the administration of these daily THC doses, the mean urinary terminal elimination half-lives averaged 50.3 ± 17.4, 44.2 ± 19.4, 64.0 ± 22.5, and 52.1 ± 21.8 hours, respectively.

3.5.6. Cannabinoid-to-Creatinine Ratio Studies

Regardless of the cutoff levels chosen for cannabinoids testing, substantial variabilities have been observed between subjects and between doses in the excretion profiles of THC-COOH. Huestis et al. *(67)* demonstrated that mean detection times in urine following smoking varied considerably between individuals even in highly controlled smoking studies. It has been documented that consecutive urine specimens may fluctuate below and above the cutoff during the terminal elimination phase when THC-COOH concentrations approach the cutoff *(67,71)*. The normalization of drug excretion to urine creatinine concentration has been well documented not only to predict new drug use but also to reduce the variability of drug measurements attributable to urine dilution *(146–150)*. Gustafson et al. *(70)* observed an up to fourfold intrasubject variation across doses and a sixfold intersubject variation for a single dose in terminal elimination half-lives. However, the authors found no significant effect of creatinine normalization on pharmacokinetic parameters, half-life, maximum excretion rate, and time to maximum excretion rate following oral THC administration. The authors also showed that the apparent urinary elimination half-life of THC-COOH prior to reaching 15 ng/mL concentration was significantly shorter than the terminal urinary elimination half-life.

3.5.7. Specimen Validity Testing

The normalization of THC metabolite concentration to urine creatinine concentration has been proven to help address the issue of fluctuating THC-COOH concentration as a result of specimen donor hydration status. In addition to physiological fluctuation, intentional dilution of urine specimens in vivo or in vitro may lower the levels of drug below the threshold for a positive screen result and thus avoid further testing *(151–154)*. Moreover, attempts to conceal drug abuse by water dilution are most likely to play a substantial role when concentrations are at or near the detection threshold, such as the terminal stages of drug eliminations *(151–153)*.

Frazer et al. *(151)* showed that cannabinoids were among the most often confirmed drug classes in diluted specimens. The authors recommended the reduction of the FN rate for DAT by incorporating lower screening and confirmation cutoff levels for diluted specimens that screened negative using the SAMHSA mandated cutoff concentrations. Nevertheless, the more direct approach is to test the samples for signs of dilution or substitution. Cook et al. *(154)* extensively reviewed the published scientific literature for the characterization of human urine for specimen validity determination in workplace drug testing. The authors developed criteria for classifying submitted urine as substituted, and the criteria were then validated by controlled dehydration study *(154,155)*.

Deliberate invalidation of the specimen by chemical adulteration has also been applied to mask urine screening *(156–160)*. Among the drugs of abuse assays, cannabinoid testing is the most sensitive to chemical additives, especially to oxidizing agents, as adulterants that may negatively affect the target analyte for drug testing. Tsai et al. *(158)* investigated the interaction of various oxidizing agents with the THC metabolites under a number of sample matrix conditions and observed a spectrum of manifestations with regard to their effects on immunoassays and GC/MS analysis. Paul and Jacobs *(160)* evaluated different oxidizing adulterants. Several oxidizing adulterants that are difficult to test by conventional urine adulterant testing methods showed considerable effects on the destruction of THC-COOH. The time and temperature for these effects were similar to those used by most laboratories to collect and test specimens, and the loss of THC-COOH was significant (>94%) in several cases.

In response to the specimen validity issues, SAMHSA and the Department of Transportation initiated the process to develop standards for testing and reporting of sample adulteration, substitution, and dilution (66 FR 43876). The revised mandatory Guidelines for specimen validity testing were published in 2004 *(92)*. Many immunoassay manufacturers also offer products or utility channels for specimen validity testing. Alternative matrices are generally perceived as less vulnerable to adulteration if the sample collection procedures are directly observed. However, there are environmental contamination and bias concerns for some of the matrices. The scenarios of passive exposure to marijuana smoking are also being investigated for hair, sweat, and oral fluid testing. The World Wide Web distributors of adulteration products for urine testing have been offering an array of adulteration products for hair and saliva /oral fluid testing. The proposed SAMHSA Guidelines provide specific information and requirements on conducting specimen validity testing for all alternative specimens submitted for mandatory drug testing programs *(91)*.

4. Conclusions

The application of cannabinoid immunoassays as the initial test remains the most economic and efficient screening tool "to eliminate negative specimens from further consideration" and "to identify the class of drugs that requires confirmatory test" *(90,91)*. The regulated cutoff levels provide a uniform approach for the mandated drug-testing programs. On the other hand, the availability of multiple cutoff choices from the immunoassay kits provides alternative means for certain drug-testing programs that require the use of cutoff levels different from regulated workplace drug testing.

Although results from urine drug testing alone are not sufficient to answer many demanding forensic and clinical questions, the detection and quantification of urinary cannabinoids have not only provided insights on cannabinoid metabolism but also played a pivotal role in overall drug-testing programs. A number of immunoassays have been developed or adapted for detecting cannabis abuse using various biological fluids and forensic matrices. The technical challenges for detecting cannabinoids in other biological matrices are higher as compared to urinalysis, and more research and development are currently ongoing in diverse fields relating to alternative specimen testing.

Regardless of the specimen type tested, it is highly recommended that presumptive positive results be confirmed to rule out issues of cross-reactivity with noncannabinoid compounds. The complexity of cannabinoid chemistry and pharmacokinetics has challenged the development of immunoassays to meet the diverse goals of detecting or deterring cannabis abuse. However, various strategies have been extensively explored for manipulating the antibody selectivity and immunoassay sensitivity and specificity. Naturally, the results for testing one specimen with different immunoassay technologies or platforms can vary to some extent because of the different antibodies and reagent systems used.

Because of the interindividual differences in metabolism, specimens that show the same apparent THC-COOH concentration as determined by an immunoassay can produce different THC-COOH concentrations as determined by GC/MS analysis. This is generally not a real issue for routine drug testing when the majority are either truly "drug-free" negative specimens (e.g., workplace testing) or high drug concentration positive specimens (e.g., criminal justice testing). For detecting clinical samples that contain cannabinoid immunoassay results between the screen cutoff and confirmation cutoff, a more specific assay may not have adequate sensitivity, whereas a more sensitive immunoassay may have a higher percentage of unconfirmed positives. A higher confirmation rate does confer efficiency and economical advantage for the process that involves large volume drug screening.

Although immunoassays lack the defined specificity of GC/MS, they remain the only practical means of conducting large-volume screening programs. For routine workplace drug testing, immunoassays work well in terms of eliminating the bulk of drug-free samples from further testing. Immunoassays are relatively easy to perform and do not require sample pretreatment for urinalysis. The values and utilities of these immunoassays have been supported by the hundreds of millions of samples tested over the past decades. In addition to qualitative screening, the assays can be run in semi-quantitative mode to provide an approximate correlation with GC/MS value and to aid in the estimation of dilution factor needed for conducting GC/MS confirmation.

In conclusion, the key factors that impact the design and performance of cannabinoids immunoassays may include (1) the chemical characteristics and pharmacokinetics of cannabinoids, (2) the analytical performance characteristics of the initial and confirmation testing for the sample matrix of interest, (3) the regulatory requirements and cutoff choices for both initial screening and confirmatory tests, (4) the analyte stability and validity of the testing specimen, (5) potential interference from structurally related compounds, and (6) the goals of drug-testing programs or the relevance to clinical decisions. The understanding of these factors, together with knowledge of the analytical screening and confirmation techniques for drug testing, are imperative for the appropriate interpretation of the drug-testing results.

References

1. National Survey on Drug Use and Health, *NSDUH*. [formerly called the National Household Survey on Drug Abuse, *NHSDA*]. (2003) (http://www.oas.samhsa.gov/nhsda.htm#NHSDAinfo).
2. Martin, B. R. and Hall, W. (1997) The health effects of cannabis: key issues of policy relevance. United Nations Office on Drugs and Crime. (1997) *UNODC Bulletin on Narcotics - 1997 Issue 1 - 005*. (http://www.unodc.org/unodc/fr/bulletin/bulletin_1997-01-01_1_page005.html).

3. United Nations International Drug Control Programme. (1997) Cannabis as an illicit narcotic crop: a review of the global situation of cannabis consumption, trafficking and production. *UNDCP Research Section,* 1997 Issue 1. (http://www.unodc.org/unodc/bulletin/bulletin_1997-01-01_1_page004.html).
4. Rowley, G. L., Armstrong, T. A., Crowl, C. P., et al. (1976) Determination of THC and its metabolites by EMIT homogeneous enzyme immunoassay: a summary report. *NIDA Res. Monogr.* **7,** 28–32.
5. Rodgers, R., Crowl, C. P., Eimstad, W. M., et al. (1978) Homogeneous enzyme immunoassay for cannabinoids in urine. *Clin. Chem.* **24,** 95–100.
6. Abercrombie, M. L. and Jewell, J. S. (1986) Evaluation of EMIT and RIA high volume test procedures for THC metabolites in urine utilizing GC/MS confirmation. *J. Anal. Toxicol.* **10,** 178–180.
7. Jolley, M. E., Stroupe, S. D., Schwenzer, K. S., et al. (1981) Fluorescence polarization immunoassay. iii. an automated system for therapeutic drug determination. *Clin. Chem.* **27,** 1575–1579.
8. Karlsson, L. and Strom, M. (1988) Laboratory evaluation of the TDx assay for detection of cannabinoids in urine from prison inmates. *J. Anal. Toxicol.* **12,** 319–321.
9. Palmer, S. M., Kaufman, R. A., Salamone, S. J., et al. (1995) Cobas Integra: clinical laboratory instrument with continuous and random-access abilities. *Clin. Chem.* **41,** 1751–1760.
10. Smith, J. and Osikowicz, G. (1993) Abbott AxSYM random and continuous access immunoassay system for improved workflow in the clinical laboratory. *Clin. Chem.* **39,** 2063–2069.
11. Ross, R., Horwitz, C. A., Hager, H., Usategui, M., Burke, M. D., and Ward, P. C. (1975) Preliminary evaluation of a latex agglutination-inhibition tube test for morphine. *Clin. Chem.* **21,** 139–143
12. Deom, A. (1984) Evaluation of a new latex agglutination inhibition test, Agglutex, for the demonstration of opiates in urine. *Ann. Biol. Clin. (Paris),* **42,** 317–319.
13. Armbruster, D. A. and Krolak, J. M. (1992) Screening for drugs of abuse with the Roche ONTRAK assays. *J. Anal. Toxicol.* **16**, 172–175.
14. Armbruster, D. A., Schwarzhoff, R. H., Hubster, E. C., and Liserio, M. K. (1993) Enzyme immunoassay, kinetic microparticle immunoassay, radioimmunoassay, and fluorescence polarization immunoassay compared for drugs-of-abuse screening. *Clin. Chem.* **39,** 2137–2146.
15. Armbruster, D. A., Schwarzhoff, R. H., Pierce, B. L., and Hubster, E. C. (1993) Method comparison of EMIT II and ONLINE with RIA for drug screening. *J. Forensic Sci.* **38,** 1326–1341.
16. Engel, W. D. and Khanna, P. L. (1992) CEDIA in vitro diagnostics with a novel homogeneous immunoassay technique. Current status and future prospects. *J. Immunol. Methods* **150,** 99–102.
17. Feldman, M., Kuntz, D., Botelho, K., et al. (2004) Evaluation of Roche Diagnostics ONLINE DAT II, a new generation of assays for the detection of drugs of abuse. *J.Anal.Toxicol.* **28,** 593–598.
18. Armbruster, D. A., Hubster, E. C., Kaufman, M. S., and Ramon, M. K. (1995) Cloned enzyme donor immunoassay (CEDIA) for drugs-of-abuse screening. *Clin. Chem.* **41,** 92–98.
19. Cleeland, R., Christenson J., Usategui-Gomez M., Heveran J., Davis R., and Grunberg E. (1976) Detection of drugs of abuse by radioimmunoassay: a summary of published data and some new information. *Clin. Chem.* **22**, 712–725.
20. Willette, R. E., ed. (1976) Cannabinoid assays in humans. *NIDA Res. Monogr.* 7. NIDA, Rockville, MD.

21. Hawks, R. L., ed. (1982) The analysis of cannabinoids in biological fluids. *NIDA Res. Monogr.* 42. NIDA, Rockville, MD.
22. Baselt, R. C. (1984) Urine drug screening by immunoassay: interpretation of results, in *Advances in Analytical Toxicology*, Vol. 1 (Baselt, R. C., ed.), Biomedical Publications, Foster City, CA, pp. 81–123.
23. Huestis, M. A. and Cone, E. J. (2004) Relationship of delta 9-tetrahydrocannabinol concentrations in oral fluid and plasma after controlled administration of smoked cannabis. *J.Anal.Toxicol.* **28,** 394–399.
24. Tobin, T., Watt, D. S., Kwiatkowski, S., et al. (1988) Non-isotopic immunoassay drug tests in racing horses: a review of their application to pre- and post-race testing, drug quantitation, and human drug testing. *Res. Commun. Chem. Pathol. Pharmacol.* **62,** 371–395.
25. Moore, K. A., Werner, C., Zannelli, R. M., Levine, B., and Smith, M. L. (1999) Screening postmortem blood and tissues for nine classes [correction of cases] of drugs of abuse using automated microplate immunoassay. *Forensic Sci. Int.* **106,** 93–102.
26. Kerrigan, S. and Phillips Jr, W. H. (2001) Comparison of ELISAs for opiates, methamphetamine, cocaine metabolite, benzodiazepines, phencyclidine, and cannabinoids in whole blood and urine. *Clin. Chem.* **47,** 540–547.
27. Niedbala, R. S., Kardos, K. W., Fritch, D. F., et al. (2001) Detection of marijuana use by oral fluid and urine analysis following single-dose administration of smoked and oral marijuana. *J. Anal. Toxicol.* **25,** 289–303.
28. Cone, E. J., Presley, L., Lehrer, M., et al. (2002) Oral fluid testing for drugs of abuse: positive prevalence rates by Intercept immunoassay screening and GC-MS-MS confirmation and suggested cutoff concentrations. *J. Anal. Toxicol.* **26,** 541–546.
29. Niedbala, S., Kardos, K., Salamone, S., Fritch, D., Bronsgeest, M., and Cone, E. J. (2004) Passive cannabis smoke exposure and oral fluid testing. *J.Anal.Toxicol.* **28,** 546–552.
30. Sharma, J. D., Aherne, G. W., and Marks, V. (1989) Enhanced chemiluminescent enzyme immunoassay for cannabinoids in urine. *Analyst* **114,** 1279–1282.
31. Willette, R. E. (1986) Choosing a laboratory. *NIDA Res. Monogra.* **73,** 13–19.
32. Finkle, B. S., Blanke, R. V., and Walsh, J. M., eds. (1990) NIDA Technical, Scientific and Procedural Issues of Employee Drug Testing consensus Report.
33. Transcript On-Site Drug Testing Workgroup Meeting, 1999. (http://workplace.samhsa.gov/ResourceCenter/r382.htm).
34. An Evaluation of Non-Instrumented Drug Test Devices, Substance Abuse and Mental Health Services Administration, Center for Substance Abuse Prevention, Division of Workplace Programs, 1999 (http://workplace.samhsa.gov/ResourceCenter/r409.htm).
35. Department of Transplantation, National Highway Traffic Safety Administration, *NHTSA*. (2000). Field test of on-site drug detection devices, DOT HS 809 192. (http://www.nhtsa.dot.gov/people/injury/research/pub/onsitedetection/Drug_index.htm).
36. Roadside Testing Assessment, *ROSITA*. (1999). Work package 2, Deliverable D2, Inventory of state-of-the-art road side drug testing equipment. (www.rosita.org).
37. Jenkins, A. J. and Goldberger, B. A., eds. (2002) *On-Site Drug Testing*, Humana Press, Totowa, NJ.
38. Buechler, K. F., Moi, S., Noar, B., et al. (1992) Simultaneous detection of seven drugs of abuse by the Triage panel for drugs of abuse. *Clin. Chem.* **38,** 1678–1684.
39. Towt, J., Tsai, S. C. J., Hernandez, M. R., et al. (1995) ONTRAK TESTCUP: a novel, on-site, multi-analyte screen for the detection of abused drugs. *J. Anal. Toxicol.* **19,** 504–510.
40. Wennig, R., Moeller, M. R., Haguenoer, J. M., et al. (1998) Development and evaluation of immunochromatographic rapid tests for screening of cannabinoids, cocaine, and opiates in urine. *J. Anal. Toxicol.* **22,** 148–155.

41. Yang, J. M. and Lewandrowski, K. B. (2001) Urine drugs of abuse testing at the point-of-care: clinical interpretation and programmatic considerations with specific reference to the Syva Rapid Test (SRT). *Clin. Chim. Acta* **307,** 27–32
42. Jehanli, A., Brannan, S., Moore, L., and Spiehler, V. R. (2001) Blind trials of an onsite saliva drug test for marijuana and opiates. *Forensic Sci. Int.* **46,** 1214–1220.
43. Gronholm, M. and Lillsunde, P., (2001) A comparison between on-site immunoassay drug-testing devices and laboratory results. *Forensic Sci. Int.* **121,** 37–46.
44. Peace, M. R., Poklis, J. L., Tarnai, L. D., and Poklis, A. (2002) An evaluation of the OnTrak Testcup-er on-site urine drug-testing device for drugs commonly encountered from emergency departments. *J. Anal. Toxicol.* **26,** 500–503.
45. Walsh, J. M., Flegel, R., Crouch, D. J., Cangianelli, L., and Baudys, J. (2003) An evaluation of rapid point-of-collection oral fluid drug-testing devices. *J. Anal. Toxicol.* **27,** 429–439.
46. Weiss, A. (1999) Concurrent engineering for lateral-flow diagnostics. *IVD Technology* **5,** 48–57.
47. Klimov, A.D., Tsai, S-C. J., Towt, J., and Salamone, S. J. (1995) Improved immunochromatographic format for competitive-type assays. *Clin. Chem.* **41**, 1360.
48. Niedbala, R. S., Feindt, H., Kardos, K., et al. (2001) Detection of analytes by immunoassay using up-converting phosphor technology. *Anal. Biochem.* **293,** 22.
49. Reynolds, L. A. (2001). What you should know about on-site saliva drug and alcohol testing. *Occup. Health Saf.* **70,** 188–190.
50. Tsai, J.S.C., Deng, D., Diebold, E., Smith, A., Wentzel, C. and Franzke, S. (2002) The latest development in biosensor immunoassay technology for drug assays. *LABOLife* **4/02**, 17–20.
51. Emergency Department Trends From DAWN: Final Estimates 1995–2002. http://dawninfo.samhsa.gov/pubs_94_02/edpubs/2002final/The DAWN Report, Major drugs of abuse in ED visits, 2002 update. http://dawninfo.samhsa.gov/pubs_94_02/shortreports/files/DAWN_tdr_MDA.pdf.
52. Quest Diagnostics' Drug Testing Index. http://www.questdiagnostics.com/employersolutions/dti_archives.html.
53. Turner, C. E., Elsohly, M. A., and Boeren, E. G. (1980) Constituents of Cannabis sativa L. XVII. A review of the natural constituents. *J. Nat Prod.* **43**, 169–234.
54. Razdan, R. K. (1987) Structure-activity relationship in cannabinoids: an overview. *NIDA Res. Monogr.* **79**, 3–14.
55. Adams, I. B. and Martin, B. R. (1996) Cannabis: pharmacology and toxicology in animals and humans. *Addiction* **91**, 1585–1614
56. Mechoulam, R. and Hanus, L. (2000) A historical overview of chemical research on cannabinoids. *Chem Phys Lipids* **108**, 1–13.
57. Martin, B. R. (2002) Identification of the endogenous cannabinoid system through integrative pharmacological approaches. *J. Pharmacol Exp Ther.* **301**, 790–796.
58. Martin, B. R. (1986) Cellular effects of cannabinoids. *Pharmacol Rev.* **38**, 45–74.
59. ElSohly, M. A., Ross, S. A., Mehmedic, Z., Arafat, R., Yi, B., and Banahan, B. F., 3rd (2000) Potency trends of delta9-THC and other cannabinoids in confiscated marijuana from 1980-1997. *J. Forensic Sci.* **45**, 24–30.
60. Ross, S. A., Mehmedic, Z., Murphy, T. P., and Elsohly, M. A. (2000) GC-MS analysis of the total delta^9-THC content of both drug- and fiber-type cannabis seeds. *J. Anal. Toxicol.* **24**, 715–717.
61. Perez-Reyes, M., Di Guiseppi, S., Davis, K. H., Schindler, V. H., and Cook, C. E. (1982) Comparison of effects of marihuana cigarettes to three different potencies. *Clin. Pharmacol Ther.* **31**, 617–624
62. Chiang, C. N. and Rapaka, R. S. (1987) Pharmacokinetics and disposition of cannabinoids. *NIDA Res. Monogr.* **79,** 173–188.

63. Perez-Reyes, M. (1990) Marijuana smoking: factors that influence the bioavailability of tetrahydrocannabinol. *NIDA Res. Monogr.* **99,** 42–62.
64. Huestis, M. A., Henningfield, J. E., and Cone, E. J. (1992) Blood cannabinoids. I. Absorption of THC and formation of 11-OH-THC and THCCOOH during and after smoking marijuana. *J. Anal. Toxicol.* **16,** 276–282.
65. Huestis, M. A., Henningfield, J. E., and Cone, E. J. (1992) Blood cannabinoids. II. Models for the prediction of time of marijuana exposure from plasma concentrations of delta 9-tetrahydrocannabinol (THC) and 11-nor-9-carboxy-delta 9-tetrahydrocannabinol (THCCOOH). *J. Anal. Toxicol.* **16,** 283–290
66. Cone, E. J., and Huestis, M. A. (1993) Relating blood concentrations of tetrahydrocannabinol and metabolites to pharmacologic effects and time of marijuana usage. *Ther. Drug Monit.* **15,** 527–532.
67. Huestis, M. A., Mitchell, J. M., and Cone, E. J. (1996) Urinary excretion profiles of 11-nor-9-carboxy-delta 9-tetrahydrocannabinol in humans after single smoked doses of marijuana. *J. Anal. Toxicol.* **20**, 441–452.
68. Huestis, M. A. and Cone, E. J. (1998). Urinary excretion half-life of 11-nor-9-carboxy-delta9-tetrahydrocannabinol in humans. *Ther. Drug Monit.* **20,** 570–576.
69. Manno, J. E., Manno, B. R., Kemp, P. M., et al. (2001) Temporal indication of marijuana use can be estimated from plasma and urine concentrations of delta9-tetrahydrocannabinol, 11-hydroxy-delta9-tetrahydrocannabinol, and 11-nor-delta9-tetrahydrocannabinol-9-carboxylic acid. *J. Anal. Toxicol.* **25,** 538–549.
70. Gustafson, R. A., Kim, I., Stout, P. R., et al. (2004) Urinary pharmacokinetics of 11-nor-9-carboxy-delta9-tetrahydrocannabinol after controlled oral delta9-tetrahydrocannabinol administration. *J. Anal. Toxicol.* **28,** 160–167.
71. Smith-Kielland, A., Skuterud, B., and Morland, J. (1999) Urinary excretion of 11-nor-9-carboxy-delta9-tetrahydrocannabinol and cannabinoids in frequent and infrequent drug users. *J. Anal. Toxicol.* **23,** 323–332
72. ElSohly, M. A. (2003) Practical challenges to positive drug tests for marijuana. *Clin. Chem.* **49,** 1037–1038.
73. Harvey, D. J. and Brown, N. K. (1991) Comparative in vitro metabolism of the cannabinoids. *Pharmacol Biochem Behav.* **40,** 533–540.
74. Yamamoto, I., Watanabe, K., Narimatsu, S., and Yoshimura, H. (1995) Recent advances in the metabolism of cannabinoids. *Int J. Biochem Cell Biol.* **27,** 741–746.
75. Matsunaga, T., Tanaka, H., Higuchi, S., et al. (2001) Oxidation mechanism of 7-hydroxy-delta 8-tetrahydrocannabinol and 8-hydroxy-delta 9-tetrahydrocannabinol to the corresponding ketones by CYP3A11. *Drug Metab Dispos.* **29,** 1485–1491.
76. Watanabe, K., Matsunaga, T., Yamamoto, I., Funae, Y., and Yoshimura, H. (1995) Involvement of CYP2C in the metabolism of cannabinoids by human hepatic microsomes from an old woman. *Biol Pharm Bull.* **18,** 1138–1141.
77. Watanabe, K., Narimatsu, S., Yamamoto, I., and Yoshimura, H. (1991) Oxygenation mechanism in conversion of aldehyde to carboxylic acid catalyzed by a cytochrome P-450 isozyme. *J. Biol Chem.* **266,** 2709–2711.
78. Alburges, M. E. and Peat, M. A. (1986) Profiles of delta 9-tetrahydrocannabinol metabolites in urine of marijuana users: preliminary observations by high performance liquid chromatography-radioimmunoassay. *J. Forensic Sci.* **31,** 695–706.
79. ElSohly, M. A. and Feng, S. (1998) Delta 9-THC metabolites in meconium: identification of 11-OH-delta 9-THC, 8 beta,11-diOH-delta 9-THC, and 11-nor-delta 9-THC-9-COOH as major metabolites of delta 9-THC. *J. Anal. Toxicol.* **22,** 329–335.
80. Feng, S., ElSohly, M. A., Salamone, S., and Salem, M. Y. (2000) Simultaneous analysis of delta9-THC and its major metabolites in urine, plasma, and meconium by GC-MS using an immunoaffinity extraction procedure. *J. Anal. Toxicol.* **24,** 395–402.

81. Gustafson, R. A., Moolchan, E. T., Barnes, A., Levine, B., and Huestis, M. A. (2003) Validated method for the simultaneous determination of Delta 9-tetrahydrocannabinol (THC), 11-hydroxy-THC and 11-nor-9-carboxy-THC in human plasma using solid phase extraction and gas chromatography-mass spectrometry with positive chemical ionization. *J. Chromatogr B Analyt Technol Biomed Life Sci.* **798,** 145–154.
82. Kemp, P. M., Abukhalaf, I. K., Manno, J. E., Manno, B. R., Alford, D. D., and Abusada, G. A. (1995) Cannabinoids in humans. I. Analysis of delta 9-tetrahydrocannabinol and six metabolites in plasma and urine using GC-MS. *J. Anal. Toxicol.* **19,** 285–291.
83. Kemp, P. M., Abukhalaf, I. K., Manno, J. E., et al. (1995) Cannabinoids in humans. II. The influence of three methods of hydrolysis on the concentration of THC and two metabolites in urine. *J. Anal. Toxicol.* **19,** 292–298.
84. Skopp, G., Potsch, L., Mauden, M., and Richter, B. (2002) Partition coefficient, blood to plasma ratio, protein binding and short-term stability of 11-nor-delta(9)-carboxy tetrahydrocannabinol glucuronide. *Forensic Sci. Int.* **126,** 17–23.
85. Skopp, G. and Potsch, L. (2004) An investigation of the stability of free and glucuronidated 11-nor-delta9-tetrahydrocannabinol-9-carboxylic acid in authentic urine samples. *J. Anal. Toxicol.* **28,** 35–40
86. Weinmann, W., Vogt, S., Goerke, R., Muller, C., and Bromberger, A. (2000) Simultaneous determination of THC-COOH and THC-COOH-glucuronide in urine samples by LC/MS/MS. *Forensic Sci. Int.* **113,** 381–387.
87. Salamone, S. J., Bender, E., Hui, R. A., and Rosen, S. (1998) A non-cannabinoid immunogen used to elicit antibodies with broad cross-reactivity to cannabinoid metabolites. *J. Forensic Sci.* **43,** 821–826.
88. Patent families for cannabinoids immunoassays (Abbott Laboratories). Representative US patents for each of the patent families include: US 5,144,030 (1992); US 5,264,373 (1993); US 5,463,027 (1995).
89. Patent families for cannabinoids immunoassays (Hoffman La Roche / Roche Diagnostics). Representative US patents for each of the patent families include: US 4,438,207 (1984); US 4,833,073 (1989); US 5,219,747 (1993); US 5,315,015 (1994); US 5,817766 (1998).
90. Mandatory guidelines for federal workplace drug testing programs (1994) *Fed. Reg.* **59,** 29908 (http://www.health.org/workplace/GDLNS-94.htm) or (http://workplace.samhsa.gov/fedprograms/MandatoryGuidelines/HHS09011994.pdf).
91. Proposed Revisions to Mandatory Guidelines for Federal Workplace Drug Testing Programs (2004) *Fed. Reg.* **69**, 19673–19732.(http://a257.g.akamaitech.net/7/257/2422/14mar20010800/edocket.access.gpo.gov/2004/pdf/04-7984.pdf).
92. Revised Mandatory Guidelines for Federal Workplace Drug Testing Programs, Specimen Validity Testing (2004) *Fed. Reg.* **69**, 19644–19673.http://a257.g.akamaitech.net/7/257/2422/14mar20010800/edocket.access.gpo.gov/2004/pdf/04-7985.pdf.
93. Badia, R., Segura, J., Artola, A., and de la Torre, R. (1998) Survey on drugs-of-abuse testing in the European Union. *J. Anal. Toxicol.* **22,** 117–126.
94. Corcione, S., Pichini, S., Badia, R., Segura, J., and de la Torre, R. (1999) Quantitative aspects of drugs of abuse in urine samples: intercollaborative studies conducted in the European Union. *Ther. Drug Monit.* **21,** 653–660.
95. Wilson, J. F. and Smith, B. L. (1999) Evaluation of detection techniques and laboratory proficiency in testing for drugs of abuse in urine: an external quality assessment scheme using clinically realistic urine samples. Steering Committee for the United Kingdom National External Quality Assessment Scheme for Drugs of Abuse in Urine. *Ann Clin. Biochem.* **36**, 592–600.
96. AGSA Swiss Working Group for Drugs of Abuse Testing Guidelines. (2003)(http://www.consilia-sa.ch/agsa/E/AGSA%20Guidelines_E_rev3.pdf).

97. Verstraete, A. G. and Pierce, A. (2001) Workplace drug testing in Europe. *Forensic Sci. Int.* **121,** 2–6.
98. EWDTS (European Workplace Drug Testing Society) Laboratory Guidelines. (2002) http://www.ewdts.org/guidelines.html.
99. Ferrara, S. D., Tedeschi, L., Frison, G., et al. (1994) Drugs-of-abuse testing in urine: statistical approach and experimental comparison of immunochemical and chromatographic techniques. *J. Anal. Toxicol.* **18,** 278–291.
100. Rowland, B. J., Irving, J., and Keith, E. S. (1994) Increased detection of marijuana use with a 50 micrograms/L urine screening cutoff. *Clin. Chem.* **40,** 2114–2115.
101. Huestis, M. A., Mitchell, J. M., and Cone, E. J. (1994) Lowering the federally mandated cannabinoid immunoassay cutoff increases true-positive results. *Clin. Chem.* **40,** 729–733.
102. Wingert, W. E. (1997) Lowering cutoffs for initial and confirmation testing for cocaine and marijuana: large-scale study of effects on the rates of drug-positive results. *Clin. Chem.* **43,** 100–103.
103. Weaver, M. L., Gan, B. K., Allen, E., et al. (1991) Correlations on radioimmunoassay, fluorescence polarization immunoassay, and enzyme immunoassay of cannabis metabolites with gas chromatography/mass spectrometry analysis of 11-nor-delta 9-tetrahydrocannabinol-9-carboxylic acid in urine specimens. *Forensic Sci. Int.* **49,** 43–56.
104. Liu, R. H., Edwards, C., Baugh, L. D., Weng, J. L., Fyfe, M. J., and Walia, A. S. (1994) Selection of an appropriate initial test cutoff concentration for workplace drug urinalysis—Cannabis example. *J. Anal. Toxicol.* **18,** 65–70.
105. Brendler, J. and Liu, R. H. (1997) Initial test cutoff selection based on regression analysis of initial test apparent analyte result vs GC/MS test analyte result—evaluation of two radioimmunoassay kits' test data. *Clin. Chem.* **43,** 688–690.
106. Cone, E. J, Johnson, R. E., Darwin, W. D., et al. (1987) Passive inhalation of marijuana smoke: urinalysis and room air levels of delta-9-tetrahydrocannabinol. *J. Anal. Toxicol.* **11,** 89–96.
107. Cone, E. J. (1990) Marijuana effects and urinalysis after passive inhalation and oral ingestion. *NIDA Res. Monogr.* **99,** 88–96.
108. ElSohly, M. A. and Jones, A. B. (1995) Drug testing in the workplace: could a positive test for one of the mandated drugs be for reasons other than illicit use of the drug? *J. Anal. Toxicol.* **19,** 450–458.
109. Lyons, T. P., Okano, C. K., Kuhnle, J. A., et al. (2001) A comparison of Roche Kinetic Interaction of Microparticles in Solution (KIMS) assay for cannabinoids and GC-MS analysis for 11-nor-9-carboxy-delta9-tetrahydrocannabinol. *J. Anal. Toxicol.* **25,** 559–564.
110. Gustafson, R. A., Levine, B., Stout, P. R., et al. (2003) Urinary cannabinoid detection times after controlled oral administration of delta9-tetrahydrocannabinol to humans. *Clin. Chem.* **49,** 1114–1124
111. Luzzi, V. I., Saunders, A. N., Koenig, J. W., et al. (2004) Analytic performance of immunoassays for drugs of abuse below established cutoff values. *Clin. Chem.* **50,** 717–722.
112. Hattab, E. M., Goldberger, B. A., Johannsen, L. M., et al. (2000) Modification of screening immunoassays to detect sub-threshold concentrations of cocaine, cannabinoids, and opiates in urine: use for detecting maternal and neonatal drug exposure. *Ann. Clin. Lab. Sci.* **30,** 85–91
113. Kintz, P., Cirimele, V., and Ludes, B. (2000) Detection of cannabis in oral fluid (saliva) and forehead wipes (sweat) from impaired drivers. *J. Anal. Toxicol.* **24,** 557–561.
114. Samyn, N., De Boeck, G., and Verstraete, A. G. (2002) The use of oral fluid and sweat wipes for the detection of drugs of abuse in drivers. *Forensic Sci. Int.* **47,** 1380–1387.
115. Moore, C. and Lewis, D. (2003) Comment on oral fluid testing for drugs of abuse: positive prevalence rates by Intercept immunoassay screening and GC-MS-MS confirmation

and suggested cutoff concentrations. *J. Anal. Toxicol.* 27, 169 (author reply, *J. Anal. Toxicol.* **27,** 170–172).
116. Spiehler, V. (2004) Comment on "An evaluation of rapid point-of-collection oral fluid drug-testing devices." *J. Anal. Toxicol.* 28, 75–76 (author reply, *J. Anal. Toxicol.* **28,** 76).
117. Sachs, H. (1997) Quality control by the Society of Hair Testing. *Forensic Sci. Int.* **84,** 145–150.
118. Jurado, C. and Sachs, H. (2003) Proficiency test for the analysis of hair for drugs of abuse, organized by the Society of Hair Testing. *Forensic Sci. Int.* **133,** 175–178.
119. Thorspecken, J., Skopp, G., and Potsch, L. (2004) In vitro contamination of hair by marijuana smoke. *Clin. Chem.* **50,** 596–602.
120. Wolff, K., Farrell, M., Marsden, J., et al. (1999) A review of biological indicators of illicit drug use, practical considerations and clinical usefulness. *Addiction* **94,** 1279–1298.
121. Cone, E. J. (2001) Legal, workplace, and treatment drug testing with alternative biological matrices on a global scale. *Forensic Sci. Int.* **121,** 7–15.
122. lan, Y. H. and Goldberger, B. A. (2001) Alternative specimens for workplace drug testing. *J. Anal. Toxicol.* **25,** 396–399
123. Armbruster, D. A., Tillman, M. D., and Hubbs, L. M. (1994) Limit of detection (LQD)/ limit of quantitation (LOQ): comparison of the empirical and the statistical methods exemplified with GC-MS assays of abused drugs. *Clin. Chem.* **40,** 1233–1238.
124. Goldberger, B. A. and Cone, E. J. (1994) Confirmatory tests for drugs in the workplace by gas chromatography-mass spectrometry. *J. Chromatogr. A* **674,** 73–86.
125. Wu, A. H. (1995) Mechanism of interferences for gas chromatography/mass spectrometry analysis of urine for drugs of abuse. *Ann Clin. Lab Sci.* **25,** 319–329.
126. Underwood, P. J., Kananen, G. E., and Armitage, E. K. (1997) A practical approach to determination of laboratory GC-MS limits of detection. *J. Anal. Toxicol.* **21,** 12–16.
127. Lehrer, M. (1998) The role of gas chromatography/mass spectrometry. Instrumental techniques in forensic urine drug testing. *Clin. Lab Med.* **184,** 631–649.
128. Haver, V. M., Romson, J. L., and Sadrzadeh, S. M. (1991) Semiquantitation of cannabinoid immunoassays? A reexamination of the EMIT 20-ng/mL assay. *J. Anal. Toxicol.* **15,** 98–100.
129. Blanc, J. A., Manneh, V. A., Ernst, R., et al. (1993) Adsorption losses from urine-based cannabinoid calibrators during routine use. *Clin. Chem.* **39,** 1705–1712.
130. Paul, B. D., McKinley, R. M., Walsh, J. K. Jr, Jamir, T. S., and Past, M. R. (1993) Effect of freezing on the concentration of drugs of abuse in urine. *J. Anal. Toxicol.* **17,** 378–380.
131. Romberg, R. W. and Past, M. R. (1994) Reanalysis of forensic urine specimens containing benzoylecgonine and THC-COOH. *J. Forensic Sci.* **39,** 479–485.
132. Dugan, S., Bogema, S., Schwartz, R. W., and Lappas, N. T. (1994) Stability of drugs of abuse in urine samples stored at -20 degrees C. *J. Anal. Toxicol.* **18,** 391–396.
133. Roth, K. D., Siegel, N. A., Johnson, R. W., Jr., et al. (1996) Investigation of the effects of solution composition and container material type on the loss of 11-nor-delta 9-THC-9-carboxylic acid. *J. Anal. Toxicol.* **20,** 291–300.
134. Moody, D. E., Monti, K. M., and Spanbauer, A. C. (1999) Long-term stability of abused drugs and antiabuse chemotherapeutical agents stored at -20 degrees C. *J. Anal. Toxicol.* **23,** 535–540.
135. Skopp, G., Potsch, L., and Mauden, M. (2000) Stability of cannabinoids in hair samples exposed to sunlight. *Clin. Chem.* **46,** 1846–1848.
136. Cone, E. J., Johnson, R. E., Paul, B. D., Mell, L. D., and Mitchell, J. (1988) Marijuana-laced brownies: behavior effects, physiologic effects, and urinalysis in humans following ingestion. *J. Anal. Toxicol.* **12,** 169–175.
137. Costantino, A., Schwartz, R. H., and Kaplan, P. (1997) Hemp oil ingestion causes positive urine tests for delta 9-tetrahydrocannabinol carboxylic acid. *J. Anal. Toxicol.* **21,** 482–485.

138. Struempler, R. E., Nelson, G., and Urry, F. M. (1997) A positive cannabinoids workplace drug test following the ingestion of commercially available hemp seed oil. *J. Anal. Toxicol.* **21,** 283–285.
139. Lehmann, T., Sager, F., and Brenneisen, R. (1997) Excretion of cannabinoids in urine after ingestion of cannabis seed oil. *J. Anal. Toxicol.* **21,** 373–375.
140. Fortner, N., Fogerson, R., Lindman, D., Iversen, T., and Armbruster, D. (1997) A marijuana-positive urine test results from consumption of hemp seeds in food products. *J. Anal. Toxicol.* **21,** 476–481.
141. Bosy, T. Z. and Cole, K. A. (2000) Consumption and quantitation of delta9-tetrahydrocannabinol in commercially available hemp seed oil products. *J. Anal. Toxicol.* **24,** 562–566.
142. Leson, G., Pless, P., Grotenhermen, F., Kalant, H., and ElSohly, M. A. (2001) Evaluating the impact of hemp food consumption on workplace drug tests. *J. Anal. Toxicol.* **25,** 691–698.
143. ElSohly, M. A., deWit, H., Wachtel, S. R., Feng, S., and Murphy, T. P. (2001) Delta9-tetrahydrocannabivarin as a marker for the ingestion of marijuana versus Marinol: results of a clinical study. *J. Anal. Toxicol.* **25,** 565–571.
144. ElSohly, M. A., Feng, S., Murphy, T. P., et al. (2001) Identification and quantitation of 11-nor-delta9-tetrahydrocannabivarin-9-carboxylic acid, a major metabolite of delta9-tetrahydrocannabivarin. *J. Anal. Toxicol.* **25,** 476–480.
145. Interpretation and clarification of listing of "tetrahydrocannabinols" in Schedule I; exemption from control of certain industrial products and materials derived from the Cannabis plant; final rules and proposed rulInterpretive rule (2001) *Fed. Reg.* **66,** 51529–51544.
146. Huestis, M. A. and Cone, E. J. (1998) Differentiating new marijuana use from residual drug excretion in occasional marijuana users. *J. Anal. Toxicol.* **22,** 445–454.
147. Lafolie, P., Beck, O., Blennow, G., et al. (1991) Importance of creatinine analyses of urine when screening for abused drugs. *Clin. Chem.* **37,** 1927–1931.
148. Fraser, A. D. and Worth, D. (1999) Urinary excretion profiles of 11-nor-9-carboxy-delta9-tetrahydrocannabinol: a delta9-THCCOOH to creatinine ratio study. *J. Anal. Toxicol.* **23,** 531–534
149. Fraser, A. D. and Worth, D. (2002) Monitoring urinary excretion of cannabinoids by fluorescence-polarization immunoassay: a cannabinoid-to-creatinine ratio study. *Ther Drug Monit.* **24,** 746–750.
150. Fraser, A. D. and Worth, D. (2003) Urinary excretion profiles of 11-nor-9-carboxy-delta9-tetrahydrocannabinol: a delta9-THC-COOH to creatinine ratio study #2. *Forensic Sci. Int.* **133,** 26–31.
151. Fraser, A. D. and Zamecnik, J. (2003) Impact of lowering the screening and confirmation cutoff values for urine drug testing based on dilution factors. *Ther. Drug Monit.* **25,** 723–727.
152. Cone, E. J., Lange, R., and Darwin, W. D. (1998) In vivo adulteration: excess fluid ingestion causes false-negative marijuana and cocaine urine test results. *J. Anal. Toxicol.* **22,** 460–473.
153. Coleman, D. E. and Baselt, R. C. (1997) Efficacy of two commercial products for altering urine drug test results. *J. Toxicol. Clin. Toxicol.* **35,** 637–642.
154. Cook, J. D., lan, Y. H., LoDico, C. P., and Bush, D. M. (2000). The characterization of human urine for specimen validity determination in workplace drug testing: a review. *J. Anal. Toxicol.* **24,** 579–588.
155. Edgell, K., lan, Y. H., Glass, L. R., and Cook, J. D. (2002) The defined HHS/DOT substituted urine criteria validated through a controlled hydration study. *J. Anal. Toxicol.* **26,** 419–423.

156. Wong, R. (2002) The effect of adulterants on urine screen for drugs of abuse: detection by an on-site dipstick device. *Am. Clin. Lab.* **21,** 37–39.
157. Pearson, S. D., Ash, K. O, and Urry, F. M. (1989) Mechanism of false-negative urine cannabinoid immunoassay screens by Visine eyedrops. *Clin. Chem.* **35,** 636–638.
158. Tsai, J. S., ElSohly, M. A., Tsai, S. F., Murphy, T. P., Twarowska, B., and Salamone, S. J. (2000) Investigation of nitrite adulteration on the immunoassay and GC-MS analysis of cannabinoids in urine specimens. *J. Anal. Toxicol.* **24,** 708–714.
159. Cody, J. T. and Valtier, S. (2001) Effects of stealth adulterant on immunoassay testing for drugs of abuse. *J. Anal. Toxicol.* **25,** 466–470.
160. Paul, B. D. and Jacobs, A. (2004) Effects of oxidizing adulterants on detection of 11-nor-delta9-THC-9-carboxylic acid in urine. *J. Anal. Toxicol.* **26**, 460–463.

Chapter 8

Mass Spectrometric Methods for Determination of Cannabinoids in Physiological Specimens

Rodger L. Foltz

1. Introduction

This chapter describes the published mass spectrometric (MS) methods that have proven most effective for quantitative measurement of Δ^9-tetrahydrocannabinol (THC) and its major metabolites in physiological specimens. Because determination of 11-nor-9-carboxy- Δ^9-tetrahydrocannabinol (THCA) in urine continues to be the most frequently used indicator of marijuana use, the first portion of the chapter will discuss methods for measurement of THCA in urine. However, the major portion of the chapter is devoted to the most recent developments for measuring THC and its metabolites in other biological specimens including blood, plasma, meconium, oral fluids, hair, and other tissues. Tables 1–7 are designed to facilitate location of references describing analytical methods involving key components for analysis of cannabinoids in various matrices.

Analysis of THC and its metabolites in biological specimens has been reviewed by Lindgren *(1)*, Foltz *(2)*, Bronner and Xu *(3)*, Goldberger and Cone *(4)*, Cody and Foltz *(5)*, and Staub *(6)*.

The selection of internal standards is an important factor in the development of quantitative assays involving MS. Because of the demand for effective internal standards for MS analysis of THC and its major metabolites, a variety of deuterium-labeled analogs have become commercially available. THC-d_3, THCA-d_3, and trideuterated 11-hydroxy-Δ^9-tetrahydrocannabinol (HO-THC-d_3) have often been used as internal

From: *Forensic Science and Medicine: Marijuana and the Cannabinoids*
Edited by: M. A. ElSohly © Humana Press Inc., Totowa, New Jersey

standards. However, cannabinoid analogs with more than three deuteriums (THC-d_6, THC-d_9, THCA-d_6, THCA-d_9, THCA-d_{10}, and HO-THC-d_6) are reported to be even more effective as internal standards *(7–10)*.

2. Determination of THCA in Urine

THCA is primarily excreted in urine as the ester-linked glucuronide conjugate. Consequently, the urine is most often subjected to mild alkaline hydrolysis to release the THCA *(11,12)*. Enzymatic hydrolysis using β-glucuronidase can also free the THCA from the conjugate, but the procedure takes considerably longer than alkaline hydrolysis *(13,14)*. After hydrolysis the urine is acidified and extracted by either liquid/liquid or solid-phase extraction (SPE). A solvent mixture of hexane and ethyl acetate, typically 7:1 (v/v), has been used most often for extraction of free THCA in urine *(11)*. A wide variety of solid-phase systems are also available for extraction of THCA in urine *(10,15–24)*, and two research groups have selectively extracted THCA from urine by means of immobilized antibodies *(8,25)*.

THCA has two polar functional groups that must be derivatized prior to gas chromatography (GC)/MS analysis. The carboxyl group and the phenolic group can both be derivatized by trimethylsilylation or by methylation. Trimethylsilylation is most often performed by adding *bis*-(trimethylsilyl)-trifluoroacetamide (BSTFA) with 1% trimethylchlorosilane (TMCS) to the dried extract and heating at approx 70°C for 20 minutes, followed by direct injection into the GC/MS system *(17,18)*. Methylation is generally performed by addition of methyl iodide in the presence of tetramethylammonium hydroxide (TMAH) in dimethyl sulfoxide *(16,26)*. Some investigators have used propyl iodide when interference problems were encountered after derivatizing with methyl iodide *(27)*; others have used a perfluorinated anhydride and a perfluorinated alcohol *(10,24,28,29)*. The latter protocol can provide increased sensitivity, particularly when the derivatives are detected by negative ion chemical ionization mass spectrometry (GC/NCI-MS; ref. *28*). However, it is important to remove the perfluorinated anhydride reagent by evaporation prior to reconstitution and injection into the GC/MS because the anhydride tends to degrade the chromatographic column.

Szirmai and co-workers compared five different methods for derivatization of THCA and two other acidic metabolites of THC in urine *(9)*. Two of the methods involved esterification of the carboxylic acid group with diazomethane followed by trimethylsilyation or trifluoroacetylation of the phenolic group; the other three methods employed (1) BSTFA alone, (2) methyl iodide-TMAH, or (3) pentafluoropropionic anhydride (PFPA) and trifluoroethanol.

Nearly all GC/MS assays for determination of THCA in urine employ fused silica capillary columns with methyl silicone or 5% phenylmethylsilicone stationary phases. Electron ionization (EI) continues to be the dominant method for ionizing derivatized THCA. With EI-MS, each of the reported THCA derivatives yields at least three ions with high relative intensities, an important benefit in forensic analyses.

The first published liquid chromatography (LC)/MS assay for determination of THCA in urine employed positive ion electrospray ionization (ESI; ref. *30*). Under selected ion monitoring the protonated molecule ion $(M + H)^+$ at m/z 345 was dominant and could be detected down to 2.5 ng/mL. Up-front collision-induced dissociation generated qualifying ions at *m/z* 327 and 299, but their ion intensities were relatively low and thereby increased the lower limit of detection to 15 ng/mL. Significantly better sensitivity has been achieved by monitoring the $(M - H)^-$ ions for THCA (*m/z* 343) and THCA-d_3 (*m/z* 346) formed by ESI *(23)*.

Weinmann and co-investigators *(21)* developed a very rapid LC/MS/MS assay for THCA in urine using negative ion atmospheric pressure chemical ionization (APCI) in combination with selected-reaction monitoring. When subjected to collision-induced dissociation, the $(M - H)^-$ ion at *m/z* 343 fragmented to abundant ions at *m/z* 325, 299, and 245. The runtime took 6 minutes, and the lower limit of quantitation was 5 ng/mL. Investigators in the same laboratory reported using positive-ion turboionspray to determine THCA and THCA glucuronide in urine by LC/MS/MS *(31)*.

Skopp and Potsch used LC/MS/MS to study the stability of THCA and THCA-glucuronide in urine and plasma stored at temperatures of –20, 4, 20, and 40°C *(32)*. The analytes and their deuterated internal standards were ionized by turboionspray, and the protonated molecule ions collisionally dissociated to abundant product ions.

Unfortunately, THCA and other cannabinoids are not as efficiently ionized by either ESI or APCI as most other drugs. Nevertheless, the advantage of not having to derivatize an analyte prior to analysis is an inducement to utilize LC/MS rather than GC/MS.

Potential problems that can occur in determination of THCA in urine include interferences *(27,33)*, adsorptive losses during storage and extraction *(12,29,34–36)*, and degradation of THCA as a result of adulteration of a urine sample *(37)*.

3. Determination of Other Cannabinoids in Urine

Although detection of THCA in urine continues to be the primary method for identifying recent use of marijuana, Manno and Manno and their co-investigators have shown that THC and other metabolites of THC are also excreted in urine as glucuronide conjugates that are not, however, as easily hydrolyzed as THCA glucuronide *(38,39)*. THC and its hydroxylated metabolites are excreted in urine primarily as ether-linked glucuronide conjugates that do not undergo hydrolysis under alkaline conditions. Enzymatic hydrolysis using β-glucuronidase from *Escherichia coli* at a pH of 6.8 is highly effective in cleaving ether-linked glucuronide conjugates. Manno et al. have used this method for quantitative analysis of cannabidiol, cannabinol, THC, and six THC metabolites in plasma and urine. After enzymatic hydrolysis, they extracted the cannabinoids with hexane:ethyl acetate (7:1), derivatized them with BSTFA, and analyzed the products by electron ionization GC/MS. Analysis of urine samples by this method proved useful for estimating the time of marijuana use *(14)*.

GC/MS analysis for 11-nor-Δ^9-tetrahydrocannabivarin-9-carboxylic acid (THCVA) has been used to determine whether the presence of THCA in a subject's urine indicates the use of marijuana or is solely the result of the use of the prescription drug Marinol® (synthetic THC; ref. *40*). Δ^9-Tetrahydrocannabivarin, a homolog of THC, is present in most marijuana and is metabolized in the body to THCVA *(41)*. Because THCVA is a homolog of THCA, the two compounds behave very similarly during extraction and derivatization but have different retention times and form abundant ions that differ by 28 amu *(40)*.

4. Determination of Cannabinoids in Blood or Plasma

Cannabinoid concentrations in urine are not very useful for determining impairment or recent use of marijuana. Therefore, in forensic cases it is important to measure cannabinoid concentrations in blood or plasma, particularly the concentrations of THC and HO-THC, the two psychoactive cannabinoids. However, analysis of cannabinoids in blood or plasma is complicated by the difficulty of separating the cannabinoids from the abundance of endogenous lipophilic and proteinaceous compounds in blood that are not generally present in urine. Furthermore, concentrations of THC and HO-THC in blood decrease rapidly after smoking marijuana or after oral ingestion of cannabinoids.

Most published methods for determination of cannabinoids in blood or plasma have not included enzymatic hydrolysis of glucuronide conjugates. However, recent studies have shown that significant but variable proportions of THC, HO-THC, and THCA are present in plasma as glucuronide conjugates *(42)*. Hydrolysis of the glucuronide conjugates is most effectively achieved using β-glucuronidase from *E. coli* *(14,42)*.

Liquid/liquid extractions have been used to separate cannabinoids from blood or plasma *(38,43–45)*. When Chu and Drummer evaluated eight different buffers and ten different solvents for extracting THC from whole blood, they obtained the best results by adding 1 mL of 1 *M* ammonium sulfate to 1 mL of blood and extraction with 7 mL of hexane *(45)*. However, because SPE is capable of achieving better selectivity, it is now more widely used for extraction of cannabinoids from blood and plasma.

D'Asaro evaluated an automated SPE system (Zymark RapidTrace™) for determining THC and THCA in whole blood *(46)*. THC-d_3 and THCA-d_3 were added to 1 mL of warm blood followed by addition of 3 mL of acetonitrile containing 10% acetone. After vortexing and centrifugation the supernatant was separated and concentrated by evaporation, then acidified with 0.1 *M* HCl and subjected to SPE. Various SPE cartridges were evaluated; the C-8 anion exchange copolymer sorbent provided the best overall recoveries and the cleanest extracts. THC and THCA were eluted at the same time and then derivatized with BSTFA and analyzed by GC/MS with electron ionization and selected-ion monitoring. The lower limits of quantitation (LOQs) were 2.0 ng/mL for THC and 1.0 ng/mL for THCA.

The combination of a liquid/liquid extraction followed by a SPE was employed by Felgate and Dinan for analysis of THC and THCA in whole blood *(47)*. After addition of deuterated internal standards to 0.5 mL of blood diluted with 1.0 mL of water and 1 mL of 1.0 phosphate buffer (pH 4.0), the diluted blood was extracted with hexane/ethyl acetate (5:1). The extract was evaporated to dryness, reconstituted with hexane, and further cleaned up by SPE using Varian Bond Elut THC cartridges. THC was eluted with hexane containing 50% toluene, and the THCA was eluted separately with hexane containing 40% ethyl acetate. The THC and THCA extracts were analyzed separately after each was derivatized with pentafluoropropanol and pentafluoropropionic anhydride. If the derivatized THC and THCA extracts were combined, sensitivity was reduced due to interferences. The GC/MS analysis, with electron ionization and selected-ion monitoring, achieved an LOQ of 1 ng/mL for each analyte.

A fully validated GC/MS assay for determination of THC, HO-THC, and THCA in serum was recently reported by Steinmeyer et al. *(48)*. Deuterated internal standards for each analyte were added to 1 mL of serum along with 0.2 mL ethanol and 2 mL 0.1 *M* phosphate buffer (pH 9.0). Samples were extracted on C18 bonded-phase adsorption cartridges. The analytes were eluted from the cartridges with acetone/methanol (1:1), and the extracts were evaporated to dryness and derivatized with tetrabutylammonium hydroxide, dimethylsulfoxide, and iodomethane. The derivatized extracts were acidified with 0.1 *M* HCl, extracted into isooctane, and analyzed by EI-GC/MS in the selected-ion monitoring mode. The LOQs in ng/mL were 0.62 (THC), 0.68 (HO-THC), and 3.35 (THCA). The method was cross-validated for analysis of liver microsomal preparations.

A method for measurement of THC and THCA in plasma was developed at the Center for Human Toxicology, University of Utah, to analyze specimens from clinical studies *(49)*. After addition of deuterated internal standards to 1 mL of plasma, 1 mL of acetonitrile was added and the samples were vortexed and centrifuged. The supernatant was separated and combined with 4 mL of 0.1 *M* acetate buffer (pH 7.0) and poured onto a conditioned CleanScreen ZSTHC020 SPE column. The column was then washed with 0.1 *M* acetate buffer and dried under vacuum. THC was eluted with hexane/ethyl acetate/ammonia hydroxide (93:5:2), and the THCA was eluted separately with hexane/ethyl acetate (70:30). The eluants containing THC and THCA were combined, evaporated to dryness, and derivatized with hexafluoroisopropanol (HFIP) and trifluoroacetic anhydride (TFAA). GC/MS analysis with negative ion chemical ionization gave abundant molecular anions for the derivatized THC (*m/z* 410) and abundant fragment ions (*m/z* 422) formed by loss of $(CF_3)_2CHOH$ from the molecular anion of derivatized THCA. LOQs were 0.5 ng/mL (THC) and 2.5 ng/mL (THCA).

Huestis et al. developed and fully validated a GC/MS assay for simultaneous determination of THC, HO-THC, and THCA in human plasma *(42)*. Their method includes enzymatic hydrolysis of glucuronide conjugates, simultaneous SPE of all three analytes in a single eluant, derivatization with BSTFA, and analysis by positive ion chemical ionization GC/MS. Ions were monitored for each analyte and internal standard: THC, *m/z* 387; THC-d_3, *m/z* 390; HO-THC, *m/z* 459; HO-THC-d_3, *m/z* 462; THCA, *m/z* 489; and THCA-d_3, *m/z* 492. Enzymatic hydrolysis with *E. coli* β-glucuronidase resulted in significantly higher concentrations of HO-THC and THCA in the eluants than could be obtained without the hydrolysis step. Extraction recoveries ranged from 67.3 to 83.5% for all three analytes. LOQs were 0.5 ng/mL for THC and HO-THC and 1.0 ng/mL for THCA.

Another method developed for analysis of clinical samples employed gas chromatography/tandem mass spectrometry (GC/MS/MS; ref. *50*). Deuterated internal standards for THC and HO-THC were added to a 2-mL aliquot of human plasma followed by 2 mL of acetonitrile and 2 mL of 0.1 *M* phosphate buffer (pH 6.0). After vortexing and centrifugation, the supernatant was transferred to a conditioned Bond Elut Certify-1 extraction column. After several washing steps the THC and HO-THC were eluted from the column with methylene chloride, derivatized by trimethylsilylation, and analyzed by GC/MS/MS using positive ion chemical ionization with ammonia as the reagent gas. The protonated molecule ions for trimethylsilylated THC (*m/z* 387) and HO-THC (*m/z* 475) were collisionally dissociated to product ions at *m/z* 293 and detected by selected-reaction monitoring. LOQs were 50 pg/mL for THC and 100 pg/mL for HO-THC.

Several preliminary efforts to measure cannabinoids in blood or plasma by LC/MS have been reported. Hughes et al. compared ESI, APCI, and atmospheric-pressure photoionization (APPI) for analysis of THC, THCA, and HO-THC in blood. APCI was more sensitive than ESI. THCA and HO-THC had better sensitivity in the negative ionization mode, while THC showed better sensitivity in the positive ionization mode. APPI was three to five times more sensitive for all three cannabinoids *(51)*. After SPE of THC, HO-THC, and THCA in blood, Mireault analyzed the extracts using an ion trap LC/MS (Finnigan LCQ) operated in the APCI mode. THC was detected using MS/MS, but HO-THC and THCA required MS/MS/MS to achieve adequate selectivity *(52)*.

5. Determination of Cannabinoids in Adipose Tissue and Other Tissues

Quantitative determination of cannabinoids in adipose tissue is even more challenging than analysis of cannabinoids in blood. Johansson et al. developed a lengthy assay for measurement of THC in human fatty tissue *(53)*. The procedure included homogenization of the fat samples with hexane:isopropanol (3:2) and sequential SPEs with Lipidex 5000 gel and a C18 resin. The extracted THC was derivatized with *N*-methyl-*N*-(*t*-butyldimethylsilyl)trifluoroacetamide (MTBSTFA), and the derivatized THC was purified by preparative HPLC using a C18 column. Finally, the purified and derivatized THC was analyzed by means of GC and high-resolution MS.

Investigators in the Department of Forensic Medicine at Kyushu University, Japan, developed a relatively simple method for determination of THC in human tissues including brain, lung, kidney, muscle, liver, spleen, and adipose tissue *(54)*. Tissue samples (0.1 g of fat or 0.5 g of the other tissues) were homogenized with 3 mL of acetonitrile. After centrifugation, the supernatant was concentrated by evaporation and mixed with 2 mL of 0.2 *M* sodium hydroxide. The aqueous solution was extracted with 3 mL of hexane:ethyl acetate (9:1); the organic extract was washed with 2 mL of 0.1 *M* HCl to remove basic compounds and then evaporated to dryness for derivatization in a solution of iodomethane, tetrabutylammonium hydroxide, and dimethyl-sulfoxide. Derivatized extracts were analyzed by GC/MS using electron ionization and selected-ion monitoring. The lower limit of detection for THC in each of the tissues examined was 1 ng/g.

6. Determination of Cannabinoids in Meconium

Clinicians are increasingly interested in determining when a newborn infant has been prenatally exposed to marijuana or other drugs of abuse. Meconium is the preferred matrix for analysis in these cases because it retains drugs and drug metabolites for a longer time than does an infant's blood or urine *(55)*.

GC/MS confirmation of THCA in meconium was first reported by Moore et al. *(56)*. The meconium was initially screened by fluorescence polarization immunoassay

(Abbott Laboratories, Abbott Park, IL). Positives were then analyzed by GC/MS. After homogenization in methanol, THCA-d_3 was added along with 11.8 *M* potassium hydroxide, and the mixture was allowed to stand for 15 minutes. After centrifugation the aqueous supernatant was diluted with deionized water and extracted with hexane:ethyl acetate (9:1) to remove lipophilic nonacidic compounds; the aqueous layer was acidified with 0.1 *N* HCl and extracted with hexane:ethyl acetate (9:1). The resulting organic layer was evaporated to dryness and derivatized with MTBSTFA. EI-GC/MS analysis monitored ions at *m/z* 572, 515, and 413 for THCA and *m/z* 575, 518, and 416 for THCA-d_3. The lower limit of detection (LOD) for THCA was 2 ng/g.

ElSohly and co-investigators extensively investigated methods of measuring THC and its metabolites in meconium *(8,55)*. They found that HO-THC and 8β,11-diHO-THC were present in significant quantities in meconium from neonates whose mothers had used marijuana and that those metabolites were mainly in the form of glucuronide conjugates. The investigators developed two different GC/MS assays for determination of cannabinoids in meconium; both included enzyme hydrolysis, but one employed liquid/liquid extraction *(55)* and the other an immunoaffinity extraction procedure *(8)*. The liquid/liquid extraction method included the following procedures: after addition of THC-d_9 and THCA-d_6 the meconium was homogenized in methanol and centrifuged, and the supernatant was evaporated to dryness. The residue was taken up in saturated monobasic potassium phosphate and extracted with chloroform. The chloroform extract was evaporated to dryness and the residue dissolved in 0.1 *M* phosphate buffer (pH 6.8) containing β-glucuronidase (*E. coli,* Type IX-A). After 16 hours at 37°C, the sample was cooled, acidified with 1 *N* HCl, and extracted with hexane:ethyl acetate (9:1). Acidic cannabinoids were removed from the organic solution by extraction into 1 *N* sodium hydroxide, reacidified, and extracted back into hexane:ethyl acetate before derivatization with BSTFA. Neutral cannabinoids remaining in the original hexane:ethyl acetate solution were subjected to further clean-up prior to derivatization with pyridine and acetic anhydride. The neutral and acidic cannabinoids were analyzed separately by GC/MS. The LODs for the THC metabolites ranged from 2 to 15 ng/g. Surprisingly, 8β,11-diOH-THC was found in the acidic fraction, along with THCA.

The second method, employing an immunoaffinity extraction, proved to be much faster and more selective than the liquid/liquid extraction method. The immunoaffinity resin was prepared by immobilization of THC antibody (Roche Diagnostic Systems, Somerville, NJ) onto cyanogen bromide-activated Sepharose 4B, and stored in 1 *M* NaCl solution containing 0.05% NaN_3. After addition of deuterated internal standards and 3 mL of methanol, the meconium (0.5 g) was homogenized and centrifuged and the supernatant was evaporated to dryness. The dried residue was extracted with 2 mL of isopropanol:water (95:5), and after centrifugation the supernatant was again separated and evaporated to dryness. The residue was taken up in 2 mL of 0.1 *M* phosphate buffer (pH 6.8) and hydrolyzed with β-glucuronidase (*E. coli*, type IX-A). The immunoaffinity-resin slurry was added to the hydrolyzed sample and poured into a frit filter cartridge and the liquid allowed to pass through under a slight vacuum. The resin was washed once with phosphate saline buffer (pH 7.0) and three times with deionized water. After the analytes were eluted with acetone and the extract evaporated to dryness, they were trimethylsilylated using BSTFA and 1% TMCS and analyzed by

EI-GC/MS with selected ion monitoring. The LODs were 1.0 ng/g for THCA and HO-THC and 2.5 ng/g for 8β,11-diHO-THC.

Authors of the above immunoaffinity procedure reported that of 24 presumptive positive meconium samples analyzed, 15 were confirmed positive for THCA and 18 were positive for HO-THC. Only three specimens were positive for 8ß,11-diHO-THC.

7. Determination of Cannabinoids in Oral Fluids

Analysis of oral fluids to detect recent use of drugs of abuse is of increasing interest because sampling is less invasive than collection of urine or blood. However, unlike most other drugs, THC gets into oral fluids primarily by direct deposition into the oral mucosa during smoking or oral ingestion, rather than being transferred from blood to saliva. Consequently, concentrations of metabolites of THC are very low and difficult to detect in this matrix.

Niedbala et al. compared results from analysis of urine and oral fluids from subjects that smoked marijuana or ingested marijuana plant material *(24)*. Oral fluid was collected using a treated absorbent cotton fiber pad affixed to a nylon stick (OraSure Technologies, Bethlehem, PA). After absorbing fluids in the mouth, the pad was placed in a preservative solution that was subsequently analyzed for THC. THC-d_3 was added to 200 μL of diluted oral fluid, and the specimen was treated with 2 mL of 0.2 *M* sodium hydroxide and extracted with 3 mL of hexane:ethyl acetate (9:1). The organic layer was washed with 3 mL of 0.1 *M* HCl to remove basic compounds and the organic layer was separated and evaporated to dryness. The dried extract was derivatized with 30 μL of BSTFA and 30 μL of ethyl acetate at 70°C for 30 minutes before analysis by GC/MS/MS using electron ionization and selected-reaction monitoring. The LOQ for THC in oral fluids was 0.5 ng/mL.

When detection of THC in oral fluids was compared to detecting THCA in urine, the probability of a positive test in oral fluids was higher in specimens collected over the first 6 hours following exposure. Subsequently, positivity in urine specimens increased and generally exceeded that of oral fluid in specimens collected after 16 hours *(24)*.

In an earlier study Menkes et al. collected oral fluids from 13 experienced users after each of them had smoked one marijuana cigarette. Each saliva sample (20–200 μL) was added to 200 μL of 8 *M* urea and extracted with 4 mL of pentane. The organic extract was evaporated to dryness, derivatized with pentafluoropropionic anhydride and analyzed by GC/MS using electron ionization and selected-ion monitoring. Concentrations of THC were compared to measurements of heart rate and intoxication over a period of 4 hours after smoking. The results indicated that salivary THC levels can be a sensitive index of recent cannabis smoking, and appear more closely linked with the effects of intoxication than do either blood or urine cannabinoid levels *(57)*.

Brodbelt and co-investigators used commercially available 30-μm poly(dimethylsiloxane) solid-phase microextraction fibers to absorb THC, cannabidiol, and cannabinol from saliva specimens collected after smoking *(58)*. One mL of saliva was diluted with 1 mL of deionized water and 0.5 mL of acetic acid. THC-d_3 was added, and the solution was transferred to a vial containing the solid-phase microextraction fibers. The fibers were subsequently transferred to a heated (270°C) injection port, which caused thermal desorption of the cannabinoids into the GC/MS. The mass spectrometer was operated in full-scan mode between 120 and 350 amu. The ions used for quantitation were THC (*m/z* 314, 299, and 231), cannabidiol (*m/z* 314 and 231), and cannabinol (*m/z* 310, 295, and 238). The range of quantitation for each cannabinoid was 5–500 ng/mL.

8. Determination of Cannabinoids in Hair

Determination of drugs in hair has continued to grow in importance; its advantages over analysis of other matrices are that it is relatively noninvasive, and drugs can be detected in hair for a much longer time period. However, cannabinoids in blood are not taken up in hair nearly as efficiently as most other drugs are. As a result, concentrations of cannabinoids in hair after smoking or ingestion of marijuana are very low and can only be detected with extremely sensitive analytical methods. Furthermore, cannabinoid metabolites such as THCA are normally present in hair at even lower concentrations than parent cannabinoids such as THC, cannabinol, and cannabidiol. This is a problem in forensic cases because passive exposure to marijuana smoke can result in external adsorption of cannabinoids to hair follicles. Consequently, a hair analysis that detects THCA provides more convincing evidence of intentional smoking or ingestion of marijuana than a hair analysis that detects THC, cannabinol, or cannabidiol. However, a strong case can be made for intentional marijuana use based on detection of THC, cannabinol, or cannabidiol if it is shown that the method of decontamination removes all externally adsorbed cannabinoids from the hair prior to hair analysis.

Most published reviews on testing for drugs in hair primarily discuss methods for analysis of basic drugs such as cocaine, opiates, and amphetamines. Authors who have reviewed analysis of cannabinoids in hair include Staub *(6)*, Sachs and Kintz *(59)*, and Baptista et al. *(60)*.

Methods for the determination of cannabinoids in hair generally include the following basic steps: (1) decontamination of hair by washing with a solvent to remove any cannabinoids adsorbed to external surfaces of the hair; (2) enzymatic or alkaline hydrolysis of the hair to facilitate extraction of the cannabinoids; (3) extraction of the digested hair; (4) derivatization of the extracted cannabinoids; and (5) analysis using GC and MS. The cannabinoids that appear to have the highest concentration in hair are THC, cannabinol, and cannabidiol. However, some of the published methods are designed to detect only THCA, for reasons stated above.

Methylene chloride has been most often used for decontaminating hair prior to digestion *(61–64)*; however, Strano-Rossi and Chiarotti reported that washing with petroleum ether was more efficient than methylene chloride for then removal of cannabinoids adsorbed to hair *(65)*. Wilkins et al. compared four different wash solvents (methylene chloride, methanol, isopropanol, and phosphate buffer) for analysis of THC in human hair from known cannabis users. The concentrations of THC were significantly lower when methylene chloride was used *(66)*.

To extract cannabinoids efficiently, the hair is first dissolved by alkaline hydrolysis or by enzymatic hydrolysis. Alkaline hydrolysis is generally favored because it can be performed very rapidly. After addition of internal standard(s) the hair is subjected to

NaOH (1–2 *N*) at 80–95°C for 10–30 minutes *(61–65,67)* or maintained at 37°C overnight *(66)*. If the assay includes determination of drugs that are degraded in the presence of strong alkali, β-glucuronidase/arylsulfatase can be used to digest the hair prior to extraction *(60)*.

Early methods for the determination of cannabinoids in hair used liquid/liquid extraction to remove cannabinoids from the hydrolyzed hair *(61–63,66,68)*; for example, after acidification, homogenized hair can be extracted with hexane:ethyl acetate (9:1 v/v; ref. *61*). A more recently published method employing enzymatic hydrolysis used a two-step liquid/liquid extraction procedure *(60)*. After adjustment of the pH to 8.5, the hydrolyzed hair sample was extracted with chloroform:isopropanol (97:3 v/v). The aqueous layer was separated, acidified with acetic acid, and re-extracted with hexane:ethyl acetate (9:1 v/v). The two organic extracts were then combined and prepared for GC/MS analysis.

Sachs and Dressler developed a very sensitive but lengthy assay for the detection of THCA in hair. The procedure involved initially extracting the hydrolyzed hair in hexane:ethyl acetate, washing the organic extract with 0.5 *M* NaOH and then with 0.1 *M* HCl, and injecting the concentrated organic extract into a high-performance liquid chromatography column. The fraction containing THCA was collected, acidified with 0.05 *M* phosphoric acid, and extracted with hexane:ethyl acetate. This extensive clean-up permitted detection of derivatized THCA at concentrations as low as 0.3 pg/mL *(67)*.

Other recently published methods have generally used SPE procedures, including solid-phase microextraction (SPME). Moore et al. used mixed-mode hydrophobic/anion exchange SPE cartridges to extract THCA from digested hair *(64)*. After conditioning the SPE cartridge, the hydrolyzed hair sample was added to the cartridge; the column was washed with deionized water (2 mL) and 0.1 *M* HCl:acetonitrile (70:30 v/v; 2 mL) and dried, after which THCA was eluted with 3 mL of hexane:ethyl acetate (75:25 v/v).

Several variations of solid-phase microextractions have recently been used to extract cannabinoids from hydrolyzed hair samples. Strano-Rossi and Chiarotti developed a relatively simple and rapid method for detection of THC, cannabinol, and cannabidiol in hair based on solid-phase microextraction and GC/MS analysis *(65)*. A commercially available 30-μm polydimethylsiloxane fiber was dipped into the neutralized hair digest for 15 minutes and then inserted directly into the injection port of the GC/MS, where the adsorbed nonderivatized cannabinoids were vaporized. The injection port temperature was 260°C; the 5% phenylmethylsilicone capillary column was maintained at 100°C for 2 minutes and then temperature-programmed to 270°C. The LODs for analysis of 50 mg of hair were 0.1 ng/mg for THC and cannabinol and 0.2 ng/mg for cannabidiol.

Musshoff et al. used two variations of a headspace solid-phase microextraction (HS-SPME) method for determination of cannabinoids in hair. With one method a 100-μm polydimethylsiloxane fiber was inserted for 25 minutes into the headspace of a heated (90°C) vial containing the digested hair *(69)*. The fiber was then exposed to the headspace in a second vial containing 25 μL of MSTFA for 8 minutes at 90°C, resulting in trimethylsilylation of the adsorbed cannabinoids. Finally, the fiber was inserted into the heated (250°C) injection port of a GC/MS, permitting the derivatized cannabinoids to be vaporized and analyzed. The reported LODs ranged from 0.05 to 0.14 ng/mg for THC, cannabidiol, and cannabinol. THCA was not detected.

Table 1
Published Methods for Mass Spectometric Analysis of Cannabinoids in Urine

Ref.	Analyte	Extraction	Derivatization	Instrumentation	Ionization	LOQ (ng/mL)	LOD (ng/mL)	Notes
29	THCA	Liq/Liq	PFPA and PFPOH	GC/MS	EI	—	—	Discusses surface adsorption problems
73	THCA	Liq/Liq	BSTFA	GC/MS	EI	—	—	Compares extraction and derivatization procedures
11	THCA	Liq/Liq	MTBSTFA	GC/MS	EI	—	0.9	Derivative is more stable than TMS derivative
74	THCA	Liq/Liq	Trimethylsilyliodide	GC/MS	EI	10	1.0	Analyzed urine collected for doping analysis
17	THCA	SPE	BSTFA	GC/MS	EI	2.0	—	Reduced solvent volume for SPE
16	THCA	SPE	Methyl iodide	GC/MS	EI	5	—	Full-scan detection on an ion trap MS
26	THCA	SPE	Methyl iodide	GC/MS	EI	—	2	Extraction uses a strong anion exchange resin
18	THCA	SPE	BSTFA	GC/MS	EI	—	—	Extraction uses 3 *M* Empore disk cartridges
20	THCA	SPE	MSTFA	GC/MS	EI	2.5	—	Compares 2 SPE and derivatization procedures
22	THCA	SPE	MSTFA	GC/MS	EI	2.0	2.0	High throughput with Cerex PolyCrom-THC SPE
9	THCA and 2 other acidic metabolites	Liq/Liq	Five procedures compared	GC/MS	EI	—	—	Compared THCA-d_3, -d_6, -d_9, and -d_{10} as internal standards

(continued)

Table 1 *(continued)*

Ref.	Analyte	Extraction	Derivatization	Instrumentation	Ionization	LOQ (ng/mL)	LOD (ng/mL)	Notes
28	THCA	Liq/Liq	PFPA and PFPOH	GC/MS	NCl	—	0.7	Compares El, PCl, and NCl mass spectra
25	THCA	*See* notes	Methyl iodide	GC/MS	EI	—	0.5	Antibody-mediated extraction
75	THCA	*See* notes	Methyl iodide	GC/MS	EI	20	0.25	Extractive-alkylation procedure
27	THCA	Liq/Liq	Propyl iodide	GC/MS	EI	0.64	0.32	Derivatization with proply preferred to methyl
8	THC and major metabolites	*See* notes	BSTFA	GC/MS	EI	—	0.5 to 2.5	Hydrolyzed with β-glucuronidase. Extracted with an immunoaffinity resin.
15	THCA	*See* notes	MSTFA	GC/MS	EI	—	—	Compares 2 SPE and 2 Liq/Liq extractions
12	THCA	SPE	BSTFA	GC/MS	EI	5	—	Automated SPE procedure
14	THC and THCA	Liq/Liq	BSTFA	GC/MS	EI	—	—	Samples hydrolyzed with β-glucuronidase
10	THCA	SPE	PFPA and PFPOH	GC/MS	EI	1.8	0.9	Automated SPE procedure
24	THCA	SPE	PFPA and PFPOH	GC/MS	EI	5.0	—	Compared oral fluid testing to urine testing
71	THCA	Liq/Liq	BSTFA	GC/MS/MS	EI	5	—	Varian Saturn 2000 ion trap
19	THCA	SPE	BSTFA	GC/MS/MS	EI	—	—	Detailed description of operating parameters

30	THCA	SPE	No derivatization	LC/MS	Pos.-ESI	2.5	—	Also tried negative ion ESI-MS
23	THCA	SPE	No derivatization	LC/MS	Neg.-ESI	—	—	Zorbax Eclipse XDB-C18 LC column
21	THCA	SPE	No derivatization	LC/MS/MS	Neg.-APCI	5	—	Short prep. and analysis time. Ret. time, 2.4 min
31	THCA and THCA-glucuronide	Liq/Liq	No derivatization	LC/MS/MS	Pos.-ESI	—	10	30 min. run time
10	THCA and THCA-glucuronide	SPE	No derivatization	LC/MS/MS	Pos.-ESI	6.0	1.4	Assay used to determine stability of THCA and THCA-glucuronide in plasma and in urine

THCA, 11-nor-9-carboxy-Δ^9-tetrahydrocannabinol; THC, Δ^9-tetrahydrocannabinol;Liq/Liq, liquid/liquid extraction; PFPA, pentafluoropropionic anhydride; PFPOH, pentafluoropropanol; GC/MS, gas chromatography/mass spectrometry; EI, electron ionization; BSTFA, bis-(trimethylsilyl)-trifluoroacetamide; MTBSTFA, *N*-methyl-*N*-(*t*-butyldimethylsilyl)-trifluoroacetamide; SPE, solid-phase extraction; MSTFA, *N*-methyl-*N*-(trimethylsilyl)-trifluoroacetamide; NCI, negative ion chemical ionization; PCI, positive ion chemical ionization; ESI, electrospray ionization; APCI, atmospheric pressure chemical ionization; LOQ, limit of quantitation; LOD, lower limit of detection.

Table 2
Published Methods for Mass Spectrometric Analysis of Cannabinoids in Plasma or Serum

Ref.	Analyte	Extraction	Derivatization	Instrumentation	Ionization	LOQ (ng/mL)	LOD (ng/mL)	Notes
38	Multiple analytes	Liq/Liq	BSTFA	GC/MS	EI	—	0.6	THC, CBD, DBN, and 5 metabolites of THC
76	THC and HO-THC	Liq/Liq	TFAA	GC/MS	NCl	0.2/0.5	—	THCA analyzed using different derivatization
	THCA		1. BF_3/MeOH 2. TFAA			0.2	—	Early use of negative ion chemical ionization
48	THC, HO-THC, and THCA	SPE	Methyl iodide	GC/MS	EI	0.6/0.7 3.4	—	Improved version of an earlier assay
82	THC, THCA, and HO-THC	SPE	PFBBr	GC/MS	NCl	0.3/0.3	—	Extractive alkylation using XAD-2 resin
			BSTFA				1.0	
49	THC and THCA	SPE	TFAA and HFIP	GC/MS	NCL	0.5/2.5	—	Fully validated assay
8	THC and major metabolites	*See* notes	BSTFA	GC/MS	EI	—	0.5–2.5	Hydrolysis with β-glucuronidase; extraction with an immunoaffinity resin; also analyzed meconium
77	THC, HO-THC, and THCA	SPE	MSTFA	GC/MS/MS	EI	2/5/8	—	Blood diluted 6:1 prior to extraction
42	THC, HO-THC, and THCA	SPE	BSTFA	GC/MS	PCl	0.5/0.5 1.0	—	Plasma hydrolyzed with β-glucuronidase. Compares concentrations with and without hydrolysis
50	THC and HO-THC	SPE	Tri-Sil TBT[a]	GC/MS/MS	PCl	0.05/0.1	0.01/0.2	Run time, 7 min

LOQ, limit of quantitation; LOD, lower limit of detection; Liq/Liq, liquid/liquid extraction; BSTFA, *bis*-(trimethylsilyl)-trifluoroacetamide; GC/MS, gas chromatography/mass spectrometry; EI, electron ionization; THC, Δ^9-tetrahydrocannabinol; HO-THC, 11-hydroxy-Δ^9-tetrahydrocannabinol; TFAA, trifluoroacetic anhydride; NCI, negative ion chemical ionization; THCA, 11-nor-9-carboxy-Δ^9-tetrahydrocannabinol; SPE, solid-phase extraction; HFIP, hexafluoroisopropanol; MSTFA, *N*-methyl-*N*-(trimethylsilyl)-trifluoroacetamide; PCI, positive ion chemical ionization.

[a]Tri-Sil TBT from Pierce Chemical Co., Rockford, IL.

Table 3
Published Methods for Mass Spectrometric Analysis of Cannbinoids in Whole Blood

Ref.	Analyte	Extraction	Derivatization	Instrumentation	Ionization	LOQ (ng/mL)	LOD (ng/mL)	Notes
78	THC	SPE	TFAA	GC/MS	NCI	1.0	—	Initial precipitation with acetonitrile
46	THC and THCA	SPE	BSTFA	GC/MS	EI	2.0/1.0	1.6/0.8	Zymark RapidTrace SPE workstation
43	THC and THCA	Liq/Liq	Methyl iodide	GC/MS	EI	1.0/0.5	—	Extract 2 mL of blood with hexane:EtOAc (9:1)
47	THC and THCA	Liq/Liq and SPE	PFPA and PFPOH	GC/MS	EI	1.0	—	THC and THCA extracts analyzed in separate runs
45	THC	Liq/Liq	PFPA and PFPOH	GC/MS	EI	1.0	—	Method fully validated; compared extraction solvents
79	THC and THCA	Liq/Liq	BSTFA	GC/MS/MS	EI	—	1.0	Multistep extraction procedure
44	THC, HO-THC, and THCA	Liq/Liq	BSTFA	GC/MS	EI	—	0.2/0.2	Evaluated several different extraction and derivatization procedures

LOQ, limit of quantitation; LOD, lower limit of detection; THC, Δ^9-tetrahydrocannabinol; SPE, solid-phase extraction; TFAA, trifluoroacetic anhydride; GC/MS, gas chromatography/mass spectrometry; THCA, 11-nor-9-carboxy-Δ^9-tetrahydrocannabinol; PFPA, pentafluoropropionic anhydride; PFPOH, pentafluoropropanol; Liq/Liq, liquid/liquid extraction; BSTFA, *bis*-(trimethylsilyl)-trifluoroacetamide; HO-THC, 11-hydroxy-Δ^9-tetrahydrocannabinol; NCI, negative ion chemical ionization; EI, electron ionization.

Table 4
Published Method for Mass Spectrometric Analysis of Cannabinoids in Tissues

Ref.	Analyte	Extraction	Derivatization	Instrumentation	Ionization	LOQ (ng/g)	LOD (ng/g)	Notes
53	THC	Liq/Liq	*t*-Butyldimethyl and SPE	GC/MS silylation	EI	0.4	—	Very lengthy procedure; uses a high-resolution mass spectrometer
54	THC	Liq/Liq	Methylation	GC/MS	EI	—	1.0	Tissue homogenized with acetonitrile

LOQ, limit of quantitation; LOD, lower limit of detection; THC, Δ^9-tetrahydrocannabinol; Liq/Liq, liquid/liquid extraction; SPE, solid-phase extraction; GC/MS, gas chromatography/mass spectrometry; EI, electron ionization.

Table 5
Published Methods for Mass Spectometric Analysis of Cannabinoids in Meconium

Ref.	Analyte	Extraction	Derivatization	Instrumentation	Ionization	LOQ (ng/g)	LOD (ng/g)	Notes
56	THCA	Liq/Liq	MTBSTFA	GC/MS	EI	—	2.0	Analyzed 100 meconium samples; 16 confirmed positive
55	THC and major metabolites	Liq/Liq	BSTFA	GC/MS	EI		2.0–15	Includes enzymatic hydrolysis; major cannabinoids in meconium are HO-
THC								and 8β, 11-diHO-THC
8	THC and major metabolites	*See* notes	BSTFA	GC/MS	EI	—	1.0–2.5	Hydrolyzed with β-glucuronidase; extracted with an immunoaffinity

LOQ, limit of quantitation; LOD, lower limit of detection; THCA, 11-nor-9-carboxy-Δ^9-tetrahydrocannabinol; Liq/Liq, liquid/liquid extraction; THC, Δ^9-tetrahydrocannabinol; MTBSTFA, *N*-methyl-*N*-(*t*-butyldimethylsilyl)-trifluoroacetamide; GC/MS, gas chromatography/mass spectrometry; EI, electron ionization; THC, Δ^9-tetrahydrocannabinol; BSTFA, *bis*-(trimethylsilyl)-trifluoroacetamide; HO-THC, 11-hydroxy-Δ^9-tetrahydrocannabinol.

Table 6
Published Methods for Mass Spectometric Analysis of Cannabinoids in Oral Fluids

Ref.	Analyte	Extraction	Derivatization	Instrumentation	Ionization	LOQ (ng/mL)	LOD (ng/mL)	Notes
58	THC	SPME	None	GC/MS	EI	10	1.0	Also analyzed cannabidiol and cannabinol
24	THC	Liq/Liq	BSTFA	GC/MS/MS	EI	0.5	0.2	Detailed description of a clinical study
57	THC	Liq/Liq	PFPA	GC/MS	EI	—	—	Chewing gum used to stimulate saliva

LOQ, limit of quantitation; LOD, lower limit of detection; THC, Δ^9-tetrahydrocannabinol; SPME, solid-phase microextraction; GC/MS, gas chromatography/mass spectrometry; EI, electron ionization; Liq/Liq, liquid/liquid extraction; PFPA, pentafluoropropionic anhydride.

24. Niedbala, R. S., Kardos, K. W., Fritch, D. F., et al. (2001) Detection of marijuana use by oral fluid and urine analysis following single-dose administration of smoked and oral marijuana. *J. Anal. Toxicol.* **25**, 289–303.
25. Lemm, U., Tenczer, J., and Baudisch, H. (1985) Antibody-mediated extraction of the main tetrahydrocannabinol metabolite from human urine and its identification by GC/MS in the sub-nanogram range. *J. Chromatogr.* **342**, 393–398.
26. Paul, B. D., Mell, L. D., Jr., Mitchell, J. M., and McKinley, R. M. (1987) Detection and quantitation of urinary 11-nor-Δ9-tetrahydrocannabinol-9-carboxylic acid, a metabolite of tetrahydrocannabinol, by capillary gas chromatography and electron impact mass fragmentography. *J. Anal. Toxicol.* **11**, 1–5.
27. Joern, W. A. (1992) GC/MS assay of the marijuana carboxy metabolite: Urine interference with the dimethyl derivative. *J. Anal. Toxicol.* **16**, 207.
28. Karlsson, L., Jonsson, J., Aberg, K., and Roos, C. (1983) Determination of Δ9-tetrahydrocannabinol-11-oic acid in urine as its pentafluoropropyl-pentafluoropropionyl derivative by GC/MS utilizing negative ion chemical ionization. *J. Anal. Toxicol.* **7**, 198–202.
29. Joern, W. A. (1987) Detection of past and recurrent marijuana use by a modified GC/MS procedure. *J. Anal. Toxicol.* **11**, 49–52.
30. Breindahl, T. and Andreasen, K. (1999) Determination of 11-nor-Δ(9)-tetrahydrocannabinol-9-carboxylic acid in urine using high-performance liquid chromatography and electrospray ionization mass spectrometry. *J. Chromatogr. B* **732**, 155–164.
31. Weinmann, W., Vogt, S., Goerke, R., Muller, C., and Bromberger, A. (2000) Simultaneous determination of THC-COOH and THC-COOH-glucuronide in urine samples by LC/MS/MS. *Forensic Sci. Int.* **113**, 381–387.
32. Skopp, G. and Potsch, L. (2002) Stability of 11-nor-Δ-9-carboxy-tetrahydrocannabinol glucuronide in plasma and urine assessed by liquid chromatography-tandem mass spectrometry. *Clin. Chem.* **48**, 301–306.
33. Brunk, S. D. (1988) False negative GC/MS assay for carboxy THC due to ibuprofen interference. *J. Anal. Toxicol.* **12**, 290–291.
34. Stout, P. R., Horn, C. K., and Lesser, D. R. (2000) Loss of THCCOOH from urine specimens stored in polypropylene and polyethylene containers at different temperatures. *J. Anal. Toxicol.* **24**, 567–571.
35. Blanc, J. A., Manneh, V. A., Ernst, R., et al. (1993) Adsorption losses from urine-based cannabinoid calibrators during routine use. *Clin. Chem.* **39**, 1705–1712.
36. Joern, W .A. (1992) Surface adsorption of the urinary marijuana carboxy metabolite: The problem and a partial solution. *J. Anal. Toxicol.* **16**, 401.
37. Tsai, J. S. C., ElSohly, M. A., Tsai, S. F., Murphy, T. P., Twarowska, B., and Salamone, S. J. (2000) Investigation of nitrite adulteration on the immunoassay and GC-MS analysis of cannabinoids in urine specimens. *J. Anal. Toxicol.* **24**, 708–714.
38. Kemp, P. M., Abukhalaf, I. K., Manno, J. E., Manno, B. R., Alford, D. D., and Abusada, G. A. (1995) Cannabinoids in humans. I. Analysis of Δ9-tetrahydrocannabinol and six metabolites in plasma and urine using GC/MS. *J. Anal. Toxicol.* **19**, 285–291.
39. Kemp, P. M., Abukhalaf, I. K., Manno, J. E., et al. (1995) Cannabinoids in humans. II. The influence of three methods of hydrolysis on the concentration of THC and two metabolites in urine. *J. Anal. Toxicol.* **19**, 292–298.
40. ElSohly, M. A., Feng, S., Murphy, T. P., Ross, S. A., Nimrod, A., Mehmedic, Z., and Fortner, N. (1999) Δ9-Tetrahydrocannabivarin (Δ9-THCV) as a marker for the ingestion of cannabis versus Marinol®. *J. Anal. Toxicol.* **23**, 222–224.
41. ElSohly, M. A., Feng, S., Murphy, T. P., et al. (2001) Identification and quantitation of 11-nor-Δ9-tetrahydrocannabivarin-9-carboxylic acid, a major metabolite of Δ9-tetrahydrocannabivarin. *J. Anal. Toxicol.* **25**, 476–480.

42. Gustafson, R. A., Moolchan, E. T., Barnes, A., Levine, B., and Huestis, M. A. (2003) Validated method for the simultaneous determination of Δ9-tetrahydrocannabinol (THC), 11-hydroxy-THC and 11-nor-9-carboxy-THC in human plasma using solid phase extraction and gas chromatography-mass spectrometry with positive chemical ionization. *J. Chromatogr. B* **798**, 145–154.
43. Kintz, P. and Cirimele, V. (1997) Testing human blood for cannabis by GC-MS. *Biomed. Chromatogr.* **11**, 371–373.
44. Goodall, C. R. and Basteyns, B. J. (1995) A reliable method for the detection, confirmation, and quantitation of cannabinoids in blood. *J. Anal. Toxicol.* **19**, 419–426.
45. Chu, M. H. C. and Drummer, O. H. (2002) Determination of Δ9-THC in whole blood using gas chromatography-mass spectrometry. *J. Anal. Toxicol.* **26**, 575–581.
46. D'Asaro, J. A. (2000) An automated and simultaneous solid-phase extraction of Δ9-tetrahydrocannabinol and 11-nor-9-carboxy- Δ9-tetrahydrocannabinol from whole blood using the Zymakr RapidTrace with confirmation and quantitation by GC-EI-MS. *J. Anal. Toxicol.* **24**, 289–295.
47. Felgate, P. D. and Dinan, A. C. (2000) The determination of Δ9-tetrahydrocannabinol and 11-nor-9-carboxy-Δ9-tetrahydrocannabinol in whole blood using solvent extraction combined with polar solid-phase extraction. *J. Anal. Toxicol.* **24**, 127–132.
48. Steinmeyer, S., Bregel, D., Warth, S., Kraemer, T., and Moeller, M. R. (2002) Improved and validated method for the determination of Δ9-tetrahydrocannabinol (THC), 11-hydroxy-THC and 11-nor-9-carboxy-THC in serum, and in human liver microsomal preparations using gas chromatography-mass spectrometry. *J. Chromatogr. B* **772**, 239–248.
49. Huang, W., Moody, D. E., Andrenyak, D. M., et al. (2001) Simultaneous determination of Δ9-tetrahydrocannabinol and 11-nor-9-carboxy- Δ9-tetrahydrocannabinol in human plasma by solid-phase extraction and gas chromatography-negative ion chemical ionization mass spectrometry. *J. Anal. Toxicol.* **25**, 531–537.
50. Nelson, C. C., Fraser, M. D., Wilfahrt, J. K., and Foltz, R. L. (1993) Gas chromatography tandem mass spectrometry measurement of Δ(9)-tetrahydrocannabinol, naltrexone, and their active metabolites in plasma. *Ther. Drug Monit.* **15**, 557–562.
51. Hughes, J. M., Andrenyak, D. M., Crouch, D. J., and Slawson, M. (2003) Comparison of LC/MS ionization techniques for cannabinoids in blood (Abstract). *J. Anal. Toxicol.* **27**, 191.
52. Mireault, P. (1998) Analysis of Δ9-THC and its two metabolites by APCI-LC/MS. ASMS Conference, Orlando, CA, (Abstract).
53. Johansson, E., Noren, K., Sjoevall, J., and Halldin, M.M. (1989) Determination of Δ1-tetrahydrocannabinol in human fat biopsies from marijuana users by GC/MS. *Biomed. Chromatogr.* **3**, 35–38.
54. Kudo, K., Nagata, T., Kimura, K., Imamura, T., and Jitsufuchi, N. (1995) Sensitive determination of Δ9-tetrahydrocannabinol in human tissue by GC/MS. *J. Anal. Toxicol.* **19**, 87–90.
55. ElSohly, M. A. and Feng, S. (1998) Δ9-THC metabolites in meconium: Identification of 11-OH-Δ9-THC, 8β,11-diOH- Δ9-THC, and 11-nor-Δ9-THC-9-COOH as major metabolites of Δ9-THC. *J. Anal. Toxicol.* **22**, 329–335.
56. Moore, C., Lewis, D., Becker, J., and Leikin, J. (1996) The determination of 11 nor-Δ9-tetrahydrocannabinol-9-carboxylic acid in meconium. *J. Anal. Toxicol.* **20**, 50–54.
57. Menkes, D. B., Howard, R. C., Spears, G. F. S., and Cairns, E. R. (1991) Salivary THC following cannabis smoking correlates with subjective intoxication and heart rate. *Psychopharmacology* **103**, 277–279.
58. Hall, B. J., Satterfield-Dover, M., Parikh, A. R., and Brodbelt, J. S. (1998) Determination of cannabinoids in water and human saliva by solid-phase microextraction and quadrupole ion trap GC/MS. *Anal. Chem.* **70**, 1788–1796.
59. Sachs, H. and Kintz, P. (1998) Testing for drugs in hair—critical review of chromatographic procedures since 1992—review. *J. Chromatogr. B* **713**, 147–161.

60. Baptista, M. J., Monsanto, P. V., Pinho Marques, E. G., et al. (2002) Hair analysis for Δ9-THC, Δ9-THC-COOH, CBN and CBD, by GC/EI-MS Comparison with GC/MS-NCI for Δ9-THC-COOH. *Forensic Sci. Int.* **128**, 66–78.
61. Cirimele, V., Kintz, P., and Mangin, P. (1995) Testing of human hair for cannabis. *Forensic Sci. Int.* **70**, 175–182.
62. Kintz, P., Cirimele, V., and Mangin, P. (1995) Testing human hair for cannabis. II. Identification of THC-COOH by GC/NCI-MS as a unique proof. *J. Forensic Sci.* **40**, 619–622.
63. Cirimele, V., Sachs, H., Kintz, P., and Mangin, P. (1996) Testing human hair for cannabis. III. Rapid screening procedure for the simultaneous identification of Δ9-tetrahydrocannabinol, cannabinol, and cannabidiol. *J. Anal. Toxicol.* **20**, 13–16.
64. Moore, C., Guzaldo, F., and Donahue, T. (2001) The determination of 11-nor- Δ9-tetrahydrocannabinol-9-carboxylic acid (THC-COOH) in hair using negative ion GC/MS and high-volume injection. *J. Anal. Toxicol.* **25**, 555–558.
65. Strano-Rossi, S. and Chiarotti, M. (1999) Solid-phase microextraction for cannabinoids analysis in hair and its possible application to other drugs. *J. Anal. Toxicol.* **23**, 7–10.
66. Wilkins, D. G., Haughey, H., Cone, E. J., Huestis, M. A., Foltz, R. L., and Rollins, D. E. (1995) Quantitative analysis of THC, 11-OH-THC, and THCCOOH in human hair by negative ion chemical ionization mass spectrometry. *J. Anal. Toxicol.* **19**, 483–491.
67. Sachs, H. and Dressler, U. (2000) Detection of THC-COOH in hair by MSD-NCI after HPLC clean-up. *Forensic Sci. Int.* **107**, 239–247.
68. Jurado, C., Gimenez, M. P., Menendez, M., and Repetto, M. (1995) Simultaneous quantification of opiates, cocaine and cannabinoids in hair. *Forensic Sci. Int.* **70**, 165–174.
69. Musshoff, F., Junker, H. P., Lachenmeier, D. W., Kroener, L., and Madea, B. (2002) Fully automated determination of cannabinoids in hair samples using headspace solid-phase microextraction and gas chromatography-mass spectrometry. *J. Anal. Toxicol.* **26**, 554–560.
70. Musshoff, F., Lachenmeier, D. W., Kroener, L., and Madea, B. (2003) Automated headspace solid-phase dynamic extraction for the determination of cannabinoids in hair samples. *Forensic Sci. Int.* **133**, 32–38.
71. Chiarotti, M. and Costamagna, L. (2000) Analysis of 11-nor-9-carboxy-Δ9-tetrahydrocannabinol in biological samples by GC/MS/MS. *Forensic Sci. Int.* **114**, 1–6.
72. Mieczkowski, T. (1995) A research note: The outcome of GC/MS/MS confirmation of hair assays on 93 cannabinoid-positive cases. *Forensic Sci. Int.* **70**, 83–91.
73. Baker, T. S., Harry, J. V., Russell, J. W., and Myers, R .L. (1984) Rapid method for the GC/MS confirmation of 11-nor-9-carboxy-Δ9-tetrahydrocannabinol in urine. *J. Anal. Toxicol.* **8**, 255–259.
74. De Cock, K. J. S., Delbeke, F. T., De Boer, D., Van Eenoo, P., and Roels, K. (2003) Quantitation of 11-nor-Δ9-tetrahydrocannabinol-9-carboxylic acid with GC/MS in urine collected for doping analysis. *J. Anal. Toxicol.* **27**, 106–109.
75. Lisi, A. M., Kazlauskas, R., and Trout, G. J. (1993) Gas chromatographic-mass spectrometric quantitation of urinary 11-nor-Δ9-tetrahydrocannabinol-9-carboxylic acid after derivatization by extractive alkylation. *J. Chromatogr.* **617**, 265–270.
76. Foltz, R. L., McGinnis, K. M., and Chinn, D. M. (1983) Quantitative measurement of Δ9-tetrahydrocannabinol and two major metabolites in physiological specimens using capillary column gas chromatography/negative ion chemical ionization mass spectrometry. *Biomed. Mass Spectrom.* **10**, 316–323.
77. Weller, J.-P., Wolf, M., and Szidat, S. (2000) Enhanced sensitivity in the determination of Δ9-tetrahydrocannabinol and two major metabolites in serum using ion-trap GC/MS/MS. *J. Anal. Toxicol.* **24**, 359–364.
78. Stonebraker, W. E., Lamoreaux, T. C., Bebault, M., Rasmussen, S. A., Jepson, B. R., and Beck, B. K. (1998) Robotic solid-phase extraction and GC/MS analysis of THC in blood. *Am. Clin. Lab.* **17**, 18–19.

79. Collins, M., Easson, J., Hansen, G., Hodda, A., and Lewis, K. (1997) GC/MS/MS confirmation of unusually high Δ9-tetrahydrocannabinol levels in two postmortem blood samples. *J. Anal. Toxicol.* **21**, 538–542.
80. Uhl, M. (1997) Determination of drugs in hair using GC/MS/MS. *Forensic Sci. Int.* **84**, 281–294.
81. Cirimele, V., Kintz, P., Majdalani, R., and Mangin, P. (1995) Supercritical fluid extraction of drugs in drug addict hair. *J. Chromatogr. B Biomed. Appl.* **673**, 173–181.
82. Rosenfeld, J. M., McLeod, R. A., and Foltz, R. L. (1986) Solid-supported reagents in the determination of cannabinoids in plasma. *Anal. Chem.* **58**, 716–721.

Chapter 9

Human Cannabinoid Pharmacokinetics and Interpretation of Cannabinoid Concentrations in Biological Fluids and Tissues

Marilyn A. Huestis and Michael L. Smith

1. Introduction

Pharmacokinetics is the study of the absorption, distribution, metabolism, and elimination of a drug in the body and how these processes change with time. Following controlled drug administration, scientists monitor the drug and its metabolites in bodily fluids and tissues to develop a pharmacokinetic profile for the animal or human being studied. After years of research, scientists have learned some important general principles about pharmacokinetic profiles. One is that, in general, pharmacokinetic profiles are similar for most animals and humans, but specific elements of the disposition of a drug in the body can differ greatly between species and between subjects within a species. Another principle is that helpful models can be developed that characterize a drug's pharmacokinetics and define parameters to describe processes such as time to peak and maximum concentrations, half-lives, volumes of distribution, and so on. Measuring these pharmacokinetic parameters facilitates comparison between and within human subjects who are examined at different times following administration of a drug. As specific examples in this chapter will convey, it is important to conduct carefully controlled studies and astutely note inter- and intrasubject similarities and differences in pharmacokinetic parameters to build databases that can be used to answer real life questions. The third principle that we will consider is that pharmacokinetic profiles change with the route of drug administration.

From: *Forensic Science and Medicine: Marijuana and the Cannabinoids*
Edited by: M. A. ElSohly © Humana Press Inc., Totowa, New Jersey

In this chapter, we describe what is currently known about the pharmacokinetics of Δ^9-tetrahydrocannabinol (THC), the principal psychoactive component of cannabis *(1,2)*. Our focus is THC because the majority of scientific studies have targeted this drug and its metabolites, although 64 different cannabinoids have been identified in the *Cannabis* plant *(3–9)*. Routes of administration and comparisons of pharmacokinetic parameters between human subjects have been published and are examined to develop a relationship to a drug's pharmacodynamic effects. In the Interpretation of Body Fluid and Hair Concentrations section of this chapter, we discuss how one uses the relationship between the pharmacokinetics of THC and its pharmacodynamic effects to interpret concentrations of cannabinoids in biological fluids and tissues with the ultimate goal of answering important social and scientific questions. Some typical questions might involve the following areas:

1. *Social scenarios*: If a man is arrested for driving erratically and triers of fact in a court of law subsequently hear testimony that his plasma concentration of THC is 2 ng/mL, can they infer that the marijuana he previously smoked contributed to his impaired driving? Should the laboratory that analyzed the plasma specimen have measured metabolites of THC to better answer this question? Could the same information be obtained by analyzing oral fluid, a specimen that can be obtained less invasively? Would analysis of the man's hair for THC help the jurors determine if he was a chronic cannabis user? These questions indicate some typical problems encountered by individuals who must evaluate human performance. Similar questions arise in workplace drug testing and death investigations.
2. *Scientific scenarios:* Scientists investigating cannabinoid mechanisms of action are also interested in their pharmacokinetics *(2)*. Sites of action are often within the brain or peripheral nerve tissues, and it is important to understand the processes and time frames for the drugs to reach and leave these sites *(10,11)*. Imaging technology measuring physiological functions such as cerebral blood flow (CBF) or other blood oxygen level-dependent function has allowed more sophisticated studies of drug uptake and distribution to cannabinoid receptor sites. It is important to relate these physiological functions to a drug's pharmacokinetic profile in plasma and other fluids *(12,13)*. Questions from these scientists might be: Do the concentrations of THC in plasma correlate with changes in CBF following cannabis use? Can measurement of THC concentrations help us to understand individual variations in CBF and effects of cannabis?

A representative clinical investigator might ask, can we use plasma cannabinoid concentrations to manage patients prescribed a cannabis preparation to treat neuropathic pain, appetite loss with AIDS wasting disease, nausea and vomiting following chemotherapy, or symptoms of multiple sclerosis? Research scientists and medical practitioners have begun to use cannabinoids to treat these and similar illnesses *(14–17)*. As with any therapeutic drug, understanding its pharmacokinetics is important in managing patients to maximize clinical effectiveness and reduce toxicity. It is also important in determining the abuse liability of a drug preparation. These and additional questions will be addressed in this chapter.

2. Cannabis Potency

Dose, chemical structure of precursors, binding of THC to macromolecules in cannabis plant material, and route of administration affect the amount of THC absorbed. The concentrations of THC in different cannabis products have been determined *(18,19)*. The most comprehensive report, by ElSohly et al., examined marijuana, hashish, and hashish oil samples seized across the United States by the Drug Enforcement Administration over an 18-year period *(20)*. THC content increased from an average of 1.5% in 1980 to 4.2% in 1997. Interestingly, THC content in hashish and hashish oil averaging 12.9% and 17.4%, respectively, did not show an increase over time. Government laboratories in the United States have confirmed this trend toward higher-potency marijuana *(21)*.

The chemical structure of cannabinoids in marijuana is also important. About 95% of THC present in marijuana plant material is in the form of two carboxylic acids that are converted to THC during smoking *(3,22)*. Scientists originally believed that if a person orally ingested marijuana without heating, very little THC would be absorbed. They had evidence that if one heated marijuana before ingestion, as occurs with marijuana brownies, significant quantities of THC were absorbed. Later studies demonstrated that an individual can also absorb THC from marijuana plants that were dried in the sun, because variable amounts of THC released by decarboxylation. Hashish and hashish oil retain much of the parent THC in a form that can be more easily absorbed, whether smoked or ingested orally.

3. Absorption

Smoking, the principal route of cannabis administration in the United States, provides a rapid and highly efficient method of drug delivery. Approximately 30% of THC in marijuana or hashish cigarettes is destroyed by pyrolysis during smoking *(23,24)*. Smoked drugs are highly abused in part because of the efficiency and speed of delivery of the drug from the lungs to the brain. Intensely pleasurable and strongly reinforcing effects may be produced because of the almost immediate drug exposure to the central nervous system. Drug delivery during cannabis smoking is characterized by rapid absorption of THC, with slightly lower peak concentrations than those found after intravenous administration *(25)*. Bioavailability of smoked THC is reported to be 18–50% partly as a result of the intra- and intersubject variability in smoking dynamics that contribute to uncertainty in dose delivery *(26)*. The number, duration, and spacing of puffs, hold time, and inhalation volume greatly influence the degree of drug exposure *(27–29)*. THC can be measured in the plasma within seconds after inhalation of the first puff of marijuana smoke (*see* Fig. 1; ref. *30*). Mean ± SD THC concentrations of 7.0 ± 8.1 and 18.1 ± 12.0 ng/mL were observed following the first inhalation of a low- (1.75% THC, approx 16 mg) or high-dose (3.55% THC, approx 30 mg) cigarette, respectively *(30)*. Concentrations increased rapidly and peaked at 9.0 minutes, berfore initiation of the last puff sequence at 9.8 minutes. Figure 2 dis-

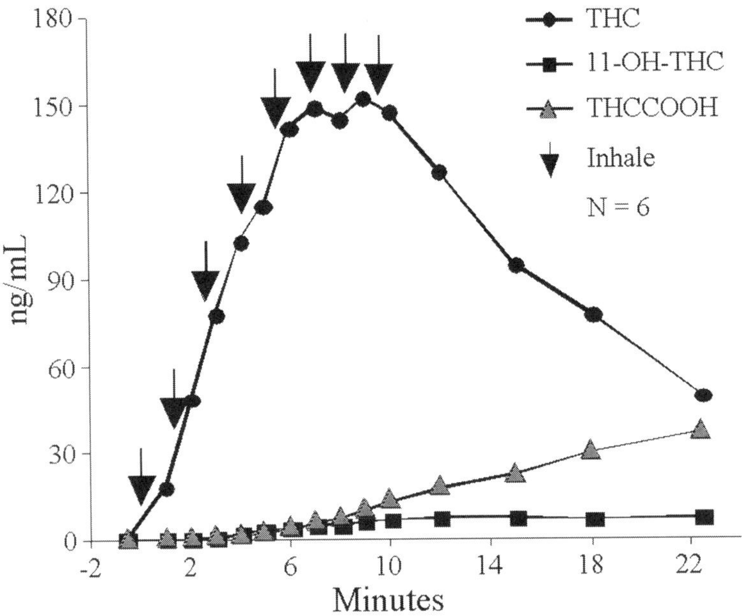

Fig. 1. Mean (*N* = 6) plasma concentrations of Δ⁹-tetrahydrocannabinol (THC), 11-hydroxy-Δ⁹-THC (11-OH-THC), and 11-nor-9-carboxy-Δ⁹-THC (THCCOOH) by gas chromatography/mass spectrometry during smoking of a single 3.55% THC cigarette. Each arrow represents one inhalation or puff on the cannabis cigarette. (From ref. *1* with permission.)

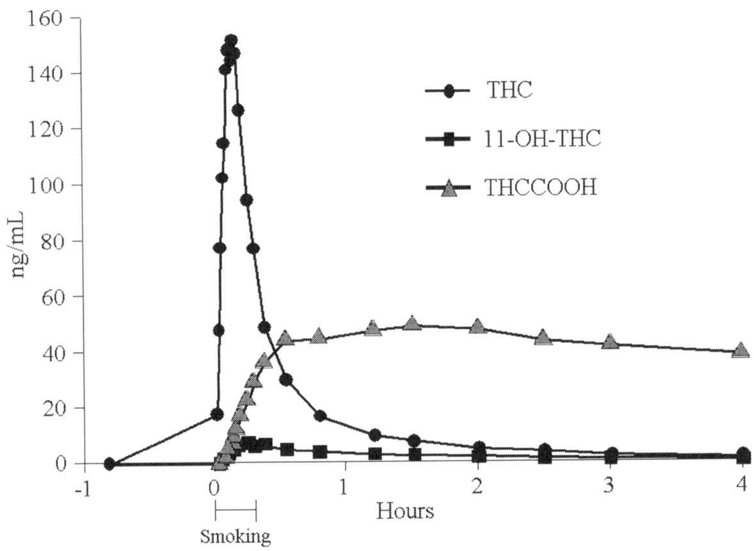

Fig. 2. Mean (*N* = 6) plasma concentrations of Δ⁹-tetrahydrocannabinol (THC), 11-hydroxy-Δ⁹-THC (11-OH-THC), and 11-nor-9-carboxy-Δ⁹-THC (THCCOOH) by gas chromatography/mass spectrometry following smoking of a single 3.55% THC cigarette. (From ref. *30* with permission.)

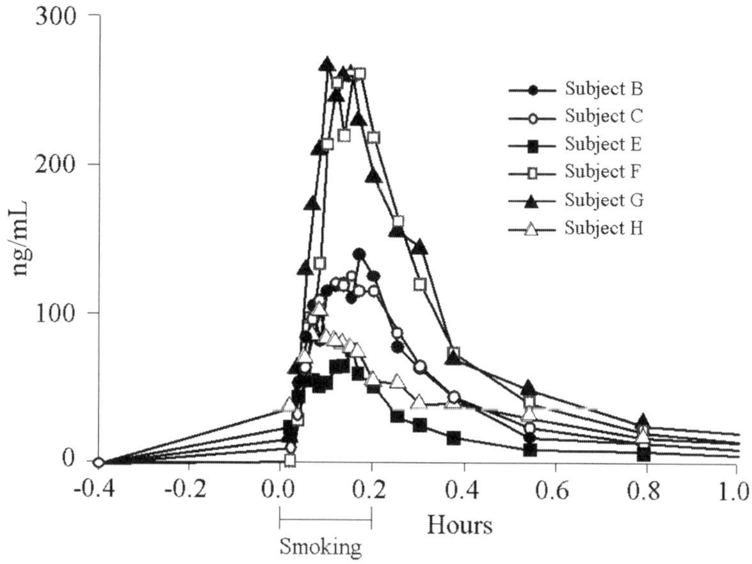

Fig. 3. Individual plasma Δ⁹-tetrahydrocannabinol (THC) time course by gas chromatography/mass spectrometry for six subjects following smoking of a single 3.55% THC cigarette. (From ref. *30* with permission)

plays mean data for a group of six subjects after paced smoking of a single 3.55% THC cigarette. The number of puffs, length of inhalation and hold time, time between puffs, and potency of the cigarette were controlled. Figure 3 shows individual THC concentration time profiles for six subjects and demonstrates the large intersubject variability of the smoked route of drug administration. Many individuals prefer the smoked route, not only for its rapid drug delivery, but also for the ability to titrate their dose.

In some studies THC was measured in blood, and expected values were found to be about half those of plasma *(31)*. Albumin and other proteins that bind THC and the poor penetration of THC into red blood cells contribute to these higher plasma concentrations. Postmortem blood is a common example where blood concentrations are routinely reported because of difficulty obtaining acceptable plasma samples. Significant differences in THC concentrations between the two fluids make it important to always be informed about which is being reported.

If cannabis is ingested orally, absorption is slower and peak plasma THC concentrations are lower *(25,32–34)*. Wall et al. found peak THC concentrations approx 4–6 hours after ingestion of 15–20 mg of THC in sesame oil *(34)*. Peak THC concentrations ranging from 4.4 to 11 ng/mL were observed 1–5 hours following ingestion of 20 mg of THC in a chocolate cookie *(25)*. Oral bioavailability has been reported to be 4–20% *(25,34)*, in part as a result of degradation of drug in the stomach *(35)*. Also, there is significant first-pass metabolism to active 11-hydroxy-Δ⁹-tetrahydrocannabinol (11-OH-THC) and inactive metabolites. Plasma 11-OH-THC concentrations range from 50 to 100% of THC concentrations following the oral route of cannabis administration compared to only about 10% after smoking *(34)*. 11-OH-THC is equipotent to THC, explaining the fact that pharmacodynamic effects after oral cannabis administration appear to be greater than those after smoking THC at the same concentrations *(25)*.

4. Distribution

THC has a large volume of distribution, 10 L/kg, and is 97–99% protein bound in plasma, primarily to lipoproteins *(36,37)*. Highly perfused organs, including the brain, are rapidly exposed to drug. Less highly perfused tissues accumulate drug more slowly because THC redistributes from the vascular compartment to tissue *(38)*. THC's high lipid solubility concentrates and prolongs retention of the drug in fat *(39,40)*. Slow release of the drug from fat and significant enterohepatic circulation contribute to THC's long terminal elimination half-life in plasma, reported as greater than 4.1 days in chronic marijuana users *(41)*. Isotopically labeled THC and sensitive analytical procedures were used to obtain this estimate of drug half-life. Use of less sensitive assays and a shorter monitoring time yield much lower estimates of terminal elimination half-life.

5. Metabolism

Hydroxylation of THC by the hepatic cytochrome P450 enzyme system leads to production of the active metabolite 11-OH-THC *(42,43)*, believed by early investigators to be the true active analyte *(44)*. When marijuana is smoked as opposed to taken orally, concentrations of 11-OH-THC are much lower (approx 10% of the THC concentration; ref. *30*). Other tissues, including brain, intestine, and lung, may contribute to the metabolism of THC, and, in these tissues, alternate hydroxylation pathways may be more prominent *(45–49)*. Further metabolism to di- and tri-hydroxy compounds, ketones, aldehydes, and carboxylic acids has been documented *(38,50)*. Oxidation of active 11-OH-THC produces the inactive metabolite, 11-nor-9-carboxy-Δ^9-tetrahydrocannabinol (THCCOOH) *(44,51)*. In a study of the pharmacokinetics of a single oral 10-mg dose of Marinol®, the concentration of inactive THCCOOH metabolite predominated from as early as 1 hour after dosing, with much lower THC and 11-OH-THC concentrations *(52)*. The inactive THCCOOH metabolite and its glucuronide conjugate have been identified as the major end products of biotransformation in most species, including humans *(50,53)*. Renal clearance of these polar metabolites is low as a result of extensive protein binding *(36)*. Plasma THCCOOH concentrations gradually increase and are greater than THC concentrations shortly after smoking (Fig. 2), whereas THC concentrations decrease rapidly after smoking cessation *(30)*. The time course of detection of THCCOOH in plasma is much longer than that of THC or 11-OH-THC.

6. Elimination

After the initial distribution phase, the rate-limiting step in the elimination of THC is its redistribution from lipid depots to blood *(54)*. Early studies showed that

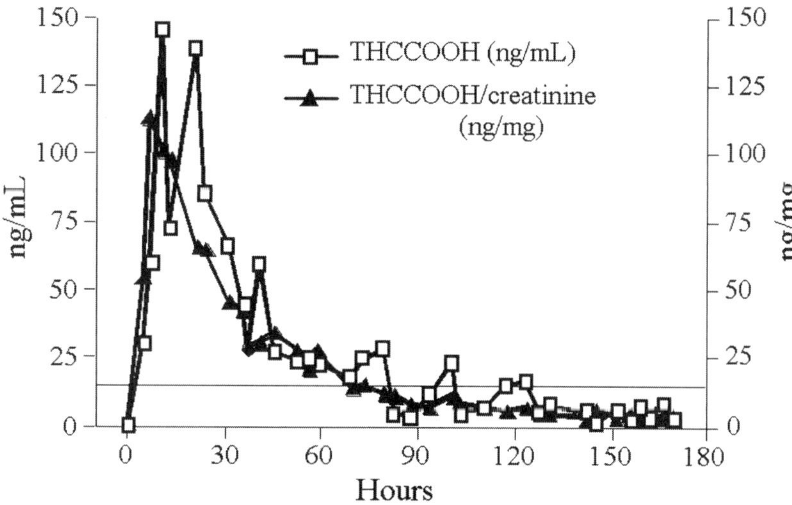

Fig. 4. Urinary excretion profile of 11-nor-9-carboxy-Δ⁹-THC (THCCOOH) as measured by gas chromatography/mass spectrometry (GC/MS) in one subject following smoking of a single 3.55% THC cigarette. The horizontal line at 15 ng/mL represents the current GC/MS cutoff used in most testing programs. The urinary THC-COOH concentrations (ng/mL) normalized to urine creatinine concentrations (mg/mL) are illustrated with closed triangles. (From ref. *89* with permission.)

15–20% of a smoked THC dose was eliminated as acidic urinary metabolites, whereas 25–30% were excreted in the feces as 11-OH-THC and THC-COOH following intravenous administration and 48–53% following oral administration *(34,38)*. Approximately 80% of the acidic urinary metabolites are estimated to be conjugated and nonconjugated THC-COOH. There appears to be no significant difference in metabolism between men and women *(34)*. A total of 80–90% of the drug is excreted within 5 days, mostly as hydroxylated and carboxylated metabolites *(38)*. Halldin et al. identified 18 acidic metabolites of THC in urine, most of which are hydroxylated or β-oxidized analogs of THC *(53)*. Many of these metabolites are conjugated with glucuronic acid, increasing the compounds' water solubility. The primary urinary metabolite is the acid-linked THCCOOH glucuronide conjugate *(55)*, whereas 11-OH-THC predominates in the feces *(38)*. Mean peak urinary concentrations of THC-COOH were 89.8 ± 31.9 ng/mL and 153.4 ± 49.2 ng/mL approx 8 and 14 hours after smoking a single 1.75 or 3.55% THC cigarette (*see* Fig. 4; refs. *56* and *57*). THC-COOH was detected in urine at a concentration greater than or equal to 15 ng/mL for 33.7 ± 9.2 hours and 88.6 ± 9.5 hours after these doses (15 ng/mL was selected for evaluation because federal drug testing programs administratively designate specimens with THCCOOH concentrations below this level as negative). When sensitive analytical procedures and sufficient sampling periods are employed, the terminal urinary excretion half-life of THCCOOH in humans has been estimated to be 3–4 days *(58)*. When THC is ingested orally, the excretion profile is similar to that following smoking *(32,59)*. Gustafson et al. studied seven subjects who received oral doses of 0, 0.39, 0.47, 7.5 (Marinol), and 14.8 mg THC per day in a double-blind, placebo-controlled, randomized study (60). THC in hemp oil or Marinol was administered in three divided daily doses at meals for 5 days. All urine specimens were collected over the 10-week study period and analyzed by several immunoassays and gas chromatography/mass spectrometry (GC/MS). Maximum THC-COOH concentrations were 5.4–38.2 ng/mL and 19.0–436 ng/mL for the two lower and two higher doses, respectively.

An important analytical study was published by Kemp et al. showing that significantly higher concentrations of THC and 11-OH-THC in urine were found when *Escherichia coli* β-glucuronidase was employed in the hydrolysis method compared with either of the common hydrolysis methods using *Helix pomatia* glucuronidase or base *(61)*. Mean THC concentration in urine specimens from seven subjects collected after each had smoked a single 3.58% marijuana cigarette was 22 ng/mL using the *E. coli* glucuronidase hydrolysis method, whereas THC concentrations using either *H. pomatia* glucuronidase or base hydrolysis methods were near zero. Similar differences were found for 11-OH-THC with a mean concentration of 72 ng/mL from the *E. coli* method and concentrations less than 10 ng/mL from the other methods. It is hoped that the finding of THC in urine may provide a reliable marker of recent cannabis use; however, adequate data from controlled drug administration studies are not yet available.

7. Interpretation of Body Fluid and Hair Concentrations

Interpreting body fluid concentrations by necessity depends on the nature of the questions that require a science-based answer; however, the most common social questions generally can be summarized as: Is the concentration of the drug in an individual's body fluid sufficiently high to indicate impairment or place them in violation of a governing policy?

Research scientists who are conducting studies to determine cannabinoid mechanisms of action or examine how cannabinoids may be used in clinical treatment also have an interest in interpreting cannabinoid concentrations in body fluids and tissues. The generic question they might ask would be: How do fluid or tissue concentrations in humans correlate with brain concentrations or with treatment outcome? To provide answers to these important social and scientific questions, we must examine more closely the kinetics of the drug in bodily fluids and tissues and how these relate to effects on the individual.

7.1. Plasma

Let us consider the specific example of a man who is stopped by a police officer for erratic driving. The driver fails a field sobriety test indicating that he is impaired, and subsequent laboratory testing determines that his plasma THC concentration is 2 ng/mL. Did the THC contribute to his impaired driving?

Plasma concentrations of drug are frequently measured in an attempt to answer this question because, in general, plasma concentrations of most drugs correlate with drug effects better than concentrations in other bodily fluids. Mason and McBay reported in 1985 that one could not predict the effects of cannabis from plasma THC concentrations *(62)*. They quoted their own study of 600 drivers killed in single-vehicle

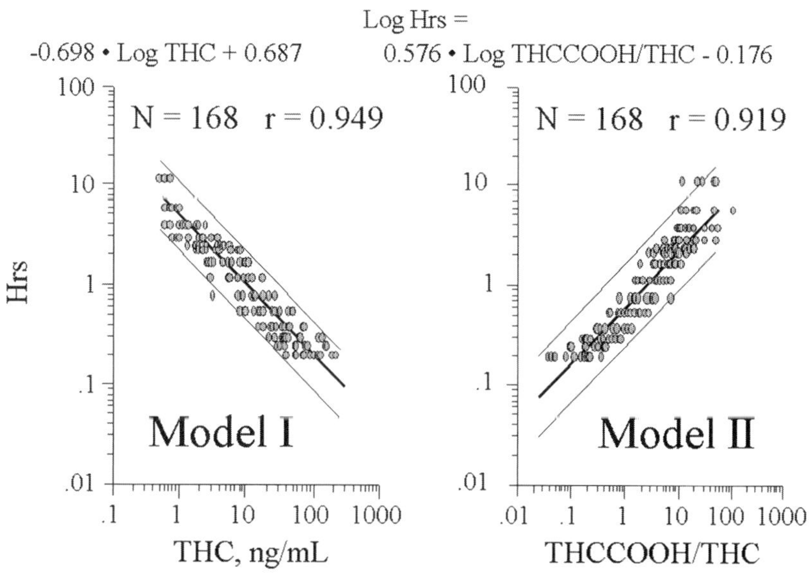

Fig. 5. Predictive mathematical models for estimating the elapsed time in hours of last cannabis use based on plasma Δ^9-tetrahydrocannabinol (THC) and 11-nor-9-carboxy-Δ^9-THC (THCCOOH) concentrations by GC/MS. (From ref. *70* with permission.)

crashes that found alcohol to be the only drug with significant adverse effects on driving *(31)*. Moskowitz, reporting during the same time frame, did not specifically address plasma concentrations of THC, but cited many studies that found a relationship between cannabis dose and performance impairment including impaired coordination, tracking, perception, and vigilance in driving simulators and on-the-road tests (63). More recent studies with carefully controlled variables and newer performance measures documented that smoking cannabis at doses of 300 μg THC/kg, or about 20 mg for the 70-kg man in our example, impaired perceptual motor speed, accuracy, and multitasking, all important requirements for safe driving *(64–66)*. The impairing effects of the 300 μg/kg dose of THC were similar to those of individuals with blood alcohol concentrations of 0.05 g/dL or greater, the legal driving limit in most European countries. When combined with alcohol, the impairing effects of THC were even greater *(66–68)*. However, most of these studies did not attempt to correlate plasma or blood THC concentrations with observed effects but demonstrated that impairment depended on the time after use, with most subjects showing no impairment 24 hours postdose. Huestis et al. performed controlled administration studies that measured plasma THC concentrations in six individuals who had smoked 15.8- and 33-mg doses of THC in marijuana *(69)*. Concentrations for plasma collected after marijuana smoking were used to construct models for predicting the time of last THC use within 95% confidence intervals (*see* Fig. 5; refs. *30, 70,* and *71*). Both Model I, which used plasma THC concentrations, and Model II, which used the ratio of THCCOOH/THC concentrations, were found to predict the time of last use in about 90% of cases from all previously published plasma concentration data, whether analysis was by radioimmunoassay (RIA), GC, or GC/MS. These mathematical models were further evaluated in another controlled drug administration study of 38 subjects, each smoking a 2.64% THC cigarette. Of these subjects, 29 smoked a second cigarette 4 hours later *(72)*. Plasma was collected immediately after the first cigarette and up to 6 hours after smoking for analysis of THC and THC-COOH concentrations ($N = 717$). Accuracy, when applying the combination of Model I and Model II's 95% confidence intervals, following the first cigarette was 99.5% (413 of 415 specimens had a THC concentration or THC-COOH/THC ratio that predicted the correct time of use within this interval) with no underestimations of time of use and maximum overestimation of 4 minutes. Accuracy when applying the combined models' 95% confidence intervals following the second cigarette was 98.6% (285 of 289 specimens) with no underestimations and the same maximum overestimation. When plasma concentrations of THC were between 0.5 and 2 ng/mL, Model I alone was 80.5% accurate, and Model II alone was 77.6% accurate. However, Model I had no underestimations, and Model II had time of use for 17 of 76 specimens underestimated with maximum errors up to 1.5 hours, indicating that Model II alone is less reliable when THC concentrations are between 0.5 and 2 ng/mL. If the models were used in combination, predicted times of use were accurate for all cases.

Both models are used frequently in courts of law in many countries to estimate elapsed time since last cannabis use in accident and criminal investigations. They allow decision makers to answer a corollary question: How accurately can you estimate the time of last use of cannabis? Officials can use this information to corroborate or discount the accused person's story. After estimating the time of last use, the time course of performance-impairment data reported in the literature is referenced to support a conclusion of possible impairment or lack of impairment. There are many laboratory, simulator, and on-the-road studies that have shown impairment in tasks required for safe driving when individuals have been under the influence of cannabis *(66,68)*, especially when cannabis is combined with ethanol *(73)*.

The onset of impairing effects of THC lags behind the increase in plasma concentration during absorption; then effects remain relatively constant as the concentration decreases dramatically because of THC distribution and metabolism *(1)*. This concentration–effect relationship, displayed in Fig. 6, is described as a counterclockwise hysteresis. As an example, one can observe two different intensities of effects for tachycardia and the visual analog scale for "feel drug" at 50 ng/mL depending on whether the individual is in the absorption or distribution phase. Plasma THC concentrations appear to be linearly related to the intensity of effects during absorption and elimination, but there is no relationship between concentration and effects during distribution. In the case of drivers, it would be rare for authorities to collect a plasma specimen prior to the initial distribution phase of THC. After smoking cannabis, absorption and distribution are complete in 45–60 minutes. It typically takes longer than this to stop the driver, perform a field sobriety test, and transport the driver to a site for drawing blood. In the scenario we are considering, it would be important to determine the time sequence of events from driving through blood collection to ensure that the driver was in the elimination phase. For instructive purposes, we will consider that the police officer testified that the time of blood collection was more than 1 hour after the driver was stopped and that the driver was under observation during this period, precluding further drug use.

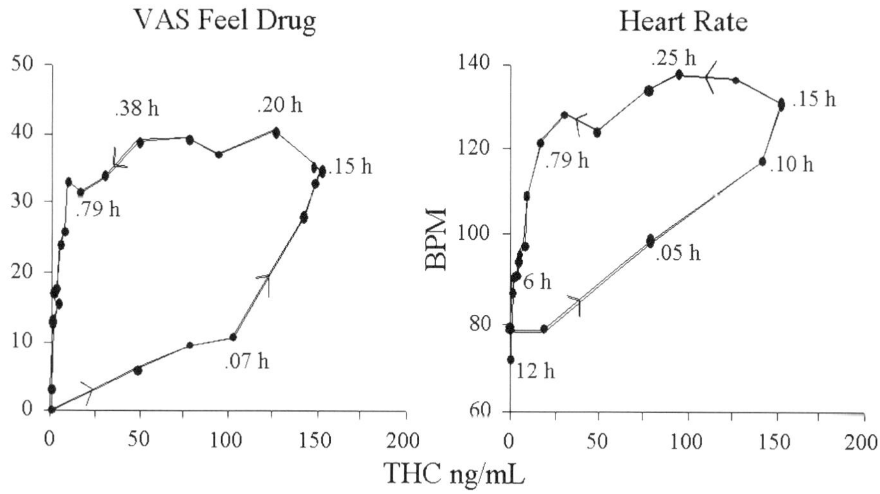

Fig. 6. Visual analog scale for "How strongly do you feel the drug now?" and heart rate (BPM, beats per minute) measures for a subject after smoking a 3.55% THC cigarette demonstrating a counterclockwise hysteresis for the concentration–effect curves.

Early epidemiological approaches relating cannabinoid plasma concentrations to accident risk yielded inconsistent results and were criticized for not including an adequate control group of drivers who were on the same roads at similar times and who did not have driving accidents *(1)*. An improved approach, responsibility analysis, independently assigns culpability for the accident and then statistically compares the odds ratio or risk that an accident could occur for individuals who had cannabinoids in their system and for those that did not. Culpability analysis proved effective for demonstrating performance impairment with alcohol, but was less successful for cannabinoids for several important reasons. In many cases blood was not drawn for cannabinoid analysis until many hours after an accident or impaired driving incident. During this time the concentration of THC in the plasma decreased rapidly, often falling below the limits of quantification (LOQs) of the methods used for analysis. In many cases, the only analyte identified in plasma was THCCOOH, the inactive metabolite with a much wider window of drug detection than parent THC. Some of the early studies only reported whether cannabinoids were present in blood or urine, not specifying whether measurable THC was found. They used analytical methods with high LOQs, i.e., small windows of detection, and were underpowered to identify increased risk because of insufficient sample size. Drummer et al. successfully employed the empirical approach of culpability analysis and found that the group of drivers who had THC present in blood were three to seven times more likely to be responsible for their accident than drivers whose blood specimens were negative for THC *(65,74)*. Those with THC blood concentrations of 5 ng/mL had the higher probability of causing the accident, with a mean odds ratio of 6.8.

With this body of scientific information, we now can answer the question of whether or not marijuana contributed to the driving impairment of the individual in our example. This individual failed the field sobriety test and had 2 ng/mL of THC in his plasma more than an hour after being stopped by the police. In this case, marijuana most likely contributed to the performance impairment. The issue of whether or not a biological test result alone can be used to document impairment is much more controversial. In many states and countries, *per se* laws have been established that state that an individual is assumed to be under the influence of cannabis if THC or, in some cases, THCCOOH is found in blood, plasma, or, sometimes, urine. The problem of drugged driving is a serious public health issue requiring additional research to link drug concentrations to ongoing impairment, to determine the best analyte and best biological fluid to monitor, and to decide whether administrative cutoff concentrations are needed.

What if the accused driver claimed that he might have unknowingly ingested food that contained cannabis? If this were true, he might be less culpable and receive less punishment. As mentioned, the ratios of 11-OH-THC to THC concentrations differ following the smoked and oral routes of administration; peak concentrations of 11-OH-THC after smoking are about 10% that of THC and approximately equal after oral administration *(1)*. If 11-OH-THC also was measured in the plasma from the driver in our example and its ratio with THC was approx 1:1, this would provide some evidence to support his story.

If we now change venues from the courtroom to the research center, we can examine how scientists use plasma concentrations to help understand the mechanisms by which cannabinoids affect brain function. Advances in brain imaging using positron emission tomography and magnetic resonance imaging have allowed investigators to observe changes in CBF as a result of THC administration *(12,75–77)*. A question relevant to this area of research might be: How do plasma concentrations of THC following administration of cannabis correlate with changes observed in the brain using imaging techniques? Mathew et al., who studied 47 subjects who received two different intravenous doses of THC or placebo, found that THC had significant effects on global and regional CBF *(13)*. Also, feeling intoxicated accounted for changes in regional CBF better than plasma levels of THC. This finding is not surprising in that the effects on the brain would be expected to have a more contemporaneous relationship with related physiological processes in the brain. However, plasma concentrations provide information about individual differences in processing the same dose of cannabis and offer additional information about the metabolites of THC, such as 11-OH-THC, which is physiologically active. It would also be interesting to examine arterial blood because it has been reported that arterial drug concentrations may be more closely related to brain function than venous concentrations *(78)*. Combining pharmacokinetic measures with brain imaging following controlled administration of cannabis is a new area of research that promises to provide interesting scientific information by examining the process of drug action from ingestion through direct physiological changes in regions of the brain.

A related question may be: What information can plasma THC concentrations give us about receptor function? Recently, cannabinoid receptors, CB_1 and CB_2, and endogenous cannabinoid neurotransmitters have been characterized, primarily from in vitro and animal studies *(79–82)*. In this line of research, cannabinoids with potential as pharmacotherapies are often evaluated by first studying their interactions with cannabinoid receptors in animals or in vitro, and then examined in human trials. SR141716 (named rimonabant), the first CB_1-selective cannabinoid receptor antagonist, was shown to block many of the effects of THC in animals *(83,84)*. In a controlled clinical study of THC's cardiovascular and subjective effects in humans, Huestis et al. found that a single 90 mg oral dose of rimonabant antagonized increases in heart rate and subjective effects following smoked cannabis *(85)*. It was important to determine whether the observed reductions in effects were a result of a receptor-mediated pharmacodynamic change or simply a pharmacokinetic interaction reducing the available THC. The investigators found that there were no statistically significant differences between peak and area-under-the-curve plasma concentrations of THC in the placebo and active rimonabant groups. Therefore, blockade of tachycardia and subjective effects by rimonabant following smoked marijuana was not a result of an alteration in THC pharmacokinetics. In addition to its role as a pharmacological tool to investigate the endogenous cannabinoid system, the antagonist appears to have potential efficacy in humans for smoking cessation *(86)* and weight loss *(87)*; phase III trials are ongoing for these medical indications. Other potential therapeutic roles for this antagonist are being actively investigated as well.

Clinical trials are evaluating the efficacy of THC, cannabidiol, and other cannabinoids in the treatment of nausea after cancer chemotherapy, appetite loss, multiple sclerosis, and neuropathic pain *(16)*. A common clinical question might be: How will monitoring plasma cannabinoid concentrations aid clinical management of these patients? As with any new pharmaceutical preparation, it is necessary to study the drug's pharmacokinetics to more clearly understand required doses, frequency of dosing, contributions of metabolites to effects or toxicity, elimination profiles, and metabolism and excretion in different populations, including newborns, children, ethnic groups, diseased individuals, and the elderly. For example, one must determine the median effective dose, ED_{50}, for these populations to assist clinicians who must prescribe doses that will be efficacious but avoid toxicity.

Another concern of clinicians prescribing medications is abuse liability. It has been shown that the route of administration affects the abuse liability of a drug *(88)*. As discussed above, inhalation of smoked cannabis, which results in rapid increases in THC concentrations, can be an effective way for individuals to titrate their THC dose, but may increase its abuse liability. Most clinical trials are evaluating oral, sublingual, or inhaler formulations to better control dose and reduce toxic side effects from smoking. This is expected to reduce the abuse liability as well. Well-designed clinical trials that include pharmacokinetic analyses in tandem with clinical assessment of patients are needed to establish the efficacy and pharmacokinetics of these new preparations and new delivery routes.

7.2. Urine

Many governmental and private organizations in the United States employ drug testing as part of their drug use-prevention programs. Urine is the biological matrix most commonly tested to identify individuals who use drugs. In 2003 it was estimated that more than 20 million urine specimens were collected for drug testing in United

States programs. Drug testing is also an important objective outcome measure of drug treatment, drug research investigating efficacy of new behavioral therapies, criminal justice, military programs, and emergency, pediatric, and geriatric medicine. A common example is judicial programs that routinely collect urine from individuals on parole. Individuals committing crimes and having a positive urine drug test may be placed in treatment while on parole if the judge believes that drug use contributed to the crime. Parolees are ordered to attend a rehabilitation program, are given a short period of time to eliminate previously self-administered drugs from their bodies, and, as a condition of continued parole, must discontinue use of prohibited drugs. To ensure compliance, treatment managers routinely have the parolee donate urine specimens, and if there is a positive urine test indicating new drug use, the donor may be sent to prison. This example sets the stage for an important social question. If a parolee who was a chronic marijuana user had a sequential set of urine tests during his first week of rehabilitation with decreasing concentrations of THCCOOH from 1000 ng/mL down to 100 ng/mL by the end of the week, and then donated a urine specimen with a concentration of 150 ng/mL, does this increase in urine concentration indicate new use in violation of his parole?

Figure 4 shows a typical urinary excretion profile for THCCOOH in an infrequent marijuana user following smoking of a single marijuana cigarette. As mentioned previously, there is great inter- and intrasubject variability in the urinary excretion of cannabinoids. Many investigators have published studies showing that in a sequential series of urine specimens from individuals who abstained from smoking cannabis, there can occasionally be urine specimens that have higher concentrations of THC-COOH than previous samples *(89–91)*. This could be a result of residual excretion of drug that has been stored in the body following chronic cannabinoid use. Most of these increases in concentration appear to be related to individuals' hydration states that are determined by fluid intake, environmental temperature, levels of activity, disease states, and a multitude of other variables. Urine may be diluted and drug concentrations reduced as a result of ordinary variations in daily activity or purposeful attempts to adulterate the sample by specimen dilution, achieved by simply drinking large quantities of fluid. In controlled studies of cocaine and cannabinoid administration followed by consumption of different amounts of liquids, investigators were able to demonstrate large reductions in urine drug concentrations. In many cases, results fell below cutoff concentrations for a positive test *(92)*.

Manno et al. first suggested that urinary THCCOOH could be normalized to urinary creatinine concentration to account for specimen dilution *(91)*. They recommended a quotient cutoff of ≥ 1.5 to identify new drug use. Huestis and Cone addressed this problem by examining more than 1800 urine specimens collected following controlled THC administration *(89)*. They found that the greatest accuracy (85.4%) in predicting new cannabis use occurred when paired specimens collected at least 24 hours apart had a quotient of ≥ 0.5 for the [THCCOOH]/[creatinine] in specimen 2 divided by the [THCCOOH]/[creatinine] for specimen 1. If the 1.5 ratio was used, as proposed by Manno, almost 30% of the cases of new drug exposure would be missed. Figure 4 shows that normalizing the THCCOOH concentration to creatinine concentrations makes the excretion pattern more predictable, i.e., it has fewer abrupt changes in the exponential decrease.

The Huestis and Cone study examined infrequent cannabis users and did not address excretion patterns that one would expect from chronic use. As mentioned, chronic users take longer than infrequent users to eliminate marijuana metabolites. This is a result of the disposition of THC into poorly perfused tissues such as fat. With chronic cannabis use, THC concentrations in these poorly perfused compartments increase, forming less accessible depots of THC in the body. Hunt and Jones demonstrated that the slow return of THC from these depots into the plasma was the rate-limiting step in the terminal elimination of THC from the body *(36)*. Fraser and Worth studied a group of 26 chronic marijuana users, testing both the Manno and Huestis criteria for new use and had a false-negative rate of 7.4% with the Huestis guideline and 24% with the Manno rule *(93)*. They extended the study to include 37 chronic marijuana users with at least 48 hours between specimens; with the ≥0.5 cutoff, new drug use was identified in 80–85% of cases *(94)*. Of course, the smaller the ratio used, the greater the potential for false-positive results. The reasons for conducting the urine test, i.e., treatment or parole, and the impact of the results on the donor guide the choice of which ratio to apply.

Based on this valuable scientific information, we can answer the question about whether the individual on parole in our example had smoked marijuana between donating the specimen containing 100 ng/mL THCCOOH and the specimen with 150 ng/mL THCCOOH. The answer is that we cannot tell if he used cannabis in violation of his conditions for parole. Additional information is needed to differentiate between new cannabis use and residual drug excretion. This spike in urine concentration would not be unusual for an individual who had complied with his treatment protocol. If the treatment center had collected the specimens at least 24 hours apart and had measured creatinine concentrations, we would have additional information to provide a more definitive answer. If the outcome of the evaluation could be used to place the individual, who was a former chronic cannabis user, in prison for continuing use after entering his rehabilitation program, the higher ratio of 1.5 might be a better choice for evaluating his urine tests. This would achieve better specificity, rather than sensitivity. In addition, more frequent monitoring may be useful if urine specimens are being collected more than 48 hours apart.

7.3. Oral Fluid

Oral fluid is composed of saliva and secretions from the nasopharyngeal area and mouth. Mechanisms of drug entry into oral fluid are not fully understood. Scientists have determined that passive diffusion from blood and tissue depots and direct entry into oral fluid following smoked, oral, sublingual, or snorted routes of drug administration are the primary sources. In rare cases (e.g., lithium), active transport mechanisms also may contribute. Some of the factors affecting how much drug enters oral fluid from the blood are the lipophilicity of the drug, the degree of plasma protein binding, the drug's pK_a, and pH differences between blood and oral fluid. In general, if the drug is not extensively bound to plasma proteins, is lipophilic, and is present in an unionized state, passive diffusion is the primary mechanism for drug entry into oral fluid. The lower pH in oral fluid as compared with blood can result in ion trapping of drugs with a higher pK_a (e.g., codeine), which has concentrations three to four times

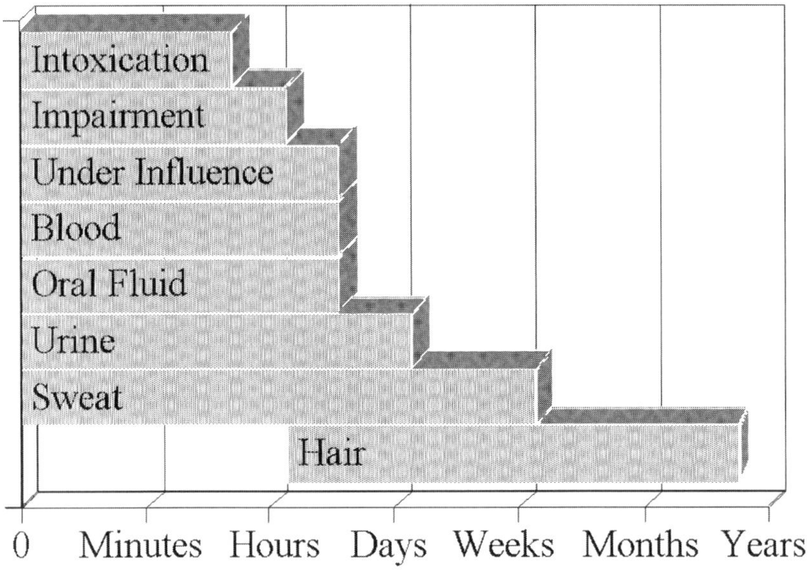

Fig. 7. General drug effects and detection time ranges in various matrices following occasional cannabinoid use. (Personal communication from Edward J. Cone, PhD.)

higher in oral fluid *(95)*. In general, detection times for drugs in oral fluid range from a few hours to 1 or 2 days following use (*see* Fig. 7).

There are few data on the disposition of cannabinoids in oral fluid following controlled cannabis administration. Scientists have known that THC is present in oral fluid since the 1970s *(96,97)*, and in the 1980s Gross et al. found that they could detect THC in saliva with RIA for 2–5 hours in 35 subjects who smoked one marijuana cigarette containing 27 mg THC *(98)*. However, the specificity of this assay was low, with frequent false-positive results. One of the first studies to examine cannabinoid concentrations in oral fluid after intravenous administration of radiolabeled THC found no radioactivity in the oral fluid, indicating that THC in oral fluid after smoking was a result of direct contamination of the oral mucosa and oral fluid in the mouth, and not from passive diffusion from plasma *(99)*. Another study examined oral fluid following the smoking of 1.75 and 3.55% marijuana cigarettes by six participants *(100)*. Specimens were collected by expectoration before and periodically up to 72 hours after smoking. All specimens were analyzed for cannabinoids using specific RIAs for THC and THCCOOH, with cutoff concentrations of 1.0 and 2.5 ng/mL, respectively. THC was detected in oral fluid for up to 24 hours after the higher dose. No specimens were positive for THCCOOH by RIA. In addition, one participant's specimen set was analyzed by GC/MS for THC, 11-OH-THC, and THCCOOH with LOQs of 0.5 ng/mL. This analysis confirmed that no measurable 11-OH-THC or THCCOOH was present throughout the time course in any of the oral fluid specimens. Niedbala et al. studied 18 subjects who were administered single doses of marijuana by smoked (20–25 mg) or oral (20–25 mg) routes *(101)*. Urine and oral fluid specimens (Intercept collection device, OraSure Technologies, Inc., Bethlehem, PA) were collected at intervals up to 72 hours. Oral fluid was screened with a cannabinoid enzyme immunoassay (Intercept Micro-Plate EIA, OraSure Technologies, Inc.) with a cutoff concentration of 1.0 ng/mL and confirmed for THC by GC tandem MS, cutoff concentration of 0.5 ng/mL. Urine was screened by cannabinoid immunoassay (Abuscreen Online, Roche Diagnostics, Inc., Indianapolis, IN) and GC-MS for THC-COOH, cutoff concentrations of 50 and 15 ng/mL, respectively. Oral fluid specimens tested positive following marijuana smoked consecutively for average periods of 13 hours. The average time of the last positive test was 31 hours. There was great individual variation, with one subject having the last positive specimen at 2 hours and another at 72 hours. The decrease in oral fluid THC concentrations during the first 2 hours appeared to parallel those published by others for plasma THC, but no plasma was collected in this study for direct comparison. Urine specimens were consecutively positive following smoking for an average of 26 hours. The average time for the last positive reading was 42 hours with ranges up to 72 hours, the last collection. In the oral ingestion study, each of three subjects ate one brownie that had been cooked with plant material containing 20–25 mg of THC. THC was present in oral fluid following this method of oral ingestion, but concentrations peaked at 1–2 hours, were low, 3–5 ng/mL, and declined rapidly to negative, typically at 4 hours.

In recent studies oral fluid has been collected in a wide variety of devices designed by different manufacturers. Unfortunately, the recovery of cannabinoids from these devices is frequently unknown, a fact that significantly affects the devices' sensitivity in detecting cannabinoid use. Another problem area is the immunoassay reagent used to screen oral fluid specimens for cannabinoids. Many of the manufacturer's reagents target THC-COOH in their antigen-antibody reactions, making the sensitivity of these tests for cannabinoid exposure unacceptably low. Kintz et al. examined oral fluid (Salivette), blood, forehead wipes, and urine from 198 injured drivers and found 22 positive by urine testing for THC-COOH *(102)*. Fourteen of these patients were also positive for THC in oral fluid, with no specimens positive for 11-OH-THC or THC-COOH at the limits of detection for their method. Samyn et al. collected urine from drivers who failed field sobriety tests at police roadblocks *(103)*. For drivers who had a positive urine test, blood specimens were collected and, following informed consent, oral fluid (Salivette) and sweat specimens were collected. Oral fluid specimens and plasma were collected from 180 drivers and analyzed by GC-MS with cutoff concentrations of 5.0 and 1.0 ng/mL, respectively. The predictive value of oral fluid compared with plasma was 90%. In a different approach, Cone et al. examined 77,218 oral fluid specimens submitted to a large drug-testing laboratory *(104)*. Using an oral fluid screening cutoff concentration for cannabinoids of 3 ng/mL and a confirmation THC cutoff concentration of 1.5 ng/mL, they found a cannabis positive rate of 3.22%, which was similar to the positive rate of 3.17% for large urine drug-testing laboratories using federally mandated cutoff concentrations. These studies have shown that measurement of THC in oral fluid compares favorably with sweat and urine testing for detecting cannabis use. Others have not found a good correlation between cannabinoid tests for oral fluid and other body fluids *(105–109)*. Some of this variability in performance may be related to differences in cutoff concentrations, different screening specificities, binding of THC by the collection devices, and large intersubject differences of cannabinoid concentrations in biological fluids. The Substance Abuse Mental Health

Services Administration, Department of Health and Human Services (SAMHSA), which regulates federal workplace drug testing in the United States, is currently proposing a screening cutoff of 4 ng/mL for cannabinoids and a confirmation cutoff of 2 ng/mL THC for oral fluid *(110)*.

Menkes et al. reported that the logarithm of salivary THC concentrations correlated with subjective effects and heart rate *(111)*. Based on all of the available data and the ease of collection of oral fluid, many states and countries are considering the use of oral fluid testing for identification of drugged drivers. A large-scale roadside evaluation of the effectiveness of oral fluid monitoring for identifying drug-impaired drivers is being conducted currently in Europe and the United States *(112,113)*.

Some organizations are interested in oral fluid testing of employees before beginning safety-sensitive work, because collection is easy and devices can give a quick screening result on-site. We will take this setting for a question regarding oral fluid testing. If a woman reports to a worksite to operate the reactor in a nuclear power station and her oral fluid screens positive for THC, is the manager justified in assigning her less sensitive duties until the test can be confirmed by a more specific method? If the woman had signed a pre-employment agreement not to use impairing drugs within 24 hours of reporting to work, did she violate her agreement, an act that could result in termination of her employment? The easy answer is that we cannot prove that she used cannabis based on a screening test. The result must be confirmed by a second method based on a different scientific principle of identification; however, it is instructive to examine the reliability of the result because many organizations would remove this person from safety-sensitive duties based on a positive screening test. The suspect employee would be returned to normal duties if the presumptive positive test was not confirmed by further laboratory testing. If the nuclear power facility had a drug policy outlining the terms and conditions for drug testing and ramifications of a positive screening and confirmation test and the woman had been informed of these regulations, then removal from a safety-sensitive position is a prudent action to take. Can we determine when the cannabinoid exposure occurred to answer the second part of the question? As mentioned above, with an oral collection device and screening and confirmation cutoffs of 1 and 0.5 ng/mL, respectively, Niedbala et al. found typical detection times of less than 24 hours, but some subjects produced a positive oral fluid specimen 72 hours after smoking *(101)*. If the confirmatory test is positive and the cutoff concentrations and methodology are the same as those used in the controlled clinical study, we may be able to limit the window of drug exposure to within the past few days. It would be important to know the collection device and the laboratory's procedures, in particular the cutoff concentrations used. Unfortunately, data from well-controlled clinical studies to aid our interpretation are limited. Oral fluid collection devices and testing methodologies differ, and their performance may not have been evaluated in controlled studies. We cannot state definitively that she violated her agreement and used cannabis within 24 hours prior to reporting for work.

There is another interesting point to consider in the interpretation of oral fluid results. Suppose the woman states that she did not use illegal drugs but that she was passively exposed to marijuana smoke when her boyfriend and two of his friends smoked cannabis in her small kitchen. Could this explain the positive oral fluid test?

Although there are limited data in the literature, Niedbala et al. reported that two subjects who did not smoke cannabis but were in the room when others smoked had some positive screening but no confirmed oral fluid cannabinoid tests *(101)*. Subsequent studies that are not yet published but were presented at the International Association of Forensic Toxicologists meeting in 2003 in Melbourne, Australia, and at a conference for Medical Review Officers (personal communication from S. Niedbala of OraSure Technologies, Inc.) conveyed the potential for passive exposure to marijuana smoke resulting in positive screening and confirmation tests. These results occurred when considerable smoke was present in small spaces, and oral fluid specimens were negative within 45 minutes of the end of exposure. This situation may be analogous to research that documented the possibility of a positive urine drug test following extensive passive exposure to marijuana smoke in a sealed experimental room *(114)*. Although a positive test was produced in this experimental setting, participants complained of noxious smoke and irritation to the eyes. Other research conducted under more realistic passive smoke conditions indicated that production of a positive urine test with currently mandated federal guideline cutoffs is highly unlikely *(115,116)*. A passive inhalation defense has rarely been accepted for a positive urine cannabinoid test. Additional research is needed to characterize the potential for positive oral fluid cannabinoid test from passive exposure. Perhaps the selection of appropriate oral fluid screening and confirmation cutoff concentrations can eliminate a positive oral fluid test from passive exposure. We lack appropriate data to answer the question of passive exposure of oral fluid at this time and must admit that additional controlled drug administration and naturalistic studies of drug in oral fluid are needed before we can definitively address the woman's claim of passive exposure.

7.4. Sweat

The substance collected for sweat testing is actually a combination of secretions onto the skin. Cannabinoids and other drugs are transported into sweat by diffusion from blood and other depots. Sweat from eccrine glands and sebum from apocrine sweat glands and sebaceous glands are the main constituents. Eccrine glands are located throughout the body near the surface of the skin, and the sweat they produce is aqueous, contains salts, is usually in the pH range of 4.0–6.0, and is produced at variable rates with an average of approx 20 mL per hour. Apocrine sweat glands are located in the shaft of the hair follicle and excrete a substance that is viscous, cloudy, and rich in cholesterol, triglycerides, and fatty acids. This secretion mixes with sebum, a similar viscous liquid rich in triglycerides and long-chain esters, from sebaceous glands in the hair bulb region. Sweat and sebum mix to form an emulsion on the skin surface. When sweat is collected for testing, this mixture is the substance absorbed onto patches. Once drugs diffuse into the glands, it is believed that eccrine sweat transports the drugs to the surface of the skin within hours, the known time frame for sweat excretion.

Two commercial collection devices are the most commonly used, the PharmChek® patch (PharmChem Laboratories, Dallas, TX), and Drugwipe® (Securetec, Ottobrunn, Germany). Some investigators have also used absorbent pads and wiped the forehead or other regions of the body, and then extracted absorbed substances from the pad. PharmChek, the only US Food and Drug Administration-approved collection device for drugs of abuse testing, has an absorbent pad covered by a tamper-resistant adhesive that is porous enough to allow the skin to breathe but protects against external contamination. Some investigators believe that it is possible to contaminate the sweat-collection pad through the adhesive cover or by insufficient cleaning of the skin surface before placement of the patch *(117,118)*. These devices provide a cumulative record of drug use over the wear time for the patch, usually 7 days, in many instances increasing the sensitivity of drug detection over other monitoring techniques. The Drugwipe device, which employs an absorbent material to wipe the skin and an immunochemical test strip for drug detection, has been evaluated in some studies *(102,107,119)*.

There are few published reports of cannabinoid concentrations in sweat following drug use. One issue is that the collection device does not accurately measure the volume of sweat collected, analogous to the case with oral fluid collection with a device rather than by expectoration. Therefore, scientists report the amount of drug collected per patch, not as a concentration of drug in sweat. Another issue is that the amount of sweat excreted and collected varies based on the amount of exercise and ambient temperature. There also are insufficient data to evaluate recovery of cannabinoids from the patch during sample preparation. Kintz et al. collected urine, oral fluid, and sweat (Drugwipe) samples from injured drivers, and then tested each by immunoassay and GC/MS. Of 22 patients who had a positive urine test, 16 also had a positive sweat test *(102)*. The amounts of THC in sweat ranged from 4 to 152 ng per pad, with no detection of 11-OH-THC or THC-COOH in any specimen at the limit of detection of the method. Samyn et al. collected blood, urine, oral fluid, and sweat (by wiping the forehead with a fleece moistened with isopropanol) from 180 drivers who failed a field sobriety test *(103)*. They reported a positive predictive value compared to plasma testing of 80% for the cannabinoid sweat test using GC/MS testing at cutoff concentrations of 5 and 1 ng/mL, respectively. In an earlier study, Samyn and Haeren found a high number of false-negative and some false-positive cannabinoid sweat testing results using a Drugwipe device *(107)*. SAMHSA has proposed guidelines for sweat cannabinoid testing using the PharmChek patch and a wear period of 7 days with a screening cutoff of 4 ng THC per patch and a confirmation cutoff of 1 ng THC per patch *(110)*.

One application of sweat testing is monitoring drug use in individuals in drug rehabilitation programs. A tamper-proof patch is often placed on the upper arm or back for 7 days, the collection pad is removed, drugs are eluted from the pad, and the extract is tested for the presence of drugs. Suppose that a sweat patch were applied to an individual who entered a drug rehabilitation program after providing a negative urine test and the patch was removed 7 days later for testing. If a THC concentration of 4 ng/patch was obtained, does this indicate that he had used cannabis after entrance into the program in violation of his treatment contract?

Based on the published information available, it is most likely that THC detected in the patch indicates cannabis use after he entered the program, assuming that the skin was properly cleaned before applying the patch and that handling procedures avoided contamination during patch removal and storage. However, no published studies have related urine THC-COOH concentrations to sweat THC patch results, making it difficult to state with certainty that the results were a result of new cannabis use. It is expected that if the THC in the sweat patch indicated drug usage just before patch application, the urine drug test also would have been positive. It might be that drug depots in the skin of heavy, chronic cannabis users could continue to excrete THC in sweat after the individual abstains from further drug use, although this hypothesis has never been tested. It is also possible that cannabinoids could remain in sebum longer than in urine since sebaceous glands often release sebum when they lyse, a process that can take up to 2 weeks. Therefore, it is possible that the THC found in the patch represented drug use before entering the program. Additional controlled drug administration and naturalistic studies of drug excretion in sweat are needed to improve the interpretation of cannabinoid sweat tests.

7.5. Hair

Drugs enter hair through several diffusion mechanisms; from the blood into the highly perfused bulb of the hair shaft, from sebum and sweat along the hair root and shaft, and from direct contact with drug in the environment *(120)*. More basic drugs are bound primarily to eumelanin through ionic interactions; little drug binds to pheomelanin *(121)*. This difference in binding properties is one explanation for higher concentrations of basic drugs in dark colored hair, which has higher eumelanin content, than in light-colored hair, which may have primarily pheomelanin or less total melanin *(122,123)*.

In general, following a single dose, basic drugs that enter hair can be detected by the most commonly used techniques 3–7 days after drug administration, peak in 1–2 weeks, and decrease thereafter *(124–126)*. Hair grows at a rate of about 1 cm per month, providing an opportunity to segment hair to determine periods of drug use over time. Studies relating time of drug use with presence in specific hair segments have had inconsistent results. Kintz et al. have utilized segmental hair analysis to indicate the time of drug exposure in drug-facilitated sexual assault *(127)*, and others have used measurement of antibiotics in hair to monitor hair growth and tie the presence of these drugs to known times of drug administration *(128)*. Other investigators administered deuterated cocaine and showed that the presence of this drug was not restricted to the appropriate hair segments but was found throughout the hair shaft *(124)*. These data are consistent with the theory that drug in sweat may bathe the hair shaft and deposit drug along the length of the hair follicle. Many drugs are well protected by hair and may be detected hundreds of years after the death of an individual *(129,130)*. Although questions remain about the different mechanisms of drug incorporation, in general, drug concentrations in hair appear to be somewhat dose related, even though the correlation is not well defined *(131)*; that is, higher and more frequent drug use is usually reflected in higher hair concentrations *(126,132)*. However, most of our knowledge about drug concentrations in hair is derived from studies of basic drugs such as cocaine, amphetamines, and opiates. There are almost no data from controlled cannabinoid administration studies to help us in our interpretation of cannabinoid hair tests. This is especially important because THC is a more neutral compound and is not thought to bind to hair through the ionic mechanisms that are important components of incorporation of basic drugs.

Furthermore, THC is present in cannabis smoke, and external contamination of hair through this mechanism is a concern. Thorspecken et al. contaminated hair with cannabis smoke, and then tried two different wash techniques to remove THC *(133)*. Their methanol and methylene chloride wash method removed most of the THC from hair that was a result of contamination. A dodecyl sulfate wash removed external contamination from all hair samples tested. Scientists have recommended testing for THC-COOH in hair as another way to address the issue of external contamination with THC; however, the concentrations of THC-COOH in hair are in the low pg/mg range, usually requiring tandem MS or special chemical ionization MS analytical techniques *(134)*. These instruments may not be available to many analytical laboratories because of the high cost of the equipment, yet the validity of testing only for THC is a highly contested issue in forensic toxicology. The concern for reducing the possibility of external contamination has motivated SAMHSA to propose guidelines that set the cutoff concentrations for cannabinoids in hair at 1 pg/mg of cannabinoids for screening and 0.05 pg/mg of THC-COOH for confirmation testing. Test results must equal or exceed these limits before one may report a hair specimen positive when collected in a workplace program *(110)*.

Another complication in determining a drug's disposition into hair and expected values after use is the variability in analytical procedures among laboratories. Different wash procedures are used to remove external contamination, different digestion procedures are employed to facilitate extraction of the drug, and different analytical procedures and instruments are utilized to identify and quantify drugs. Our understanding of recovery of cannabinoids incorporated into authentic users' hair is poor. Scientists can measure the efficiency of extraction methods when cannabinoids are spiked into hair, but this technique probably does not adequately reflect the extraction of drug incorporated into hair following cannabis use. Cannabinoid measurements are further complicated by the very low concentrations of drug in hair. Jurado et al. found THC and THC-COOH concentrations in hair of cannabis and hashish users that ranged from 0.06 to 7.63 ng/mg and 0.05 to 3.87 ng/mg, respectively *(135)*. Cirimele et al. found lower concentrations for THC and THC-COOH of 0.26–2.17 and 0.07–0.33 ng/mg of hair, respectively, in 43 subjects who had died from fatal heroin overdoses *(134,136)*. Other investigators have found much lower concentration ranges, often in the pg/mg range *(137)*. Testing differences and difficulties in analyzing very low concentrations often result in a wide range of reported concentrations, as documented by Jurado et al. in a quality control study that had 18 laboratories analyze the same lot of hair samples and found a 93% coefficient of variation *(138)*.

Let us consider the question regarding the individual accused of using cannabis before driving that resulted in a plasma THC concentration of 2 ng/mL. Suppose this man claimed that someone put the cannabis in his food just before driving and that he had not knowingly used cannabis in the past year. If a hair specimen were submitted for testing to support his contention and the analysis for cannabinoids were negative, could the man legitimately use this information to support his claim that he did not smoke cannabis during the past year? To answer this question, we must first understand the pharmacokinetics of cannabinoid disposition into hair. How extensive was the laboratory's wash procedure, what analytes were targeted, what laboratory procedures were used, and what were the cutoff concentrations? The cutoff concentrations for the laboratory procedure are critical because for many laboratories cannabinoid cutoff concentrations are close to the limit of detection. If we find that the laboratory procedures were valid and cutoff concentrations similar to those recommended by SAMHSA, we can make some assessments. For example, the driver might not have been a chronic user of cannabis. However, we cannot say that the negative hair test supports his assertion that he never used cannabis during the past year except unknowingly when someone put cannabis in his food the day he was arrested. The low concentrations of THC and metabolites in hair and the lack of published dose–response data following controlled administration of cannabis will not allow us to answer the question. The best answer to the original question is that the negative hair result is supporting evidence that he is not a chronic cannabis user.

Let us suppose that the test had been positive. Could the prosecution use this information to support their claim that the man had used cannabis prior to this most recent incident, indicating a lie that would reflect poorly on his integrity and make his story about unknowing ingestion less credible? Once again the procedures and cutoff concentrations are important, but for instructive purposes we will assume they are reliable and similar to the proposed guidelines. As mentioned, we do not have data from studies following controlled administration of cannabis to assist in interpreting the positive hair test result. However, the studies on cocaine, codeine, and other basic drugs show that drugs or metabolites do not appear for at least 3–7 days when the hair is cut, not plucked, and usually appear later if the hair testing method has removed external contamination from sweat. If THC follows similar kinetics, its presence, along with the presence of other cannabinoids such as cannabinol, cannabidiol, and THC-COOH, would support the contention that the man had used cannabis, but not specifically on the day of his arrest. What about the possibility of external contamination? The presence of THC-COOH makes external contamination less likely because it indicates that the drug was actually metabolized by the body. There are no data to indicate that THC-COOH is present in cannabis smoke. Also, if appropriate wash procedures were used, external THC contamination would be less likely and the evidence of drug use stronger *(133)*. The answer to the original question would be that the presence of cannabinoids and specifically THC-COOH in the man's hair is supporting evidence that he used cannabis prior to the day he was stopped for driving erratically; this evidence would not lend support to a case of impairment at the time of arrest.

8. Final Thoughts

The information in this chapter demonstrates that the disposition and time course of cannabinoid analytes into different biological fluids and tissues is critical for interpreting drug test concentrations and answering related scientific and social questions. Each matrix has advantages and limitations. Blood or plasma interacts with cells throughout the body, including the central nervous system; cannabinoid concentrations in these biofluids more closely relate to drug effects, but the window of drug detection is usually limited to hours. Urine, a depot for waste, has an analysis time frame of days for detecting drug use and provides important information about drug metabolism, but concentrations of urine cannabinoids are difficult to relate to effects of the drug. Oral fluid appears to absorb THC directly from contact with cannabis and is a convenient fluid for detecting recently smoked cannabis. Concentrations of drugs in sweat are difficult to determine as a result of problems obtaining an accurate volume of excreted sweat, but detecting drugs in sweat patches or wipes has important applications for detecting drug use occurring over 1–2 weeks. Drugs appear to be more stable in hair and have larger windows of detection, from weeks to years. Analysis of each of these matrices offers unique scientific information. Knowledge of the disposition of drugs and metabolites in these fluids and tissues after controlled drug administration provides a powerful pharmacokinetic database for scientists who are called upon to give science-based answers to important questions that have a major impact on our society.

ACKNOWLEDGMENTS

The authors wish to thank Beverly Cepl, Karen Schaeffer, David Darwin, Deborah Price, and Insook Kim, Ph.D., for providing assistance with the reference material for the manuscript.

REFERENCES

1. Huestis, M. A. (2002) Cannabis (marijuana)—effects on human behavior and performance, in The Effects of Drugs on Human Performance and Behavior (Farrell, L. J., Logan, B. K., and Dubowski, K. M., eds.), Central Police University Press, Taipei, pp. 15–60.
2. Grotenhermen, F. (2003) Pharmacokinetics and pharmacodynamics of cannabinoids. *Clin. Pharmacokinet.* **42**, 327–360.
3. Turner, C. E., ElSohly, M. A., and Boeren, E. G. (1980) Constituents of cannabis sativa L. XVII. a review of the natural constituents. *J. Nat. Products* **43**, 169–234.
4. Turner, C .E., Hadley, K. W., Fetterman, P. S., Doorenbos, N. J., Quimby, M. W., and Waller, C. (1973) Constituents of Cannabis sativa L. IV: Stability of cannabinoids in stored plant material. *J. Pharm. Sci.* **62**, 1601–1605.
5. Turner, C. E., Bouwsma, O. J., Billets, S., and ElSohly, M. A. (1980) Constituents of cannabis sativa L. XVIII-electron voltage selected ion monitoring study of cannabinoids. *Biomed. Mass Spectrom.* **7**, 247–256.
6. Turner, C. E. (1983) Cannabis: the plant, its drugs, and their effects. *Aviat. Space Environ. Med.* **54**, 363–368.
7. ElSohly, H. N., Boeren, E. G., Turner, C. E., and ElSohly, M. A. (1984) Constituents of cannabis sativa L. XXIIII: Cannabitetrol, a new Polyhydroxylated cannabinoid, in *The Cannabinoids: Chemical, Pharmacologic and Therapeutic Aspects* (Agurell, S., Dewey, W. L., and Willette, R. E., eds.), Academic Press, Inc., Orlando, FL, pp. 89–96.
8. Turner, C. E., Hadley, K., and Fetterman, P. S. (1973) Constituents of cannabis sativa L. VI: Propyl homologs in samples of known geographical origin. *J. Pharm. Sci.* **62**, 1739–1741.
9. Hemphill, J. K., Turner, J. C., and Mahlberg, P. G. (1980) Cannabinoid content of individual plant organs from different geographical strains of cannabis sativa L. *J. Nat. Products* **43(1)**, 112–122.

10. Iversen, L. (2003) Cannabis and the brain. *Brain* **126**, 1252–1270.
11. Roth, M. D., Baldwin, G. C., and Tashkin, D. P. (2002) Effects of delta-9-tetrahydrocannabinol on human immune function and host defense. *CPL* **121**, 229–239.
12. Salmeron, B. J. and Stein, E. A. (2002) Pharmacological applications of magnetic resonance imaging. *Psychopharmacol. Bull.* **36**, 102–129.
13. Mathew, R. J., Wilson, W. H., Turkington, T. G., et al. (2002) Time course of tetrahydrocannabinol-induced changes in regional cerebral blood flow measured with positron emission tomography. *Psychiatry Res. Neuroimaging* **116**, 173–185.
14. Kumar, R. N., Chambers, W. A., and Pertwee, R. G. (2001) Pharmacological actions and therapeutic uses of cannabis and cannabinoids. *Anaesthesia* **56**, 1059–1068.
15. Pertwee, R. G. (2002) Cannabinoids and multiple sclerosis. *Pharmacol. Ther.* **95**, 165–174.
16. Mechoulam, R. and Hanu, L. (2001) The cannabinoids: an overview. Therapeutic implications in vomiting and nausea after cancer chemotherapy, in appetite promotion, in multiple sclerosis and in neuroprotection. *Pain Res. Manag.* **6**, 67–73.
17. Baker, D., Pryce, G., Giovannoni, G., and Thompson, A.J. (2003) The therapeutic potential of cannabis. *Lancet Neurol.* **2**, 291–298.
18. Ross, S. A., Mehmedic, Z., Murphy, T. P., and ElSohly, M. A. (2000) GC-MS analysis of the total delta-9-THC content of both drug- and fiber-type cannabis seeds. *J. Anal. Toxicol.* **24**, 715–717.
19. Pitts, J. E., Neal, J. D., and Gough, T. A. (1992) Some features of Cannabis plants grown in the United Kingdom from seeds of known origin. *J. Pharm. Pharmacol.* **44**, 947–951.
20. ElSohly, M. A., Ross, S. A., Mehmedic, Z., Arafat, R., Yi, B., and Banahan, B. F. III (2000) Potency trends of delta-9-THC and other cannabinoids in confiscated marijuana from 1980-1997. *J. Forensic Sci.* **45**, 24–30.
21. Drug Enforcement Administration (2003) Illegal drug price and purity report. *DEA-02058* **April**, 1–16.
22. Claussen, U. and Korte, F. (1968) Concerning the behavior of hemp and of delta-9-6a,10a-trans-tetrahydrocannabinol in smoking. *Justus Liebigs. Ann. Chem.* **713**, 162–165.
23. Abrams, R. M., Davis, K. H., Jaeger, M. J., and Szeto, H .H. (1985) Marijuana smoke production and delivery system, in *Marihuana '84 Proceedings of the Oxford Symposium on Cannabis* (Harvey, D. J., Paton, S. W., and Nahas, G. G., eds.), IRL Press Limited, Oxford, pp. 205–209.
24. Davis, K. H., McDaniel, I. A., Cadwell, L. W., and Moody, P. L. (1984) Some smoking characteristics of marijuana cigarettes, in *The Cannabinoids: Chemical, Pharmacologic, and Therapeutic Aspects* (Agurell, S., Dewey, W. L., and Willette, R. E., eds.), Academic Press, Orlando, FL, pp 97–109.
25. Ohlsson, A., Lindgren, J. E., Wahlen, A., Agurell, S., Hollister, L. E., and Gillespie, H.K. (1980) Plasma delta-9-tetrahydrocannabinol concentrations and clinical effects after oral and intravenous administration and smoking. *Clin. Pharmacol. Ther.* **28**, 409–416.
26. Agurell, S., Halldin, M., Lindgren, J. E., et al. (1986) Pharmacokinetics and metabolism of delta1-tetrahydrocannabinol and other cannabinoids with emphasis on man. *Pharmacol. Rev.* **38**, 21–43.
27. Azorlosa, J. L., Heishman, S. J., Stitzer, M. L., and Mahaffey, J. M. (1992) Marijuana smoking: effect of varying delta 9-tetrahydrocannabinol content and number of puffs. *J. Pharmacol. Exp. Ther.* **261(1)**, 114–122.
28. Heishman, S. J., Stitzer, M. L., and Yingling, J. E. (1989) Effects of tetrahydrocannabinol content on marijuana smoking behavior, subjective reports, and performance. *Pharmacol. Biochem. Behav.* **34**, 173–179.
29. Tinklenberg, J. R., Melges, F. T., Hollister, L. E., and Gillespie, H. K. (1970) Marijuana and immediate memory. *Nature* **226**, 1171–1172.

30. Huestis, M. A., Henningfield, J. E., and Cone, E. J. (1992) Blood cannabinoids. I. Absorption of THC and formation of 11-OH-THC and THCCOOH during and after smoking marijuana. *J. Anal. Toxicol.* **16**, 276–282.
31. Mason, A. P. and McBay, A. J. (1984) Ethanol, marijuana, and other drug use in 600 drivers killed in single-vehicle crashes in North Carolina, 1978-1981. *J. Forensic Sci.* **29**, 987–1026.
32. Law, B., Mason, P. A., Moffat, A. C., Gleadle, R. I., and King, L. J. (1984) Forensic aspects of the metabolism and excretion of cannabinoids following oral ingestion of cannabis resin. *J. Pharm. Pharmacol.* **36**, 289–294.
33. Ohlsson, A., Lindgren, J. E., Wahlen, A., Agurell, S., Hollister, L. E., and Gillespie, H.K. (1981) Plasma levels of delta-9-tetrahydrocannabinol after intravenous, oral and smoke administration. *NIDA Monograph* **34**, 250–256.
34. Wall, M. E., Sadler, B. M., Brine, D., Taylor, H., and Perez-Reyes, M. (1983) Metabolism, disposition, and kinetics of delta-9-tetrahydrocannabinol in men and women. *Clin. Pharmacol. Ther.* **34**, 352–363.
35. Perez-Reyes, M., Timmons, M. C., Davis, K. H., and Wall, E. M. (1973) A comparison of the pharmacological activity in man of intravenously administered delta-9-tetrahydrocannabinol, cannabinol and cannabidiol. *Experientia* **29**, 1368–1369.
36. Hunt, C. A. and Jones, R. T. (1980) Tolerance and disposition of tetrahydrocannabinol in man. *J. Pharmacol. Exp. Ther.* **215**, 35–44.
37. Kelly, P. and Jones, R. T. (1992) Metabolism of tetrahydrocannabinol in frequent and infrequent marijuana users. *J. Anal. Toxicol.* **16**, 228–235.
38. Harvey, D. J. (2001) Absorption, distribution, and biotransformation of the cannabinoids, in *Marijuana and Medicine* (Nahas, G. G., Sutin, K. M., Harvey, D. J., and Agurell, S., eds.), Humana Press, Totowa, NJ, pp. 91–103.
39. Johansson, E., Noren, K., Sjovall, J., and Halldin, M. M. (1989) Determination of delta-1-tetrahydrocannabinol in human fat biopsies from marihuana users by gas chromatography-mass spectrometry. *Biomed. Chromatogr.* **3**, 35–38.
40. Kreuz, D. S. and Axelrod, J. (1973) Delta-9-tetrahydrocannabinol: localization in body fat. *Science* **179**, 391–393.
41. Johansson, E., Agurell, S., Hollister, L. E., and Halldin, M. M. (1988) Prolonged apparent half-life of delta-1-tetrahydrocannabinol in plasma of chronic marijuana users. *J. Pharm. Pharmacol.* **40**, 374–375.
42. Iribarne, C., Berthou, F., Baird, S., et al. (1996) Involvement of cytochrome P450 3A4 enzyme in the N-demethylation of methadone in human liver microsomes. *Chem. Res. Toxicol.* **9**, 365–373.
43. Matsunaga, T., Iwawaki, Y., Watanabe, K., Yamamoto, I., Kageyama, T., and Yoshimura, H. (1995) Metabolism of delta-9-tetrahydrocannabinol by cytochrome P450 isozymes purified from hepatic microsomes of monkeys. *Life Sci.* **56**, 2089–2095.
44. Lemberger, L., Silberstein, S. D., Axelrod, J., and Kopin, I. J. (1970) Marihuana: studies on the disposition and metabolism of delta-9-tetrahydrocannabinol in man. *Science* **170**, 1320–1322.
45. Ben-Zvi, Z., Bergen, J. R., Burstein, S., Sehgal, P. K., and Varanelli, C. (1976) The metabolism of delta-tetrahydrocannabinol in the rhesus monkey, in *The Pharmacology of Marihuana* (Braude, M. C. and Szara, S., eds.), Raven Press, New York, pp. 63–75.
46. Greene, M. L. and Saunders, D. R. (1974) Metabolism of tetrahydrocannabinol by the small intestine. *Gastroenterology* **66**, 365–372.
47. Krishna, D. R. and Klotz, U. (1994) Extrahepatic metabolism of drugs in humans. *Clin. Pharmacokinet.* **26**, 144–160.
48. Watanabe, K., Tanaka, T., Yamamoto, I., and Yoshimura, H. (1988) Brain microsomal oxidation of delta-8- and delta-9-tetrahydrocannabinol. *Biochem.and Biophys. Res. Commun.* **157**, 75–80.

49. Widman, M., Nordqvist, M., Dollery, C. T., and Briant, R. H. (1975) Metabolism of delta-1-tetrahydrocannabinol by the isolated perfused dog lung. Comparison with in vitro liver metabolism. *J. Pharm. Pharmacol.* **27**, 842–848.
50. Harvey, D. J. and Paton, W. D. M. (1984) Metabolism of the cannabinoids. *Rev. Biochem. Toxicol.* **6**, 221–264.
51. Mechoulam, R., BenZvi, Z., Agurell, S., et al. (1973) Delta-6 tetrahydrocannabinol-7-oic acid, a urinary delta-6-THC metabolite: isolation and synthesis. *Experientia* **29**, 1193–1195.
52. Sporkert, F., Pragst, F., Ploner, C. J., Tschirch, A., and Stadelmann, A. M. (2001) Pharmacokinetic investigations and delta-9-tetrahydrocannabinol and its metabolites after single administration of 10 mg Marinol in attendance of a psychiatric study. The Annual Meeting of The International Association of Forensic Toxicologists, Prague, Czech Republic, Abstract P62.
53. Halldin, M. M., Widman, M., Bahr, C. V., Lindgren, J. E., and Martin, B. R. (1982) Identification of in vitro metabolites of delta1-tetrahydrocannabinol formed by human livers. *Drug Metab. Dispos.* **10**, 297–301.
54. Garrett, E. R. and Hunt, C. A. (1977) Pharmacokinetics of delta-9-tetrahydrocannabinol in dogs. *J. Pharm. Sci.* **66**, 395–407.
55. Williams, P. L. and Moffat, A. C. (1980) Identification in human urine of delta-9-tetrahydrocannabinol-11-oic glucuronide: a tetrahydrocannabinol metabolite. *J. Pharm. Pharmacol.* **32**, 445–448.
56. Huestis, M. A., Mitchell, J. M., and Cone, E. J. (1996) Urinary excretion profiles of 11-nor-9-carboxy-Δ^9-tetrahydrocannabinol in humans after single smoked doses of marijuana. *J. Anal. Toxicol.* **20**, 441–452.
57. Huestis, M. A. and Cone, E. J. (1998) Urinary excretion half-life of 11-nor-9-carboxy-delta-9-tetrahydrocannabinol in humans. *Ther. Drug Monit.* **20**, 570–576.
58. Johansson, E. and Halldin, M. M. (1989) Urinary excretion half-life of delta1-tetrahydrocannabinol-7-oic acid in heavy marijuana users after smoking. *J. Anal. Toxicol.* **13**, 218–223.
59. Cone, E. J., Johnson, R. E., Paul, B. D., Mell, L. D., and Mitchell, J. (1988) Marijuana-laced brownies: Behavioral effects, physiologic effects, and urinalysis in humans following ingestion. *J. Anal. Toxicol.* **12**, 169–175.
60. Gustafson, R. A., Levine, B., Stout, P. R., et al. (2003) Urinary cannabinoid detection times after controlled oral administration of delta-9-tetrahydrocannabinol to humans. *Clin. Chem.* **49**, 1114–1124.
61. Kemp, P. M., Abukhalaf, I. K., Manno, J. E., et al. (1995) Cannabinoids in humans. II. The influence of three methods of hydrolysis on the concentration of THC and two metabolites in urine. *J. Anal. Toxicol.* **19**, 292–298.
62. Mason, A. P. and McBay, A. J. (1985) Cannabis: pharmacology and interpretation of effects. *J. Forensic Sci.* **30**, 615–631.
63. Moskowitz, H. (1985) Marijuana and driving. *Accid. Anal. Prev.* **17**, 323–345.
64. Kurzthaler, I., Hummer, M., Miller, C., et al. (1999) Effect of cannabis use on cognitive functions and driving ability. *J. Clin. Psychiatry* **60**, 395–399.
65. Ramaekers, J. G., Berghaus, G., van Laar, M., and Drummer, O. H. (2004) Dose related risk of motor vehicle crashes after cannabis use. *Drug Alcohol Depend.* **73**, 109–119.
66. O'Kane, C. J., Tutt, D. C., and Bauer, L. A. (2002) Cannabis and driving: a new perspective. *Emerg. Med.* **14**, 296–303.
67. Lukas, S. E. and Orozco, S. (2001) Ethanol increases plasma delta-9-tetrahydrocannabinol (THC) levels and subjective effects after marihuana smoking in human volunteers. *Drug Alcohol Depend.* **64**, 143–149.
68. Ramaekers, J. G., Robbe, H. W., and O'Hanlon, J. F. (2000) Marijuana, alcohol and actual driving performance. *Hum. Psychopharmacol.* **15**, 551–558.

69. Huestis, M. A., Sampson, A. H., Holicky, B. J., Henningfield, J. E., and Cone, E. J. (1992) Characterization of the absorption phase of marijuana smoking. *Clin. Pharmacol. Ther.* **52**, 31–41.
70. Huestis, M. A., Henningfield, J. E., and Cone, E. J. (1992) Blood cannabinoids. II. Models for the prediction of time of marijuana exposure from plasma concentrations of delta-9-tetrahydrocannabinol (THC) and 11-nor-9-carboxy-delta-9-tetrahydrocannabinol (THCCOOH). *J. Anal. Toxicol.* **16**, 283–290.
71. Cone, E. J. and Huestis, M. A. (1993) Relating blood concentrations of tetrahydrocannabinol and metabolites to pharmacologic effects and time of marijuana usage. *Ther. Drug Monit.* **15**, 527–532.
72. Huestis, M. A., Zigbuo, E., Heishman, S. J., et al. (2002) Determination of time of last exposure following controlled smoking of multiple marijuana cigarettes. Annual Meeting of the Society of Forensic Toxicologists, Dearborn, MI, Abstract 26.
73. Robbe, H. W. and O'Hanlon, J. F. (1993) *Marijuana and Actual Driving Performance*, U.S. Department of Transportation/National Highway Traffic Safety Administration Report, November, pp. 1–133.
74. Drummer, O. H., Gerostamoulos, J., Batziris, H., et al. (2004) The involvement of drugs in drivers of motor vehicles killed in Australian road traffic crashes. *Accid. Anal. Prev.* **36**, 239–248.
75. Wilson, W., Mathew, R., Turkington, T., Hawk, T., Coleman, R. E., and Provenzale, J. (2000) Brain morphological changes and early marijuana use: a magnetic resonance and positron emission tomography study. *J. Addict. Dis.* **19**, 1–22.
76. Mathew, R. J., Wilson, W. H., Coleman, R. E., Turkington, T. G., and DeGrado, T. R. (1997) Marijuana intoxication and brain activation in marijuana smokers. *Life Sci.* **60(23)**, 2075–2089.
77. Gatley, S. J., Lan, R., Volkow, N. D., et al. (1998) Imaging the brain marijuana receptor: development of a radioligand that binds to cannabinoid CB1 receptors in vivo. *J. Neurochem.* **70**, 417–423.
78. Evans, S. M., Cone, E. J., and Henningfield, J. E. (1996) Arterial and venous cocaine plasma concentrations in humans: relationship to route of administration, cardiovascular effects and subjective effects. *J. Pharmacol. Exp. Ther.* **279**, 1345–1356.
79. Martin, B. R., Mechoulam, R., and Razdan, R. K. (1999) Discovery and characterization of endogenous cannabinoids. *Life Sci.* **65**, 573–595.
80. Pertwee, R. (1993) The evidence for the existence of cannabinoid receptors. *Gen. Pharmacol.* **24(4)**, 811–824.
81. Devane, W. A., Hanus, L., Breuer, A., et al. (1992) Isolation and structure of a brain constituent that binds to the cannabinoid receptor. *Science* **258**, 1946–1949.
82. Mechoulam, R., Shabat, S. B., Hanus, L., et al. (1996) Endogenous cannabinoid ligands—chemical and biological studies. *J. Lipid Mediators Cell Signal.* **14**, 45–49.
83. Rinaldi-Carmona, M., Barth, F., Heaulme, M., et al. (1995) Biochemical and pharmacological characterization of SR141716A, the first potent and selective brain cannabinoid receptor antagonist. *Life Sci.* **56**, 1941–1947.
84. Aceto, M. D., Scates, S. M., Lowe, J. A., and Martin, B. R. (1996) Dependence on delta^9-tetrahydrocannabinol: studies on precipitated and abrupt withdrawal. *J. Pharmacol. Exp. Ther.* **278**, 1290–1295.
85. Huestis, M. A., Gorelick, D. A., Heishman, S. J., et al. (2001) Blockade of effects of smoked marijuana by the CB1-selective cannabinoid receptor antagonist SR141716. *Arch. Gen. Psychiatry* **58**, 322–328.
86. Cohen, C., Perrault, G., Voltz, C., Steinberg, R., and Soubrie, P. (2002) SR141716, a central cannabinoid (CB1) receptor antagonist, blocks the motivational and dopamine-releasing effects of nicotine in rats. *Behav. Pharmacol.***13**, 451–463.

87. LeFur, G., Arnone, M., Rinaldi-Carmona, M., Barth, F., and Heshmati, H. (2001) SR141716, a selective antagonist of CB1, receptors and obesity. Annual Meeting of the International Cannabinoid Research Society, El Escorial, Spain, Abstract 101.
88. Preston, K. L. and Jasinski, D. R. (1991) Abuse liability studies of opioid agonist-antagonists in humans. *Drug Alcohol Depend.* **28**, 49–82.
89. Huestis, M. A. and Cone, E. J. (1998) Differentiating new marijuana use from residual drug excretion in occasional marijuana users. *J. Anal. Toxicol.* **22**, 445–454.
90. Lafolie, P., Beck, O., Blennow, G., et al. (1991) Importance of creatinine analyses of urine when screening for abused drugs. *Clin. Chem.* **37**, 1927–1931.
91. Manno, J. E., Ferslew, K. E., and Manno, B. R. (1984) Urine excretion patterns of cannabinoids and the clinical application of the EMIT-d.a.u. cannabinoid urine assay for substance abuse treatment, in *The Cannabinoids: Chemical, Pharmacologic, and Therapeutic Aspects* (Agurell, S., Dewey, W. L., and Willette, R. E., eds.), Academic Press, Orlando, FL, pp. 281–290.
92. Cone, E. J., Lange, R., and Darwin, W. D. (1998) In vivo adulteration: excess fluid ingestion causes false-negative marijuana and cocaine urine test results. *J. Anal. Toxicol.* **22**, 460–473.
93. Fraser, A. D. and Worth, D. (1999) Urinary excretion profiles of 11-nor-9-carboxy-delta-9-tetrahydrocannabinol: a delta-9-THCCOOH to creatinine ratio study. *J. Anal. Toxicol.* **23**, 531–534.
94. Fraser, A. D. and Worth, D. (2003) Urinary excretion profiles of 11-nor-9-corboxy-delta-9-tetrahydrocannabinol: a delta-9-THC-COOH to creatinine ratio study #2. *Forensic Sci. Int.* **133**, 26–31.
95. Kim, I., Barnes, A. J., Oyler, J. M., et al. (2002) Plasma and oral fluid pharmacokinetics and pharmacodynamics after oral codeine administration *Clin. Chem.* **48**, 1486–1496.
96. Just, W. W., Werner, G., Erdmann, G., and Wiechmann, M. (1975) Detection and identification of delta-8- and delta 9-tetrahydrocannabinol in saliva of man and autoradiographic investigation of their distribution in different organs of the monkey. *Strahlentherapie-Sonderbande* **74**, 90–97.
97. Maseda, C., Hama, K., Fukui, Y., Matsubara, K., Takahashi, S., and Akane, A. (1986) Detection of delta-9-THC in saliva by capillary GC/ECD after marihuana smoking. *Forensic Sci. Int.* **32**, 259–266.
98. Gross, S. J., Worthy, T. E., Nerder, L., Zimmermann, E. G., Soares, J. R., and Lomax, P. (1985) Detection of recent cannabis use by saliva delta-9-THC radioimmunoassay. *J. Anal. Toxicol.* **9**, 1–5.
99. Hawks, R. L. (1984) Developments in cannabinoid analyses of body fluids: implications for forensic applications, in *The Cannabinoids: Chemical, Pharmacologic, and Therapeutic Aspects* (Agurell, S., Dewey, W., and Willette, R., eds.), Academic Press, Orlando, FL, pp. 123–134.
100. Huestis, M. A., Dickerson, S., and Cone, E. J. (1992) Can saliva THC levels be correlated to behavior?, in American Academy of Forensic Science Annual Meeting, Fittje Brothers, Colorado Springs, CO, p. 190.
101. Niedbala, R. S., Kardos, K. W., Fritch, D. F., et al. (2001) Detection of marijuana use by oral fluid and urine analysis following single-dose administration of smoked and oral marijuana. *J. Anal. Toxicol.* **25**, 289–303.
102. Kintz, P., Cirimele, V., and Ludes, B. (2000) Detection of cannabis in oral fluid (saliva) and forehead wipes (sweat) from impaired drivers. *J. Anal. Toxicol.* **24**, 557–561.
103. Samyn, N., De Boeck, G., and Verstraete, A. G. (2002) The use of oral fluid and sweat wipes for the detection of drugs of abuse in drivers. *J. Forensic Sci.* **47**, 1380–1387.
104. Cone, E. J., Presley, L., Lehrer, M., et al. (2002) Oral fluid testing for drugs of abuse: positive prevalence rates by intercept immunoassay screening and GC-MS-MS confirmation and suggested cutoff concentrations. *J. Anal. Toxicol.* **26**, 541–546.

105. Gronholm, M. and Lillsunde, P. (2001) A comparison between on-site immunoassay drug-testing devices and laboratory results. *Forensic Sci. Int.* **121**, 37–46.
106. Jehanli, A., Brannan, S., Moore, L., and Spiehler, V. R. (2001) Blind trials of an onsite saliva drug test for marijuana and opiates. *J. Forensic Sci.* **46**, 1214–1220.
107. Samyn, N. and van Haeren, C. (2000) On-site testing of saliva and sweat with Drugwipe and determination of concentrations of drugs of abuse in saliva, plasma and urine of suspected users. *Int. J. Leg. Med.* **113**, 150–154.
108. Yacoubian, G. S., Jr., Wish, E. D., and Perez, D. M. (2001) A comparison of saliva testing to urinalysis in an arrestee population. *J. Psychoactive Drugs* **33**, 289–294.
109. Walsh, J. M., Flegel, R., Crouch, D. J., Cangianelli, L., and Baudys, J. (2003) An evaluation of rapid-point-of-collection oral fluid drug-testing devices. *J. Anal. Toxicol.* **27**, 429–439.
110. Substance Abuse and Mental Health Services Administration. (2004) http://workplace.samhsa.gov/.
111. Menkes, D. B., Howard, R. C., Spears, G. F., and Cairns, E. R. (1991) Salivary THC following cannabis smoking correlates with subjective intoxication and heart rate. *Psychopharmacology* **103**, 277–279.
112. ROSITA (2004) http://www.rosita.org. Rosita website.
113. Steinmeyer, S., Ohr, H., Maurer, H. J., and Moeller, M. R. (2001) Practical aspects of roadside tests for administrative traffic offences in Germany. *Forensic Sci. Int.* **121**, 33–36.
114. Cone, E. J., Johnson, R. E., Darwin, W. D., et al. (1987) Passive inhalation of marijuana smoke: urinalysis and room air levels of delta-9-tetrahydrocannabinol. *J. Anal. Toxicol.* **11**, 89–96.
115. Hayden, J. W. (1991) Passive inhalation of marijuana smoke: a critical review. *J. Substance Abuse* **3**, 85–90.
116. Mule, S. J., Lomax, P., and Gross, S. J. (1988) Active and realistic passive marijuana exposure tested by three immunoassays and GC/MS in urine. *J. Anal. Toxicol.* **12**, 113–116.
117. Kidwell, D. A., Holland, J. C., and Athanaselis, S. (1998) Testing for drugs of abuse in saliva and sweat. *J. Chromatogr. B Biomed. Sci. Appl.* **713**, 111–135.
118. Crouch, D. J., Cook, R. F., Trudeau, J. V., et al. (2001) The detection of drugs of abuse in liquid perspiration. *J. Anal. Toxicol.* **25**, 625–627.
119. Kintz, P. (1996) Drug testing in addicts: a comparison between urine, sweat, and hair. *Ther. Drug Monit.* **18**, 450–455.
120. Cone, E. J. (1996) Mechanisms of drug incorporation into hair. *Ther. Drug Monit.* **18**, 438–443.
121. Borges, C. R., Roberts, J. C., Wilkins, D. G., and Rollins, D. E. (2003) Cocaine, benzoylecgonine, amphetamine, and N-acetylamphetamine binding to melanin subtypes. *J. Anal. Toxicol.* **27**, 125–134.
122. Cone, E. J., Darwin, W. D., and Wang, W. L. (1993) The occurrence of cocaine, heroin and metabolites in hair of drug abusers. *Forensic. Sci. Int.* **63**, 55–68.
123. Rollins, D. E., Wilkins, D. G., Krueger, G. G., et al. (2003) The effect of hair color on the incorporation of codeine into human hair. *J. Anal. Toxicol.* **27**, 545–551.
124. Henderson, G. L., Harkey, M. R., Zhou, C., Jones, R. T., and Jacob, P. III (1996) Incorporation of isotopically labeled cocaine and metabolites into human hair: 1. Dose-response relationships. *J. Anal. Toxicol.* **20**, 1–12.
125. Cone, E. J. (1990) Testing human hair for drugs of abuse. I. Individual dose and time profiles of morphine and codeine in plasma, saliva, urine, and beard compared to drug-induced effects on pupils and behavior. *J. Anal. Toxicol.* **14**, 1–7.

126. Joseph, R. E., Jr., Hold, K. M., Wilkins, D. G., Rollins, D. E., and Cone, E. J. (1999) Drug testing with alternative matrices II. Mechanisms of cocaine and codeine deposition in hair. *J. Anal. Toxicol.* **23**, 396–408.
127. Kintz, P., Cirimele, V., Jamey, C., and Ludes, B. (2003) Testing for GHB in hair by GC/MS/MS after a single exposure. Application to document sexual assault. *J. Forensic Sci.* **48**, 195–200.
128. Miyazawa, N. and Uematsu, T. (1992) Analysis of ofloxacin in hair as a measure of hair growth and as a time marker for hair analysis. *Ther. Drug Monit.* **14**, 525–528.
129. Baez, H., Castro, M. M., Benaventa, M. A., et al. (2000) Drugs in prehistory: chemical analysis of ancient human hair. *Forensic Sci. Int.* **108**, 173–179.
130. Springfield, A. C., Cartmell, L. W., Aufderheide, A. C., Buikstra, J., and Ho, J. (1993) Cocaine and metabolites in the hair of ancient Peruvian coca leaf chewers. *Forensic. Sci. Int.* **63**, 269–275.
131. Goldberger, B. A., Darraj, A. G., Caplan, Y. H., and Cone, E. J. (1998) Detection of methadone, methadone metabolites, and other illicit drugs of abuse in hair of methadone-treatment subjects. *J. Anal. Toxicol.* **22**, 526–530.
132. Cairns, T., Kippenberger, D. J., and Gordon, A. M. (1997) Hair analysis for detection of drugs of abuse, in *Handbook of Analytical Therapeutic Drug Monitoring and Toxicology* (Wong, S. H. Y. and Sunshine, I., eds.) CRC Press, New York, pp. 237–251.
133. Thorspecken, J., Skopp, G., and Potsch, L. (2004) In vitro contamination of hair by marijuana smoke. *Clin. Chem.* **50**, 596–602.
134. Kintz, P., Cirimele, V., and Mangin, P. (1995) Testing human hair for cannabis II. Identification of THC-COOH by GC-MS-NCI as a unique proof. *J. Forensic Sci.* **40**, 619–622.
135. Jurado, C., Menendez, M., Repetto, M., Kintz, P., Cirimele, V., and Mangin, P. (1996) Hair testing for cannabis in Spain and France: is there a difference in consumption? *J. Anal. Toxicol.* **20**, 111–115.
136. Cirimele, V., Kintz, P., and Mangin, P. (1995) Testing human hair for cannabis. *Forensic Sci. Int.* **70**, 175–182.
137. Cairns, T., Kippenberger, D. J., Scholtz, H., and Baumgartner, W. A. (1995) Determination of carboxy-THC in hair by mass spectrometry, in *Hair Analysis in Forensic Toxicology: Proceedings of the 1995 International Conference and Workshop* (de Zeeuw, R. A., Al Hosani, I., Al Munthiri, S., and Maqbool, A., eds.), The Organizing Committee of the Conference, Abu Dhabi, pp. 185–193.
138. Jurado, C. and Sachs, H. (2003) Proficiency test for the analysis of hair for drugs of abuse, organized by the Society of Hair Testing. *Forensic Sci. Int.* **133**, 175–178.

Chapter 10

Medical and Health Consequences of Marijuana

Jag H. Khalsa

1. Introduction

Marijuana is the most frequently used illegal drug in the world today. Some 146 million people, or 3.7% of the population 15–64 years of age, consumed cannabis in 2001–2003 *(1)*. In the United States, 95 million Americans over the age of 12 have tried marijuana at least once. In 2002, an estimated 15 million Americans had used the drug in the month before a survey *(2)*, representing 6.2% of the population age 12 years and older. Marijuana was used either alone or in combination with other drugs by 75% of the current illicit drug users. Approximately 2–3 million new users of marijuana are added each year, with about 1.1% becoming clinically dependent on it *(3)*. In the case of young people, according to a recent survey of high school students known as Monitoring the Future, supported by the US National Institute on Drug Abuse (NIDA) and conducted yearly, at least 19% of 8th graders had tried marijuana at least once and 18% of 10th graders were "current" drug users (i.e., had used the drug within the past month before the survey). Among 12th graders, nearly 48% had tried marijuana at least once, and approx 21% were "current" marijuana users *(4)*. Marijuana use by young people has increased or decreased at various times during the last decade, possibly as a result of its potency, which has been on the rise, although nonsignificantly—from a 3% concentration of Δ^9-tetrahyrocannabinol (THC; marijuana's active chemical constituent) in 1991 to 4.4% in 1997—possibly because of changes in the perceptions of youths about marijuana's dangers or other unknown factors. Research suggests that marijuana use usually peaks in the late teens to early 20s, and then declines in later years *(5)*.

From: *Forensic Science and Medicine: Marijuana and the Cannabinoids*
Edited by: M. A. ElSohly © Humana Press Inc., Totowa, New Jersey

Marijuana use has been reported to cause adverse psychosocial and health consequences. The psychosocial consequences of marijuana use—such as dropping out of school, poor school performance, antisocial and other behaviors of youth—have been the subjects of many publications. Therefore, this chapter presents current research on the medical and health consequences of marijuana use *(6)*, including the adverse effects on the immune, cardiopulmonary/respiratory, hepatic, renal, endocrine, reproductive, and central nervous systems, genetic aspects, and general health. The chapter also includes a brief discussion of the treatment of marijuana dependence, the carcinogenic potential of marijuana, and motor effects with respect to driving performance and traffic accidents.

Marijuana use is associated with a myriad of pharmacological effects that may be attributable to THC as well as to some of its less psychoactive chemical constituents, known as cannabinoids and endocannabinoids: the latter have been observed in the central and peripheral nervous systems, as well as in the immune, cardiovascular, and reproductive systems. However, the physiological roles of these cannabinoids have not yet been fully defined. Evidence suggests that endocannabinoids are involved in the amelioration of pain, blocking of working memory, enhancement of appetite and suckling, cardiovascular modulation including blood pressure lowering during shock, and embryonic development. They may also be of importance in psychomotor control and in the regulation of some immune responses *(7)*.

The acute effects of marijuana use may include euphoria, anxiety, and panic, especially in naïve users; impaired attention, memory, and psychomotor performance; perceptual alterations; intensification of sensory experiences, such as eating, watching films, listening to music; increased risk of psychotic symptoms, especially among those who are already vulnerable because of a personal or family history of psychiatric/psychological problems *(8)*; and possibly increased risk of motor accidents, especially if used concomitantly with alcohol *(9)*.

2. Immune System Effects

Marijuana impairs cell-mediated and humoral immunity in rodents and decreases resistance to bacterial and viral infections; noncannabinoids in cannabis smoke impair alveolar macrophages *(10)*. However, the few nonhuman animal studies that found adverse immunological consequences of marijuana have not been replicated in humans *(11)*. There is no conclusive evidence to suggest that use of marijuana impairs immune function, as measured by number of T-cell lymphocytes, B-cell lymphocytes, macrophages, or levels of immunoglobulin *(11)*. No epidemiological data or data from case reports suggest that marijuana is immunotoxic or that it increases the risk of exacerbating other bacterial or viral diseases in marijuana users. Two recent prospective studies of HIV infection in homosexual men showed no clear association between marijuana use and increased risk of progression to AIDS *(12,13)*. Kaslow and colleagues *(13)* conducted a prospective study of progression to AIDS among HIV-positive men in a cohort of 4954 homosexual and bisexual men. Marijuana use did not predict an increased rate of progression to AIDS among men who were HIV positive, nor was marijuana use related to changes in a limited number of measures of immunological functioning. Thus, although persons infected with HIV have been advised to avoid marijuana, this advice appears to be reasonable as a general health precaution. The fact that Marinol (dronabinol, THC) has been approved by the US Food and Drug Administration for the treatment of anorexia associated with weight loss in patients with AIDS and the nausea and vomiting associated with cancer chemotherapy shows that Marinol does not impair the immune system significantly and does not exacerbate bacterial or viral infections. It is not known whether studies have been conducted in this area.

3. Cardiopulmonary/Cardiorespiratory Effects

Marijuana use is associated with serious cardiovascular consequences. Acutely, marijuana increases heart rate, supine blood pressure, and, after higher doses, orthostatic hypotension; it increases cardiac output, decreases peripheral vascular resistance, and dose-dependently decreases maximum exercise performance. With prolonged exposure, supine blood pressure falls, orthostatic hypotension disappears, blood volume increases, heart rate slows, and circulatory responses to exercise diminish, which is consistent with the centrally mediated, reduced sympathetic and enhanced parasympathetic activity in animals. These studies were reviewed by Jones *(14)*, who cautioned that although marijuana's cardiovascular effects do not seem to cause serious health problems for young, healthy users, marijuana smoking by older people with cardiovascular disease poses greater risks because of the resulting increased cardiac work, increased catecholamines, carboxyhemoglobin, and hypotension. On the basis of results from a NIDA-funded study in which more than 65,000 medical charts of enrollees in the Kaiser Permanente Hospital system were reviewed for medical consequences of marijuana use, Sidney *(15)* reported no clear temporal association of marijuana use with hospitalizations from cardiovascular disease. On the other hand, marijuana use was associated with an increased number of hospitalizations for respiratory and pulmonary complications, injuries, and slightly increased mortality (discussed in the next paragraph).

Regarding the pulmonary/respiratory consequences, chronic heavy smoking of marijuana is associated with increased symptoms of chronic bronchitis, coughing, production of sputum, and wheezing *(16,17)* and with impairment of pulmonary function, pulmonary responsiveness, and bronchial cell characteristics in marijuana-only smokers. Tashkin and co-workers *(17)* further show that chronic marijuana smoking is associated with poorer lung function and greater abnormalities in the large airways of marijuana smokers than in nonsmokers. In 1997, Tashkin and colleagues *(18)* reported that the rate of decline in respiratory function over 8 years among marijuana smokers did not differ from that in nonsmokers of any substance—marijuana or tobacco. However, in another cohort there was a greater rate of decline in respiratory function among marijuana-only smokers than in tobacco-only smokers *(19)*. Both studies showed that long-term smoking of marijuana increased bronchitis symptoms. Starr and Renneker *(20)* also reported that marijuana smokers show significantly higher levels of cytological components in the sputum when compared with sputum from tobacco smokers. According to Tashkin and colleagues *(21)*, marijuana smoking may predispose individuals to pulmonary infection, especially patients whose immune defenses are already compromised by HIV infection and/or cancer and related chemotherapy. They report that THC produces a concentration-dependent reduction in T-cell proliferation and interferon-γ production via a CB_2 receptor-dependent pathway. At the level of gene expression, THC increased expression of Th1 cytokines (interferon- γ/interleukin [IL]-2) and reduced expression of Th2 cytokines (IL-4/IL-5). Tashkin and colleagues *(20)* caution that suppression of cell-mediated immunity by THC may place marijuana smokers at risk for infection or cancer. Caiaffa and colleagues *(22)* reported that the incidence of bacterial pneumonia was almost four times higher in HIV-seropositive subjects than among HIV-negative subjects; smoking illicit drugs (marijuana, cocaine, or crack) had the strongest effect on risk of bacterial pneumonia among HIV-seropositive intravenous drug users with a previous history of *Peumocystic carinii* pneumonia. On the other hand, results from a NIDA-funded, randomized, prospective, controlled clinical trial, in which HIV-infected patients on antiretroviral therapy smoked one marijuana cigarette (containing 3.9% THC) three times daily for 21 days, Brendt and colleagues *(23)* showed no significant changes in naive/memory cells, activated lymphocytes, B-cells, or natural killer cell numbers that could be directly attributed to the administration of cannabinoids. Thus, there were no untoward effects of cannabinoids on immune system function in HIV patients in this short trial *(23)*.

Polen et al. *(24)* identified marijuana use as a risk factor for ill health. They examined the health effects of smoking marijuana by comparing the medical experience of daily marijuana smokers who never smoked tobacco (n = 452) with a demographically similar group of nonsmokers of either substance (n = 450). Frequent smokers had a small but significant increased risk of outpatient visits for respiratory illness (relative risk = 1.19; 95% confidence interval = 1.01, 1.41), injuries (relative risk = 1.32; confidence interval = 1.10, 1.57), and other types of illnesses compared with nonsmokers. The authors concluded that daily marijuana smoking was associated with an elevated risk of health care use for various health problems. There was an increased rate of presentation for respiratory conditions among marijuana-only users, although its significance remains uncertain because infectious and noninfectious respiratory conditions were aggregated. Nevertheless, marijuana use was associated with increased respiratory/pulmonary complications and increased rates of hospitalizations for such complications among chronic marijuana smokers *(12,24)*.

Marijuana smoking produces histopathological changes that precede lung cancer, and long-term marijuana smoking may increase the risk of respiratory cancer *(25)*. Johnson and colleagues *(26)* presented case histories of four men with multiple, large, upper-zone lung bullae but otherwise relatively preserved lung parenchyma. Each had a history of significant exposure to marijuana. In three of the four cases, the tobacco smoking had been relatively small, suggesting a possible causal role for marijuana in the pathogenesis of this unusual pattern of bullous emphysema. aWengen *(27)* reported a case series of 34 young patients (between 20 and 40 years of age) with squamous cell carcinomas of the oral cavity in association with chronic smoking of marijuana (unfortunately the abstract reviewed did not provide the length of marijuana or other drug use). In another report, Caplan and Brigham *(28)* reported on two cases of squamous cell carcinoma of the tongue in men who chronically smoked marijuana but had no other risk factors such as smoking of tobacco or chronic use of alcohol. Caplan *(29)* also reviewed 13 reports of cancer of the mouth and larynx among chronic marijuana smokers in Australia and the United States in the last 5 years. Five of the cases had no other risk factors, and all were young. Caplan hypothesized that deep inhalation leads to earlier deposition of particulate matter as a result of turbulence and internal impaction. These reports of cancers in young individuals are of concern because such cancers are rare among adults under the age of 60, even those who smoke tobacco and drink alcohol *(30)*, and also because smoke from each marijuana cigarette contains more carcinogenic chemical constituents, such as benzopyrene, than smoke from a tobacco cigarette *(31)*. Thus, although no epidemiological studies show a causal relation between lung disease, including cancer, and marijuana use, the available evidence suggests that marijuana use may increase the risk of cancer and significant adverse respiratory/pulmonary consequences.

4. Hepatic and Renal Consequences

No significant reports of hepatic effects in humans have been reported that could be attributed to the use of marijuana. In the case of renal effects; a few case reports show that use of marijuana could cause reversible renal consequences such as impaired renal function *(32)*, acute renal infarction *(33)*, or renal insufficiency *(34)*.

5. Endocrine Effects

Marijuana use affects endocrine and reproductive functions as well, inhibits the secretion of gonadotropins from the pituitary gland, and may act directly on the ovary or testis. Although the effects are subtle, it is important to determine the true incidence of hypothalamic dysfunction, metabolic abnormalities, and mechanism of action of marijuana from well-designed studies *(35)*. Cannabinoids affect multiple reproductive functions, from hormone secretion to birth of offspring *(36)*. Schuel and colleagues reported that endocannabinoid anandamide signaling regulates sperm functions required for fertilization in the human reproductive tract and that abuse of marijuana could affect these processes *(36)*. Chronic administration of high doses of THC lowers testosterone secretions; impairs semen production, motility, and viability; and disrupts the ovulatory cycle in animals *(37)*. Furthermore, according to Harclerode *(38)*, THC lowers testosterone levels by lowering luteinizing hormone and follicle-stimulating hormone. Marijuana depresses the levels of prolactin, thyroid function, and growth hormone while elevating adrenal cortical steroids. Chronic exposure of laboratory animals (rats, mice, and monkeys) to marijuana altered the function of several accessory reproductive organs. Reduced testosterone levels leads to reduced testicular function and reduced prostate and seminal vesicle weights. Chronic administration of marijuana also produces testicular degeneration and necrosis in dogs *(39)*.

In 1986, Mendelson and colleagues *(40)* reported that marijuana smoking suppressed luteinizing hormone levels in normal women but not in menopausal women *(41)*. Barnett et al. *(42)* showed that testosterone levels were depressed both after smoking one marijuana cigarette and after intravenous infusion of THC. This antiandrogenic effect of marijuana appears to occur through action on the hypothalamic–pituitary–

gonadal axis (37) or, in part, from inhibition of androgen action at the receptor level *(43)*. Besides a single case of retarded growth in a 16-year-old marijuana smoker *(44)*, no epidemiological studies or reports show that marijuana impairs sexual maturation and reproduction in humans.

6. Birth and Later Developmental Outcomes

Marijuana administration at high doses can produce teratogenic effects in mice, rats, rabbit, and hamsters. In humans, although far from definitive, evidence from longitudinal studies with women who abused marijuana during pregnancy suggests that prenatal exposure to marijuana is related to some aspects of postnatal developmental deficits in the offspring *(45)*.

Two major studies, both funded by NIDA, have followed women who smoked marijuana during pregnancy to examine the developmental consequences of marijuana use on the offspring. The study by Fried and colleagues at the University of Ottawa, Canada *(46,47)*, examined the developmental consequences of marijuana in a cohort of Canadian, mostly Caucasian women. Another study by Day and colleagues *(48)*, at the University of Pittsburgh, examined the consequences of prenatal marijuana in mainly poor African American women who smoked marijuana during pregnancy. Such use was reported to be associated with fetal growth retardation, as shown by reduction in birthweight, reduced length at birth, and reduced gestation period; the latter may be a result of the hormonal effects of marijuana. Fried *(46,47)* found that in the newborns, marijuana use by the mother was associated with mild withdrawal symptoms and some autonomic disruption of nervous system state regulation. Between 6 months and 3 years of age, after controlling for confounders, no behavioral consequences of prenatal marijuana exposure were observed among the children. At 4 years of age, no differences were observed between exposed and nonexposed children on global tests of intelligence, but differences were observed in verbal ability and memory. Impairment *of* verbal ability, memory, and sustained attention were also seen at 5 and 6 years of age. The pattern of results suggested an association of prenatal marijuana exposure with impaired "executive functioning"—the latter thought to be a marker of prefrontal lobe functioning that may not be apparent until 4 years of age.

Day and co-workers *(48)* reported similar findings of impaired cognition in children who were exposed prenatally to marijuana. Recently, Goldschmidt and colleagues *(49)* reported significant effects on academic achievement in 10-year-old children who had been exposed to prenatal marijuana. However, it is important to note that the cognitive effects of prenatal exposure to marijuana on the offspring are quite complex, in that marijuana exposure appears to be associated with impairment of particular aspects of intelligence, such as tasks that require visual analysis, visual memory, analysis, and integration among children 9–12 as well as 13–16 years of age *(50)*. By comparison, prenatal exposure to tobacco affects the overall IQ and verbal functioning aspects of cognitive performance. By using the newer imaging techniques, Smith et al. *(51)* reported that, with increased exposure to prenatal marijuana, there was a significant increase in neural activity in bilateral prefrontal cortex and right premotor cortex during response inhibition. There was also an attenuation of activity in the left cerebellum with increased prenatal exposure to marijuana when challenging the response inhibition neural circuitry. Prenatally exposed offspring had significantly more commission errors than nonexposed participants, but all participants were able to perform the task with more than 85% accuracy. These findings suggest that prenatal marijuana exposure is related to changes in neural activity during response inhibition that may last into young adulthood *(51)*.

7. Effects on the Brain: Cognitive, Psychological, and Mental Consequences

Research by Pope and Yurgelum-Todd *(52)*, Kouri et al. *(53)*, Solowij et al. *(54)*, and Block and Ghoneim *(55)* has shown that chronic use of marijuana was associated with impairment of cognition, particularly affecting short-term memory and executive functioning in humans; and this impairment did not recover after abstaining from heavy use of marijuana (up to 5000 times in a lifetime) for at least 24 hours *(52)*, 7 days *(56)*, or 6 weeks *(54)*. However, in the study of Pope and colleagues *(57)*, the subjects did recover after 28 days of abstinence from marijuana use. In studies by Pope and colleagues *(52,56,57)*, the subjects smoked marijuana up to 5000 times in their lifetime (8-15 years), whereas in the study by Solowij et al. *(54)*, the subject had smoked approx 6 g of marijuana each day for about 17 years. Many other older studies have also reported that marijuana use is associated with impairment of short-term memory and not "old" memory.

Pope and Yurgelum-Todd *(52)* found that heavy use of marijuana is associated with cognitive impairment in college undergraduate students. The researchers enrolled two groups of students—65 "heavy users" (38 male, 27 female), who had smoked marijuana a median of 29 days in the past 30 days (range 22–30) and who also displayed cannabinoids in their urine, and 64 "light users" (31 male, 33 female), who had smoked a median of 1 day in the previous 30 days (range 0–9) and who displayed no urinary cannabinoids. All of the subjects were assessed by several neuropsychological tests when they were abstinent from marijuana and other drug use for at least 19 hours. The outcome measures were general intellectual functioning, abstraction ability, sustained attention, verbal fluency, and ability to learn and recall new verbal and visuospatial information. Heavy users displayed significantly greater impairment than light users in attention/executive functions, as evidenced by greater perseverations on card sorting and reduced learning of word lists. These differences remained after controlling for potential confounding variables, such as estimated levels of premorbid cognitive functioning, and for use of alcohol and other substances in the two groups. It is not clear whether this cognitive impairment is a reslut of a residue of drug in the brain, a withdrawal effect from the drug, or a frank neurotoxic effect of the drug.

Similarly, Fletcher and colleagues *(58)* reported cognitive impairment from chronic marijuana use, but in older subjects. They studied two cohorts of older chronic cannabis-using and cannabis-nonusing adult men. Both cohorts were comparable in age and socioeconomic status. Polydrug users and users who tested positive for use of cannabis at the time of cognitive assessment after a 72-hour abstention period were excluded. The older cohort (17 users, 30 nonusers; mean age 45 years) had consumed cannabis for an average of 34 years; the younger cohort (37 users and 49 nonusers; mean age 28 years) had consumed cannabis for an average of 8 years. Each subject received measures of short-term memory, working memory, and attentional skills. Results showed that the older chronic users performed more poorly than older nonusers on two short-term memory tests involving lists of words and on selective and divided attention tasks associated with working memory. No significant differences were apparent between younger users and nonusers. The authors concluded that long-term cannabis use was associated with disruption of short-term memory, working memory, and attention skills in older long-term cannabis users.

Crowley and colleagues *(59)* examined 89 seriously delinquent, drug-dependent adolescent males 2 years after their admission to a residential treatment program. All had at least three lifetime symptoms of conduct disorder. Of these boys, 82% were dependent on alcohol and 81% were dependent on cannabis, and many also were dependent on a wide variety of other substances. The boys were very aggressive by history, and more than half had committed a crime in the past month. Many of them also had major depression and/or attention deficit hyperactivity disorder (ADHD) at the time of admission. Nearly half had been in jail or detention just before admission. When followed up 2 years later, the boys showed highly significant reduction in antisocial and criminal acts. Both major depression and ADHD had nearly disappeared. About 40% of the group had achieved high school graduation or GED equivalency at the time of follow-up. However, the number reporting recent drug use had changed little, although the prevalence of heavy daily use had significantly declined. Research shows that seriously delinquent adolescents who are heavily involved in drug-taking behavior can improve in antisocial behaviors and depression after treatment. But the authors emphasize the need for more research on effective treatments for the drug dependence commonly found among delinquents.

Crowley and colleagues *(60)* carried out a study to determine the consequences of marijuana use among adolescents. The subjects were 165 male and 64 female 13- to 19-year-old patients recruited from a university treatment program for delinquent, substance-involved youths who had been referred for substance use and conduct problems (usually from social service or criminal justice agencies). The admission criteria were one or more dependence diagnoses and three or more lifetime conduct disorder symptoms (stealing, lying, running away, physical cruelty). The diagnoses were: substance dependence, 100%; conduct disorder, 82%; major depression, 17.5%; and ADHD, 14.8%. Standardized diagnostic interview instruments were used for substance dependence, psychiatric disorders, and patterns of substance abuse. Results showed that of the 229 teens, 220 had dependence on at least one nontobacco substance and 9 were dependent on tobacco with abuse of other substances. On average the youths were dependent on 3.2 substances, with marijuana and alcohol producing the most cases. Among the marijuana-dependent teens, 31.2% reported at least daily use of marijuana in the previous year. The rate of progression from first to regular marijuana use was as rapid as tobacco progression and more rapid than that of alcohol, indicating potent reinforcing effects of marijuana. Most patients described serious problems from marijuana: more than 80% of male and 60% of female patients met criteria for marijuana dependence, 66% of marijuana-dependent patients reported withdrawal, and more than 25% had used marijuana to relieve withdrawal symptoms (e.g., irritability, restlessness, insomnia, anorexia, nausea, sweating, salivation, elevated body temperature, tremor, and weight loss) that were clinically significant. About 85% said that marijuana interfered with their responsibilities at school, at work, or at home or endangered them while, for example, driving. Finally, the patients reported that in most cases, conduct problems arose before marijuana use, which typically began around the time of appearance of the third conduct disorder symptom. In summary, among adolescents with conduct problems, marijuana is not benign; moreover, its use by susceptible youths may be considered unsafe. It was stated that marijuana potentially reinforced marijuana taking, producing both dependence and withdrawal *(59,60)*.

Although "cannabis psychotic disorder" with delusions or with hallucinations is recognized in the *Diagnostic and Statistical Manual of Mental Disorders*, 4th ed., relatively little information is available on this disorder. Gruber and Pope *(61)* reviewed 395 eligible charts of the 9432 admissions at two psychiatric centers between April 1991 and October 1992 and October 1989 and November 1992, respectively, seeking cases of cannabis-induced disorders. There were no convincing cases of a cannabis-induced psychotic syndrome. The authors also reviewed published studies on the subject. There were 10 series of 10 or more cases, all describing primarily cannabis-induced psychotic syndromes. None of the 10 studies was performed in the United States; only two have been published in the last 10 years, neither of which supported the existence of a distinct cannabis-induced psychosis. Furthermore, most studies were retrospective and uncontrolled. The overall evidence from both reviews was insufficient to prove that marijuana alone can produce a psychotic syndrome in previously asymptomatic individuals, and further research is needed to validate the diagnosis of cannabis psychosis *(61)*. On the other hand, more recent and excellent reviews by Zammit and colleagues *(62)*, Aresneault et al. *(63)*, and Smit et al. *(64)* show that marijuana use is causally associated with the development of psychosis. For example, Zammit and colleagues concluded that cannabis use is associated with an increased risk of developing schizophrenia, consistent with a causal relation, and that this association is not explained by the use of other psychoactive drugs or personality traits relating to social integration. Aresneault et al. *(63)* also stated that on an individual level, cannabis use increases the risk at least twofold in the relative risk for later schizophrenia, while at the population level, elimination of cannabis would reduce the incidence of schizophrenia by approx 8% assuming a causal relationship. Similarly, Smit and colleagues *(64)* also suggested a relationship between cannabis use and schizophrenia. The reader is further directed to these excellent reviews on marijuana and psychosis.

8. Marijuana Dependence

Animal and human studies show that marijuana can produce tolerance and dependence. Lichtman and Martin *(65)* have shown that abstinence leads to clinically significant withdrawal symptoms that can be precipitated by treating the marijuana-dependent animals with a cannabinoid receptor antagonist, SR14176A. The most prominent signs of marijuana withdrawal in rats were wet-dog shakes; less frequent signs included grooming, retropulsion, and stretching; while the most prominent signs in the mice were head shakes and paw tremors. Similarly, mice exposed repetitively to marijuana smoke exhibit a dependence syndrome similar to that produced by THC. The development of cannabinoid or marijuana dependence in laboratory animals was consistent with marijuana dependence in humans *(57,66)*. Moreover, marijuana dependence is much more similar than dissimilar to other forms of drug dependence *(67)*. In humans, daily marijuana smoking in healthy individuals produces dependence, as demonstrated by withdrawal symptoms such as increased irritability and anxiety and decreased food intake. Furthermore, some aspects of marijuana dependence can be treated. During marijuana abstinence, sustained-release bupropion increases ratings of irritability, depression, and stomach pain and decreases food intake compared with placebo, suggesting ineffectiveness, whereas nefazodone was effective in decreasing anxiety during marijuana withdrawal compared with placebo. Nefazodone also did not alter the ratings of irritability and misery during withdrawal *(66–68)*.

Withdrawal of marijuana after chronic use leads to "inner unrest," increased activity, irritability, insomnia, and restlessness in humans *(69)*. Common symptoms reported were hot flashes, sweating, rhinorrhea, loose stools, hiccups, and anorexia. These symptoms were reduced by resumption of marijuana use *(70)*. Studies from Sweden have shown that chronic marijuana users seeking treatment became dependent on marijuana and were unable to give up its use *(71)*. Further epidemiological evidence *(72,73)* also supports the observation that chronic marijuana use produces dependence, the consequences of which are the loss of control over their drug use, cognitive and motivational impairments that interfere with occupational performance, lowered self-esteem and depression, and the complaints of spouses and partners.

In terms of marijuana-associated amotivational syndrome, the available evidence is equivocal. Research is needed to study this rare, inadequately defined, and insufficiently studied clinical consequence of prolonged heavy marijuana use.

9. Genetic Effects

Research shows a more than threefold and more than twofold increase over nonsmoking pregnant women in mutations of the hypoxanthine phosphoribosyl transferase (*hprt*) gene in among pregnant women who smoked marijuana and cigarettes, respectively, early in their pregnancies and before *(74)*. Authors indicated that these observations from a preliminary study suggest that marijuana smokers may have an elevated risk of cancer. For pregnant marijuana smokers, there is also concern about the possibility of genotoxic effects on the fetus, resulting in heightened risk of birth defects or childhood cancer.

The role of genetics in marijuana abuse was suggested by the studies of Tsuang and colleagues *(75–77)*. In a twin study of drug abuse, 4000 pairs of twins—monozygotic and dizygotic—were assessed for drug abuse and dependence. They showed that marijuana use was affected to a great extent by genetic factors. The common or family environment made a significant contribution to the use of marijuana. Initiation of marijuana use could be influenced by characteristics of the environment (drug availability, peer groups) and the characteristics of the individual (personality). For the continuation of drug use, other individual characteristics, such as physiological and subjective reactions to the drugs, may be important. Furthermore, among the marijuana users, suspiciousness and agitation appeared to be genetically related, whereas the pleasant psychological effects appeared to be mediated by the twins' shared environment, and not by genes. Using this twin model, additional studies are underway to examine the medical and health consequences, including psychiatric consequences, of drug abuse and genetic influences on drug use/abuse and associated conduct disorders and antisocial behaviors in childhood and later in adults.

10. Marijuana and Health

Sidney *(15)* and Polen et al. *(24)* at Kaiser Permanente HMO reviewed the medical charts of approx 65,000 patients and showed that, after adjusting for gender, age, race, education, marital status, and alcohol use, frequent marijuana smokers (duration of marijuana use between 5 and 15 years) had an increased risk of making outpatient visits for respiratory illness, injuries, and "other" illnesses compared with nonsmokers. In addition, the relative risk of cervical cancer among women who used marijuana but never smoked tobacco was 1.42 compared with those who used marijuana. However, there was no increased risk for other cancers in association with marijuana use. There was an increased risk of mortality associated with ever using marijuana among men, AIDS (probably reflective of lifestyles), injury/poisoning, and other causes of death, whereas among marijuana using women, there was a decreased risk for mortality.

11. Marijuana and Cancer

It is currently unclear whether long-term smoking of marijuana causes cancer. As mentioned above, marijuana smoke contains more carcinogenic chemical constituents than tobacco smoke *(31)*; thus, one might expect to see more cases of lung cancer than with tobacco smoking. However, no significantly large number of cases of lung cancer or other cancers has been reported in marijuana smokers, possibly because no such studies have ever been conducted. Recently, after controlling for age, sex, race, education, alcohol consumption, pack-years of cigarette smoking, and passive smoking, Zhang and colleagues *(78)* reported that the risk of squamous cell carcinoma of the head and neck was increased with marijuana use in a strong dose–response pattern. The researchers also suggested that marijuana use might interact with mutagenicity and other risk factors to increase the risk of head and neck cancer. However, the investigators noted that the results should be interpreted with some caution in drawing causal inferences because of certain methodological limitations, especially with regard to interactions between marijuana smoking and concomitant use of alcohol and tobacco. On the other hand, on the basis of a large case–control study of head, neck, or lung cancer in marijuana smokers, Hashibe et al. *(79)* reported that although the use of tobacco and alcohol was associated with these cancers, the use of marijuana was not associated with these cancers in young adults.

12. Marijuana and Highway Accidents

The published evidence suggests that marijuana use may impair motor performance. In a recent review, Ramaekers and colleagues *(80)* report that both epidemiological and experimental studies show that marijuana use is associated with motor accidents. Further, they state that combined use of THC and alcohol produced severe impairment of cognitive, psychomotor, and actual driving performance in experimental studies and sharply increased the crash risk in epidemiological analyses. Significantly increased rates of motor vehicle injuries resulting in hospitalization have also been reported among marijuana users *(81)*. Despite many reports in the published literature, the incidence and prevalence of accidents causally related to marijuana use are not known. More research is needed to establish a causal association between marijuana use and traffic accidents.

13. Summary

For the past several years marijuana has been the most commonly abused drug in the United States, with approx 6% of the population 12 years and older having used the drug in the month before interview. The use of marijuana is not without significant health risks. Marijuana is associated with effects on almost every organ system in the body, ranging from the central nervous system to the cardiovascular, endocrine, respiratory/pulmonary, and immune systems. Research shows that in addition to marijuana abuse/dependence, marijuana use is associated with serious health consequences in some studies with impairment of cognitive function in the young and old, fetal and developmental consequences, cardiovascular effects (heart rate and blood pressure changes), respiratory/pulmonary complications such as chronic cough and emphysema, impairment of immune function, and risk of developing head, neck, and/or lung cancer. In general, acute effects are better studied than those of chronic use, and more studies are needed that focus on disentangling effects of marijuana from those of other drugs and adverse environmental conditions. More research is needed in the following areas: (1) the general health consequences of marijuana use, neurocognitive effects of chronic marijuana use by adolescents and young adults using traditional as well as newer imaging techniques; marijuana dependence in animal models and humans; marijuana effects in various human diseases (endocrine, pulmonary/respiratory diseases; immune dysfunction-related infections); effects of chronic marijuana use on sleep disorders; drug interactions between marijuana and medications used in the treatment of mental disorders or other diseases; effects of acute and chronic marijuana use on the reproductive system; and functional assays to study neuropsychiatric/behavioral effects; (2) in the cardiovascular area, the effects of chronic marijuana use and atherosclerotic events (effects on clotting mechanisms; lipid metabolism) and endothelial function; arrhythmic effects of chronic marijuana use; effects on body weight resulting from plasma fluid retention (renal effects via renin–angiotensin–aldosterone system); and long-term effects on coronary output using noninvasive techniques; (3) future pulmonary and cancer studies addressing lung immunity among chronic marijuana smokers; incidence, prevalence, and underlying pathophysiology (molecular/genetic basis) of head and neck cancer and other cancers (cervix, prostate) associated with chronic marijuana use; population epidemiological studies; and tumor registries to determine whether chronic marijuana smoking is associated with cancers; and finally (4) training for new investigators and those from other disciplines to conduct research on the medical and health consequences of marijuana.

References

1. *2004 World Drug Report*, United Nations, Office of Drugs and Crime. Oxford University Press, Oxford, UK.
2. Substance Abuse and Mental Health Services Administration *(2004) National Household Survey on Drug Abuse, Main Findings, 2004*, Rockville, MD, US Department of Health and Human Services.
3. Wagner, F. A. and Anthony, J. C. (2002) From first drug use to drug dependence: developmental periods of risk for dependence upon marijuana, cocaine, and alcohol. *Neuropsychopharmacol*ogy **26**, 479–488.
4. 2003 Monitoring the Future, National Survey Results on Drug Use, National Institutes of Health, Department of health and Human Services; conducted by the University of Michigan's Institute for Social Research, National Institute on Drug Abuse, Bethesda, Maryland. The latest data are available at www.drugabuse.gov.
5. Chen, K. and Kandel, D. B. (1998) Predictors of cessation of marijuana use: an event history analysis. *Drug Alcohol Depend.* **50(2)**, 109–121.
6. Khalsa, J., Genser, S., Francis, H., and Martin, B. R. (2002) Medical and health consequences of marijuana. *J. Clin. Pharmacol.* **42 (11, Suppl.)**, 7s–10s.
7. Mechoulam, R., Parker, L. A., and Gallily, R. (2002) Cannabidiol: An over view of some pharmacological aspects. *J. Clin. Pharmacol.* **42 (11, Suppl.)**, 11s–19s.
8. Hall, W., Solowij, N., and Lemon, J. (1994) The health and psychological consequences of cannabis use, National Drug Strategy Monograph Series no.25, Canberra; Australian Government Publishing Service, 1994.
9. Hall, W. and Solowij, N. (1998) Adverse effects of cannabis use. *Lancet* **352**, 1611–1616.
10. Munson, A. E. and Fehr, K. O. (1983) Immunological effects of cannabis, in *Cannabis and Health Hazards, (*Fehr K. O. and Kalant H., eds.), Addiction Research Foundation, Toronto, Canada, pp. 257–253.
11. Hollister, L.E. (1992) Marijuana and immunity. *J. Psychoactive Drugs.* **24,** 159–164.
12. Coates, R. A., Farewell, V. T., Raboud, J., et al. (1990) Cofactors of progression to acquired immunodeficiency syndrome in a cohort of male sexual contacts of men with human immunodeficiency virus disease. *Am. J. Epidemiol.* **132**, 717–722.
13. Kaslow, R. A., Blackwelder, W. C., Ostrow, D. G., et al. (1989) No evidence for a role of alcohol or other psychoactive drugs in accelerating immunodeficiency in HIV-1-positive individuals. A report from the Multicenter AIDS Cohort Study. *JAMA* **261(23)**, 3424–3429.
14. Jones, R. T. (2002) Cardiovascular system effects of marijuana. *J. Clin. Pharmacol.* **42 (11, Suppl.)**, 58s–63s.
15. Sidney, S. (2002) Cardiovascular complications of marijuana use. *J. Clin. Pharmacol.* **42 (11, Suppl.)**, 64s–70s.
16. Bloom, J. W., Kaltenborn, W. T., Paoletti, P., Camilli, A., and Lebowitz, M. D. (1987) Respiratory effects of non-tobacco cigarettes. *Br. Med. J. Clin. Res. Ed.* **295(6612)**, 1516–1518.
17. Tashkin, D. P., Fligiel, S., Wu, T. C., et al. (1990) Effects of habitual use of marijuana and/or cocaine on the lung. *NIDA Res. Monogr.* **99**, 63–87.
18. Tashkin, D. P., Simmons, M. S., Sherrill, D. L., and Coulson, A. H. (1997) Heavy habitual marijuana smoking does not cause accelerated decline in FEV1 with age. *Am. J. Respir. Crit. Care Med.* **155**, 141–148.
19. Sherrill, D. L., Kryzanowski, M., Bloom, J. W., and Lebowitz, M. D. (1991) Respiratory effects of non-tobacco cigarettes: a longitudinal study in general population. *Int. J. Epidemiol.* **20**, 132–137.
20. Starr, K. and Renneker, M. (1994) A cytologic evaluation of sputum in marijuana smokers. *J. Family Practice* **39(4)**, 359–363.

21. Tashkin, D.P., Baldwin, G.C., Sarafian, T., Dubinett, S., and Roth, M.D. (2002) Respiratory and immunologic consequences of marijuana smoking, *J. Clin. Pharmacol.* **42(11, Suppl.)**, 71s–81s.
22. Caiaffa, W. T., Vlahov, D., Graham, N. M., et al. (1994) Drug smoking, Peneumocystis carinii pneumonia, and immunosppression increase risk of bacterial pneumonia in human immunodeficiency virus-seropositive injection drug users, Am. J. Respir. Crit. Care Med. **150(6 Pt. 1)**, 1493–1498.
23. Brendt, B. M., Higuera-Alhino, D., Shade, S. B., Herbert, S. J., McCune, J. M., and Abrams, D. I. (2002) Short-term effects of cannabinoids on immune phenotype and function in HIV-1-infected patients. *J. Clin. Pharmacol.* **42 (11, Suppl.)**, 82s–89s.
24. Polen, M. R., Sidney, S., Tekawa, I. S., Sadler, M., and Friedman, G. D. (1993) Health care use by frequent marijuana smokers who do not smoke tobacco. *Western J. Med.* **158**, 596–601.
25. Fligiel, S. E., Roth, M. D., Kleerup, E. C., Barsky, S. H., Simmons, M. S., and Tashkin, D. P. (1997) Tracheobronchial histopathology in habitual smokers of cocaine, marijuana, and/or tobacco. *Chest* **112(2)**, 319–326.
26. Johnson, M. K., Smith, R. P., Morrison, D., Laszlo, G., and White, R. J. (2000) Large lung bullae in marijuana smokers. *Thorax* **55**, 340–342.
27. aWengen, D. F. (1993) Marijuana and malignant tumors of the upper aerodigestive tract in young patients. *Laryngorhinootologie* **72(5)**, 264–267.
28. Caplan, G. A. and Brigham, B. A. (1990) Marijuana smoking and carcinoma of the tongue. Is there an association? *Cancer* **66**, 1005–1006.
29. Caplan, G. A. (1991) Marihuana and mouth cancer. *J. Royal Soc. Med.* **84,** 386.
30. Tashkin, D. P. (1993) Is frequent marijuana smoking harmful to health? *Western J. Med.* **158,** 635–637.
31. Novotny, M., Lee, M. L., and Bartle, K. D. (1976) A possible chemical basis for the higher mutagenicity of marijuana smoke as compared to tobacco smoke. *Experentia* **32(3)**, 280–282.
32. Vupputuri, S., Batuman, V., Muntner, P., et al. (2004) The risk for mild kidney function decline associated with illicit drug use among hypertensive men. *Am. J. Kidney Dis.* **43(4)**, 629–635.
33. Lambrecht, G. L., Malbrain, M. L., Coremans, P., Verbist, L., and Verhaegen, H. (1995) Acute renal infarction and heavy marijuana smoking. *Nephron* **70(4)**, 494–496.
34. Farber, S. J. and Huertas, V.E. (1976) Intravenously injected marihuana syndrome. *Arch. Intern. Med.* **136(3)**, 337–339.
35. Brown, T. T. and Dobs, A. S. (2002) Endocrine effects of marijuana. *J. Clin. Pharmacol.* **42 (11, Suppl.)**, 90s–96s.
36. Schuel, H., Burkman, L. J., Lippes, J., et al. (2002) Evidence that anandamide-signaling regulates human sperm functions required for fertilization. *Mol. Reprod. Dev.* **63(3)**, 376–387.
37. Bloch, E. (1983) Effects of marijuana and cannabinoids on reproduction, endocrine function, development and chromosomes, in *Cannabis and Health Hazards* (Fehr, K. O and Kalant, H., eds.), Addiction Research Foundation, Toronto.
38. Harclerode, J. (1984) Endocrine effects of marijuana in the male: preclinical studies. *NIDA Res. Monogr.* **44**, 46–64.
39. Dixit, V. P., Gupta, C. L., and Agarwal, M. (1977) Testicular degeneration and necrosis induced by chronic administration of cannabis extract in dogs. *Endocrinologie* **69(3)**, 299–305.
40. Mendelson, J. H., Mello, K., Ellingboe, J., Skupny, A. S., Lex, B. W., and Griffin, M. (1986) Marijuana smoking suppresses luteinizing hormone in women. *J. Pharmacol. Exp. Ther.* **237(3)**, 862–866.

41. Mendelson, J. H., Cristofaro, P., Ellingboe, J., Benedikt, R., and Mello, N. K. (1985) Acute effects of marihuana on luteinizing hormone in menopausal women. *Pharmacol. Biochem. Behav.* **23(5)**, 765–768.
42. Barnett, G., Chiang, C. W., and Licko, V. (1983) Effects of marijuana on testosterone in male subjects. *J. Theor. Biol.* **104(4)**, 685–692.
43. Purohit, V., Ahluwalia, B. S., and Vigersky, R. A. (1980) Marihuana inhibits dihydrotestosterone binding to the androgen receptor. *Endocrinology* **107(3)**, 848–850.
44. Copeland, K. C., Underwood, L. E., and Van Wyck, J. J. (1980) Marijuana smoking and prepubertal arrest. *J. Pediatrics* **96**, 1079–1080.
45. Khalsa, J. H. and Gfroerer, J. (1991) Epidemiology and health consequences of drug abuse among pregnant women. *Sem. Perinatol.* **15(4)**, 265–270.
46. Fried, P. A. (1995) The Ottawa prenatal prospective study (OPPS): methodological issues and findings—it's easy to throw the baby out with the bath water. *Life Sciences*. **56**, 2159–2168.
47. Fried, P. A. (1995) Prenatal exposure to marihuana and tobacco during infancy, early and middle childhood: effects and an attempt at synthesis. *Arch. Toxicol. Suppl.* **17**, 233–260.
48. Day, N. L., Richardson, G. A., Goldschmidt, L., et al. (1994) Effect of prenatal marijuana exposure on the cognitive development of offspring at age three. *Neurotoxicology & Teratology.* **16(2)**, 169–175.
49. Goldschmidt, L., Richardson, G. A., Cornelius, M. D., and Day, N. L. (2004) Prenatal marijuana and alcohol exposure and academic achievement at age 10. *Neurotoxicol. Teratol.* **26**, 521–532.
50. Fried, P. A., Watkinson, B., and Gray, R. (2003) Differential effects on cognitive functioning in 13- to 16- year-olds prenatally exposed to cigarettes and marihuana. *Neurotoxicol. Teratol.* **25(4)**, 427–436.
51. Smith, A. M., Fried, P. A., Hogan, M. J., and Cameron, I. (2004) Effects of prenatal marijuana on response inhibition: an fMRI study of young adults. *Neurotoxicol. Teratol.* **26(4)**, 533–542.
52. Pope, H. G., Jr, Gruber, A. J., and Yurgelum-Todd, D. (1995) The residual neuropsychological effects of cannabis:the current status of research. *Drug Alcohol Depend.* **38**, 25–34.
53. Kouri, E., Pope, H. G., Jr., Yurgelun-Todd, D., and Gruber, S. (1995) Attributes of heavy vs. occasional marijuana smokers in a college population. *Biol. Psychiatry* **38**, 475–481.
54. Solowij, N., Grenyer, B. F., Chesher, G., and Lewis, J. (1995) Biopsychological changes associated with cessation of cannabis use: a single case study of acute and chronic cognitive effects, withdrawal and treatment. *Life Sci.* **56(23/24)**, 2127–2134.
55. Block, R. I. and Ghoneim, M. M. (1993) Effects of chronic marijuana use on human cognition. *Psychopharmacol*ogy **110**, 219–228.
56. Pope, H. G., Jr. and Yurgelun-Todd, D. (1996) The residual cognitive effects of heavy marijuana use in college students. *JAMA* **275(7)**, 521–527.
57. Harrison, G. P. Jr., Gruber, A. J., Hudson, J. I., Huestis, M. A., and Yiurgelun-Todd, D. (2002) Cognitive measures in long-term cannabis users. *J. Clin. Pharmacol.* **42 (11, Suppl.)**, 41s–47s.
58. Fletcher, J. M., Page, J. B., Francis, D. J., et al. (1996) Cognitive correlates of chronic cannabis use in Costa Rican men. *Arch. Gen. Psychiatry* **53,**1051–1057.
59. Crowley, T. J., Mikulich, S. K., Macdonald, M., Young, S. E., and Zerbe, G .O. (1998) Substance-dependent, conduct-disordered adolescent males: severity of diagnosis predicts two-year outcome. *Drug Alcohol Depend.* **49(3)**, 225–237.
60. Crowley, T. J., MacDonald, M. J., Whitmore, E. A., and Mikulich, S. K. (1998) Cannabis dependence, withdrawal, and reinforcement among adolescents with conduct symptoms and substance use disorders. *Drug Alcohol Depend.* **50 (1)**, 27–37.

61. Gruber, A. J. and Pope, H. G. (1994) Cannabis psychotic disorder: Does it exist? *Am. J. Addict.* **1(1)**, 72–83.
62. Zammit, S., Allebeck, P., Andreasson, S., Lundberg, I., and Lewis, G. (2002) Self-reported cannabis use as a risk factor for schizophrenia in Swedish conscripts of 1969: historical cohort study. *Br. Med. J.* **325**, 1199.
63. Arseneault, L., Cannon, M., Witton, J., and Murray, R. M. (2004) Causal association between cannabis and psychosis: examination of the evidence. *Br. J. Psychiatry* **184**, 110–117.
64. Smit, F., Bolier, L., and Cuijpers, P. (2004) Cannabis use and the risk of later schizophrenia: a review. *Addiction* **99(4)**, 425–430.
65. Lichtman, A. H. and Martin, B. R. (2002) Marijuana withdrawal syndrome in the animal model. *J. Clin. Pharmacol.* **42 (11, Suppl.)**, 20s–27s.
66. Budney, A. J. and Moore, B. A. (2002) Development and consequences of cannabis dependence. *J. Clin. Pharmacol.* **42 (11, Suppl.)**, 28s–33s.
67. Haney, M. (2002) Effects of smoked marijuana in healthy and HIV + marijuana smokers. *J. Clin. Pharmacol.* **42 (11, Suppl.)**, 34s–40s.
68. Haney, M., Hart, C. L., Vosburg, S. K., et al. (2004) Marijuana withdrawal in humans: effects of oral THC or divalproex. *J. Neuropsychopharmacol.* **29(1)**, 158–170.
69. Jones, R. T. and Benowitz, N. (1976) The 30-day trip-clinical studies of cannabis tolerance and dependence, in *Pharmacology of Marijuana*, Vol. 2 (Braude, M. C. and Szara, S., eds), Academic Press, New York.
70. Jones, R. T., Benowitz, N., and Herning, R. I. (1981) The clinical relevance of cannabis tolerance and dependence. *J. Clin. Pharmacol.* **21**, 143s–152s.
71. Tunving, K., Lundquist, T., and Ericksson, D. (1988) "A way out of fog": an outpatient program for cannabis abusers, in *Marijuana: An International Research Report, (*Chesher, G., Consroe, P., and Musty, R., eds.), Australian Government Publishing Service, Canberra, pp. 207–212.
72. Robins, L. N. and Regier, D. A. (eds) (1991) *Psychiatric Disorders in America,* MacMillan, New York, Free Press.
73. Anthony, J. C. and Helzer, J. E. (1991) Syndromes of drug abuse and dependence, in *Psychiatric Disorders in America* (Robins, L. N. and Regier, D. A., eds), Free Press, MacMillan, New York.
74. Ammenheuser, M. M., Berenson, A. B., Babiak, A. E., et al. (1998) Frequencies of hprt mutant lymphocytes in marijuana-smoking mothers and their newborns. *Mutat. Res.* **403(1–2)**, 55–64.
75. Tsuang, M. T., Llyons, M., Isen, S., Goldberg, J., and True, W. (1993) Heritability of initiation and continuation of drug use. *Psychiatr. Genet.* **3(3)**, 141.
76. Tsuang, M. T., Lyons, M. J., Harley, R. M., et al. (1999) Genetic and environmental inflences on transitions in drug use. *Behav. Genet.* **29(6)**, 473–479.
77. Lyons, M. J., Toomey, R., Meyer, J. M., et al. (1997) How do genes influence marijuana use? The role of subjective effects. *Addiction* **92(4)**, 409–417.
78. Zhang, Z. F., Morgenstern, H., Spitz, M. R., et al. (1999) Marijuana use and increased risk of squamous cell carcinoma of the head and neck. *Cancer Epidemiol. Biomarkers Prev.* **8**, 1071–1078.
79. Hashibe, M., Ford, D. E., and Zhang, Z. F. (2002) Marijuana smoking and head and neck cancer. *J. Clin. Pharmacol.* **42 (11, Suppl.)**, 103s–107s.
80. Ramaekers, J. G., Berghaus, G., van Laar, M., and Drummer, O. H. (2004). Dose related risk of motor vehicle crashes after cannabis use. *Drug Alcohol Depend.* **73**, 109–119.
81. Gerberich, S. G., Sidney, S., Braun, B. L., Tekawa, I. S., Tolan, K. K., and Quesenberry, C. P. (2003) Marijuana use and injury events resulting in hospitalization. *Ann. Epidemiol.* **13**, 230–237.

Chapter 11

Effects of Marijuana on the Lung and Immune Defenses

Donald P. Tashkin and Michael D. Roth

1. Introduction

Cannabis has been used as a drug for thousands of years, but marijuana smoking has become prevalent in Western society only during the last 40 years *(1,2)*. An annual survey conducted in the United States from 1975 to 2002 documented that marijuana is now the second most commonly smoked substance after tobacco *(1,2)*. Marijuana smoke, like tobacco smoke, is generated by the pyrolysis of dried plant leaves. As a result, it shares thousands of chemical features in common with tobacco smoke, including qualitatively similar amounts of carbon monoxide, cyanide, acrolein, benzene, vinyl chlorides, aldehydes, phenols, nitrosamines, reactive oxygen species (ROS), and a variety of polycyclic aromatic hydrocarbons *(3,4)*. The primary distinction between marijuana and tobacco is the presence of Δ^9-tetrahydrocannabinol (THC) and other cannabinoids in *Cannabis* vs the presence of nicotine in tobacco *(3,4)*. Although the hazardous effects of tobacco smoking have been extensively documented and include emphysema, chronic obstructive pulmonary disease (COPD), heart disease, and risk for developing several different types of cancer, studies on the health effects of marijuana smoking are less abundant. The common perception is that marijuana smoke is less toxic and that smoking a few marijuana joints per day has far fewer consequences than smoking a pack of tobacco cigarettes *(5)*. However, the lack of filtering and differences in the smoking technique associated with marijuana use result in an approximately fourfold greater deposition of tar particulates in the lung than occurs from smoking similar amounts of tobacco *(6)*. In addition, the concentration of pro-carcinogens such as benz-[α]-anthracene and benzo-[α]-pyrene are up to twofold higher in marijuana tar *(3,7)*. The presence of irritants and pro-carcinogens in mari-

From: *Forensic Science and Medicine: Marijuana and the Cannabinoids*
Edited by: M. A. ElSohly © Humana Press Inc., Totowa, New Jersey

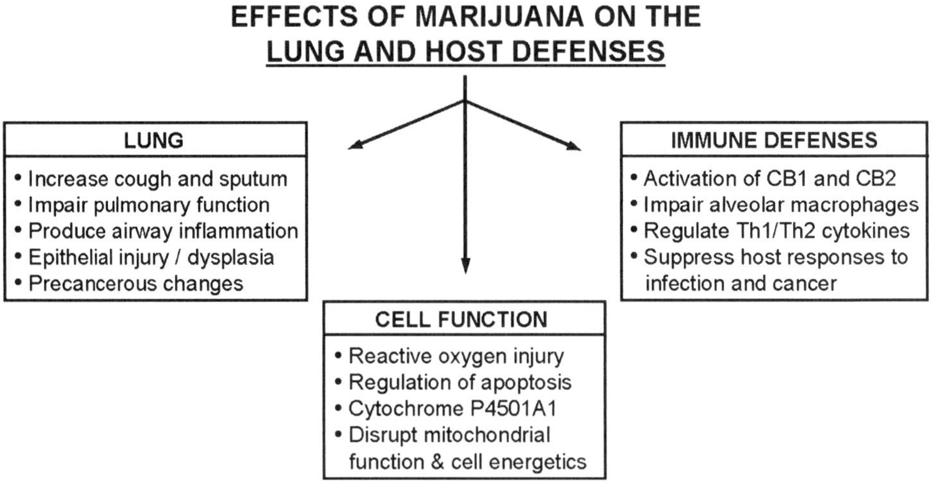

Fig. 1. Habitual marijuana smoking delivers toxic smoke components and high concentrations of tetrahydrocannabinol to the lung with subsequent effects on the lung, respiratory cell function, and host immune defenses.

juana smoke and the enhanced deposition of these in the lung during smoking suggest that habitual smoking of marijuana might result in a spectrum of respiratory consequences similar to those described for tobacco smoking. Moreover, THC has recently been shown to exert potent biological effects on lung epithelial cells and on the immune system *(8–10)*. Consequently, it is possible that regular exposure to marijuana smoke, a large proportion of which is THC, might predispose to lung injury, pulmonary infections, and/or tumor growth. This chapter reviews the current knowledge concerning the pulmonary and immune consequences of marijuana smoking and THC, as briefly outlined in Fig. 1.

2. Acute Effects of Marijuana on Airway Physiology

Although anecdotal reports dating back to the 19th century suggested a therapeutic role for marijuana in the relief of asthma, formal experiments first documented this effect in the 1970s. Smoke from marijuana cigarettes was found to produce short-term bronchodilation both in healthy individuals *(11,12)* and in patients with asthma *(13)*. This bronchodilator effect was clearly attributable to the presence of THC, because oral administration of synthetic THC also produced a dose-dependent bronchodilatation *(11)*. Recently, a potential mechanism for this effect on bronchomotor tone was identified. Cannabinoid type 1 (CB_1) receptors were found on axon terminals of postganglionic parasympathetic nerve fibers in rat lung. These nerve terminals are in close proximity to airway smooth muscle *(14)*. In the guinea pig airway, stimulation of these receptors by the endogenous cannabinoid anandamide resulted in dose-dependent relaxation of capsaicin-contracted airway smooth muscle, whereas anandamide caused dose-dependent bronchoconstriction in vagotomized preparations in which airway smooth muscle was maximally relaxed *(14)*. These observations suggest that the endogenous cannabinoid system may play a regulatory role in the bidirectional control of airway smooth muscle tone.

From a clinical standpoint, however, smoking marijuana does not have a therapeutic role in obstructive airways diseases such as asthma. Despite its short-term bronchodilator properties, the long-term pulmonary consequences of marijuana smoking include airway inflammation, edema, and mucus hypersecretion *(5)*. On the other hand, the development of aerosolized preparations of pure THC for inhalation *(15)* could produce local physiological effects with a rapid and reproducible onset of action. However, inhalation of pure THC has been shown to induce bronchospasm in individuals with airways hyperreactivity because of local irritant effects *(16)*. THC can also disrupt mitochondrial function and the generation of adenosine triphosphate (ATP) in airway epithelial cells, as well as promote necrotic cell death *(8,17)*. These toxic effects occur rapidly, and the impact of THC on mucociliary function and noxious lung injury can be significant.

3. Effects of Habitual Marijuana Exposure on the Lung

3.1. Animal Studies

Several long-term animal exposure studies (dog, rat, monkey) have demonstrated extensive inflammatory changes in small airways (bronchioles) and focal inflammation within the lung parenchyma, as well as proliferative alterations in alveolar epithelium *(18–20)*. On the other hand, a carefully conducted study in rats in which animals were exposed to increasing concentrations of marijuana or tobacco smoke for 1 year demonstrated morphological and physiological changes of emphysema (decreased alveolar surface area and reduced lung elastic recoil) in the tobacco-exposed rats but not in the animals exposed to a similar quantity of marijuana *(21)*. The results of these animal studies are difficult to extrapolate to humans because of differences in exposure of different regions of the respiratory system to the inhaled smoke as well as species differences.

3.2. Human Studies

3.2.1. Older Studies on the Effects of Cannabis on Respiratory Disorders and Lung Function

Several older human studies conducted in the 1970s yielded conflicting results concerning the impact of regular cannabis use on clinical features of chronic respiratory disease and/or lung function *(22–25)*. These results are difficult to interpret because the studies were mostly small in scale, cross-sectional in design, and subject to selection bias. In addition, many of them failed to control adequately for the important confounding effect of concomitant tobacco use.

3.2.2. Newer Studies on the Pulmonary Consequences of Marijuana Use

Three relatively large-scale, controlled observational studies of the pulmonary consequences of regular use of marijuana have been conduced since 1980. One longitudinal cohort study reported on a convenience sample of heavy habitual smokers of marijuana alone (MS; $N = 144$) or with tobacco (MTS; $N = 134$), regular smokers of

Table 1
Pulmonary Consequences of Habitual Marijuana Use

- Increased prevalence of acute and chronic bronchitis *(26,28,30)*
- Inconsistent evidence of mild, progressive airflow obstruction *(26–31)*
- Visual evidence of airway inflammation (mucosal erythema, edema, and increased secretions) that correlates with inflammatory findings on airway biopsy *(5)*
- Histopathological alterations in tracheobronchial epithelium and subepithelium, including squamous metaplasia, basal cell hyperplasia, goblet cell hyperplasia, loss of ciliated surface epithelium, basement membrane thickening, epithelial inflammation, cellular disorganization, and increased nuclear-to-cytoplasm ratio *(35,36)*
- Overexpression of epidermal growth factor receptor and Ki-67, a nuclear marker of cell proliferation, by bronchial epithelial cells suggesting dysregulated growth and a risk for progression to bronchogenic carcinoma *(36)*
- Epidemiological evidence of increased risk for both bacterial and opportunistic pneumonia in HIV-seropositive individuals *(83–85)*

tobacco alone (TS; $N = 80$), and nonsmokers of either substance (NS; $N = 99$) recruited from the greater Los Angeles area *(26,27)*. A second cohort study reported on a random stratified sample of young residents of Tucson, AZ *(28,29)*. The third study was a population-based approach employing a birth cohort of individuals residing in Dunedin, New Zealand *(30,31)*. Results of these studies have revealed a number of adverse pulmonary consequences of habitual marijuana use (Table 1).

3.2.2.1. Respiratory Symptoms

All three studies reported comparable results with respect to the association between regular marijuana smoking and chronic respiratory symptoms: the prevalence of chronic cough and/or sputum and wheeze was significantly higher in the marijuana smokers than in the nonsmokers, indicating a link between regular marijuana use and symptoms of chronic bronchitis. In the Los Angeles study, the incidence of acute lower respiratory infections was also higher in both MS and TS than NS, and the prevalence of chronic respiratory symptoms was comparable between MS and TS without evidence of additive effects in those who smoked both substances *(26,27)*. However, an additive adverse effect of combined marijuana and tobacco smoking was suggested in the Tucson study *(28,29)*.

3.2.2.2. Lung Function

The Los Angeles study failed to reveal any association between marijuana smoking and abnormalities on pulmonary function tests including sensitive tests of small airway function, the major site of involvement in COPD, and the diffusing capacity for carbon monoxide, a sensitive physiological indicator of emphysema. Moreover, no impact of even heavy regular smoking of marijuana alone (average of three joints per day) was found on the annual rate of change in the forced expiratory volume in 1 second (FEV_1), an indicator of obstructive lung disease. In contrast, TS from the same cohort study demonstrated an accelerated rate of loss of FEV_1 *(27)*, consistent with the known predisposition of tobacco smokers to the development of COPD. These findings, therefore, did not support the concept that marijuana smoking leads to the development of COPD and are consistent with the results of the rat exposure experiments cited above. In contrast, both the Tucson study and the Dunedin study did find evidence of mild airflow obstruction in association with marijuana use *(28,30)*, and the airflow obstruction progressed over time in the continuing marijuana users *(29,31)*. In contrast to the Los Angeles study, these two reports suggest that regular use of marijuana may be a risk factor for the subsequent development of COPD.

A specialized test of lung function that serves as a measure of alveolar epithelial permeability was carried out in a subset of the participants in the Los Angeles study *(32)*. This test measures the rate of clearance from the lung of a radiolabeled small molecule (^{99m}Tc-DTPA) after inhalation. Elimination of the ^{99m}Tc-DTPA through the normally tight junctions between adjacent alveolar epithelial cells is accelerated in the presence of epithelial cell injury. Interestingly, while the results of this test were abnormal in regular tobacco smokers, consistent with tobacco-related lung injury, findings in the regular smokers of marijuana only (MS) were similar to those in nonsmoking healthy control subjects (NS). These negative results parallel the findings of a normal diffusing capacity for carbon monoxide in the MS and provide further evidence of disparate effects of marijuana and tobacco on lung function.

Thus, the available evidence is mixed and contradictory with regard to the possible link between marijuana and COPD. Clearly, further research is required to resolve these conflicting findings.

3.2.2.3. Effects on Airway Injury and Bronchial Epithelial Pathology

A subset of MS, TS, MTS, and NS from the Los Angeles cohort underwent fiberoptic bronchoscopy during which videotapes of the tracheobronchial airway mucosa were recorded and a series of mucosal biopsies obtained. The videotapes were reviewed in a blinded manner for the presence and degree of airway injury according to a semiquantitative scoring system ("bronchitis index"; ref. *5*). Visual evidence of airway injury among the MS comparable to that noted in the TS was identified with abnormal scores for mucosal erythema, swelling, and increased secretions as compared to control NS. These visual abnormalities were corroborated by histopathological alterations on the mucosal biopsies in which an increased number and size of submucosal blood vessels, submucosal edema, and hyperplasia of the mucus-secreting surface epithelial cells (goblet cells) were observed. These findings indicate that regular smoking of marijuana by young adults leads to the same frequency, type, and degree of aiway inflammation as that seen in the lungs of regular tobacco smokers, despite a marked difference in the number of cigarettes smoked for the two types of substances (~3 joints per day in the MS vs 22 tobacco cigarettes per day in the TS).

It is possible that the presence of THC in marijuana smoke directly contributes to this higher than expected degree of airway injury. During smoking, THC is concentrated in the particulate phase of the smoke and deposited onto the respiratory mucosa. To examine its potential impact on cell function, endothelial cells (ECV 304 cell line), lung tumor cells (A549 cell line), and primary human airway epithelial cells were exposed in vitro to either purified THC or to smoke from marijuana cigarettes *(8,17,33,34)*. Exposure to whole marijuana smoke stimulated the formation of more ROS than did exposure to the same amount of tobacco smoke. Furthermore, the magnitude of ROS was directly proportional to the concentration of THC in the cigarettes

(33). Marijuana smoke exposure was also associated with a reduction in intracellular glutathione and a toxic effect on mitochondial electron transport, resulting in ATP depletion *(8,33,34)*. Mitochondrial dysfunction was observed with both purified THC and with the tar extracts from marijuana cigarettes, but not when cells were exposed to extracts from placebo marijuana smoke (not containing THC) or regular tobacco smoke. ATP depletion may impair important energy-dependent functions, including ciliary activity, phagocytosis, and normal fluid and electrolyte transport. Another potential consequence of mitochondial toxicity is an inhibition of apoptosis and the promotion of necrotic cell death, a pattern observed when respiratory epithelial cells are exposed to THC in vitro *(17,34)*. The shift from apoptotic to necrotic cell death has been shown in animal models to disrupt normal epithelial defenses and promote inflammation and infection. Further studies are required to determine the relevance of these toxic cellular effects of THC to the degree of lung injury observed in marijuana smokers.

Bronchial mucosal biopsies were also obtained during fiberoptic bronchoscopy from 40 MS, 31 TS, 44 MTS, and 53 NS as part of their participation in the Los Angeles study *(35)*. Light microscopy revealed extensive histopathological abnormalities in the epithelium of the MS, including goblet cell hyperplasia, reserve cell hyperplasia, squamous metaplasia, cellular disorganization, nuclear atypia, increased mitotic index, increased nuclear/cytoplasmic ratio, and inflammatory changes. These abnormalities were comparable to those noted in the TS, and the data suggested additive changes resulting from habitual use of both substances in the MTS. Some of these histological alterations are associated with the subsequent development of bronchogenic carcinoma in tobacco smokers *(36)*.

Immunohistology was used to examine bronchial biopsies from 52 of the previously mentioned subjects for abnormal expression of genes involved in the pathogenesis of lung cancer, including overexpression of epidermal growth factor receptor (Fig. 2), a pathway that promotes autonomous cell growth, and Ki-67, a nuclear proliferation protein involved in cell replication *(36)*. Results of these immunohistochemical studies revealed marked overexpression of epidermal growth factor receptor and Ki-67 among the MS compared to the NS and even numerically greater expression than was noted in the TS, with the suggestion of additivity in the MTS. Together with the aforementioned light microscopic changes, these findings suggest that regular marijuana smoking damages the airway epithelium, leading to dysregulation of bronchial epithelial cell growth and potentially malignant transformation.

3.2.2.4. Effects on Alveolar Macrophages

Alveolar macrophages (AM) are key immune effector cells in the lung that protect against infection and other noxious insults. AM were recovered by bronchoalveolar lavage during the bronchoscopy studies performed on subjects studied in Los Angeles. The number of AM recovered from MS was approximately twice that from NS, whereas the yield of AM from TS and MTS was three and four times that of NS, respectively, indicating an additive effect of the two substances on either AM recruitment to, and/or replication in, the lung (Table 2; Fig. 3; refs. *37* and *38*). The increased accumulation of AM in the lungs of MS may be viewed as an inflammatory response to chronic low-grade lung injury from habitual exposure to irritants, including oxyradicals, within the smoke of marijuana. Ultrastructural examination of AM

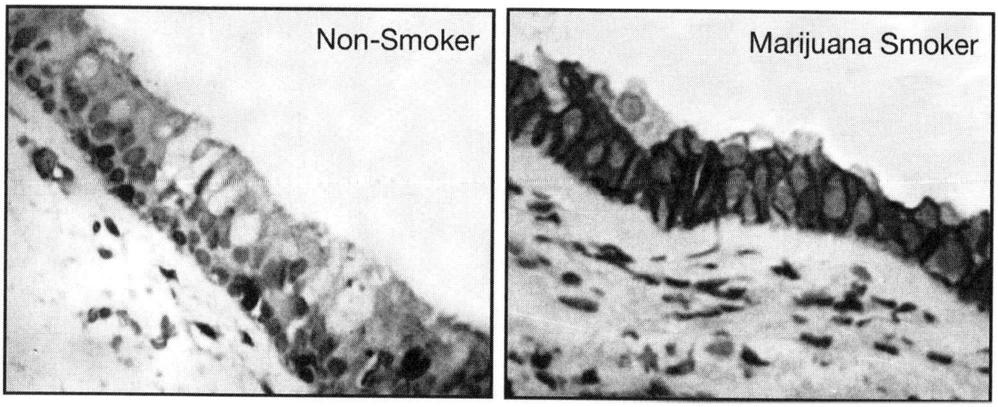

Fig. 2. Habitual marijuana smoking is associated with abnormal expression of epidermal growth factor receptor (EGFR), a growth factor receptor that promotes autonomous cell growth. Airway mucosal biopsies were obtained from a cohort of nonsmokers and smokers of marijuana alone, tobacco alone, or both marijuana and tobacco, and evaluated for EGFR expression by immunohistology. Compared to the limited basal staining present in normal epithelium **(left panel)**, biopsies demonstrated diffuse and dark staining of epithelial cells in 58% of marijuana smokers **(right panel)** and in 89% of those who smoked both marijuana and tobacco (not shown).

Table 2
Effects of Marijuana on Human Alveolar Macrophages

- Increased number of alveolar macrophages recovered by bronchoalveolar lavage from habitual marijuana smokers compared to nonsmokers *(37,38)*
- Increased size of intracytoplasmic inclusions *(39)*
- Impaired ability to kill *Candida albicans (40)* and *Candida pseudotropicalis (41)*
- Impaired phagocytosis and killing of *Staphylococcus aureus (41,42)*
- Decreased respiratory burst activity (superoxide anion production) under both basal and stimulated conditions *(40)*
- Limited tumoricidal activity against tumor cell targets in vitro *(41)*
- Reduced production of proinflammatory cytokines (tumor necrosis factor-α, interleukin-6, and granulocyte macrophage–colony-stimulating factor [GM-CSF]) when stimulated by bacterial lipopolysaccharide *(41)*
- Inability to express inducible nitric acid synthase or produce nitric oxide upon exposure to pathogenic bacteria, largely reversed by stimulation with proinflammatory cytokines such as GM-CSF and interferon-γ *(42)*

recovered from MS revealed large irregular-shaped cytoplasmic inclusions that most likely contain particulates from marijuana tar, possibly including metabolites of THC and other cannabinoids *(39)*. AM from TS also show abnormal cytosolic inclusion bodies, and the number of these inclusions is dramatically increased in smokers of both marijuana and tobacco *(39)*. It seems plausible that the presence of a large number of abnormal inclusion bodies within the cytoplasm of AM from smokers of marijuana and/or tobacco might interfere with the function of these important immune effector cells.

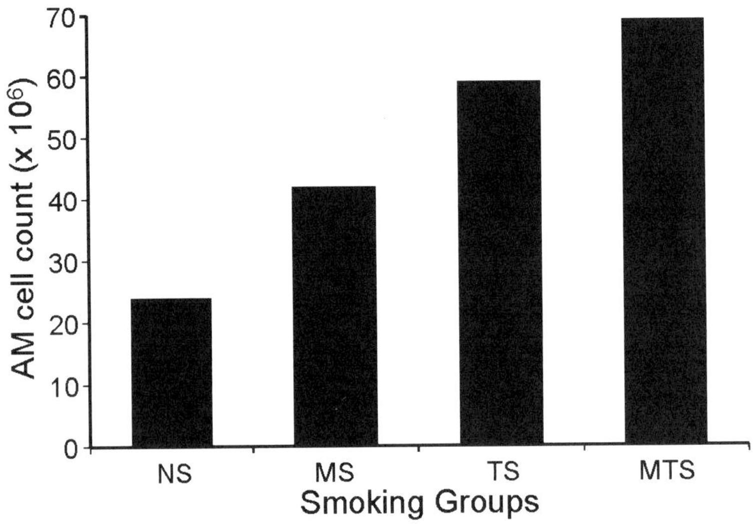

Fig. 3. The number of alveolar macrophages (AM) increases in response to smoking. Bronchoalveolar lavage was used to recover AM from the lungs of nonsmokers (NS) and smokers of marijuana alone (MS), tobacco alone (TS), or both marijuana and tobacco (MTS). The number of AM recovered from MS was approximately twice that from NS, while the yield of AM from TS and MTS was three and four times that of NS, respectively, indicating an additive effect of the two substances on the recruitment and/or replication of macrophages in the lung.

The function of AM recovered from a subset of MS, TS, MTS, and NS was systematically evaluated ex vivo with respect to their phagocytic and killing activity for fungi and bacteria, their production of reactive oxygen and nitrogen intermediates during incubation with fungal or bacterial microorganisms, their ability to produce pro-inflammatory cytokines when stimulated, and their cytotoxic activity against tumor cell targets. Briefly, findings from these studies showed the following: (1) an impairment in fungicidal activity against *Candida albicans* and *Candida tropicalis* when AM from both MS and TS were compared to AM collected from control NS *(40,41)*; (2) impairment in phagocytosis and killing of the pathogenic bacterium, *Staphylococcus aureus*, by AM from MS but not TS *(41)*; (3) a reduction in basal superoxide production by AM from MS (in contrast to an increase in basal superoxide generation by AM from TS) and an apparent attenuation by AM from marijuana smokers of the stimulated production of superoxide by AM from concomitant smokers of both tobacco and marijuana *(40)*; (4) an impairment in the generation of nitric oxide by AM from MS (but not TS) that parallels their impairment in bactericidal activity *(42)*; (5) a reduction in production of pro-inflammatory cytokines, tumor necrosis factor (TNF)-α and granulocyte macrophage–colony-stimulating factor (GM-CSF), by AM from MS when stimulated with bacterial lipopolysaccharide *(41)*; and (6) an impairment in tumoricidal activity by AM from MS *(41)*. A more detailed description of the effects of marijuana and THC on the function of AM and other immune cells and the likely clinical consequences of these immunological effects is provided below.

Table 3
Evidence Supporting Carcinogenic Effects of Marijuana

- Increased concentrations of pro-carcinogenic polycyclic aromatic hydrocarbons (PAHs), including benzo-[α]-pyrene, in the tar phase of marijuana smoke compared to tobacco smoke *(3,4,7)*
- Fourfold increase in lung deposition of tar from marijuana smoke as compared to tobacco smoke mainly as a result of the differences in cigarette filtration and smoking technique *(6)*
- Activation of the cytochrome P4501A1 gene by THC, potentially enhancing the transformation of PAHs into active carcinogens *(7)*
- Accelerated malignant transformation in hamster lung explants exposed to marijuana smoke for up to 2 years *(43)*
- Premalignant histopathological alterations in bronchial biopsies from smokers of marijuana only, including metaplastic and dysplastic changes in the bronchial epithelium *(35)*
- Overexpression of cell proteins associated with malignant transformation in the bronchial epithelium of habitual smokers of marijuana *(36)*
- Systemic administration of Δ^9-tetrahydrocannabinol accelerates the growth of non-small-cell lung cancer cells implanted into immunocompetent mice *(44)*
- Case series reporting a disproportionately high percentage of chronic marijuana smokers in young patients (<45 years) diagnosed with upper airway or lung cancer *(45–49)*
- Conflicting case–control studies demonstrating either a significantly increased risk *(51)* or no increased risk *(52)* of upper airway cancer in association with marijuana smoking
- Evidence from a case–control study of an increased risk for developing lung cancer in association with the combined use of cannabis (hashish) and snuff (tobacco), but not with hashish alone *(53)*

4. Potential Effects of Marijuana on Respiratory Carcinogenesis

Several lines of evidence suggest that marijuana smoking may be a risk factor for the development of respiratory cancer (Table 3). First, the tar phase of marijuana smoke contains more of some pro-carcinogenic polycyclic aromatic hydrocarbons, including benz[α]pyrene, than the tar collected from tobacco cigarettes *(3,4,7)*. Second, because of the manner in which marijuana cigarettes are smoked, approximately fourfold more of the particulate phase of the smoke (tar) is deposited in the human respiratory tract than occurs during tobacco smoking *(6)*. This enhanced lung deposition during marijuana smoking, combined with the high concentration of known carcinogens in marijuana smoke, significantly magnifies the level of exposure to carcinogens from each marijuana cigarette. Third, THC can interact with the aryl hydrocarbon receptor and, independent of other components in the smoke, activate transcription of cytochrome P4501A1 *(7)*. Cytochrome P4501A1 is involved in the biotransformation of polycyclic aromatic hydrocarbons into active carcinogens and plays a central role in the development of lung cancer. Fourth, hamster lung explants exposed to marijuana smoke for up to 2 years exhibited abnormalities in cell growth and accelerated malignant transformation *(43)*. Fifth, bronchial biopsies from habitual marijuana smokers overexpressed surrogate endpoint markers of pretumor progression, as already described *(36)*. Sixth, non-small-cell lung cancer cell lines implanted into immunocompetent mice displayed accelerated growth when the animals were given intraperitoneal injections of THC *(44)*. Tumors and splenic tissue from these THC-treated mice overproduced immunosuppressive cytokines (interleukin [IL]-10 and transforming growth factor [TGF]-β) and underproduced immunostimulatory cytokines (IL-2 and interferon [IFN]-γ) compared with vehicle-treated mice. When the tumor growth experiments were repeated in the presence of a selective CB_2 antagonist, SR144528, the augmentation of tumor cell growth by THC was blocked. These findings suggest that THC accelerates tumor growth by a cytokine-dependent and CB_2 receptor-mediated mechanism that impairs the development of antitumor immunity.

Although strongly suggesting that marijuana smoking is carcinogenic, these findings are not definitive proof that it is a clinically significant cancer risk factor. Additional support for this conclusion is provided by several small case series, each reporting an unusually high proportion of marijuana smokers among young individuals (<40–45 years) in whom respiratory tract cancers have been diagnosed *(45–49)*. The few controlled epidemiological studies that have addressed this issue, however, have revealed conflicting results. A large cohort study of participants in a health maintenance organization (n = 65,000) failed to show an association between marijuana smoking and the development of tobacco-related cancers *(50)*. Interpretation of this study was limited by the fact that the participants were relatively young at the end of follow-up and relatively few cancers had therefore developed *(50)*. A case–control study (n = 173 head and neck cancer cases, 176 controls) found that a history of daily or near-daily marijuana smoking was associated with a 2.6-fold greater risk (95% confidence interval [CI] 1.1–6.6) for developing head and neck cancer after controlling for other known risk factors, such as tobacco smoking and alcohol use *(51)*. Moreover, a dose–response relationship was noted, and the risk of marijuana smoking for the development of cancer was even higher among younger individuals (<55 years). In contrast, however, another case–control study of 407 cases of oral squamous cell cancer and 615 controls failed to find an association with marijuana use (odds ratio [OR] = 0.9, CI 0.6–1.3), even among younger, heavier, and longer-term marijuana smokers *(52)*. A case–control study conducted in Morocco, including 118 lung cancer cases and 235 controls, found that the combined use of hashish and snuff was associated with a 6.67-fold greater risk (95% CI 1.65–26.90) for developing lung cancer, while the risk was much lower for the use of hashish without snuff (1.93-fold [95% CI 0.57–6.58]), suggesting possible synergism between the effects of cannabis and tobacco on respiratory carcinogenesis *(53)*. A recently published case–control study of risk factors for oral cancer in young people (≤45 years) from the United Kingdom, which included 116 cases of squamous cell cancer of the oral cavity and 207 matched controls, failed to implicate cannabis use as a risk factor *(54)*. On the other hand, a recently reported population-based case–control study of incident cases of cancers of the lung (n = 611) and upper aerodigestive tract (oral cavity, pharynx, and esophagus) (n = 601), along with 1040 cancer-free population controls, from Los Angeles County did not find any positive association between marijuana use (including heavy lifetime use, i.e., a cumulative total of ≥10,950 joints) and the risk of lung or upper aerodigestive tract cancers after controlling for potential confounders (including tobacco use) *(54a)*. Moreover, no interactions were observed between the effects of marijuana and tobacco. These results suggest that any possible association between marijuana use and respiratory cancer may be below practically detectable limits for typical levels of marijuana use.

5. Effects of Marijuana and THC on Immune Defenses

5.1. Cannabinoid Receptors on Peripheral Blood Leukocytes

Marijuana smoking and purified THC were first proposed as immune modulators in the 1970s when abnormal leukocyte proliferation was observed in spleen cells collected from THC-treated animals *(55)* and in peripheral blood mononuclear cells collected from a sample of chronic marijuana smokers *(56)*. However, similar findings were not reported in other clinical studies *(57,58)*, and it was not until the discovery of the two different cannabinoid receptors that interactions between cannabinoids and the immune system began to be investigated in detail *(59–62)*. Both CB_1 and CB_2 are seven transmembrane G protein-coupled receptors that block forskolin-induced accumulation of intracellular cyclic adenosine 3',5'-monophosphate (cAMP) when activated *(63)*. They have also been linked to a number of other signaling events, including changes in intracellular calcium, protein kinases, and nuclear factor for immunoglobulin κ chain (NF-κB). Whereas CB_1 receptors are expressed at high levels in the central nervous system and mediate the psychotropic and behavioral effects associated with marijuana use, CB_2 receptors are expressed mainly in peripheral tissues and primarily by leukocytes. Of the two cannabinoid receptor subtypes, messenger RNA (mRNA) encoding for the CB_2 receptor is present in mouse spleen at levels 10- to 100-fold higher than those of mRNA encoding for CB_1 *(62,64)*. The CB_2 receptor is also preferentially expressed in human leukocytes, where mRNA encoding for it is present at approximately threefold higher levels than mRNA encoding for CB_1 *(65)*. Within human leukocytes, B-cells express several-fold higher levels of CB_2 receptor protein than monocytes, which express higher levels than those found in T-cells *(62,65,66)*. The presence of these two receptor subtypes and their differential expression in the brain (CB_1) and on immune cells (CB_2) suggests that endogenous cannabinoids are part of a unique neuroimmune axis.

To determine if cannabinoid receptors are activated on leukocytes in response to marijuana use, researchers from the University of South Florida and from the UCLA School of Medicine collected and examined peripheral blood samples from habitual marijuana users and nonsmoking control subjects *(65)*. mRNA encoding for both CB_1 and CB_2 were evaluated by reverse transcriptase-polymerase chain reaction (RT-PCR) assays. A consistent and significant increase in expression of mRNA encoding for both CB_1 and CB_2 was observed in blood cells collected from marijuana smoking subjects, consistent with drug-induced receptor stimulation and potential regulation of host immune defenses *(65)*. There is also evidence that activation of immune cells regulates expression of cannabinoid receptors in a reciprocal manner. When human B-cells were activated via their cell surface CD40 receptors, a reproducible increase in CB_2 receptor mRNA and cell surface protein occurred within 24 hours, with transcripts encoding for CB_2 increasing six- to eightfold *(67)*. Gardner et al. *(68)* carried out similar studies using human peripheral blood T-cells. T-cells activated with an immobilized anti-CD3 monoclonal antibody that activates the T-cell receptor were

Table 4
Associations Among Marijuana, THC, and Altered Immune Defenses

- Human leukocytes express type 1 and type 2 cannabinoid receptors (CB_1 and CB_2), with expression of CB_2 higher than expression of CB_1 *(59–62,64–68)*
- mRNA encoding for both CB_1 and CB_2 was found to be increased in peripheral blood leukocytes collected from marijuana smokers when compared to samples collected from nonsmokers, suggesting cannabinoid receptor activation in response to marijuana smoking *(65)*
- Systemic administration of Δ^9-tetrahydrocannabinol (THC) to mice decreased the production of T-helper type 1 (Th1) cytokines (interleukin [IL]-2, interferon [IFN]-γ) and increased the production of Th2 factors (IL-4, IL-10, and transforming growth factor [TGF]-β), resulting in a suppression of T-cell immunity and increased susceptibility to opportunistic infections and the growth of implanted cancer cells *(44,74,75)* Epidemiological studies suggest an increased risk for bacterial pneumonia, opportunistic infections, and Kaposi's sarcoma in HIV-seropositive individuals who smoke marijuana compared to individuals who do not *(83–85)*
- Alveolar macrophages (AM) recovered from the lungs of habitual marijuana smokers were found to be deficient compared to AMs recovered from the lungs of nonsmokers or tobacco smokers in their production of inflammatory cytòkines, phagocytosis, antibacterial killing, and capacity to produce both superoxide anion and nitric oxide *(40–42)*
- The inability of marijuana-exposed AM to express nitric acid synthase (iNOS) and kill pathogenic bacteria was reversed by treatment with granulocyte macrophage–colony-stimulating factor and IFN-γ *(42)*
- Human T-cells exposed to THC in vitro produced less IL-2 and IFN-γ, but more IL-4, resulting in an imbalance between Th1 and Th2 cytokines and an inhibition of T-cell activation *(86)*

examined for changes in their expression of CB_2 receptor protein by Western blots. T-cell activation was associated with an upregulation of CB_2 and with the induction of TGF-β, an effect enhanced by THC in a CB_2-dependent manner. Collectively, these studies demonstrate the potential for a bidirectional interaction between cannabinoid receptor expression and human B- and T-cell activation. Comprehensive reviews of the interaction between cannabinoids and immune function and the role of cannabinoid receptors in this process were recently published by several authors, including Klein *(10,69,70)*, Cabral and Dove Pettit *(71)*, Salzet *(72)*, and Berdyshev *(73)*. Rather than recapitulating these reviews, the following sections focus on evidence linking THC to immune regulation in drug-exposed animals and in human cells exposed to either purified THC in vitro or in vivo following marijuana use (Table 4).

5.2. THC Alters Cytokine Balance and Suppresses Host Immunity in Animal Models

Two well-designed mouse models have provided important insight into the potential impact of THC on immune responses *(44,74,75)*. In one study, BALB/c mice were treated with a single intravenous dose of THC (4 mg/kg) before infection with a sublethal inoculation of *Legionella pneumophila*, a facultative intracellular bacterium that produces pneumonia in susceptible patients *(74)*. When challenged 3–4 weeks later with a lethal inoculation of *L. pneumophila*, control mice survived and demonstrated *L. pneumophila*-specific T-cell proliferation and cytokine production. In contrast, a high percentage of mice pretreated with THC during the immunization phase died following rechallenge, and their T-cells failed to proliferate in response to *L. pneumophila* antigen in vitro. T-cells, and the cytokines that they produce, serve as critical regulators of cell-mediated immunity. T-cells producing type 1 cytokines (Th1), including IL-2 and IFN-γ, stimulate macrophage and T-cell effector function and promote cell-mediated immunity *(76)*. In contrast, T-cells producing primarily type 2 cytokines (Th2), such as IL-4 and IL-10, suppress cell-mediated immunity and promote humoral and allergic responses. Hypothesizing that THC might mediate its adverse effects by disrupting Th1/Th2 balance, additional experiments were performed. Exposure to THC was found to downregulate the production of antilegionella antibody of the immunoglobulin-G $(IgG)_{2a}$ subclass, associated with cell-mediated immunity, and increase antibody of IgG_1 subclass, associated with a Th2 response *(74)*. In vitro, control splenocytes activated with immobilized anti-CD3 antibody secreted primarily IFN-γ with little IL-4. However, splenocytes activated in the presence of THC produced less IFN-γ, and more IL-4 in a dose-dependent manner. The capacity for THC to block immunity against *L. pneumophila*, promote an immunoglobulin serotype switch from IgG_{2a} to IgG_1, and alter the balance of memory T-cells producing Th1 and Th2 cytokines, provided the first evidence that cannabinoids and cannabinoid receptors might act as Th2 inducers.

In follow-up experiments, THC was examined for its impact on cytokine production during the initial immunization phase *(75)*. Consistent with its role as a Th2 inducer, pretreatment with THC resulted in lower serum concentrations of IL-12 and IFN-γ within hours after sublethal infection with *L. pneumophila*. THC also stimulated splenocytes to secrete higher levels of IL-4. Additional experiments revealed a downregulation in the expression of mRNA encoding for the IL-12 receptor and thus a coordinated suppressive effect of THC on the production and function of Th1-inducing cytokines. Employing the same model, mice were treated with either CB_1 or CB_2 selective receptor antagonists (SR141716A or SR144528, respectively) before administration of THC. Administration of either receptor antagonist blocked the effects of THC on the production of Th1 cytokines, suggesting that both cannabinoid receptors participate in the immunological consequences mediated by THC *(75)*. Because CB_1 receptors are expressed primarily in the central nervous system, it was hypothesized that ligation of CB_1 receptors by THC acts on the hypothalamic–pituitary–adrenal axis, resulting in secondary immunoregulation by corticosteroids *(77)*. Corticosteroids are known to regulate Th1/Th2 balance, favoring the development of Th2 responses *(78)*. Alternatively, because both CB_1 and CB_2 are expressed on leukocytes, THC might mediate its effects directly by either one or both of these receptors.

The second animal model was developed by Zhu et al. *(44)* to examine the effects of THC on the host response to a tumor challenge. Immune function plays a central role in limiting tumor growth *(79)*, and disruption of Th1/Th2 cytokine balance by the tumor plays an opposing role in promoting tumor growth *(80)*. As such, it was hypothesized that the regulatory effects of THC on Th1/Th2 balance, with a decrease in Th1-cells and an increase in Th2-cells, might disrupt host antitumor immunity and promote tumor growth. Mice were treated with daily intraperitoneal injections of THC (5 mg/kg) for 4 days each week and then challenged with subcutaneous tumor implants. As hypothesized, mice receiving THC experienced a more rapid rate of tumor growth. By the end of 5–6 weeks, tumors in control animals had grown to 3000–4000 mm^3 in size, whereas tumors implanted into animals treated with THC averaged 12,000–13,000 mm^3. Similar results were observed in two different lung cancer models, one employing Line 1 alveolar cell carcinoma implanted into BALB/c mice and the other using Lewis lung carcinoma cells implanted into C57Bl/6 mice. Because there was no direct effect of THC on the proliferation of either tumor in vitro, and administration of THC had no effect when tumors were implanted into immunodeficient mice, these studies suggested that THC enhanced tumor growth by disrupting immune function in vivo. As reported in the *L. pneumophila* model, splenocytes from THC-treated mice produced less IFN-γ. Zhu et al. *(44)* also examined splenocytes for their production of IL-10, a regulatory Th2 cytokine *(81)*, and TGF-β, another immunosuppressive factor known to downregulate the production of IFN-γ *(82)*. Production of both IL-10 and TGF-β were increased roughly twofold in the spleen and at the tumor site in animals receiving THC. More importantly, administration of neutralizing antibody specific for either IL-10 or TGF-β completely neutralized the impact of THC on tumor growth. These studies demonstrated for the first time that THC can regulate antitumor immunity by increasing the production of suppressive cytokines. Finally, blocking studies with SR144528, a selective CB_2 receptor antagonist, confirmed a receptor-mediated pathway.

5.3. Impact of THC on Human Immune Responses and T-Cell Activation

In addition to animal models, there are several epidemiological studies suggesting that marijuana smoking can predispose to the development of opportunistic infections and cancer. Tindall et al. *(83)* collected careful drug use histories from 386 HIV-positive individuals and observed a significantly more rapid progression from HIV infection to AIDS in those who smoked marijuana. Similarly, Newell and associates *(84)* found marijuana use to be associated with the acquisition of opportunistic infections and/or Kaposi's sarcoma in patients with HIV (OR 3.7). Caiaffa et al. *(85)* also observed that the smoking of illicit drugs, including marijuana and/or cocaine, was statistically associated with the development of bacterial pneumonia in HIV-positive individuals (OR 2.24). More recently, marijuana use was identified in one large study as an independent risk factor for the development of head and neck cancer *(51)*.

To evaluate the impact of THC on human immune responses, Yuan et al. *(86)* purified T-cells from the blood of healthy volunteers and stimulated them ex vivo with antigen-presenting cells in the presence or absence of THC. THC inhibited T-cell proliferation in a dose-dependent manner, with 5 μg/mL inhibiting activation by an average of 53% (range 28–79%) compared with control cells. Hypothesizing that this effect was associated with a change in the balance of Th1 and Th2 cytokines, supernatants were harvested from the T-cell cultures and examined for the presence of IFN-γ and IL-4. IFN-γ concentrations were reduced on average by 50%, whereas IL-4 levels were increased on average to 110%, resulting in a significant shift in Th1/Th2 cytokine

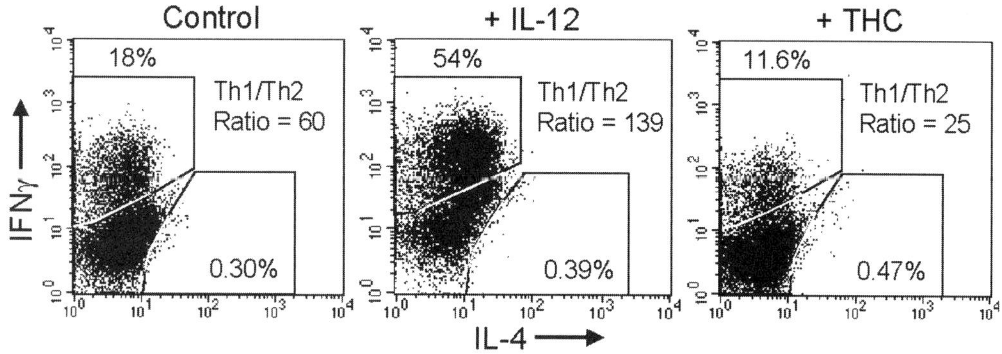

Fig. 4. Tetrahydrocannabinol (THC) shifts the capacity for activated T-cells to produce T-helper type 1 (Th1) and T-helper type 2l (Th2) cytokines. Purified human T-cells were activated with a combination of monoclonal antibodies directed against the T-cell receptor (CD3) and costimulatory molecules (CD28) in the presence of control medium **(left panel)** or medium supplemented with interleukin (IL)-12 (10 ng/mL, **middle panel**) or THC (5 μg/mL, **right panel**). Cells were permeabilized, and the production of interferon (IFN)-γ, a Th1 cytokine, and IL-4, a Th2 cytokine, was detected in each cell by flow cytometry. IL-12 increased the Th1/Th2 ratio, whereas THC decreased the production of IFN-γ and the Th1/Th2 ratio.

balance similar to that observed in animal models *(44,74,75)*. When examined at the single cell level, THC decreased both the number of T-cells producing IFN-γ and the average cytokine production per cell (Fig. 4). $CD4^+$ and $CD8^+$ T-cells were both equally suppressed. The impact of THC on the subsets was also examined at the level of mRNA expression using a ribonuclease protection assay to simultaneously assay for both Th1 (IL-2, IFN-γ) and Th2 (IL-4, IL-5) cytokines. Consistent with the results obtained by enzyme-linked immunosorbent assay and single cell analyses, mRNA encoding for IFN-γ and IL-2 was reduced by 21–48% in cells treated with 5 μg/mL THC, and mRNA encoding for IL-4 and IL-5 was increased by 1.5- to 11.2-fold. Pretreatment with SR144528, a CB_2-selective antagonist, prevented the majority of the THC-mediated effects, whereas there was little response to AM251, a selective CB_1 antagonist. This work suggests a strong correlation between murine models and human studies, with THC acting via cannabinoid receptors to suppress antigen-specific T-cell activation and skew responding T-cells toward a Th2 profile *(86)*.

As in the mouse model by Zhu et al. *(44)*, THC also upregulates the production of TGF-β when human T-cells are activated by immobilized anti-CD3 *(68)*. TGF-β, although not a classic Th2 cytokine, inhibits T-cell proliferation, suppresses production of IL-2 and IFN-γ, and antagonizes the activation of both lymphocytes and monocytes. As little as 50 ng/mL of THC increased the production of TGF-β two- to threefold, and 5 μg/mL of THC increased the release of TGF-β protein fivefold. To evaluate the role of cannabinoid receptors in this response, human T-cells were pretreated with either pertussis toxin, forskolin, or methylxanthine before activation in the presence of THC. Inactivation of G protein-coupled receptors by pertussis toxin, activation of adenyl cyclase by forskolin, and inactivation of phosphodiesterase activity by methylxanthine all blocked the capacity for THC to induce TGF-β consistent with signaling via cannabinoid receptors. Selective CB_1 or CB_2 receptor antagonists were then used to confirm that signaling was mediated via the CB_2 receptor. It is entirely possible that upregulation of TGF-β by THC mediates many of its immunological consequences on human cells, as it does on mouse cells, but experiments to test this hypothesis have not yet been carried out.

5.4. Immunological Suppression of Alveolar Macrophages in the Lungs of Habitual Marijuana Smokers

The finding that peripheral blood leukocytes collected from marijuana smokers express higher than normal levels of CB_1 and CB_2 mRNA *(65)*, and that THC mediates distinct immunoregulatory effects when cultured with human leukocytes in vitro *(68,86)*, provide only indirect evidence that marijuana smoking is associated with immunological consequences. The most compelling and direct evidence is provided by studies with AM recovered directly from the lungs of habitual marijuana users (Table 2; refs. *41* and *42*). AM are the primary immune cells residing in the distal air spaces of the lung, where they take up and retain large amounts of inhaled tar *(39)*. As previously described, AM recovered from the lungs of marijuana smokers were found to be significantly impaired in their ability to secrete pro-inflammatory cytokines and to phagocytose and kill *S. aureus*, whereas AM from tobacco smokers performed normally in these studies *(41)*. It is very likely that THC, which is present only in the tar generated from marijuana smoke, accounts for these functional abnormalities.

THC can alter specific cytoskeletal components involved in phagocytosis (tubulin and actin) and inhibit macrophage-mediated phagocytosis in vitro *(87)*. In addition to producing defects in phagocytosis, THC can also impair the production of nitric oxide (NO), a reactive nitrogen intermediate that serves as an important effector molecule in bacterial killing *(88)*. Using murine macrophage cell lines, several investigators have demonstrated that THC suppresses lipopolysaccharide-induced production of NO and subsequent antibacterial or antitumor activity *(89–91)*. This effect is mediated by cannabinoid receptors, involves inhibition of both cAMP and the NF-κB/Rel family of transcription factors, and blocks the induction of mRNA encoding for inducible nitric oxide synthase (iNOS) *(91)*.

Inhaled THC appears to mediate the same effects in the lungs of marijuana smokers. The etiology for this antimicrobial deficit was first suggested by inhibitor studies using N^G-monomethyly-L-arginine monoacetate (NGMMA), an inhibitor of NOS *(41)*. The addition of NGMMA to cultures containing AM from nonsmokers and tobacco smokers inhibited their antibacterial killing activity, but this compound had no effect when added to cultures containing AM from marijuana smokers. *S. aureus*, and its isolated cell wall constituent protein A, are known to induce NO when used to stimulate murine cells in vivo and/or in vitro *(92,93)*. The investigators hypothesized that *S. aureus* induced iNOS when added to cultures with AM from nonsmokers or smokers of tobacco only, resulting in potent antimicrobial activity, but not when added to cells recovered from marijuana smokers. To test this hypothesis, they used semi-quantitative RT-PCR to measure mRNA levels encoding for iNOS in resting AM and following co-culture with *S. aureus (42)*. Release of NO was also determined by the accumulation of nitrite in the culture supernatant, and the impact on bacterial killing was also measured. Exposure to *S. aureus* induced the expression of iNOS and the production of nitrite in AM from control smokers and tobacco-only smokers, but not in AM from marijuana smokers. Resting macrophages must be primed with inflammatory cytokines, such as TNF-α, IFN-γ, or GM-CSF, in order to upregulate expression of iNOS. Interestingly, production of NO and restoration of efficient antimicrobial killing by cells from MS were restored following the addition of these pro-inflammatory cytokines (IFN-γ or GM-CSF) to the *S. aureus* killing assay. In contrast, the addition of cytokines had no effect on the expression of iNOS or bacterial killing when added to cells from nonsmokers or smokers of tobacco only. These findings suggest that impairment in the bactericidal activity of AM from marijuana smokers was a result of a THC-related inhibition of key pro-inflammatory cytokines that are needed, in turn, to induce iNOS. Consistent with this hypothesis, Baldwin et al. *(41)* found that lipopolysaccharide, a bacterial wall component involved in macrophage activation, failed to stimulate normal release of TNF-α, IL-6, or GM-CSF from AM recovered from the lungs of marijuana smokers. AM recovered from tobacco smokers produced normal levels of these cytokines and, as reported above, exhibited normal induction of NO and normal antibacterial activity. The clinical implications of these findings are that regular marijuana smoking may compromise the lung's defense against infection by impairing the antimicrobial function of AM and the production of pro-inflammatory cytokines required for immune activation.

6. Summary

The smoke generated during the pyrolysis of cannabis contains not only a high concentration of THC, but also a large number of toxic gases and particulates similar to tobacco smoke. The effects on the lung are therefore complex. Whereas THC can produce short-term bronchodilation by relaxing airway smooth muscle, heavy habitual smoking of marijuana is associated with mainly adverse pulmonary consequences. These include symptoms of acute and chronic bronchitis, endoscopic evidence of airway injury, lung inflammation, and extensive histopathology and immunohistological evidence of dysregulated growth of the tracheobronchial epithelium. These damaging effects of marijuana smoking are magnified by (1) its high concentration of polycyclic aromatic hydrocarbons (which act as pro-carcinogens), (2) the enhanced deposition of tar because of the manner in which marijuana is smoked, and (3) the biological effects of THC on respiratory epithelial cells, which include oxidant stress, mitochondrial dysfunction, induction of cytochrome P4501A1, and inhibition of apoptosis. These features raise concerns that marijuana smoking may predispose to respiratory malignancy. However, epidemiological evidence linking marijuana use and respiratory cancer is at present inconclusive. Moreover, in contrast to the known relationship between regular tobacco smoking and the development of COPD, cohort studies have yielded inconsistent findings with the respect to the impact of regular smoking of marijuana on the development of chronic airways obstruction. Habitual use of marijuana has also been shown to produce abnormalities in the structure and function of AM, key cells in the lung's immune defense system. Specifically, AM from regular marijuana users are impaired with respect to antimicrobicial and tumoricidal activity, production of immunostimulatory cytokines, and generation of iNOS and NO, an important effector molecule in microbial killing. These changes in AM are consistent with the effects observed when immune cells are exposed to THC in vitro and in vivo in animal models. Both CB_1 and CB_2 receptors are expressed on immune cells and blood samples collected from marijuana smokers suggest that these receptors are stimulated by marijuana smoking. Acting primarily through CB_2, THC suppresses T-cell activation and alters the production of cytokines, resulting in a predominance of immunosuppressive factors such as IL-10 and TGF-β and a reduction of immunostimulatory cytokines including IL-2, IL-12, and IFN-γ. In animal models THC impairs the immune response to both opportunistic infections and cancer. Epidemiological studies suggest that marijuana smoking may have similar immunosuppressive effects in humans. Taken together, these findings may have important clinical implications, including the possibility of (1) an increased risk of opportunistic infections, especially in already immunocompromised patients as a result of AIDS, organ transplantation, or chemotherapy for cancer and (2) an increased risk of developing respiratory tract cancer, possibly in synergism with the risk from concomitant tobacco use. However, results of epidemiological studies are thus far mixed with regard to the actual occurrence of these potential clinical consequences of marijuana on the lung and host immune defenses. Other epidemiological study designs or approaches may be necessary to clarify whether marijuana is truly associated with these risks.

Acknowledgment

Research and writing supported by the National Institute on Drug Abuse grant #R37 DA03018.

References

1. Johnston, L. D., O'Malley, P. M., and Bachman, J. G. (2003) *Monitoring the Future: National Survey Results on Drug Use, 1975–2002. Volume I: Secondary School Students* (NIH Publication No. 03-5375), National Institute on Drug Abuse, Bethesda, MD.
2. Johnston, L. D., O'Malley, P. M., and Bachman, J. G. (2003) *Monitoring the Future: National Survey Results on Drug Use, 1975-2002. Volume II: College Students and Adults Ages 19-40* (NIH Publication No. 03-5376), National Institute on Drug Abuse, Bethesda, MD.
3. Hoffmann, D., Brunneman, D. K., Gori, G. B., and Wynder E. L. (1975) On the carcinogenicity of marijuana smoke. *Recent Adv. Phytochem.* **9**, 63–81.
4. Lee, M. L., Novotny, M., and Bartle, K. D. (1976) Gas chromatography/mass spectrometric and nuclear magnetic resonance spectrometric studies of carcinogenic polynuclear aromatic hydrocarbons in tobacco and marijuana smoke condensates. *Anal. Chem.* **48**, 405–416.
5. Roth, M. D., Arora, A., Barsky, S. H., Kleerup, E. C., Simmons, M., and Tashkin, D. P. (1998) Airway inflammation in young marijuana and tobacco smokers. *Am. J. Respir. Crit. Care Med.* **157**, 928–937.
6. Wu, T-C., Tashkin, D. P., Djahed, B., and Rose, J. E. (1988) Pulmonary hazards of smoking marijuana as compared with tobacco. *N. Engl. J. Med.* **318**, 347–351.
7. Roth, M. D., Marquez-Magallanes, J. A., Yuan, M., Sun, W., Tashkin, D. P., and Hankinson, O. (2001) Induction and regulation of the carcinogen-metabolizing enzyme,

CYP1A1, by marijuana smoke and Δ⁹-tetrahydrocannabinol. *Am. J. Respir. Cell Mol. Biol.* **24**, 1–6.

8. Sarafian, T. A., Kouyoumjian, S., Khoshaghideh, F., Tashkin, D. P., and Roth, M. D. (2003) Delta 9-tetrahydrocannabinol disrupts mitochondrial function and cell energetics. *Am. J. Physiol. Lung. Cell. Mol. Physiol.* **284**, L298–306.
9. Roth, M. D., Baldwin, G. C., and Tashkin, D. P. (2002) Effects of delta-9-tetrahydrocannabinol on human immune function and host defense. *Chem. Phys. Lipids* **121**, 229–239.
10. Klein, T. W., Newton, C., and Friedman, H. (1998) Cannabinoid receptors and immunity. *Immunol. Today* **19**, 373–381.
11. Tashkin, D. P., Shapiro, B. J., and Frank, I. M. (1973) Acute pulmonary physiologic effects of smoked marijuana and oral Œ"⁹-tetrahydrocannabinol in healthy young men. *N. Engl. J. Med.* **289**, 336–341.
12. Vachon, L., Fitzgerald, M. X., Solliday, N. H., Gould, I. A., and Gaensler, E. A. (1973) Single-dose effect of marihuana smoke. Bronchial dynamics and respiratory-center sensitivity in normal subjects. *N. Engl. J. Med.* **288**, 985–989.
13. Tashkin, D. P., Shapiro, B. J., and Frank, I. M. (1974) Acute effects of smoked marijuana and oral Œ"⁹-tetrahydrocannabinol on specific airway conductance in asthmatic subjects. *Am. Rev. Respir. Dis.* **109**, 420–428.
14. Calignano, A., Katona, I., Desarnaud, F., et al. (2000) Bidirectional control of airway responsiveness by endogenous cannabinoids. *Nature* **408**, 96–101.
15. Wilson, D. M., Peart, J., Martin, B. R., Bridgen, D. T., Byron, P. R., and Lichtman, A. H. (2002) Physiochemical and pharmacological characterization of a Delta(9)-THC aerosol generated by a metered dose inhaler. *Drug Alcohol Depend.* **67**, 259–267.
16. Tashkin, D. P., Reiss, S., Shapiro, B. J., Calvarese, B., Olsen, J. L., and Lodge, J. W. (1977) Bronchial effects of aerosolized Œ"⁹-tetrahydrocannabinol in healthy and asthmatic subjects. *Am. Rev. Respir. Dis.* **115**, 57–65.
17. Sarafian, T. A., Tashkin, D. P., and Roth, M. D. (2001) Marijuana smoke and Delta(9)-tetrahydrocannabinol promote necrotic cell death but inhibit Fas-mediated apoptosis. *Toxicol. Appl. Pharmacol.* **174**, 264–272.
18. Roy, P. E., Magnan-Lapointe, F., Huy, N. D., and Boutet, M. (1976) Chronic inhalation of marijuana and tobacco in dogs: Pulmonary pathology. *Res. Commun. Chem. Pathol. Pharmacol.* **14**, 305–317.
19. Rosenkrantz, H. and Fleischman, R. W. (1979) Effects of cannabis on lungs, in *Advances in the Biosciences* (Nahas, G. G. and Paton, W. D. M., eds.), Pergamon Press, Oxford, pp. 279–299.
20. Fliegiel, S. E. G., Beals, T. F., Tashkin, D. P., et al. (1991) Marijuana exposure and pulmonary alterations in primates. *Pharm. Biochem. Behavior* **40**, 637–642.
21. Huber, G. L. and Mahajan, V. K. (1987) The comparative response of the lung to marihuana or tobacco smoke inhalation, in *Marijuana: An International Research Report. Proceedings of Melbourne Symposium on Cannabis, 2–4 September, 1987* (National Campaign Against Drug Abuse Monograph Series No. 7), (Chesher, G., Consroe, P., and Musty, R. eds.), Australian Government Publishing Service, Canberra, pp. 19–24.
22. Chopra, G. S. (1973) Studies on psycho-clinical aspects of long-term marihuana use in 124 cases. *Int. J. Addict.* **8**, 1015–1026.
23. Hall, J. A. S. (1975) Testimony in marijuana-hashish epidemic and its impact on United States security, in *Hearings of the Committee on the Judiciary, U.S. Senate*: Government Printing Office, Washington, DC, pp. 147–154.
24. Boulougouris, J. C., Panayiotopoulos, C. P., Antypas, E., Liakos, A., and Stefanis, C. (1976) Effects of chronic hashish use on medical status in 44 users compared with 38 controls. *Ann. NY Acad. Sci.* **282**, 168–172.
25. Cruickshank, E. K. (1976) Physical assessment of 30 chronic cannabis users and 30 matched controls. *Ann. NY Acad. Sci.* **282**, 162–167.

26. Tashkin, D. P., Coulson, A. H., Clark, V. A., et al. (1987) Respiratory symptoms and lung function in habitual, heavy smokers of marijuana alone, smokers of marijuana and tobacco, smokers of tobacco alone, and nonsmokers. *Am. Rev. Respir. Dis.* **135**, 209–216.
27. Tashkin, D. P., Simmons, M. S., Sherrill, D., and Coulson, A. H. (1997) Heavy habitual marijuana smoking does not cause an accelerated decline in FEV_1 with age: a longitudinal study. *Am. J. Respir. Crit. Care Med.* **155**, 141–148.
28. Bloom, J. W., Kaltenborn, W. T., Paoletti, P., Camilli, A., and Lebowitz, M. D. (1987) Respiratory effects of non-tobacco cigarettes. *Br. Med. J.* **295**, 1516–1518.
29. Sherrill, D. L., Krzyzanowski, M., Bloom, J. W., and Lebowitz, M. D. (1991) Respiratory effects of non-tobacco cigarettes: A longitudinal study in general population. *Int. J. Epidemiol.* **20**, 132–137.
30. Taylor, D. R., Poulton, R., Moffitt, T. E., Ramankutty, P., and Sears, M. R. (2000) The respiratory effects of cannabis dependence in young adults. *Addiction* **95**, 1669–1677.
31. Taylor, D. R., Fergusson, D. M., Milne, B. J., et al. (2002) A longitudinal study of the effects of tobacco and cannabis exposure on lung function in young adults. *Addiction* **97**, 1055–1061.
32. Gil, E., Chen, B., Kleerup, E., Webber, M., and Tashkin, D. P. (1995) Acute and chronic effects of marijuana smoking on pulmonary alveolar permeability. *Life Sci.* **23/24**, 2193–2199.
33. Sarafian, T. A., Magallanes, J. A., Shau, H., Tashkin, D., and Roth, M. D. (1999) Oxidative stress produced by marijuana smoke. An adverse effect enhanced by cannabinoids. *Am. J. Respir. Cell Mol. Biol.* **20**, 1286–1293.
34. Sarafian, T. A., Kouyoumjian, S., Tashkin, D., and Roth, M. D. (2002) Synergistic cytotoxicity of Delta(9)-tetrahydrocannabinol and butylated hydroxyanisole. *Toxicol. Lett.* **133**, 171–179.
35. Fligiel, S. E. G., Roth, M. D., Kleerup, E. C., Barsky, S. H., Simmons, M. S., and Tashkin, D. P. (1997) Tracheobronchial histopathology in habitual smokers of cocaine, marijuana and/or tobacco. *Chest* **112**, 319–326.
36. Barsky, S. H., Roth, M. D., Kleerup, E. C., Simmons, M., and Tashkin, D. P. (1998) Similar molecular alterations in bronchial epithellium are observed in habitual smokers of marijuana, cocaine and/or tobacco. *J. Natl. Cancer Inst.* **90**, 1198–1204.
37. Barbers, R. G., Gong, H. Jr., Tashkin, D. P., Oishi, J., and Wallace, J. M. (1987) Differential examination of bronchoalveolar lavage cells in tobacco cigarette and marijuana smokers. *Am. Rev. Respir. Dis.* **135**, 1271–1275.
38. Barbers, R. G., Evans, M. J., Gong, H. Jr., and Tashkin, D. P. (1991) Enhanced alveolar monocytic phagocyte (macrophage) proliferation in tobacco and marijuana smokers. *Am. Rev. Respir. Dis.* **143**, 1092–1095.
39. Beals, T. F., Fligiel, S. E. G., Stuth, S., and Tashkin, D. P. (1989) Morphological alterations of alveolar macrophages from marijuana smokers. *Am. Rev. Respir. Dis.* **139 (Pt. 2)**, A336.
40. Sherman, M. P., Campbell, L. A., Gong, H. Jr., Roth, M. D., and Tashkin, D. P. (1991) Respiratory burst and microbicidal characteristics of pulmonary alveolar macrophages recovered from smokers of marijuana alone, smokers of tobacco alone, smokers of marijuana and tobacco and nonsmokers. *Am. Rev. Respir. Dis.* **144**, 1351–1356.
41. Baldwin, G. C., Tashkin, D. P., Buckley, D. M., Park, A. N., Dubinett, S. M., and Roth, M. D. (1997) Habitual smoking of marijuana and cocaine impairs alveolar macrophage function and cytokine production. *Am. J. Respir. Crit. Care Med.* **56**, 1606–1613.
42. Shay, A. H., Choi, R., Whittaker, K., et al. (2003) Impairment of antimicrobial activity and nitric oxide production in alveolar macrophages from smokers of marijuana and cocaine. *J. Infect. Dis.* **187**, 700–704.

43. Leuchtenberger, C. and Leuchtenberger, R. (1976) Cytological and cytochemical studies of the effects of fresh marihuana cigarette smoke on growth and DNA metabolism of animal and human lung cultures, in *The Pharmacology of Marijuana* (Braude, M. C. and Szara, S., eds.), Raven Press, New York, pp. 595–612.
44. Zhu, L. X., Sharma, S., Stolina, M., et al. (2000) Delta-9-tetrahydrocannabinol inhibits antitumor immunity by a CB2 receptor-mediated, cytokine-dependent pathway. *J. Immunol.* **165**, 373–380.
45. Taylor, F. M. (1988) Marijuana as a potential respiratory tract carcinogen: a retrospective analysis of a community hospital population. *South. Med. J.* **81**, 1213–1216.
46. Donald, P. J. (1991) Advanced malignancy in the young marijuana smoker. *Adv. Exp. Med. Biol.* **288**, 33–56.
47. Sridhar, K. S., Raub, W. A., Jr., Weatherby, N. L., et al. (1994) Possible role of marijuana smoking as a carcinogen in the development of lung cancer at a young age. *J. Psychoactive Drugs* **26**, 285–288.
48. Endicott, J. N., Skipper, P., and Hernandez, L. (1993) Marijuana and head and neck cancer. *Adv. Exp. Med. Biol.* **335**, 107–113.
49. Fung, M., Gallagher, C., and Machtay, M. (1999) Lung and aero-digestive cancers in young marijuana smokers. *Tumori* **85**, 140–142.
50. Sidney, S., Beck, J. E., Tekawa, I. S., and Quesenberry, C. P., Jr. (1997) Marijuana use and cancer incidence. *Am. J. Public Health* **87**, 585–590.
51. Zhang, Z. F., Morgenstern, H., Spitz, M. R., et al. (1999) Marijuana use and increased risk of squamous cell carcinoma of the head and neck. *Cancer Epidemiol. Biomarkers Prev.* **8**, 1071–1078.
52. Rosenblatt, K. A., Doody, D. R., Dawn Fitzgibbons, E., Daling, J. R., and Schwartz, S. M. (2001) Marijuana use is no associated with the risk of oral squamous cell carcinoma: Results for a population-based study. *Proc. Am. Assoc. Cancer Res.* **42**, 887 (abstr).
53. Sasco, A. J., Merrill, R. M., Dari, I., et al. (2002) A case-control study of lung cancer in Casablanca, Morocco. *Cancer Causes Control* **3**, 609–616.
54. Llewellyn, C. D., Linklater, K., Bell, J., Johnson, N. W., and Warnakulasuriya, S. (2003) Squamous cell carcinoma of the oral cavity in patients aged 45 years and under: a descriptive analysis of 116 cases diagnosed in the South East of England from 1990 to 1997. *Oral Oncol.* **39**, 106–114.
54a. Tashkin, D. P., Zhang, Z-F., Greeland, S., Cozen, W., Mack, T. M., and Morgenstern, H. (2006) *Proc. Am. Thorac. Soc.* **3,** A777.
55. Nahas, G. G., Zagury, D., Schwartz, I. W., and Nagel, M. D. (1973) Evidence for the possible immunogenicity of delta 9-tetrahydrocannabinol (THC) in rodents. *Nature* **243**, 407–408.
56. Nahas, G. G., Suciu-Foca, N., Armand, J-P., and Morishima, A. (1974) Inhibition of cellular mediated immunity in marihuana smokers. *Science* **183**, 419–420.
57. Lau, R. J., Tubergen, D. G., Barr, M., Jr., Domino, E. F., Benowitz, N., and Jones, R. T. (1976) Phytohemagglutinin-induced lymphocyte transformation in humans receiving delta 9-tetrahydrocannabinol. *Science* **192**, 805–807.
58. Rachelefsky, G. S., Opelz, G., Mickey, M. R., et al. (1976) Intact humoral and cell-mediated immunity in chronic marijuana smoking. *J. Allergy. Clin. Immunol.* **58**, 483–490.
59. Matsuda L. A., Lolait, S. J., Brownstein, M. J., Young, A. C., and Bonner, T. I. (1990) Structure of a cannabinoid receptor and functional expression of the cloned cDNA. *Nature* **346**, 561–564.
60. Bouaboula, M., Rinaldi, M., Carayon, P., et al. (1993) Cannabinoid-receptor expression in human leukocytes. *Eur. J. Biochem.* **214**, 173–180.
61. Munro, S., Thomas, K. L., and Abu-Shaar, M. (1993) Molecular characterization of a peripheral receptor for cannabinoids. *Nature* **365**, 61–65.

62. Galiegue S., Mary, S., Marchand, J., et al. (1995) Expression of central and peripheral cannabinoid receptors in human immune tissues and leukocyte subpopulations. *Eur. J. Biochem.* **232**, 54–61.
63. Howlett, A. C. (1995) Pharmacology of cannabinoid receptors. *Annu. Rev. Pharmacol. Toxicol.* **35**, 607–634.
64. Schatz, A. R., Lee, M., Condie, R. B., Pulaski, J. T., and Kaminski, N. E. (1997) Cannabinoid receptors CB1 and CB2: a characterization of expression and adenylate cyclase modulation within the immune system. *Toxicol. Appl. Pharmacol.* **142**, 278–287.
65. Nong, L., Newton, C., Cheng, Q., Friedman, H., Roth, M. D., and Klein, T. W. (2002) Altered cannabiniod receptor mRNA expression in peripheral blood mononuclear cells from marijuana smokers. *J. Neuroimmunol.* **127**, 169–176.
66. Marchand, J., Bord, A., Penarier, G., Laure, F., Carayon, P., and Casellas, P. (1999) Quantitative method to determine mRNA levels by reverse transcriptase-poymerase chain reaction from leukocyte subsets purified by fluorescence-activated cell sorting: application to peripheral cannabinoid receptors. *Cytometry* **35**, 227–234.
67. Carayon, P., Marchand, J., Dussossoy, D., et al. (1998) Modulation and functional involvement of CB2 peripheral cannabinoid receptors during B-cell differentiation. *Blood* **92**, 3605–3615.
68. Gardner, B., Zhu, L. X., Sharma, S., et al. (2002) Autocrine and paracrine regulation of lymphocyte CB2 receptor expression by TGF-β. *Biochem. Biophys. Res. Commun.* **290**, 91–96.
69. Klein, T. W., Friedman, H., and Specter, S. (1998) Marijuana, immunity and infection. *J. Neuroimmunol.* **83**, 102–115.
70. Klein, T. W, Newton, C. A., and Friedman, H. (2001) Cannabinoids and the immune system. *Pain Res. Manag.* **6**, 95–101.
71. Cabral, G. A. and Dove Pettit, D. A. (1998) Drugs and immunity: cannabinoids and their role in decreased resistance to infectious disease. *J. Neuroimmunol.* **83**, 116–123.
72. Salzet, M., Breton, C., Bisogno, T., and Di Marzo, V. (2000) Comparative biology of the endocannabinoid system possible role in the immune response. *Eur. J. Biochem.* **267**, 4917–4927.
73. Berdyshev, E. V. (2000) Cannabinoid receptors and the regulation of immune response. *Chem. Physics Lipids* **108**, 169–190.
74. Newton, C. A., Klein, T. W., and Friedman, H. (1994) Secondary immunity to *Legionella pneumophila* and Th1 activity are suppressed by delta-9-tetrahydrocannabinol injection. *Infect. Immun.* **62**, 4015–4020.
75. Klein, T. W., Newton, C. A., Nakachi, N., and Friedman. H. (2000) Delta-9-tetrahydrocannabinol treatment suppresses immunity and early IFN-gamma, IL-12, and IL-12 receptor beta2 responses to *Legionella pneumophila* infection. *J. Immunol.* **164**, 6461–6466.
76. Mosmann, T. R. and Coffman, R. L. (1989) TH1 and TH2 cells: different patterns of lymphokine secretion lead to different functional properties. *Annu. Rev. Immunol.* **7**, 145–173.
77. Manzanares, J., Corchero, J., and Fuentes, J.A. (1999) Opioid and cannabinoid receptor-mediated regulation of the increase in adrenocorticotropin hormone and corticosterone plasma concentrations induced by central administration of delta(9)-tetrahydrocannabinol in rats. *Brain Res.* **839**, 173–179.
78. Elenkov, I. J., Webster, E. L., Torpy, D. J., and Chrousos. G. P. (1999) Stress, corticotropin-releasing hormone, glucocorticoids, and the immune/inflammatory response: acute and chronic effects. *Ann. NY Acad. Sci.* **876**, 1–11.
79. Sogn, J. A. (1998) Tumor immunology: the glass is half full. *Immunity* **9**, 757–763.
80. Huang, M., Wang, J., Lee, P., et al. (1995) Human non-small cell lung cancer cells express a type 2 cytokine pattern. *Cancer Res.* **55**, 3847–3853.

81. Mosmann, T. and Moore, K. W. (1991) The role of IL-10 in cross-regulation of TH1 and TH2 responses. *Immunol. Today* **12**, A49–A53.
82. De Visser, K. E. and Kast, W. M. (1999) Effects of TGF-β on the immune system: implications for cancer immunotherapy. *Leukemia* **13**, 1188–1199.
83. Tindall, B., Cooper, D. A., Donovan, B., et al. (1988) The Sydney AIDS Project: development of acquired immunodeficiency syndrome in a group of HIV seropositive homosexual men. *Aust. NZ J. Med.* **18**, 8–15.
84. Newell, G. R., Mansell, P. W., Wilson, M. B., Lynch, H. K., Spitz, M. R., and Hersh, E. M. (1985) Risk factor analysis among men referred for possible acquired immune deficiency syndrome. *Prev. Med.* **14**, 81–91.
85. Caiaffa, W. T., Vlahov, D., Graham, N. M., et al. (1994) Drug smoking, Pneumocystis carinii pneumonia, and immunosuppression increase risk of bacterial pneumonia in human immunodeficiency virus-seropositive injection drug users. *Am. J. Respir. Crit. Care Med.* **150**, 1493–1498.
86. Yuan, M., Kiertscher, S. M., Cheng, Q., Zoumalan, R., Tashkin, D. P., and Roth, M. D. (2002) Δ^9-Tetrahydrocannabinol regulates Th1/Th2 cytokine balance in activated human T-cells. *J. Neuroimmunol.* **133**, 124–131.
87. Tang, J. L., Lancz, G., Spector, S., and Bullock, H. (1992) Marijuana and immunity: tetrahydrocannabinol-mediated inhibition of growth and phagocytic activity of the murine macrophage cell line, P388D1. *Int. J. Immunopharmacol.* **14**, 253–262.
88. Nathan, C. F. and Shiloh, M. U. (2000) Reactive oxygen and nitrogen intermediates in the relationship between mammalian hosts and microbial pathogens. *Proc. Natl. Acad. Sci. USA* **97**, 8841–8848.
89. Burnette-Curley, D., and Cabral, G. A. (1995) Differential inhibition of RAW264.7 macrophage tumoricidal activity by delta 9 tetrahydrocannabinol. *Proc. Soc. Exp. Biol. Med.* **210**, 64–76.
90. Coffey, R. G., Snella, E., Johnson, K., and Pross, S. (1996) Inhibition of macrophage nitric oxide production by tetrahydrocannabinol *in vivo* and *in vitro*. *Int. J. Immunopharmacol.* **18**, 749–752.
91. Jeon, Y., Yang, K. H., Pulaski, J. T., and Kaminski, N. E. (1996) Attenuation of inducible nitric oxide synthase gene expression by delta 9-tetrahydrocannabinol is mediated through the inhibition of nuclear factor-kappa B/Rel activation. *Mol. Pharmacol.* **50**, 334–341.
92. Cunha, F. Q., Moss, D. W., Leal, L. M., Moncada, S., and Liew, F. Y. (1993) Induction of macrophage parasiticidal acitivy by *Staphylococcus aureus* and exotoxins through the nitric oxide synthesis pathway. *Immunology* **78**, 563–567.
93. Sasaki, S., Miura, T., Nishikawa, S., Yamada, K., Hirasue, M., and Nakane, A. (1998) Protective role of nitric oxide in *Staphylococcus aureus* infection in mice. *Infect. Immun.* **66**, 1017–1022.

Chapter 12

Marijuana and Driving Impairment

Barry K. Logan

1. Effects of Marijuana

After alcohol, marijuana is the most popular recreational drug in North America. Its effects are largely predictable in type, but not in degree, although they do appear in a roughly dose-dependent manner. The effects discussed here make a very convincing case for the potential for marijuana to impair driving, although as noted, the extent to which that potential is realized in a given case will be related to many other factors.

1.1. Getting "High"

People variously use marijuana for its exhilarating, relaxing, hallucinogenic, antinausea, and soporific effects.

Marijuana is most frequently smoked and less frequently eaten in baked goods or drunk as an infusion. Cannabis products, including marijuana, hashish, and hashish oil, can be ingested orally, in tea, or baked into brownies. The effect profile from oral ingestion is much longer, taking longer for the drug to be absorbed and for the active Δ^9-tetrahydrocannabinol (THC) to be distributed. The drug is likely subject to enterohepatic cycling when orally ingested, further complicating its kinetics. Metabolite concentrations are often highly elevated. It is not uncommon for the acute effects to last for 24 hours following oral ingestion. Oral use is also more frequently associated with adverse effects, such as paranoia, panic, depression, and irritability. Currently available tests for blood or urine will not allow discrimination of the route of administration.

Following smoking, marijuana effects appear within 5–10 minutes. The lower-grade effects are remarkably similar to those resulting from alcohol consumption: relaxation, social disinhibition, and talkativeness. This disinhibition leads to users perceiving the drug effects as being mildly stimulatory at low doses. Users report the

From: *Forensic Science and Medicine: Marijuana and the Cannabinoids*
Edited by: M. A. ElSohly © Humana Press Inc., Totowa, New Jersey

experience as producing a general sense of well-being, which can rise to the level of exhilaration or euphoria. It is described as a blissful state of reverie, fantasy, free-flowing thought, and clarity. The senses are heightened, with colors, smell, touch, taste, and body perception being enhanced. Cravings for food are common. Bouts of uncontrollable spontaneous laughter or giggling are regularly seen, with even common events appearing to be funny or amusing.

The perceptual effects of marijuana use have an association with driving impairment at least in part as a result of their distracting nature. The degree to which someone is absorbed in his or her drug experience will affect his or her inclination to engage fully in other demanding tasks such as driving. The degree of effect will differ from individual to individual and can be significantly affected by the setting.

1.2. Physiological Effects

The physiological effects of marijuana use are more tenuously related to driving; however, they are useful indicators in assessing a person for recent marijuana use. THC is a vasodilator, and within minutes of smoking marijuana, peripheral vasodilation leads to a precipitous drop in blood pressure and a reflex increase in heart rate. Users can feel dizzy or faint until homeostasis is restored. The dilatory effects of the drug on the capillaries in the sclera produce a distinctive reddening of the eyes, giving them a bloodshot appearance. Users usually report a dry throat and mouth. Among the other effects on the eyes are loss of convergence or ability to cross, hippus (an intermittent change in the size of the pupil occurring without external stimuli), and rebound dilation following changing light conditions, in which the pupil size will oscillate before stabilizing. Nystagmus, or the ability of the eye to track smoothly, is affected by marijuana and becomes more prominent under conditions of very high or repeated dosing.

Although these effects are not indicators of impairment *per se*, this characteristic set of symptoms can be relied on by police officers or medical personnel to make a connection between an individual's appearance of intoxication and recent marijuana use.

1.3. Cognitive and Psychomotor Effects

Driving is a complex task requiring the integration of various cognitive and psychomotor skills. Cognitive skills are those related to the processes of knowing, thinking, learning, and judging. For driving, these effects include memory, perceptual skills, cognitive processing and task accuracy, reaction time, and sustained and divided attention.

Impairment of short-term memory and learning impairment following marijuana use is probably the most frequently reported and validated behavioral effect of marijuana use, and one for which there is the most consistent evidence. The link between memory impairment and driving impairment is, however, difficult to make convincingly. The strongest argument is the contribution of memory impairment to focus and selective attention. A clear recollection of recent events contributes to organizational and planning ability and promotes goal-directed behavior and action, allowing the subject to devote available cognitive capacity more efficiently to the driving task.

The user's perception is altered with respect to the passage of time, which appears to pass more quickly relative to real time. Impairment in perception of speed and distance may be related to the time distortion. Laboratory studies have shown that cannabis users lose the perceptual ability to identify simple geometric figures within more complex patterns when intoxicated. Such perceptual changes can influence a person's normal driving behavior in a potentially unsafe way.

Simple tests of cognitive processing such as measures of associative ability (e.g., digit symbol substitution, Stroop color word test) have been shown to be adversely affected by acute cannabis use resulting in greater numbers of errors. The effect when compared to moderate doses of alcohol, however, is small.

Reaction time effects are also present and are more significant at higher doses, but they are generally small compared with those observed with moderate doses of alcohol. Impairment indicators are more prominent in complex rather than simple reaction time tests, and subjects tend to perform more slowly and make more errors.

Driving is a divided-attention task, and as such, laboratory assessments of divided and sustained attention performance have been scrutinized for evidence of effects. These tests show consistently that the greater the demands on cognitive processing ability, the more complex the tasks, and the more tasks to be attended to, the poorer marijuana-dosed subjects performed. This has important implications for marijuana and driving impairment and explains the findings in some of the on-road driving studies discussed later.

Driving demands various levels of attention, cognitive capacity, and psychomotor ability, depending on factors such as weather, road conditions, vehicle condition, other road user behavior, lighting, and city vs highway driving. The threshold demands of driver performance for satisfactory vehicle operation might be within the subject's ability under normal driving conditions, but if the demands change unexpectedly, or emergencies arise, or there is a confluence of demands occurring at once (merging traffic, signal failure, unfamiliar neighborhood, road construction, etc.), the driver's ability is surpassed and errors arise that result in a crash or bring the driver to the attention of the police. Peak cognitive impairment effects are reported to occur roughly 40–60 minutes following smoking and typically last for about 2–3 hours.

1.4. Hallucinations

The effects noted on heightened awareness of colors, smell, touch, and taste can be enhanced to the point where they constitute hallucinations—perceptions of things or sensations that do not exist. Objects can appear to "melt" or to lose or change form. Synesthesias can occur in which, for example, sound or music can trigger visual or olfactory sensations. In most marijuana users who do experience these, they are more correctly characterized as pseudohallucinations in that the user is aware that the perception is unreal even while experiencing it. Nevertheless, hallucinations of any kind are distracting and absorbing and, when they occur, will impair attention and focus.

Infrequently, flashbacks are reported where individuals will re-experience or vividly recall the experience of a previous marijuana "trip." This can be triggered by environmental cues or by readministration of marijuana or some other psychoactive drug.

1.5. Other Adverse Reactions

Although many of the effects discussed above have the potential to be detrimental to driving, the adverse affects considered here are those not sought by the recreational marijuana user (a "bad trip"). They are atypical, but can be related to the user's underlying frame of mind or mood, and are most commonly reported by naïve users. These include dysphoria, fearfulness, extreme anxiety, mild paranoia, and panic. When this occurs, its relationship to impairment of driving is clear. Typically at higher doses or in naïve users, sedation or sleepiness becomes a significant factor, and presumably users already tired would be more susceptible to this effect.

1.6. Discussion

Based on the above considerations, it is clear than in many respects marijuana has the ability to produce effects—both sought-after and incidental—that can affect the balance of skills and abilities needed to drive safely. These effects can vary in magnitude, but frequently when compared with effects of moderate dosing with alcohol (e.g., the presumptive level for intoxication in many US states of 0.08 g ethanol/100 mL blood), the impairing effects are less severe, even after the use of typical user-preferred doses. Additionally, the consistent observation that the impairing effects of marijuana after moderate use will dissipate in 2–3 hours limits the likelihood of police contact or crash involvement if the driver allows some time to pass between marijuana use and driving. The related ability of marijuana users to recognize the drug effect and take a less risky course of action also contributes positively to harm reduction.

On balance, the empirical evidence suggests that impairment observed following recent marijuana use can very reasonably be ascribed to the drug. This is most likely when the drug use, if moderate, is within 3 hours of driving. Beyond this time frame, however, light to moderate marijuana use under normal demands of driving does not consistently generate impairment in driving skills that would come to the attention of the police or result in increased risk of crash involvement.

2. Evidence of Marijuana Intoxication

2.1. Diagnosis of Marijuana Use: Physiological and Psychomotor Effects

According to the Drug Recognition Expert evaluation matrix used by police officers, characteristic symptoms of marijuana use include a lack of horizontal or vertical gaze nystagmus, pupil size dilated to normal, a lack of pupillary convergence, and pupils normally reactive to light. Pulse is usually elevated within the first few hours following use, and blood pressure is correspondingly elevated. Body temperature will typically be normal. Speech may be slow or slurred, and muscle tone will be normal. Other clues include stale breath; sometimes users will have flakes or residue of marijuana in the mouth or a green discoloration of the tongue. The taste buds may be elevated as a result of irritation from the hot smoke. The user's eyes will typically be bloodshot because of the vasodilatory effects of THC on the capillaries of the sclera. The face may be similarly flushed, and subjects may be diaphoretic. Nystagmus is not typically present, although some studies do suggest an association between acute marijuana use and nystagmus.

Subjects may have short attention spans, express hunger (THC is an appetite stimulant), and giggle or laugh. If acutely intoxicated, users may also seem dazed, disengaged, or unconcerned. Because of the short distribution half-life of THC, users may also appear to sober up or improve in their performance and coordination during the first hour or two in custody.

Field sobriety tests have been criticized for having been validated for alcohol and not for other drugs. The tests, however, are considered tests of impairment; that is, they are tests that a normal sober person can perform without much difficulty, but that a person impaired in cognitive and psychomotor skills cannot. Any errors in the test may therefore be considered indicators of impairment irrespective of its cause. A careful validation of the tests for marijuana has recently been performed in 40 subjects. Papafotiou et al. *(1)* evaluated the efficacy of the standardized field sobriety three-test battery on marijuana smokers. They applied the three tests—horizontal gaze nystagmus, walk and turn, and one-leg stand—at 5, 55, and 105 minutes after smoking a placebo, 1.74%, or 2.93% THC content marijuana cigarette. The data are summarized in Table 1.

The study showed dose-dependent increases in rates of impairment in the subjects, with the most pronounced effects closest to smoking. It also confirmed low rates of failure of 2.5–7.5% in nonintoxicated subjects. After 100 minutes, symptoms of impairment were beginning to diminish. The authors also noted a fourth category of head movements and jerks. Adding the head movements and jerks observations improved the diagnostic value of the tests by 5–20% and should be considered for future inclusion in a battery of tests for drug impairment.

Individually, the walk-and-turn test elicited significant differences in performance between the marijuana and placebo conditions, but misses heel to toe, improper turn, and incorrect number of steps appeared almost as often in the placebo session as they did in the THC conditions and are therefore likely to be observed irrespective of drug consumption. Balance and ability to focus attention were impaired at all three time points. Of the three tests, the one-leg stand was the most significant at all three time points, with poorer performance being significantly related to the level of THC at all testing times, as was performance on all of the scored signs of this test except for hopping at Time 3.

Overall, when impairment caused by drugs including marijuana is present, it apparently can be detected by the tests currently in widespread use by police officers. It is likely that these tests can be further refined to increase their effectiveness and sensitivity.

2.1.1. Toxicological Tests

Marijuana use can be demonstrated by a chemical or toxicological test. Toxicological tests for detection of marijuana use currently include hair, urine, blood, sweat, and oral fluid. Hair marijuana tests offer the possibility of looking at marijuana exposure over the time period during which the hair was growing. Hair grows at a rate of about 1 cm a month, and most commercial vendors offering hair testing will test a 3-cm (~3 month) section closest to the scalp. Upon request, a longer length can be tested, in sections if necessary, to assess patterns of use over the lifetime of the growth of the hair. This test has little applicability in assessing intoxication at any particular point in

Table 1
Relationship Between Time After Smoking, Average Blood THC Concentration (ng/mL), and Percentage of Subjects Considered Impaired Under Standardized Field Sobriety Tests (SFSTs)[a]

	Time 1 (0–5 min)		Time 2 (50–55 min)		Time 3 (100–105 min)	
Dose	Blood THC	% impaired	Blood THC	% impaired	Blood THC	% impaired
Placebo	0	2.5	0	7.5	0	5
1.74% THC	55.5	23	6.8	23	3.7	15
2.93% THC	70.6	46	6.2	41	3.2	28

THC, Δ^9-tetrahydrocannabinol.

[a]Time 1, 0 min after smoking for blood sampling and 5 min for SFSTs; Time 2, 50 min after smoking for blood sampling and 55 min for SFSTs; Time 3, 100 min after smoking for blood sampling and 105 min for SFSTs.

From ref. *1*.

time, however, as would be relevant in an impaired driving investigation. If the subject's prior marijuana use became an issue, this approach could offer some qualitative insight.

2.1.1.1. Toxicological Evidence: Urine

As discussed in Chapters 5 and 9, THC is metabolized to 11-OH-THC and 11-carboxy-THC (THC-COOH). The latter compounds are glucuronidated and excreted in the urine. Substantial variation exists in the excretion patterns of marijuana metabolites in subjects' urine. THC metabolites appear in the urine in detectable amounts within 30–90 minutes following smoking, but they may not reach the levels needed to cause a positive response at typical thresholds used for screening. Many laboratories use the 50 ng/mL screening cutoff mandated for federal workplace urine drug testing, but one study showed that first void urine specimens after smoking a single 3.55% THC marijuana cigarette quantitated below that threshold in five of six subjects, at times ranging from 1 to 4 hours (mean 3.0 hours; ref. *2*). In the same subjects, each smoking an identical 3.55% THC cigarette, peak urine concentrations varied considerably (29–355 ng/mL, mean 153 ng/mL), as did the time to peak (5.6–28 hours, mean 13.9 hours). Similarly, urine specimens were confirmed positive by gas chromatography/mass spectrometry at a 15 ng/mL cutoff for 57–122 hours following this single use (mean 89 hours or 3.7 days). The same authors have reported similar results in other subjects *(3)*. Using a lower threshold, for example, 20 ng/mL, was shown to be more effective in identifying use for a longer period of time and presumably for earlier detection of use in urine samples.

Other workers have evaluated the time it took for urine samples to test consistently negative in chronic marijuana users *(4)*. These authors identified an extreme case of a subject who took 77 days to produce 10 consecutive negative urine samples screened at a 20 ng/mL cutoff. Of the 86 subjects evaluated, the mean time to the end of their consecutive positive results at that threshold was 27 days.

There are significant implications following from these and similar studies for the use of urine as the specimen in a driving-under-the-influence-of-drugs (DUID) setting. A specimen taken up to 3 hours after smoking marijuana may test negative for cannabinoids, depending on the screening threshold used and the potency of the marijuana smoked, even though the subject would have experienced the peak effect within a few minutes and would have been under the influence of marijuana at the time of driving or arrest. Also, following single acute use by naive users, urine concentrations may peak, then drop below detectable levels over the space of a few hours. Conversely, the presence of marijuana metabolites in a subject's urine may have resulted from drug use several days earlier, considerably after the impairing effects of the drug have passed.

In summary, a positive urine test for THC-COOH cannot be used to infer either intoxication or marijuana use within any forensically useful time frame. At best, if coupled with objective observations of physiological signs and symptoms of marijuana use and documentation of psychomotor impairment, it can substantiate an opinion that observed impairment was a result of marijuana use.

2.1.1.2. Toxicological Evidence: Blood

Blood or plasma* analysis of THC provides the most direct toxicological evidence of recent marijuana use and, consequently, of intoxication. There are several approaches to the interpretation of blood toxicological data.

2.1.1.2.1. THC and THC-COOH Concentrations

Because the effects of marijuana use have a relatively rapid onset when smoked, users can titrate the effects against the rate of administration to maximize the desirable drug effects while minimizing the adverse effects. Various studies have attempted to identify a "user-preferred" dose of marijuana. These have established a typical user-preferred dose of about 300 μg/kg, or about 21 mg in a 70-kg (154-lb) individual *(7)*. In terms of what this translates to in marijuana cigarettes, that will depend on the THC content of the marijuana and the individual's smoking technique, with more efficient absorption achieved with deeper inhalation and breath holding.

For context, a standard National Institute on Drug Abuse marijuana cigarette (weight 558 mg) having 3.58% THC content would deliver 20 mg of THC, although not all of that may be bioavailable, depending on the subject's smoking technique. Plasma concentrations of THC and THC-COOH from one study with different levels of dosing are shown in Table 2.

Current street marijuana strength can vary considerably, from essentially zero to 20% THC content or more; consequently, predicting THC concentration or impairment based on a history of how many "joints" were smoked is inadvisable.

Peak blood or plasma THC concentrations occur within a few minutes of the end of smoking and begin a rapid decline as the drug distributes from the central compartment into tissues. There is widespread agreement that the peak effects of the drug occur after the blood concentration has peaked and begun to decline. Plasma THC concentrations of 2–3 ng/mL (equivalent to whole blood concentrations of 1–1.5 ng/

---

*Most pharmacokinetic studies have made measurements of THC and its metabolites in plasma, whereas in a forensic context whole blood is the most commonly analyzed specimen. The plasma–to–whole blood ratio for cannabinoids is approx 2:1 *(5,6)*; therefore, when comparing whole blood concentrations to plasma concentrations, the plasma concentrations should be divided by 2.

Table 2
Mean, Median, and Range of THC and THC-COOH Concentrations in Plasma of 14 Subjects Under Various Dosing Conditions

		100 μg/kg		200 μg/kg		300 μg/kg	
		t = 35	t = 190	t = 35	t = 190	t = 35	t = 190
THC	Mean	7.9	0.7	12.0	1.0	16.1	1.5
	Median	6.5	0.9	10.0	1.1	15.8	1.5
	Range	0.8–17.2	0.0–1.3	1.5–27.1	0.0–2.7	4.7–30.9	0.4–3.2
THC-COOH	Mean	8.2	4.1	12.2	7.61	15.3	10.0
(ng/mL)	Median	7.4	4.1	11.2	6.4	13.0	8.2
	Range	1.4–19.4	0.0–12.0	2.0–37.2	0.0–32.2	4.2–39.6	1.5–36.3

THC, Δ^9-tetrahydrocannabinol; THC-COOH, 11-carboxy-THC.
From ref. *1*.

mL) were linked by several authors to recent use (within 6–8 hours) and consequently potential impairment of some psychomotor functions *(8–10)*. Other authors have suggested that whole blood concentrations of 1.6 ng/mL or greater may cause psychomotor effects.

Detection of THC-COOH in the absence of any detectable parent drug is a not infrequent finding in DUID cases. This emphasizes the importance of using appropriate cutoffs for confirmatory testing, which should be of the order of 1 ng/mL or less for both THC and THC-COOH. Assuming that those thresholds are observed, data such as those in Table 2 and in other work suggest that even following acute impairing doses of marijuana, concentrations of THC are likely to become undetectable within 3 hours following use, whereas THC-COOH may persist longer. In chronic users, THC concentrations of 2 ng/mL have been shown to persist for more than 12 hours.

These limitations highlight the importance of obtaining a timely blood sample when investigating cases of impaired driving attributed to marijuana use.

2.1.1.2.2. THC:THC-COOH Ratio

As noted previously, peak psychomotor and cognitive effects following marijuana use occur within the first hour after smoking, a time interval during which the THC concentration is falling rapidly and THC-COOH is beginning to appear as a result of oxidative metabolism. Several studies *(2,6,10)* suggest that following single acute administration, THC-COOH concentrations will surpass THC concentrations within 30–45 minutes following initiation of use (*see*, e.g., the patterns in Table 2). Consequently, THC/THC-COOH ratios of greater than 1 suggest use within the prior hour, the period during which effects are likely to be greatest.

In practice, in a DUI setting, the likelihood of obtaining a specimen during the hour following initiation of smoking is small because of the time taken to investigate, assess, and obtain a sample from a subject.

Algorithms for predicting time of marijuana use based on both THC concentrations and the THC/THC-COOH ratio have been described *(9,11)*. Although preliminary data suggest that these models are accurate in predicting a likely time interval for

Table 3
Distribution of THC and THC-COOH Concentrations in Forensic Serum Specimens (n = 212)[a]

Level (ng/mL)	<0.5	0.5–3.0	3.0–5.0	5.0–7.0	7.0–9.0	>9.0
THC	32%	55%	9%	2%	2%	0.5%
THC-COOH	26%	42%	18%	8%	2%	4%

THC, Δ^9-tetrahydrocannabinol; THC-COOH, 11-carboxy-THC.
[a]The corresponding whole blood concentrations would be approximately half the reported serum amount.
From ref. *13*.

last use following single acute moderate doses, they have not been extensively evaluated in chronic users and have not been evaluated with THC concentrations of less than 2 ng/mL, precluding their use in many DUID cases. Although these models may be informative for evaluation of cases, readers are urged to exercise caution in their application in a forensic setting because their limitations are still debated *(12)*. More extensive evaluation of this approach in chronic users is promising and warrants further study.

In a report of a gas chromatography/mass spectrometry method for the simultaneous determination of THC and THC-COOH in serum *(13)*, this method was applied to serial samples from subjects smoking 300 μg of THC/kg body weight and to 212 forensic serum specimens, including driving cases. The samples from the smoking study showed that THC concentrations in serum had fallen below 5 ng/mL (equivalent of 2.5 ng/mL in blood) in 33% of subjects within 100 minutes, and in 92% of subjects within 160 minutes following smoking. The distribution of concentrations of THC and THC-COOH in the forensic cases is shown in Table 3 and illustrates that delays between the time of driving and the time of sample collection can result in undetectable THC concentrations. Of these cases, 87% have blood equivalent THC concentrations of less than 1.5 ng/mL.

2.1.1.3. Toxicological Evidence: Oral Fluid (Saliva)

Oral fluid (saliva) is receiving a lot of scrutiny for its efficacy in detecting marijuana usage at the time of driving. Oral fluid is a plasma ultrafiltrate produced through the parotid and other glands in the mouth. Many water-soluble drugs appear in this ultrafiltrate and can be detected by on-site immunoassays. Because of its lipophilicity, THC does not readily transfer from the blood to the oral fluid, but contamination of the oral cavity during smoking, from the smoke and possibly from marijuana debris from the cigarette, can result in a positive test within 30–90 minutes of use.

Oral fluid testing is still somewhat controversial. Many of the devices currently being sold are not consistently reliable, are subject to operator error, and are not comprehensive in terms of the drugs they test for. Additionally, the role of roadside testing is still a subject of debate. Because the tests are not comprehensive, drivers who appear impaired should be arrested regardless of the results of the roadside test, making it somewhat superfluous. The presence of the drug must still be confirmed by forensically acceptable techniques, requiring resampling or preservation of the roadside sample and subsequent laboratory tests.

2.1.1.4. Summary

Blood concentrations of both THC and THC-COOH drop precipitously in the first few hours following smoking, because these substances partition into fatty compartments. It is recommended that blood or plasma concentrations of THC and THC-COOH be interpreted with caution. Under most circumstances, detection of parent THC will reflect recent use, meaning within the last few hours, making the likelihood of impairment within that time frame that much greater. More distant, higher-intensity marijuana use cannot be ruled out, however, when THC is detected, and under that pattern of use impairment may persist longer than the 2–3 hours typical of the low- to moderate-dose administration. Detection of THC-COOH in the absence of the parent drug (i.e., <2 ng/mL) tends to suggest more distant use (>2 hours). It should go without saying that the screening threshold and confirmatory test sensitivity of the analytical laboratory must be taken into consideration when evaluating these results.

3. Epidemiology of Marijuana and Driving

A thorough review of epidemiological studies related to marijuana in various driving populations was done recently by Huestis *(14)*, and we will not attempt to replicate that in this chapter. The focus of this discussion is on studies that have attempted to relate marijuana use to risk of accident involvement or accident culpability.

A survey of many of the studies cited by Huestis shows various rates of marijuana positivity in impaired drivers, fatally injured drivers, drivers injured in motor vehicle accidents, and commercial vehicle operators. The rates of positivity vary depending on whether blood or urine was tested, whether the parent or metabolite was tested for, whether the samples were provided voluntarily or following arrest, the sensitivity of the testing method, and whether the study group was selected out (e.g., only subjects without alcohol tested). In spite of these variables, in the fatally injured driving population overall, 10–20% of drivers test positive for cannabinoids, whereas in the arrest population rates are between 15 and 60%, suggesting a significant role for marijuana use.

None of these studies has control data, however, that would show the rate of marijuana use in the local driving population not killed or injured in a collision, such that a comparative rate or odds ratio for fatal accident involvement could be calculated. Another limiting factor was that in some studies urine was tested, and, as noted above, urine can test positive for marijuana use for a few days following use, while the impairing effects last only for a few hours.

These studies do uniformly find evidence, however, that there is widespread use of marijuana in all these driving populations. In nonselected populations (e.g., all fatally injured drivers, trauma patients), the incidence of cannabinoid positives was typically between 5 and 20%, and in selected populations (e.g., young males, fatally injured drivers) the rate was as high as between 15 and 60%.

A recent voluntary test of commercial vehicle operators in Washington and Oregon *(15)* showed a marijuana-positive rate of 5%, in spite of a 19% refusal rate in what is a heavily regulated industry with mandatory random testing. A similar survey done in 1988 showed 15% of tractor trailer drivers positive for cannabinoids, suggesting some improvement following the introduction of testing *(16)*.

3.1. Assessment of Relative Crash Risk Following Marijuana Use

Studies that have assessed crash responsibility offer more insight into the quantitative relationship between marijuana usage and crash involvement. An excellent review of culpability studies has recently been published *(17)*. The general design of these studies is to compare rates of drug use in at-fault drivers vs no-fault drivers and compute the ratio, with values greater than 1.0 indicating increased rates of risk. The 95% confidence interval is also computed, and when the range includes 1.0, the difference in responsibility rates is not significant at the $p = 0.05$ level.

In most of these studies, authors validate their data set and methodology by assessing odds ratios for alcohol. The relationship between alcohol and risk of crash involvement has been well established, most famously in the 1960 Grand Rapids Study. In each case the method showed the expected significant relationship at the $p = 0.05$ (95% confidence interval) level between alcohol positivity and greater odds of crash involvement.

The data from studies that made odds ratio assessments based on the presence of the inactive THC-COOH metabolite uniformly failed to show significant differences at the $p = 0.05$ level in rates of accident involvement for the drug-positive drivers. This can be rationalized in terms of the fact that the metabolite is inactive and that in most cases urine was being tested. Bearing this in mind, together with the fact that urine can test positive for the metabolite for many hours or even days after the effect has passed, its detection in urine is not a good surrogate for impairment, and the negative findings are not surprising.

Studies assessing crash risk based on parent THC in blood are more informative. One study of 2500 injured drivers *(18,19)* showed a trend towards increasing odds ratio with increasing THC concentration (although not significant at $p = 0.05$) and found that culpable drivers had a higher mean THC concentration ($p = 0.057$). This suggests a dose-dependent increase in risk, with the threshold for significance being somewhere above 2 ng/mL THC. One limitation of the Hunter study is the lack of control of the interval between driving and when the sample was collected. Intervals of an hour or less between the driving and the time the sample was collected would cause appreciable decreases in THC concentration.

In a cohort of 3398 fatally injured drivers *(20)*, the authors avoid this limitation because absorption of THC will stop at the time of death. Those data showed an odds ratio of 2.7 in cases in which THC was detected and 6.6 when the THC concentration was greater than 5 ng/mL.

Several studies have evaluated crash risk in drivers positive for both alcohol and marijuana (THC or THC-COOH). Table 4 shows that irrespective of whether the parent drug or metabolite was measured, when combined with alcohol the odds ratio for crash involvement was between 3.5 and 11.5 (significant in all cases, $p = 0.05$) and compared to alcohol positive cases was still significant, with an odds ratio of 2.9.

Taken together, these data represent strong evidence for a concentration-dependent (and consequently dose-dependent) relationship between THC and risk of crash involvement and enhanced risk for any use of marijuana when combined with alcohol.

Table 4
Summary of Odds Ratio of Becoming Involved in Fatal or Injurious Traffic Accidents Under the Influence of Cannabis, Alcohol, or Their Combination as Reported in Culpability Studies

Substance	Authors	Odds ratio	95% CI
Drug-free cases		1.0	
Alcohol	Terhune and Fell *(21)*	5.4*	2.8–10.5
	Williams et al. *(22)*	5.0*	2.1–12.2
	Terhune et al. *(23)*	5.7*	5.1–10.7
	Drummer *(24)*	5.5*	3.2–9.6
	Hunter et al. *(18)*	6.8*	4.3–11.1
	Lowenstein and Koziol-Mclain *(25)*	3.2*	1.1–9.4
	Drummer et al. *(20)*	6.0*	4.0–9.1
THC-COOH	Terhune and Fell *(21)*	2.1	0.7–6.6
	Williams et al. *(22)*	0.2	0.2–1.5
	Terhune et al. *(23)*	0.7	0.2–0.8
	Drummer *(24)*	0.7	0.4–1.5
	Hunter et al. *(18)*	0.9	0.6–1.4
	Lowenstein and Koziol-Mclain *(25)*	1.1	0.5–2.4
TCH (range: ng/mL)			
<1.0	Hunter et al. *(18)*	0.35	0.02–2.1
1.10–2.0		0.51	0.2–1.4
>2.0		1.74	0.6–5.7
1–100	Drummer et al. *(26)*	2.7*	1.02–7.0
5–100		6.6*	1.5–28.0
Alcohol/THC or THC-COOH	Williams et al. *(22)*	8.6*	3.1–26.9
	Terhune et al. *(23)*	8.4*	2.1–72.1
	Drummer *(24)*	5.3*	1.9–20.3
	Hunter et al. *(18)*	11.5*	4.6–36.7
	Lowenstein and Koziol-Mclain *(25)*	3.5*	1.2–11.4

Significant changes in OR indicated as follows: *<0.05.
THC-COOH, 11-carboxy-THC; THC, Δ^9-tetrahydrocannabinol.
From ref. *11*.

4. Marijuana and On-Road Driving Studies

The above considerations suggest that in addition to the empirical intoxicating properties of marijuana, there is epidemiological and behavioral evidence that it can cause impairment in the first few hours following use. Assessments of psychomotor performance following marijuana use have been performed, and these have been reviewed recently by Ramaekers et al. *(17)*. These studies support the idea that dose-dependent impairments in psychomotor performance and cognition appear immediately following marijuana administration, peak after the blood concentration peaks, and persist for 3–4 hours. Although there is a relationship between many of these tasks and the driving task, the clearest means of assessing the actual effects of marijuana on drivers is to measure their performance in actual on-road driving following marijuana administration. A number of such studies have been done.

4.1. Study of Klonoff et al. (27)

Conducted in Vancouver, British Columbia, in the early 1970s, drivers were dosed with 4.9 or 8.4 mg of THC by smoking. This represents 70 and 120 μg/kg, respectively, in a 70-kg person, compared with the 300 μg/kg described by Robbe and O'Hanlon *(7)* as the user-preferred dose, so both should be considered relatively low-dose conditions compared to normal patterns of use. Following drug administration, drivers drove both on a closed traffic free course and on the streets of downtown Vancouver during peak traffic hours. Driving performance was rated subjectively by a professional driving examiner. Researchers found subtle differences between the marijuana and placebo conditions and noted some bidirectional changes in performance. Sixty-four volunteers drove the driving course. There was a trend towards a greater number of subjects, demonstrating poorer performance going from placebo to low dose to high dose, with 73% of the high-dose subjects demonstrating a decline in performance. However, 23% of subjects demonstrated an increase in performance in the high-dose condition, with 14% showing significant improvement.

Thirty-eight subjects participated in the on-street driving. Similarly, although 79% of subjects demonstrated a decline in driving performance, 16% demonstrated improved performance even in the high-dose condition.

The components of driving that were most affected by marijuana following the high dose were judgment, care while driving, and concentration. Minimally affected were factors such as general driving ability, speed, confidence, and aggression, and cooperation and attitude were unaffected. Unusual behaviors documented in drivers after marijuana use included missing traffic lights or stop signs, passing without sufficient caution, poor anticipation or handling of the vehicle with respect to traffic flow, inappropriate awareness of pedestrians or stationary vehicles, and preoccupation and lack of response at green lights.

Although the tendency was toward deterioration in driving performance with increasing dose of marijuana, the trend was not uniform. The authors struggled to explain the bidirectional changes in performance and hypothesize that interindividual differences in response can outweigh dose-related effects, and that subjects can recognize impairment and compensate, and in some cases overcompensate, resulting in improvement.

Caution should be exercised in applying the results of this study to users engaging in more demanding driving and also to drivers using higher doses and more potent marijuana.

4.2. Study of Robbe and O'Hanlon (7)

The most comprehensive work on marijuana in actual on-road driving has been done at the University of Maastricht in the Netherlands, beginning with this report. The authors first made an assessment of the dose of marijuana preferred by users, so that appropriate doses could the assessed for their effects on driving. Twenty-four subjects who used the drug more than once a month and less than daily and who had driven within an hour of marijuana use within the last year were assessed. Their average preferred dose to achieve the desired psychological effect was 20.8 mg, which after adjustment for body weight was 308 µg/kg, with no significant difference for males and females.

Subjects were tested on a closed driving course with doses of 0, 100, 200, and 300 µg/kg THC. Interestingly, 40–60% of the subjects indicated that they would have been willing to drive for unimportant reasons shortly after smoking the two highest doses. Driver performance was assessed by measurement of standard deviation of lateral position (SDLP), an index of weaving that has been validated for alcohol and other drugs as a measurement of deterioration of driving performance.

There was dose-dependent deterioration in SDLP. Driving performance decrement persisted undiminished for 2 hours following drug administration, even after perceived "high" and heart rate had declined. It also persisted even as measured plasma THC concentrations fell, but SDLP was not quantitatively related to plasma THC or THC-COOH concentrations. Drivers accurately assessed their performance as being poorer than normal under the two highest-dose conditions. Quantitatively, the decrement in SDLP was equivalent to blood alcohol concentrations (BACs) of 0.03–0.07 g/100 mL.

Having determined the scale of the performance decrement, the researchers decided it was safe to evaluate driving performance on open highways around other vehicles under the same dosing conditions. Subjects were again dosed with 0, 100, 200, and 300 µg/kg THC. SDLP as an index of weaving and a car-following test where the subjects had to maintain headway with a lead vehicle were conducted. This phase confirmed the dose-dependent deterioration in SDLP, with the lower doses producing impairment less than 0.05 g/100 mL and the highest dose producing impairment marginally above that. The subjects rated their performance as worse than normal at the two highest doses, but still expressed a willingness to drive.

The final phase of the study involved more demanding urban city driving, and consequently only the placebo and lowest dose were administered because the prior two phases had shown significant impairment in the two highest-dose conditions. In this phase the driver's performance was compared against other drivers dosed to a 0.05 g/100 mL BAC. The alcohol condition produced the expected deterioration in driving performance, but the 100 µg/kg THC dose produced no measurable decline in urban city driving performance. Interestingly, the alcohol-impaired drivers reported no perceived deterioration in performance even while it was evident to the observers, whereas the subjects receiving the low-dose THC reported feeling impaired even while no impairment could be measured. This echoes the experience of Klonoff's study that users were compensating and often overcompensating for their perceived impairment.

Most importantly, this careful work demonstrates that although marijuana has the ability to impair under certain conditions, and does so in a dose-dependent manner, the degree of impairment associated with a user-preferred dose of 300 µg/kg produced impairment equivalent to BACs of 0.03–0.07 g/100 mL. Additionally, it confirmed the lack of correlation between plasma THC concentrations and the level of impairment.

4.3. Study of Lamers and Ramaekers (28)

In this study, performed at the same institute and using the same methodology, researchers assessed the combined effects of alcohol and marijuana using 0.04 g/100 mL BAC and 100 μg/kg THC on urban city driving. Additionally, using a head-mounted eye movement-recording system, the subjects' visual search or side glances were assessed.

This study confirmed that low doses of marijuana, or alcohol at the 0.04 g/100 mL concentration, when taken alone, did not impair city driving or performance or interfere with visual search frequency at intersections. When alcohol and THC were taken in combination, however, visual search frequency decreased by about 3%. The study also confirmed the finding of previous work that subjects did not feel impaired when using alcohol, even when impairment was present, but did feel impaired after marijuana use even when no impairment was measurable. The subjects' ability to recognize their impairment from marijuana was abolished, however, when it was consumed in conjunction with alcohol.

5. Conclusions

The material reviewed in this chapter highlights the challenges of assessing driving impairment caused by marijuana. Epidemiologically, there is evidence for dose-dependent increases in crash risk with increasing blood THC concentration. There is good evidence that the prevalence of cannabinoids in the system of injured, killed, and arrested drivers is higher than the incidence in the population at large. Empirically, the drug produces effects on cognition and psychomotor performance, which have the potential to impair driving ability, and users recognize the presence of that impairment and can even compensate accordingly. There is good evidence that there is a significant dose–response relationship between marijuana use and the degree of impairing effects. On the other hand, the passage of time between driving or involvement in a crash limits our ability to get an accurate measurement of the THC concentration at the time of driving. More complex tasks are more sensitive to the effects of marijuana and increase the likelihood that that the impairment will become significant and observable.

Studies of driving behavior have been conducted with typical user-preferred doses and show that the effects, at least on the alcohol-impairment scale, are mild to moderate and are affected by the dose, the time since use, the users' perception of the effect, and their degree of compensation or overcompensation for those effects.

In short, the assessment of the role of marijuana use in a crash or impaired driving case must be made with caution and will be most defensible when all available information is considered, including the pattern of driving, recent drug use history or admission to marijuana use, an appearance of impairment, performance in field sobriety tests, the presence of physiological signs and symptoms of marijuana use, and toxicological test results of blood or serum samples.

6. General Readings

1. Couper, F. J. and Logan, B. K. (2004) Drugs and Human Performance Fact Sheets. NHTSA DOT HS 809 725.
2. *Drugs and Drug Abuse* (2002) Addiction Research Foundation, Toronto.
3. Huestis, M. A. (2002) Cannabis (marijuana)—effects on human performance and behavior. *Forensic Sci. Rev.* **14**, 15–59.

References

1. Papafotiou, K., Carter, J. D., and Stough, C. (2004) An evaluation of the sensitivity of the Standardised Field Sobriety Tests (SFSTs) to detect impairment due to marijuana intoxication. Psychopharmacology (Berl). Dec 24 (published online).
2. Huestis, M. A., Mitchell, J. M., and Cone, E. J. (1996) Urinary excretion profiles of 11-nor-9-carboxy-delta 9-tetrahydrocannabinol in humans after single smoked doses of marijuana. *J. Anal. Toxicol.* **20**, 441–452.
3. Huestis, M. A., Mitchell, J. M., and Cone, E. J. (1995) Detection times of marijuana metabolites in urine by immunoassay and GC-MS. *J. Anal. Toxicol.* **19**, 443–449.
4. Ellis, G. M. Jr, Mann, M. A., Judson, B. A., Schramm, N. T., and Tashchian, A. (1985) Excretion patterns of cannabinoid metabolites after last use in a group of chronic users. *Clin. Pharmacol. Ther.* **38**, 572–578.
5. Owens, S.M., McBay, A.J., Reisner, H.M., and Perez-Reyes, M. (1981) 1251 radioimmunoassay of delta-9-tetrahydrocannabinolin blood and plasma with a solid-phase second-antibodyseparation method. *Clin. Chem.* **27**, 619.
6. Skopp, G., Potsch, L., Mauden, M., and Richter, B. (2002) Partition coefficient, blood to plasma ratio, protein binding and short-term stability of 11-nor-delta(9)-carboxy tetrahydrocannabinol glucuronide. *Forensic Sci. Int.* **126**, 17–23.
7. Robbe, H. W. and O'Hanlon, J. F. (1993) Marijuana and Actual Driving Performance. DOT HS 808 078. US Department of Transportation, National Highway Traffic Safety Administration.
8. Barnett, G. and Willette, R. E. (1989) Feasibility of chemical testing for drug impaired performance, in *Advances in Analytical Toxicology*, (Baselt, R.C., ed.), Yearbook Medical Publishers, Chicago, IL, p. 218.
9. Huestis, M. A., Henningfield, J. E., and Cone, E. J. (1992) Blood cannabinoids. II. Models for the prediction of time of marijuana exposure from plasma concentrations of delta 9-tetrahydrocannabinol (THC) and 11-nor-9-carboxy-delta 9-tetrahydrocannabinol (THCCOOH) *J. Anal Toxicol.* **16**, 283–290.
10. Mason, A. P. and McBay, A. J. (1985) Cannabis; Pharmacology and interpretation of effects. *J. Forensic Sci.* **30**, 615–631.
11. Peat, M. A. (1989) Distribution of delta-9-tetrahydrocannabinol and its metabolites, in *Advances in Analytical Toxicology II* (Baselt, R. C., ed.), Book Medical Publishers, Chicago, IL, pp. 186–217.
12. Bogusz, M. (1993) Concerning blood cannabinoids and the effect of residual THCCOOH on calculated exposure time. *J. Anal. Toxicol.* **17**, 313–316.
13. Moeller, M. R., Doerr, G., and Warth, S. (1992) Simultaneous quantitation of delta-9-tetrahydrocannabinol (THC) and 11-nor-9-carboxy-delta-9-tetrahydrocannabinol (THC-COOH) in serum by GC/MS using deuterated internal standards and its application to a smoking study and forensic cases. *J. Forensic Sci.* **37**, 969–983.
14. Huestis, M.A. (2002) Cannabis (marijuana)—effects on human performance and behavior. *Forensic Sci. Rev.* **14**, 15–59.
15. Couper, F. J., Pemberton, M., Jarvis, A., Hughes, M., and Logan, B. K. (2002) Prevalence of drug use in commercial tractor-trailer drivers. *J. Forensic Sci.* **47**, 562–567.
16. Lund, A. K., Preusser, D. F., Blomberg, R. D., and Williams, A. F. (1988) Drug use by tractor-trailer drivers. *J. Forensic Sci.* **33**, 648–661.
17. Ramaekers, J. G., Berghaus, G., van Laar, M., and Drummer, O. H. (2004) Dose related risk of motor vehicle crashes after cannabis use. *Drug Alcohol Depend.* **73**, 109–119.
18. Hunter, C. E., Lokan, R. J., and Longo, M. C. (1998) The prevalence and role of alcohol, cannabinoids, benzodiazepines and stimulants in non-fatal crashes. Forensic Science, Department for Administrative and Information Services, Adelaide, South Australia.

19. Longo, M. C., Hunter, C. E., Lokan, R. J., White, J. M., and White, M. A. (2000) The prevalence of alcohol, cannabinoids, benzodiazepines and stimulants amongst injured drivers and their role in driver culpability: part II: the relationship between drug prevalence and drug concentration, and driver culpability. *Accid. Anal. Prev.* **32**, 623–632.
20. Drummer, O. H., Gerostamoulos, J., Batziris, H., et al. (2004) The involvement of drugs in drivers of motor vehicles killed in Australian road traffic crashes. *Accid. Anal. Prev.* **36**, 239–248.
21. Terhune, K. W. and Fell, J.C. (1982) The role of alcohol, marijuana and other drugs in the accidents of injured drivers. (Tech. Rep. under Contract No. DOT-HS-5-01179). Calspan Field Services Inc., Buffalo, NY.
22. Williams, A. F., Peat, M. A., Crouch, D. J., Wells, J. K., and Finkle, B. S. (1985) Drugs in fatally injured young male drivers. *Public Health Rep.* **100**, 19–25.
23. Terhune, K. W., Ippolito, C. A., Hendriks, D. L., and Michalovic, J. G. (1992) The incidence and role of drugs in fatally injured drivers. National Highway Traffic Safety Administration, Final Report under Contract No. DTNH 22-88-C-07069.
24. Drummer, O. H. (1994) Drugs in drivers killed in Australian road traffic accidents. Victorian Institute of Forensic Pathology, Institute of Forensic Medicine, Monash University, Melbourne, Australia (report no. 0594).
25. Lowenstein, S. R. and Koziol-Mclain, J. (2001) Drugs and traffic crash responsibility: a study of injured motorists in Colorado. *J. Trauma* **50**, 313–320.
26. Drummer, O. H., Gerostamoulos, J., Batziris, H., et al. (2003) The incidence of drugs in drivers killed in Australian road traffic crashes. *Forensic. Sci. Int.* **134**, 154–162.
27. Klonoff, H. (1974) Marijuana and driving in real-life situations. *Science* **186**, 317–324.
28. Lamers, C. T. and Ramaekers, J. G. (2001) Visual search and urban driving under the influence of marijuana and alcohol. *Hum. Psychopharmacol.* **16**, 393–401.

Chapter 13

Postmortem Considerations

Steven B. Karch

1. Introduction

The prevalence of marijuana smoking among adults in the United States has remained stable, at approx 4%, for the last decade *(1)*. Even that low rate (four times as many Americans smoke cigarettes) still translates into more than 6 million active users. In 2002, an estimated 19.5 million Americans aged 12 years or older admitted to having used illicit drugs during the month before the survey interview, and that number translates into 8.3% of the population over the age of 12 (Fig. 1). Of these individuals, 75% reported using marijuana, and 72 million individuals report having smoked marijuana at least once in their life *(2)*. Given the surprisingly large number of users, it is quite surprising to see how little has been written about marijuana toxicity. Reports of acute life-threatening illness, or at least reports emanating from the offices of medical examiners, are extraordinarily rare.

There is, however, no doubt that marijuana smoking does have measurable cardiovascular effects, and cardiovascular disease is the principal cause of death in the United States. (Surprisingly, cardiovascular disease is the third leading cause of death for children under age 15 *[3]*, accounting for at least one in five deaths [approx 2500 deaths per day].) Coronary heart disease alone is the single largest killer of Americans, and stroke is the third. Each year, about 700,000 people experience a new or recurrent stroke. About 500,000 of these are first attacks, and 200,000 are recurrent. Stroke accounted for more than one of every 15 deaths in the country in 2001. In total, cardiovascular disease killed 931,108 Americans in 2001 (compared with 553,768 deaths from cancer, 101,537 accidental deaths, 53,852 deaths from Alzheimer's disease, and 14,175 from HIV).

Because the number of marijuana smokers is very large, it is inevitable that there would be overlap between the two groups. The difficulty for pathologists is deciding

From: *Forensic Science and Medicine: Marijuana and the Cannabinoids*
Edited by: M. A. ElSohly © Humana Press Inc., Totowa, New Jersey

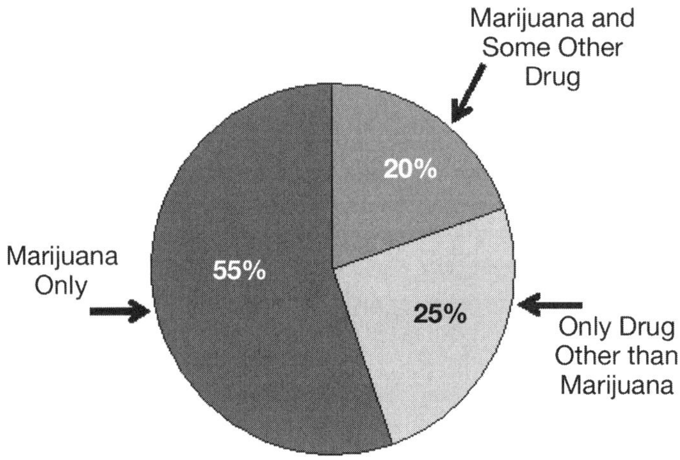

Fig. 1. Current breakdown of illicit drug use in the United States.

when an individual with cardiovascular disease has died "from" their marijuana smoking or "with" marijuana smoking. Currently available diagnostic techniques do not permit making such distinctions. This chapter reviews what is known about the cardiovascular consequences of marijuana smoking, with special emphasis on marijuana as a triggering factor for plaque rupture and sudden cardiac death. Evidence for other marijuana-related illnesses and medical effects will be reviewed, as will postmortem testing methodologies.

2. Pharmacokinetics and Pharmacodynamics

A brief overview of aspects relevant to death investigation is provided here. Δ^9-Tetrahydrocannabinol (THC) is highly lipophilic and essentially water insoluble *(4)*. It is destroyed by exposure to heat and is also photolaible *(5)*. These physical properties have considerable relevance to the storage and testing of postmortem specimens. It has never been proven that overdose has caused the death of humans, dogs (in oral doses of up to 3000 mg/kg), or monkeys (in oral doses up to 9000 mg/kg; ref. *6*).

Most (>90%) THC is distributed to the plasma, with 10% in red blood cells *(7)*. Almost all of the THC in plasma is protein bound, mainly to lipoproteins, but also to albumin *(8)*. These physical properties must be considered when making postmortem measurements; postmortem measurements are conducted on whole blood, but the pharmacokinetic data sometimes used to interpret these concentrations are based on measurements made using plasma obtained from the living.

THC is extremely lipophilic, but, because of strong protein binding, it has a relatively small apparent plasma volume of 2–4 L, at least initially *(9)*. The steady-state volume of distribution is much higher (10 L/kg; ref. *10*). Plasma THC levels decline very rapidly because tissue uptake is so rapid. Only small amounts (probably <1%) reside in the brain during periods of peak psychoactivity *(11)*. This seemingly paradoxical finding is explained by the brain's very high blood flow and the ease with which THC enters and departs cells *(12)*. With repeated use, THC accumulates in less vascular tissue, especially body fat *(13)*. This property makes fat a useful alternative matrix for testing *(14)*.

Maximum plasma concentrations occur within minutes of smoking, and psychological effects become apparent within a few seconds to a few minutes. Maximum psychological effects are observed after 15–30 minutes, and these taper off within 2–3 hours. When taken orally there is a delay of 30–90 minutes before the onset of psychotropic effects, and these effects remain relatively constant for 2–3 hours. The psychological effects then dissipate slowly over the following 4–12 hours *(15)*.

3. Cardiovascular Effects

THC, the major psychoactive component of *Cannabis sativa*, like anandamide, the endogenous cannabinoid ligand, activates G protein-coupled receptors in the heart, brain, and periphery. Two distinct types of cannabinoid receptors have been identified: CB_1 and CB_2. Activation of peripheral CB_1 receptors elicits profound coronary and cerebral vasodilatation *(16)*. In vitro studies have shown that this response is a result of direct receptor activation and that the process occurs independently of the sympathetic nervous system *(17)*. In animal models, the predictable result is hypotension.

In humans the vascular response is a largely dose-dependent increase in heart rate, usually accompanied by a mild increase in systolic pressure, although orthostatic hypotension is a recognized complication in occasional users. Studies with human volunteers have shown that complete tolerance to the tachycardiac and blood pressure effects develops and that electrocardiographic alterations produced by marijuana smoking are minimal *(18)*.

Whether or not these recognized cardiovascular effects are sufficient to actually trigger myocardial infarction is still debated, although there is ample evidence for concern. The acute onset of coronary syndromes is thought to result from the disruption of vulnerable plaque. Vulnerable plaques are not necessarily the largest plaques (i.e., they do not cause clinically significant obstruction of large epicardial arteries) but, rather, are comprised of thin-capped, lipid-rich lesions that may be located in second-order vessels. "Triggers," whether intense athletic activity, marijuana smoking, or even intense sexual activity, result in homodynamic forces that can disrupt the thin fibrous cap, probably because changes in arterial pressure disrupt the underlying vulnerable plaque *(19)*.

Epidemiological evidence supports the triggering theory. Investigators in the Myocardial Infarction Onset Study interviewed 3882 patients (1258 women) hospitalized with acute myocardial infarction *(20)*. Of these, 124 (3.2%) reported smoking marijuana in the prior year, 37 within 24 hours and 9 within 1 hour of the onset of symptoms. As is true for most patients with coronary artery disease, marijuana users were more likely to be men (94 vs 67%, $p < 0.001$), more likely to be current cigarette smokers (68 vs 32%, $p < 0.001$), and more likely to be obese (43 vs 32%, $p = 0.008$). The risk of myocardial infarction onset in the marijuana smokers was elevated 4.8 times over baseline (95% confidence interval 2.4–9.5) in the 60 minutes after marijuana use, dropping to a relative risk of 1.7 in the second hour, after which no increase risk was apparent.

The authors of the study concluded that smoking marijuana was a rare trigger of acute myocardial infarction. A number of other "triggers" for myocardial infarction have been identified *(21,22)*. These include heavy physical exertion, mental stress, particulate air pollution, and sexual activity. The increased relative risk associated with sexual activity is comparable to that associated with marijuana smoking—roughly double the relative risk of acute myocardial infarction in healthy individuals or even in patients with a prior history of angina or those with prior infarction.

Although the relative risk for infarction is definitely increased, the absolute risk of marijuana-triggered infarction is extremely low because the baseline risk of infarction is low for most individuals. The increased risk is transient, probably because marijuana-induced changes in pulse and blood pressure changes are transient, if they occur at all. Tolerance to vascular effects rapidly emerges in chronic marijuana smokers. These factors must be given due weight in any cause of death determination.

4. Other Medical Effects

Chronic marijuana smoking is clearly related to lung injury, although there is nothing diagnostic about the resultant pattern of injury *(23)*. Because of the way marijuana is smoked, more particulate matter is generated than by smoking tobacco, which means that damage to the respiratory tract is more likely than with tobacco smoking. The effects of cannabis and tobacco smoking are additive and independent. The resultant histopathological effects include changes consistent with acute and chronic bronchitis but are in no way diagnostic. In the only published autopsy series, lungs were examined in 13 known marijuana smokers with sudden death. Decedents ranged in age from 15 to 40 years. There were accumulations of pigmented monocytes within the alveoli and variable, spotty, infiltrates of monocytes and lymphocytes within the intersititum. The study authors suggest that the degree of infiltrate was dose-related, with heavier smokers having heavier infiltrates *(24)*.

Alveolar macrophages recovered from the lungs of marijuana smokers have a decreased ability to release pro-inflammatory cytokines and nitric oxide and are less effective at killing bacteria. THC alters human immune responses. Lymphocytes of marijuana smokers contain increased amounts of messenger RNA encoding for both type 1 and 2 cannabinoid receptors. THC suppresses T-cell proliferation, inhibits the release of interferon-γ, and alters the production of T-helper cytokines *(25)*. Habitual exposure to THC impacts human cell-mediated immunity and host defenses, but there is little evidence to support the notion that, like tobacco smoking, cannabis exposure actually causes malignancy. In fact, there is equally good evidence that, as a group, cannabinoids induce tumor regression in rodents. The mechanism of cannabinoid antitumoral action in vivo is as yet unknown, but it may involve the direct inhibition of vascular endothelial cell migration and survival as well as decreased expression of pro-angiogenic factors (vascular endothelial growth factor and angiopoietin-2) and matrix metalloproteinase-2 found within tumors.

5. Postmortem Measurements

Forensic pathologists occasionally screen for THC and its metabolites, but only if impairment is an issue or, in the rare episode of atherosclerotic sudden cardiac death, where "trigger" factors are being sought. Routine screening for cannabanoids is, however, not considered cost-effective (an important issue for medical examiner's offices). When nonspecific populations have been screened, results have generally mirrored patterns of drug abuse within the rest of the population. Of 500 sequential specimens screened by the Medical Examiner's Office in Maryland, 63 (13%) were initially positive by enzyme multiplied immunoassay technique, and 58 of those (12%) were confirmed positive *(26)*.

6. Cause-of-Death Determination

There are no unique or diagnostic lesions associated with acute THC toxicity. It is not even clear what the clinical signs of massive overdose would be. Pathological abnormalities identified in chronic users are likely to be a consequence of chronic polydrug abuse and are nonspecific. The question to be answered by forensic pathologists is whether marijuana use has "triggered" an episode of myocardial infarction or sudden cardiac death, but answers are unlikely to be forthcoming. "Trigger" theories can only be applied in situations in which coronary artery disease is already established, which almost surely means that the decedent will be in an older age group, the very group most likely to experience myocardial infarction in the first place.

Blood and tissue measurements of THC are of little or no diagnostic value in cause-of-death determination and are seldom measured. Even when postmortem blood concentrations are measured, a number of toxicological issues make interpretation of these measurements difficult. Perhaps the greatest impediment to interpretation is that all published studies (and formulas for predicting time of use) are based on measurement made in plasma *(27,28)*. Even in the living, relating measurement made in whole blood to measurements made in plasma is problematic. When THC, 11-OH-THC, and THC-COOH concentrations were measured in the plasma and whole blood taken from eight chronic marijuana smokers, the values of the plasma-to-whole blood distribution ratios were very similar, and the individual coefficient of variation was relatively low. These results suggest that plasma levels could be calculated from whole blood concentrations by taking into account a multiplying factor of 1.6. Unfortunately, similar attempts with postmortem "blood" resulted in a distribution of cannabinoids between whole blood and "serum" that was scattered over too wide a range to be of any forensic value; the Huestis models could not be applied *(29)*.

Tolerance to the vascular—and many of the psychological—effects of marijuana smoking rapidly emerges, and even in the living, plasma concentrations do not predict pulse or blood pressure *(18)*. Slow diffusion of THC from plasma into body fat and reentry into the blood is a constant ongoing process. Within 6–8 hours after use, plasma THC concentrations drop below 2 μg/L, and then continue to decrease somewhat more slowly. After smoking cigarettes containing 16 mg (low dose), levels fall below 0.5 μg/L (the limit of detection for most laboratories) after 7.2 hours *(27,28)*. When the dose is doubled, plasma concentration remained above 0.5 for an average of 12.5 hours, and THC-COOH remained detectable for an average of 3.5 days.

With higher doses and long-term use, substantial amounts of THC and its metabolites accumulate in deep body stores *(30)*. After death these stores are slowly released. Although there exist a host of reliable methods for THC extraction *(31)* and quantitation *(32)*, THC's large volume of distribution virtually guarantees that postmortem redistribution will occur, which means that postmortem THC concentration measurements are of even less use than antemortem measurements, which is to say not at all.

References

1. Compton, W. M., Grant, B. F., Collier, J. D., Glantz, M. D., and Stinson, F. S. (2004) Prevalence of marijuana use disorders in the United States: 1991-1992 and 2001-2002. *JAMA* **291**, 2114–2121.
2. Substance Abuse and Mental Health Service Administration. (2003) *Results: 2002 National Survey on Drug Use & Health (NSDUH)*, in NHSDA Series H-22, DHHS Publication NO SMA 03-3836, O.o.A. Studies, Rockville, MD.
3. American Heart (2004) *American Heart Association's Heart Disease and Stroke Statistics—2004 Update*, in *Stats2004, NRO3*, Dallas.
4. Garrett, E. R. and Hunt, C. A. (1974) Physiochemical properties, solubility, and protein binding of delta9-tetrahydrocannabinol. *J. Pharm. Sci.* **63**, 1056–1064.
5. Agurell, S. and Leander, K. (1971) Metabolism of cannabis. VIII. Stability, transfer and absorption of cannabinoid constituents of cannabis (hashish) during smoking. *Acta Pharm. Suec.* **8**, 391-402.
6. Thompson, G. R., Rosenkrantz, H., Schaeppi, U. H., and Braude, M. C. (1973) Comparison of acute oral toxicity of cannabinoids in rats, dogs and monkeys. *Toxicol. Appl. Pharmacol.* **25**, 363–372.
7. Widman, M., Agurell, S., Ehrnebo, M., and Jones, G. (1974) Binding of (+)- and (minus)-delta-1-tetrahydrocannabinols and (minus)-7-hydroxy-delta-1-tetrahydrocannabinol to blood cells and plasma proteins in man. *J. Pharm. Pharmacol.* **26**, 914–916.
8. Wahlqvist, M., Nilsson, I. M., Sandberg, F., and Agurell, S. (1970) Binding of delta-1-tetrahydrocannabinol to human plasma proteins. *Biochem. Pharmacol.* **19**, 2579–2584.
9. Wall, M. E., Sadler, B. M., Brine, D., Taylor, H., and Perez-Reyes, M. (1983) Metabolism, disposition, and kinetics of delta-9-tetrahydrocannabinol in men and women. *Clin. Pharmacol. Ther.* **34**, 352–363.
10. Lemberger, L., Tamarkin, N. R., Axelrod, J., and Kopin, I. J. (1971) Delta-9-tetrahydrocannabinol: metabolism and disposition in long-term marihuana smokers. *Science* **173**, 72–74.
11. Gill, E. W. and Jones, G. (1972) Brain levels of delta1-tetrahydrocannabinol and its metabolites in mice—correlation with behaviour, and the effect of the metabolic inhibitors SKF 525A and piperonyl butoxide. *Biochem. Pharmacol.* **21**, 2237–2248.
12. Chiang, C. N. and Rapaka, R. S. (1987) Pharmacokinetics and disposition of cannabinoids. *NIDA Res. Monogr.* **79**, 173–188.
13. Kreuz, D. S. and Axelrod, J. (1973) Delta-9-tetrahydrocannabinol: localization in body fat. *Science* **179**, 391–393.
14. Levisky, J. A., Bowerman, D. L., Jenkins, W. W., Johnson, D.G., and Karch, S. B. (2001) Drugs in postmortem adipose tissues: evidence of antemortem deposition. *Forensic Sci. Int.* **121**, 157–160.
15. Grotenhermen, F. (2003) Pharmacokinetics and pharmacodynamics of cannabinoids. *Clin. Pharmacokinet.* **42**, 327–360.
16. Wagner, J. A., Jarai, Z., Batkai, S., and Kunos, G. (2001) Hemodynamic effects of cannabinoids: coronary and cerebral vasodilation mediated by cannabinoid CB1 receptors. *Eur. J. Pharmacol.* **423**, 203–210.
17. Sidney, S. (2002) Cardiovascular consequences of marijuana use. *J. Clin. Pharmacol.* **42(11 Suppl.)**, 64S–70S.

18. Benowitz, N. L. and Jones, R. T. (1975) Cardiovascular effects of prolonged delta-9-tetrahydrocannabinol ingestion. *Clin. Pharmacol. Ther.* **18**, 287–297.
19. Servoss, S. J., Januzzi, J. L., and Muller, J. E. (2002) Triggers of acute coronary syndromes. *Prog. Cardiovasc. Dis.* **44**, 369–380.
20. Mittleman, M. A., Lewis, R. A., Maclure, M., Sherwood, J. B., and Muller, J. E. (2001) Triggering myocardial infarction by marijuana. *Circulation* **103**, 2805–2809.
21. Mittleman, M. A., Maclure, M., Nachnani, M., Sherwood, J. B., and Muller, J.E. (1997) Educational attainment, anger, and the risk of triggering myocardial infarction onset. The Determinants of Myocardial Infarction Onset Study Investigators. *Arch. Intern. Med.* **157**, 769–775.
22. Mittleman, M. A. and Siscovick, D. S. (1996) Physical exertion as a trigger of myocardial infarction and sudden cardiac death. *Cardiol. Clin.* **14**, 263–270.
23. Barsky, S. H., Roth, M. D., Kleerup, E. C., Simmons, M., and Tashkin, D P. (1998) Histopathologic and molecular alterations in bronchial epithelium in habitual smokers of marijuana, cocaine, and/or tobacco. *J. Natl. Cancer Inst.* **90**, 1198–1205.
24. Morris, R. R. (1985) Human pulmonary histopathological changes from marijuana smoking. *J. Forensic Sci.* 3**0**, 345–349.
25. Roth, M. D., Baldwin, G. C., and Tashkin, D. P. (2002) Effects of delta-9-tetrahydrocannabinol on human immune function and host defense. *Chem. Phys. Lipids* **121**, 229–239.
26. Isenschmid, D. S. and Caplan, Y. H. (1988) Incidence of cannabinoids in medical examiner urine specimens. *J. Forensic Sci.* **33**, 1421–1431.
27. Huestis, M. A., Henningfield, J. E., and Cone, E. J. (1992) Blood cannabinoids. II. Models for the prediction of time of marijuana exposure from plasma concentrations of delta 9-tetrahydrocannabinol (THC) and 11-nor-9-carboxy-delta9-tetrahydrocannabinol (THCCOOH). *J. Anal. Toxicol.* **16**, 283–290.
28. Huestis, M. A., Henningfield, J. E., and Cone, E. J. (1992) Blood cannabinoids. I. Absorption of THC and formation of 11-OH-THC and THCCOOH during and after smoking marijuana. *J. Anal. Toxicol.* **16**, 276–282.
29. Giroud, C., Menetrey, A., Augsburger, M., Buclin, T., Sanchez-Mazas, P., and Mangin, P. (2001) Delta(9)-THC, 11-OH-delta(9)-THC and delta(9)-THCCOOH plasma or serum to whole blood concentrations distribution ratios in blood samples taken from living and dead people. *Forensic Sci. Int.* **123**, 159–164.
30. Leuschner, J. T., Harvey, D. J., Bullingham, R. E. S., and Paton, W. D. M. (1986) Pharmacokinetics of delta 9-tetrahydrocannabinol in rabbits following single or multiple intravenous doses. *Drug Metab. Dispos.* **14**, 230–238.
31. Nyoni, E. C., Sitaram, B. R., and Taylor, D. A. (1996) Determination of delta 9-tetrahydrocannabinol levels in brain tissue using high-performance liquid chromatography with electrochemical detection. *J. Chromatogr. B Biomed. Appl.* **679**, 79–84.
32. Moffat, A., Osselton, D., and Widdop, B. (eds.) (2004) *Clarke's Analysis of Drugs and Poisons in Pharmaceuticals, Body Fluids and Postmortem Material*, 3rd ed., Vol. 2, Pharmaceutical Press, London, pp. 740–743.

Chapter 14

Cannabinoid Effects on Biopsychological, Neuropsychiatric, and Neurological Processes

Richard E. Musty

1. Introduction

There have been several reviews of the therapeutic potential of both natural and synthetic cannabinoids *(1,2)*. These reviews strongly suggest potential therapeutic effects of cannabinoids in motivational processes and their associated disorders (hunger, appetite, pain), psychological disorders (anxiety, depression, bipolar disorder, schizophrenia, alcohol dependence), and central nervous system (CNS) disorders (vomiting and nausea, spasticity, dystonia, brain damage, epilepsy). This chapter, for the most part, covers developments since these reviews were published.

2. Hunger and Appetite

Cannabis was reported to be an appetite stimulant as early as 1845 by Donovan *(3)*, suggesting that it might be used for anorexia nervosa. Although it is common knowledge that cannabis stimulates hunger, very little research has been accomplished over subsequent years. Van Den Broek et al. *(4)* administered 9-aza-cannabinol to sheep intravenously and found that feeding behavior was increased along with a decrease in gastric secretion.

Foltin et al. *(5)* tested nine normal subjects in a live-in laboratory setting. He found that administration of two or three active marijuana cigarettes (1.84%) during a time when subjects could smoke in a social setting increased caloric intake as a result of between-meal snack food, but not during regular meals. These data seem to be the

From: *Forensic Science and Medicine: Marijuana and the Cannabinoids*
Edited by: M. A. ElSohly © Humana Press Inc., Totowa, New Jersey

most objective test of the appetite/hunger-stimulating effects of cannabinoid agonists (*see also* ref. *6*).

Beal et al. *(7)* examined the effects of dronabinol on 94 late-stage AIDS patients who received dronabinol orally 2.5 mg twice daily (90%) or 2.5 mg once daily (10%) for 12 months. Appetite was measured using a visual analog scale for hunger. They found an increase in appetite of 48.6–76.1%, which peaked at 4 months, after which dronabinol induced appetite increases of at least double that at baseline and stable weight for the remaining months. These data seem to suggest that dronabinol stimulates appetite and leads to maintained weight in advanced AIDS patients. Further research in this area is certainly needed, especially in patients earlier in the progression of the disease.

2.1. Appetite Supression

Sanofi-Aventis *(8)* reported the following concerning the effects of the cannabinoid type 1 (CB_1) receptor antagonist SR141716, now known as rimonabant (also Acomplia™).

The results of a 2-year phase III study in 3040 patients with rimonabant (Acomplia), the first in a new class of therapeutic agents called selective CB_1 blockers, demonstrate that the benefits achieved with rimonabant 20 mg at the end of the first year of the study were sustained in the second year of therapy with a good safety and tolerability profile vs placebo. Patients treated with rimonabant 20 mg for 2 years experienced a reduction in body weight and in waist circumference, demonstrating a significant reduction in abdominal fat, a key marker for cardiovascular disease. Patients treated with rimonabant 20 mg over the 2-year period also achieved a significant increase in high-density lipoprotein (HDL) cholesterol (good cholesterol), a reduction in triglycerides, and an improvement in insulin sensitivity. The RIO–North America study is the largest of all rimonabant studies presented to date. The results from this study are consistent with the findings from two previous large-scale studies on rimonabant–RIO-Lipids and RIO-Europe–communicated earlier this year and add to the ever-growing body of evidence supporting the drug's efficacy and tolerability profile. Rimonabant is currently being developed for the management of cardiovascular risk factors, including reduction of abdominal obesity, improving lipid and glucose metabolism, and as an aid to smoking cessation.

Obesity is a major public health burden and one of the most frequent causes of death worldwide, mainly through cardiovascular disease. Obesity is typically measured by body mass index. However, recent findings have shown that visceral (abdominal) fat (simply measured by waist circumference) is a better predictor for heart attack than weight or body mass index. Forty-four percent of adult Americans have a waist circumference size exceeding the at-risk level (40 in. for men and 35 in. for women). Visceral fat is associated with the cause of metabolic risk factors such as dyslipidemia or insulin resistance that may lead to diabetes, heart attack, stroke, and other cardiovascular disease. Reducing abdominal fat is a recognized priority for preventing cardiovascular disease.

RIO–North America was a phase III, multinational multicenter, randomized, double-blind, placebo-controlled trial comparing two fixed-dose regimens of rimonabant (5 and 20 mg once daily) to placebo for a period of 2 years. The study was conducted in 3040 patients at 72 centers in the United States and Canada.

The objectives of the trial were to assess the effect of rimonabant on weight loss over a period of 1 year and to determine the ability of rimonabant to prevent weight regain during a second year of treatment. The study objectives also included an assessment of improvement in risk factors associated with abdominal obesity (as measured by waist circumference), such as dyslipidemia, glucose metabolism, and the metabolic syndrome, and an evaluation of the safety and tolerability of rimonabant over a period of 2 years.

After a screening period of 1 week, patients were prescribed a mild hypocaloric diet (designed to reduce daily caloric intake by 600 kcal from the patient's energy requirements) and entered a 4-week single-blind placebo run-in period. Afterward, patients were randomly allocated to one of the three treatment groups: placebo or rimonabant 5 or 20 mg for 52 weeks of double-blind treatment using a randomization ratio of 1:2:2.

After the first year of treatment, patients who received rimonabant 5 or 20 mg were rerandomized to either the same dose of rimonabant or placebo using a randomization ratio of 1:1 for an additional 52-week treatment period (the placebo group remained on placebo during the second year).

2.2. Rio–North America Findings

The findings show that 2-year treatment with rimonabant 20 mg significantly lowered weight, reduced abdominal fat, diminished cardiovascular risk factors, and decreased metabolic disorders in this patient population. Waist circumference, a simple measure of abdominal fat, in patients treated with rimonabant 20 mg for the full 2-year period was reduced by 8 cm (3.1 in.) vs 4.9 cm (1.9 in.) for rimonabant 5 mg and 3.8 cm (1.5 in.) in the placebo group ($p < 0.001$). Of the patients who received treatment with rimonabant 20 mg throughout the 2-year period, 62.5% lost more than 5% of their initial body weight vs 36.7% of those on rimonabant 5 mg and 33.2% of those on placebo ($p < 0.001$). In the same period, 32.8% of patients treated with rimonabant 20 mg lost in excess of 10% of their initial body weight vs 20% of those on rimonabant 5 mg and 16.4% of patients on placebo ($p < 0.001$).

Metabolic parameters were also significantly improved in patients treated with rimonabant 20 mg throughout the 2-year period, with HDL cholesterol increased by 24.5% in the rimonabant 20 mg group vs 15.6 and 13.8% in the rimonabant 5 mg and placebo groups, respectively ($p < 0.001$). Triglycerides were reduced by 9.9% in patients treated with rimonabant 20 mg throughout the 2-year period vs 5.9 and 1.6% in the rimonabant 5 mg and placebo groups, respectively ($p < 0.05$).

Although diabetic patients were not included in the study, patients on rimonabant 20 mg had significantly improved their insulin sensitivity compared to those on rimonabant 5 mg and on placebo. The effect of rimonabant on HDL cholesterol, triglycerides, fasting insulin, and insulin sensitivity (as measured by homeostasis model assessment) appeared to be twice that which would be expected from the degree of weight loss achieved (all $p < 0.05$). Of particular note is that the number of patients diagnosed with metabolic syndrome at baseline and treated with rimonabant 20 mg over the 2-year study period was reduced by more than one third ($p < 0.001$). Metabolic syndrome encompasses a series of serious health risks or conditions that increase a person's chance to develop heart disease, stroke, and diabetes.

2.3. A Good Safety and Tolerability Profile

Rimonabant 20 mg proved to be safe and tolerable vs placebo throughout the 2-year study period. Side effects were mainly minor and short-lived. Overall discontinuation rates for adverse events in the first year of the study were 7.2, 9.4, and 12.8% in the placebo, rimonabant 5 mg, and rimonabant 20 mg groups, respectively. The discontinuation rates for patients randomly assigned to continue their first-year treatment for a second year were 6.7, 8.3, and 6.0% in the placebo, rimonabant 5 mg and 20 mg groups, respectively. No differences were noted in the three groups with regard to scores measured by the Hospital Anxiety Depression scale. In this trial and in two preceding studies, rimonabant was also shown to have no significant electrocardiogram or heart rate changes.

2.4. Rimonabant and the Endocannabinoid System

The Endocannabinoid (EC) System is a newly discovered physiological system in the body that is believed to play a key role in the central and peripheral regulation of energy balance, glucose and lipid metabolism, as well as in the control of tobacco dependence. CB_1 receptors are found in the brain as well as in peripheral tissues of the body, such as adipocytes (or "fat cells"), which are associated with lipid and glucose metabolism. Excessive food intake or chronic tobacco use results in an overactive EC system. This can trigger a cycle of increased eating and fat storage or, in the case of smoking, sustained tobacco dependence.

Rimonabant is the first in a new class of drugs called CB_1 blockers. By selectively blocking both centrally and peripherally the CB_1 receptors, rimonabant modulates the overactive EC System. The results have been seen in reducing cardiovascular risk factors through reduction in abdominal fat and a corresponding improvement in metabolic parameters that is beyond that expected through weight reduction.

The new clinical results from the RIO–North America study further suggest that rimonabant may become an important tool in the cardiovascular risk factor reduction armamentarium.

LeFur *(6)* reviewed a number of findings that support the effects of the mechanisms by which rimonabant acts:

1. CB_1 receptors are located in brain areas associated with hunger and appetite.
2. "Endocannabinoids may tonically activate the CB_1 receptors to maintain food intake, and increase the incentive value of food as well as reinforcing the rewarding effects of nicotine involving the brain reward circuits..."
3. In mutant obese mice, rimonabant decreased food intake and led to a sustained loss in body weight.
4. Rimonabant had no effect in CB_1 receptor knockout mice, confirming the fact that CB_1 receptors are necessary for the action of this drug.

To conclude, it seems that cannabinoid agonists increase hunger and appetite, whereas antagonists decrease appetite and hunger. There seems to be significant promise for both stimulating appetite and decreasing it. If these results continue to show promise, medications of significant value might be developed.

3. Pain

In a review, Walker et al. *(9)* concluded that cannabinoids suppress nociceptive neurotransmission, synthetic agonists are as potent as morphine, there are both direct effects on spinal cord, the periphery, and the brain.

Bicher and Mechoulam *(10)* found that Δ^9-tetrahydrocnnabinol (THC) and Δ^8-THC (ip) were about half as effective as morphine (sc) on three tests of analgesia: the hot plate test, the acetic acid writhing test, and the tail flick test. In a review of human anecdotal studies and controlled studies *(11)*, pain relief has been reported anecdotally as well as in controlled studies. Of the four double-blind placebo-controlled studies reviewing THC administration for cancer pain, THC was effective at 15 and 20 mg in one study and in the second study was more effective than placebo and THC for postoperative pain: levonatradol was effective at 1.5–3 mg, and THC was not effective at doses of 0.22 and 0.44 mg/kg (pain after extraction of impacted molar teeth). In a questionnaire study, Dunn and Davis *(12)* reported that patients who smoked cannabis found relief from phantom limb pain. In a single case report, Finnegan-Ling and Musty *(13)* reported that THC p.o. was more effective than conventional pain medications, including opiates and nonsteroidal anti-inflammatory drugs.

Very few studies have examined the effects of extracts with a low THC/cannabidiol (CBD) ratio or experimentally varied pure THC and CBD mixtures. Sofia et al. *(14)* conducted a comparison of the pain-relieving effects of Δ^9-THC, a crude marihuana extract (CME), cannabinol (CBN), CBD, morphine SO-4, and aspirin (all po). They used the acetic acid induced writhing test, the hot plate test, and the Randall–Selitto paw pressure tests in rats. Δ^9-THC and morphine were equipotent in all tests except that morphine was significantly more potent in elevating pain threshold in the uninflamed rat hind paw. In terms of Δ^9-THC content, CME was nearly equipotent in the hot plate and Randall–Selitto tests, but was three times more potent in the acetic acid writhing test. On the other hand, CBN, like aspirin, was only effective in reducing writhing frequency in mice (three times more potent than aspirin) and raising the pain threshold of the inflamed hind paw of the rat (equipotent with aspirin). CBD did not display a significantly analgesic effect in any of the test systems used. The results of this investigation seem to suggest that both Δ^9-THC and CME possess analgesic activity similar to morphine, whereas CBN appears to be a nonanalgesic at the doses used. Only one human case study that used an extract with known amounts of THC, CBD, and CBN *(15)* has been published prior to reports with orally administered extracts. The extract contained THC (5.75%), CBD (4.73%), and CBN (2.42%). They administered an oral extract to a person with chronic abdominal pain associated with familial Mediterranean fever in a 6-week randomized placebo-controlled study. Both normal use of morphine and escape use (dosing when an acute attack of pain occurs) were significantly reduced. Self-reports on the visual analog scale also demonstrated significant reductions in perception of pain.

Recently there have been several studies suggesting therapeutic potential for CB_1 and CB_2 agonists.

Dogrul et al. *(16)* reported that diabetic neuropathic pain is common and is resistant to morphine treatment. Streptozotocin (200 mg/kg) was used to induce diabetes in mice, which were tested between 45 and 60 days after onset of diabetes. Antinociception was measured using the radiant tail flick test, Von Frey filaments, and the hot-plate test, respectively. Tactile allodynia but not thermal hyperalgesia was found. WIN 55-212-2a, a cannabinoid receptor agonist that acts in the CNS but is not inhibited by the CB_1 antagonist AM 251, produced a dose-dependent decrease in allodynia at doses of 1, 5, and 10 mg/kg.

Ibrahim et al. *(17)* tested the effects of AM 1241 (a selective CB_2 receptor agonist) on experimental neuropathic pain in rats. Tactile hypersensitivity and thermal hypersensitivity were induced by ligation of L5 and L6 spinal nerves. AM 1241 dose-dependently reversed hypersensitivity. When tested in CB_1 knockout mice using the same ligation procedure, AM 1241 was effective in reducing pain sensitivity, suggesting that this peripherally active agonist blocks neuropathic pain. The authors suggest that CB_2 receptor agonists, devoid of CNS activity, are predicted to be effective without the CNS side effects of centrally acting cannabinoid agonists.

Johanek and Simone *(18)* examined whether or not cannabinoids attenuated hyperalgesia produced by a mild heat injury to the glabrous hind paw and if the antihyperalgesia was receptor-mediated. Mild heat injury (55°C for 30 seconds) to one hind paw was given to anesthetized rats. Fifteen minutes after injury, decreased withdrawal latency to radiant heat and increased withdrawal frequency to a von Frey monofilament (200 mN force) delivered to the injured hindpaw was observed. Intraplantar injection of vehicle or the agonist WIN 55,212-2 (1, 10, or 30 μg in 100 μL) decreased heat and and mechanical hyperalgesia in a dose-dependent fashion, whereas the inactive enantiomer WIN 55,212-3 did not. The CB_1 receptor antagonist AM 251 (30 μg) co-injected with WIN 55,212-2 (30 μg) decreased the antihyperalgesic effects of WIN 55,212-2,.and CB_2 receptor antagonist AM 630 (30 μg) co-injected with WIN 55,212-2 decreased the antihyperalgesic effects of the agonist. Injection of WIN 55,212-2 into the contralateral paw did not change heat-injury-induced hyperalgesia. These results suggest that antihyperalgesia was mediated by peripheral mechanisms. The authors conclude, like Ibrahim *(17)*, that this reduction of hyperanalgesia may be peripheral.

Nackley et al. *(19)* examined the effects of CB_2-selective cannabinoid agonist AM1241 on activity in spinal wide dynamic range neurons by transcutaneous electrical stimulation urethane-anesthetized rats during either carrageenan inflammation or not. Intravenous administration decreased activity in wide dynamic range neurons induced by stimulation. This effect was blocked by the CB_2 antagonist SR144528 but not by the CB_1 antagonist SR141716A. In addition, activity of nonnociceptive neurons recorded in the lumbar dorsal horn was not affected by AM1241.

In a recent report, Chichewizc and Welch *(20)* found that Δ^9-THC (20 mg/kg) and morphine (20 mg/kg) induced analgesia in both vehicle-treated and morphine-tolerant mice. In both groups analgesia was equally effective, "indicating that analgesia produced by the combination is not hampered by existing morphine treatment (no cross tolerance to the combination)." Mice were tested with Δ^9-THC (20 mg/kg) and morphine (20 mg/kg) twice daily for 6.5 days and tested for tolerance, and on day 8, Δ^9-THC tolerance was observed, but morphine tolerance did not occur. These results suggest that low-dose combinations of Δ^9-THC and morphine might prevent morphine tolerance. The authors conclude that combinations of these drugs may be useful in chronic pain patients over morphine administration alone.

In summary, animal research indicates that there are potential effects on the control of pain at many different levels of analysis. Some of these results are supported by human studies, to be discussed later. Others must await clinical trials, assuming toxicity and safety standards are met.

3.1. Human Studies

Brenneisen et al. *(21)* administered multiple does of either THC capsules (Marinol®) or THC hemisuccinate suppositories at 24-hour intervals to two patients who had spasticity due to organic damage. They found that the oral bioavailability was 45–53% compared with the rectal route of administration, because the oral route involves less absorption and higher first-pass metabolism. Both patients experienced lower pain (self-rated) and decreased spasticity and rigidity as measured by the Ashworth Scale and walking ability. Passive mobility also improved. Using physiological and psychological testing, no differences were found in cardiovascular functioning, ability to concentrate, or mood. Finally, the comparative effectiveness of the oral form of administration was 25–50% of the rectal route.

Wade et al. *(22)* conducted a study testing the effects of plant-derived CME, administered by buccal spray. Using a double-blind drug and placebo, single-patient randomized crossover design, patients were administered the extracts THC, CBD, 1:1 CBD:THC by self-titration to doses providing symptom relief with the lowest possible unwanted side effects. Doses to achieve relief were highly individual, ranging from 2.5 to 120 mg in a 24-hour period. Patients included 18 with multiple sclerosis (MS), 4 with spinal cord injury, and one each with brachial plexus damage *(7)* and limb amputation. Pain relief was measured using visual analog scales. THC, CBD, and the combination were significantly superior to placebo. Impaired bladder control, muscle spasms, and spasticity were improved by CME in some patients with these symptoms.

Brady et al. *(23)* tested the effects of cannabis-based medicinal extracts in patients with advanced MS who had developed troublesome lower urinary tract symptoms. Using an open-label design, THC and CBD (2.5 mg of each per oral spray) for 8 weeks followed by THC only (2.5 mg THC per oral spray) for a further 8 weeks and then into a long-term extension were taken by the patients. Fifteen patients were evaluated using the following measures: urinary frequency and volume charts, incontinence pad weights, cystometry and visual analog scales for secondary troublesome symptoms. Significant decreases in urinary urgency, the number and volume of incontinence episodes, frequency nocturia, and daily total voided occurred in patients. Self-assessment of spasticity, pain, and quality of sleep improved continuously for a 35-week period with both extracts.

Burstein et al. *(24)* reported that ajulemic acid, also known as CT-3 and IP-751, derived from the major metabolite of THC, had many of the properties of the nonsteroidal anti-inflammatory drugs and is apparently free of the intoxicating effects of THC. In healthy patients and those with neuropathic pain, no psychotropic effects were found. In short-term trials of 1 week, pain was reduced in patients with neuropathic pain using a visual analog scale. Neither normal subjects nor pain patients experienced any signs of either dependence or withdrawal. These data suggest that ajulemic acid has therapeutic potential in the treatment of chronic pain.

Zajicek et al. *(25)* evaluated the effects of THC (Marinol) and a cannabis extract (oral Cannador, a capsule with THC and an unstated amount of cannabidiol) in patients with MS in a multicenter randomized placebo-controlled trial. They found no effects on the Ashworth Scale in the 611 patients in the trial, but objective improvement in mobility and reduction in pain occurred. One problem with this study is that both THC and Cannador are poorly absorbed, which might explain the differences between buccal spray administration and oral administration.

Svendsen et al. *(26)* tested the effects of dronabinol in patients with MS in a randomized double-blind placebo-controlled crossover trial for 3 weeks followed by a 3-week washout period, then crossover to either drug or placebo for the final 3 weeks. Twenty-four patients were enrolled through an outpatient clinic. Drug doses were adjusted to a maximum dose of 10 mg daily. Using a numerical pain scale, scores were significantly measured during the last week of treatment when compared with the placebo condition. Dizziness occurred frequently during the first week of treatment. Although the authors comment correctly that pain reduction was moderate in this study, the design of the study did not allow patients to self-titrate doses of dronabinol, probably minimizing the efficacy of pain reduction achieved by the patients.

In summary, it seems that cannabinoid agonists have potential for therapeutic use in pain and MS. This is supported by the reports of GW Phamaceuticals discussed in the next section.

4. Various Potential for Natural Cannabinoids

GW Pharmaceuticals *(27)* has an ambitious program testing a natural cannabinoid mixture, Sativex® (THC:CBD ratio 1.1), in the form of an oral spray. Applications for regulatory approval have been approved in Canada for neuropathic pain and for symptoms of MS. Regulatory findings will be submitted in the United Kingdom. Figure 1 shows the drug-development progress as of mid-2004. Note that Sativex is presently in phase III trials for spinal cord injury and bladder dysfunction and in phase II trials for diabetic neuroropathy. High-THC extracts are in various stages of development for several types of pain. In addition, extracts high in CBD are also in various stages of development.

5. Psychological Disorders (Anxiety, Depression, Bipolar Disorder, Schizophrenia, Alcohol Dependence)

5.1. Anxiety

In a review, Musty *(28)* concluded that for CB_1 antagonists, it seems that the preponderance of the data suggest that these compounds are anxiolytic. Agonists, on the other hand, seem to have biphasic effects: low doses seem to be anxiolytic, high doses anxiogenic. In addition, it seems that the context is important. Further research is needed to sort out the differences among various studies, but it is clear that both antagonists and agonists on the CB_1 receptor have anxiolytic properties. Standardization of testing procedures across laboratories might be helpful, the problem being that

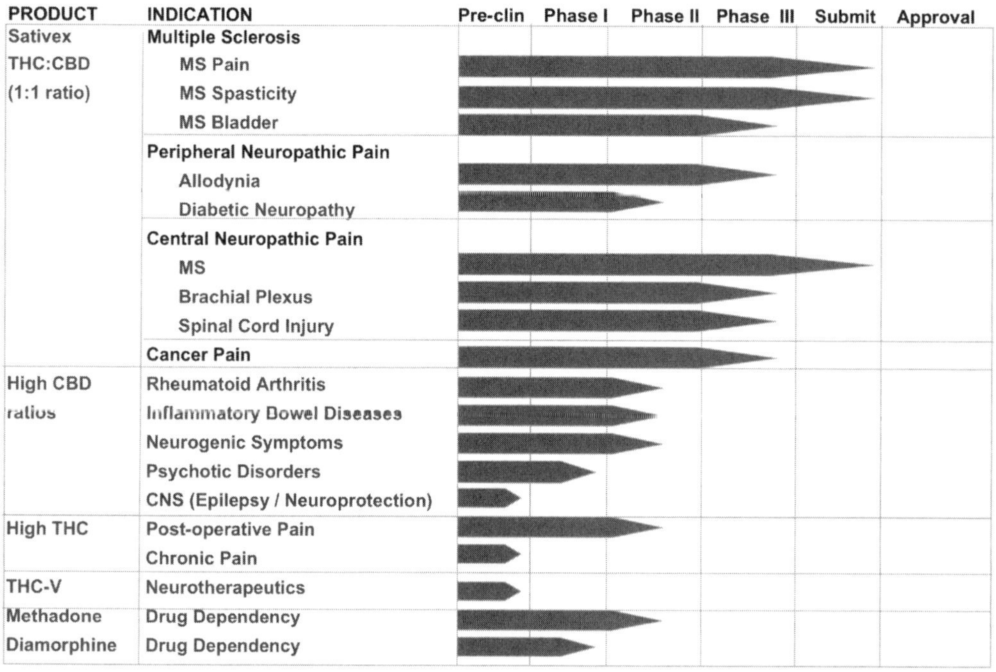

Fig. 1. Progress on preclinical and clinical trails of cannabinoid products by GW Pharmaceuticals.

there are many variables that have not been explored with behavioral methods used to test for anxiolytic properties. Because it is widely known that activation and inactivation of CB_1 receptors has a multitude of modulatory effects on neurotransmitter systems, it would be advantageous for researchers to examine what changes in neurotransmitter activity occur in conjunction with the pharmacological effects conserved in the types of studies. There seems to be quite a convergence between animal research and human research, strongly suggesting that CBD is a true anxiolytic. Given the fact that this drug has no psychoactivity in terms of intoxication and is very safe, it seems important to pursue the potential of CBD with vigor, with further behavioral pharmacological studies, mechanistic studies employing neuropharmacological methods, and clinical studies.

5.2. Depression

In a review by Musty *(11)*, the following summaries of research on depression, bipolar disorder, schizophrenia, and alcohol dependence are presented:

In a study of normal subjects, Musty *(29)* found a positive correlation on the depression scale of the Minnesota Multiphase Personality Inventory with feelings of euphoria after smoking marijuana, while there was no correlation between anxiety (hysteria scale) and somatic concerns (hypochondriasis scale) with feeling euphoric, suggesting an antidepressive effect from marijuana use. Schnelle et al. *(30)*, in a survey of 128 patients in Germany, reported 12% used marijuana for relief of depression.

Consroe et al. *(31)* found that depression was reduced in patients with MS in a self-report questionnaire. In another self-report study *(32)* of patients with spinal cord injuries, similar reductions in depression were reported. In cancer patients Regalson *(33)* found that THC relieved depression in advanced cancer patients. Finally, Warner et al. *(34)* found reported relief from depression in a survey of 79 mental patients. At present, there are very few data supporting the hypothesis that cannabinoids might relieve depression, but tests of both agonists and antagonists of the CB_1 receptor are clearly indicated to test this hypothesis.

Since the Musty review *(11)*, Musty et al. *(35)* discovered that cannnabichromene selectively blocks behavioral despair in a mouse model of depression. This is a novel finding in that there has been very little work published on the effects of cannnabichromene.

5.3. Bipolar Disorder

Grinspoon and Bakalar *(36,37)* presented six case studies of people with bipolar disorder using cannabis to treat their symptoms. Some used it to treat mania, depression, or both. They stated that it was more effective than conventional drugs or helped relieve the side effects of those drugs. One woman found that cannabis curbed her manic rages. Others described the use of cannabis as a supplement to lithium (allowing reduced consumption) or for relief of lithium's side effects.

These clinical observations are important leads to the potential use of cannabinoids for manic depressive disorder and suggest that clinical trials should be conducted.

5.4. Schizophrenia

5.4.1. Animal Studies

Zuardi et al. *(38)* tested the effects of CBD and haloperidol in a model that predicts antipsychotic activity in rats. Apomorphine induces stereotyped sniffing and biting. Both drugs decreased the frequency of these behaviors. CBD did not induce catalepsy, even at very high doses, although haloperidol induced catalepsy. The authors conclude that CBD has a pharmacological profile similar to the atypical antipsychotic drugs.

Musty et al. *(2)* tested the effects of the of the CB_1 receptor antagonist SR141716 in two animal models of schizophrenia. In the first, ibotenic acid lesions of the hippocampus were made in neonatal rats, which results in a brain degeneration pattern similar to that observed in schizophrenics as well as abnormal play behavior in an anxiety-provoking environment. In a second model, ketamine-induced enhancement of prepulse inhibition was tested. In both of these tests, SR141716 reversed the abnormal behavior. These findings in animal models are consistent with the hypothesis that CB_1 receptor antagonists have antipsychotic activity.

5.4.2. Human Studies

The use of cannabis has been associated with exacerbation of symptoms of schizophrenia *(39)*, but other reports suggest that the use of cannabis helped patients manage their symptoms of schizophrenia, but several studies have shown potential symptom-relieving effects of cannabis use.

Peralta and Cuesta *(40)* studied 95 schizophrenics who had used cannabis in the last year. They found lower scores in the schizophrenics on delusions and alogia scales of Andreasen's Scales for the Assessment of Positive and Negative Symptoms, suggesting that cannabis may affect the negative symptoms of schizophrenia. In a sample of community-based mentally ill patients, Warner et al. *(34)* reported fewer hospital admissions and fewer symptoms of anxiety, depression, and insomnia among users preferring marijuana.

Zuardi and Morais et al. *(41)* reported an experiment in a single case, in which the patient was being treated with haloperidol. The medication was stopped as a result of side effects followed by a return of symptoms, leading to hospitalization. At this point the patient was given placebo medication for 4 days, after which she was administered CBD (two doses per day) on an increasing dose schedule up to 750 mg/dose until the 26th day. This was followed by 4 days of placebo and finally by a return to haloperidol for 4 weeks. Interviews were conducted and videotaped, which was followed by rating of interviews using the Brief Psychiatric Rating Scale (BPRS) and the Interactive Observation Scale for Psychiatric Patients (IOSPP). A psychiatrist rated the patient, blind to treatment conditions on the BPRS, and nurse assistants independently, and blind to treatment conditions rated the patient on the IOSPP. Comparing placebo to the CBD condition, Hostility–Suspiciousness dropped by 50% of the BPRS maximum scale score, Thought Disturbance by 37.5%, Anxiety–Depression by 43.7%, Activation by 41.6%, and Anergia by 31.3%. During 4 days of placebo that followed, all four scale scores increased somewhat. The patient was then returned to haloperidol treatment, and the subsequent scores were close to those with CBD treatment. This experiment demonstrates that antagonists of the CB_1 receptor are candidates for testing in human schizophrenia.

5.5. Alcohol Dependence

Musty *(42)* found that CBD, Δ^9-THC, and clonidine reduced body tremor and audiogenic seizures during alcohol withdrawal in C57Bl6J mice forced to become alcohol tolerant on a liquid diet containing alcohol. Equivalent reductions in tremors and seizures were found with clonidine. Grinspoon and Bakalar *(36)* reported two cases of individuals who used marijuana to deal with alcohol dependence.

References

1. Musty, R. E. (2004) Natural cannabinoids: interactions and effects, in *The Medicinal Use of Cannabis and the Cannabinoids* (Guy, G. W., Whittle, B. A., and Robson, R. J., eds.), Pharmaceutical Press, London, pp.165–204.
2. Musty, R. E., Deyo, R. A., Baer, J. L., Darrow, S. M., and Coleman, B. (2000) Effects of SR141716A on animal models of depression. 2000 Symposium on the Cannabinoids, International Cannabinoid Research Society, Burlington, VT, p. 109.
3. Donovan, M. (1845) On the physical and medicinal qualities of Indian hemp *(Cannabis indica)*; with observations on the best mode of administration, and cases illustrative of its powers. *Dublin J. Med. Sci.* **26**, 368–402, 459–461.
4. Van Den Broek, G. W., Robertson, J., Keim, D. A., and Baile, C. A. (1979) Feeding and depression of abomasal secretion in sheep elicited by elfazepam and 9-aza-cannabinol. *Pharmacol. Biochem. Behav.* **11**, 51–56.

5. Foltin, R. W., Brady, J. V., and Fischman, M. W. (1986) Behavioral analysis of marijuana effects on food intake in humans. *Pharmacol. Biochem. Behav.* **25**, 577–582.
6. LeFur, G. (2004) Clinical results with rimonabant in obesity, in 14th Annual Symposium on the Cannabinoids. International Cannabinoid Research Society, Burlington, VT, p. 67.
7. Beal, J. E., Olson, R., Lefkowitz, L., et al. (1997) Long-term efficacy and safety of dronabinol for acquired immunodeficiency syndrome-associated anorexia. *J. Pain Symptom Manage.* **14**, 7–14.
8. Pi-Sunyer, F. X., Aronne, L. J., Heshmati, H. M., Devin, J., Rosenstock, J., RIO-North America Study Group. (2006) Effect of rimonabant, a cannabinoid-1 receptor blocker, on weight and cardiometabolic risk factors in overweight or obese patients: RIO-North America: a randomized controlled trial. *JAMA* **295,** 761–775.
9. Walker, J. M., Strangman, N. M., and Huang, S. M. (2002) Cannabis as analgesics, in *Biology of Marijuana.* (Onaivi, E., ed.), Taylor and Francis, New York, pp. 573–590.
10. Bicher, H. I. and Mechoulam, R. (1968) Pharmacological effects of two active constituents of marihuana, *Arch. Int. Pharmacodynam.* **172**, 24–31.
11. Musty, R. E. (2002) Cannabinoid therapeutic potential in motivational processes, psychological disorders and central nervous system disorders, in *Biology of Cannabis* (Onaivi, E., ed.), Taylor and Francis, New York, pp. 45–74.
12. Dunn, M. and Davis, R. (1974) The perceived effects of marijuana on spinal cord injured males. *Paraplegia* **12**, 175.
13. Finnegan-Ling, D. and Musty, R. E. (1994) Marinol and phantom limb pain: a case study. Paper presented at the International Cannabis Research Society, July 21–23, L'Esterel, Quebec, Canada.
14. Sofia, R. D., Vassar, H. B., and Knobloch, L. C. (1975) Comparative analgesic activity of various naturally occurring cannabinoids in mice and rats. *Psychopharmacologia* **40**, 285–295.
15. Holdcroft, A., Smith, M., Jacklin, A., et al. (1997) Pain relief with oral cannabinoids in familial Mediterranean fever. *Anaesthesia* **52**, 483–486.
16. Dogrul, A., Gul, H., Yildiz, O., Bilgin, F., and Guzeldemir, M. E. (2004) Cannabinoids blocks tactile allodynia in diabetic mice without attenuation of its antinociceptive effect. *Neurosci. Lett.* **368**, 82–86.
17. Ibrahim, M. M., Deng, H., Zvonok, A., et al. (2003) Activation of CB2 cannabinoid receptors by AM1241 inhibits experimental neuropathic pain: pain inhibition by receptors not present in the CNS. *Proc. Natl. Acad. Sci.* **100,** 10529–10533.
18. Johanek, L. M. and Simone, D. A. (2004) Activation of peripheral cannabinoid receptors attenuates cutaneous hyperalgesia produced by a heat injury. *Pain* **109**, 432–442.
19. Nackley, A. G., Zvonok, A. M., Makriyannis, A., and Hohmann, A. G. (2004) Activation of cannabinoid cb2 receptors suppresses c-fiber responses and windup in spinal wide dynamic range neurons in the absence and presence of inflammation. *J. Neurophysiol.* **92,** 3562–3574.
20. Chichewizc, D. L. and Welch, S. (1999) *Symposium on the Cannabinoids*, International Cannabinoid Research Society, Burlington, VT, p. 66.
21. Brenneisen, R., Egli, A., ElSohly, M. A., Henn, V., and Spiess, Y. (1996) The effect of orally and rectally administered delta 9-tetrahydrocannabinol on spasticity: a pilot study with 2 patients. Int. *J. Clin. Pharmacol. Ther.* **34**, 446–452.
22. Wade, D. T., Robson, P., House, H., Makela, and Aram, P. (2003) A preliminary controlled study to determine whether whole-plant cannabis extracts can improve intractable neurogenic symptoms. *J. Clin. Rehab.* **17**, 21–29.
23. Brady, C. M., DasGupta, R., Dalton, C., Wiseman, O. J., Berkley, K. J., and Fowler, C. J. (2004) An open-label pilot study of cannabis-based extracts for bladder dysfunction in advanced multiple sclerosis. *Mult. Scler.***10**, 425–433.

24. Burstein, S. H., Karst, M., Schneider, U., and Zurier, R. B. (2004) Ajulemic acid: a novel cannabinoid produces analgesia without a "high." *Life Sci.* **75**,1513–1522.
25. Zajicek, J., Fox, P., Sanders, H., et al. (2003) Cannabinoids for treatment of spasticity and other symptoms related to multiple sclerosis (CAMS study): multicentre randomised placebo-controlled trial. *Lancet* **362**,17–26.
26. Svendsen, K. B., Jensen, T. S., Bach, F. W., Svendsen, K. B., Jensen, T. S., and Bach, F. W. (2004) Does the cannabinoid dronabinol reduce central pain in multiple sclerosis? Randomised double blind placebo controlled crossover trial. *BMJ* **329**, 253.
27. GW Pharmaceuticals (2004) http://www.gwpharm.com/research_pipeline.asp
28. Musty, R. E. (2005) Cannabinoids and anxiety, in *Cannabinoids as Therapeutics* (Mechoulam, R., ed.), Birkhauser Verlag, Basel, pp. 141–148.
29. Musty, R. E. (1988) Individual differences as predictors of marihuana phenomenology, in *Marihuana: An International Research Report* (Chesher, G., Consroe, P., and Musty, R., eds.), Australian Government Publishing Service, Canberra, pp. 201 207.
30. Schnelle, M., Grotenhermen, F., Reif, M., and Gorter, R. W. (1999) Ergebnisse einer standardisierten Umfrage zur medizinischen Verwendung von Cannabisprodukten im deutschen Sprachraum [Results of a standardized survey on the medical use of cannabis products in the German-speaking area]. *Forsch. Komplementarmed. Suppl.* **3**, 28–36.
31. Consroe, P., Musty, R. E., Tillery, W., and Pertwee, R. (1997) Perceived effects of cannabis smoking in patients with multiple sclerosis. *Eur. Neurol.* **38**, 44–48.
32. Consroe, P., Tillery, W., Rein, J., and Musty, R. E. (1998) Reported marijuana effects in patients with spinal cord injury. *1998 Symposium on the Cannabinoids*, International Cannabinoid Research Society, Burlington, VT, p. 64.
33. Regelson, W., Butler, J. R., Schultz, J., et al. (1976) Δ^9-Tetrahydrocannabinol as an effective antidepressant and appetite stimulating agent in advanced cancer patients, in *Pharmacology of Marijuana* (Braude, M. C. and Szara, S., eds.), Raven Press, New York, pp. 763–776.
34. Warner, R., Taylor, D., Wright, J., et al. (1994) Substance use among the mentally ill: prevalence, reasons for use, and effects on illness. *Am. J. Orthopsychiatry* **64,** 30–39.
35. Musty, R. E. and Deyo, R. A. (2003) Cannabichromene (CBC) extract alters Behavioral Despair on the Mouse Tail Suspension test of depression, 2003 Symposium on the Cannabinoids, Burlington, VT. International Cannabinoid Research Society, p. 146.
36. Grinspoon, L. and Bakalar, J. B. (eds.) (1997) *Marihuana, the Forbidden Medicine,* rev. ed., Yale University Press, New Haven, CT.
37. Grinspoon, L. and Bakalar, J. B. (eds.) (1993) *Marihuana, the Forbidden Medicine*, Yale University Press, New Haven, CT.
38. Zuardi, A. W., Rodrigues, J. A., and Cunha, J. M. (1991) Effects of cannabidiol in animal models predictive of antipsychotic activity. *Psychopharmacology* **104**, 260–264.
39. Negrete, J.C., Knapp, W.P., Douglas, D. E., and Smith, W. B. (1986) Cannabis affects the severity of schizophrenic symptoms: results of a clinical survey. *Psychol. Med.* **16,** 515–520.
40. Peralta, V. and Cuesta, M. J. (1992) Influence of cannabis abuse on schizophrenic psychopathology. *Acta Psychiatr. Scand.* **85,**127–130.
41. Zuardi, A. W., Morais, S. L., Guimaraes, F. S., and Mechoulam, R. (1995) Antipsychotic effect of cannabidiol. *J. Clin. Psychiatry* **56**, 485–486.
42. Musty, R.E. (1984) Possible anxiolytic effects of cannabidiol, in *The Cannabinoids* (Agurell, S., Dewey, W., and Willette, R., eds.), Academic Press, New York, pp. 829–844.

Index

AcompliaTM, *see* Rimonabant
Acquired immunodeficiency syndrome (AIDS), marijuana effects on progression, 238, 239
Acute coronary syndrome, marijuana as trigger, 297, 298
Addiction,
  endocannabinoid system in addiction to other drugs, 133–135
  marijuana withdrawal management, 132, 133
  neural pathways, 113
  opioid receptors in cannabinoid dependence, 133, 134
  tolerance and dependence, 113, 114, 245, 246
Adipose tissue testing,
  mass spectrometry, 184
  rationale, 297
2-AG, *see* 2-Arachidonoyl glycerol
AIDS, *see* Acquired immunodeficiency syndrome
Alcohol,
  dependence and marijuana management, 313
  endocannabinoid system and intake, 134
  marijuana combination and impairment, 213
Alcohols, *Cannabis* composition, 36
Alkaloids, *Cannabis* composition, 29
Alveolar macrophage, marijuana effects, 258–260, 268, 269
AM 1241, analgesia, 308
Amygdala, CB1 receptors, 109
Analgesia,
  cannabinoid agonist studies, 307–309
  cannabinoid receptor agonists, 130–132
  CB_1 receptors, 112, 113, 130–132
  endogenous cannabinoid system, 130
  human studies of THC, 309, 310
  pain pathways, 110, 112
  THC efficacy, 307
Anandamide,
  neuromodulation, 97–99
  synthesis, 98, 127
Anxiety, cannabinoid antagonist studies, 310, 311
Apigenin, pharmacology, 40
Appetite,
  cannabinoid effects, 303, 304
  endogenous cannabinoid system in homeostasis, 128, 129
  rimonabant and suppression, 304, 305
  THC effects, 129
Arachidonoyl ethanolamide, neuromodulation, 97–99
2-Arachidonoyl glycerol (2-AG),
  neuromodulation, 97–99
  synthesis, 98
  vasodilatation, 116

B-cell, cannabinoid effects, 263, 264
Bipolar disorder, marijuana effects, 312
Blood pressure, cannabinoid effects, 115, 116, 239
Blood testing,
  cause-of-death determination, 299
  driving impairment testing,
    11-carboxy-THC, 283, 284

THC, 283, 284
THC/11-carboxy-THC ratio, 284, 285
interpretation of plasma tests, 212–217
mass spectrometry, 182–184, 192, 193
Bupropion, marijuana withdrawal studies, 132

Cannabichromene,
antidepressant activity, 312
biosynthesis, 7
features, 18
Cannabicyclol, features, 22
Cannabidiol (CBD),
anxiolytic activity, 311
biosynthesis, 7
features, 18, 19
indica content, 11
medical marijuana content, 11, 12
pharmacology and activity, 39
schizophrenia studies, 312, 313
Cannabidiolic acid, features, 18, 19
Cannabielsoin, features, 22
Cannabigerol,
biosynthesis, 7
features, 18
Cannabigerovan, biosynthesis, 7
Cannabinodiol, features, 23
Cannabinoid receptors,
agonist studies of analgesia, 307–309
antagonists, *see* Rimonabant
CB_1 receptors,
addiction role, 113, 114
cardiovascular system, 116
distribution, 101, 126
knockout mice, 101, 112, 117, 133
limbic system, 109, 110
motor function, 103, 104, 106, 107
peripheral blood leukocyte expression, 263, 264, 298
signaling, 99–101, 127
splice variants, 99
types, 99, 126, 127, 297
Cannabinoid test system, features, 150, 151
Cannabinol,
analgesia, 307
features, 23
Cannabis, *see also* Indica,
chemical fingerprinting for source identification, *see* Chemical fingerprinting, *Cannabis*
color spot tests, 42
compound biosynthesis, 6, 7
domestication and dispersal, 8, 9, 14
drugs-of-abuse testing, *see* Immunoassays, *Cannabis*; Mass spectrometry
ecology, 1, 2
epidemiology of use, 237, 253, 286, 295
life cycle, 1, 2
medical marijuana, *see* Medical marijuana
microscopy, 41, 42
origin, 8
production,
drug breeding, 9, 10
field crop, 2, 4
greenhouse and grow room, 4, 5
resin gland anatomy and development, 5, 6
species taxonomy, 9
Cannabis psychotic disorder, features, 245
Cannabitriol, features, 24
Cannachromavarin, biosynthesis, 7
Carbohydrates, *Cannabis* composition, 30, 31
Cardiovascular disease, epidemiology, 295
CB_1 receptor, *see* Cannabinoid receptors
CBD, *see* Cannabidiol
CEDIA, *see* Cloned enzyme donor immunoassay
Cervical cancer, risks in marijuana users, 247
Chemical fingerprinting, *Cannabis*,
age and sex of plants, 61
chemometrics, 53, 54
compounds of interest, 54, 55
daughter plants grown in a different region, 61
experimental design, 56, 57
extraction, 57, 58
gas chromatography/mass spectrometry, 58
hashish analysis, 62
indoor versus outdoor plants, 60, 61
multivariate data analysis, 58, 59
overview, 51–53
phase II study, 59–63
prospects, 63, 64
storage condition effects, 61

Cloned enzyme donor immunoassay (CEDIA), principles, 148
Cognitive function, marijuana effects, 243–245, 278, 279
Color spot tests, *Cannabis*, 42
Cytokines, cannabinoid effects, 264–266, 270

DAT, *see* Drugs-of-abuse testing
Dependence, *see* Addiction
Depression, marijuana effects, 311, 312
Dihydrotestosterone, marijuana smoke condensate antagonism, 94
DNA testing, *Cannabis*, 43
Driving impairment,
  alcohol and marijuana combination, 213
  cognitive effects of marijuana, 278, 279
  epidemiology of marijuana and driving, 286
  field sobriety testing, 280, 281
  hallucinations, 279
  highway accident studies, 247, 248
  on-road driving studies, 288–291
  physiological effects of marijuana, 277, 278
  psychomotor effects of marijuana, 278, 279
  relative crash risk assessment following marijuana use, 287
  toxicological tests,
    blood, 283–295
    oral fluid, 285, 286
    overview, 281, 282
    urine, 282, 283
Dronabinol, appetite induction, 304
Drugs-of-abuse testing (DAT), *see* Immunoassays, *Cannabis*
Drugwipe®, sweat testing, 223, 224

ELISA, *see* Enzyme-linked immunosorbent assay
Emesis, THC prevention, 129
EMIT, *see* Enzyme-multiplied immunoassay technique
Enzyme-linked immunosorbent assay (ELISA), principles, 149
Enzyme-multiplied immunoassay technique (EMIT), principles, 147
Estrogen receptor, marijuana smoke condensate interactions, 93, 94

Fatty acids, *Cannabis* composition, 32–34
Flavonoids, *Cannabis* composition, 31, 32
Fluorescence polarization immunoassay (FPIA), principles, 147, 148
FPIA, *see* Fluorescence polarization immunoassay

Gas chromatography/mass spectrometry (GC/MS),
  adipose tissue testing, 184
  blood testing, 182–184, 192, 193
  chemical fingerprinting of *Cannabis*, 58
  chemometrics, 53, 54
  hair testing, 187, 188, 197–199
  immunoassay comparison, 161, 163, 164, 169
  meconium testing, 184–186, 195
  oral fluid testing, 186, 187, 196
  phytocannabinoid analysis, 40, 42
  urine testing, 180, 181, 189–191
GC/MS, *see* Gas chromatography/mass spectrometry

Hair testing,
  external contamination, 226
  growth rate of hair, 225, 281
  interpretation, 225–227
  mass spectrometry, 187, 188, 197–199
Hallucinations, marijuana induction, 279
Head and neck cancer, marijuana smoking risks, 247
Heredity, marijuana effects, 246, 247
High-performance liquid chromatography (HPLC), phytocannabinoid analysis, 42, 43
Hippocampus,
  CB1 receptors, 109
  memory role, 108, 109
HPLC, *see* High-performance liquid chromatography
Hydrocarbons, *Cannabis* composition, 28
Hypothalamus,
  CB_1 receptors, 110
  functions, 109, 110

Immune system,
cannabinoid modulation, 116, 117
marijuana effects,
alveolar macrophages, 258–260, 268, 269
cytokine response to THC, 264–266, 270
overview, 239, 239
T-cell activation, 266–268
peripheral blood leukocytes and cannabinoid receptor expression, 263, 264, 298
Immunoassays, *Cannabis*,
cannabinoid test system, 150, 151
cannabinoid-to-creatinine ratio studies, 167
evaluation,
cutoff concentrations, 159–161
efficiency, 159
gas chromatography/mass spectrometry comparison, 161, 163, 164, 169
general evaluations, 159
sensitivity, 159
specificity, 159
hemp products, 166
heterogeneous competitive immunoassays, 148, 149
homogenous competitive immunoassays, 147, 148
immunogen strategies for antibody generation, 155–157
overview, 147
point-of-collection immunoassays, 150
regulations and guidelines, 157, 158
specimen validity testing, 167, 168
stability of cannabinoids, 164, 166
THC medications, 166, 167
THC pharmacokinetics and metabolite analysis, 151–155
Indica,
features, 10
sativa hybrids, 11
taxonomy, 9

Ketones, *Cannabis* composition, 36
KIMS, *see* Kinetic interaction of microparticles in solution
Kinetic interaction of microparticles in solution (KIMS), principles, 148

Lung cancer, marijuana smoking risks, 240, 241, 247, 261–263
Lungs, *see* Pulmonary function, marijuana effects
Luteinizing hormone, marijuana effects, 241

Marijuana smoke condensate, *see* Smoke condensate
Marijuana, *see Cannabis*
Mass spectrometry (MS),
adipose tissue testing, 184
blood testing, 182–184, 192, 193
gas chromatography coupling, *see* Gas chromatography/mass spectrometry
hair testing, 187, 188, 197–199
marijuana smoke condensate analysis, 68–72
meconium testing, 184–186, 195
oral fluid testing, 186, 187, 196
phytocannabinoid analysis, 40, 42
urine testing, 180, 181, 189–191
Meconium testing, mass spectrometry, 184–186, 195
Medical examiner,
cause-of-death determination, 299, 300
THC screening, 298, 299
Medical marijuana,
abuse liability, 217
breeding, 13, 14
genetic modification, 13
sources and features, 11, 12
Morphine, THC combination for analgesia, 308
Motor function,
marijuana effects on driving, 278, 279
neuroanatomy,
basal ganglia, 103, 104, 106, 107
CB_1 receptors, 103, 104, 106, 107
cerebellum, 103, 104, 106, 107
cortical areas, 101–103
MS, *see* Mass spectrometry
Myocardial infarction, marijuana as trigger, 297, 298

Nabilone, emesis prevention, 130
Naloxone, marijuana withdrawal studies, 133, 134

Nefazodone, marijuana withdrawal management, 132
Noladin ether, neuromodulation, 97–99
Nor-9-carboxy-Δ9-tetrahydrocannabinol (THCA),
  deuterated analogs, 179, 180
  mass spectrometry,
    blood testing, 182–184
    hair testing, 187, 188, 199
    meconium testing, 184–186
    urine testing, 180, 181

Oral fluid testing,
  driving impairment testing, 285
  interpretation, 219–223
  mass spectrometry, 186, 187, 196
Oropharyngeal cancer, *see* Head and neck cancer

Pain, *see* Analgesia
Peripheral blood leukocytes, cannabinoid receptor expression, 263, 264, 298
Pharmchek® patch, sweat testing, 223
Phenols, *Cannabis* composition, 35, 35
Phytocannabinoids, *see specific compounds*
Pirouette, chemometrics, 53
Plasma, *see* Blood testing
Postmortem redistribution, THC, 299, 300
Pregnancy, marijuana effects, 242, 243
Prolactin, marijuana effects, 241
Pulmonary function, marijuana effects,
  acute effects, 254, 255
  airway injury and bronchial epithelial pathology, 257, 258, 298
  alveolar macrophages, 258–260
  animal studies, 255
  human study overview, 255, 256
  lung function testing, 256, 257
  overview, 239, 240, 253, 254
  respiratory symptoms, 256

Radioimmunoassay (RIA), principles, 148, 149
Reproductive function, marijuana effects, 241
Resin gland, anatomy and development, 5, 6
RIA, *see* Radioimmunoassay
Rimonabant,
  appetite suppression, 304, 305
  cannabinoid receptor antagonism, 217, 306
  drug dependency studies, 133, 134
  safety and tolerability, 306

Saliva, *see* Oral fluid testing
Sativex®, indications and clinical trials, 309, 310
Schizophrenia, marijuana studies,
  animal studies, 312
  human studies, 312, 313
Serum, *see* Blood testing
Smoke condensate,
  behavioral activity, 72, 92
  dihydrotestosterone antagonism, 94
  estrogen receptor interactions, 93, 94
  fractionation and analysis, 68–72
  mutagenicity, 92, 93
  preparation, 67, 68
  pulmonary hazards, 93
  table of compounds, 73–92
SR141716, *see* Rimonabant
Sweat testing, interpretation, 223

Tachycardia, cannabinoid induction, 116, 239
T-cell,
  cannabinoid receptor expression, 263, 264, 298
  THC effects,
    activation, 266–268
    T-helper balance and cytokine expression, 264–266
Teratogenicity, marijuana, 242
Terpenes,
  biosynthesis, 6
  Cannabis composition, 28
  medical value, 7, 8, 40
  types, 28, 29
Testicular function, marijuana effects, 241
Testosterone, marijuana effects, 241
Δ8-Tetrahydrocannabinol,
  analgesia, 307
  features, 21

Δ9-Tetrahydrocannabinol (THC),
  appetite effects, 129
  biosynthesis, 7
  deuterated analogs, 179, 180
  emesis prevention, 129, 130
  hemp seed product content, 27
  isomers, 38
  metabolism,
    absorption, 207, 209, 210
    distribution, 210, 296
    elimination, 210–212
    ingestion versus smoking, 216
    metabolism, 151–155, 210
    pharmacodynamics, 296, 297
    pharmacokinetics, 151–155, 296, 297
    social and scientific questions, 206
  potency trends, 25–27
  release, 207
  synergy with other *Cannabis* compounds, 39
Δ9-Tetrahydrocannabinolic acids, types and features, 19, 20
THC, *see* Δ9-Tetrahydrocannabinol
THCA, *see* Nor-9-carboxy-Δ9-tetrahydrocannabinol
Thin-layer chromatography (TLC), phytocannabinoid analysis, 40, 42
TLC, *see* Thin-layer chromatography

Urine testing,
  driving impairment testing, 282, 283
  interpretation, 217–219
  mass spectrometry, 180, 181, 189–191

WIN 55,212-2, analgesia, 308